VERMONT

Numbered Highways

INTERSTATE LEGEND

○━━━ COMPLETED HIGHWAY AND INTERCHANGE

▦▦▦ UNDER CONSTRUCTION

▬ ▬ ▬ APPROXIMATE LOCATION

SCALE OF MILES

0   8   16   24   32

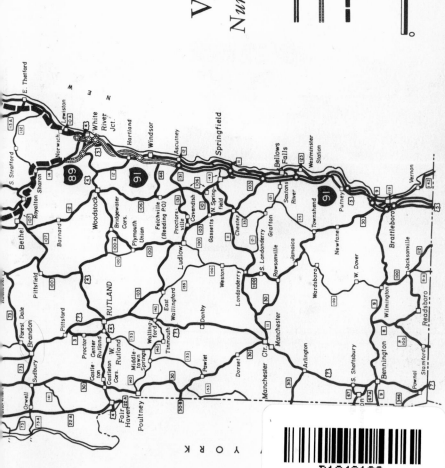

VERMONT

A Guide to the Green Mountain State

THE NEW AMERICAN GUIDE SERIES

VERMONT

A Guide to the Green Mountain State

SECOND EDITION

REVISED AND ENLARGED

EDITED BY RAY BEARSE

ILLUSTRATED WITH MAPS AND PHOTOGRAPHS

HOUGHTON MIFFLIN COMPANY BOSTON

The Riverside Press Cambridge

1966

First Printing R

Acknowledgments

U.S. SENATOR GEORGE AIKEN, hill farmer and writer; Harold Arthur, Burlington attorney and former governor; Miss Elaine Atkins, former publisher-editor of the *Montpelier Evening Argus;* Robert S. Babcock, former lieutenant governor and political scientist; Grace Bearse, Boston, Mass.; Percy F. Bearse, Brandon Development Association information specialist and my father; the late Charles H. Brown, former Speaker of the House, and at his untimely death, Secretary of Civil and Military Affairs; Walter Cabell, chief state game warden and authority on wildlife and poachers' techniques; Robert Candy, public relations director, Vermont Fish and Game Department; George Davis, former director, Vermont Fish and Game Department; Ralph Flanders, former U.S. Senator and onetime president, Federal Reserve Bank of Boston, and leading U.S. machine-tool authority; Wilder Foote, Camden, Maine, former publisher-editor, *Brandon Union, Middlebury Register* and *Bristol Herald,* personal aide to the late Secretary of State Edward Stettinius and retired Information Director, United Nations; Stephen Greene, Brattleboro publisher and bookseller; Walter Hard, Manchester bookseller and poet; Walter Hard, Jr., longtime editor of *Vermont Life;* Governor Philip Hoff; Robert Ingram, director, U.S. Weather Bureau, Burlington; Mrs. Arthur Landon, public relations director, Brandon Development Association; Robert Lautzenheiser, Vermont climatologist, U.S. Weather Bureau, Boston, Mass.; Miss Dorothy Lyman, public relations director, Vermont Highway Dept.; John and Elsie Masterson, writers and innkeepers, Blueberry Hill, Goshen; Gerald McLaughlin, senior news editor, *Connecticut Valley Times-Reporter;* Aldo Merusi, city editor, *Rutland Herald;* Peter and Samuel Miller, Miller and Co., Montpelier; Robert Mitchell, publisher, *Rutland Herald;* District Supervisor, Paul S. Newcomb, Green Mountain National Forest, Rutland; Professor Andrew Nuquist, Political Science Department, University of Vermont, and authority on Vermont town government; Geoffrey Orton, public relations director, Vermont Development Commission; Carl Parsons, Manchester bookseller; former Commissioner Raymond S. Rowley, Vermont State Department of Agriculture; the late Vilhjalmur Stefansson; his widow Evelyn, Washington, D.C., and former Stefansson Arctic Collection librarian,

Baker Memorial Library, Dartmouth College; Wynn Underwood, Middlebury attorney and historian; Dr. Richard Wood, director, Vermont Historical Society, Montpelier; L. P. Yale, bureau chief, Associated Press, Boston, and my former AP colleagues.

Special thanks are due my friends and editors at Houghton Mifflin, including Lovell Thompson, vice-president; Craig Wylie, managing editor; Mrs. Ruth Hapgood who checked hundreds of small but important details; Laurette Murdock, copy editor, who was faced with the onerous task of copy editing more than 900 manuscript pages; and David Harris for handling the many chores involved in production. My friends and Weston neighbors including Ray Austin, J. Alan Chalmers, William and Ann Kemsley, Sam Lloyd, Norman Knapp, Mary and Peg Miller, Vrest Orton, Mr. and Mrs. Mark Robbins, Chace Sherman, Jack Straw, Ruth Thomas, Clark Voorhes, Ashael Waite, and Mrs. Rachel Wood, have been most helpful. Mrs. Thomas M. Kugeman, Weston, and Fritz Pruyn, Manchester, rendered invaluable assistance and advice.

RAY BEARSE

Weston, Vermont
October 1965

Preface to the Second Edition

THIS NEW EDITION of *Vermont: A Guide to the Green Mountain State* is a complete revision of the earlier book, with many new chapters and much new material. The section on Geology has not been revised. Vermont's geology has not changed much during the past thirty years.

Where the original edition was divided into descriptions of the cities and larger towns and tours of the countryside, the present book treats places alphabetically. More than fifty towns and over one hundred villages and settlements have been added to the descriptions in the original edition. Every city, town and major settlements within towns are listed in alphabetical order and are cross-indexed. For instance, Forestdale is a settlement in the town of Brandon. Look under "Forestdale" and you will find the cross-reference "See Brandon."

Vermont: A Guide to the Green Mountain State, American Guide Series, first edition, was produced during the mid-1930's by writers, reporters and editors of the Federal Writers' Project of the Works Progress Administration under the general direction of the late Harry Hopkins. The Federal Writers' Project — there was an art project, too — was a New Deal brain child, designed to give creative and productive employment to unemployed writers and editors.

Only a large-budget government agency, with knowledge rather than profit as the motivation, could afford the large staffs necessary for research, writing and editing of even a single volume — and there were more than fifty books in the series.

Dana Doten was director of the Federal Writers' Project in Vermont. In his preface to the original edition, he described the editorial process that produced the most concrete and enduring of WPA projects:

> None of this is individual procedure; it is laid out according to the standard plan for all state guidebooks in the American Guide Series. Standard likewise have been the organization and carrying out of the work.
>
> Nobody in his senses would attempt to explain how writers work. But some light can be thrown upon the way in which the material for

this volume was assembled so that it could be worked upon. A score or more of research workers scattered throughout the state were engaged for over a year in gathering data and in forwarding it to Montpelier. A handful of editors in the central office sifted and checked and revised this accumulation. A still smaller group took the results in hand and in mind and went out on the road, covering every foot of the tours (in some cases driving over sections three or four times), and returned to piece together the mosaic of the tour descriptions. A great amount of independent research by the editors was, of course, also required before any final copy could be produced. And the contributions of voluntary assistants and consultants (of which, fortunately, almost every town furnished generous examples) had to be incorporated. But even then it sounds simpler than it was.

If a book cannot stand on its own feet, it is certainly not to be justified for its by-products. At the same time, no volume like the present can come into being without a variety of corollary results. And of the many such, I believe two definitely significant. One is the indication, which strengthens with each new publication of the American Guide Series, that writing can be nationally fostered, that literature will ultimately repay, as other arts have for centuries, what governments choose to expend upon it. The other result likewise is to be thought of as applying nationally. It lies in the impact which this work has inevitably made upon the minds of the writers themselves. If great writing must be rooted in the soil, if genuine creation must grow out of the artist's intense identification with his background, is it too optimistic to expect that these state books will help to prepare at least a few writers who, in the years to come, can write more deeply of America through knowing their parts of America deeply?

Director Doten noted that hundreds of Vermonters had volunteered information. He then made the following specific acknowledgments:

We are under personal obligation to those whose connection with the work has been an especially intimate one. Among them are Mr. Charles Crane, of Montpelier; Professor Hugh S. Morrison, of Dartmouth College; Mr. Dorman B. E. Kent, of Montpelier; Mr. Vrest Orton, of Weston; Mr. Harrison J. Conant, State Librarian; Professor Arthur Wallace Peach and Professor K. R. B. Flint, of Norwich University; and Mrs. Mabel W. Mayforth of Barre.

Several of the essays have been in whole or in part contributed by consultants. The essay on agriculture was almost entirely the work of Dr. John A. Hitchcock of the Vermont Experiment Station; the natural setting essay was written by Dr. Robert K. Doten, formerly of the Geology faculty of the Massachusetts Institute of Technology. Mr. Raymond E. Bassett, of Burlington, supplied valuable material for the transportation article, and Miss Elin Anderson, formerly of the Eugenics Survey in Vermont, provided a summary of several years of research for the essay on racial elements. Finally, the share which Mrs. Dorothy Canfield Fisher, of Arlington, has had in the Guide is only partially indicated by her own essay, "Vermonters." She has taken an active interest in the work through all its stages, has been a steady friend and perceptive critic. This volume was prepared under the editorial supervision of Joseph Gaer, Editor-in-Chief of the New England Guides and Chief Field Supervisor of the Federal Writers' Project.

R. B.

Contents

PART ONE. *Vermont: The General Background*

Illustrations

Maps

All of the maps in this book, except those of Montpelier and Bennington, are based on maps supplied through the courtesy of the Vermont Department of Highways and the State of Vermont.

How To Use This Guide

THE first and second parts of this volume are a guide to Vermont history, natural resources, recreation and the general background of the state.

The third or gazetteer section includes data on Vermont's 238 towns, eight cities and several gores, grants, unorganized towns, and a number of the prominent geographical features. The communities are listed alphabetically. Many Vermont towns (known as townships in other states) have several settlements.

Each settlement, village or town is listed alphabetically. The information for all of the communities or settlements in a town are listed under the town or city's name. Forestdale — a settlement in Brandon Town — is listed under Forestdale where the cross-index notation reads FORESTDALE (see BRANDON). Some towns have as many as eight settlements.

Each noteworthy settlement is described. Some place names shown on the various maps may include no more than two or three houses. The tourist upon arriving in one of these "settlements" will frequently find it difficult to determine just what the place is. There may be no sign indicating that the settlement is "Goose Green" or "Goshen Corners." You can always ask a resident.

The cross-index saves time and confusion. You will discover that while East Middlebury lies within Middlebury town, East Haven is more than 100 miles from either West Haven or Fair Haven, both separate towns.

Many cities like Rutland and Barre abut towns of the same name. Thus we have Rutland City, Rutland Town, Center Rutland, West Rutland and Mill Village. Rutland City, a community with a city form of government, is surrounded by Rutland Town which has a town government. Center Rutland and Mill Village are settlements in Rutland Town. West Rutland is a town separate from either Rutland City or Rutland Town. Each community is listed separately and is cross-indexed for easy reference.

In each instance where there are several settlements within one town the chief village or settlement is described first. The remaining settlements or villages are listed thereafter in alphabetical order.

Ski Areas: Some ski areas are listed under the name of the town in which the area is located. Others are listed under the name of the largest nearby community. All areas, regardless of where they are listed, are cross-indexed.

State Parks and Forests: These are usually listed under the name of the town they are located in. Some of these larger areas which spread into several towns are described under their respective names. All others are cross-indexed.

ABBREVIATIONS

R.D.   Rural Delivery. When R.D. is followed by the name of a city or town, it means that the community is served by Rural Delivery mail service from the town mentioned. Example: GOSHEN, Brandon R.D. means that Goshen is served by a rural carrier out of the Brandon post office.

Stage   Many small towns which have no railroad or bus service are served by the local rural mail carrier who totes passengers for a small fee.

VAH   Vermont Agricultural Host sign means that the farm or business on which the sign is posted welcomes interested visitors.

VHS   Vermont Historic Site marker posted by the Vermont State Board of Historic Sites.

General Information

Nickname: Green Mountain State
Area: 9609 square miles — ranks 43rd.
Population: 389,881 (1960)–409,000 (1965 est.) — ranks 47th.
Motto: Freedom and Unity
Flower: Red Clover
Tree: Sugar Maple
Bird: Hermit Thrush
Animal: Morgan Horse
Song: "Hail Vermont"
Union Admission: March 4, 1791 (14th state)
Average Annual Income: $2121 (compared to New England average of $2766 and U.S. average of $2449).
Motor vehicle registrations: 163,190
Drivers' licenses: 193,807.
Maps: Secure the official Vermont Highway Map published jointly by the Vermont Highway Department and the Vermont Development Commission either by writing to the Commission at Montpelier or picking one up at information booths scattered throughout the state. The Highway Department, for a small fee, can furnish a detailed highway map of each county.
Airlines: Northeast, formerly Boston & Maine Airline (Boston–Barre/Montpelier–Burlington) and Mohawk Airlines (N.Y.–Rutland–Burlington). Nonscheduled airports with limited facilities are listed in Chapter 10.
Highways: Two major highways run north and south (US 5, US 7), and two run east to west (US 2, US 4). Interstate 91 when completed will follow US5. Interstate 89 beginning at northwest corner will follow US 7 to Burlington and then swing southeast along present US 2 to Barre and southeast to join Interstate 91 at White River Junction. Vt. 100 runs north and south through center of state and leads to most major ski areas. There are no public toll roads. Vermont State Police troopers patrol highways.
Railroads: Central Vermont Ry. (CVR); Vermont Railway (Vt. Ry.); Boston & Maine R.R. (B & M); Canadian Pacific R.R. (CPR); Delaware and Hudson R.R. (D & H); Maine Central R.R. (MCR);

Canadian National Grand Trunk (CNGT); St. Johnsbury & Lake Champlain Ry. (St. J & LC); Hoosac Tunnel & Wilmington R.R. (HT & W); Clarendon & Pittsford R.R. (C & PRR); Montpelier & Barre R.R. (M & BRR). On account of the state's topography most of the railroads run north to south; rail connections east to west are scanty and poor. CVR is a subsidiary of Canadian National.

Taxes: State income tax. No sales tax (as of 1966). Gas tax: $0.065 per gallon. Inheritance, meal, room, and poll taxes.

Climate and Equipment: Temperature subject to abrupt and drastic changes in any season. Summer nights are invariably cool, sometimes quite cold, and topcoats are often required. In spring and fall the days are apt to be intermittently cool and warm, with topcoats a necessity. The highways are kept open throughout the winter, but sudden storms may cause temporary blockades, and winter travelers should note weather reports.

Accommodations: Hotels and inns in cities and larger towns and resort areas. Motels or cabins along roads most traveled by tourists. Not many motels have swimming pools. Air conditioning is rarely found because it is not very often needed. Some ski resort areas are keeping open in the summer though many such places are closed in the spring and fall. Write Vermont Development Commission for current list of tourist accommodations.

Motor Vehicle Laws (digest): Maximum speed for pleasure cars, 50 mph. unless otherwise posted. A speed of 55 or 60 mph. is permitted on newer sections of some state highways. Interstate Highways have 65 mph. maximum and 40 mph. minimum speeds. Pleasure vehicles with trailers or semi-trailers; 45 mph. maximum speed. Full reciprocity granted to nonresidents except when their vehicles are operated for hire between points within the state. Minimum age for drivers: Children under 12 are not permitted to drive on public highways but they can operate farm tractors on highway within limits of farm; minimum age for learner's permit, 15 years; junior operator's license, 16 years; senior operator, 18 years. All vehicles manufactured after May 1955 must be equipped with directional signals. All Vermont-registered motor vehicles must be inspected during May and October at approved inspection stations.

Liquor Regulations: Vermont towns and cities have local option. Each community at regularly scheduled town meetings or elections votes "wet" or "dry." The larger "wet" communities usually have a state liquor store for fortified wines and spirits. Grocery and other stores may be licensed to sell beer and light wines. Sunday beer sales are permitted.

Class of Licenses

First Class: Beer and wine on premises.
Second Class: Beer and wine off premises.
Third Class: Spirituous liquors on premises.
State Stores: Spirituous liquors off premises.

Beer to 6 percent and wines to 14 percent sold by privately owned package stores and on-premise licensees. Fortified wines over 14 percent and spirituous liquors sold by state-owned package stores and third-class licensees for on-premise consumption.

Hours of Sale

State Stores: 10 A.M. to 6 P.M. Eastern Standard Time, or Daylight Saving Time if prevailing. Saturdays — 10 A.M. to 8 P.M. Closed on Holidays and Sundays.

On-premise Licensees: 8 A.M. to 1 A.M. Eastern Standard Time except Saturdays and Sundays. Sunday hours — 12 noon to 9 P.M. (Eastern Standard Time). Saturday hours — 8 A.M. to 12 P.M. (Eastern Standard Time). Third-class license holders, employing three or more entertainers, may serve liquor until 2 A.M., Monday–Friday.

PART ONE

Vermont:
The General Background

I

Vermonters

(*This chapter is a slightly abridged version of Chapter 29 in Charles Miner Thompson's* Independent Vermont.)

VERMONT'S early settlers won a place for their state in the Union but their troubles were not over. They had the qualities needed to overcome difficulties. The old discipline of the frontier, the old struggles for their land and for their independence, were no longer afflicting them, but they had left their deep imprint on character. Their experience had made them strong, and the ceaseless training of a lovely but exacting land was enough to keep them so. A mountainous country that, although it had rich pockets and rich stretches of fertile soil and abundant rain, also had long, rigorous winters and a short growing season; it exacted hard and resolute labor to make it yield its none too lavish rewards.

Vermont is a land that, like all lands that reward nothing except persistent industry, wins the love of the men who conquer it — like Scotland, like Switzerland, like Finland. Their beauty awakens love, their challenge invites conquest. They create character in the citizen. The Vermonters have vivid traditions and tenacious standards. They are proud of them and sedulously hand them on to their children and to the newcomers among them. One story, the thrilling though historically incorrect *Green Mountain Boys* of D. P. Thompson, which every Vermont boy reads, has done yeoman's service in making their home the object of a romantic regard. The Vermonters are proud, quite justly, of their state, and proud to think of themselves as Vermonters; they know their own genealogies and the genealogies of others. Mrs. Dorothy Canfield Fisher noted that, as is natural in the people who bred the Morgan horse, they thoroughly believe in heredity and in the value of deriving from good stock. One result of their common traditions and standards and their common feeling of quasi relationship is that they have a sense of intimate union. In the unitedness of the people, the smallness of the population — many an American city has a larger — the excellent roads and the automobile play a large part. The leading men in all parts of the state know one another. The wide and intimate knowledge that they have of one another accounts, at least in part, for the cleanness of Vermont politics and the intelligence and character of the public men, for it places a formidable stumbling-block in the path of any stupid, demagogic, or dishonest candidate for public office; he cannot successfully assume a virtue if he has it not.

TODAY'S VERMONTER

Can we draw a passable picture, a rough sketch in outline, of the present Vermonter that will be recognized as his likeness? Such a man plainly has characteristics that may be safely attributed to the forces of heredity and environment. Let us see if we can detect some of them. Certainly one of them is a stubborn independence. Vermonters have marked self-reliance. They are little influenced, I think, either in conduct or in opinion by other people. Among the children of an earlier generation one of the commonest defiances that they hurled at one another was, "You can't run me!" I do not know whether Vermont children are so vocal in their independence now,[1] but I do believe that the remark expresses a feeling common to all Vermonters, child or adult, male or female. They all are inclined to shake off any control but such as they voluntarily accept, as, for example, when they take a job. If a Vermonter wants your advice, he will ask for it, and until he does, you had better keep your thoughts to yourself. Vermonters do not like meddlers, even governmental. I think that their dislike of dictation, so resented throughout their earlier history, has lost little of its intensity.

However, if you do not bother Vermonters, they will not bother you. They are tolerant of almost everything except aggression. Tolerance, of course, goes with individualism. If you are constantly with men of strong personal opinions, opposed to your own, the only course open to you, if you want a peaceful life, is to take a "live and let live" position, to acknowledge that if you have a right to your opinion and a right to rule your own conduct, so has the other fellow. If you have not enough opinions in common with him to leave an ample field for pleasant talk, you let him alone. You do not quarrel with him unless the matter is serious, unless it touches your rights in some way that seems to you important. For the Vermonter, as I know him, is not quick tempered. However, he does stick to his opinion, or an adopted course of action, with an admirable tenacity, not to say stubbornness.

Another quality of the ordinary Vermonter is respect for money. No one knows better than he what a dollar costs in work and in

[1] They still are! (ed. note.)

self-denial. If he has a little, he is proud of it, not as one who is purse-proud, but for the qualities that it shows he has — industry, thrift, and shrewdness — and for the same reason he admires other men who have it. To him having money means character. The "eccentric" in this respect is the man who, as the Vermonters describe him, is "tighter than the bark on a tree," the man who has turned the virtue of thrift into a vice. There are not many such men, and they are not admired. To the pioneers financial independence was the almost universal goal; they taught their children both by precept and practice to prize it.

Another quality that, like the Vermonters' respect for money, is the natural result of pioneer conditions in a difficult country is their realistic outlook on life. They have had to face facts, exceedingly stubborn facts. They have learned not to believe in short cuts to success, luck, easy money, cerulean prospects, even when held out by government. The Vermonter fears the politician bearing gifts and examines them closely to see that they are real gifts and not something that will bring to the donor a concealed advantage, political power, perhaps, more valuable than the gifts. He puts his hope of financial security rather in spending less than he earns, in thrifty, not to say close, management. It is surprising how often he wins it.

Not only the pioneer hardships, but the early struggles of the state to maintain itself, taught the people to take punishment, whether in their public or private affairs, without a whimper.

Vermonters showed the same stoical spirit, and cheerful courage in the great flood of 1927. That catastrophe did enormous damage, caused great public and private losses. They acted like the quiet, uncomplaining, undaunted folk that they are. No one gave up, or grew unduly discouraged. They merely set to work. In time, they knew, they would regain their wonted level of prosperity. They made no appeal for help to the national government. They took the calamity in the same resolute, fighting spirit in which their fathers took the burning of a village by raiding French and Indians. As their ancestors simply rebuilt their village and calmly went on with their dangerous lives, so without undue fuss they repaired the damage and made things better than they had been before, so that another flood, if one came, could do a minimum of mischief.

There are instances of their courage under private affliction that are more notable, perhaps, than their endurance of public calamity, and of course seldom known to the public. I know one man, for example, whose little business in a little village could be supposed not to bring in enough money to supply his own modest needs, whose achievement it was to pay heavy bills for the care of a wife afflicted with a weary chronic disease and at the same time to give his son not only collegiate but professional education. You would never know the facts from anything that he ever said, and his neighbors, Vermonters like himself, seemed to regard his fierce economy as creditable indeed, but as hardly more than a man ought to do at least for his wife, though sending boys to college may have seemed to some of them an extravagance.

It is not strange that men whom life has so well disciplined, who are so little likely to take their hands from the plow once they have grasped it, and moreover with a long tradition of war going back to the landing of the Pilgrims — and even farther, for more than one of Cromwell's troopers came to settle in the land — have made good soldiers. Vermonters have fought well in every war in which the United States has taken part, not only on land but on sea; for, surprisingly enough, the state has given one admiral and ten rear admirals to the United States Navy. In fact, until the draft began to do the work of the recruiting officer, the number of Vermonters enlisting has been markedly large in proportion to the population. And here, I think, is the proper point at which to say that the native stock has not deteriorated. Let me enforce that opinion with that of the late William S. Rossiter, the statistician. In 1911 he published a careful, thorough study of the people of Vermont. These are his concluding words: "The rare quality of the settlers has proved for the later generations an inheritance as valuable as a strong constitution to the individual; after half a century of population drain there remains surprising vitality." What Rossiter wrote in 1911, we can confidently repeat today.

GREEN MOUNTAIN HUMOR

There is one characteristic of Vermonters that is hard to trace to any influence of the pioneers; that is, their humor. We know little of the jokes current in the early years, but in general we do know that pioneer humor is boisterous, extravagant, and obvious. B. H. Hall in his *History of Eastern Vermont* mentions a popular wit, a certain Peter Parker of Ira, and quotes two of his tales. One is that familiar antique, the story of the two snakes that seizing each the other's tail swallowed until both had disappeared. The second is the story of the duel to the death that Peter Parker boasted he had had with a British giant. The fight, he relates, took place on the top of a small but steep hill, at the base of which a crowd gathered to watch. It was fought with sabers. It ended when Peter with a mighty blow severed the giant's head from his body and sent it rolling and bounding down the hill toward the spectators. As it came, they heard it shout in a clear, powerful voice, "Well done, Peter Parker!" Later humor naturally does not always have an undercurrent of serious feeling and often is quite as extravagant as either of Peter Parker's two stories.

Here, for example, is a witticism of the whimsical sort that I know is authentic, for I heard it myself. A man was getting into his car after eating a notably large trout dinner at the small inn beside the small lake in which he and some friends had been successfully fishing. One of them shouted this jocular question after him: "Say, Nat, think you can drive that car home after eating all them trout?" "I guess so," was the instant retort, "if all them trout don't head back toward the lake."

Another remark that I heard shows the gift for vivid phrasing that many Vermonters have. In my boyhood a buffalo robe was in every sleigh, and its condition accurately marked the owner's relative prosperity. The robe of the well-to-do man was superb, soft and silky with its deep, rich fur; the poor man's robe was rusty and dull and had many a leathery patch from which the fur was quite worn away. A man described the people of a hill village where getting a living was hard in this memorable phrase, "They hain't got much fur on their buffalers up that way." Nothing could have told you more about them. But I am not sure he was conscious of his own wit: he may merely have been giving a bit of significant information. Like any other person who thinks pictorially, he may have merely been using the picture with which his observation had provided him.

Vermonters have an alert eye for the humors of character. If you have any fault or oddity, they are sure to detect it, and unless it is quite beyond the pale, will laugh at it with tolerant understanding. They take especial joy in anecdotes of sharp trading. The gleanings that I get at such times are mainly tales that would make you think that everyone was trying to bilk his neighbor. The tales are told, however, with no idea of maligning the honesty either of the town or of the state. The tellers think them amusing, as they are, and tell them, not as facts on which they expect you to build unfavorable generalizations, but as tales of individuals, who are not representative. They know that the majority of their people are excellent persons; the only trouble with them is that they give small occasion for amusing comment.

A magazine for which I once worked was always at great pains not to print anecdotes that were likely to offend any racial or other special groups. There were two racial groups that never showed any sensitiveness to jests based on their national peculiarities. They were the Scotch and the Yankees. They were as ready to laugh at them as any disinterested reader. The people of whom that can be said are plainly sure of themselves and of their standing in the world. They have no inferiority complex.

Just as the maple sugar of Vermont tastes different from maple sugar made elsewhere, so the Vermonter himself is a recognizable variant of the species Yankee. He reveals himself shyly but most distinctly in his humor. That gets its special tang — as indeed his whole character does — from the peculiar conditions under which he spends his life, but that man is bold who thinks he is expert enough in matching shades so to differentiate the Vermonter from the rest of the Yankee family that everyone can recognize his special blend of color. All that anyone can surely affirm is that the distinction really represents a difference.

Of course there are in Vermont, as everywhere, shiftless and even vicious people, but there are not many, not enough, I'm sure, to count greatly in any appraisal of the character of the people as a whole. In proportion to the population the state has placed the names of more men in *Who's Who* than any other state in the Union.

YESTERYEAR

My boyhood was spent in Vermont and of late years I have visited it regularly and have driven not only over its main highways but over its back roads among the hills, and I hope I have kept my eyes open. I think that I can best illustrate the changes that have taken place in my old home if I sketch first the little village in which I grew up as a boy and the relatively large town that I found when age brought me back to it, and then contrast the two.

In summer the streets and roads were thick with dust, a cloud of which followed every carriage or farm wagon that went over them. But facing the streets were many good houses, shaded with arching elms. Indeed, certain streets had a distinctly aristocratic look. It had at first a "union" school and later a parochial school that drew the French and the Irish boys, of whom there were many then, away from companionship with us Yankees, to the loss, I believe, of both groups. Of course, in so small a place they could not be wholly segregated, but the Yankee boys did get the idea that their former playmates were in some way different and alien. There was a single railway station, then always called the "depot," to which the villagers still resorted to see the train come in, and in front of which there was an old stagecoach or so, with haggard horses waiting for possible travelers to nearby hamlets in the hills — where perhaps a sawmill and a half-dozen houses clustered round a "general" store. On other days than Saturday, on which the farmers generally did their trading, the streets were stretches of hot and sleepy solitude. There was good water power, and several mills that did a thriving business. The shops had satisfactory earnings. Living was cheap.

It was a county town with a substantial, well-built courthouse; many people visited us when court was in session. Numerous lawyers, among whom were two or three judges, lived in the village and had their offices over the shops. There were also several men who had held state office in Washington. There was no public supply of water; each house had its water butt at the end of the sink in the kitchen, into which a bubbling stream of pure, cold water danced up from the lead pipe at the bottom. Each denomination had its own church, and there were two ministers at least who were superior men. But in that sternly prohibition community there were for each church two or three secret drinking places to which there was much furtive resort. There was still a rigorous Puritanism. There was little recreation. There were church "sociables" now and then and at the town hall there was an occasional minstrel show, ventriloquist, magician, or a phrenologist. But even so, I could not as a boy see that the men had much fun. When the boys became men they literally laid aside childish things; they abjured all sports and became sober citizens; dignity would not permit them to share in any wholesome outdoor sports. For business reasons they could not afford not to seem serious. They played no tennis and no golf, games, indeed, that were not known at that time. Pool and billiards were not respectable, and as for baseball, the best the men could do was to stand for a while and with wistful eyes watch some twelve-year-olds play a game of "one-old-cat." Almost the only fun — except for him who could afford to drive a fast horse — that my boy's eyes could see was once or twice in a season to go on a fishing trip. For several days before they went, I used to hear their cronies asking with a grin whether they were sure they had "the right kind of bait" — a question the meaning of which I soon found out. Both men and women played old-fashioned whist.

Perhaps the limited amusements made the men devote themselves more sedulously to business. At any rate, many of them accumulated money. The industrious ones when they left school started as clerks in one of the village shops or banks, and then plodded on to higher positions and better pay. They married, bought a house and a horse and buggy, and in the long summer evenings drove with their wives down the river road, the only level one. They never had large pay, but by living simply — the wife kept the house with the help of a hired girl who was more often a companion than a servant; the husband took care of the horse and worked in the garden — they saved money and invested it in local enterprises or in mortgages that they knew all about. When the men died, seldom less than eighty years old, they were worth from twenty to sixty thousand dollars. They took pride in the village; they were prominent at town meeting. Their judgment on mortgages was notably sound; their cautious enterprise helped the village to become a city.

Up and down the valley of the river and the valleys of its tributaries and also on the arable uplands lived the farmers. Many of them were well-to-do; men who not only were skilled in raising crops, but who had native business acumen. But there were too many farmers, and of course the submarginal land fell into the hands of the less competent men. The higher you got into the hills, the oftener you saw small farms that were obviously unproductive, the oftener was the ground rough and stony, the buildings in bad repair if not actually in danger of collapse.

Here and there you would find a district school at a "central" point, which too often meant distant from everyone. They were in bad repair, ill-painted, ill-lighted, and with most uncomfortable seats. The teachers, often young girls awaiting marriage, or young men trying to earn a little money for college expenses, were without any special training and often without any natural aptitude for their tasks. What the teaching was like, the reader can learn by reading Mason Stone's comprehensive history of education in Vermont.

Life was often drab, laborious, and deadening, both in the village and on the farms among the hills. Not all the district schools were bad; ambitious pupils often made good use of them and afterwards of the many excellent "academies" and "seminaries" scattered over the state, and of the three colleges. On a walking trip, some time in the late eighties or early nineties of the last century, my companion and I stopped in early afternoon where a farmer was hitching his horse into a "democrat" wagon in front of the barn. We asked him if we could buy a meal at this house. He gave us a shrewd look. "Why, I guess so," he said, with a little chuckle; "wait till I see what the womenfolks say." The family had had its dinner and the table had to be reset for us. She gave us a good meal and asked if we thought a quarter apiece was too much. We had no quarrel with the price. But what I remember best is that while waiting in the sitting room we saw on the table three of the best magazines of the day — *Harper's*, I think, the *Atlantic*, and the *Century*. In many a farmhouse, I am sure, we should have found signs as convincing of intellectual alertness and good literary taste. Not only the ladies of the village, you see, but also the ladies of the hills read with intelligent judgment.

That was the old village and the county that I used to know. The present city has three times its population; has hard-surfaced streets and electric lighting. New streets go back and forth along the steep sides of the hills and the lines of houses rise picturesquely tier on tier one above the other. The public schools — substantial brick buildings of modern design — have increased from one to four. The hotels are good. Liquor is sold no longer clandestinely, but during limited hours at a state agency of which the patronage is not excessive; there is a public library intelligently and helpfully run; the churches look as if they were well supported; there are two "movie" theaters. The handsome old houses still stand along the elm-lined streets, though some have been replaced with buildings — gasoline stations, for example — that lack their dignity and charm. The lawns are well kept, and the place abounds in flower gardens. There's an attractive recreation park that contains not only an excellent diamond and roofed grandstand, but a commodious swimming pool and locker house. Another park on a high hill provides not only attractive picnic places but a superb view of the Green Mountains. There are two golf courses, one of which is accompanied with good tennis courts.

IT'S BETTER TODAY

The farmhouses on the good land, whether in valley or on upland, have always looked well and now are no longer shamed by the windowless houses and the broken-backed barns of "abandoned farms." There are not so many farmers, to be sure, but to all appearances few if any of them work on stony land at a hopeless task. There has been a wise and successful effort to discourage farming on submarginal land. Useful timber has taken the place of the inferior farm and the whole state looks the better for having given up trying to get figs from thistles. I have heard it said that too many farmers limited the products of their farms to whole milk, which brought unsatisfactory returns, but if so, the Vermont farmer, though his natural persistence inclines him to cling to a course he has adopted, does abandon it *once* he is convinced that the difficulty is not merely of the moment. He always finds the proper remedy in the end.

Farmhouses are more attractive than in the past. Front yards once knee-deep in grass with no path to the door are now neatly mown and adorned with flowers. There are even occasional rock gardens. Good roads and automobiles have had much to do with this improvement. There are people now to see and admire. The old dull loneliness has gone. The dirt roads at their best are delightful to ride over, a macadam road is usually not far from anyone. Every now and then you will find in a spot of special beauty the generally modest but always trim house of a summer resident. But what has pleased me most is the schools. They, too, have lost their battered, indigent look.

The summer residents have done much to bring about a more active social life. A Vermonter once remarked in town meeting that summer people would be "at least" financially beneficial; he plainly thought they could hardly be beneficial in any other way. Vermont, however, has wisely done its best to attract people of moderate means and simple tastes who will not regard their country neighbors as an inferior class. The over-rich, ultra-fashionable, who would disdainfully keep to themselves, would not please the independent, self-respecting Vermonter. Their coming would be no less than a major misfortune. For the most part the summer residents have been attracted to the state by its beauty, by the chance it offers of living simply and wholesomely, by a real liking and respect for the people whose friends they have become. Working with the permanent residents, they have done much to vary and brighten the routine of life; they have awakened interest in all sorts of things; like folk dancing, amateur acting, community music, and household industries.

BUREAUCRACY

Vermonters have other problems than the summer visitors, of course, but I am confident that such people as they can solve them. Vermont is bothered by the tendency of the government, both local and national, to take control in various fields that we used to think were the individual's sole concern. There are things, of course, that the individual cannot do, but I should hate to see him leaving to the state anything that with a little gumption he could do himself.

The growth of bureaucracy shows more plainly in Montpelier, the capital. In the old days the legislature met every other year — as it does now, for that matter — got through its modest business in a few weeks, and dispersed. Between sessions, the beautiful statehouse stood undisturbed and somnolent except for an assistant librarian in the state library to attend to the wants of the lawyers — the books were mainly lawbooks — who occasionally visited it, and for the sergeant-at-arms and the janitor who cared for the building and kept a kindly and indulgent eye on the children who came to look at the butterflies, the stuffed birds and beasts in the Historical Society's museum.

There has been a striking change. The statehouse is now stuffed with officials and their clerks, and it has been not only enlarged to some extent, but supplemented with handsome state buildings.

The national government has its own crowd of employees, mostly in rented quarters. To one who remembers the old simplicity this crowd raises a doubt whether there is not some overgrowth of paper workers. I do not think that the activities of the national government need cause much worry. So far as my observation goes, Vermonters regard them at best with skeptical tolerance, and certainly with a tinge of suspicion. They want no external interference with their affairs; in the notable instances in which the national government has tried to get independent control of the resources of the state, they have vigorously rebelled. Flood control, a measure that sought to give the national government rule over water power, aroused great antagonism. Mr. R. C. Overton, Fellow in American History at Harvard University, wrote a clear and vigorous paper on the legal and political aspects of the plan. I quote the final sentence: "I do not believe that the accumulation of undefined powers in a few hands will long be tolerated in the United States. And I am certain that it will not be tolerated by the people of Vermont." And so am I. The people of the state still keep their old dislike of being "run." Perhaps, however, they will not be so careful to watch their own bureaucracy, since they think that they are not being run by them, but are running them. Still, they are a shrewd people, jealous of their own liberty of action, a fact that encourages their friends to believe that they will not fail to stop every unnecessary extension of power, every growth of unnecessary expenditure. They should keep the power and the purse strings in their own care. For bureaucracy, in its natural capacity to spread, resembles the pretty daisies that spoil the mowing and that are quite as hard to get rid of.

Two other subjects to worry Vermonters: the decline in the numbers of the native stock, and the racial cleavage that, though slight, still exists between them and the foreign-born. I do not think that the old stock will die out, and in time the foreign-born will become Vermonters. Vermont has always been able to mold those who live in it into its own spiritual image. The fact is that no one not a Vermonter in heart, if not in birth, can live and be happy in it. The French Canadians and the Italians already have some of the valued traits of the Yankee; they are hardworking and thrifty, and besides each has aptitudes that it would do almost any Yankee good to acquire. Both gain from intermarriage. The French Canadians are the more clannish, and are supported by their fellows in Canada, from whom come their customs and ideas. The races can blend, and once blended form an even stronger and more gifted race. Dr. Claude M. Fuess, headmaster of Phillips Andover Academy, and biographer of Calvin Coolidge, thinks that in spite of all difficulties, the races will mingle in time if we "leave the matter to Cupid." If that fusion should happen, perhaps the people in the hills would be more joyous, more social, more given to singing and dancing, to music and the arts generally, without losing their common sense, sane humor, and strength of character. And Vermont would still be Vermont. If the native stock prefers to solve the problem in another way, all that it has to do is to have more children and teach them to love the state of their birth. It should be easier to hold them in the state. There are few wholesome attractions in the cities that young people cannot find nowadays in Vermont.

2

Geography and Topography

VERMONT — New England's second largest state — ranks forty-third among American states. Only New Hampshire, Massachusetts, New Jersey, Hawaii, Connecticut, Delaware and Rhode Island are smaller. Vermont, with an area of 9609 square miles including a reported 440 square miles of water, is the only New England state without Atlantic Ocean coastline.

The Green Mountain State is bounded on the north by Canada's Quebec Province, on the south by Massachusetts, along the east by New Hampshire's Connecticut River and on the west by Lake Champlain, the Poultney River and the Taconic Mountains along the New York State frontier.

The Connecticut River boundary is about 200 miles long while the Vermont-Quebec frontier extends for about 90 miles. The Massachusetts border is about 40 miles long. Only New Hampshire and Idaho have shorter international boundaries with Canada. It is 159 jet miles between the Massachusetts and Canadian frontiers.

The highest elevation is Mount Mansfield (4393 ft.) and the lowest is Lake Champlain (95 ft.). The approximate geographical center of the state is about 4.5 miles south-southeast of Roxbury Village in Washington County.

Vermont has six major natural physiographic provinces: (1) Green Mountains (2) Taconic Mountains (3) Valley of Vermont (4) Vermont Lowland and Lake Champlain (5) Vermont Piedmont and (6) Northeast Highlands.

THE GREEN MOUNTAINS

The Green Mountains — very few peaks are barren — which dominate the state are a northern link of the Appalachian Mountain System which extends from Alabama to the Gulf of Saint Lawrence. The Hoosac Mountains of Massachusetts become the Green Mountains which in turn become the Sutton Mountains at the Vermont-Quebec frontier. The range varies from 20 to 36 miles in width.

The Green Mountains, a single range for more than 60 miles, splits into three ranges in the vicinity of Pico Peak in Sherburne Town.

The First Range is the short Hogback Range beginning about Brandon Town and extending west of and parallel to the Main Range through the towns of Leicester, Salisbury, Middlebury, Bristol and into Monkton. The average elevation of the Hogbacks is less than 2000 feet.

The Second or Main Range continues north to Lincoln Town and then courses northeastward to the Canadian frontier. This range contains the state's highest peaks (south to north): Stratton (3839 ft.), Shrewsbury (3737 ft.), Killington (4241 ft.), Pico Peak (3967 ft.), Mount Abraham (4052 ft.), Mount Ellen (4135 ft.), Camel's Hump (4083 ft.), Mount Mansfield's Chin (4393 ft.), and Jay Peak (3861 ft.). The average elevation of the highest peaks is nearly 4000 feet while the average elevation of all peaks in the Main Range is 3200. There are 80 peaks in the state with elevations above 3000 and 21 peaks exceed 3500. There are six peaks with elevations above 4000 feet.

The Main Range is cut through at Bolton by the Winooski River which rises far to the east beyond both the Main and Third Ranges. The Main Range, in less than four miles, drops from 4083 feet at Camel's Hump to almost sea level at Bolton Gorge.

The Lamoille River cuts through the Main Range at an elevation of 500 feet where Vt. 115 crosses the Lamoille River Bridge.

The Green Mountains are also cut through at several places by gaps or notches. Some were cut with water and others — the high dry ones — by wind. Major passes, gaps or notches include:

US 2 at Sherburne Pass (2190 ft.); Vt. 73 at Brandon Gap (2184 ft.); Vt. 125 at Middlebury Gap (2149 ft.); Lincoln–Warren road at Lincoln Gap (2424 ft.); McCullough Highway at Appalachian Gap (2365 ft.); Huntington Gap — no road — (2217 ft.); Wind Gap — no road — (2800 ft.); Vt. 108 at Smugglers' Notch (2162 ft.) and Hazen's Notch (alt. 1700).

Talc, asbestos and verde antique marble are the principal mineral products of the Main Range. Forest products are an important local economic factor.

Most of the Green Mountain National Forest's 580,000 acres lie on the slopes and peaks of the Main Range. The 260-mile Long Trail for hikers covers the major peaks of the Main Range from the Massachusetts to the Canadian line.

Major ski areas including Stowe, Mad River, Glen Ellen, Sugarbush,

Pico, Killington and Big Bromley are on the slopes of the Main Range. High elevations with prolonged heavy snow cover is the decisive factor here.

The Third Range begins at Stockbridge and continues north to Canada. Physiographers believe the Third Range was once continuous but some millions of years back the Lamoille River slashed its way through the Third Range in the Hyde Park region. The northern section is now the Lowell Mountains of which the northernmost portion is named Worcester, Northfield and Braintree ranges after the respective towns.

The highest Worcester peak is Mt. Hunger (3286 ft.) while Mount Adams (3236 ft.) is the highest Northfield Range peak. Rochester Mountain (2952 ft.) has the maximum elevation in the Braintree Range.

Former Vermont State geologist Elbridge Churchill Jacobs said the Green Mountains were folded and first elevated about 350 million years ago. Ethan Hitchcock reported that the Green Mountains were probably once as high as the Alps. Another geologist noted the world's scenery — including the Green Mountains — has remained about the same for the past fifty-eight million years.

TACONIC MOUNTAINS

The Taconic Mountains emerge from the New York Highlands along the Hudson, cross northwestern Connecticut, range along the Massachusetts–New York border and cross into Vermont as the Taconics. The range follows the Vermont–New York border for nearly 80 miles and ends in Sudbury near Brandon.

Major peaks along the crestline (south to north) include: Mount Anthony (2345 ft.), Equinox (3816 ft), Owls Head (2535 ft.), Dorset Peak (3804 ft.), Tinmouth Mountain (2847 ft.), Biddie's Knob (2020 ft.) and Government Hill (1075 ft.).

Most Taconic streams flow into the St. Lawrence via Lake Champlain. The Batten Kill — one of America's famous trout streams — the Hoosic and Walloomsac flow into the Hudson.

The Taconics are estimated to have been first formed about four hundred and fifty million years ago. Vermont's position as the nation's second largest slate producer is solely due to the deposits in the Taconics. Marble is also quarried in these ancient hills.

The average elevation of the Taconics is generally too low for the creation of a major ski area.

VALLEY OF VERMONT

This is the floor of the narrow valley lying between the base of the Taconics on the west and the Green Mountains on the east. The Valley of Vermont is a northern and narrower extension of Stockbridge Valley in Massachusetts. US 7 runs north and south along the valley's floor. The valley begins at the Massachusetts-Vermont line and runs north to Brandon where it widens into the Vermont Lowlands along Lake Champlain's coastal plain.

The valley's most important river — also the longest in the state — is the Big Otter, also known as Otter Creek even though it is a river and not a creek. There is no through-running river in the valley. The Otter and the Batten Kill originate within a few rods of each other in Mt. Tabor Town but the elevation is such that the Otter flows north into Lake Champlain and the Batten Kill southwesterly into the Hudson River.

The valley in the West Rutland–Proctor area contains one of the richest and most productive marble deposits in the United States. Marble for the U.N. building in New York, the Supreme Court Building in Washington, Roosevelt's tombstone at Hyde Park and for many other buildings and monuments came from the valley's quarries and marble mills.

The old Carnegie Steel Company once mined manganese in Wallingford. A century ago the night skies over the valley were aglow from blast furnaces processing iron ore from valley mines. Bennington's famous stoneware pottery was made from the valley's large china clay (kaolin) deposits.

One out of every eight Vermonters lives in the valley which includes Rutland and Bennington, resort villages like Brandon and Manchester.

The Red Sandrock Hills extend along the coastal plain from Addison north to St. Albans. Snake Mountain in Addison is the highest (1271 ft.) and the hills decrease as the ridges run north. The so-called "Mallet's Bay Marble" (actually a red dolomite) and much of the red building stone used in Burlington came from these hills. These hills account for the beauty of such prominences as Red Rocks, Rock Point and Mallet's Bay.

VERMONT LOWLANDS AND LAKE CHAMPLAIN

The Taconics terminate at Brandon and here the Valley of Vermont widens into the Vermont Lowlands known to natives and tourists alike as the Champlain Valley. The Vermont Lowlands, together with the St. Lawrence Valley, are the northern terminus of the long corridor — the Great Valley — that extends southward through the Hudson Valley of New York, the Wallkill Valley of New Jersey, the Lebanon Valley of Pennsylvania, Cumberland Valley of Pennsylvania and Maryland, Shenandoah of western Virginia, the Valley of eastern Tennessee into the Coosa Valley of Georgia and Alabama.

The Vermont Lowlands–Lake Champlain area is bounded by the Green Mountains on the east and the Adirondacks on the west. The valley opens out toward its northern end from its lowest base, the Valley of Vermont. Its average width is 20 miles.

One of every five Vermonters lives in the Champlain Valley either in the state's largest and most beautiful city, Burlington, in smaller St. Albans, in a college town like Middlebury, in Vergennes — one of the nation's smallest and oldest cities — or in rural towns like Cornwall, Whiting, Shoreham and Sudbury.

The gentle rolling meadows provided forage for Merinos when Vermont was a leading sheep state. Here are most of the state's commercial apple orchards and many of its largest dairy herds.

Five of Lake Champlain's 107 miles extend into Canada. The lake's water area covers about 435 square miles and the 12 largest islands occupy about 55 square miles. Vermont owns 322 miles of the Lake and New York 191 and Canada has only 17 square miles. The average level of the lake is 92 feet above sea level while the deepest sounding of 390 feet was made two miles offshore at Split Rock Point.

The lake flows from south to north so when a Vermonter — or even a Yorker — speaks of "down Champlain" he means "up north" or when speaking of "up Champlain" he means "down south." Champlain flows through the Richelieu River and is connected with the Hudson River via the Lake Champlain Barge Canal.

The major islands are Isle La Motte, North Hero and South Hero. There are about 80 islands in the lake but many are really nothing more than large boulders projecting above the surface.

The state's four principal rivers, Otter, Lamoille, Missisquoi and Winooski drain into the lake.

THE VERMONT PIEDMONT

"Piedmont" as the name implies means "foot of the mountains" and the Vermont Piedmont is the eastern foot of the Green Mountains for about 100 miles beginning where Saxtons River enters the Connecticut River to the Essex County line. Here the Piedmont leaves the Connecticut River Valley and continues northward in an inverted V toward the Canadian frontier.

The Vermont Piedmont is the northern extension of the 14 terraces comprising the New England peneplain of the Connecticut which eventually drops to Long Island Sound.

The Piedmont is drained by two great water systems. Lower Piedmont rivers and the Passumpsic flow into the Connecticut while upper Piedmont rivers drain into the St. Lawrence via Lakes Champlain or Memphremagog.

The Saxtons, Williams, Black, Ottauquechee, White, Ompompanoosuc, Waits, Wells and Passumpsic drain into the Connecticut. The Winooski, Lamoille and Missisquoi with headwaters in the Piedmont cut directly through the Green Mountains and across the Vermont Lowland into Lake Champlain and into the St. Lawrence via the Richelieu River. The Barton, Black (northern) and Clyde drain into the St. Lawrence via Lake Memphremagog.

This is Vermont's lake country. Lake Willoughby in Westmore is considered by many far traveled visitors to have one of the finest settings of any lake anywhere. Other lakes: Caspian in Greensboro, Lakes Fairlee and Morey in Fairlee, Crystal Lake in Barton, Seymour Lake in Morgan and the many lakes and ponds in Calais.

The Granite Hills near Barre contain the state's great granite quarries. Copper is mined in Vershire.

One out of every three Vermonters lives in the Piedmont cities Barre, Bellows Falls, Montpelier, Newport, St. Johnsbury, Springfield, White River Junction or in villages like lovely Woodstock, Pomfret or Craftsbury Common.

THE NORTHEAST HIGHLANDS

This area, usually known as the Northeast Kingdom, is essentially Essex County with its 16 towns, two gores and a grant covering 611 square miles and is mostly mountainous terrain. The mountains are isolated monadnocks — peaks composed of harder geologic materials than the surrounding country which has been worn down to the status of valleys or flatlands.

This highly glaciated region is an extension — cut by the Connecticut River — of New Hampshire's White Mountain upthrust. The Highlands — except Lake Averill which drains into Memphremagog en route to the St. Lawrence — drain into the Connecticut River. The Nulhegan — familiar to readers of Kenneth Roberts' *Northwest Passage* and the exploits of Major Robert Rogers and his green-stained buckskin-clad Rangers — is the major stream. Other streams include the Paul and the Willard.

Maidstone — a lovely English name — and the Averill lakes are the largest bodies of water within the region.

Timber is the region's prime product and much of the area is owned or controlled by large paper companies like Brown. The granite deposits will probably not be developed until the Granite Hills in the Barre area have been emptied of their vast reserves.

The towns here are small and, until 1964, two towns had no electricity. Residents are mostly employed by the big paper companies. Farms are scarce.

LAKES AND PONDS

Lake Champlain, 107 miles long and constituting for nearly 100 miles the western boundary of Vermont, is jointly owned by Vermont, New York, and Quebec Province. Lake Memphremagog, the second largest lake in which Vermont has an interest, forms part of the northern boundary of the state; about one-quarter of its 60 square miles of area is in Vermont, and the rest in Quebec. The largest natural body of water entirely within the state is Lake Bomoseen in Castleton, with an area of eight square miles. The highest considerable body of water is Sterling Pond in Stowe, lying at an elevation of 3200 feet.

Most of Vermont's more than 400 lakes and ponds owe their origin to the great ice sheet which once covered the state, and which formed them by scouring out hollows in the rocks and damming up stream valleys with rock waste (glacial drift). A number, however, have an origin independent of any glacial action. Thus, Lake Champlain occupies the western portion of the great Champlain Valley, a structural feature formed in early geological times by the downfaulting of its western margin. Picturesque Lake Willoughby rests in a U-shaped trough formed by the downfaulting of a block of the earth's crust between Mounts Hor and Pisgah; the ice sheet somewhat modified the form of this trough and, by damming up the southern end, gave rise to the lake in its present form. Lake Dunmore and Silver Lake occupy synclinal folds in rocks, and are retained by glacial gravels.

RIVERS

The rivers of the state, besides adding greatly to its scenic beauty, are important as sources of hydroelectric power and because of the fact that, aside from the Champlain Valley, their valleys contain the bulk of the arable lands of the state.

The Connecticut River, forming the entire eastern border, is the largest and most important, but is actually under the control of New Hampshire since the boundary line follows the low-water mark on the stream's western side. Otter Creek, rising in Mt. Tabor Town and flowing 75 miles northward to empty into Lake Champlain about eight miles west of Vergennes, is the longest river within the state. The Batten Kill, rising in Dorset and flowing southward, and the Walloomsac south of it, occupy the Valley of Vermont. In general, because of the central mass of the Green Mountains, Vermont rivers flow down the eastern slopes into the Connecticut or down the western into Lake Champlain. Three streams are interesting exceptions to this rule, in that they rise to the east of and flow directly through the Green Mountains to Lake Champlain. The Missisquoi, Lamoille, and Winooski are apparently "antecedent" rivers — that is, they ran in their present courses before the Green Mountains were formed, and were able to cut down their valleys rapidly enough to maintain them against the rising mountains. The great valley of the Winooski where it cuts through the main range is nearly 4000 feet deep, and equals in scenic grandeur many western canyons.

3

Geology

THE scenery of any area, as well as the economic life of its inhabitants, is in the last analysis dependent upon its geological history. Hence it is felt that the following sketch of the geology of the state will help the visitor in understanding the Vermont of today.[1]

Although representatives of the three great rock types (igneous, sedimentary, and metamorphic) occur in the state, the metamorphic (schists, slates, gneisses) are the most common, forming the bedrock of most of the state, with the exception of the Champlain Valley and the Granite Hills. The rocks of the Champlain Valley are almost entirely sedimentary, largely limestones and shales with some sandstones and conglomerates. The Granite Hills, together with certain mountains such as Ascutney and Monadnock, are the principal examples of igneous rocks.

In general, the various rock formations may be considered as occurring in a series of north-south trending belts of differing widths. Each band may consist of several more or less closely related rock types, and individual bands may not continue the entire length of the state; but the following generalizations are useful in outlining the distribution of rocks. Beginning at the Connecticut River in the east and proceeding westward, the rocks encountered are as follows:

1. A belt of schist of variable width from the Canadian line south to Bellows Falls. In this are found the copper deposits of Strafford and Vershire.

2. A narrow belt of slate, not more than a mile or two wide, extending from Burke to the Massachusetts line.

3. A wide belt, up to 20 miles or more across, consisting of a number of types of schists, extending the length of the state. The granite batholith of the Granite Hills has been intruded into this formation.

4. A second narrow belt of dark slate, up to three miles wide, from Lake Memphremagog through Bethel.

---

[1] Those interested in more detailed accounts of the geology and natural resources of Vermont are advised to consult the volumes of the biennial *Reports of the State Geologist on the Mineral Industries and Geology of Vermont,* which may be found in most of the larger libraries.

5. A wide belt of schists and gneisses forming the main chain of the Green Mountains and extending the length of the state. Some 30 miles wide in the north, it gradually narrows to 18 in the south. It consists of a number of types of metamorphic rocks, including much chlorite and mica schist highly contorted, and encloses the lenses of altered intrusives forming the talc, verde antique, and asbestos deposits of the state.

6. West of the mountains, and in part forming their western foot-hills, is a belt of sedimentary rocks, strongly folded near the mountains, which underlies much of the Champlain Valley. It is composed of an eastern conglomerate and a western silicious limestone member in the northern half of the state. These die out in the south, and are replaced by a variety of sedimentary beds.

7. West of the last belt and following rather closely the eastern shore of the lake is a belt of red sandstones, shales, and dolomites, forming the Red Sandrock Hills.

8. Finally, forming the islands in Lake Champlain and on places its eastern shore, is a series of flat-lying shales and limestones. The forces forming the Taconic Mountains to the south of the valley changed (metamorphosed) these rocks into slates and marbles.

In addition very extensive deposits of sands and gravels are scattered everywhere throughout the state, representing the material left on the retreat of the great ice sheet of the Glacial Period.

No rocks as old as the ancient Archean formations of the Adiron-dack Mountains of New York State are definitely known in Vermont, though it is possible that some of the intensely metamorphosed schists and gneisses of the Green Mountain core may be of this age. The known geological history of the Vermont area began in early Paleozoic times with the invasion of the Lower Cambrian sea into the area now forming the Champlain Valley. This was probably the result of the downfaulting of a crustal block along the eastern margin of the Adirondack Massif initiating the structural lowland of the Champlain Valley, which has continued in existence in one form or another to the present. Sands, clays, and dolomitic muds washed from the ad-jacent land areas accumulated to the depth of several thousand feet in the sea thus formed, and later became the rocks whose remnants now form the red sandrock and other cambrian formations of the valley.

Toward the close of the Cambrian there was some uplift and con-sequent erosion, but in early Ordovician times there was again sub-sidence and a renewal of sedimentation. The Ordovician seas appear to have covered at one time or another nearly the entire area now included within the state of Vermont, for rocks carrying fossils of that age are found in both the eastern and western sides of the state and it seems probable that some of the schists of the Green Mountain core are their metamorphic equivalents, as are the slates and marbles of the Taconic area. The limestones of this age in the northern part of the Champlain Valley carry in places an abundant fossil fauna. Thus, some of the beaches on Grand Isle are covered with fossil brachiopods which have weathered out of the limestone outcrops, while a fossil coral reef on Isle La Motte furnishes one of the earliest examples of Colonial corals.

GREEN MOUNTAIN UPLIFT

The close of the Ordovician marked the end of any important sedimentation in the Vermont area, as far as is now known. Strong compressive forces, apparently acting from the east, produced sharp folds in the sediments of the Taconic area, giving birth to the Taconic Mountains and at the same time causing some folding and uplift along the Green Mountain axis. In the Champlain Valley area these crustal forces found relief through the development of the Champlain overthrust rather than through folding of the rocks. This overthrust extends from Canada along the eastern shore of the lake nearly to the New York line and brought Cambrian rocks over the younger Ordovician. During this overthrusting, cubic miles of rock were moved bodily westward for miles. The thrust plane is beautifully exposed at Rock Point just north of Burlington, where the red Cambrian formations may be seen resting on black Ordovician shale.

In late Paleozoic times, probably in connection with renewed mountain-building activity at the close of the Devonian, came the implacement of granitic batholiths whose exposed upper portions now form the Granite Hills. Other bodies of igneous rocks, such as the syenitic intrusive stocks of Mts. Monadnock and Ascutney, were presumably formed at about the same time.

At the close of the Paleozoic came the great mountain-building period known as the Appalachian Revolution, which affected the entire Appalachian region of North America and in the Vermont area raised the Green Mountain region into a lofty mountain range and produced the very intense crushing and metamorphism of its rocks.

An interesting illustration of the tremendous stresses to which the rocks involved in these mountain-building movements were subjected may be seen in the spontaneous explosive splitting of quarry blocks at some of the marble quarries. In spite of the immense period of time which has elapsed since the stresses were imposed, enough residual strain remains to cause these great solid blocks of rock to split asunder. A somewhat similar case is a common experience in the granite quarries, where great blocks freed except on the under side suddenly snap loose with a sharp report.

No Mesozoic history is recorded in the Vermont area, but in the early Tertiary (Eocene) deposits of clays of various types, including small bodies of bog iron and manganese, ores and beds of lignite were formed. These are now found along the Champlain Valley from Colchester south to Bennington. The lignite beds, known as the Brandon lignites, though actually occurring at Forestdale three miles north, were discovered while digging for clay and were at one time exploited as a substitute for coal. The lignites are of interest in that they contain a rich fossil flora consisting of several hundred species of fruits and nuts of tropical and subtropical plants. It thus appears that a warm climate prevailed at that time, in this part of the state at least.

THE SCENERY CHANGES

Sometime between the formation of the Brandon lignite and the Pleistocene a revolutionary change in climate occurred, bringing on the great Pleistocene Glacial Age with conditions similar to those in the Antarctic today. The changes produced in the scenery of Vermont during the Glacial Period were probably greater than during any other period of similar length. A great ice sheet advancing southward from Labrador covered the country with thousands of feet of ice, overriding even the highest mountains. This mass of slowly moving ice carried away the soil and loosened rock and gouged out the solid rocks, rounding off the hills and widening and deepening the valleys. Its great weight caused a subsidence of the land, so that at the close of the period the Vermont area was five hundred or six hundred feet lower than it is today and the waters of the melting ice, augmented by an invasion of the sea, covered much of the State, leaving the mountains standing as islands. Relieved of its ice load, the land gradually rose until the present level was reached, while the flood waters drained off and the streams re-established themselves. During a long period the Champlain Valley was filled by a sea hundreds of feet deep, which reached well up on the western foothills of the mountains and formed arms running far up the river valleys. Incoming streams built extensive deltas where they entered this sea, and as it gradually receded successive deltas were formed, each farther out from the mountain front, until at the present day they are being formed in Lake Champlain. Remnants of these ancient deltas, forming level sand and gravel plains and flat-topped terraces, may be seen today at many places along the Champlain Valley and the valleys entering it. Marine fossils have been found on many of them, sometimes several hundred feet above present sea level. They are found at various elevations, as can be seen by anyone traveling up the Winooski Valley, particularly in the vicinity of Richmond. The Burlington Airport and the village of Bristol are built on such plains. Similar formations exist in the eastern part of the state, where several large glacial lakes were formed with the melting of the ice.

Rounded and grooved ledges, polished rock surfaces, ice-born boulders (erratics), and great deposits of unsorted sands, clays, and gravels (glacial till) throughout the state are further evidences of the former presence of the ice. The steep escarpment on the southern end of the summit of Camel's Hump is the result of the "plucking" action of the ice. The damming of the normal drainage by glacial drift, and the floods of water resulting from the melting of the ice, caused the erosion of deep gashes in the rocks — as at Williamstown and North-field Gulfs — and produced the potholes and water-worn forms of the rocks on the sides of many of the valleys high above even the flood stages of the present.

4

Vermont Weather

"A VERMONT year is nine months winter and three months of damn poor sleddin'," commented an old Vermont hill farmer whose grandfather had survived 1816, better known as "eighteen hundred and froze to death."

Weatherwise, 1816 was Vermont's worst year. It snowed even in July and August. There was a frost every month. Crops failed. Cow critters died. Vermonters who stuck it out did so on a diet which included boiled thistles and fried weeds. It was even a poor year for maple sap and wild honey.

Most Vermonters are fair weather prophets. They have to be. Weather is far more vital to rural folk — particularly those paid by the hour — than to city dwellers to whom inclement weather is but an inconvenience. Farmers, farm workers, loggers and even mill workers who "commute" — that's an "Un-Vermont" word — balance the TV weatherman's forecast with their own weather sagacity.

Vermonters have few if any original weather prophesies. Favorites like

> *Evening red and morning gray*
> *Sends the traveler on his way.*
> *Evening gray and morning red,*
> *Stays the traveler home in bed*

are standard forecasting equipment.

The weather, however, has contributed to several once popular Vermont expressions — possibly they originated elsewhere.

"Independent as a hog on ice" means that a man is not independent. Another — and somewhat more explicit version. "As independent as a hog on ice with his tail froze in."

"Cold as the north side of a January tombstone by starlight" describes subzero weather.

CLIMATOLOGICAL DIVISIONS

Climatologists divide Vermont into three major climatological divisions or provinces: Western, Northeastern and Southwestern.

These divisions take into account various local modifying factors.

The Western division includes Green Mountains' crestline, the Valley of Vermont, Taconic Mountains, the Vermont Lowland and Lake Champlain areas.

This division is least affected by the maritime features of the Atlantic Ocean. It is more affected by Lake Champlain and the warm moist air masses traveling up through the Great Valley from the Gulf of Mexico.

The Northeastern division includes the eastern slopes of the Green Mountains, the Northeast Highlands and the northern section of the Vermont Piedmont.

The Southeastern Division includes the lower portion of the Vermont Piedmont along the Connecticut River Valley and the eastern slopes of the Green Mountains in the southeastern corner of the state.

TEMPERATURES

The hottest recorded day in Vermont's history was July 4, 1911, when the mercury reached 105°F. at Vernon. Vermont, together with Maine and Connecticut, tie for third place with the lowest maximum temperatures. Rhode Island is second with a maximum of 102°F. while Alaska and Hawaii, each with a maximum record temperature of 100°F. tie for first place.

Vermont's coldest recorded day was December 30, 1933, when the U.S. Weather Bureau station at Bloomfield reported a —50°F. Only eleven other states including New York have recorded a lower minimum temperature. New Mexico, Utah and Nevada have also recorded a —50°F. minimum.

The state's summer climate is comfortable. Hot, humid days are rare. Summer afternoon temperatures average about 80°F. while night temperatures are in the comfortable 50°–60°F. range. Summer temperatures tend toward much greater uniformity throughout the state — except for extremes of altitude — than winter temperatures. The mercury, at most U.S. Weather Bureau climatological data reporting stations, rarely passes the 90°F. mark on more than ten days in any one year.

Winters are cold but periods of prolonged cold are infrequent. The first subzero day — high mountains excepted — usually comes about mid-December. Rarely does the temperature drop below the zero mark after late February. The daily winter temperature range averages about 20° compared to the average summer daily range of 20° to 30°.

The temperature range for different areas in the state, however, is somewhat greater in winter than in summer.

GROWING SEASON

The growing season — the number of days between the last day in spring with a 32°F. minimum and the first day in late summer or early fall with a 32°F. minimum — is of great importance to Vermont farmers — and to the purchasers of Vermont farm produce which can be killed by freezing temperatures.

The growing season in the Western and much of the Southeastern Divisions averages 130–150 days between frosts. The between-frosts season of the Northeastern Division and in the southern section of the Western Division averages 100–130 days. In a few communities along the upper slopes of the higher Green Mountains the season may be as short as 80 days. Fortunately, little agriculture is carried out in this region.

PRECIPITATION

Vermont's precipitation usually comes at the right time; enough rainfall for crops and sufficient snow to bring in skiers' dollars — $40,000,000 in 1965.

Average annual rainfall varies from about 30 inches in the Western and Northeastern Divisions to about 45 inches in the Southeastern. Heaviest annual rainfall — 55 inches — has been reported from the Searsburg station. Vermont's wettest known twenty-four hours was November 2–3, 1927, when more than 8 inches was reported by most U.S. Weather Bureau precipitation recording stations. During the same twenty-four hours Somerset station reported 8.77 inches. Measurable precipitation is reported 120 to 160 days a year.

Prolonged droughts and widespread floods are infrequent. Vermont State Climatologist Robert E. Lautzenheiser, director, U.S. Weather Bureau, Boston, Mass., in his excellent monograph *Climate of Vermont* reported major floods in 1801, 1826, 1830, 1886, 1895, 1897, 1909, 1913, 1927, 1936 and 1927.

A four-year-long drought apparently ended in the fall of 1965. Addison County, a dairy region, was declared a disaster area and received federal aid.

SNOWFALL

Snow in today's Vermont is more blessed than cussed. Even Vermonters not remotely connected with the ski-tourist industry are aware of the benefits from the millions which pour into the economy from the wallets of visiting skiers.

Ski area operators have found, after some costly experience, that the one place to ensure season-long snow for their clients is the crestline and upper slopes of the Green Mountains. The Stowe-Mansfield area — the state's first successful high country resort — clings to the upper slopes of Vermont's highest peak, Mt. Mansfield (alt. 4393). The more recent multi-million dollar ski areas followed Stowe's lead. Glen Ellen, Killington, Mad River, Sugarbush and Stratton areas have their summits at or around the 4000-foot level.

The annual snowfall at this elevation averages 100–120 inches. Average snowfall throughout the Champlain Valley and the Valley of Vermont averages 55–65 inches annually. That altitude, i.e. topographical variations, does make a difference is shown by the Weather Bureau's report from two stations. Bennington (alt. 672) has 55 inches annual average while Somerset (alt. 2000) fifteen miles distant, averages 120 inches plus annually.

There is a much greater annual and area variation with snowfall than rainfall. The maximum monthly snowfall recorded at Burlington as 34.3 inches was obtained in February but in 1957 only 1.3 inches fell that month. A single snowfall of more than 20 inches is rare even at the highest elevations. The number of days with 1.04 or more inches of snow varies between 20 and 40. During the average winter most of the state will have several snowstorms, each with 5 or more inches of snow.

The heaviest reported snowstorm was the "Great Blizzard of 1888" when 40–50 inches fell in the southwestern part of the state while the southeastern section received 39–50 inches. Drifts reaching 40 feet were reported.

When snow comes in late November or early December it usually stays until the spring thaws. Snow is usually the deepest just before the thaws in late February. Maximum snow depth is normally reached at the highest elevations during mid-March.

WIND, STORMS AND SUNSHINE

Many Vermonters were surprised to read in the paper, September 24, 1938, that a hurricane had hit the state. Just about everybody knew there had been a "damned high wind" the night before, but no living Vermonter remembered a "hurry-cane." They only happened in Florida and other foreign places. The last previous Vermont hurricane occurred in the early 1830's.

Hurricanes that strike New England rarely touch Vermont because such tropical disturbances lose force very rapidly once they move inland. Vermont's last storm approaching hurricane force was in late November, 1951.

Tornadoes hit Vermont, but today, no Vermonter — or anybody else — remembers the state's most memorable tornado, June 23, 1782. Entering the state near Bennington, it traveled northeastward and crossed the Connecticut into New Hampshire at Weathersfield. So much of the state is sparsely settled that tornadoes generally strike and pass unnoticed.

The Weather Bureau reports that 75 percent of the state's tornadoes occur between May 13 and September 15. This is the summer tourist season, so it is probably just as well that most of them are not observed. Nearly 80 percent occur between 2 and 7 P.M. June, before the tourists arrive, and July, when they are here, are the peak months. Average arrival time is 5–6 P.M.

Vermont has reported thunderstorms in all twelve months — even December — but the 20–30 storms a year usually occur between late spring and early fall. Rarely are thunderstorms attended by hail. When hail occurs it is generally confined to a small area.

Little data is available on the number of days of sunshine but an average of 50 percent places Vermont's occurrence of sunshine below that of St. Petersburg, Florida, but higher than St. Petersburg, Russia.

5

Wildlife and Plants

VERMONT'S mammals, past and present, range from the mastodon (prehistoric elephant) to the pigmy shrew weighing less than a one-cent piece. Elk, woodland caribou, moose and apparently the panther have vanished from the state. Black bear and deer are the only remaining so-called big game.

Bats: There are 2000 separate species of bats in the world but only the eastern, little brown, red and silver-haired are usually found in Vermont.

Cats: The panther, also known as the mountain lion, puma, cougar, catamount and painter, is occasionally reported to roam the state but the last catamount known to have been killed within the state was taken about 1900. The Boston Museum of Science offers $100 reward for concrete evidence of any catamount in Vermont or any New England state. Other Vermont cats include the Canadian lynx and the bobcat (bay lynx or wildcat).

Shrews: pigmy, masked, water, short-tailed.

Weasels: short-tailed weasel, marten, fisher, mink, striped skunk and wolverine (rare).

The coyote is returning to northern Vermont.

Red foxes are plentiful.

Squirrels: red (spruce), gray, eastern chipmunk and woodchuck (groundhog).

Mice and rats: white-footed mice, bog lemmings, meadow vole (mice), red-banded vole, pine vole, Norway rat, house mice, woodland mice and muskrats.

The beaver has come back in Vermont to such an extent that its dams frequently flood roads and pastures.

The porcupine is too familiar to Long Trail travelers. It gnaws sweaty axe handles and chews up huts and cabins.

The varying hare (snowshoe rabbit) is a favorite small game animal.

Deer: the whitetail deer, aside from domesticated cattle and horses, is Vermont's most plentiful hoofed critter. The whitetail and black bear are the state's only legal big game animals. Indiscriminately slaughtered for more than a century, the deer was considered extinct by 1865 when a ban was placed on deer hunting. Seventeen deer, purchased with private funds, were released in Rutland County in 1878. Deer hunting was legalized in 1898. There has been a deer season ever since. Except for a special one-day season in 1961 it has been illegal to shoot does — or bucks with horns less than three inches long — since 1920. The annual legal deer harvest is about 12,000. Many game biologists urge an annual season on does. The latter have been protected for so many years that there is now an unbalanced and unhealthy ratio between does and bucks. During severe winters, like that of 1962–63, there is not sufficient food for all the state's deer. Biologists noted that in 1963, two years after the one-day doe season, there were plenty of young fawns. This indicated that an excessive number of does were not killed on the one-day season. In the late summer and fall of 1965 orchardists in southern Vermont complained that the deer were "too damn plentiful" in that they were destroying crops.

Fish and Game Department officials and biologists hope that the legislature will eventually give the department permission to set the deer season and establish biologically sound regulations.

FISH

Nearly all north temperate zone fresh-water fish are found in Vermont. There are several kinds of trout: speckled (brook), lake (longe), golden (indigenous to Lake Averill), and three introduced varieties — rainbow, brown and landlocked salmon. It is to the propagation and protection of the trout, or *salmonidae,* that the Fish and Game Service, through its hatcheries and rearing pools, has devoted its chief energies for several years. Other important game and food fishes in Vermont waters include the wall-eyed pike, pickerel, catfish (bullpout), perch and bass.

TREES AND PLANTS

Trees are scenically and economically the most important Vermont plants. Most ancient are the conifers, of which 15 varieties are found. The most valuable commercially is the white pine, depicted on the state seal. The red spruce is the most abundant and valuable spruce. It is largely responsible for the dark green of Vermont's wooded mountains. Common deciduous trees include: several varieties of maple, elm, birch, oak, hickory, ash, cherry, and butternut.

There are 81 distinct fern species in Vermont. Mount Mansfield and nearby Smuggler's Notch are the best territory for these plants. Here, as early as 1807, Pursh discovered the graceful shield fern called Braun's holly fern (*Aspidium aculeatum braunii*); and about seventy years later the botanist Pringle, in an intensive survey of the region, discovered three other species of fern not previously found in this country. Many interesting varieties of fern also grow on the limestone cliffs in the western part of the state. In the southern part of Rutland County, ferns are gathered on a commercial scale and stored in refrigeration for winter use.

There are 130 species of the grass family and 192 of the sedge family in Vermont. The former group is valuable for fodder; the latter, in general, is not. Both groups include many remarkably graceful varieties that approach the beauty of ferns.

Of the flower-producing plants found in the state, no enumeration can be attempted here, though careful botanical studies of Vermont's flora may be consulted in any good Vermont library. There are 1482 species, classified under 481 genera and 101 families. More than half the species are included in a relatively few families: the conifers, grasses, and sedges, already mentioned; the orchid family, whose 43 species include the beautiful lady's-slipper; the rose family, of which there are more than 80 species; the pea family, whose 46 species include the various types of clover; the heath family, which includes the arbutus and several of our edible berries; and the buttercup family, which includes the springtime anemone and the marsh marigold or cowslip.

Many Vermont floral species have a state-wide distribution; others are found in limited areas. About 30 species grow only on the summits of mountains; about fifty only in swampy bogs. There is in general a considerable difference between the flora of eastern and western Vermont, due to the lower altitude and clay and calcareous soils of the Champlain Valley and to the fact that many species have apparently been unable to cross the barrier of the central range of the Green Mountains.

6

Eskimos and Indians

THAT Vermont may once have been the home of Eskimos will come as no surprise to those Vermonters who have survived winters with minimum temperatures ranging well below those usually encountered by Eskimos now resident along the Arctic coast of Canada, Greenland and Alaska.

Traces of alleged Eskimo culture have been found in several places. Similar traces have been found in other portions of New England, New York and Quebec Province south of the St. Lawrence River.

The next Vermonters — like the Eskimos, also migrants from Asia — were the Pre-Algonkians. (?? B.C.–2000 B.C. ?). Whale-tail ceremonial artifacts have been unearthed along Otter Creek. Pre-Algonkian fish lures and sinkers have been found in the vicinity of Hubbardton village. The Pre-Algonkian people were pushed out of Vermont by the "Old Algonkians."

The Old Algonkians (2000 B.C.–A.D. 1300) left pottery and hunting and fishing implements in Vermont and in every other state east of the Mississippi River and north of the Carolina-Tennessee region.

Some of the best Old Algonkian artifacts were found in 1933–34 near Orwell. Others were found near Swanton in the 1870's. The late John Huden, a student of Vermont Indian lore, suggested that "further archaeological research would reveal many other Old Algonkian and Pre-Algonkian sites in Vermont."

RECENT ALGONKIANS

The recent Algonkians (A.D. 1200–1790) and the Iroquois Confederacy were the Indians encountered by Vermont discoverer Samuel de Champlain.

The Algonkians were the largest, though loosely knit, American Indian group. Algonkians lived in an area roughly bounded by Newfoundland and the Shining Mountains (the Rockies) and from Canada's Churchill River to Pamlico Sound in the Carolinas. It is reported that the various subgroups or tribes from the different regions could understand each other's language.

The Abnakis (Abenakis, Quabenaki, Waubanakee, etc.) were a truly small tribe living in Maine between the Saco and St. John rivers. Abnaki reportedly means "People of the East" or "Dawn People." Abnaki, however, became the general term for all Algonkians living in northern Vermont, New Hampshire and Maine. Their known Vermont range was along Lake Champlain from Otter Creek, or possibly Chimney Point, north to Missisquoi Bay; along the Connecticut River from the present Canadian boundary south to Ottauquechee River; in the vicinity of Lakes Bomoseen and Memphremagog.

The Mohicans (Mahicans) called variously "Wolf People," "People of the Ebbing Tide" or "River Folk," long resident in the Hudson River Valley, were dispersed during the 1600's by the advent of the Dutch and English. The Mohawks (sometimes confused with Mohicans) drove the Mohicans from the Hudson northeastward into the Hoosic Valley. Mohicans settled around Pownal, West Arlington, Fair Haven, Lake Bomoseen, Lake Hortonia. Some settled at the mouth of the Winooski and about Missisquoi Bay.

The Obom Sawin (Bomaseens or Bomzeens) were a small band of Algonkians, either Maine Abnakis or Mohicans (possibly a mixture of both) who lived around Lake Hortonia and Lake Bomoseen. Chief Bomoseen had lived in what is now Norridgewock, Maine.

IROQUOIS

The "People of the Long House" or "People of the Extended Lodge" — Iroquois to the white man — had settled in central and eastern New York by 1550. The people of the Five Nations (six after 1712) included: Cayugas (Swamp Dwellers), Mohawks (Wolves), Onondagas (We of the Hills), Oneidas (Beacon Rock People) and Senecas (Stone People). Confederation members spoke a similar but not identical language. The Five Nations became the Six Nations when the Tuscaroras migrated from the Carolinas to join their Iroquois kinsmen in about 1712.

New York State was the focal point of Iroquois settlement and rule but these able warriors, through the competent use of bow and tomahawk together with first-rate chiefs and strategists, once dominated nearly all New England, and along the Atlantic seaboard to the Carolinas and inland to Mississippi.

ADDER VS. ALGONKIAN

"Iroquois" is an Algonkian epithet meaning "real adder" or the Snake People.

The Algonkian-Iroquois feud resulting in the French-Algonkian *vs.* the English-Iroquois coalition eventually meant the end of New France.

The exact origin of the Algonkian-Iroquois feud is unknown. When in 1535 Jacques Cartier first visited Hochelaga, later Mount Royal or Montreal, Iroquois occupied the area. Seventy-four years later when Samuel de Champlain arrived the Algonkians had replaced the Iroquois. The two great Indian units were engaged in bitter warfare. Champlain's reluctant assistance to his Algonkian allies placed the Iroquois squarely on the British side in the 150-year-long fight for domination of the continent.

Both Algonkian and Iroquois used Vermont as a hunting ground and at least as a temporary residence. The Algonkians eventually won. Vermont Indian students Daniel Pierce Thompson and Rowland Robinson noted that the Indian names of geomorphological features are Algonkian.

INDIAN TRAILS

Vermont, during the seventeenth century and first six decades of the eighteenth century, was notable as an Indian route rather than a residence. Sporadic settlement attempts by the French, Dutch and English failed. Only a few Indians lived here during this bloody era. Vernon, in the southeastern corner, was the home of some Squakheags whose principal village was Northfield, Massachusetts. Chief Gray Lock, of the Waranokes along the Bay State's Westfield River, moved his people to Montreal and then to Missisquoi Bay. He became the terror of the northern Massachusetts frontier. Bay Staters were so impressed with this able Indian fighter that they later named their state's highest peak in his honor.

Major Indian trails crossing Vermont were originally used by Iroquois and Algonkians to visit or raid Massachusetts and Hudson or Mohawk River Indians. After the advent of the white man, the trails were primarily used for raiding English settlements. The English, on rare occasions, used the same trails for pursuing captive-laden raiders or for scouting expeditions against the French in Montreal.

The main trail overland led from Indian villages around Montreal to the Richelieu River, then up Lake Champlain past Alburg, Isle La Motte, South Hero and Colchester Point. Here the raiders could canoe up the Winooski and then portage to the headwaters of one of the several major streams leading into the Connecticut. This route was known to the Massachusetts settlers as the "French Trail."

Some raiders continued up Lake Champlain to Thompson's Point (Ferrisburg) and thence up the Otter. The "Wantasiquet Path" was a portage over the Green Mountains from the Otter to the West River and then down to the Connecticut near Fort Dummer (Brattleboro).

Other travelers canoed up the Otter to its Mill River tributary and then portaged over the Mountains to the Black River and down to the Connecticut River near Ascutney. This was the "Ascutney Trail."

Raiders or travelers to the Mohawk Valley continued past Thompson's Point and Chimney Point and then over to the future site of Fort Carillion (called by the English, Fort Ticonderoga). It was a short portage to Lake George (the French had a more romantic and beautiful name: Lac St. Sacrement). The Kayadrosseras Trail ran from the foot of Lake George to the Mohawk River near Amsterdam via Glen Falls. "Kayadrosseras" may have been the English corruption of the Iroquois term "Caniade ro seras," meaning "lakes linked together."

THE DEERFIELD RAID

The winter of 1704 was one of the coldest experienced along the northern Massachusetts frontier. Neither cold nor deep snow kept Major Hertel de Rouville with 200 French soldiers and 140 Christian Indians from raiding Deerfield, Massachusetts. The Deerfield Raid was one of the most famous and successful raids ever made by Indians against white settlements.

Most of Deerfield was burned. Forty-nine residents including two children of the Reverend John Williams, one of New England's leading Congregationalist clergymen, were killed. One hundred and nineteen captives were taken. Not all prisoners reached Montreal. Preacher Williams' wife was tomahawked a few days' travel from Deerfield. Babies were an impediment to travel. An Indian picked up Williams' few weeks old baby and bashed its head against a tree. Wolves were the undertakers.

The returning raiders split into two groups at the confluence of the White and Connecticut Rivers. The Reverend Mr. Williams' detachment walked over the frozen White River to the First Branch, crossed the height of land, then went down the Stevens Branch to the Winooski and out to Lake Champlain and down the lake to Canada. The "Long Walk" from Deerfield to Canada took about four weeks.

(The Stevens Branch was named after a disappointed lover whose body was found along its banks by twelve-year-old Daniel Pierce Thompson, a century after the Deerfield Raid).

Williams, his young sons Stephen and Samuel were later exchanged and returned home to Deerfield. His daughter Eunice, aged seven or eight at the time of her capture, was converted to Catholicism and later married an Indian. The Reverend Mr. Williams had his tribulations but out of this Harvardman's captivity and sorrow came *The Redeemed Captive Returning to Zion.* It is one of the best accounts ever written by a former Indian captive.

Vermont, like Kentucky, could have been well called "Kan-tu-kee" or "Dark and bloody ground."

LAST DAYS OF THE REDMAN

Vermont's first settlers, other than those at Fort Dummer, had no Indian troubles until the Revolution when British-financed Tories and Indians raided Neshobe (now Brandon) and Royalton.

In 1960 thirty Indians were living in Vermont. This represented a substantial decrease from the fifty-seven listed in the 1950 census. The late President Calvin Coolidge, hardly a braggart, was fond of pointing out that he had Indian as well as Yankee blood.

7

Historical Highlights

SAMUEL DE CHAMPLAIN (1567–1635), the French explorer, was the first white man known to have seen any part of the country that now comprises the state of Vermont. This was in 1609, when, coming from Canada, he went up the long lake that now bears his name and with his Algonkian allies engaged in successful battle with the Iroquois. By incurring then the undying enmity of the latter tribe, Champlain paradoxically laid the basis for the ultimate loss of French control of the region at the same time that he temporarily established it. For the proud Iroquois never forgave the nation that first humiliated them with "white man's lightning," and they relentlessly pursued the French along the "Great Warpath" — between the Hudson and the St. Lawrence — until the latter bowed in ultimate defeat to the British a century and a half later.

The first attempted settlement within the limits of the present state was also French and of a military nature, though motivated in part by religious zeal. In 1666, Captain La Mothe built a fort and a shrine to Sainte Anne on Isle La Motte in Lake Champlain, but the settlement was short-lived. In 1690, Captain Jacobus de Warm and a party from Albany, New York, established an outpost at what is now Chimney Point, in Addison Township, but this settlement ended with the military emergency that had brought it into being. Throughout the seventeenth and well into the eighteenth century, Vermont was a no man's land, a passageway for French and Indian raiding parties seeking to harass the English settlements to the south and east. Furthermore, lying as it did between the two great natural water routes of the northeast, the Connecticut River and Lake Champlain, the territory possessed a strategic importance that was early recognized.

SETTLEMENT

To protect its western settlements, Massachusetts, in 1724, established Fort Dummer, near present Brattleboro, the site being a part of the "Equivalent Lands," the soil but not the jurisdiction of which Massachusetts had ceded to Connecticut in 1715 in return for lands already settled by Massachusetts that a new survey had located in Connecticut. This is accepted as the first permanent settlement on Vermont soil; the first one in or near which white men have lived continuously from its founding to the present day. In 1731, France built a fort at Crown Point and a small village opposite on the Vermont side, but though extensive grants were allotted, the French made little attempt at the actual settlement of the region, all claims to which they formally relinquished to Great Britain by treaty in 1763.

The British monarchs, however, did not await this formality before granting with royal largess the land that is now Vermont. In fact, the clouded and turbulent early history of this state and the very methods by which it became an independent territorial unit and then a state were dependent not upon the fact that the land had not been granted, but rather upon the fact that it had been granted too many times; in terms of maddening ambiguity; by kings and governors who knew not what they were giving; and often to land speculators who cared little under whose jurisdiction their grants lay. In the commission which King George issued to Benning Wentworth as governor of New Hampshire on July 3, 1741, the New Hampshire territory was defined as extending "due West Cross the said River [Merrimack] till it meets with our other governments." But the eastern limits of the Province of New York had never been publicly proclaimed by the King. As Timothy Walker said in 1778: "The King had never told his Governor of New Hampshire, in express terms, how far west he should go, and there stop, nor his Governor of New York how far east he should go and then cease." But Governor Benning Wentworth was a shrewd, aggressive man, whose policy was always to go as far as possible in any direction in the interests of himself and his province. On September 6, 1744, the Crown, acting upon a report of the Privy Council that "the same is now within the District of New Hampshire," had ordered the Governor of New Hampshire to move the Assembly to provide for the maintenance of Fort Dummer, which was west of the Connecticut River. He therefore assumed — not without expectations of being challenged — that the Province of New Hampshire extended as far westward as did Massachusetts and Connecticut. On that assumption he granted on January 3, 1749 (O.S.), to himself and several of his Portsmouth neighbors, the town of Bennington, the western border of which was an extension north of the line between Massachusetts and New York. Governor George Clinton of New York soon informed Governor Wentworth that he was making grants outside his jurisdiction, since the great grant made in 1664 by Charles II to his brother James, Duke of York, expressly included "all the land

from the west side of the Conectecutte River to the East side of
De la Ware Bay." He added that Connecticut's western border had
been fixed where it was long ago to the satisfaction of both parties, but
that Massachusetts' claims, like New Hampshire's, rested on "intru-
sion." Governor Wentworth, in reply, suggested that the matter be
referred to the Crown, His Majesty's decision to be final for both
parties, and Governor Clinton agreed. Wentworth continued, however,
to make grants in what is now Vermont to the number of sixteen
before 1754, though none so far west as Bennington. In 1754, war
with France broke out; the Vermont territory was again open to
invasion from the north and was not in demand; and the whole matter
rested.

WENTWORTH CARRIES ON

After the capture of Ticonderoga and Crown Point by the British in
1759, Governor Wentworth continued his grants, making as many as
sixty in one year, until he had ultimately portioned out a very large
part of what is now Vermont, then known as the New Hampshire
Grants. The King and his Council were slow to act, though frequently
besought by clever New York spokesmen; but at last, in his famous
order of July 20, 1764, His Majesty declared "the Western Banks of
the River Connecticut to be the Boundary Line between the said two
Provinces of New Hampshire and New York." Thereupon New York
immediately assumed that "to be" was retroactive, declared all of
Wentworth's grants to be null and void, and began to make new
grants to new grantees of lands already held under the New Hampshire title. The dynamite, fifteen years in the mixing, was now ready.

The King's decision was not known in the disputed territory until
the summer of 1765. From that time until the battle of Lexington,
the future state of Vermont was the scene of an important part of
Colonial history that has been much romanticized and much misun-
derstood, especially in its motives. The settlers on the New Hampshire
Grants were fearful for their land titles and in most instances unable
to repurchase them by payment of additional fees to New York. Many
of them were deeply in debt and about to lose their hard-won possessions by legal processes anyway. For this reason the first outbreaks of
actual violence against New York consisted of the breaking up of the
Cumberland County Court at Windsor in 1770, and armed resistance
to a sheriff's posse at Bennington in 1771. The seizure of the courthouse at Westminster by one hundred armed men on March 13, 1775,
resulting in the death of two of the rebels, has been extravagantly

called the Westminster Massacre. It has also been designated the first engagement of the American Revolution by persons who failed to understand that the insurrection was against the authority and practice of the Province of New York, not against the British Crown, to which, as a matter of fact, the insurgents were in the very process of making a direct appeal.

GREEN MOUNTAIN BOYS

On the western side of the state, resistance to New York authority was more widespread, better organized, and even bolder. Here the "Green Mountain Boys," organized by Ethan Allen in 1770–71, persistently harassed and persecuted grantees of land in Vermont under New York title and even carried their depredations into the Province of New York itself. There was little of the heroic in these attacks, usually rendered safe by surprise and numbers. That most of the men in these groups thought themselves wronged is understandable, but they were aggressive outlaws from the only duly constituted government in the Colonies at that time. Nevertheless, the fact that there was a closely knit fighting group in this region, ready to respond at a minute's notice to the call of rousing if not always disinterested leaders, was one so fortuitously auspicious to the Colonial cause in the immediately ensuing struggle that posterity has not been entirely wrong in glossing over the real reasons for its being there.

Between 1765 and 1775 there had been, on both sides of the state, several conventions, the records of which are unfortunately incomplete, made up of delegates chosen from the Committees of Safety in the various towns. The most significant of these conventions was the so-called fourth Cumberland County Convention at Westminster on April 11, 1775; for it was there that the delegates voted to petition the Crown of England for a new and separate province and designated a committee to prepare the petition. The fact that this committee never functioned was due to the receipt of some startling news from a little place called Lexington, Massachusetts.

"AWAY WITH THE LOBSTERBACKS"

The American Revolution had begun. The inhabitants of the New Hampshire Grants ceased their hostile actions against New York and, for a time at least, lost most of their hostile feeling. Not to have done so would have considerably retarded the Colonial cause and might have altered the subsequent history of the state.

On May 10, 1775, less than a month after Lexington and Concord, Ethan Allen, who had been joined by Benedict Arnold, crossed Lake Champlain with eighty-three followers and captured Fort Ticonderoga, at that time the largest and most impregnable fortification in this country, without resistance from a sleeping British force of not more than fifty men. (Seventeen years earlier four thousand Frenchmen under Montcalm had successfully repelled sixteen thousand British assailants.) It was utterly in keeping with the man — and the most zealous debunkers have not been able to establish proof to the contrary — that Allen should have demanded the fort's surrender "In the name of the Great Jehovah and the Continental Congress" — "in spite of the fact," as a later critic has said, "that he held a commission from neither source." The capture of Ticonderoga, followed on the 12th by the taking of the fort at Crown Point by Seth Warner, deprived the British of what, properly garrisoned, might have been an important northern base during the ensuing struggle; and it supplied Washington with nearly one hundred and fifty cannons by means of which he was able to drive the British from Boston the next winter; but its most important result was the thrill that ran through all the Colonies at the news of it and that made it one of the major factors in turning a local Massachusetts affray into a united American cause.

LONE PINE REPUBLIC

The idea of making a separate state of the New Hampshire Grants occurred to many individuals long before it was mentioned in any official document. But it was certain to gain wider favor when the national Declaration of Independence, of July 4, 1776, abrogated all allegiance to Great Britain. The New Hampshire Grants were no longer a part of New York, many of their inhabitants argued, since the grant of 1664 by Charles II was now nullified. A continuation of this line of reasoning would also have rendered null the township grants under Benning Wentworth and left the territory, governmentally speaking, in that "state of nature" in which one of its spokesmen maintained it actually to be. There were many, however, and among them some of the ablest men in the Grants, especially in the eastern townships, who sincerely believed that it was both unfair and unwise to wage a separate fight for independence from New York at a time when all the Colonies were engaged — or should have been — in winning their common independence from a common enemy. But the aggressive faction prevailed and, as when any bold venture meets with lasting success, made heroes of its leaders.

In treating this early period of Vermont history, it is often impossible to learn the absolute truth, for the truth rests not in documents and records, but in the collective mental and emotional reactions of the men and women of Vermont at that time. These reactions were never completely unified, were frequently the result of misunderstanding and personal motives, and can never be entirely recaptured. History can be too realistically as well as too romantically written. Most histories of Vermont have erred not in making its founders and early leaders heroes — that they surely were — but in making them perfect ones. Vermont's early history, in the form familiar to "every schoolboy," consists of a small group of glamorous incidents including the Green Mountain Boys' defense of their land titles against the threat of the Yorkers, the indomitable Ethan Allen's capture of Ticonderoga, and the crucial battle of Bennington, which affected Saratoga, which in turn determined the fate of the nation. If these passages of Vermont history appear to some to be understressed in this brief account, it is not because their importance is not recognized, but rather because that importance is so universally known and accepted that it has seemed wiser to attempt to delineate broadly the background and moving causes than merely to assert it again.

In a series of conventions (none of them wholly representative) the ideas of independence were gradually articulated. Dr. Thomas Young, then of Philadelphia, a shrewd, learned, and liberal man, convinced those interested in forming a new State that they would be admitted to representation in the general Congress as soon as they had done so. It was Young also who by addressing these men as "the inhabitants of Vermont" caused that name to be adopted, in June, 1777, though Verd-Mont had been suggested several years before as a suitable name for the region. A final impetus to secession was given by the publication, on April 22, 1777, of the new Constitution of New York State, which, in a number of ways, was extremely distasteful to an overwhelmingly large majority of the men on the New Hampshire Grants, including many who up to that time had been stubbornly loyal.

At last, in Windsor, in a convention that lasted six days, July 2–8, 1777, seventy-odd delegates asserted again the independence of Vermont (the state had declared its independence the previous January at Westminster) and unanimously adopted a constitution for the state's government. It is unlikely that this task would have been completed had not a violent thunderstorm, following close upon the receipt of the news on July 8 of the evacuation of Ticonderoga, forced the convention to remain in Windsor long enough for a final reading and acceptance of the draft of the constitution. It is even less likely that the work of this convention would have been accomplished, in the face of danger from Burgoyne's rapidly approaching army, had its delegates known that on June 30 the petition and aspirations to statehood of the New Hampshire Grants had been peremptorily if not contemptuously rejected by the Continental Congress.

From July 8, 1777, to March 4, 1791, Vermont was a completely independent but tottering republic. Many within the confines of the new country, especially in the southeastern part, refused to recognize its authority and remained stubbornly loyal to New York. Another cause of dissension and ill feeling was the annexation of sixteen towns in western New Hampshire whose inhabitants desired them to become a part of Vermont. The annexation was not permanent.

The first general election in the new republic was held March 3, 1778; the General Assembly convened March 12 to count the votes for state officers; and the next day — Friday the 13th — the government was inaugurated, with Governor Chittenden at its head. Ethan Allen was not more perfectly suited to lead the men of Vermont under arms than was Thomas Chittenden to be the head of its body politic. For eighteen years this unlearned, uneloquent, informal one-eyed giant of a man governed the people of this state, most of whom felt, with Ethan Allen, that Tom Chittenden was bound to be right even when he couldn't tell why.

The idea of ultimate union with the other thirteen states was in the mind of most Vermonters from the time when statehood was first achieved. Those states, however, had more urgent matters to consider, and were, furthermore, antagonized by Vermont's revolt from New York authority during such crucial times and by the fact that, valuable as its services had been at Ticonderoga, Crown Point, Hubbardton, and Bennington, the state had taken almost no aggressive part in the later stages of the Revolution, although it maintained and garrisoned a series of forts within its own borders as a northern line of defense. So withdrawn was Vermont from the struggle — and the struggle from Vermont — that the British actually approached some of its leaders in an attempt to align the state with their cause and make it a Crown dependency. But while there were many Tories in Vermont, as elsewhere, they certainly never constituted a majority of the population; and later historians have seen in its passive and ambiguous attitude a conscious and extremely strategic policy by which the British were restrained from launching through its territory an offensive against the Colonies to the south. Vermont maintained its independence for nearly fourteen years, longer, in fact, than it desired to, and during that time it performed the acts of a sovereign government, including issuing bills of credit, coining money, regulating weights and measures, establishing post offices, naturalizing citizens of other states and countries, and corresponding with foreign governments.

THE 14TH STAR

The story of the admission of Vermont into the Union is one of long delays and mutual misunderstandings. Vermont was led to believe that it would be admitted long before it was, and each disappointment strengthened its feeling of independence and endangered the balance of the chip on its shoulder. George Washington seriously believed that it would be necessary to subdue Vermont with arms, as his long and justly famous letter of February 11, 1783, to the President of Congress makes clear. Happily Washington was for once wrong. Vermont steadily gained the friendly confidence of neighboring states. The ancient dispute with New York over land grants was settled forever in 1790 for $30,000. Vermont ratified and adopted the Constitution of the United States at Bennington in January, 1791. And on March 4 of the same year, Congress unanimously passed an act for the admission of Vermont into the Union as the fourteenth state and the first one to be added to the original thirteen. Vermont's little home-built Ship of State — buffeted by storms beyond its control, endangered by dissension and even mutiny among the crew, sometimes unwisely but always daringly manned — was safe in harbor at last. Vermont has retained and maintained in significant ways its own inviolable identity, but the most distinctive as well as the most tempestuous period of its history ended when it became one of the United States of America.

PROGRESS (1790–1812)

In the thirty years since 1760, Vermont had developed from a wilderness inhabited by 300 people to a sovereign state with a population of 85,425. The two decades following its admission to the Union brought the greatest increase in population that the state has ever known: from 85,425 in 1790 to 154,465 in 1800 to 217,895 in 1810. No other northern or eastern state showed so large an increase by percentage during this period. Many of the new immigrants came, as in the earliest days, from southern New England. The country was still largely agricultural, and Vermont seemed to offer an opportunity somewhat similar to that presented by the West at a later period. For this reason many of the newcomers settled in the relatively undeveloped northern sections of the state.

During the same two decades six new counties and fifty-one townships were settled. By 1810 the state had assumed very much the geographical division that obtains today, with the exception of a few towns and Lamoille County, which was created in 1835. The constitution underwent its last general revision in 1793, the permanent capital was established at Montpelier in 1805, and a State House was built there in 1808. The University of Vermont was opened in 1800, and the first bank was chartered in 1806.

In this period of general stabilization and creation of institutions necessary for a socially as well as a politically independent State, Vermont also achieved the highest degree of economic self-sufficiency that it has ever known. The Embargo Act that preceded the War of 1812 stimulated the establishment of more small factories, mills, and forges than can ever exist here again under modern methods of production and distribution. In 1810, for example, there were one hundred and twenty-five distilleries in the state; in 1850 there were none.

WAR OF 1812

With the declaration of war against Great Britain in 1812, Vermont again became a frontier State to a hostile country. An invasion of this country from Canada — and one seemed inevitable — was to be anticipated through Vermont. Panic seized the inhabitants of the northern part of the state, and frenzied preparations were made to resist an attack. In this crisis Vermonters reverted more or less to the attitude that had been forced upon them during the Revolution. Late in 1813, Governor Martin Chittenden, son of the first governor, issued a proclamation ordering the Vermont Militia stationed at Plattsburgh to return home, declaring: "the military strength and resources of this State must be reserved for its own defence and protection exclusively excepting in cases provided for by the Constitution of the U. States; and then under orders only from the Commander-in-chief." As a result of this proclamation, resolutions were introduced into the National Congress requesting the Attorney General of the United

States to institute prosecution against Governor Chittenden, but they were tabled.

Much less easy to condone than an imperfect conception of the responsibilities of union was the wholesale smuggling which was carried on between Vermont and Canada and which federal officers, despite several violent affrays, were unable to halt. In 1814, Sir George Prevost, Governor General of Canada, reported: "two-thirds of the army in Canada are at this moment eating beef provided by American contractors, drawn principally from the States of Vermont and New York." And General Izard of the American army reported to the Secretary of War: "were it not for these supplies [Vermont cattle] the British forces in Canada would soon be suffering from famine."

Oddly enough, however, it was as the base of the naval activities of Macdonough's fleet on Lake Champlain that Vermont was most vitally involved in this struggle. The "poor forlorn looking squadron" chose Shelburne as winter quarters in 1812–13. After an unsuccessful engagement the next June and two British raids by water on Burlington and Swanton in August, Macdonough chose the small city of Vergennes, on the navigable Otter Creek, as the place in which to winter (1813–14), and above all to add to, his fleet. In the yards at Vergennes new ships, of Vermont timber, were constructed in record time: ships without which the decisive battle of Plattsburg, which gave America control of Lake Champlain as completely as Perry's victory had given it control of Lake Erie, could not have been won in the following September. This battle saved Vermont from immediate British occupation, and Vermonters appropriately played an important part in the land engagement that accompanied the naval victory. The state had redeemed itself — if it can be called redemption to have rendered, however tardily, wholehearted support to what Woodrow Wilson termed a "clumsy, foolhardy, haphazard war."

SOCIAL FERMENT (1815–1861)

The year 1816, "the famine year," or "eighteen hundred and froze to death," brought the greatest physical hardships that the inhabitants of this state as a whole have ever known. On June 8 a foot of snow fell and blew into drifts two and three feet high. There was a little snow in July and August and a heavy frost on September 10. Almost no crops were harvested that fall. Much of the livestock in the state perished, the hay crop having failed. Nettles, wild turnips, hedgehogs, and other crude substitutes for ordinary fare kept all but a few of the human inhabitants from starvation, but the suffering was so intense that the year proved a vital factor in greatly increasing the emigration from Vermont to the lands of promise in the West, particularly Ohio — an exodus that was duplicated in all the New England states.

Beginning in the 1820's, the Anti-Masonic movement colored and disturbed the political and emotional life of Vermont to an almost incredible extent. Not limited to this state, it was more dominant here than anywhere else in this part of the country, and Caledonia County was the acknowledged center of the movement in New England. Masons were excluded from jury service and town offices, Masonic clergymen were driven from their pulpits, and members of families were irrevocably alienated from one another. In 1831 Governor Palmer was elected on an Anti-Masonic ticket and was re-elected in the three succeeding years. In 1832, Vermont was the only state to cast its votes for the Anti-Masonic presidential candidate, William Wirt. Many Masons withdrew from the order, and in 1834 all the lodges in Washington and Windham Counties were voluntarily dissolved by their members. The Burlington *Sentinel* (1835) charged that, Anti-Masonry being about to expire, its supporters were preparing to leap upon "the hobby of anti-slavery." Again in 1837, Senator Wright of New York, a former Vermonter, in a long letter addressed to the people of this state, expressed apprehension that the distraction of Anti-Masonry would be succeeded "by some other exciting topic or political hobby, like Anti-Slavery or modern Abolitionism." It may be true that the training in agitation afforded by this earlier fury contributed appreciably to the persistence and effectiveness of the later crusade. But the hatred of slavery in Vermont, which never ceased to grow in intensity during the next twenty-five years, was not bounded by party lines and sprang from a belief too deep-rooted and long-cherished to be rightly called a hobby.

It was the desire of Vermonters during the earliest years of this period to check the further growth of slavery rather than to abolish it. In 1837, resolutions by the Vermont Legislature were presented to the National Senate protesting against the annexation of Texas and, further, "against the admission into the Union of any State whose Constitution tolerates domestic slavery." Senator King of Alabama called these resolutions "an infamous libel on, and an insult to, the South." Calhoun, in a personal letter, referred to the Vermont Resolutions as "the first move from a State" and "a new and bold move from a higher quarter." Congress responded to these and similar resolutions by passing the famous "Gag Laws," which seemed to Vermonters to violate the sacred right of petition. In his address to the 1844 legislature Governor Slade maintained that the annexation of Texas would constitute "a new Union" and one with which Vermont should "have no connection."

THE MEXICAN WAR

Vermonters had little enthusiasm for the Mexican War, feeling as they did that it was being fought to add slave territory to the country. On June 1, 1846, Governor Slade proclaimed, "the voluntary service of those who may be disposed to engage in this war will be accepted to an extent sufficient to form one battalion of five companies of infantry," which must certainly be one of the faintest calls to arms ever officially issued. Not all Vermonters were so lukewarm, however. Truman Ransom resigned the presidency of Norwich University to become a major in, and later lieutenant colonel in command of, the Ninth Regiment. He was killed at Chapultepec, at the capture of which two members of the single Vermont company, Sergeant Major Fairbanks and Captain Kimball, were the first to reach the roof of the Bishop's Palace and lower the Mexican colors.

Some Vermonters, including Regular Army career officers, received their pre–Civil War combat training during the Mexican affair. Major General Ethan Allen Hitchcock was one of the Mexican War's ablest general officers. Bennington native Colonel Martin Scott died while leading his troops. Benjamin S. Roberts became a brigadier general during the Civil War as did Seminole War veteran John W. Phelps of Guilford.

"THE WRATH TO COME"

The Vermont legislature continued to make annual resolutions protesting the practice of slavery and to send copies of them to the legislatures of all the other states. Almost every southern state at one time or another returned equally dogmatic replies, some of which violated dignity if not sobriety. A resolution offered in the Georgia legislature in 1856 proposed to transmit to the governor of Vermont a former pro-slavery resolution enclosed in a leaden bullet, the addition of gunpowder and a coil of rope being later suggested. Another Georgia resolution requested President Pierce to employ enough able-bodied Irishmen to dig a ditch around Vermont and float "the thing" into the Atlantic Ocean. The *Richmond* (Va.) *Enquirer* in 1856

spoke of Vermont as "Always foremost in the path of infamy."
Throughout the nation Vermont became the variously regarded symbol
of an unyielding determination that slavery must be abolished forever
from all parts of the United States.

The abrogation of the Missouri Compromise relative to Nebraska
ruined the Whig Party in the nation, and in 1856 gave control of
Vermont to the new anti-slavery Republican Party, which has dominated it ever since. In the election of 1860 Lincoln received four times
as many votes in Vermont as did Stephen A. Douglas (1813–1861),
though Douglas was the first native-born Vermonter ever to be nominated for the presidency and campaigned in this state in person. Thus
ruthlessly did the people of Vermont subjugate all other emotions and
considerations to upholding what they believed to be the right side of
the cause that was about to disrupt the nation.

BULL RUN TO APPOMATTOX

The Civil War, to many Vermonters, was almost a holy war. It
was a war to end the hated institution of human slavery. The Allen
(after Ethan, of course) Grays of Brandon were one of the first militia
companies in the Union to answer the President's call for volunteers.

The war's northernmost shoot-out occurred October 19, 1864, in St.
Albans when Captain Bennett Young, C.S.A., and twenty-one members of the "Secesh" Army — escapees from Yankee prison camps
and helped no doubt by Copperheads — raided the city. (See ST.
ALBANS.)

At Gettysburg, General George Stannard (1820–1886), born in
Georgia, Vermont, and his 16th Vermont Regiment broke General
George Pickett's gallant charge — the high tide of the Confederacy.

Bethel-born General Stephen Thomas (1809–1903), of the Old
Vermont Brigade, was the hero of Cedar Creek.

Union Cavalry chief "Fighting Phil" Sheridan rode a Vermont-
sired Morgan on his soul-stirring, troop-rallying ride to Winchester.
That was the same day Young's raiders — armed and equipped in
Canada — hit St. Albans.

William Scott, the weary "Sleeping Sentinel" known by every
schoolboy to have been saved from a firing squad by President Lincoln's kindly intervention, was a native Vermonter. Scott, the best-
known Yankee private in the Civil War, was later killed in combat at
Lee's Mill, Virginia.

Stannard, Thomas, Scott and 34,325 other Vermonters entered the

Union Army directly from Vermont. Five thousand, one hundred and twenty-eight Vermonters were killed in action, died from wounds received in battle, from disease or in Rebel prison camps like Libby and Andersonville.

Thousands of native Vermonters enlisted from Michigan, Wisconsin, Ohio or other states to which they had migrated. Vermont contributed $9,323,407 to war funds.

The Reverend Harkness Gray, a native Vermonter and longtime U.S. Senate chaplain, was one of four preachers who officiated at President Lincoln's funeral services.

Vermont sculptor Larkin Mead was selected to design the figures on Lincoln's tomb in Springfield.

Vermonter Charles Tinker, War Department (1861–65) telegrapher, a friend of Lincoln, was the first to tell the President he had been renominated by the Republican Party.

Danville native Thaddeus Stevens, a Pennsylvania congressman, and militant abolitionist leader, sabotaged Lincoln's postwar plans for peacefully restoring the former Confederate states to their rightful place in the union.

DOLDRUMS (1865–1898)

Between 1866 and 1870, Vermont was the base of operations against Canada by the Fenians, the Irish enthusiasts who aimed to take Canada away from the British Empire. Although there was some private sympathy with these ill-organized and abortive Fenian raids, they were, of course, not publicly countenanced or officially approved. (See FRANKLIN.)

Between the Civil and Spanish-American Wars, Vermont remained in a condition that must be called relatively static, if not sluggish. The War Between the States had taken a heavy toll from farms, hamlets, and cities of the men who would have been most energetic in all kinds of private and civic enterprises. The desertion of the hill farms, one of the state's most vital problems until the recent reclamation of many of them as summer homes, was well under way. Sheep raising had ceased to be of real importance in the state's agriculture, and the transition to dairying was progressing slowly. There was no appreciable growth in population.

Vermonters were making history. Senator Justin S. Morrill, with a record of almost forty-four continuous years of service in the House and Senate, conceived and brought to passage the Morrill Act, which through governmental aid led directly to the establishment of our entire present system of state-supported agricultural, scientific, and industrial schools of college rank. Senator George F. Edmunds was the author of the Electoral Commission Bill and the Senate member of the commission established by it that averted what at least threatened to be another civil upheaval over the Hayes-Tilden (1876) election. He was the author of the vital parts of the Sherman Anti-Trust Bill, and his name was twice (1880 and 1884) placed in nomination for the presidency. Judge Luke Poland, who served at various times as a member of both national houses, rendered a great and unique service to his country by making the first revision of the laws of the United States ever attempted. In 1874, Congress accepted without a single amendment or reservation his decisions as to the incompatibility of some of its own enactments that had successively overlapped one another for nearly a century.

In 1880, Chester A. Arthur was elected Vice-President, and upon President Garfield's death in September, 1881, he succeeded to the presidency. He was the first native Vermonter to hold either office. (See FAIRFIELD.)

In 1888, Levi P. Morton, a native Vermonter who had been United States Minister to France under Garfield, was elected Vice-President, with President Benjamin Harrison, in securing whose nomination the Republican delegation from Vermont had taken the lead.

"REMEMBER THE MAINE"

The Spanish-American 1898 summer fracas has been called by some Vermonters — with limited justification — the "Vermont-Spanish War."

The war's two great naval heroes, Commodore George Dewey and Captain Charles Clark, were Montpelier and Bradford natives. The U.S. Army's commanding general in Cuba was potbellied, tough, able General William Shafter, a Michigan native of Vermont-born parents. Major Henry B. Hersey, a peacetime balloonist, was aide to the war's most prominent non-Vermonter, Lieutenant Colonel Theodore Roosevelt. Another Rough Rider was Vermonter Wallace N. Batchelder.

Vermont's U.S. Senator, Colonel Redfield Proctor, marble tycoon, former governor, U.S. Secretary of War under Benjamin Harrison, junketed to Cuba and reported his observations on Spanish despotism in a Senate speech which historian Woodrow Wilson later termed "one of those rare utterances which have really shaped public policies."

Theodore Roosevelt, then Assistant Secretary of the Navy, told Vermonters in 1901, "I knew that when Senator Proctor made that speech, with his influence, there could be but one possible outcome, and the next morning I started to find the quickest way to get to the front."

In late 1897 Roosevelt and Proctor had successfully contrived to get Commodore Dewey, then outranked by seven senior officers, placed in command of the Navy's Asiatic Squadron. Dewey, knowing what was expected of him, made his ships combat-ready.

Meanwhile, the battleship USS *Maine* blew up in Havana Harbor, February 15, 1898; 246 officers and enlisted men were killed. The hero of the occasion was, of course, a Vermonter. Cadet Jonas Hannibal Holden, assistant navigator and Number 1 man in his Annapolis graduating class, took command of Captain Sigbee's gig (small boat) and rescued many shipmates struggling in the water.

War with Spain was declared April 19 and orders were cabled to Dewey at Hong Kong to "Take Manila."

> *Oh! Dewey was the morning*
> *Upon the first of May.*
> *Oh! Dewey was the victor*
> *Down in Manila Bay.*
> *Dewey were those Spaniards' eyes,*
> *Those orbs of black and blue.*
> *Do we feel discouraged?*
> *We do not feel we do.*

Thus in doggerel and Dewey's historic phrase, "You may fire when you are ready, Gridley," is celebrated Dewey's signal victory. The Spanish fleet was sunk, destroyed or captured. Spanish forts at Cavite were tossed in as a bonus. Not one American was killed and no ships were lost or even seriously damaged.

Possibly the most single important event of the war was the 14,900 nautical mile race of Captain George Clark and his battleship the USS *Oregon* from San Francisco to a rendezvous with the American fleet off Cuba. The necessity of Clark's journey down the West Coast of South America, through the raging Strait of Magellan and up the southern continent's East Coast, sounded loud and clear the immediate necessity for a Panama Canal.

The 1st Vermont Volunteer Infantry saw no combat. Mustered into service three days after the declaration of war, troops gathered at Camp Olympia — named after Dewey's flagship — adjacent to Fort Ethan Allen. Troops left Camp Olympia May 21 for Chickamauga Park, Tennessee. They returned to Vermont, August 21. Twenty-seven Vermonters died of illness and disease in Tennessee.

BOXER REBELLION

The brief, bloody Boxer Rebellion of 1900 produced two public heroes; both were Vermonters. The Boxers, a secret Chinese society dedicated to ousting all "foreign dogs," killed the German minister. Foreigners, including American nationals, barricaded themselves in legation compounds at Peking. Nearly 20,000 American, British, French, Japanese and Russian troops marched to relieve the beleagured makeshift garrison.

Colonel Emerson H. Liscum, a Regular Army man who fought through the Civil War, Indian Wars, Spanish-American War — he was brevet brigadier general of volunteers in the Philippine Insurrection — was killed leading his command, 9th U.S. Infantry, in the successful attack on Tientsin.

The first man to scale the high wall at Peking was Private Calvin P. Titus, former boy bugler with Vermont troops in the Spanish-American War. Titus then enlisted in the Regular Army. He was awarded the Congressional Medal of Honor for his inspiring action at Peking and was appointed to West Point.

Today, Old Soldier Titus, living out his sunset years midst honorable, exciting memories in California, is the oldest living Congressional Medal of Honor holder.

TEDDY, TAFT AND THE PROFESSOR

Vice-President Theodore Roosevelt was attending a meeting of the Vermont Fish and Game League on Isle La Motte when he was told President McKinley had been shot in Buffalo. This was but one of many visits the former Rough Rider made to Vermont. Vermonters, in 1904, voted overwhelmingly to return Republican Roosevelt to the White House but in 1912 they gave President Taft — son of Vermont-born Alphonso Taft — an edge of less than 2000 votes.

During the Roosevelt-Taft era many Vermonters were awarded substantial political plums. Iowa's Governor Leslie Shaw, a native Vermonter, was Secretary of the Treasury — Vermonters are frugal — under TR. Rough Rider Roosevelt named Charles H. Darling of Bennington to the President's old seat as Assistant Secretary of the Navy. It was Darling who arranged for Commander Robert E. Peary's leave of absence from the Navy so the Pennsylvanian could make a dash for the North Pole.

The 1904 legislature passed a 5 percent inheritance tax, created a medical and dental registration board and made child labor illegal in mills but not on farms. Most legislators were either farmers or from rural areas.

The 1906 legislature voted to allow women the right to run for town clerk, town treasurer, town superintendent of schools or for trustee of public libraries.

Prohibition was a major Vermont topic for many years prior to the adoption of the unsuccessful 18th Amendment. Local option was Vermont's democratic solution. Liquor sales were permitted in those towns which voted to allow liquor sales. The number of towns approving liquor sales decreased at every election.

The 1905 legislature passed the Perry Prohibition Amendment with a referendum provision attached. Vermont voters in 1906 defeated the proposed Perry Prohibition Amendment by a nearly 2–1 margin. After the 18th Amendment was repealed Vermonters once again voted for local option and this system remains in effect.

Immediately after Mexican bandit Pancho Villa raided Columbus, N.M., President Wilson ordered the mobilization of National Guard units. The 1st Vermont Infantry mustered in at Fort Ethan Allen, June 18, 1916, and entrained for Eagle Pass, Texas, where it arrived July 2. It was the first complete National Guard unit to reach the U.S.–Mexican frontier. The National Guardsmen's pay from the War Department was so low that Governor Gates called a special session of the legislature which voted to pay each soldier an additional $10 a month.

The guardsmen returned to Vermont in late September after having successfully guarded the frontier. Villa was busy elsewhere eluding the pursuing troopers of the Regular Army's 3rd Cavalry from Fort Ethan Allen.

President Woodrow Wilson sometimes summered in Cornish, N.H., but often crossed the Connecticut River through the covered bridge to collect his mail in Windsor. When he took the steamcars for

Washington a few Vermonters gathered at the railroad station to see the Democrat on his way out of the state.

"OVER THERE"

Several weeks before the federal government declared war on Imperial Germany the Vermont legislature appropriated $1,000,000 for war purposes. This act not only won wide acclaim but spared Vermont the financial embarrassment many states later found themselves in.

The War Department refused to let Vermonters serve together as a state unit. About 2000 officers and men of the 1st Vermont Regiment served with the 26th "Yankee Division" and were among the first National Guard troops to engage in combat. Many Vermonters served with the much decorated 101st Ammunition Train. The exact numbers of Vermonters who served in World War I is difficult to determine. Many native Vermonters enlisted in other states while some had enlisted in the Canadian Army as early as 1914. The Adjutant General's Office reported that at least 16,000 Vermonters were in the service and that more than half served overseas. Killed in action and from wounds received in battle: 642.

Burlington native Admiral Henry T. Mayo was Commander-in-Chief of the Atlantic Fleet. The first known native Vermonter reported killed in action was George H. Marchessault of St. Albans who fell May 13, 1915, while serving with His Majesty's Canadian Forces. Corporal Leonard A. Lord of Swanton, killed at Apremont, April 17, 1918, was the first Vermonter to enlist in his native state, to die in action.

"KEEP COOL WITH COOLIDGE"

In 1920, native Vermonter Calvin Coolidge was nominated and elected Vice-President of the United States on the Republican ticket with Warren G. Harding. In August 1923, President Harding died after a short illness, and Coolidge succeeded to the presidency. He was visiting his aged father at his home in Plymouth, Vermont, when the news of Harding's death reached him, and he was sworn into the presidency by his father that night by the light of a kerosene lamp. This scene, so homely and so typically democratic, captured the imagination of the American people as no other connected with the presidency had since the days of Abraham Lincoln. Not since Lincoln, in fact, had there been a President so essentially homespun as Coolidge was. Those commentators who have expressed the belief that Calvin Coolidge's Yankee terseness, simple ways, and oft-repeated love of both the rigors and the beauties of his native state were a part of a sustained political pose are deluded by their own sophistication. In 1924, Coolidge was elected President, the first Vermonter ever to achieve that honor, though Chester A. Arthur, like Coolidge himself, had succeeded to the presidency.

Vermonter Coolidge was the most popular GOP president in American history. Let the record speak: Coolidge in his 1924 race against Democrat John Davis racked up a 2–1 popular vote margin. The popular vote was Coolidge: 15,725,016 — Davis: 8,385,586. Electoral vote, Coolidge: 382 — Davis: 136. Roosevelt's most popular vote percentage was considerably less than dour "Silent Cal's" impressive 2–1 margin.

November, 1927, brought the worst flood that Vermont has ever known. Whole sections of towns and villages were swept away, sixty lives were lost, roads and railroads were in places obliterated, and millions of dollars' worth of damage was done. To prevent a recurrence of this catastrophe, the Washington government built flood-control dams in strategic areas.

DEPRESSION YEARS

Many Vermonters, like millions of other Americans, were forced to accept federal government handouts and jobs during the long depression years. Local welfare agencies found the need for food, clothing, medical assistance and money so great that they had to accept outside assistance. Many Vermonters, especially older folk, became eager supporters of the Townsend Plan which promised "Thirty Dollars Every Thursday."

The federal government with its many projects left a permanent mark, most of it good, upon the state. Ski trails built by the CCC (Civilian Conservation Corps) formed the basis for much of the state's present-day winter tourist industry. Everyone benefited, even if only indirectly from the Gypsy Moth and Blister Rust Control projects. Many cities and larger towns benefited from PWA Projects like post office and other public buildings. Schools were built or expanded with PWA funds. Flood control dams were constructed. Writers and painters were given creative employment. These benefits were secondary to the primary object of giving employment — and a measure of self-respect — to many Vermonters.

In 1936, Vermont gained national notice by declining the Green Mountain Parkway, which the federal government at an expense of $18,000,000 proposed to establish as a National Park running the whole length of the state, with a motor highway, a bridle path, and a foot trail. The creation of the Parkway was contingent upon the conveying by Vermont to the United States of approximately 35,000 acres of land, to be governed and administered by Congress. The Parkway was defeated by a popular referendum.

In the presidential election of 1936, Vermont was one of only two states that returned a Republican plurality, adding its three electoral votes for Alfred M. Landon to the five from Maine. The parallel with 1912, when Vermont and Utah stood alone for Taft, and with 1832, when Vermont was the only state to support the Anti-Masonic candidates, is notable and gives evidence that in recent times as in its earliest days Vermont has retained that spirit of independence which has brought it both great praise and great obloquy, but which has always, whatever the issue, been the dominating force behind its history.

The great New England hurricane of September 1938 cut a narrow swath through the state. No lives were lost but property damage was estimated at several million dollars. It was the state's first hurricane in more than a century.

WORLD WAR II

Vermont's overwhelmingly Republican legislature decided in September 1941 that President Roosevelt's acts including Lend Lease were acts of war and that the United States would soon be involved. Three months before Pearl Harbor the legislature officially declared "a state of belligerency with Germany."

Before the Selective Service Act went into effect, the former Republic of Vermont contributed more volunteers to the Armed Forces than any other state including the former Republic of Texas. Many Vermonters had enlisted in the Canadian forces as early as the fall of 1939.

More than 25,000 Vermonters were estimated to have served in World War II. The outstanding Vermonter was probably the late Marine Corps General Merritt Edson of "Edson's Raiders." Vermont's machine tool industry played an important role in winning the war.

SINCE V-J DAY

Vermont since World War II has elected the first Democratic congressman in more than a century. In 1962 the state had its first Democratic governor since the Civil War.

Major problems in the postwar era: (1) Shortage of jobs for high school graduates. Too many leave the state. (2) Refusal of the legislatures to appropriate adequate funds for general educational needs. In 1963 one legislator when queried on his refusal to see that teachers received a pay increase said, "Teachers are already working, aren't they? If you give a cow more hay she don't give more milk. Why pay teachers more money?"

Skiing has become a large source of revenue for the state. Even though outsiders — and most Vermonters — think of the state primarily as an agricultural area, a greater percentage of its income is now derived from industry.

During the mid-1960's many small industries — often branch plants of large corporations — attracted by reasonable taxes, a healthy climate, good recreational facilities and a good labor supply, moved into Vermont. The trend will probably continue.

"ALL THE WAY WITH LBJ"

Bay State–born Philip H. Hoff, in 1962, became the state's first Democratic governor since 1853. In that year no candidate received a majority vote and even though Whig candidate Erastus Fairbanks received more popular votes the contest was decided by the legislature, which elected Democrat John S. Robinson. No Democrat had been elected governor since the formation of the Republican party during the 1850's.

Hoff's 1962 plurality over one-term incumbent F. Ray Keyser was a scant 1348 votes. Hoff's 1964 plurality soared to nearly 50,000 votes over GOP Lieutenant Governor Ralph Foote. Hoff had the highest popular vote, by more than 14,000, of any governor in the state's history, regardless of party.

Vermont remained loyal to the GOP standard from the party's inception until Goldwater proved too much for too many Vermonters. Vermont, despite great affection for TR, voted against the 1912 Bull

Moosers. Even Maine backslid from GOP ranks that year. Vermont and Maine bucked the 1936 Roosevelt landslide.

Lyndon B. Johnson carried Vermont by even a greater majority than did Governor Hoff. The tall Texan took Vermont by a 2:1 majority.

8

Merinos, Morgans, Maple Syrup and Milk

VERMONT, known for its Merino sheep, Morgan horses, maple syrup and milk, also produced Joshua Stoddard, inventor of the horse-drawn hayrake and Charles Deere of Moline steel plow fame.

Vermont's settlement, attended by dissension, controversy and confusion, did not provide a favorable climate for a "stable" agriculture until the state entered the Union in 1791. Vermont's population increased from 85,425 in 1790 to 154,465 in 1800. A century passed before it doubled again. The strictly pioneer economy in which each household produced its own food and clothing had just about ended by 1790. An extensive trade with Portland, Boston and New York City was developing and there was trading with Montreal and Quebec City.

Earliest export items were pot and pearl ash, by-products of land-clearing operations. Long before 1840 potash manufacture had been replaced by a highly diversified agriculture. Potatoes were sold to starch factories. Rye and corn were purchased by whiskey distilleries. Beef cattle, however, was the basis of Vermont farming.

GRAIN AND MEAT

Green Mountain cowboys, most of them afoot rather than on horseback, trail-drove tens of thousands of beef critters to Boston and New York between 1790 and 1820. An 1806 Vermont gazetteer estimated that cowboys drove up to 15,000 head annually to the Boston market. These cowboys drank rum in taverns instead of redeye neat as did later cowboys in Dodge and other trail towns. These mountain cowboys were more often barefoot than booted and spurred but they were tough just the same.

Some beef, but more often pork, mutton, butter, cheese, grain and maple sugar and syrup were freighted out in winter on sleds drawn by four to eight great draft horses.

Except for the past sixty years when milk has been the state's number one farm crop, Vermont agriculture has never maintained a stable position. Many changes have also occurred within the milk industry and these changes are continuing today.

Hardly has one farming system become established before it has given way to another. Vermont farmers are conservative and they did not ask for the changes but the necessity for change was thrust on them by outsiders. Each generation has seen a different farming type prevail. The self-sufficient agriculture of the pioneers gave way to the mixed beef and grain farming of their sons. The next generation saw Merino sheep dominate Vermont agriculture.

SHEEP

The shift from beef to sheep was partly due to increasingly sharper competition from other states in Vermont's own Boston and New York markets. Western York State and Ohio Country produce flowed in an ever increasing stream into Atlantic seaboard cities. This flow was greatly accelerated by the opening of the Erie Canal in 1825.

The textile industry's rapid advance in southern New England provided a market within easy traveling distance of western Vermont's rolling verdant pasturelands. Way back in 1798 sheep had been described to Vermont farmers as "universally acknowledged to be the most useful" domestic animal. Some Green Mountain pioneers raised sheep to provide both wool and mutton for home consumption. Later, farmers exported winter-killed frozen mutton to seaboard cities but it remained for the Merino sheep — famous for its durable wool — to place Vermont among the leading wool-producing states of the young nation. (See WEATHERSFIELD on introduction of Merinos.)

Sheep raising reached its peak between 1830 and 1840 but continued to dominate the state's agriculture until after the Rebellion. Some sheep raisers went hog wild over sheep prices. Many a farmer paid up to $5000 for a first-rate ram. The railroads arriving in Vermont during the late 1840's gave sheepmen easier and quicker access to an already nearby market. The extension of railroads into the vast free grazing areas of the mountain West spelled trouble. Wyoming and Montana sheepmen, who managed to survive ambushes and rimrocking by their cattlemen enemies, sent cheap wool east where it largely displaced the more expensive Vermont product.

DAIRY PRODUCTS

The twenty years following the Rebellion was another transitional period; this time from sheep to dairy produce. Two factors were important: advent of horse-drawn machinery; industrial growth of the Northeast.

Scattered boulders, steep hillsides, small irregular fields were not serious obstacles to the scythe and bull rake. The mowing machine, industrial competition in the labor market and the move westward resulted in the transfer of much tilled land to pasture and in a large reduction of the labor force. These changes led to the combination of small farms into larger farms and in some cases to the complete abandonment of farms. The process, slow and painful, is continued today.

When competition rendered sheep raising unprofitable, Vermonters turned to butter and cheese manufacture. The state already had some dairy cows but the change from sheep to dairying was more than a decrease in sheep and an increase in dairy cows. In earlier years dairy products had been primarily for home consumption. Beef cattle were partly descended from stock brought in by early settlers and partly Shorthorns (Durhams). There were a few Devons.

Dairy cow breeding stock (Ayrshire, Holstein, Jersey) was introduced during the 1860–70 decade. Development was rapid. Jerseys were the dominant breed. Some — usually Jersey owners — say that this gentle animal transformed Vermont into a dairying state.

Butter shipments to city markets increased rapidly. St. Albans shipments tripled between 1852 and 1871, rising from 1,149,225 pounds to 3,270,182 pounds annually. St. Albans cheese shipments rose from 600,000 to more than 2,000,000 pounds annually and then decreased to an annual average of 400,000 pounds.

Butter and cheese were delivered weekly to buyers at the railroad. Milk was set in shallow pans and skimmed with a large clamshell. Butter was hand churned. There was a steady growth in the number of creameries. Cheese factories were built in considerable numbers but cheese never approached creameries in economic importance.

The centrifugal cream separator came to Vermont in 1884. It gave further impetus to the butter factory system. At first separators were designed only for use in creameries. For a few years farmers delivered whole milk instead of cream. The production of home dairy-size separators swung the balance the other way. From 1900 to 1910 most Vermont milk was separated on the farm and the cream was sold to creameries.

WHITE GOLD

Vermont farmers had seen western beef, wool and grain force a switch in their produce. No sooner had the shift to dairy products commenced than similar produce from the Midwest began to appear in ever increasing quantities in eastern markets.

Again Vermont farmers shifted. The change from cream sales to milk sales, while less drastic than previous transitions, required many adjustments. By the mid-1930's Vermont was supplying Boston with more than 50 percent of its milk. Yorkers also purchased large quantities of Vermont milk.

FARMING TODAY

Vermont agriculture is undergoing a transition. Today's trend is toward fewer but larger farms. In thirty years farms decreased from about 36,000 to 12,000. Today's farms, however, produce about 50 percent more milk than did the 36,000. The hired farmhand is slowly disappearing. Farm employment dropped from more than 35,000 in the mid-1940's to less than 20,000 in the mid-1960's — nearly a 50 percent decline.

A larger slice of the agricultural income per capita comes from dairying than in any other state. Milk production steadily increases despite fewer farms. The total acreage remains about the same. Nearly 35 percent of Vermont dairy farmers milk 20 cows or less. This small operation is becoming increasingly unprofitable. The requirement by large dairy companies and creameries for bulk milk deliveries in tank trucks rather than in the traditional 40-quart cans means that farmers must install a stainless steel bulk tank. This switch costs at least $2500 for the smallest farm. Many small farmers are selling out to a bigger operator. Today's Vermont farm family, with the help of mechanical aids, can handle a farm twice the size that their parents could run during the mid-1930's.

Approximately one out of four New England farm acres is in Vermont, nearly 3,000,000 acres. The $20,000 average value of Vermont farms is below the New England average of $25,000 but more than Maine's low of $15,000. Connecticut farms average nearly $50,000.

Vermont farms with an average of about $80 per acre is the lowest per acre value in New England. Connecticut averages nearly $450 per farm acre. New England farms average $150 per acre. Vermont farms average about 200 acres.

About one-half of Vermont's farm acreage — excluding forests — is so stony that it is difficult or impossible to till and harvest with machinery. Productivity is limited and much of the land is suitable for pasturage — and some is mighty poor.

Approximately 35 percent of farm acreage has some stones but can be tilled or harvested with machinery. This land has medium production capabilities.

The remaining 15 percent is smooth land with fertile soil, has high production capabilities.

Vermont farmers in the mid-1960's were selling about $100,000,000 of milk annually to the New York and Boston markets. Cattle, calves, eggs, chickens and minor produce account for nearly $20,000,000 annually.

Hay, with annual sales averaging more than $3,000,000 annually, is the major field crop. Potatoes bring in slightly less than $1,000,000 annually.

Maple syrup and sugar — one out of every four gallons of American-produced maple syrup comes from Vermont — averages better than 500,000 gallons annually. Income: about $2,500,000. Apples, fruits and berries bring in about the same amount.

Vermonters have developed a new farm crop — bird's-foot trefoil.

9

Industry

ALTHOUGH industry by the mid-1960's had replaced farming as Vermont's prime source of income, the state has always been more important as a producer of inventors and designers than in industrial output. It seems fitting that U.S. Patent Number 1 was issued to Vermonter Samuel Hopkins. The 1790 patent, signed by George Washington, covered a pearl-ash manufacturing process.

Nearly every American for generations previous to present teen-agers has thrilled to the delightful music of the steam calliope, other-wise known as the American steam piano. This and the horsedrawn hayrake were invented by Pawlet's Joshua Stoddard. Gardner Q. Colton and Horace Wells invented laughing gas. William W. Chandler invented the first railroad refrigerator car.

It will probably never be decided at this late date whether Orange A. Smalley or Thomas Davenport or both of them working together invented the electric motor. They were both Vermonters and so was Wareham Chase of Calais, unaware of Smalley or Davenport's work, who invented an electric motor. His work may have preceded theirs.

For more than a century the leading American manufacturers of scales have been the Howe (now Howe-Richardson) of Rutland and Fairbanks (Fairbanks-Morse) of St. Johnsbury. Francis Strong of Pittsford invented the Howe Scale and Thaddeus Fairbanks of St. Johnsbury designed the first Fairbanks Scale.

Three rifles, mostly in the hands of civilians, decimated the Indians and settled the hash of many a western outlaw. The Sharps rifle, first built in Windsor, and later in Connecticut under the super-vision of native Vermonter Richard Lawrence, was primarily respon-sible for wiping out the buffalo, the main source of hides and food for the Plains Indians.

The Henry rifle — our first commercially successful repeating rifle and the predecessor of the Winchester M66, also a Henry design — were invented by Windsor-trained Benjamin Henry. Oliver Winchester was not a firearms designer but a promoter who switched manufacture from shirts to shooting irons. Rebels called the Henry rifle "that damned Yankee rifle that you load on Sunday and shoot all week."

Today, a century later, Winchesters are still making history, under the ownership of John and Spencer Olin, sons of Vermonter Franklin Olin, founder of one of the world's great industrial empires — Olin Mathieson Chemical Corporation.

The Remington Rolling block rifle — Nelson Story and a few cowhands armed with Vermonter Leonard Geiger's invention held off several thousand Sioux warriors on the first trail drive from Texas to Montana — played a substantial role in the Winning of the West.

Samuel Colt was not a Vermonter but his firm's number one competitor, a century ago as now, was Smith & Wesson, co-founded by Vermonter Horace Smith.

Today, several thousand Vermonters working at General Electric's Burlington plant are manufacturing the world's fastest firing cannon for our Air Force jets.

Some Vermonters have been leading manufacturers in their selected fields: George H. Coates was the world's leading manufacturer of clippers for human and horse hair; onetime Vermont governor and U.S. Senator Carroll S. Page was the world's largest dealer and processor of hides; Wells native Marcellus E. Wheeler was once the world's foremost fertilizer dealer and processor. This position is now held by a subsidiary of the Vermonter-founded Olin Mathieson Chemical Corporation. Charles H. Deere of Derby, designer of the Moline steel plow, was the world's largest plow manufacturer. Jearum Atkins invented a device which revolutionized the manufacture of mechanical reapers.

Silas Harris of Shaftsbury invented the carpenter's square. Bradford farmer James Wilson made the first geographical globes in North America. Quimby Backus designed and manufactured the famed Backus heater which heated many a grange hall and country church. Philo P. Stewart designed and manufactured America's best-selling woodburning kitchen and parlor stoves — the Stewart.

Vermonters are a frugal people. Salisbury's Silas Herring designed the first practical fire- and burglar-proof safe to protect their savings.

INDUSTRY TODAY

Trees, aside from people, are Vermont's most important economic resource. Trees or wood products are injecting about $125,000,000 annually into Vermont's economic bloodstream. Lumber and wood products account for nearly $20,000,000. Pulp and paper products account for about $30,000,000 more. The remainder is paid out in wages to loggers; profits to lumbermen and woodlot owners (including cities and towns). Many small-town Vermonters make a living trucking logs to sawmills and woodworking plants. The economic mainstay in many communities is the local wood products plant. The management of the Green Mountain National Forests pays into the till of each town located within its borders a substantial percentage of the fees received from lumbermen who cut specified trees within the forest.

Vermont, reported Geoffrey Orton of the Vermont Development Commission, in 1965 manufactures 10 percent of all the machine tools made in the United States. One out of every three dollars brought into Vermont by the sale of manufactured products comes from the manufacture and sale of machine tools. Lathes, grinders and gear shapers are among Vermont's products so vital to nearly all American industry. Nearly 90 percent of the gears in American automobiles are made on machines manufactured by Springfield's Fellows' Gear Shaper Company.

The names of Springfield and Windsor are synonymous throughout the world with quality specialized machine tools, some of which are unobtainable elsewhere. Firms in these communities largely produce machines designed by native or locally trained mechanical geniuses like: Adna Brown, W. LeRoy Bryant, E. R. Fellows, former U.S. Senator Ralph Flanders, James Hartness, Fred Lovejoy and Amasa Woolson.

Vermont industry during the mid-1960's annually manufactured more than $100,000,000 worth of machinery. This represents more than one-third of the state's total value of manufactured goods. Machinery accounted for more than $50,000,000; machine tools nearly $40,000,-000 and electrical machinery production exceeded $11,000,000.

Food processing and manufacture — largely of Vermont-produced items — brings in $40,000,000 annually. This includes: milk processing, cheese and ice cream manufacture, maple syrup processing (largely for cigarette manufacturers) and cereal products like nationally sold Maltex.

Many national firms have established one or several plants in the state: General Electric (4), Tampax, International Business Machines, American Optical and Union Carbide. The latter firm makes all Eveready batteries in its St. Albans plant.

MINES AND QUARRIES

Vermont leads the nation in production of marble and granite. It ranks high in talc and slate production. Barre area granite is widely used for tombstones. Many an American finally rests under a headstone of granite hewn from the hard hills. Granite is also used as a building stone.

Vermont Marble Company's marble has been used in the United States Supreme Court building in Washington, the UN building in New York and in many other public buildings. The Proctors who founded the Vermont Marble Company nearly a century ago, and still control it, were once very influential in Vermont and national politics.

Vermont mines produce about 95 percent of the nation's asbestos output. This represents less than 10 percent of the national asbestos requirements.

Iron ore was once mined in the Valley of Vermont. An old iron furnace can still be seen in the Forestdale section of Brandon. Iron stoves, railroad car carriages and other iron products were once made here.

Manganese, silver, and reportedly gold, have been mined in Vermont.

Vermont, no longer an active copper ore–producing state, once produced 40 percent of the nation's copper.

Horace Austin Warner Tabor — sometimes called "Haw" from his first three initials but better known to the world as "Silver Dollar" Tabor — is probably the best-known Vermonter with a mining connection. He wasn't a miner but he did better than most miners did from the mines. While operating a Colorado mining town general store he grubstaked prospectors in return for a share in future strikes, if any. Some of his grubstake miners made a strike. Silver Dollar became the wealthiest man in Colorado. His faithful wife died, he married a dance hall girl, blew his millions on such lavish charities as the Denver Opera House. Silver Dollar died broke about the turn of the century. His widow, known to millions of newspaper readers as "Baby Doe," died a pauper in 1935 in a miserable shack.

Highways and Skyways

VERMONTERS, rather than Vermont, have played a major role in the development of continental transportation. Probably no other state can equal Vermont's record as a producer of railroad presidents and railroad executives. Let the record speak: three Vermonters were president of the Atchison, Topeka & Santa Fe Railroad while a fourth was its receiver and longtime chairman of the board. Vermonters have been president of the New York Central, Erie, Baltimore & Ohio, Chicago & Northwestern, Denver & Rio Grande, Mexican Central, Troy & Boston, Boston & Maine, Arkansas Central, Barre & Chelsea, Grand Trunk, Wabash, Gulf, Mobile & Northern, Illinois Central, Fort Worth & Rio Grande, Northern Missouri, Fort Wayne & Chicago, Terre Haute, Alton & St. Louis, Ohio & Mississippi, Great Northern and others.

Vermonters have served in major positions like vice-president, general superintendent, chief counsel or surgeon. Milton's Don Juan Whittemore, for instance, was chief engineer of the Chicago, Milwaukee and St. Paul for fifty-one years.

Charles B. Holmes of Springfield, long known as the "Street Railway King of America," was president of street railways lines in Chicago, Moline and many other cities. Dorset's Benjamin Field was co-founder with George Pullman of the first sleeping car manufacturing company in America. John A. Hill from Bennington edited *Locomotive Engineering* and was a leading authority on the subject. Orange native Frank P. Sargent was long head of the Brotherhood of Locomotive Firemen. John Converse, of Burlington, was president of the Baldwin Locomotive Works for many years.

Some Vermonters weren't content to wait for the railroad to come to their adopted state or territory. Burlington's William Hepburn Russell was co-founder of the "Pony Express" while another Vermonter was a co-founder of the famed Wells, Fargo Company. David M. Means designed the first Cadillac car while Bennington's John F. Winslow, first American to manufacture Bessemer process steel, built the U.S. Navy's first ironclad ship, the *Monitor*. Traveler Arthur Jackson was president and founder of the International Good Roads and Automobile Association, a forerunner of the present-day automobile associations. Colonel Nelson H. Jackson of Burlington was the first man to drive an automobile across the United States. That was in 1903, the car was a Winton and the trip, much of it across roadless territory, took 70 days.

HIGHWAYS

Vermont's small area; its four-season attraction to tourists; its location as a main thoroughfare between eastern seaboard cities and Montreal; its increasing appeal to city folk as an ideal weekend home throughout the year, has resulted in a greatly expanded highway program. Thanks to the development of the annual $35,000,000 ski business most Vermont roads are kept open through the year. It was not always this way. In the early days Vermont's mountains and sparsely populated rural districts were all but inaccessible and remained rural and sparsely populated because they were so. Travel was afoot or horseback, and produce was arduously transported in oxcarts. Existing roads were rough and tortuous, following brooks and rivers through wasteful miles of curves because bridges could not be built and maintained, but seldom swerving aside for mountains. Vermonters were aware of the need for adequate travel and commercial highways long before they acquired them. In 1763, judicious Jacob Bayley petitioned New Hampshire for aid in building a road from Dover, New Hampshire, to the newly opened territory around Newbury.

Vermont's first real roads were of military origin. Crown Point Military Road, built by axemen for Lord Jeffrey Amherst in 1759–60, entered the state at Springfield, crossed it on a northwestern slant, and left it at Chimney Point, just across Lake Champlain from its Crown Point, York Province, terminus. It was the old "corduroy" construction — a type used by Vermont backwoodsmen — in which the trunks of small trees were laid crosswise in the path by felling them. A similarly constructed path was General Moses Hazen's Military Road, built in the summer of 1779 for a second proposed Yankee invasion of Canada. Beginning at Newbury, it extended northwest through Caledonia and Orleans Counties, to end near scenic Hazen's Notch (Vt. 58) in Westfield. Neither road completely fulfilled its military objective but they remained the chief travel routes in their section for many years. Vt. 103 and part of US 7 follow in part the Old Crown Point Road.

Privately constructed and operated turnpikes with tollgates often made needed highways possible which towns could not afford to construct. Turnpikes facilitated the early establishment (1801) of stagecoach lines. From the end of the eighteenth century until nearly 1850 these roads were maintained on a toll basis. When popular resentment forced abandonment of toll charges, many turnpikes were purchased and operated by towns. These were forerunners of today's "Freeways." Some roads, constructed to avoid turnpike toll charges, were termed "shun-pikes."

WATER ROUTES

Early Vermonters showed even more interest and initiative in the development of water routes and shipping techniques than they did in highways. This was natural. Vermont's first visitor Samuel de Champlain came via canoe. Lake Champlain and the Connecticut were important routes both in winter and summer for raiding and counter raiding whites and Indians.

Capt. Samuel Morey of Fairlee whose work was barely antedated by John Fitch, operated a steamboat on the Connecticut and Lake Morey in 1793 or fourteen years before Yorker Robert Fulton steamed up-Hudson to Albany. In 1808, less than a year after the successful operation of Fulton's *Clermont,* the steamboat *Vermont* — the second steamship in the world to be put into regular commercial operation — was launched on Lake Champlain. Others soon followed. The last Lake Champlain excursion steamer, the *Ticonderoga,* remained in operation into the mid-1950's. It can be inspected by visitors to the Shelburne Museum.

STEAM CARS TO DIESELS

Boston and New York's competition for trade with the newly opened West was the main reason for Vermont's first railroad — the Vermont Central . This competition was dated from the 1825 opening of the Erie Canal. Northern New York, Boston and Vermont capitalists thought to fight the Erie by constructing a Boston–Ogdensburg, N.Y. canal. The advent of the railroads ended this plan. Part of the canal survey, however, was utilized in selecting the Vermont Central's route. The VC was regarded by its builders not as a Vermont line, but as a link in a Boston–Great Lakes area trunk line. Ground was broken at Northfield, January 1846. The first passenger train from White River Junction to Bethel ran June 26, 1848. In 1850 the company went into receivership — an ill omen for many Vermont railroads in the coming century — and united with the Vermont and Canada Railroad. Today the Central Vermont, a Canadian National Railways subsidiary, is an important connection between transcontinental trunk lines of the Canadian government owned parent corporation and U.S. Atlantic seaboard cities.

The Vermont Central's route and some of its early financial troubles show that personalities, local pride and executive willfulness sometimes replaced logic in laying out our early railroad routes. Montpelier and Barre were left off the main line of the Vermont Central because Governor Paine — also a railroad company official — was determined to include his home town, Northfield, on the route. He also established the company's head offices and built a too elaborate depot for such a small town. Paine was probably closer to being a crook than any other governor in the history of this relatively corruption-free state.

Burlington, the largest city in the state, was left off the main line because Burlington men involved in Lake Champlain shipping quite accurately predicted the northern Vermont farm products they had been shipping via water to Albany and New York City would be diverted by rail to Boston.

The second Vermont railroad, the Lake Champlain and Connecticut River, later the Rutland and now in an amputated form the Vermont Railway, was first to reach Burlington (see MT. HOLLY). Burlington's water shippers welcomed the L.C. & C.R. because while it did not tap their trading area it did open up new territory to the south.

The Rutland Railway, after a long series of financial difficulties, ended passenger service in the mid-1950's. Management, at the time of a strike in 1961, announced that the Rutland would permanently cease operations. Thus western Vermont was without a railroad (except Delaware & Hudson freightline to Rutland from Whitehall, N.Y.) for the first time in more than a century.

Philip Hoff, Vermont's first Democratic governor in more than a century, persuaded the 1963 legislature to purchase the Rutland's trackage from Burlington to White Creek, N.Y. (near Bennington). Cost: $1,800,000. The road leased to a short-line operator from Rhode Island was back in business in 1964 under the name Vermont Railway. Headquarters was moved from Rutland to Burlington.

Vermont's third railroad, the Passumpsic and Connecticut Rivers Railroad, whose route followed the Connecticut River from about the Massachusetts line, has been largely taken over by the financially troubled Boston & Maine Railroad and by the very solvent Canadian Pacific Railroad.

The St. Johnsbury and Lake Champlain Railroad (St. J & LC) locally known from its initials as the "St. Jesus and Long Coming" is a freight line which wanders across the northern section of the state. The Canadian National Grand Trunk and the Maine Central also operate within the state.

Vermont's most interesting railroad — it pays dividends — is the Hoosac Tunnel & Wilmington known variously by its HT & W initials as the Hog Tied & Wobbly; Hot Tea & Whiskey, Halibut Tuna & Whale; Hard Tack & Wine; Hungry Tired & Weary and Horses' Walk & Trot, but better known throughout the realm of railroading and to natives as the Hoot Toot & Whistle.

The Hoot Toot & Whistle during its prime decades ran a full 24 miles along its then narrow gauge 3-foot wide track from Hoosac Tunnel, Massachusetts, to Wilmington, Vermont. Today its standard gauge 4-foot, 8½-inch wide track runs a scant 10.9 miles from Hoosac Tunnel to Readsboro, Vermont. Its freight cars haul goods to the Yankee Atomic Plant at Monroe Bridge, Massachusetts. The road once paid a $30 dividend for every mile of track. Passenger traffic has unfortunately ceased.

The Clarendon & Pittsford and the Montpelier and Barre are freight lines used for hauling marble and granite. Many short lines like the West River Railroad, the White River Railroad and the Montpelier & Wells River have been abandoned.

Vermont railroads owned by large companies and which are but a link in a trunk line have generally remained solvent or at least are continuing in operation. The Rutland while it had to maintain large amounts of equipment could not charge sufficiently high rates for its relatively short length. Local business was not enough. Competition from trucks was another factor in its decline.

Vermont's rail track mileage reached a peak of 1100 miles in 1910 when railroad trackage construction ceased. By the mid-1960's about 600 miles were left.

The electric railroad came and went within less than a fifty-year span. The first one in 1893 replaced a horse-car line between Burlington and Winooski. More than forty years have passed since trucks and busses replaced the trolley in Burlington, Montpelier, Rutland, Barre and other communities.

AVIATION

Vermont, lacking large population centers, was much later than other eastern states in developing commercial aviation facilities. The first airplane flight in the state was at St. Johnsbury in 1910. Two airlines serve Vermont: Mohawk Airlines and Northeast Airlines.

Local airports with limited facilities are located at: Bennington, Bristol, Canaan (Bunnell Farm), Colchester (Champlain), East Berkshire, Manchester (Equinox), Waitsfield (Estey), Fair Haven, Springfield (Hartness), Worcester (Maxham), Middlebury, Coventry (Newport), Thetford (Post Mills), St. Albans and St. Johnsbury.

TODAY'S HIGHWAYS

Vermont has nearly 14,000 miles of highway: 2000 miles of state (numbered highways other than Interstate) roads; 2500 miles of town roads partially maintained by state funds and more than 9000 miles of town roads.

About 75 miles — or more than one-fourth of the planned system — of Interstate Routes had been completed by 1964. Interstate 89, from Burlington to Montpelier, was opened in late 1964. Interstate 91 was open from the Massachusetts line to a point several miles north of Bellows Falls in Rockingham Town. Interstate 189, a feeder route from US 7 to Interstate 89, is completed. Planned Interstate Routes in Vermont, when completed by 1970 will total 321.2 miles. The federal government will pay 90 percent of the estimated $400,000,000 cost.

Interstate 89 will connect with New Hampshire at White River Junction and run northwesterly to connect with Canadian highways north of St. Albans; Interstate 91 will connect with Massachusetts and run almost due north to connect with Canadian highways north of the Newport area, and Interstate 93 will connect a second New Hampshire highway to Route 91 in the St. Johnsbury area, making a clear travel route to Canadian destinations. Thirty-seven turn-outs and picnic areas are planned along its 321-mile length. Landscaping, blending with natural beauty, enhances the Interstate system.

In the mid-1960's Vermont's total highway mileage was basically classified: paved, 4267.2; gravel, 7238.6; graded and drained, 1333.9 and unimproved 816.6 miles.

II

Racial Elements

VERMONTERS are, and always have been, predominantly of English stock. The state, today, has one of the smallest percentages of foreign-born residents of any American state. Only one out of ten Vermonters was born outside the United States.

The state has less than 1000 non-whites. The last U.S. census reported 789 non-whites including 422 males and 367 females. There are 519 Negroes, 30 Indians, 79 Japanese, 68 Chinese and 66 miscellaneous. The non-white population was 559 in 1950. The largest increase was among the Japanese.

The state was settled during the latter half of the eighteenth century by Protestants from Massachusetts, New Hampshire, New York, and above all, Connecticut, who were mainly of English extraction. The lack of new lands to develop and the absence of large manufacturing centers have left the state relatively unaffected by the waves of foreign immigration that have swept over almost every settled section of the country since 1830. During the past hundred years foreign-born persons have constituted, on an average, from 10 to 13 percent of the total population of the state. The considerable variation over different periods of the ethnic origin of this foreign element can be explained partly, if not chiefly, by the affinity that undoubtedly exists between certain racial groups and certain types of labor.

In 1850, there were approximately 15,000 Irish in Vermont, this number constituting nearly half of the foreign-born and 5 percent of the total population. They outnumbered all other groups among the laborers who built the first railroads in the state and operated the mills and quarries of that period. In these occupations they were long ago replaced by other peoples. More thoroughly than any other race, the Irish have become assimilated and now occupy many positions of executive or political responsibility.

FRENCH CANADIANS

Since 1900 the largest single important group has been the French Canadian. As early as the 1830's this element began replacing the

Yankee farmers in the northernmost tier of counties; today they constitute approximately one-quarter of the population there (including second generation) as compared with 13 percent of the state's total. In some towns they outnumber the inhabitants of English stock, and in several the parts of the Roman Catholic service that are not in Latin are conducted in French as well as in English. Since 1860 this group has also come in increasing numbers to the larger towns and cities of northern Vermont, in particular to Burlington and Winooski.

Recent immigrants are for the most part concentrated in the manufacturing and quarry towns. In the mills and machine shops of Windsor County — in Windsor, Springfield and Ludlow — there is a considerable foreign element, largely Slavic. In the Rutland County quarry towns — Proctor, West Rutland, and Poultney — Poles, Czechs, and Russians have been joined by Austrians and Swedes. In Poultney, Castleton, and Fair Haven, Welsh settlements keep alive their own traditions and maintain their racial customs as strictly as the Welsh always do, wherever they settle. Beautiful music, for instance, is still heard in Welsh churches in this section.

In Barre, heart of the granite region, Scots and Italians predominate. Barre Scots are largely from Aberdeen, an important granite district. The Italians, many of whom are highly skilled stonecutters, are mostly from north Italy's quarry areas.

Forming a thin crescent from Andover on the east to Sandgate on the west is a sprinkling of Finns who have eagerly bought farms, many of them abandoned, in this area. Many Finns came from New Hampshire mill cities to which they, or their parents, originally immigrated. Their settling in Vermont constitutes a real reversion to the soil.

To summarize: the largest foreign-born group in Vermont is the French Canadians. The next largest is the non-French Canadians. No other foreign-born group constitutes so much as 1 percent of the total.

The concentration of these foreign-born groups in a relatively few towns, cities, and localities has undoubtedly retarded their assimilation. It is also partly responsible, no doubt, for the fact that the foreign elements in Vermont have made no appreciable contribution to arts or manners and no changes in the ways of living — or of thinking — of Vermonters. Still the members of the second generation, those of mixed or foreign parentage, through education and imitation have in most instances become scarcely distinguishable from their companions whose forebears for many generations have lived in the state.

The fact that many foreign-born Vermont residents are Roman Catholics and that the Yankee is Protestant has been, and still remains one of the strongest (if not the strongest) barriers to Yankee-foreigner marriages. The new liberal policy of the Catholic Church under Pope Paul may possibly alter the old demarcation between Protestant-Catholic marriages. Probably more second-generation Protestant Swedes and Scots, along with non-French Canadians, marry Yankees than they do members of their own nationality.

12

"Oh Promised Land!"

THE first known Christian service, conducted within the confines of the present state of Vermont, was held about 1665 when the French established Fort St. Anne on Isle La Motte. During its short existence this post was visited by Quebec's Bishop Laval. He was the first reported Catholic bishop to visit what is now the United States. The first Catholic church was built in Burlington in 1832.

The first reported Protestant service in Vermont was conducted in March, 1704 at the confluence of the Connecticut and Williams Rivers in Rockingham by the Reverend John Williams. Preacher Williams, pastor of the Deerfield (Massachusetts) Congregational Church and one of New England's leading clergymen, was on his way to two years captivity in Canada as a prisoner of the French. Williams and his family had been taken prisoner during the previous month's raid on Deerfield.

A Congregational chaplain was stationed at Fort Dummer, now Brattleboro, in 1728. The first organized Congregational Church in the state was established in Bennington in 1762.

The first Baptist Church in Vermont was organized in Shaftsbury in 1768 but a settled pastor was not available until 1782. The Free Will Baptists, as distinguished from the regular Baptists, organized their first Vermont church at Stafford in 1793. There were nine members.

Methodism reached Vermont in 1788 when the Reverend Freeborn Garrettson rode the circuit out of Cambridge, N.Y. The first Methodist church building was erected in Danby about 1793.

The Reverend Hosea Ballou organized the first Vermont Universalist Church in Barnard about 1794. The state's first Unitarian Church, organized by dissident Congregationalists, was established in Burlington in 1810.

A few Presbyterian Churches — similar to the Congregational Church except the deacon's role is fulfilled by Presbyters — were organized by the early Scottish settlers in Caledonia County. Today, there are Welsh Presbyterian and Welsh Congregational Churches in Rutland County's slate mining area.

The first settled Episcopal clergymen in Vermont were the Reverend

Bethuel Chittenden in Tinmouth (1774) and the Reverend Reuben Garlick. These early preachers each served several churches in the area which is now the Diocese of Vermont. Arlington was settled largely by Episcopalians.

The Seventh-Day Adventists, who worship on Saturday because according to their interpretation of the Bible it is the seventh day of the week and therefore designed for rest and worship, organized churches in Sutton and Wolcott about 1845.

CONGREGATIONALISM

At the time of Vermont's early settlement the Congregational Church was the only church recognized by New England's ecclesiastical and political powers. This church, organized in Scrooby, England, during the 1580's by the "Separatists," came to Plymouth with the Pilgrims, and its Calvinist doctrines were rigidly enforced for many years by Boston Puritans. Rhode Island's Quakers were considered outcasts from decent society save on those occasions when Rhode Island's troops were needed to help put down Indian uprisings.

Massachusetts and Connecticut (Maine was part of Massachusetts until 1820) residents were taxed to support the Congregational Church and its clergymen.

The religion, or lack of it, of Vermont's early settlers largely depended on where they came from and their amount of worldly goods. Eastern Vermont, along the Connecticut River Valley, was generally settled by staid citizens from valley towns down in Connecticut or from a similar background in Massachusetts.

These settlers were usually Congregationalists, provident and conservative in matters social, economic and political. During Vermont's fight with York Province over land titles most eastern Vermonters preferred to make peace with the Yorker landlords.

Western Vermonters, though there were Congregationalists among them, were of a different breed. Many walked to Vermont carrying only a smooth-bore musket, axe and an iron cooking pot. A few were comfortably off but most of them, like their covered wagon counterparts of a century later, had little to lose but their debts. Vermont offered an opportunity to start anew on cheap land.

General Ethan Allen, the taker of Ticonderoga, and legendary leader of the Green Mountain Boys, was a rebel in religion as in politics. An uneducated but clear thinker, when unbefuddled by vast quantities of rum and hard cider, he issued in 1784 *Reason the Only*

Oracle of Man. This was the first attack on Christian doctrines to be published in America.

THE SECOND COMING

During the 1830's and 1840's the millennium or the Second Coming of Christ — the Second Advent — was the major theme of the many religious sects temporarily popular among Vermonters. Some sects were created in Vermont while others were but the local manifestation of a larger unit. Vermont-originated sects like the Millerites had substantial followings outside the state.

William Miller (1782–1849), born in Pittsfield, Massachusetts, migrated in 1786 to Poultney. Miller decided the world would be destroyed in 1844. Previous Yankee prophets had predicted that Gabriel's Horn would sound in 1866. Miller's "revelation" came in 1818 but his first public prediction appeared in the Brandon *Vermont Telegraph* in May 1832. Miller's prophesies might have come to naught but for Boston preacher Joshua V. Hines. A quick and devoted convert to Millerism, Hines focused national attention on the Vermonter's prophesies through continual front-page stories in the Boston *Sign of the Times* and the New York *Midnight Cry.*

Millerism received no support from Congregationalists but the more emotional Methodists and Baptists swelled the rapidly growing ranks of Father Miller's flock. Miller made no predictions as to the exact date but his followers finally set October 20, 1844.

Millerites began immediate preparations for "going up." Many gave away their worldly belongings and purchased white robes for their "trip." As midnight of the fateful day approached, many Millerites climbed mountains "so the trip to heaven would be shorter." Down in Boston the trees on the Common sagged under the weight of heaven-seeking Millerites gathered on the branches.

An enterprising Rutland Millerite, eager to facilitate ascension, attached a large pair of wood and canvas wings to his shoulders. At the first stroke of midnight the would-be heavenly traveler took off from the peak of his barn roof. He plummeted groundward and suffered a broken leg and many bruises.

Midnight came and passed and with its passing the Millerites, as an organized religious sect, passed out of existence.

BIBLE COMMUNISM

In the beginning Putney residents thought John Humphrey Noyes (1811–1886) was a likely young man. A native of Brattleboro and a graduate of that Congregational stronghold, Yale; his father had been a U.S. Congressman and he was a cousin of President-to-be Rutherford Hayes.

Noyes was primarily concerned with attaining a more perfect society through both religious and economic means. He preached and practiced "Bible Communism." Noyes believed that only through community ownership of property and with equal division of labor for the community could man achieve social, economic and religious perfection.

Noyes and his followers practiced what Vermonters called — after they found out about it — "wife swapping." Noyes, according to his interpretation of the Scriptures, said the usual husband-wife relationship was immoral.

In 1847 Noyes was charged with adultery. He posted bond and with his followers fled to Oneida, New York, where the fugitives re-established their community.

Noyes organized the Oneida Community plated silverware company which more than a century later is one of the major manufacturers of silverware in the United States.

The Oneida Community was the only financially successful community or "commune" of the several hundreds which were organized in the United States during the mid-nineteenth century.

The Great Revival Era of the 1830's and 1840's ended when people joined the Abolition Crusade. At the beginning of the era most churches were unenthusiastic about outright abolition. Brandon editor Orson S. Murray of the *Vermont Telegraph* was expelled from the Baptist Church in 1841 because he insisted that the church should take a forthright stand for the immediate abolition of slavery. Five years later every Protestant Church in the state had joined the anti-slavery crusade.

After the Great Rebellion Vermonters were "too tuckered out" by the war and the thirty preceding years of intense emotionalism to get excited about anything. Revivalism returned in the late 1890's.

MORMONS

Joseph Smith (1805–1844) of Sharon and Brigham Young (1801–1877) of Whitingham, were the only native Vermonters to create a major religion.

Smith's family migrated to Palmyra, New York. There in 1830, Joseph was reported to have unearthed the Golden Plates of Nephi on which were inscriptions that provided the foundation of the Mormon Church — officially, the Church of Jesus Christ of Latter-Day Saints.

Smith and his followers encountered violent opposition from Gentiles — nonbelievers — when it was discovered that a basic tenet of the new church permitted a male Mormon to have several wives at the same time.

Persecution led the Prophet Joseph and his followers to Kirtland, Ohio; Independence, Missouri and to Nauvoo, Illinois. Irate — and possibly jealous — menfolk shot and killed Joseph and his brother Hyrum while they were lodged in the Carthage jailhouse. A polished granite shaft has been erected at Smith's birthplace. The statue has one foot of height for each of Smith's thirty-eight years.

Mormonism, but for one man, might have been buried with the Smith brothers or degenerated into small bickering claques without influence. Mighty empire builder Brigham Young rallied his people, led them across the Great American Plains, over the Rockies, down into the Valley of the Great Salt Lake, to establish a new Canaan in the wilderness. Young and his followers founded the state of Deseret — now Utah. Good Vermont Yankee that he was, Young adopted as territorial (state) emblem that symbol of industry — the beehive.

As long as church members practiced plural marriage Utah was denied statehood. Following the elimination of plural marriage, Utah was admitted to the Union as the forty-fifth state in 1896.

CHURCHES TODAY

The Congregational Church, today, despite inroads in the past two hundred years by Methodists, Baptists, Universalists and Unitarians, is the dominant religion in the state.

Vermont has 238 organized towns and eight cities. There are 186 Congregational Churches. Many of the smaller towns with populations of 50 or less have no churches but in most instances where there is only one church it is usually a white-spired Congregational Church.

Today, the Green Mountain State is the most "Congregational" of all states. There are more Congregationalists per thousand residents than in any other state. Massachusetts and Connecticut, both former strongholds of Congregationalism, have slipped behind owing to the large influx of foreign-born residents.

Statistically, Vermont has about 130,000 Roman Catholics and about 30,000 Congregationalists. Statistics, however, are misleading. Congregationalists only count as members those who have actually undergone the simple membership rituals. Many Congregational Churches can, on any given Sunday, count more nonmembers among the congregation than members. Congregationalism is as much a way of life and philosophy as a religion. The Catholic Church includes in its count children and those who do not attend church.

In 1957 the Congregational Christian Church united with the Evangelical and Reformed Churches on a nationwide basis. Members in 39 Congregational Churches voted to remain separate. The combined church is now called United Church of Christ but most Vermonters even though they voted union consider themselves Congregationalists.

The Roman Catholic Church in Vermont has a bishop in Burlington who presides over the Vermont diocese. The Vermont diocese is under the jurisdiction of the Boston archdiocese. There are 94 parish churches in the state along with 47 missions. Fourteen of the 58 chapels have resident chaplains. There are eight parochial schools.

Cities are the strongholds of Catholicism. There are a number of French Catholic churches in which many of the members do not speak or understand English. These are immigrants from French Canada rather than Old France. There are a few Polish Catholic Churches.

13

Government

VERMONT, forty-seventh state in population, has the third largest state legislative body in the United States. The Senate has 30 members and the House of Representatives 246 members. Each town or city, regardless of its population, be it Stratton with 41 residents or Burlington with more than 35,000 population, has one representative. Under this system it is possible for 12 percent of the state's voters to elect a majority in the lower house. This imbalance of representation exists in many states (see Chapter 8).

Legislators and state officials are elected for two-year terms. The legislature meets in January in odd-numbered years. Members receive $80 a week during the session. The increasing complexity of state business has brought under discussion the possibility of annual legislative meetings. Another proposed change is the election of all constitutional officials and legislators for a four-year term.

THE GOVERNOR'S CHAIR

One-eyed Tom Chittenden, a tavern keeper who served nineteen gubernatorial terms, may well have been the state's greatest governor. He served through most of Vermont's hectic lean dangerous years as an independent republic and beyond into the anti-democratic Federalist era of the hated Sedition Laws. He was also Vermont's first governor.

Governors from Tom Chittenden in 1778 through the thirty-third, Peter Washburn in 1870, served one-year terms. No other governor has served one-fourth as long as did Tom Chittenden. Banker John E. Weeks of Salisbury was the first of the two-year governors to serve two full terms (1927–31). Twelve governors have served since Weeks established the precedent and seven have been elected to two full terms.

A Vermont governor has no Executive Mansion. He makes about 100 major appointments. His lieutenant governor may be a member of the opposite party. It has been proposed that this untenable situation be corrected.

The lieutenant governor may or may not be a member of the same party as the governor. A constitutional amendment will be passed one of these years making it mandatory for the lieutenant governor to be a member of the same party as the governor. It has also been proposed that the governor, lieutenant governor, other elected state officers, legislators and state senators be elected for a four-year rather than a two-year term.

A TYPICAL LEGISLATOR

The average age of house members during a recent session was 60.7 years. The youngest was but 21 and the oldest was aged 84. The typical member was Protestant, probably one of 71 Congregationalists though he might have been one of 50 Methodists, 21 Baptists or 14 Episcopalians. Of his fellow 245 legislators, 238 stated their religious preference. Of those, 192 were Protestants, 45 Catholics and one Mormon. Of the 21 Protestants who did not state their denomination some were undoubtedly Congregationalists though a few may have been freethinkers. It's poor politics to admit you are a freethinker. There was one Quaker and one Community Church member.

This was a conservative legislature. Its occupational makeup included 72 retired people, 45 farmers and 24 farmers with part-time jobs off the farm. There were 24 housewives 12 of whom had other jobs. There was one peace officer.

Lone representatives of their trade or profession included: a newsman, legal secretary, day laborer, geologist, horse trader, minister, mechanic, writer, peddler and a wrecker. Seven attorneys sat in this session.

REAPPORTIONMENT

A series of complicated legal and political maneuvers led to a U.S. Supreme Court order for the legislature to reapportion itself on a more representative basis. Under the more than century-old apportionment system, every city and town, regardless of size, has been entitled to one legislator. Stratton with a population of 41 had one vote and so did Burlington with more than 35,000 residents. One Stratton resident carried as much legislative weight as 853 Burlington voters.

Conservative Republicans, better known as Tories, came mostly from small towns, many with populations of less than 100. After futilely fighting reapportionment — most of them would lose their seats and paychecks — they fought hard for a minimum reapportionment of 210 seats. Liberal Republicans, Independents and Democrats supported Governor Hoff's proposed 150-seat legislature.

Reapportionment of the 30-member senate was also ordered in the court's decision.

THE JUDICIARY

The Vermont Supreme Court, unlike that of neighboring York State, is not a lower court, but is the state's highest court. The chief justice and four associate justices are elected biannually by a joint session of the legislature. The Supreme Court must sit at least five times a year in Montpelier. They may hold special sessions in Montpelier or wherever necessary.

SUPERIOR COURT

The chief superior judge and his five associates are elected biannually by a joint legislative session. There are six superior court districts. The first superior court judge elected becomes the chief superior judge. If the office becomes vacant during his tenure the second judge elected becomes a chief superior judge. Each superior court judge is a judge of chancery. The chief superior judge assigns his associates to serve as judges of a particular county and to sit as a judge in chancery.

COUNTY COURTS

Municipal courts in smaller county seats are also the county court. The chief judges of the county courts, however, are the state's chief superior court judge and his five associates. Each county judge has two assistant judges, formerly known as "side judges." These side judges are not lawyers but laymen, elected to advise the county judge. The latter can rule on points of law but side judges can overrule his decisions. Side judges date back to the eighteenth century when Vermonters distrusted lawyers and judges. Many Vermonters still do, so they continue to elect side judges as a layman's check on potential judicial hornswoggling.

Chancery court judges are superior court judges sitting unflanked by side judges.

There are 20 probate judges with at least one in each county. They are elected by popular vote.

MUNICIPAL JUDGES

Municipal judges are state judges. Seventeen judges are assigned to the 14 counties and some cities. A municipal judgeship is a part-time occupation. Governor Hoff in the mid-1960's continued to fight — and with considerable support — to reorganize the municipal court system into five districts with eight full-time judges.

WHAT IS A TOWN?

Vermont towns were originally supposed to contain 36 square miles or 23,040 acres. Most towns contain considerably less. The variation was caused by conflicting land grants, primitive survey equipment and techniques and by rugged terrain.

Non-Yankees are often confused by Vermonters' interpretation of "town." Legally and geographically, a Vermont town includes not only a village, or villages, but all the countryside including mountains, hills, meadows, forest lands, pastures and swamps. Such legal and geographic areas are usually called townships in other states. A village within a town may or may not be incorporated. An incorporated village can raise monies through bond issues. More than one village within a town may be incorporated. In this case each would have its own corporation.

All Vermonters, except city residents, live in a town even though their home may be in an isolated rural area. A village becomes a town when a rural resident, who lives also in a town, says "I'm going to town" — meaning that though he's already in a town he is going to the village which may or may not be the chief settlement of the town. A New Yorker "on the town" is having a good time. A Vermonter "on the town" has taken the Pauper's Oath or is receiving some form of relief.

LOCAL GOVERNMENT

Vermont has 238 organized towns and eight cities. There are five unorganized towns. Averill, Lewis and Ferdinand were chartered but the small populations never organized a town government. Glastenbury and Somerset were declared unorganized towns by the 1937 legislature. Legal voters, if any, in unorganized towns, grants and gores, cast their vote in state and national elections in the nearest town. The affairs of unorganized towns, grants and gores are conducted by a supervisor.

Town affairs are conducted by three selectmen, one of whom is elected at every town meeting. Today, larger towns like Brandon and Springfield employ a professional town manager. Some town managers serve two towns. He is responsible to the selectmen who are in turn answerable to the voters. Town offices, in most towns, are a part-time job. Town records and town transactions are recorded by the town clerk. Town officers include: treasurer, grand juror, listers and moderator. The latter is chairman of the town meeting. A "lister" is a tax assessor. There is a school board and a road commissioner.

There are several town government modifications. In some instances the entire town (known as townships in many states) is incorporated while in other instances only the village — usually the chief settlement in a town — is incorporated. The village corporation members — the voters — can raise monies through taxes or bond issues for projects within the designated village area. Town residents outside the village boundaries who do not benefit from the village services are thus not taxed for the services.

Brattleboro has representational town government. The town is divided into units. The voters in each unit elect a representative to the annual town meeting. Smaller towns — some only have a dozen or so voters — usually conduct all of the town's business which requires voting at the annual town meeting where voice votes are taken on all issues. In some larger towns all business is conducted via the Australian ballot. Towns like Brandon use both the Australian ballot and voice vote. The method of voting depends on the issues involved.

The town meeting in which each voter can voice his own opinions is considered the very essence of American democracy. Unfortunately, this is not always true. In some towns, notably the smaller ones, a small minority often manipulate town affairs to suit their own purposes.

CITIES

Barre, Burlington, Montpelier, Newport, Rutland, St. Albans, Vergennes and Winooski are Vermont's eight cities. Population is not the determining criteria for switching from a town to city status. Vergennes, America's third oldest incorporated city, is smaller than several Vermont towns. Brattleboro is larger than most Vermont cities but its residents prefer representative town meetings. St. Johnsbury was once granted, by the legislature, the chance to become a city but voters still prefer town government.

Many Vermonters, whose town could become a city, prefer the more direct democracy of the town meeting to the less personal city government administered by a mayor and council.

Some confusion is created by the existence of two communities with seemingly the same name. Rutland City is surrounded by Rutland Town. Rutland City has a mayor while the larger but sparsely populated Rutland Town has its own town government. Center Rutland is the chief settlement within Rutland Town. West Rutland is a separate town with its own government.

THE COUNTY

Vermont has 14 counties. All counties except Bennington have one county seat, known as a shire town. A shire town is still a town even if it is a city. Bennington and Manchester are half shire towns. Court sessions alternate between towns.

County government, in recent years, has played a decreasing role in the life of Vermonters. However, this may change if the proposed merger — or modification thereof — of several towns into one is eventually approved by some future legislature and by the voters themselves. Regional divisions may replace counties.

County elective offices include: probate court judge, assistant judges of the county court, county clerk, state's attorney, high bailiff — he can arrest the sheriff — treasurer and sheriff. Since the formation of the Vermont State Police some twenty years ago, the sheriff has lost much of his power. Today, he is primarily a process server. He names his own deputies.

14

Education

TIMOTHY DWIGHT, the first white child born in Vermont, had three descendants who became presidents of Yale. This may have been significant because Vermont became one of the nation's leading producers of future college presidents, college founders and educators.

Justin Morrill, senator and congressman for forty-four years, wrote, sponsored, and cashed in all his political checks, to ensure passage of the Land Grant College Acts of 1862 and 1890. Millions of Americans owe their college education to these two legislative acts.

Every American student for nearly 150 years has been influenced by the blackboard introduced by Concord, Vermont schoolmaster Samuel Reed Hall. He also wrote the first teacher's manual.

Hall is credited with founding the first normal school — teachers college — in America. He did found one but Jacob Eddy had established a similar one in Danby nearly forty years earlier.

Philosopher John Dewey (1859–1952) of Burlington was the "Father of Modern Education."

"BEACON IN THE WILDERNESS"

Vermont-born Congregational missionaries Philo Stewart and John Jay Shipherd decided the Ohio frontier needed a college. Neither had any money, a common affliction of clergymen then as now, but Stewart designed an improved stove. He came back to Vermont and secured backers for its manufacture. Shipherd remained to combat the devil.

Stewart stoves were probably America's most widely used wood stoves. Stewart poured a substantial share of his profits into the establishment and operation of Oberlin College — one of our finest colleges.

The number one man in Iowa's history is Josiah Grinnell (1821–1891) from New Haven. He was the first president of Iowa (now Grinnell) College. The Reverend George "Pearly" Gates, a fiddle-footed educator, moved from Vermont to Iowa where he was president of Iowa College. He moved to the presidency of Pomona College in California and then to the same position in Fiske College for Negroes.

Carleton (formerly Northfield) College and the James Boys —
Jesse and Frank, not Henry and William — made Northfield, Min-
nesota famous. The first president was James Strong from Brownington.

The most influential pre–Civil War southern educator was probably Alonzo Church, University of Georgia president for thirty years.
He taught many secession leaders. This Brattleboro native, educated
at Middlebury College, died while his sons and sons-in-law were
fighting for the Confederacy.

Milo P. Jewett and his well-heeled friend Matthew Vassar founded
a girls' college on the Hudson. Vermonter Jewett was the first president. James Kendrick from Poultney was another Vassar president.

Pioneer female educator Emma Hart Willard commenced her work
at the Middlebury Female Academy in 1807. She moved west to
Troy, N.Y. in 1821 and opened her famed school which is very much
alive today.

Susan Mills of Enosburg moved to Oakland, Calif., established
Mills College and retired after nineteen years as president at the age
of eighty-three. It has long been considered as one of the finest
women's colleges in the West.

RUM, DRUM AND A BIBLE

"A gradus ad parnasseum, a bible, a drum and 500 gallons of New
England rum," were toted by the Reverend Eleazer Wheelock when he
came upriver from Connecticut to found Vermont's first college —
Dartmouth.

Dartmouth was Vermont's only college during that era when what
is now Hanover, N.H., was then Dresden, Vt. Hanover or Dresden
was one of 16 New Hampshire and 14 York State towns whose residents preferred Vermont Republic's democratic government to their
own autocratic state governments. Vermont, seeking full membership
as an American state, reluctantly removed the 30 towns from the
realm of the tottering republic.

The Vermont Republic's 1777 Constitution provided for the establishment of a state university and for a "common school" — grammar school — in each county. Fourteen years passed before Ira Allen
could persuade the legislature to establish the University of Vermont.
Nine more years passed before the school commenced instruction.

Dartmouth, which received aid from Vermont's official coffers, was
considered a Vermont college long after Dresden had reluctantly

returned to the embrace of the Granite State. This is probably the only instance where a state legislature officially appropriated funds for the support of a college in another state, and is still remembered by grateful Dartmouth which grants full scholarships to students from Wheelock, Vermont.

THE U.V.M.

The University of Vermont — all Vermonters call it the U.V.M. from "University of Verde Mont" — accepted its first students in 1800. President Daniel C. Sanders (Harvard '88) and one tutor constituted the entire faculty for the college's first eight years. The first graduating class in 1804 had four members.

The University's Medical School, established in 1822 (discontinued 1836–1853) has long been rated "A" by the American Medical Association.

Vermont Agricultural College — not to be confused with the Vermont Agricultural and Technical Institute in Randolph — was organized under U.S. Senator Justin Morrill's (R–Vt.) Land Grant College Act of 1862, in 1864. V.A.C. and the U.V.M. were combined in 1865. V.A.C./U.V.M. operates an experimental station in cooperation with the U.S. Department of Agriculture. The school and station publish and translate into readable English results of their experiments and research.

The U.V.M. today has the medical college, an engineering college, College of Arts and Sciences, education and nursing schools. It has a summer school, and recently night classes were instituted for adults. The U.V.M. in the mid-1960's has 4500 students. The instructor-student ratio is a favorable 1–8.

The University, beautifully situated on a plateau, overlooks Lake Champlain and the Adirondacks.

MIDDLEBURY

The Reverend Timothy Dwight, president of Yale, with the help of Addison County's shrewd Sheriff Gamaliel Painter, founded Middlebury to combat the Deism of the Allen-founded U.V.M. even though the Allens never had anything to do with the operation of the Burlington school. Brothers Ethan, Levi, Heman, Heber and Zimri were dead and gunrunner Ira was languishing in a French jailhouse when the U.V.M. commenced instruction.

Vermont novelist Daniel Pierce Thompson was an early Middlebury graduate.

Middlebury's reputation has been enhanced through its summer language schools. There are German, Russian, French, Italian and Spanish schools where students spend the summer speaking only their major language. The college maintains the Bread Loaf Summer School of English and sponsors the Bread Loaf Writers' Conference. The college in the mid-1960's has about 1300 students. The instructor-student ratio is 1–11.

NORWICH

Norwich, the oldest private military academy in the United States, was founded in 1819 as "The American Literary, Scientific and Military Academy" by Norwich native Captain Alden Partridge (West Point 1806). The school was moved to Middletown, Conn., in 1825. Partridge moved back to Norwich in 1826 and reopened his school as a preparatory school for Wesleyan College. In 1835 the preparatory school became Norwich College under the sponsorship of the Universalist Church. Captain Partridge was president.

Captain Partridge expressed the belief that the system of education in the United States was "defective" in that: "First: It is not sufficiently practical nor properly adapted to the duties an American citizen may be called upon to discharge. Second: Another defect is the entire neglect in all our principal seminaries of physical education, of the cultivation and improvement of the physical powers of the student." The routine and training of Norwich have consistently tried to remedy these "defects" ever since.

The college buildings burned in 1866 and a delegation from Northfield, Vermont, invited the school to that town. College officials immediately accepted. The school, today, is Norwich University. Norwich, despite its youth, supplied the Union Army with more than 500 officers. A proportionate number has been furnished in more recent conflicts. Norwich for many years was the chief source, outside of West Point, for horse cavalry officers and engineers. The student body in the mid-1960's was about 1000 with an instructor-student ratio of 1–13.

OTHER COLLEGES

Bennington College, women only, founded in 1932, has achieved an international reputation for its teaching methods and liberal student rules. The Bennington College School of the Dance is held during the summer.

The aims of the college, explicitly stated and dominating its whole system of operation, are to encourage voluntary self-dependent education throughout life; to develop permanent intellectual interests; to train students for social co-operation and responsibility; and, finally, to fit each student's course of study as far as possible to her individual tastes, talents, and needs. The academic year is divided into two parts by a winter recess of two months which students are urged to treat as a field period for observation and investigation correlated with their work on the campus.

Bennington in the mid-1960's has 350 students with an instructor-student ratio of 1–7.

Goddard College (1863) in Plainfield, a four year liberal arts college with about 300 students in the mid-1960's, allows students a great deal of freedom in both their private and academic life. The student-teacher ratio is about 1–100. The school is expected to enlarge its plant and double its student body before 1970. Goddard students, faculty and administration hope the school will not lose its unique personality during the enlarging process.

St. Michael's College, in Winooski, was established in 1904 by the Fathers of St. Edmund, whose schools in France had been confiscated. During its early years, made difficult by insufficient funds, the school was of the Continental preparatory school type. In 1913 it was incorporated as St. Michael's College. During the mid-1960's "St. Mike's" has about 1000 students with an instructor-student ratio of 1–13. Trinity (1925) is a Catholic women's college in Burlington.

Two small liberal arts colleges, Marlboro (1947) in Marlboro near Brattleboro and Windham (1951) in Putney, have been established. Rudolf Serkin presides over Marlboro's annual summer Music Seminar and festival.

State-operated teachers' colleges include: Castleton (1867), Johnson (1866) and Lyndon (1921). The Vermont Agricultural and Technical Institute (1867) was formerly the Randolph Normal and Vermont Agricultural Schools.

Vermont has Green Mountain Junior College (1834) in Poultney; Vermont Junior College (1834) in Montpelier, and Champlain Junior College in Burlington. The latter is essentially a business college. Bennington, Burlington, Montpelier and Rutland have business schools.

PUBLIC SCHOOLS

The 1777 Vermont Constitution provided for the establishment of a grammar school (grades 1–8) in every county. During the late eighteenth century and throughout the early nineteenth century Vermonters who wanted a high school education usually paid tuition to attend one of the numerous academies or seminaries. The first academy, Clio Hall, was founded 1780 in Bennington. In 1850 there were 66 and eleven years later there were 109 academies, seminaries and free public schools. Some academies and seminaries were operated and supported by various religious — usually Protestant — denominations.

Vermont, a century ago, had about 2500 school districts. Each district had at least one school. Some towns with only a few hundred population had 10 schools, most, if not all, being one-room school (grades 1–8) houses. Travel was difficult over blizzard-drifted or through axle-deep mud-bogged roads.

Today, the number of districts, is rapidly decreasing. Few one-room school houses remain. Towns which have not replaced several one-room schools with one central elementary school usually bus their students to a neighboring town.

In 1965 Landgrove, Londonderry and Weston voted to create the first regional elementary school district in the state. Similar schools will no doubt be created.

In 1965 all but nine of the 238 towns had at least one elementary school.

Regional high schools like Otter Valley High in Brandon which serves Brandon, Pittsford and several other towns are increasing. The formation of these regional schools brings many students nearer to membership in a 100–student graduating class. This is what Dr. James Bryant Conant considers the minimal size for effective teaching.

ADMINISTRATION

Schools are maintained by locally elected school boards. Regional schools are operated by board members elected from and representing the various towns taxed for the school. Where several schools exist in one town the board may hire a superintendent to oversee general operations.

The state department of education is operated by a board whose members are named by the governor. The department establishes curricula standards and standards for new construction or improved school structures. The state may pay up to 30 percent of the construction costs of a new school building.

The state, aided in some instances by federal funds, grants monies for educating handicapped children, vocational training or arts and crafts instruction. It supervises state teachers colleges and makes grants for special projects. It also establishes and supervises the maintenance of teaching standards.

The state finances and operates the Brandon Training School, an institution which attempts to train, and in some instances provide part-time employment for, mentally defective children or adults with retarded minds.

PRIVATE AND PAROCHIAL SCHOOLS

Vermont in the mid-1960's has 25 private schools or academies including 10 Roman Catholic parochial schools and about 80 high schools.

The Putney School (1935) was founded along experimental lines. Its emphasis upon individual needs and aptitudes of its students, the two long vacation periods, and its consistent attempt to correlate textbook learning with extracurricular experience make it more or less the secondary school counterpart of Bennington College. Members of the school and the local residents maintain an unusually close relationship. Students, for instance, who raise animals on the school farm, as many do, are almost invariably members of the Putney 4-H Club. The autumn Harvest Festival is a community gathering in the best and fullest sense of the phrase. The tuition fee provides one summer every two years in Europe, where students live in typical homes with associates of their own age.

In the mid-1960's Vermont elementary schools have about 55,000 students with 2200 teachers. There are about 26,000 high school students with 1400 teachers.

15

Architecture

THE varied developments in early American architecture made a belated appearance in a region as remote from fashionable centers as
Vermont was. At a time when the seacoast towns were well settled
and displaying developed styles of architecture, Vermont was still a
frontier state. However, it was not a too-distant frontier and the first
frame structures were based on examples of well-developed styles in
the nearby coastal areas. For the most part its buildings are variants
on the purest types of the styles they represent, and it is in these variations that we discern the ingenuity, individuality and general good
taste of the designers, builders, and original owners.

In a sense Vermont may be said to have leaped the usual transitional
stages, and elements characteristic of very primitive New England
Colonial work are rarely found here. There are no second-story over-
hangs, and a gambrel roof is very exceptional. The first buildings
among the heavily forested hills of Vermont were naturally of rough-
hewn logs. None of these shelters, forts or houses remains, and it is
not recorded where or when the first frame structure in the area was
built. Probably it did not antedate by many years the Henry House,
in North Bennington, which is said to date from 1763. The Old
Constitution House in Windsor, 1772, is an early example of frame
construction, a long, narrow two-story building with a steeply pitched
gable roof. The Congregational Church at Chester dates from 1773,
while the Rockingham Meeting House, built in 1787, is a landmark
in the history of the architecture of the state. It also is a two-story
frame clapboard structure, having seven bays, a modillioned cornice,
and a gable roof. The simplicity of the building emphasizes the
decorative note in the cornice — undoubtedly Vermont's conservative
acknowledgment of the greater elegancies that were flowering elsewhere in late eighteenth century New England Colonial work. In
1784, the Old Center Meeting House was built in Hartford, while the
Old South Church in Windsor dates from 1798. Both are frame
structures.

Early Vermont farmhouses, invariably of wood, were built primarily
to meet utilitarian requirements. The great body of this work consisted
of simple buildings, adapted to rural purposes, and displaying little or

no influence of any formal style. The older houses are plain story-and-a-half structures of wood with rough pine floorboards, crude fireplaces, usually closed up now, handwrought iron hinges, and worn flagstone entrance steps. Many of those built later, between 1800 and 1825, are of a more spacious type, comfortable and attractive. The earlier practice of connecting house, barns, and shed — a concession to the rigors of winter — was later abandoned in the interests of sanitation, but many examples of this "continuous architecture" remain.

The type of house found near Bennington is similar to that built in great numbers in the North Connecticut Valley. They are narrow and rectangular in plan but well proportioned. An early and interesting, though not a typical, example is the Colonel Johnson House built in 1775 in Newbury. Considering the date, it is surprising to find quoined corners, a modillioned cornice, and a paneled entrance doorway, refinements customary in the earlier New England settlements, but not widely used in Vermont until about 1800.

Excellent examples of early, more typical houses are the Richardson House built in 1787, the Hutchinson House, now the White Cupboard Inn, dating from 1794, and the Benjamin Swan House, 1801, all in Woodstock. In general they combine spaciousness with simplicity, although in the Hutchinson House there are a few sophisticated touches such as the pillared side porch and the circular louvered openings in the gable end.

ASHER BENJAMIN

With the admission of the state to the Union in 1791, there began a period of prosperity which was reflected in architecture. It was also a time coincidental with the maturing of the first native architects, for Charles Bulfinch in Boston, Samuel McIntire in Salem, and Asher Benjamin in Greenfield were consolidating the New England tradition at the high point of its development. No buildings in their entirety in Vermont are attributed to Bulfinch or McIntire, but it is certain that their influence was vital. In connection with the Unitarian Church (1816), Burlington, it is recorded that Bulfinch and Peter Banner, architect of the Park Street Church, Boston, both received fees for professional services. Benjamin lived for several years in Windsor and did considerable work there (see WINDSOR). His influence is further reflected in the Congregational churches in Bennington and Middlebury, the designer of both, Lavius Fillmore, having obviously studied Benjamin's celebrated handbooks. It was shortly before 1800 that the publications issued by the Adam brothers began to circulate among the architects on this side of the Atlantic. Benjamin, a skillful carpenter, drew freely from these publications for the details in his books, such as 'Country Builder's Assistant, Fully Explaining the Best Methods for Striking Regular and Quirked Mouldings' (1805).

DAKE

In listing names that influenced the course of architecture in Vermont we must include that of Thomas Royal Dake, who went to Castleton about 1807 and worked there for nearly half a century (see CASTLETON). Though he was entirely original at times, as in the Cole House (1833), Dake showed the influence of Bulfinch and McIntire and, like them, of the Adam brothers. The Ransom House (1840) in Castleton, a favorite photographic subject today, is one of his late experiments, an adaptation of the temple façade to residential purposes. It is more or less duplicated in the Ebenezer Wilcox House at Orwell. Both houses display the architectural oddity of five Ionic columns on the entrance façade. This results in a column in the center — a free interpretation indeed of the classic formula.

Characteristic details that are found in Vermont work previous to the Greek Revival of 1820 include beaded corner boards as well as beaded corners on columns, wood quoins, small triglyphs in the frieze, and modillioned and dentiled cornices. The more elaborate houses of this period show the Adam influence in the use of delicately carved festoons, urns, and rosettes. There are many examples of the triple-arched window, as well as the Palladian motif, on houses and churches. Graceful adaptations of the motif to house entrances were made, the Palladian side windows forming the side lights for the arched doorway. Interiors received their share of attention as good details of wood mantels and wall paneling indicate.

"Maple Grove" (1804) in Randolph Center is a graceful example of the work at this time. The detail of the cornices, the delicate fanlight and nice disposition of carved ornament on the white exterior are matched by the elaborate ceiling-high paneled mantels within. The Isaac Bayley House (1800) in Newbury is a good example of the almost flat roof, circled by a white balustrade with finial posts. The parlor interior is distinguished by arched alcoves at the sides of the fireplace.

NATIVE MATERIALS

With Vermont notable as a source of such staple building materials as marble, granite, and slate, it is natural to look for evidence of their use. Wood, of course, was plentiful and was the most widely employed of the native materials. Mainly in modern work, however, is marble or granite used and only in the southwest part of the state, adjacent to the quarries, is slate freely used for roofs. Here most roofs are slate, the use of the material extending even to the covering of such a utilitarian structure as an icehouse. Clay for brick was not plentiful and its use in consequence was somewhat restricted. Some of the old taverns, however, of one hundred years ago were built of brick and there are outstanding examples of more formal work such as the church at Weathersfield Center (1821) that indicate the skill and taste governing the use of this material.

It is regrettable that green and red slate have not been widely utilized in home construction. Poultney's new post office (1962) is an excellent example of what can be done with slate. Chester Depot (Vt. 103) has several houses more than a century old built from a stone quarried locally.

Grassemount (1804) in Burlington, now a women's dormitory at the University of Vermont, is a fine, well-known example. Though marred by later additions, the charm of its detail remains in the arched insets of pink brick around the windows, the second-story pilasters, and the columned cupola encircled by a white balustrade. The Bailey House (1823), in Woodstock, illustrates how the well-balanced proportions of the Georgian house are often nicely accented by the pattern of the fenestration. In Norwich is the Constant Murdock House, dating from 1788 and probably the earliest preserved example of the pure Georgian mode in the State.

GREEK REVIVAL

Vermont, as has been said, reflected the trends in the neighboring States in her own way. The Greek Revival did not flourish in Vermont in the sense of a frequent and complete use of the forms of the style. It left its mark in a general way in its effect on details and general proportions used on houses whose essential form belonged to an earlier period. In many of the churches the classic flavor did not extend beyond the Greek Doric columns of the portico. In the State

Capitol building in Montpelier an effort was made to extend the idiom to the entire building (see MONTPELIER). The work of Dake in Castleton in the Greek Revival style has been discussed above.

Domestic architecture in this state since 1850 has followed no very set pattern. There were fewer great private fortunes amassed here during the latter half of the nineteenth century than in most northern and eastern states, and consequently fewer baroque mansions in the General Grant "gingerbread" manner. Occasionally one may be seen, however, with wide lawns and a weather-vaned coach house, dominating a village in ornate ugliness. The preservation and restoration, during recent years, of the earlier and simpler houses of Vermont have exerted an appreciable influence on suburban building, much of which has followed the Colonial or Dutch Colonial style of small, neat, unpretentious houses.

PUBLIC BUILDINGS

The chief public buildings of Vermont other than the churches are the town halls and the county courthouses. In several instances one structure first served the community as a church and then as a town hall, or vice versa (see GEORGIA, LOWELL, RICHMOND, ROCKINGHAM). The predominant style of Vermont courthouses is either semi-ecclesiastical or, in a few counties, that of the Greek Revival. Of the latter type the Windham County Courthouse, at Newfane, is the most representative example, an almost pure expression of the Doric mode except for the domed cupola. It is a beautiful building.

The great variety of treatment of church towers and spires is a characteristic element of the Vermont scene. In contrast with the rolling green and blue of the Vermont hills these white sentinels provide the needed accent to the serenity of the landscape. A square tower rising from the front of the church, terminating in a belfry surmounted by a spire, was the most common form. The First Congregational Church (1806) in Bennington and the Old South Church (1798) in Windsor are excellent examples. The cone-shaped spire is used with good effect on the Congregational Church, Middlebury (1806–1809). Very occasionally a drastic departure from the form was ventured as in the Old Round Church, actually sixteen-sided, built in Richmond in 1813. It is a two-story frame structure surmounted at its center by an open octagonal belfry and lantern, with bell-shaped roof. The interiors of the churches were for the most part plain to the point of severity, and the infrequent original pulpit compositions as in the Federated Church (1833) in Castleton were limited by an aestheticism rooted in a moral distrust of the ornate. Fortunately the basement vestry, which despite its varied functional value has marred the lines of so many later churches, occurred very seldom in the earlier ones.

For the formal student of American architecture, therefore, Vermont is not the happy hunting ground that states settled and built up earlier can justly claim to be. For the informal observer, however, almost every section of the state preserves at least a few old houses and churches in the building of which individuality and ingenuity combined to produce something of lasting beauty.

The rapidly increasing popularity of weekend homes for skiers has resulted in the construction of many A-frame houses together with modified chalets and contemporary design homes with one wall of insulated glass panels and sliding doors. More expensive year-round homes have been developed along similar lines. Wide expanses of insulated glass are ideal for viewing Vermont's year-round beauty and scenery. Many city folk now building Vermont homes have discovered that well-designed contemporary homes are much better adapted to Vermont living than reproductions of older houses. Each dwelling type was adapted to the customs of the times.

COVERED BRIDGES

Vermont's covered wooden bridges are a major tourist attraction and a source of pride to many Vermonters. There are nearly 100 public, private and railroad covered bridges in the state, and most of them are well past the century mark in years. Fire, flood, highway modernization programs and, formerly, neglect, are major causes for the decreasing number of bridges.

Vermont, however, has more covered bridges than all of the other New England states together. The covered bridge in Old Sturbridge Village, Massachusetts, was built in Vermont where it was used for many years before being dismantled, toted to the Bay State and re-erected there.

Covered bridges, contrary to local legend, were not built to provide cover for courtin' couples during inclement weather — Vermonters are too practical and thrifty — but to provide protection for the wooden-planked roadway.

Vermont's first known covered bridge — and the first bridge to cross the Connecticut River anywhere along its length — was built by Colonel Enoch Hale in Bellows Falls in 1785. The bridge, 365 feet long with its planked roadway 50 feet above water, was replaced by Nathaniel Tucker's bridge in 1840. The Tucker bridge, still sturdy, was replaced in 1930.

Steel and concrete bridges are frequently destroyed by heavy floods. Covered wooden bridges are often re-useable. The Hammond Bridge (1843) and the neighboring Gorham Bridge in Pittsford floated nearly two miles downstream during the devastating 1927 flood. Both bridges were floated back to their original positions and are still used today.

Pittsford-born Nicholas M. Powers (1817–1897) was America's greatest covered bridge designer and builder. He built scores of bridges not only in New England but throughout the East. He designed and supervised the construction of the famous North Blenheim, N.Y., bridge and the Havre-de-Grace Maryland bridge.

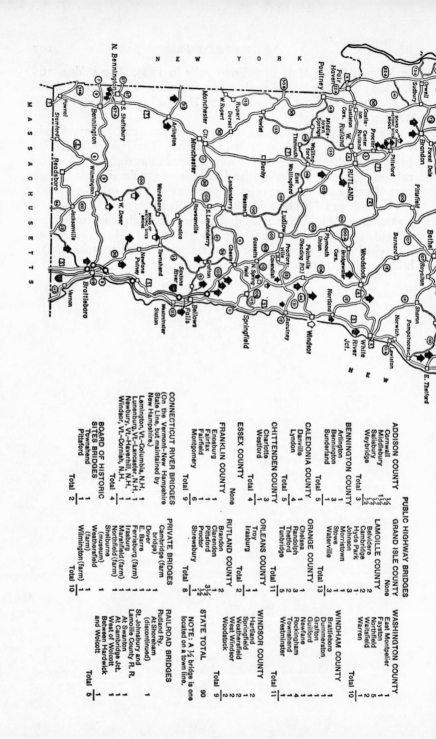

PUBLIC HIGHWAY BRIDGES

ADDISON COUNTY
Cornwall — ½
Middlebury — 1½
Salisbury — ½
Weybridge — ½
Total — 3

BENNINGTON COUNTY
Arlington — 1
Bennington — 3
Sunderland — 1
Total — 5

CALEDONIA COUNTY
Danville — 1
Lyndon — 4
Total — 5

CHITTENDEN COUNTY
Charlotte — 3
Westford — 1
Total — 4

ESSEX COUNTY
None

FRANKLIN COUNTY
Enosburg — 1
Fairfax — 1
Fairfield — 1
Montgomery — 3
Total — 6

GRAND ISLE COUNTY
None

LAMOILLE COUNTY
Belvidere — 2
Cambridge — 2
Hyde Park — 1
Johnson — 3
Morristown — 1
Stowe — 3
Waterville — 1
Total — 13

ORANGE COUNTY
Chelsea — 1
Randolph — 3
Thetford — 1
Tunbridge — 5
Total — 10

ORLEANS COUNTY
Troy — 1
Irasburg — 1
Total — 2

RUTLAND COUNTY
Brandon — 2
Clarendon — 1
Pittsford — 3½
Proctor — ½
Shrewsbury — 1
Total — 8

PRIVATE BRIDGES
Cambridge (farm bridge) — 1
Dover — 1
E. Barre — 1
Ferrisburg (farm) — 1
Irasburg (farm) — 1
Marshfield (farm) — 1
Northfield (farm) — 1
Shelburne (museum) — 1
Weathersfield (farm) — 1
Wilmington (farm) — 1
Total — 10

WASHINGTON COUNTY
East Montpelier — 1
Fayston — 1
Northfield — 5
Waitsfield — 2
Warren — 1
Total — 10

WINDHAM COUNTY
Brattleboro — 1
Dummerston — 1
Grafton — 1
Guilford — 1
Newfane — 4
Rockingham — 2
Townshend — 4
Westminster — 1
Total — 15

WINDSOR COUNTY
Hartland — 2
Springfield — 1
Weathersfield — 2
West Windsor — 2
Woodstock — 2
Total — 9

STATE TOTAL — 90

NOTE: A ½ bridge is one located on a town line.

RAILROAD BRIDGES
Rutland Ry.
At Shoreham (discontinued) — 1
St. Johnsbury and
Lamoille County R. R.
At Swanton — 1
At Cambridge Jct. — 1
West of Wolcott — 1
Between Hardwick
and Wolcott — 1
Total — 5

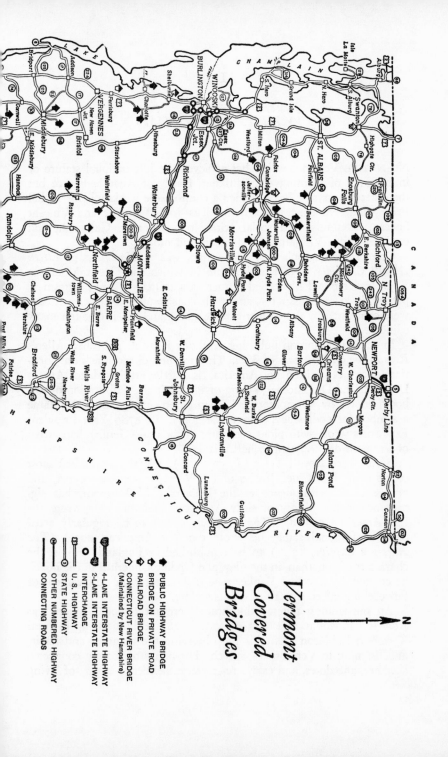

Vermont
Covered
Bridges

PUBLIC HIGHWAY BRIDGE
BRIDGE ON PRIVATE ROAD
RAILROAD BRIDGE
CONNECTICUT RIVER BRIDGE
(Maintained by New Hampshire)

4-LANE INTERSTATE HIGHWAY
2-LANE INTERSTATE HIGHWAY
INTERCHANGE
U. S. HIGHWAY
STATE HIGHWAY
OTHER NUMBERED HIGHWAY
CONNECTING ROADS

16

Writers and Artists

NO NATIVE Vermont writer has achieved the international stature or immortality of Hemingway, Faulkner, Hardy or Anatole France but the quiet countryside has provided a comfortable workshop for Nobel Prize winner Sinclair Lewis, journalists John Gunther and Vincent Sheean, economist and social critic John Kenneth Galbraith, and explorer-writer Vilhjalmur Stefansson and others.

One of the nation's first best sellers was *A Narrative of Ethan Allen's Captivity,* a hair-raising tale in which the Green Mountain Boys' leader noted his varied virtues as a military genius, statesman, patriot, hero and tosspot — and with considerable truth. Americans were captivated by the former captive's tales and ran it through many editions.

In 1784 Bennington publisher Anthony Haswell published Allen's *Reason the Only Oracle of Man.* This, the first direct attack on Christian doctrines written in America, is partly attributed to Allen's Deistic friend Dr. Thomas Young of Philadelphia. Publication of this book, known by Vermonters as "Ethan Allen's Bible," made his name a symbol for godlessness among the godly. In 1789 Yale President Ezra Stiles wrote with pious certainty: "Feb. 13 — Genl. Ethan Allen of Vermont died & went to hell this day."

Boston-born Royall Tyler (1757–1820), a Vermont resident most of his adult life, Chief Justice of the Vermont Supreme Court, and professor of jurisprudence at the University of Vermont, has significance in the history of early American literature. He wrote the first American comedy (*The Contrast,* 1786) to be regularly acted on a professional stage; he wrote the first American novel (*The Algerine Captive,* 1797) to be republished in England; and in the characters of Jonathan, in the play, and Updike Underhill in the novel, he created the first real Yankee type in literature: an achievement of far-reaching effect, though of dubious glory.

An outstanding nineteenth-century Vermont regional writer was Rowland E. Robinson (1833–1900). Born and brought up in rural Vermont, Robinson spent his life observing the manners and habits and listening to Vermonters' speech. His books of loosely connected sketches, anecdotes, and essays re-create authentically a way of living and a way of speaking that have disappeared forever. Not a first-flight creative artist, Robinson nevertheless left us books that are readable and frequently rereadable because of the warm humanity of the characterizations, the pervading love of nature expressing itself with careful accuracy, and the vanished rhythms of Yankee speech. Those who believe that uniformity in national life and language is achieved only at the heavy cost of the charm that lies in differences should read at least one Robinson book. They will find there the most complete record we shall ever have of a little corner of American civilization that was both colorful and unique.

THE THOMPSONS

Even more popular than Robinson's books in their day were the historical romances of Daniel P. Thompson (1797-1868), of which *The Green Mountain Boys* is by far the best. Unreliable in the factual details of their historical background, they were emotionally accurate, and their honest native melodrama served to keep alive in the Vermont consciousness a number of Vermont heroes whose exploits have proved much less exciting material in the hands of later and more scholarly historians. Van Wyck Brooks has said of *The Green Mountain Boys:* "It was a home-grown product, if ever literature saw one, as unpretentious as a log-cabin, but it was built on such a good model that no faults of style or execution counted in the final result . . . This was a Yankee tale as brisk and wholesome as any mountain ballad. It was a border-song in prose."

Daniel Greenleaf Thompson (1850-1897), son of Judge Thompson, wrote seven volumes. Charles Miner Thompson (1864-1941), grandson of Judge Thompson, longtime editor of *The Youth's Companion,* wrote *Independent Vermont* the best single book anybody has yet written on Vermont as an independent republic.

Longtime Portland, Ore., resident Stewart Holbrook, until his death in 1964, was Vermont's best-known contemporary writer. Informal historian Holbrook exploring the backwaters and byways of American history wrote delightful, witty and informative books like *Iron Brew, Holyoh Mackinaw, Ethan Allen, Murder Out Yonder, Little Annie Oakley and Other Rugged People, Lost Men of American History, Dreamers of the American Dream,* and others including *The Columbia* for the Rivers of America Series. *Age of The Moguls* was a best seller.

Calvin Coolidge, whose autobiography revealed less of the man than any autobiography ever published, may have been Vermont's highest paid writer. After he wrote his biography he liked to tell leading American writers "I get a dollar a word."

Manchester druggist and proprietor of the Johnny Appleseed Bookshop Walter Hard and his wife Margaret wrote *This Is Vermont*. Poet Hard also wrote *The Connecticut* for the Rivers of America series. He is a regular verse contributor to the *Rutland Herald*. His son Walter, Jr., is the able editor of *Vermont Life*, the state-sponsored quarterly which ranks among the best of such publications.

Vermonter Charles Crane, now deceased, returned home after years abroad as a foreign correspondent of the Associated Press. He wrote *Let Me Show You Vermont* which is probably the best interpretation ever written of the state. He also wrote the excellent *Winter In Vermont*. New York Times man R. L. Duffus wrote *Williamstown Branch,* a story of his Vermont boyhood. Thomas E. Ripley, of the Rutland marble sawmill Ripleys, wrote *Vermont Boyhood*. New Yorker Frederic Van de Water, a successful slick magazine novelist, moved to Vermont in the early 1930's. He wrote *Reluctant Republic,* a fastmoving informal history of the state's early years. Van de Water has since written several novels about the same era. His *Home in the Country* is a beautifully written account of the writer's family seeking a refuge and finding it here in Vermont. City folk thinking about moving to Vermont should read this book.

Louise Andrews Kent is known to tens of thousands of readers of the *Ladies' Home Journal* for her Mrs. Appleyard books. Mrs. Kent has written more than a dozen children's books but is best known for her books which combine comments on Vermont country life with excellent recipes. Notable are her *Winter Kitchen* and *Summer Kitchen* written in collaboration with her daughter Elizabeth Kent Gay. The Appleyard Center of her books is said to bear a resemblance to Kent's Corner in Calais, Vermont. She writes the food department for *Vermont Life,* and many of these recipes are to be found in her recent *Vermont Year Round Cookbook*.

Burlington resident Ralph Nading Hill has written several volumes about Vermont, including *The Winooski* for the Rivers of America series and *Contrary Country*.

In Bennington County formerly lived three women writers of distinction whom Robert Frost once called Vermont's "three verities": Dorothy Canfield Fisher, "wise and a novelist"; Zephine Humphrey (Fahnestock), "mystic and an essayist"; and Sarah Cleghorn, "saintly and a poet." Their untimely demise was greatly lamented far beyond the state. The profound social sympathy that permeated their work is proof that Vermont is not an artist's ivory tower, not a "colony," but a vantage point from which the world's injustices are to be battled, not ignored.

Novelist Pearl Buck is a Vermont resident.

POETS

San Francisco native Robert Frost, a longtime summer Vermonter, was the only poet ever elected Vermont's Official Poet Laureate, by the legislature. Frost lived in several Vermont towns before he decided on Ripton near Middlebury College's Bread Loaf School of English. The traits that most clearly distinguish Frost's verse; his terseness, dry piercing wit, oblique approach to a moral conclusion, his fusion into poetry of the tempo and inflections of living speech, his solid good sense — all mark him as the heir to an intellectual and spiritual heritage that is utterly Yankee, if not exclusively Vermont.

Vermonters usually don't pay much attention to literary folk, resident or summertimers, but they were proud of Robert Frost, one of their own kind, who articulated what many believed and lived.

Vermont's first poet Thomas Rowley (1721–1796) came to Danby from Connecticut. He played an active role in the struggle for independence and statehood. Rowley's verses — almost wholly on contemporary political themes — may not, as has been said, "set the mountains on fire," but their rugged swing fired the hearts of the Green Mountain boys in their heavy moments.

During the nineteenth century, Vermont, like the rest of the country, produced too many versifiers who published in newspapers and cheaply printed volumes their uninspired sentimental mush. Vermont poets who rose several notches above the usual mediocrity included Julia C. Dorr (1825–1913) and newsman Charles Gamage Eastman (1813–1860), uncritically dubbed "The Burns of New England."

Newsman John Godfrey Saxe (1816–1887) was Vermont's best and most widely known nineteenth-century poet. Saxe during the mid-nineteenth century was one of the nation's most popular poetry readers. He was especially popular before college audiences and his works appeared in the nation's popular magazines. His *Poems* went through more than forty editions.

The most popular native Vermont poet of the present century is probably Daniel Cady (1861–1934). Cady, a man of considerable scholarship, in his later years wrote more serious verse but fame rests on his four volumes of *Rhymes of Rural Vermont*. It is easy to patronize these poems but it is very foolish to do so. They are the equal of any dialect verse written in America with the exception of James Russell Lowell's works. As regards subject matter and diction, they have as much right to critical consideration as have many of the most popular poems of Rudyard Kipling. The comprehensiveness with which they covered the homely aspects of Vermont country life makes them the poetic counterpart of Robinson's works, with much of the same value.

Walter Hard's books, including *Salt of Vermont* and *Some Vermonters,* preserve in free-verse form some of the same tradition. Hard's major emphasis, however, is upon the collective Vermont personality and quirks of Yankee character.

Unrelated to Robert Frost by family or style of verse, Frances Frost of St. Albans wrote articulate verse, often akin to that of Emily Dickinson in concentration and economy.

A growing number of well-known writers are making Vermont either their summer or their permanent home. Though not native sons and daughters, if these people choose Vermont as their inspiration and workshop, they belong — in a sense — to this state in a more significant way than they could be said to do from the mere accident of birth here.

ARTISTS

Vermont has produced few artists of national reknown but the state for many years has been a favorite place for landscape painters. Middlebury's Arthur K. Healy's refreshing light airy landscapes have received national recognition. Italian-born Luigi Lucioni is probably the best-known painter of Vermont landscapes. His work is admired by many for its "photographlike" qualities. Many native and summer visitor painters exhibit their works in Manchester's annual Southern Vermont Artists Exhibition.

Many magazine and book illustrators have found Vermont a good place to live and work. Norman Rockwell, famed for his *Saturday Evening Post* covers, lived for many years in Arlington. Many of the figures he portrayed on *Post* covers were his Vermont friends and neighbors. Hamilton Greene is another Vermont resident whose illustrations appear in national periodicals. William Schaldach, noted for his fishing pictures, is a former Vermont resident.

Montpelier's Thomas Waterman Wood (1823–1903) was probably the best-known nineteenth-century painter of Vermont scenes. He left money to establish the Wood Art Gallery whose prime function is to insure perpetual display of the painter's work.

William Morris Hunt (1824–1879), born and buried in Brattleboro, though not a great American painter, was one of the most influential. Hunt rescued from discouragement and obscurity, broken only by the critics who had ridiculed his "clodhoppers," Jean François Millet, the French artist whose paintings ("The Angelus," "The Sower," "The Reaper") have in recent decades been almost too popular in this country. Hunt owned Millet originals including "The Sower," for which Millet accepted sixty dollars. After helping Millet establish the Barbizon school of painting in France, Hunt opened his own school in Boston, where for a time he occupied much the same position in American portraiture that Sargent held later. In 1875 he executed two large murals for the Assembly chamber of the Capitol at Albany, New York, considered the most important American murals until they were surpassed by Sargent's in the Boston Public Library. They have unfortunately been quite ruined by the dampness of the walls upon which, unlike Sargent's work, they were directly painted.

Richard Morris Hunt (1827–1895), William Morris Hunt's younger brother, was a very fashionable American architect. He did Newport residences for Cornelius Vanderbilt, Mrs. William K. Vanderbilt, and Oliver Belmont. He did the New York City town houses of Elbridge T. Gerry, John Jacob Astor, and William K. Vanderbilt, the latter, at Fifth Avenue and Fifty-second Street, being generally regarded as the apogee of the architectural exhibitionism of nineteenth-century multimillionaires. Hunt's public works included the Tribune Building (1873), among the first of the elevator office buildings; the Administration Building of the Columbian Exposition; the central portion of the Metropolitan Museum of Art; the National Observatory, in Washington; and the base of the Statue of Liberty. He was a native of Brattleboro.

Sculptor Larkin Mead (1835–1910), though born in Chesterfield, N.H., grew up in Brattleboro and considered it his home. He came to public notice through the "Recording Angel," which he sculptured in snow on New Year's Eve, 1856, at Linden and Main Streets. Rain and cold preserved the iced statue for several days, and — snow sculpture not being the common thing it now is — newspaper reporters came from Boston to write about it. James Russell Lowell celebrated it in a poem, "A Good Word for Winter." Mead later did several replicas in marble of what was originally an artistic prank. His best-known Vermont work is his colossal statue of Ethan Allen (1861) in the Capitol portico at Montpelier, which he duplicated for the Hall of Statuary in Washington. He did the original figure of Ceres on the Vermont Capitol dome. After the Civil War, during which he was a staff artist for *Harper's Weekly,* he lived for several years in Italy, where he married — despite the Pope's disapproval and refusal of dispensation — a celebrated Italian beauty, Marietta de Benvenuti. In Italy he did most of the actual work on his most ambitious piece, the Lincoln Memorial at Springfield, Illinois, completed in 1883.

William Rutherford Mead (1846–1928) Larkin's younger brother, was a distinguished American architect. A member of McKim, Mead, and White, he made the basic designs for many public buildings, including the Capitol at Providence, Rhode Island, and the Boston Public Library. He became president of the American Academy at Rome in 1909 and was its guiding spirit for eighteen years. Elinor Mead, a sister of Larkin and William, was an artist of some reputation and wife of William Dean Howells, the novelist and editor of the *Atlantic Monthly.*

Hiram Powers (1805–1873), born on a Woodstock hill farm, was the most famous mid-nineteenth-century American sculptor. His "Greek Slave" (1843) engaged the attention of the American public as no other statue ever has done before or since. The original was sold in England, but Powers made eight marble copies of it, one of which is now in the Corcoran Gallery, in Washington. His 150 busts included historical characters and the great personages of his own day. The National Capitol has his bust of Marshall and the statues of Franklin and Jefferson. The latter part of his life was spent in Florence, where Nathaniel Hawthorne said the life of two continents flowed through his studio. Powers' son, Preston, a sculptor of considerable talent, executed the Jacob Collamer statue in the National Capitol.

CONTEMPORARY ARTISTS

Dartmouth's recently retired Artist-in-Residence, Paul Sample, lives and paints in Norwich, Vermont. His most famous Vermont painting is the great mural in the National Life Insurance Company's national headquarters building in Montpelier.

Churchill Ettinger of Weston is probably America's best-known sporting artist. He is noted for his etchings. He has done many sporting watercolors and oils.

Many young artists — and some with growing reputations — are associated with colleges like Bennington.

Rockport, Massachusetts, artist Aldro Hibbard is known for his photograph-like Vermont landscapes. His oil, "The Little Village of Weston," is an excellent portrayal of the classic Vermont hill town.

17

Keeping Posted

VERMONT'S newspapers and other communications media have never exerted appreciable influence outside the state. Vermont, however, has either produced or trained some of the nation's most influential newsmen and editors, including founders and editors of the New York *Times,* New York *Tribune,* New York *World,* New York *Daily News,* Chicago *Tribune,* Milwaukee *Sentinel* and the Detroit *Free Press.* Three Vermonters were editors of *Harper's Magazine.* Two editors and one assistant editor of the *Youth's Companion* were Vermonters.

New Hampshire–born Horace Greeley (1811–1872) learned his trade as a printer's devil in an East Poultney printing shop. Greeley's fellow apprentice was Poultney native George Jones (1811–1896). Greeley founded the New York *Tribune* while Jones, together with Vermont-educated Henry J. Raymond (1820–1869), founded the New York *Times.*

VERMONT WEEKLIES

The Scourge of Aristocracy and Repository of Important Political Truth was neither a Bolshevik propaganda pamphlet by Leon Trotzky nor an anarchist tract by Pierre Proudhon. It was a Vermont newspaper published by fiery two-fisted Matthew Lyon (1750–1822), onetime Green Mountain Boy and anti-Federalist Vermont Congressman. Lyon's published comments about President John Adams brought his arrest and conviction under the unconstitutional "Alien and Sedition" law.

Lyon, during his four month's confinement, was re-elected to Congress. When the presidential election of 1800 was thrown into the House of Representatives, Lyon cast the vote which decided the outcome in favor of Thomas Jefferson. Lyon later became a Congressman from Kentucky and still later from Arkansas.

The *Vermont Gazette* or *Green Mountain Post Boy* was the first newspaper known to have been printed within the present boundaries of Vermont. It was published in Westminster in 1781 by Alden and Judah Spooner and Timothy Green, all formerly of Norwich, Connecticut. The paper existed until 1783 when the press was moved to

Windsor where Alden Spooner and George Hough commenced publication of the *Vermont Journal and Universal Advertiser*. This paper exists today as the *Vermont Journal*. It has undergone several management changes and was once published in Woodstock and for some years was known as the Windsor *Journal*.

Henry Oscar Houghton (1823–1895), a native of Sutton who founded the Houghton Mifflin publishing house and the Riverside Press, is the authority for the statement that the press on which Vermont's first newspaper was printed was also the first printing press in the United States. It was brought to the colonies in 1638 by America's first printer, Stephen Daye of Cambridge, Massachusetts. The first book printed in the colonies — the now immensely valuable *Bay State Psalm Book* — was printed on this press which is now in the Vermont Historical Society's museum in Montpelier.

Vermont's second newspaper, the *Vermont Gazette or Freeman's Depository,* was established in Bennington by Anthony Haswell. British-born Haswell learned his trade in Boston and Worcester under Isaiah Thomas, publisher of the "seditious" *Massachusetts Spy*. Some *Gazette* readers — there weren't many — swapped farm produce and firewood for their subscription.

James Lyon, son of the contumacious Matthew, established *The Farmer's Library of Vermont's Political and Historical Register* in Rutland in 1793. The paper was purchased by the Reverend Samuel Williams in 1794 and the name was changed to the Rutland *Herald* or *Vermont Mercury*. The Rutland *Herald,* a national award winning newspaper, is now published as a daily.

The *Green Mountain Freeman,* established in 1844 as a Montpelier weekly, was published and edited for a time by Judge Daniel Pierce Thompson (1795–1868), "novelist, historian, student and gentleman."

Orson S. Murray, of the *Vermont Telegraph* in Brandon, was the state's most vigorous editor during his eight-year reign (1835–1843). Murray, the local or Vermont agent for numerous national and regional reform societies, readily espoused any cause which remotely promised to better his fellow man. Murray in turn championed anti-Masonry, women's rights, prohibition, abolishment of capital punishment, no smoking and finally vegetarianism.

Vermont's most recent weekly editor to achieve high rank was Wilder Foote (1905–19—). Bay Stater Foote after graduation from Harvard worked for the Boston *Herald* and in the Boston Bureau of the Associated Press. He purchased the Brandon *Union* in 1930 and some years later the Middlebury *Register* and Bristol *Herald*. Foote attracted national attention with his first-rate column "Beyond Main Street" which was devoted to national and international affairs. He sold the papers — all since deceased — and went to Washington in 1940, where he served as personal assistant to Secretary of State Edward Stettinius. The former Brandon editor attended the Roosevelt-Stalin-Churchill conference at Yalta. After World War II he served as chief of information for the United Nations until his retirement.

The following weekly newspapers are currently published in Vermont: Bradford *United Opinion,* Bristol *Herald,* Chelsea–South Royalton edition of the *White River Herald* (Chelsea), Enosburg Falls *Standard, Suburban List* (Essex Junction), Fair Haven *Era, Twin State News* (Groton), Hardwick *Gazette, Essex County Herald* (Island Pond), Jericho *Reporter,* Manchester *Journal,* Addison *Independent* (Middlebury), Morrisville *News and Citizen,* Northfield *News and Advertiser,* Poultney *Herald, White River Valley Herald* (White River Junction), Richford *Journal-Gazette,* Randolph, Bethel and Rochester edition of the *White River Valley Herald* (Rochester), St. Albans *Leader,* Swanton *Courier,* Vergennes *Enterprize and Vermonter, Vermont Standard* (Woodstock).

Vermont's only Sunday newspaper is the *Vermont Sunday News,* published by William Loeb, in Burlington. Loeb also publishes the St. Albans (Daily) *Messenger.*

One of the finest and most popular publications issued by any state is *Vermont Life,* a quarterly, published by the Vermont Development Commission since 1946. It is read by most Vermonters, who are proud of it, and there are subscribers in Moscow, Russia, and Moscow, Vermont. *Vermont Life* contains many four-color illustrations of Vermont's scenery and people at work and play. Recreation through the four seasons and places to visit are regular features.

DAILY NEWSPAPERS

Vermont has two morning newspapers. The Burlington *Free Press,* established in 1827, has been published daily — except Sundays — since 1848. The Rutland *Herald,* established in 1794, has published daily — except Sundays — since 1861. The *Connecticut Valley Times-Reporter* commenced publication in October 1965.

The *Herald* for many years has won the annual Ayer Award for the best makeup of papers in its circulation classification. Former editor Howard K. Lindley is reported to have been the inspiration for

Doremus Jessup, the antifascist Vermont editor in Sinclair Lewis' novel *It Can't Happen Here.*

The *Herald* has received numerous cups and awards. Considering its handling of international, national, state and local reporting together with outstanding progressive editorials, it is one of America's best daily papers.

Vermont's first new morning daily paper to be established in more than a century is the *Connecticut Valley Times-Reporter* which commenced publication in Springfield in October, 1965. Former *Life* magazine foreign correspondent and onetime Vermont State Senator Harold Raynolds, Jr., took his *Bellows Falls Times* (Rockingham), *Springfield Reporter, Vermont Journal* (Woodstock) and the *Vermont Tribune* (Ludlow) and converted them into a daily morning paper. Editorial, news, advertising and production offices are located in Springfield while remaining departments are located in Bellows Falls. The *Times-Reporter* is the first Vermont daily to be reproduced by offset printing methods. The newspaper's stiffest competition comes from the Rutland *Herald's* Windsor County edition. Former Rutland *Herald* city editor Gerald McLaughlin, onetime *Time* Vermont correspondent, and longtime *Springfield Reporter* editor, was named senior news editor. Former *Bennington Banner* managing editor Tyler Resch was named managing editor.

Vermont's evening newspapers — daily except Sunday — include: Bennington *Banner,* Brattleboro *Reformer, Times-Argus* (Barre-Montpelier), St. Albans *Daily Messenger,* St. Johnsbury *Caledonian.*

White River Junction (Hartford) has the *Valley News* which is published across the Connecticut River in West Lebanon, New Hampshire.

With the passing of the Burlington *Daily News* in the early 1960's Vermont no longer has a community with two daily newspapers. There is not sufficient advertising revenue or reader interest. Many Vermonters, of course, read a local daily and either a Boston, New York, Albany or Montreal daily.

The recent merger of the Barre *Times* and the Montpelier *Argus* marked the passing of a longtime feud between the two papers of neighboring cities. The *Argus,* for many years the only Democratic paper in the state, was founded by Hiram Atkins in 1863. His descendant Miss B. Elaine Atkins was the paper's last editor and publisher. She bossed an all-woman news staff. The Rutland *Herald* purchased the *Argus* in 1964.

RADIO

Vermonter Calvin Coolidge was the first President to speak on the radio. Pioneer radio manufacturer Atwater Kent was a Vermonter who left $30,000 to restore the Kent Tavern in Kent's Corner in Calais.

Most of the state's radio stations are "dawn to dusk" operations. Current stations: WSNO (Barre) 1450 kc., WBTN (Bennington) 1379 kc., WTSA (Brattleboro) 1450 kc., WKVT (Brattleboro) 1490 kc., WVMT (Burlington) 620 kc., WDCT (Burlington) 1400 kc., WDEV (Waterbury) 550 kc., WSYB (Rutland) 1380 kc., WHWB (Rutland) 1000 kc., WWSR (St. Albans) 1420 kc., WTWN (St. Johnsbury) 1430 kc., WSKI (Montpelier-Barre) 1240 kc., WIKE (Newport) 1490 kc., WCFR (Springfield) 1480 kc.

TELEVISION

Vermont's lone television station is WCAX-TV (Channel 3), a CBS affiliate in Burlington. The antenna is located on Mt. Mansfield, the state's highest peak.

Vermonters, depending on their location and antennas, can pick up programs from Mt. Washington, Montreal, Plattsburgh, Schenectady and Northfield, Mass. Cable TV brings in Boston and Manchester, N.H., channels.

An attempt to establish a nonprofit educational television station in the state failed in the 1965 legislature.

COMMUNICATIONS

Communication methods are of prime importance to newsmen. Vermonters have always been in the forefront, either in devising new communication methods or in operating and improving existing techniques.

Burlington-born William H. Russell (1812–1872) was a co-founder of the legendary Pony Express. Matt Bushnell Jones was president of the New England Telephone and Telegraph Company. Harry Bates Thayer was an early president of the American Telephone and Telegraph Company. Ohio-born but longtime Vermont resident and philanthropist Theodore Vail was another A.T. & T. president.

Sir Curtis Miranda Lampson, a native of New Haven, was knighted by Queen Victoria for his role in laying the Transatlantic cable. Albert Chandler was president of the American Postal Telegraph Company.

PART TWO

Recreation

18

Hunting

VERMONTERS hunt over three basic terrains: (1) the rolling meadows and flatlands of the Valley of Vermont, Lake Champlain lowlands and that portion of the Connecticut River Valley within the state, (2) the forested slopes of the Green Mountains and Taconic ranges, and (3) boulder-strewn pastures and orchards of abandoned hill farms and cut-over woodlands.

Vermont farmers are hospitable folk, but they have to work hard for the little cash return from their small submarginal hill farms. Many of them have lost cattle during the deer season, and have had unwelcome guests litter their land with trash and leave cattle gates open. Ask permission before you shoot.

DEER

In 1897 the legislature ended thirty-two years of no deer hunting, and there have been deer seasons ever since. Vermont has had a bucks-only law for the past forty years.

A minor exception to the bucks-only law occurred in 1961 in specified areas when deer hunters were allowed to take one doe on the final day of the deer season.

Two southeastern counties, Windham and Windsor, have regularly produced the biggest annual deer harvest. Rutland County usually holds third place. The kill in these three counties usually accounts for nearly half of the state's total deer kill.

The towns of Rupert, Pawlet, Hubbardton, Rochester and Norwich are in the best deer-hunting areas. A town-by-town and year-by-year search of Fish and Game Service records since 1897 shows the following other towns and counties have been among producers of highest deer kills: Addison County, Ripton and Granville; Bennington County, Arlington and Dorset; Lamoille County, Stowe; Orange County, Newbury and Thetford; Rutland County, Castleton; Washington County, Berlin; Windham County, Newfane and Jamaica; Windsor County, Windsor, Norwich, Chester, Bethel, and Bridgewater.

Essex County in the extreme northeastern corner of the state has a substantial deer population. Owing in part to its distance from major metropolitan areas and to easier accessibility of good hunting areas farther south, the hunting pressure is quite light.

There are three types of deer hunting in Vermont: (1) still-hunting in mountainside forests, (2) drives through woods and swamps, and (3) long-range shots in the rolling meadows of the Valley of Vermont and the Champlain Valley.

The regular sixteen-day deer season opens the second Saturday in November. Sunday hunting is permitted. Deer must have horns at least three inches long. The use of dogs is prohibited and so is the use of autoloading rifles with magazine capacity of more than six shots. Kills must be immediately tagged and transported. All kills must be reported to the nearest game warden within 48 hours.

BOW SEASON

A special 16-day bow season opens the second Saturday in October. The limit is one deer of either sex. A special bow-and-arrow deer license is required in addition to the regular hunting license. Bow hunters who have bagged a deer cannot hunt during the regular deer season. Arrows must have at least a 7/8-inch head.

WOODCHUCK SHOOTING

Vermont woodchuck shooting begins in mid-April and continues through the first frost, usually mid-September. Just before the first and second hay mowings, meadow grass is too tall, but mountain pastures provide season-long shooting.

There is good chuck shooting all over Vermont. The best is found in creek and river meadows, mountain pastures, along stone walls by fields of clover and alfalfa, abandoned apple orchards, and deserted hill farms.

BEAR HUNTING

About half the state's black bear harvest is killed in November, the deer-hunting month. Rutland, Addison, Essex, Orleans, and Windham are the best bear-hunting counties. Most bear kills in recent years have come from the towns of Ripton, Granville, Granby, Eden, Montgomery, Chittenden, Huntington, Starksboro, Warren, and Rochester.

Most of these towns, also among the best deer areas, are on the slope of the Green Mountains. Black bear, though formerly on the state's bounty list, is now protected in all counties from December 1 through August 31. A person who takes a black bear must report his kill to a town clerk or game warden within 48 hours.

The bay lynx, commonly called bobcat or wildcat, is a predator. To collect the $10 bounty, a successful bobcat hunter must report his kill within 10 days to the nearest game warden. The warden will remove both ears, ruining the hide for taxidermy. Most out-of-state hunters, and many residents, prefer to forego the bounty and retain the complete hide.

SMALL GAME

Red fox and raccoon provide late fall sport. Coon, usually taken with guns, dogs, and lights, is the only game animal which can be legally hunted between sunset and sunrise.

There are few thrills like listening to the baying of coon hounds in the crisp clear air of a Vermont autumn evening. There is a limit of 25 coons for the season, which opens August 1 and closes December 31. There is no limit on the red fox, which can be hunted with a gun anytime during the year. Fox hunting with gun and dogs is limited to October through February.

The snowshoe hare — Vermont's only rabbit until the 1830's — since the advent of the more prolific cottontail, has been confined to the cedar swamps of the lowlands and the evergreen-clad slopes of the mountains. The five-month season opens October 1, and the bag limit of either snowshoes or cottontails is three a day.

GROUSE

The "pa'tridge," as Vermonters call ruffed grouse, is the state's number one game bird. State game ecologists estimate that grouse are more plentiful today than in Ethan Allen's era, because grouse prefer the mixed cover of cut-over timberlands to the virgin forests of the eighteenth century. Cedar swamps and abandoned apple orchards on deserted farms are also favorite haunts of this hardy bird which has managed to survive winters of 40° below zero. The daily bag limit of four has been in effect since 1874, but the month-long season has been extended to five weeks. The season now opens in late September and closes the Wednesday before the deer season opens. Season limit is 25 birds.

Ringneck pheasant shooting is spotty. Shooting has little effect on the overall annual mortality rate. Inadequate cover and insufficient food means fewer birds. Stocking under such circumstances is somewhat futile, report game biologists. Both cocks and hens can be taken during October. Daily limit: two birds.

Lake Champlain, 107 miles long and 1/4 mile to 12 miles wide, provides breeding grounds for mallard, black duck, teal and wood duck. These are augmented by migrating waterfowl.

Eagles, hawks and owls are protected.

STATE WATERFOWL AREAS

Vermont has been a leader among the Atlantic Flyway Council states in developing waterfowl management areas. The Dead Creek Waterfowl Area of 2037 acres, in the towns of Panton, Addison and Bridport, contains a true marsh with adjacent farmland where crops pleasing to waterfowl are planted. Other waterfowl development areas purchased include Little Otter Creek Area (838 acres) and Dead Creek Area (1000 acres). These are managed to insure good public shooting and breeding grounds. Roads and parking places are being constructed along their periphery.

Distances in Vermont are short and hunters will find good accommodations and food at reasonable prices almost anywhere. The Vermont State Development Commission, Montpelier, will furnish on request a list of hotels, motels, and other accommodations.

DETERMINING GAME PROSPECTS

Game wardens — about thirty are strategically located throughout the state — are always a well-informed source on game prospects. Their names, addresses, and telephone numbers are listed in the booklet *Vermont Fish and Game Laws,* which can be obtained from the town clerk where you purchase your hunting license or from the Fish and Game Service, Montpelier.

Vermont's best deer country is a 5-hour drive from New York City, 4 hours from Boston, and 10 hours from Washington. The state is served by airlines from Boston to Montpelier and Burlington and from New York to Rutland and Burlington.

A nonresident hunting license in Vermont costs $22. A nonresident small-game license covering all game except bear and deer costs $10.50. The nonresident bow-and-arrow license is $3.50. A nonresident hunting and fishing license costs $26. No special licenses or fees are required for hunting in the Green Mountain National Forest. A resident license is $2.25. A resident bow-and-arrow license is $1.00. A resident hunting and fishing license is $3.50. A resident trapping license is $1.75. A non-resident trapping license costs $50.

19

Fishing

VERMONT fishing is many things to many fishermen: a bass plug plopping into the weeds of a warm-water pond; wild antics of a bucking brookie; a screaming reel as a walleye plunges bottomward; drowsy warmth of an ice fisherman shanty; playing a rainbow into the shallows and waiting net; the smell of frying bass at a campfire beside a Long Trail pond.

Vermont's lakes, ponds and streams are fished annually by more than 150,000 fishermen and the number is increasing. About one out of two fishermen holds a nonresident license.

The Vermont Fish and Game Department is stocking the state's waters with more than 6,000,000 fish annually. Nearly 50 percent are at least legal size. This percentage will be increased. Many remote ponds and lakes — like those in Essex County — which are reachable by foot trails only, are stocked with fingerlings dropped from low-flying aircraft.

The F & G Department has already acquired more than 100 access areas on lakes, streams and ponds throughout the state. More will be acquired as funds become available. The department has no powers of condemnation or eminent domain. Owners of desirable sites must be willing to sell and at a price the department can afford. These areas insure fishermen and boat owners of public access areas along the state's best boating and fishing areas.

Vermont-bound fishermen should secure a free copy of *Vermont Fishing Access Areas and Impoundments* available from the Vermont Fish and Game Department, Montpelier, Vt.

License Fees: resident, $1.75; nonresident, season, $6.25; nonresident, three consecutive days, $2.25; nonresident, 14 consecutive days, $4.25.

The *Vermont Fishing Guide,* a large map folding to handy pocket-size, is indispensable to anyone fishing Vermont waters — and that includes Vermonters, who all too often devote their entire fishing career to a limited number of favorite "hot spots." This guide shows many of the state's 400 lakes and ponds and several hundred streams. The species of fish found in various locations along the streams and in the lakes and ponds are indicated on the map. The guide contains current general information, data on stream, pond and lake fishing, ice fishing, camping along fishing waters, fishing access areas, fish culture and stocking along with the aforementioned illustrated species distribution. The guide is free.

Obtain a free *Syllabus of Fish and Game Laws* from either the Department or the town clerk where you purchase your license. Write the Department and ask for a list of their free literature on Vermont fish and fishing.

Visitors are welcome at the state fish hatcheries in Bald Hill, Bennington, Canaan, Morgan, Roxbury and Salisbury. The Department cooperates extensively with the federal government-operated hatcheries at Pittsford, St. Johnsbury and York Pond (West Milan, N.H.)

LAKE AND POND FISHING

More than 400 lakes and ponds give Vermont fishermen plenty of angling choice. Most waters have public access to them.

Lake Champlain, over 100 miles long in Vermont, offers a wide variety of fishing. Ling, bowfin and sturgeon from prehistoric times to limited muskie, salmon, trout and abundant warm-water species, yellow perch, walleyed pike, sauger or sand pike, largemouth and smallmouth bass, pickerel, northern pike, bullheads and catfish, plus numerous species of minnows and panfish may all be found in Champlain. A Vermont license is needed on this side of the deep water channel, buoy marked; a New York license on the west side.

Winter fishing is popular and productive on most Vermont lakes and ponds which are not listed as closed waters. Hundreds of shanties dot the ice. Other hardy souls fish in the open using jigs, whips, jacks, and tie-ups. Smelt are caught in most of the larger lakes even though the species is not indicated on the map.

Motor boats should be registered. (A booklet on this law as well as applications for registering are available from the Department of Public Safety, Marine Division, Montpelier.)

STREAM FISHING

The *Vermont Fishing Guide,* a remarkably candid publication despite its official status comments on river and stream fishing:

Slow winding meadow brooks with undercut banks where fat square-tails hide are still plentiful in Vermont. Or perhaps the wild brook with its intermittent beaver ponds are to your liking. A word of warning about beaver ponds. After a few years, usually the beaver pond fills with sediment, temperatures rise, and fishing falls off. However, further up the same flowage you might well strike excellent fishing and in some places heavy spring run-offs appear to remedy the problem. These ponds hold up year after year.

Frankly, however, all is not on the rosy side. As in most places, man has often abused his rich natural endowment. Our streams in many areas bring this sharply into focus. Vermont has made and is making good progress in abating pollution. But too often fields run to the stream's edge, cattle trails crosshatch the grassed banks to the water. Erosion has eaten away the soil until the stream lies divorced from its sheltering banks amid sun-baked ledge and rubber. Water temperatures now run high. In other places huge unmarketable trees crowd the banks and suck the life-blood from the stream which now becomes a trickle or dries up in late summer. Abuse of privilege has led to a good deal of posting in some areas and greed has influenced additional posting. Courtesy seeking landowner permission, sporting salesmanship and promotion can help in all instances but particularly on the posting.

20

General Recreation

SKIING

VERMONT, site of the nation's first ski tow (Suicide Six, Woodstock, 1933–34) and the leading ski state east of the Rockies, offers both the longest and highest ski lifts in the East. There are more than 40 ski areas from deluxe accommodation resorts favored by TV and film stars to simple community affairs patronized largely by local families on weekends.

Each resort has at least one lift or tow ranging from the old-fashioned rope tow powered by an automobile engine to three passenger-enclosed gondolas. Ski areas provide trails for the novice, intermediate and expert skier. There are gentle open slopes and plunging trails. Many areas have special slopes for children.

Resort accommodations may include expensive suites and one-sex bunkhouses. There are tiny snack bars in one-room warming huts and expensive restaurants featuring European cuisine prepared by imported chefs. Outdoor heated swimming pools are featured at some resorts.

"Learn to Ski Weeks" are becoming popular at many ski areas. Two meals a day, room, ski lessons and use of lifts are usually included in prices ranging from $75 to $150. The price varies with the type of accommodation.

Weekend or week-long skiers can, at many resorts, attend ski classes or take individual instruction. Area ski shops usually sell or rent equipment.

Affluent skiers can fly from New York or Boston to Burlington or Rutland. Taxi service is provided from both airports to nearby ski areas like Stowe, Pico or Killington. Vermont roads are kept open all winter long to facilitate approach by automobile. There is direct train and/or bus service from New York and Boston to many ski areas.

Vermont high country skiing usually lasts from December into April. In some years there is late May skiing at Stowe. The major ski developments like: Big Bromley, Glen Ellen, Mad River, Magic Mountain, Mount Snow, Pico–Killington, Stowe–Spruce Mountain, Stratton Mountain and Sugarbush are in the heavy snow belt (120 inches) country. Other areas usually have good skiing during the mid-winter season with 50 to 75 inches of snow.

Skiers can purchase all necessary equipment at ski resort shops. Rentals are available. Nearly all ski areas have Ski (safety and rescue) Patrols. The Brattleboro Patrol, founded before World War II, is one of the oldest in the country.

Information: New Yorkers can receive daily Vermont Snow condition reports by phoning COlumbus 5-1450. Canadians can phone UNiversity 1-0195 in Montreal, Quebec. Cleveland residents should phone 781-1840.

Write the Vermont Development Commission for a current copy of *Ski Vermont*. Each area will send its own material upon request.

STATE PARKS AND FORESTS

There are 61 state forests and state forest parks in Vermont with a total of nearly 100,000 acres. State forests were provided for by legislative acts in 1908 and state forest parks — usually called state parks — were provided for by a legislative act in 1921. Many of the parks and forests started with a gift of land to which the state had added by purchasing additional acres.

Park and forest facilities may include: picnic tables, fireplaces, tent sites, three-side log leantos — camp trailer sites, bathing beaches, bathhouses, boat landing and launching, fishing, hunting, foot trails, scenic roads and scenic views. Few parks or forests contain all these facilities. Picnic tables and fireplaces are standard equipment at nearly all parks and many forests. Parks without facilities are those recently acquired which are currently undergoing development. Some state forests, usually those reachable only by trails, have little or no developed facilities.

All state parks and forests are listed alphabetically in the gazetteer section of this book. Forests and parks whose names do not indicate the town they are located in are listed by name and then cross-indexed to the town of their location. Exceptions are major state forest recreation areas like Calvin Coolidge State Forest which are listed and described under their respective names.

"WHAT DOES IT COST?"

A fee of 25 cents per person — without or with car — is collected upon entering the park or forest.

A tent site or camp trailer site without or with a tent platform: $1 per night per adult (minimum charge $2 per night); Green Mt. leanto, $1.50 per night per adult (minimum charge, $3 per night). There is no charge for children under eighteen who are part of a family unit.

The minimum campsite fee is charged Boy Scouts, Girl Scouts, 4-H Clubs or other youth groups. Where there are more than five youths in a group the rate is 40 cents per night for camp and camp trailer sites or 60 cents per night for leantos. No weekly rates. Checkout time is noon.

Reservations are usually required before Labor Day. None are required after Labor Day. Reservations made between January 1 and May 1 should be mailed to the Department of Forests and Parks, Montpelier. Reservations made after May 1 — you may be too late — should be mailed directly to the caretaker of the forest or park you are interested in. The mailing address is included with the description of each park or forest.

At state parks or forests with a bathhouse a 10 cent fee is charged for the clothes basket, locker room. (Fees subject to change.)

PARK HOURS

Parks are open to the public between 10 A.M. to 9 P.M. from the Sunday preceding Memorial Day through Labor Day. Camping parties with permits are excepted. Ski tow areas close at 5 P.M.

CAMPFIRE PERMITS

No fire shall be built at any time on state land except in fireplaces at designated picnic areas and campsites. Firewood is furnished at some picnic and camp areas. Where wood is not furnished only dead trees shall be used. No trees are to be cut. It is strictly prohibited to peel birch trees for their bark.

Campers and picnickers may use gasoline or gas stoves and charcoal grills provided proper precautions are taken.

CAMP TRAILERS

No provisions are made at parks or forests for regular trailers. Camp trailers can be used in certain areas provided the trailer fits into the allotted space. Camp trailer sites are available at: Allis, Ascutney, Bomoseen, Brighton, Button Bay, D.A.R., Emerald Lake, Fort Dummer, Gifford Woods, Grande Isle, Groton, Molly Stark and at Smuggler's Notch, Mount Mansfield.

NO FLOWER PICKING

The Vermont state laws expressly prohibit the picking of plants or flowers found within state parks or forests. Flowers and plants on state property, the legislators believe, are there for everyone to enjoy.

ANTI-LITTER LAW

Vermonters, the good ones anyway, are proud of their state's beauty. There is a $50 fine for throwing trash out of car windows — and this includes empty cigarette packages. The fine also applies to failing to pick up a camp or picnic site.

THE LONG TRAIL

The Long Trail is a 261-mile (some say 259) trail which runs over the peaks of the main Green Mountain range from the Massachusetts border near Williamstown north to the U.S. Canadian frontier. There are about 170 miles of side and approach trails. The entire Long Trail system now includes about 425 miles. The Green Mountain Club maintains 175 miles of the main Long Trail and 80 miles of side trails. The remainder of the Long Trail and side trails — those sections lying within the Green Mountain National Forest — are maintained by U.S. Forest service personnel.

On March 11, 1910, twenty-three hiking enthusiasts, headed by James P. Taylor, then principal of Vermont Academy at Saxtons River, met at Burlington and formed the Green Mountain Club, the purpose of which was to build a foot trail over the main range of the Green Mountains from Massachusetts to the Canadian Line. Small at first, and financially handicapped, the group gradually acquired a larger membership, including many persons outside the state. Those who were unable to contribute money gave of their time, the actual construction of the Trail being done largely by volunteer labor. Early progress was impeded by the necessity of clearing away each year's undergrowth from the completed parts of the Trail. In several places completed stretches were abandoned for a higher location, a discouraging process at the time, but one that resulted in a scenic gain. The 261-mile "Footpath in the Wilderness" was finished in 1928, and the Green Mountain Club, which maintains and publicizes it, is now on a solid financial basis, with more than 1500 paid memberships.

The Trail is divided into five main sections. The northernmost division, from the Canadian Line to Johnson, was the last to be built. This is probably the wildest part of the route and is distinguished by the view from Jay Peak, the highest mountain in northern Vermont, and the crossing of Hazens Notch.

The second section, from Johnson to Camel's Hump, is the most strenuous, crossing six major mountains, including Mansfield, the highest mountain in the state, which with its huts is a favorite stopping place.

The section from the south bank of the Winooski River in Bolton to Lincoln Gap at Lincoln Warren Pass is called the Monroe Skyline in honor of the late Professor Will Monroe who did so much to construct the Long Trail.

The Presidential Section is included in that portion of the trail which runs south from Lincoln Gap to Sherburne Pass, ten miles east of Rutland. The beautiful log Long Trail Lodge, located here, was formerly the Green Mountain Club's clubhouse. It is now a commercial venture.

The fifth section runs south from Sherburne Pass to the Massachusetts frontier and crosses through some of the wildest areas in the state.

Free shelters are maintained every few miles either by the Green Mountain Club or the U.S. Forest Service. Most shelters are of the three-sided log Adirondack type. These are equipped with bunks, open fireplaces and in some instances stoves. Drinking water is always handy. Some huts are enclosed.

The Trail is more often taken from south to north. By traveling in this direction, hikers achieve a scenic climax in the vistas of the Adirondacks, Lake Champlain, and the White Mountains that occur throughout the northern sections, though the smooth timbered hills of the southern end and the prospects of the Taconics to the west have their own distinctive, if less spectacular, beauty.

GREEN MOUNTAIN NATIONAL FOREST

Details will be found under Part III (see Green Mountain National Forest p. 247).

BOATING

Vermont's 400 lakes and ponds including Lake Champlain, the nation's third largest natural freshwater lake outside of the Great Lakes, provide sailing, power boating, canoeing, fishing and winter ice yachting opportunities.

Public agencies maintain 13 launching sites on the Vermont side of Lake Champlain. Another 13 sites are privately operated for the public. There are at least 16 state maintained launching sites on other lakes.

The Fish and Game Department has secured about 100 access areas on lakes, streams and ponds. Shoreline property costs are sharply increasing. The Fish and Game Department with its very limited funds, is attempting to secure as many suitable access areas as possible before land prices climb too high. The department has no power of eminent domain nor can it institute condemnation proceedings.

The many rivers and streams including Otter Creek — the state's longest river — offer combined opportunities for canoeing, fishing and camping. Canoes can be launched nearly anywhere along the hundreds of miles of streamside. The annual National White Water Canoe Contest is held, usually in late spring, along the White River.

(Write for *Vermont Boating Map and Guide* published by the Vermont Development Commission and *Access Areas and Maps* published by the Fish and Game Department.)

GOLF

Vermont has 38 golf courses including 24 nine-hole links and 14 eighteen-hole courses. Four nine-hole courses were recently expanded to 18 holes. Most communities are within 30 minutes drive from a country club. For current information write either directly to the club or to the Vermont Development Commission, Montpelier, Vermont.

Eighteen-hole courses: Bennington, Burlington, Fairlee, Manchester, Orleans, Rutland, St. George, Springfield, Stowe, Vergennes, Warren, Williston, Woodstock.

Nine-hole courses: Barre, Barton, Bradford, Brandon, Brattleboro, Castleton, Colchester, Dorset, Greensboro, Middlebury, Montpelier, Morristown, Newport, Northfield, Poultney, Proctor, Richford, Randolph, Rockingham, St. Albans, St. Johnsbury, Waterbury, Windsor.

A description of each course including facilities will be found under the respective cities and towns.

Courses are being constructed at the Mt. Snow and Stratton ski areas and in the Windham–Andover area.

PART THREE

*Main Street
and Village Green*

Main Street
and Village Green

ACKWORTH (see BRISTOL)
ADAMANT (see CALAIS)

ADDISON COUNTY (Area 756 sq. miles. Population 20,076). Shire
town: Middlebury, organized 1785. Includes: Addison, Bridport, Bristol,
Cornwall, Ferrisburg, Goshen, Granville, Hancock, Leicester, Middlebury,
Monkton, New Haven, Orwell, Panton, Ripton, Salisbury, Shoreham,
Starksboro, Vergennes, Waltham, Weybridge, Whiting.

ADDISON, 5–A (Addison County, Vt. 17 and Vt. 22A; alt. 280, pop.
645; 25,027 area; Vergennes R.D.). Includes: Addison Four Corners,
West Addison and Chimney Point.

ADDISON (Four Corners) is a little plains settlement built at the crossroads (Vt. 17 and 22A) around a fenced green which fronts the *Baptist
Church* (1816), a simple white structure, and the *Grandview Grange*.
In the background are sweeping meadows, Lake Champlain, and the
serrated wall of the Adirondacks. An incongruous note is struck here
in this quiet crossroads village — a machine gun is mounted on the
World War I Memorial in the peaceful green.

South of Addison, Vt. 22A passes an orchard with long straight rows
of apple trees spread over level acres, and the twisted gray tentacles of
stump fences are seen along the highway. *Snake Mountain* (R), whose
elevation of 1271 feet is distinctive in this region, dominates the scene
for miles, its long ridge curling against the eastern horizon.

The *Bigelow House* is a good example of the region's well-made
brick homesteads, large and trim-lined in faded red brick, with the
habitual end chimneys of its period, early nineteenth century. *The
Stone Houses* uphold the tradition of the section for combining prac-
ticality with beauty in building. These stone houses are testimonials of
the thrift, labor, and craft of past generations.

West of Addison, Vt. 17 traverses a level open countryside of sweeping plains and broad meadows typical of western Addison County. The
air is imbued with a fresh new quality; the nearness of Lake Champlain
is felt in the atmosphere.

WEST ADDISON (Vt. 17) is a few houses along the road.

John Strong Mansion (open July 1–Sept. 1) was purchased in 1934 by the Daughters of the American Revolution, Vermont Chapter, and is maintained by them. The Georgian style mansion, a fine structure, was built in 1796–98 of bricks made on the farm of John Strong, who was a prominent figure in the early affairs of town and state. The handsome brick house stands on the site of an earlier home of John Strong, a wooden house built before the Revolution and burned by the British on their big drive down the lake in 1777. The present mansion has an entrance hall of beautiful design, and the interior contains many points of interest: corkscrew hinges on some of the doors; skillfully built-in shutters; old fireplaces with iron back walls; stenciled floors; and an artfully concealed hiding place in the massive chimney, entered by a secret panel in the kitchen, and large enough to conceal six or seven people.

John Strong, a native of Connecticut, was one of the first three settlers and his son, John, was the first white child of Anglo-American parentage born in Addison County. A general in the Vermont militia, Strong was a member of the Convention that approved for Vermont the Constitution of the United States. Five generations of Strongs lived in the mansion.

Crown Point Military Road Marker (on Vt. 17, southside, 1.3 m. west of the John Strong Mansion) indicated the northern limit of that important trail through the wilderness which was followed by scouts, soldiers, and pioneer settlers and extended from Charlestown, N.H. (Old No. 4), to this point. The road was built in 1759 under General Amherst to connect the waterways of the Connecticut and Lake Champlain. The country road that branches left from this junction follows the course of the historic old Crown Point Road to Bridport, and here can be conjured pictures of the strange lonely people who tramped along it in those eighteenth century days — lean, wiry frontier scouts in buckskin; grim, plodding settlers bearing all their earthly possessions; smart, red-coated Britishers and ragged, starving soldiers with powder stains on their gaunt cheeks; Indians in war paint moving silently as shadows; Rogers Rangers in greenish buckskin, lithe, bronzed men who were themselves almost like Indians in their woodcraft, tireless endurance, and ruthless methods of fighting.

CHIMNEY POINT (8.0 m. west of Addison on Vt. 17) is a promontory in Lake Champlain where the Lake Champlain Bridge spans the narrowed waters to connect Vermont with New York State. Chimney Point is generally accepted as the spot where Samuel de Champlain stood on July 30, 1609, and gave his name to the beautiful inland sea stretching before him. Champlain crossed the lake to Chimney Point, after defeating the Iroquois Indians in a battle fought on the western shore, a battle of far-reaching consequences as proved in later warfare, for the powerful Iroquois were ever afterward hostile to the French. As early as 1690, Jacobus de Warm, heading a French expedition from Albany, built a small fort here. The first lasting settlement was made in 1730 by a little band of French colonists who came up the lake and repaired the old De Warm fort. Around their fortress, which they called Fort de Pieux, a settlement grew up to become one of the important early French possessions in the New World. The French deserted the village in 1759 before the threat of an Indian invasion, and in 1760 raiding Mohawks devastated the settlement completely. The grim picture of chimneys rising from blackened ruins resulted in the present name, Chimney Point. Many cellar holes of the ancient French town are still visible. Where Champlain landed after blasting the Iroquois and where French trappers and hunters built up a stronghold that was ultimately destroyed by painted Mohawks, there is today a concrete highway curving toward a handsome steel bridge over the peaceful lake.

The *Barnes House* (visitors welcome) stands on the site of the old De Warm fort and contains one wall of stone, two and one-half feet thick, which is thought to be a wall of the original fortress. In the construction of this house, by the grandfather of the present owner, bricks were brought across the lake from the ruins of Fort St. Frederic to build a wall enclosing the shell of the ancient stone blockhouse on Chimney Point. For nearly 100 years this structure served as an inn, and as the *Old Captain Hendee House* figures prominently in *The Green Mountain Boys* written by Judge Daniel P. Thompson. Here in the taproom, according to the story, Ethan Allen and Seth Warner were surprised by the British and narrowly escaped capture.

The house is now a veritable treasure vault of historical relics. In the taproom, where the Green Mountain Boys once lounged to talk and plan over their rum, is the old bar and liquor cabinet with Waterford decanters; old Normandy inn chairs; collections of Indian, French, and English relics, such as arrowheads, cannon balls, parts of firearms, silver shoe buckles, buttons, insignia, etc. The keel and ribs of Arnold's flagship *Congress* salvaged from Buttonmould Bay (see PANTON) are kept here, along with small articles recovered from the wreckage, including an early hand grenade with wooden fuse plug. In another part of the house is one of the most beautiful and best equipped ancient fireplaces to be found in America, and a great oven believed to be from Fort de Pieux. There are old kitchen utensils of all sorts, oil lamps, cones of Waterford and Sandwich glass, and a heating stove long enough to take four-foot sticks and extended through a partition to heat two rooms. Among the Indian implements are serrated points, peculiar to the Oregon Indians, and obsidian points which are identified with far western tribes, making it a matter of conjecture as to how such arrow-heads reached the shores of Champlain.

LAKE CHAMPLAIN BRIDGE is operated by the States of Vermont & New

York Lake Champlain Bridge Commission. The more than $1,000,000 cost was amortized from toll receipts. New York, the larger and wealthier state, paid 60 percent of the construction cost. The opening of the bridge, August 27, 1929, created a new and important route for interstate traffic, providing the first roadway across the lake, and supplementing the many existing ferries. This handsome steel structure has proved a vital gateway for traffic entering New England.

Just across the bridge, in New York, are the *Crown Point Fort Ruins,* remnants of the second most important fortification on the lake. Here in 1731 the French built Fort St. Frederic, which for twenty-four years remained their most extreme outpost in the Colonies, until in 1755 they established Fort Carillon twelve miles south on the lakeshore at Ticonderoga. In 1759, the French evacuated before the advance of General Amherst's superior forces, blowing up part of the fortifications as they left. Amherst took possession, made repairs, and left a small garrison there, calling it Fort Amherst. The British held the fort until 1775 when Colonel Seth Warner of the Green Mountain Boys captured it without bloodshed. An important vantage point on the Champlain waterway, this stronghold changed hands several times, apparently without a gun being fired in its defense.

D.A.R. STATE PARK (Vt. 17; 85 acres; Vergennes R.D. 4), given to people of Vermont in 1949 by Daughters of American Revolution, Vermont Chapter. Park has Revolutionary war associations (see description of John Strong Mansion above). Picnic area and park shelter located on bluff overlooking Lake Champlain. Facilities: picnic tables and fireplaces, tent sites, lean-tos, camp trailers, bathing, boating, fishing, refreshments.

VAH (Addison), Champlain Valley Farms, Erwin Clark. Bird's-foot trefoil and dairy farm (Holstein cattle).

AITKEN STATE FOREST (see MENDON)

ALBANY, 2–D (Orleans County, Vt. 14; alt. 900, pop. 560; 17,631 acres). Includes: Albany Center, East Albany, South Albany.

ALBANY (Center, pop. 169), a pleasant village on the Black River (north), was chartered as Lutterloh, the present name being adopted in 1815. The village is set on a long sloping plain with a wooded ridge offering shelter on the west. The *Town Hall* and *Library* are housed in an old white church building, with a belfry and built-on entry hall. Beside the line of gasoline pumps fronting the village stores, a row of Lombardy poplars serves to relieve the drabness of the street. The atmosphere is a solid hinterland one. An annual event that gives vivid expression to this back-country air is the Albany Fair held here each September in the heart of the village, with Main St. serving as midway and racetrack combined. Extensive potato raising is carried on here.

Between Albany and Irasburg, the highway overlooks the meandering bends of the Black River weaving an intricate pattern through a valley supporting good farm sites. Two tiny ponds lie below the highway and the lowlands in this section are widely known duck-hunting grounds.

EAST ALBANY (on unnumbered road south of Irasburg, Irasburg R.D.) is a small settlement around a Catholic Church (nonresident pastor).

SOUTH ALBANY (on unnumbered dirt road north of East Craftsbury) is another tiny settlement with a general store.

ALBURG, 1–A (Grand Isle County, US 2 and Vt. 78; alt. 123, pop. 1123; 17,366 acres). Includes: Alburg village, Alburg Center, Alburg Springs, East Alburg, South Alburg, Windmill Point. Alburg Official Information Booth (near American Legion bldg.).

ALBURG village (US 2; alt. 123, pop. 426) is believed to be a contraction — or corruption — of Allenburg (after Ethan and/or Ira Allen). Much of the town's importance was lost when the Rutland Railway ceased operations in this area. The Central Vermont joined the Rutland RR here. It is thought that the Abnaki Indians originally occupied the area. Alburg is the only town of any size on the islands. The village street is well shaded by elms, with flowerbeds brightening the general dullness. Stone houses, characteristic of the islands, are seen here and there, and apple trees along the roadside hint of the extensive orchards that lie southward.

The *Stone House* was built in 1823 and once served as a tavern known as Motte's Inn. It is representative of the century-old stone structures so prevalent throughout Grand Isle County, which are generally built of field stone with cornerstones of cut rock or granite, and differ from the slab stone buildings of southern Vermont.

U.S. Customs and Port of Entry is located in Alburg. The East Alburg Springs station is under the direct jurisdiction of the Alburg Port of Entry.

ALBURG CENTER (US 2; alt. 140; Alburg R.D.), the original settlement of Alburg town, is a straggling hamlet with leafy boughs arching the highway, undistinguished except for a handsome *Stone House,* which once was used as a tavern. In early times a tannery was operated across the street from this house, where the farmers brought hides to be cured. After the process was finished a visiting cobbler went around to each home in the vicinity, outfitting every family with shoes handmade from the cured hides. Itinerant tailors also made the rounds in the spring after sheep-shearing time. Following the Embargo of 1808, smuggling was carried on in Alburg, as in other border towns of Vermont. In the wintertime contraband goods were sledded over the ice;

one Alburg smuggler was plunged into the water and lost his load when the ice broke, but managed to save himself and the horses. His clothing froze so stiff that he was unable to walk or mount a horse, and of necessity threw himself down in his icy armor, clutched the whiffletree, and let his horses drag him to the settlement.

ALBURG SPRINGS (3.0 m. north of Alburg Center off Vt. 78) has a U.S. Customs station and an immigration service officer on duty. Alburg, with its once famed mineral springs, was a pleasant health and vacation resort until the two hotels burned and mineral springs lost much of their previous popularity. This small settlement has a fine sandy beach, good bathing facilities and excellent fishing (Lake Champlain). There is a fine view across the narrow bay to the mainland with the Green Mountains across the eastern horizon.

EAST ALBURG (Vt. 78; alt. 116; Alburg R.D.) is reached after crossing through a low swampy region alongside a calm creek filled with water lilies and overhung with dense vegetation. The whole scene is reminiscent of the mysterious Louisiana bayous. At the end of the bayou is a beautiful house of brownstone, shaded, secure and trim. East Alburg's center is a rustic circle of small wooden houses and a tiny unused depot. The settlement spreads along the shores of Missisquoi Bay like a Maine seacoast village with vine-covered porches and slanting shingled roofs. A railroad bridge crosses to the mainland (Swanton) and in 1937 the old Alburg-Swanton ferry was replaced with a more efficient but less colorful bridge.

SOUTH ALBURG (junction US 2 and Vt. 129) was formerly known as Isle La Motte (RR) station. The commercial aspect of service stations and lunchrooms is somewhat relieved by rows of straight shiny-leafed Lombardy poplars.

WINDMILL POINT (northern terminus of US 2 in Vt.). This is the site of the Alburg–Rouses Point $1,000,000 bridge (1937).

On September 3, 1776, prior to the battle of Valcour Island, Arnold anchored in the shelter of Windmill Bay, at which time the British occupied Isle-aux-Têtes, a few miles to the north. On September 6 a landing party was dispatched to Windmill Point, where it was attacked by Indians. The Americans fought their way back to the boat, but three were killed and six wounded in the savage skirmish. The survivors rowed furiously back to the ships, exchanging riflefire with the Indians as they went. A few cannonballs from the fleet sent the redmen scattering into the woods. From 1783 to 1796 the British kept a heavily armed gunboat stationed off the Point to control this extreme northern end of the lake.

ALBURG COUNTRY CLUB (Vt. 129, 6 m. south of Alburg village) (9 holes); Range: 165–570 yds. Par 36. Total: 3300 yds. Rolling terrain. No hills. Facilities: clubhouse, restaurant, sandy swimming beach. Additional 9 holes planned.

ALFRECHA (see CLARENDON)
ALLIS STATE PARK (see BROOKFIELD)
AMSDEN (see WEATHERSFIELD)

ANDOVER, 9–C (Windsor County, off Vt. 11, west of Chester; alt. 1165, pop. 215; 16,534 acres). R.D. and Star routes from Chester and Ludlow. Includes Peaseville and Simonsville.

PEASEVILLE, a small rural settlement, has a *Community Church* (non-resident pastor) and three cemeteries. East Hill Farm is a boys' and girls' camp.

SIMONSVILLE (Vt. 11, lies 10 m. west of Chester; alt. 1161) is a tiny settlement with two bridges over the swift-running pebbly mountain stream that bends through the little village in white-rippled flow. Trim stone walls follow the curving line of the street and mark the watercourse. The little white *Church* with blunted tower is neatly built in a style similar to the Peru church. *Rowell's Inn* was built in 1820 by Simons, who gave his name to the community. Constructed of red brick kilned on the farm, the building served as an inn and store, and retains such early features as the many fireplaces, Christian doors, and the third-floor ballroom. A double porch now fronts the first two floors, with a third smaller porch opening from the ell. In early automobile days, this inn was a stopover on the "Ideal Tour" between Manchester, Vt., and the White Mountains of New Hampshire.

The *Parsonage* stands in the attractive sturdiness of red brick, made locally in Simonsville, and is early nineteenth century, having been used as a parsonage since its construction.

ARLINGTON, 10–B (Bennington County, US 7 and Vt. 313; alt. 691, pop. 1605; 22,758 acres). Vt. Transit bus service and Vt. Ry. Includes: East Arlington and West Arlington.

ARLINGTON (US 7, alt. 691) is another beautifully kept summer village, having more of the simple natural charm of Vermont towns and less of the polish that is Manchester's. The home of Vermont's pioneer leaders in the early times of strife, Arlington clings to a character and quality indigenous to Vermont, in spite of its attractiveness as a summer retreat. There is a similarity in the two towns, but the difference between them is vast. Arlington's appeal is unpretentious, inherently Vermont. Lacking the well-groomed sheen of Manchester, it is more homelike, more representative of the state.

Arlington was first settled in 1763, and the names of prominent pioneers are closely linked with the town's early history, in spite of which Arlington was known as a hotbed of Tory sympathizers in those trying times. Remember Baker was an early town clerk and miller; Thomas Chittenden lived here during the Revolution; Ethan Allen once resided here, and here his first wife and two children are buried. It is believed locally that these Green Mountain Boys were attracted to Tory Hollow, as Arlington was then called, by the very predominance of Loyalist and Church of England feeling, in order to keep an eye on the goings on. Nevertheless, the pattern of early social life in the community was shaped by Tory Anglicanism, and it was to enjoy the more gracious amenities permitted by their faith that the first families had deserted the puritanical rigors of Connecticut. Nowhere else in eighteenth century Vermont were there Maypoles and Christmas trees. In 1777, the town clerk, a Tory named Isaac Bisco, is said to have destroyed the town records and fled to Canada, thus depriving historians of much important lore. Afterwards Bisco claimed that he had buried the records in a kettle, but they were never found. The landscape depicted on the Vermont State Seal can be seen by looking west from the *Site of the Chittenden House* (Depot St. near RR Station). The legend is that a British officer visiting Chittenden was so impressed by the western vista from his room that he engraved it on a horn drinking cup, and his engraving, with minor changes, was later adopted for the state seal.

Martha Canfield Library (east side of US 7 in village) is an old red brick structure, originally the home of the Canfield family who were among Arlington's earliest settlers. Some 7500 volumes are available here. Novelist, short story writer, critic and Book-of-the-Month Club judge Dorothy Canfield Fisher was probably Arlington's most beloved twentieth century resident. Though not a Vermont native—her ancestors moved to Kansas where she was born—Mrs. Fisher was rarely thought of as a "foreigner." For many years she was considered the leading interpreter of Vermonters and their somewhat contrary characteristics.

If Mrs. Fisher was the town's most beloved resident, then for many years magazine illustrator Norman Rockwell was probably its best-known resident. Rockwell portrayed many local characters on numerous *Saturday Evening Post* covers. Rockwell has denied reports that he moved from Arlington some 50 miles south to Massachusetts "because the Vermont winters were too cold."

St. James Church Cemetery (1830), a somber stone building with crenellated tower, is evidence of the survival of Arlington's Episcopalianism. Its walled graveyard is one of the oldest and most interesting in the State, containing many queer old headstones with curious inscriptions. Mary Brownson, Ethan Allen's first wife is buried here. Church and cemetery set a note of quiet reverence for the thick-shaded village street.

Studio Tavern occupies the site where Ethan and Ira Allen lived during the hectic early days, and the office established by them here was virtually the capital of the Republic of Vermont. Here it was that Ethan's famous treatise *Oracles of Reason* (1784) was largely composed. This volume, strongly rationalist in tone, added the title "Anti-Christ of Vermont" to Ethan's other designations ("Robin Hood of Vermont," etc.).

EAST ARLINGTON (1 m. east off US 7; alt. 740) is a sprawling rural suburb of Arlington proper, touched with a careless rusticity. The *Site of Remember Baker's Mill* is that of the present Lawrence Mill. Baker built his mill, one of the earliest in the state, in 1764. *Green Mountain House,* formerly an old tavern, is now occupied by a feed store. The *Hard House,* one of the older houses in town, is supposed to have been the home for some time of Shays, the leader of Shays' Rebellion, after he fled from Massachusetts.

WEST ARLINGTON (3.6 m. west on Vt. 313 off US 7; alt. 595) lies along the shaded banks of one of America's finest trout streams, the *Batten Kill.* Lumberyards with orange mounds of sawdust and stacks of boards are the hamlet's distinguishing characteristic. A general store and a *Methodist Church* are the settlement's community structures. Broom handles are made here.

ASCUTNEY(ville) (see WEATHERSFIELD)
ASCUTNEY STATE PARK (see WINDSOR)

ATHENS, 9–D (Windham County, 7 m. north of Townshend on Vt. 35; alt. 360, pop. 142; 8307 acres. Bartonsville R.D.). This tiny town has no village or stores but there is a *Methodist Church* and a library.

AVERILL, 1–F (Essex County, Vt. 114; alt. 1744, pop. 16; 24,534 acres) was chartered in 1762 but has never been organized as a town. Its affairs come under the direction of a supervisor who lives in Island Pond. The 16 residents are mostly concerned with the operation of Hortense Quimby's two outfits: *Quimby's Inn* on *Great Averill Lake* (847 acres), *Quimby's Club & Cottages* on *Forest Lake* (62 acres) and *Little Averill Pond* (428 acres). The one general store and *Quimby's Club & Cottages* are actually located just over the line in neighboring Norton but the P.O. address is Averill. This is one of the most isolated and beautiful areas in the state. The fishing and hunting are excellent.

AVERY'S GORE, 1–F (Essex County, 10,625 acres) has no public roads and no known residents. The gore's affairs are supervised by an Island Pond resident.

AVERY'S GORE (Franklin County) had no public roads or reported residents when it ceased to exist. The 1963 legislature divided the gore's acreage between Bakersfield and Montgomery.

BAILEY'S MILLS (see READING)

BAKERSFIELD, 2–C (Franklin County, Vt. 108; alt. 762, pop. 644; 24,545 acres; St. Albans stage) is a village of one unusually long street lying along a broad plateau. Toward the southern end is a rectangular white-fenced Common. Behind the Common is a neat cemetery, and bordering it on the southern side are two red brick churches and the town hall. Bakersfield has long been an educational center for this region. Bakersfield Academy was founded in 1840, the first building being the brick structure that now serves as a Catholic church. Union Institute was founded in 1854. Neither of these schools is now in existence. *Brigham Academy,* just north of the Common, was established in 1878 by Peter Bent Brigham, a native of Bakersfield and founder of the well-known Boston hospital that bears his name.

Bakersfield was named for Joseph Baker, the first settler, who purchased the township in 1791 for slightly more than one hundred times as much as Manhattan Island is alleged to have cost the Dutch. The graph of the town's industrial activity follows what constitutes the norm for countless small Vermont towns: a sharp rise during the first half of the nineteenth century to indicate a gristmill, a sawmill, a potash factory, a carding mill, and a tannery; a steady decline since, to indicate the passing of these localized ventures to larger industrial centers. Today dairying and lumbering are the basic industries. Bakersfield is now a typical northern New England residential village, pervaded with quietude.

BALTIMORE, 8–D (Windsor County, north of Vt. 10 near Springfield; alt. 1067, pop. 88; 3190 acres; Chester Depot R.D.). In area, this tiny town of less than a hundred souls and without stores, churches or a library, is the second smallest in the state. Only St. George is smaller.

BARNARD, 7–D (Windsor County, Vt. 12; alt. 1334, pop. 435; 28,674 acres) Woodstock Stage. Includes: Barnard village and East Barnard.

BARNARD is a drowsy village located at the outlet of beautiful Silver Lake, upon the shores of which, slightly removed from the village, are a growing number of summer cottages. Once a commercially thriving community, Barnard is now chiefly noted as a haven of seclusion. The last panther killed in Vermont was shot in Barnard in

1881 and is preserved at the State House in Montpelier. Unfortunately no such tangible proof remains to authenticate the legend that on June 17, 1775, when Barnard was settled, the pioneers distinctly heard the cannons of Bunker Hill, more than 100 miles away.

Nobel Prize (1930) winning novelist Sinclair Lewis (1885–1951) and his journalist wife Dorothy Thompson (1894–1961) lived in *Twin Farms* during the 1930's. Miss Thompson and her third husband, Maxim Kopf, the Czech painter, are buried in the Barnard cemetery. Vincent Sheean is a former Barnard resident.

Site of *Fort Defiance* is marked by a bronze tablet. The fort was a garrisoned stronghold during the town's early history.

SILVER LAKE STATE PARK (West shore of Silver Lake, Vt. 12; alt. 1305; 26 acres) was given in 1954 by Mr. and Mrs. John H. McDill, Miss Catherine Field, Mrs. Margaret Crosby. Facilities: picnic tables and fireplaces, bathing, boating, fishing, refreshments.

BARNARD GULF, about 5 miles long, is a lovely winding wooded road of great scenic beauty. It lies between Barnard and Propper, a settlement in Woodstock town, along Vt. 12.

BARNET, 4–E (Caledonia County, US 5; alt. 425, pop. 1445; 27,605 acres). CP/RR. Includes: Barnet village, East Barnet (Inwood), West Barnet, McIndoe Falls and Passumpsic.

BARNET was settled in 1770, the first house in town, and in Caledonia County, being built by Elijah Hall at the foot of picturesque *Stevens Falls*. Caledonia, the ancient Roman name for Scotland, was given to the county in honor of Harvey and Whitelaw, leaders of the Scottish settlers here. Barnet and Ryegate share the distinction of being the only towns in Vermont founded by colonists from across the Atlantic. Most of the pioneer settlers of Barnet have descendants living here today.

Barnet is a side-hill village, spread from low river flats to a slanting plateau. Attractive yards and flower gardens add color to the homely wooden houses, and a sense of well-being is merged with Scottish thrift and security. In 1771, Colonel Hurd, as agent of the Stevens brothers, built a mill at the falls here. Two sturdy Scots, Stevenson and Cross, clubbed a bear to death in a hand-to-hand battle in 1776. Henry Stevens, founder of the Vermont Historical Society and head of the department of Americana in the British Museum, was born here. Another native son was Horace Fairbanks (Governor of Vermont, 1876–78).

EAST BARNET, also known as Inwood, is a railroad station on the CP/RR. East Barnet is near the junction of the Passumpsic with the Connecticut. A tragic episode in the flight of Rogers' Rangers took place at the mouth of the Passumpsic. Lord Amherst dispatched a small party from Charlestown, N.H., with provision-laden canoes to meet Rogers' force returning from Canada after their amazing expedition against the St. Francis Indians. The rescue party camped at the mouth of the Passumpsic. In the morning they heard rifle fire up the river, and fearing the approach of savages, they fled back downstream. Rogers and some of his starving men were encamped but a few miles upstream at this time, counting on the supplies they felt sure would be awaiting them. Reaching the river mouth about noon, the half-dead Rangers found the campfire abandoned by the rescue party, its ashes still warm; but not a crumb of food was left behind. Already reduced to a state of famished despair, several of the men died before the next day. Major Rogers, a man of great resourcefulness and indomitable spirit, built a raft and selected three men to accompany him. Before leaving, Rogers showed the rest of the party how to eke a subsistence from groundnuts and lily roots until he should send help and supplies. The four raftsmen then pushed off on the start of their long perilous float down the Connecticut. The men watching from the shore stood in silence, like skeletons in tattered green buckskin, bent in the middle by the pangs of hunger. The voyage was successful, and somehow or other, after the most frightful hardships and suffering, most of the men finally reached Charlestown.

FIFTEEN-MILE FALLS DAM. From East Barnet on a country road is the mammoth *Fifteen-Mile Falls Dam* (open to inspection; free guide service furnished), 2.6 m., known as Comerford Station in honor of the president of the Connecticut River Power Company. This 216,000 horsepower hydroelectric plant, constructed 1928–30, was then the largest in New England. Stretching 1600 feet across the Connecticut, the 175-foot-high concrete dam creates a lake seven miles long. The 850-foot spillway is on the Vermont side.

WEST BARNET, a straggling little village with an air of rustic languor, is enlivened a part of each year by the summer activity around Harvey Pond. South of West Barnet is the *Old Covenanter Church*, only meetinghouse in the state where the Covenanter faith is still preserved. This plain weatherbeaten structure marks the last survival in Vermont of that severe and uncompromising form of church service and church government which the first settlers of this region transplanted intact from Scotland (see EAST CRAFTSBURY). To this day instrumental music is forbidden in the service, and only psalms may be sung, hymns being of profane origin. Since the Constitution of the United States does not specifically acknowledge the power of the Almighty, members of this faith are forbidden to vote or otherwise participate in public affairs. Disenfranchisement, rather than the

Thetford — the Connecticut River. *Ewing Galloway*

A roundup in Wilmington. *Ewing Galloway*

East Corinth, hill town. *Ewing Galloway*

Moretown — a mountain farm off Vt. 100. *Vermont Development Department*

Sleighbells in the air. *Arthur Griffin*

Mt. Mansfield's "Chin" photographed from the "Nose"
Vermont Development Department

A view of Lake Champlain from Mt. Philo State Park

Vermont Development Department

Street scene in Peacham. *Claire Griffin*

rigid moral code, proved the chief cause of the decline of the Covenanter Church.

MCINDOE FALLS (alt. 441), a little village in the center of a dairying district, has a well-kept street running between shaded lawns and flowerbeds. The angular brown-painted *House,* with its tall wooden columns, is a landmark of hybrid architecture.

PASSUMPSIC (alt. 531), a small village in Barnet Town on the banks of the river for which it was named, is shaded by elms and maples and hemmed in by uneven hills. The trim wooden homes of this dairying community wear an agreeable suburban aspect.

BARRE CITY, 5–D (Washington County, US 302 and Vt. 14; alt. 609, pop. 10,385; 2570 acres). Barre & Montpelier RR. Vt. Transit bus.

GREATER BARRE includes Barre city and the settlements of East Barre, South Barre, Graniteville and Websterville, which lie within Barre town. The two are separate political and geographical areas but for all economic and social purposes are a single unit. Most granite quarries are in Barre Town.

Barre Area Information: Official Information Booth (west side of the Park opposite City Hall).

Bus Station: Peter George Store, 102 North Seminart St. Vermont Transit (Interstate) and Twin City Bus Co. (local service).

Airport: Barre-Montpelier (located in Berlin Town). Northeast Airlines (Boston-Burlington). Charter service.

Railroad: Barre & Montpelier/RR depot.

Accommodations: Hotels, motels, tourist homes, cabins.

Nearest Ski Area: Barre Skyline (inside city limits).

Country Club: Barre Country Club, 9 holes.

Schools: Public grammar, junior and senior high schools; Marian High School (parochial).

Churches: Protestant including Christian Science, Catholic.

Newspaper: Times-Argus (daily except Sunday).

Hospital: Barre City.

State Police Outpost: K Troop. Phone: GR6–4166.

Radio Station: WSNO (1450 kc.).

"Granite Center of the World"

Barre is so charged with aggressive activity as to seem curiously misplaced in its setting of green hills moulded roughly around the valley of the Stevens and Jail Branches of the Winooski. This aliveness is without question due to the granite industry, which dominates Barre from the stark gray quarries on Millstone Hill to the long, somber sheds on the river flats. Something of this aggressive spirit, however, came with the first settlers. In March 1793, the town was organized under the charter name of Wildersburgh, but the pioneers held that name to be too "uncouth," and in September a town meeting was held to choose another. It is legendary that this meeting reached a white heat. Two Massachusetts men, Thompson of Holden and Sherman of Barre, stood out for the names of their respective home towns until words were no longer strong enough. Thompson knocked his opponent down with a solid smash, and jumped on him to finish the bout. But as they thrashed and plunged about, collecting slivers from the barn floor, Sherman slugged Thompson until the latter rolled away groaning, and lay still. Sherman then sprang to his feet and panted: "There, by God, the name is Barre!" And Barre the name has been ever since.

From the air (the city is on the main route of Northeast Airlines) Barre appears as a cluster of dwellings and long sheds by the railroad, with the shattered mass of Millstone Hill, great slices of which have been devoured by fifty years of quarrying, completely dominating the settlements along the riverbanks.

Main Street, a long thoroughfare, is paved with granite blocks and lined on either side with close-set places of business, dingy buildings masked by colored fronts, gilt signs, and show windows. To enter this long narrow stretch from the open countryside is to come suddenly upon a virile little city transplanted from some busier section to the heart of rural Vermont. Here and there grave century-old brick houses of Georgian Colonial style overlook the noisy flow of traffic. The green triangle of City Park, ranged around with the granite and brick of public buildings, churches, and school, is a brief respite from undiluted commercialism. The statue of Robert Burns, which looks down upon the park from the High School grounds, is effective symbolism for a city where Scotch granite workers form a strong element. The survival of the philosophy of "a man's a man for a' that" is evidenced by Barre's former election and re-election of Vermont's only Socialist mayor. Rising southeast from this central plaza is the Trow Hill section, where attractive homes rest comfortably on terraced streets and lawns. Architecturally the city is conspicuous for the absence of granite buildings, being thus in contrast to the towns in Vermont's marble belt where local stone has served excellently for civic construction. Also notable is the fact that, though the Italian and Scotch races here predominate, neither Catholic nor Presbyterian churches are prominent.

Granite cutters are well paid for their work, which requires extreme skill, and is also hazardous. Notoriously a free-spending and pleasure-seeking people, the stoneworkers are largely responsible for the vigor of Barre life. The swift circulation of money, the swarming streets and stores, the whole fast and lusty tempo that sets Barre apart from the rest of Vermont, is created by the hardworking, hard-playing stonecutters. It is characteristic of many busier towns in the state to relapse into quiet with nightfall, but not so Barre. Darkness falling from the hills is defied by the lighted length of Main Street; cars and people moving ceaselessly under the blaze of neon signs; restaurants, shops, and beer taverns bright and crowded; and the counterpoint of cash-register bells against the music of radio and phonograph.

Granite cutters were not always so well paid. During the depression Barre was the scene of violence and labor strife. In 1936 the Communist Party candidate for President, Earl Browder, received 405 votes out of 107,552 presidential votes in the state. Rhode Island, in that same election, gave Browder 411 votes out of 288,991 votes. These revealing figures are probably accounted for by the fact that during the height of the long strike when strikers' families were starving and many homes had no heat and clothing was scarce, the Communist Party in Boston, Mass., rushed truckloads of food and clothing to the strikers.

Situated close together near the geographical center of the state, Vermont's twin cities, Barre and Montpelier, are natural and inevitable rivals, and offer a striking study of contrasts in appearance, character, and tone. Barre, forceful and arrogant, displays the haste and tension of a modern industrial community; Montpelier, serenely indifferent, is a true Vermont town, sleeping in the shadow of the hills.

In early time, three straggling villages grew up in Barre. Twingville, at the northern end, was built around the foundry of Joshua Twing, established in 1833. Gospel Village clustered about the first Congregational Church erected in 1808. Jockey Hollow, a flat section at the southern end of town, was used by pioneer sportsmen for the training of race horses, and here began the sporting and gaming so prevalent in present-day Barre. As the town grew, the three villages merged.

The granite industry was started soon after the War of 1812 by two returned soldiers, Robert Parker and Thomas Courser, who opened the first quarry on Cobble Hill. The stone from early quarries was used for millstones, doorsteps, posts, and window lintels. A finer grade of granite was found on Millstone Hill, to which quarrying activities were transferred and where they remain today. From the quarries on Millstone, granite for the construction of the State Capitol was hauled to Montpelier by oxteam (1833–37). It is in the field of monumental stone, however, that Barre granite excels, because of its beauty and flawless texture. The granite comes in two principal shades, with many variations: the "light" is nearly white, and the "dark" is a soft blue-gray that takes a high polish. The Joseph Smith Monument (see SHARON), a shaft 38½ feet in height, dedicated to the founder of Mormonism, is an example of the unblemished monoliths taken from the quarries on Millstone Hill.

Between 1880 and 1890 the population of Barre jumped from 2060 to 6812, the most rapid advance ever made by a Vermont town in a decade, and directly traceable to the granite quarries, which brought an influx of Italian, Scotch, and some Scandinavian stoneworkers. The extension of the Central Vermont Railway from Montpelier to Barre in 1875 aided this boom in granite. A natural result was the flourishing of all other branches of business and trade. In 1894 Barre was chartered as a city.

Focal points for most Barre visitors are tours of granite quarries and a granite plant.

What To See and Do

1. *Rock of Ages Granite Quarry Tour* (free) takes visitors to the brink of the "world's largest granite quarry." This 100-year-old, 350 feet deep quarry covers more than 20 acres. Free granite specimens are given all visitors.

2. *Rock of Ages Craftsmen Center* (free) has a guided tour through the "world's largest modern granite manufacturing plant." Visitors are invited to use the free picnic and camp grounds in the park adjacent to the plant.

3. *John Shelby's Maple Museum,* W. Patterson St. (off Washington St. US 302 or Ayers St. off South Main St. Vt. 14). Free guided tour of maple syrup and sugar processing plant. (open May 1st–Oct. 15).

4. The *Robert Burns Memorial Statue* faces the central plaza from the Spaulding High School grounds, a graceful and dignified figure on a beautiful base, considered a notably fine example of granite carving. J. Massey Rhind of Edinburgh, Scotland, designed the statue, and Samuel Novelli, Barre craftsman, did the carving. Rhind, disappointed in not doing the actual carving himself, died in 1936 without ever seeing the finished piece. The panels in the base, depicting scenes from Burns's poetry, were modeled by James King and cut by a Barre artisan, Eli Corti. The memorial, presented by the Scotsmen of the city, was unveiled in 1899.

5. *Youth Victorious,* City Park, carved by Gino Tosi, local stonecutter, from the design made by H. P. Jennewein. The central figure is a kneeling man, representing youth victorious, but supplicating even in victory. The symbolism is unusual in the treatment of a war memorial.

6. *Aldrich Public Library,* City Park, a square brick building with large windows and ornamental entrance portico, was dedicated in 1908.

7. The *Wheelock House,* 145 N. Main St. (*private*), 1823–25, a red-brick Georgian house with granite trim and four high chimneys, stands with gable end and arched sentinel window facing the street. The entrance is beautifully detailed; delicate leaded glass fanlight and side-lights frame the door, and mouldings harmonize with the slender Ionic columns. The granite arch and monolithic pilasters reveal sensitive hand-tooling. The structure maintains its dignity in the midst of the commercial hurly-burly that surrounds it.

8. The *Paddock House,* 188 S. Main St. (private), red brick on a granite foundation, was built in 1814 for Robert Paddock, the farmer-doctor who was Barre's first physician (an early job was removing the splinters from the combatants in the memorable fist fight). This is the best of the Georgian houses; the lines are right, and the white trim is in pleasing contrast with the red brick. The entrance has four graceful pilasters and

an attractive fanlight. Dr. Paddock charged from 25¢ to $1 for making calls, depending on the case and the distance traveled.

9. *VAH* — Granite City Cooperative Creamery. Milk processing, ice cream and dairy product manufacture.

10. *VAH* — Windy Wood Farm, Donald W. Smith. Orchard and dairy products.

BARRE SKYLINE SKI AREA (inside city limits off US 2), 60-acre ski area; 1950-ft. Pomalift ride to summit; 500-ft. and 800-ft. rope tows. Trails for tots, novices, intermediates and experts. 35-meter jump. Night skiing 7 to 10 P.M. Lodge with fireplace and restaurant. Ski patrol and first aid. Accommodations at nearby motels and hotels. A community project with moderate rates. *Information: Phone* GRanite 6-4694.

BARRE COUNTRY CLUB (4.5 m. from Barre off Vt. 14); 9 holes. Range: 135-520 yds.; par 72. Hilly terrain and wide fairways. Facilities: clubhouse, lockers, lunch and suppers, pro, golf shop, caddies.

BARRE TOWN (Washington County, US 302; Vt. 14 and 110; alt. 609, pop. 4580; 17,298 acres). Vt. Transit bus. Includes: Barre village, East Barre, Graniteville, South Barre and Websterville.

EAST BARRE (alt. 1128) is situated on an S-curve in the highway at a high elevation surrounded by higher forested hills. In the vicinity of the granite quarries, it is but natural that this village should emphasize the industrial aspects. The houses are scattered on a broken sloping terrain.

East Barre Dam was finished in 1935 as part of the Winooski Flood Control Project instituted by the federal government to prevent further flood damages in the Winooski Valley. The work was done by CCC under the direction of U.S. Army Engineers, and the great northern dam was completed in time to protect Barre, Montpelier, and other towns of the valley during the 1936 flood. On the Jail Branch of the Winooski, normally little more than a brook, this massive dam, with its tremendous bulk of earth fill reinforced by stone rip-rapping, and its huge spillways, seems ridiculously out of proportion to the meager flow of water in the dry seasons. But in floodtime the Jail Branch, like all the other deceptive-looking little streams, rises with incredible wrath, and habitually unleashed its power to join the torrent of the Winooski in wreaking havoc and destruction. In March, 1936, the East Barre Dam proved conclusively that it can control the Jail Branch at its worst.

GRANITEVILLE (alt. 1137), another quarry town, has great gaping chasms cut deep and wide in the rock deposits that have made Barre world-famous. The village, based on a common foundation, is closely unified and compact, as an isolated encampment might be in wartime.

SOUTH BARRE (alt. 740), is a residential suburb of Barre. The *Denison Smith House,* built in 1805, is of white wood with an overornate façade. The Palladian window above the fine arched entrance is the only one in the vicinity. The windows, slightly recessed in arched panels, are harmonious with the details of the doorway. Four plain pilasters, the Doric frieze with triglyph motif, and the modillion cornice produce a richness of design. The *South Barre Recreation Field* across the Stevens Branch of the Winooski River has a baseball field, tennis courts, playground, and swimming pool.

WEBSTERVILLE (alt. 1400) is a quarry town on the heights overlooking Barre and the distant panoramic grandeur of mountain chains. The road winds into Websterville past great gray mounds of waste rock, high walls of granite-block, and a deep abandoned quarry hole. The wooden homes are scattered about on the slope, and the *Quarries* now being worked lie at the summit above the village. Here, under mighty boom derricks and a complex overhead pattern of guy wires, vast open pits have been cut more than 200 feet deep in solid rock, the great blocks of granite drilled out and hoisted to the surface to be loaded on flatcars and taken down the steep looping railroad to the Barre finishing plants. The view southward from this lofty hilltop overlooks the Gargantuan pits of the Graniteville quarries. Everywhere on the upland stretches are the rearing gray piles of waste granite that barricade the countless abandoned quarries. Deserted quarry holes filled with spring water make good swimming holes.

BARTON, 2–E (Orleans County, US 5, Vt. 12, Vt. 16 and Vt. 58; alt. 931, pop. 3066; 24,622 acres). CP/RY. Vt. Transit bus. Includes: Orleans and Willoughby.

BARTON occupies the valley north of Crystal Lake, spreading from eastern hill slopes across the broad valley floor to the west. A good part of the village lies at a lower level than the lake. The long unshaded Main St., which US 5 follows, winds in gradual descent northward between a railway embankment and dwellings and scattered stores. At the foot of Main St., the north end of the village clusters about a triangular Common surrounded by stores, the red brick post-office building, and a modern municipal building with a false façade. Much more attractive are the outlying residential sections on hillside and plain, shaded by maples and tall elms. Once a lively industrial village, Barton has lapsed into relative inactivity, with Crystal Lake its main attraction as a summer playground. With many community activities, Barton keeps up a brave front, but the industrial backbone is gone.

Ranged along Church St. are the Barton Library, the brick Methodist Church, Barton Academy in red brick, and the gray wooden Congregational Church. When the hill behind the Academy was leveled an Indian burial ground was uncovered. *Roaring Brook Park,* an attractive fairgrounds at the western edge of town, is the site of Orleans County Fair (August); it has one of the best half-mile racetracks in the State. An unusual annual event in Barton (Wednesday following the fair) is a summertime sugaring-off party, with snow carefully preserved for the occasion.

The town was named for Colonel William Barton, grantee and first settler, although the charter was granted in the name of Providence. Early settlers resented Colonel Barton, and he was jailed for a minor debt. The Revolutionary veteran remained in jail, so the story goes, until Lafayette's visit in 1825. Lafayette remembered Barton as a good soldier, and on hearing of his plight, the Marquis immediately had him set free. At the Common in Barton is the junction with Vt. 12.

ORLEANS lies low in the valley where the Barton and Willoughby Rivers unite on their way to Memphremagog, and is sheltered by ridged slopes. Springing from the sound substructure of the woodworking industry here is a progressive alertness and community spirit seldom found in villages of like size. A broad level green flanks the four-lane Main St., with the railroad depot, tracks, and a furniture factory forming an incongruous background. Large wooden business blocks face the park and depot, and the railroad bisects Main St. The village center is huddled about a small oval green with a cement base and iron fountain; the *Municipal Building,* a modern brick structure with tapestried front, houses village offices, a banquet hall, theater, Masonic lodge, and National Guard barracks. The outlying residential districts are more pleasant, spreading from the valley bottom to terraced hill slopes. Along with civic consciousness, Orleans has achieved state-wide fame for her championship high school basketball teams. Samuel Read Hall, pioneer educator and founder of the first normal school, is buried here (see CONCORD, and Education).

Settled as Barton Landing about 1821, the village adopted the name Orleans in 1909, not wishing to appear in any way subsidiary to Barton. The rivalry between these neighboring villages has been intense, and many an athletic contest between the two has been marked by fist fights and riots. Orleans grew up quickly around the furniture factory; veneer and wooden heels are also turned out by Orleans mills. For many years the village has been the industrial nucleus of the section. The southern end of the village is bordered by the uniform yellow frame houses, company-built to house the mill workers.

WILLOUGHBY (Kimball), formerly South Barton, is a little mill village with faded wooden houses irregularly grouped on the uneven terrain. Between Willoughby and Barton, the highway skirts the western shore of *Crystal Lake,* which lies in the ridged shelter of *Brooks Mountain* (alt. 1400) at the southern end of Barton village. This charming little body of water has an excellent bathing beach across the north end, and facilities for boating and water sports. One detachment of Rogers' Rangers, ragged, starving, and harried by Indian pursuers, camped here on their flight from Canada. The quiet shores were a haven of rest after their hardships in the wilderness, and the fish taken from the lake eased the pain of their hunger. The fine fishing still exists, with bass, lake trout, and salmon being caught. An auto road leads over Brooks Mountain to the summer cottages along the eastern shore. The Barton Winter Circus, an annual event with all winter sports and an air meet, features horse racing on the ice of the lake.

CRYSTAL LAKE STATE PARK, US 5 (1937); 0.5 m. long white sand beach. Facilities: picnic tables and fireplaces, bathing, boating, fishing, refreshments.

BARTON COUNTRY CLUB (1 m. north of Barton off US 5); 9 holes. Range: 154–525 yds.; par 36. Hilly terrain, woods, unseen greens. Facilities: clubhouse, showers, soft drinks. Open to public except on special tournament days.

ORLEANS COUNTRY CLUB (off Vt. 58 about 1 m. from Orleans towards Willoughby); 18 holes. Range: 135–515 yds.; par 72. Rolling terrain. Facilities: clubhouse with showers, golf shop, pro, caddies, food.

BARTONSVILLE (see ROCKINGHAM)
BASIN HARBOR (see FERRISBURG)
BEECHER'S FALLS (see CANAAN)
BEEMAN'S CORNERS (see ORWELL)
BELLOWS FALLS (see ROCKINGHAM)
BELMONT (see MT. HOLLY)

BELVIDERE, 2–C (Lamoille County, Vt. 109 and Vt. 118; alt. 702, pop. 155; 19,582 acres). Includes: Belvidere Center, Belvidere Corners, Belvidere Junction.

BELVIDERE CENTER is a few houses scattered along a valley floor. There is a white *Community Church* (1872) and a 2-story wooden schoolhouse.
BELVIDERE CORNERS has two houses and three barns.
BELVIDERE JUNCTION has several houses and a town hall.

BELVIDERE MOUNTAIN (see EDEN)

BENNINGTON COUNTY (Area 661 sq. miles. Population 25,088).
Shire towns: Bennington and Manchester. Organized 1779. Includes:
Arlington, Bennington, Dorset, Glastenbury (unorganized), Landgrove,
Manchester, Peru, Pownal, Readsboro, Rupert, Sandgate, Searsburg,
Shaftsbury, Stamford, Sunderland, Winhall, Woodford.

BENNINGTON, 10–B (Bennington County half-shire town, with Man-
chester, US 7 and Vt. 9, Molly Stark Trail); alt. 672, pop. 13,002; 23,040
acres. Includes three incorporated villages: Bennington village, North
Bennington, Old Bennington.
   Information: Bennington Official Information Booth (215 South St.,
US 7). July-Aug., weekdays: 8:30–7:30; Sundays and holidays: 1–5.
   Bus Depot: Vermont Transit.
   Railroad: VT/Ry (freight only).
   Hospital: H. W. Putnam Memorial.
   Newspaper: Bennington *Evening Banner.*
   Radio: Station WBTN (1370 kc.) Catamount Broadcasters.

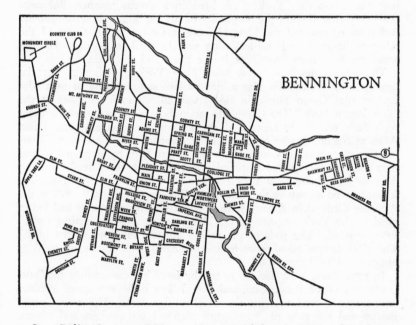

   State Police Outpost: C Troop (South Shaftsbury), Phone: Bennington
5421.
   State Liquor Store.
   Annual Events: Bennington (Battle) Day, Aug. 16.

Bennington, the first town chartered west of the Connecticut River by New Hampshire (1749), took the Christian name of Governor Benning Wentworth, who subsequently issued charters covering most of the territory now included in Vermont. Situated on the New York frontier, Bennington naturally became the focal point in the strife between the New Hampshire Grants and the "Yorkers," and was the background against which the opening scenes of Vermont history were enacted. The name of the town is most widely known in connection with the battle of Bennington (1777), which did much toward breaking Burgoyne's dominance in the northern theater of the Revolutionary War.

The Green Mountain Boys

Settlement was begun by Capt. Samuel Robinson of Hardwick, Mass., who was attracted by the site when he camped here on his return from the French and Indian War. In 1761, Robinson led a half-dozen families to settle along the broad terrace of the slope now known as Monument Avenue. When New York surveyors came trespassing on Robinson's land, he immediately chopped their surveying-chain in two with his hoe; but when the "Yorkers" desisted in a decent manner, Robinson graciously offered them the hospitality of his log house. In 1766, Samuel Robinson represented the New Hampshire Grants in the Court of the King of England, and the following year he died in London. His descendants have been prominent in the town and the state.

Throughout the controversy with New York, Bennington was the headquarters of the New Hampshire faction, and the band of men who became the "Green Mountain Boys" was known in York State as the "Bennington Mob." The Green Mountain Boys were organized in 1770, with Seth Warner as captain of the Bennington company, and Ethan Allen as colonel in command of all the companies in the Grants. Their meeting-place was the Green Mountain Tavern kept by Stephen Fay, and over the sign they placed a stuffed catamount with bared teeth, snarling defiance toward the New York border. The most historic Vermont inn, it came to be known as the Catamount Tavern (see below). When the Attorney General in Albany warned Allen that his followers had better yield to the York proprietors, for "Might often prevails against right," Ethan replied, "The gods of the valleys are not the gods of the hills!" The York lawyer asked what he meant; Allen said, "Come up to Bennington and we'll show you."

In 1771, New York decided to test by force her case against the "outlaw mobsters" of Bennington, and Sheriff Ten Eyck with three hundred armed men moved to seize the Breakenridge farm. The news spread swiftly and the men of Bennington snatched up muskets and pistols, swords and scythes, clubs and pitchforks to rally to the aid of Breakenridge. They met the Yorkers at the covered bridge beyond the threatened farm, and before their menace Ten Eyck and his posse fell back toward Albany. The old covered bridge is still standing (see below). There were many other skirmishes between the Yorkers and the Green Mountain Boys. When Tory John Munroe's crew captured Remember Baker of Arlington, ten Bennington horsemen pounded after in mad pursuit and rescued Baker before the Yorkmen could get him over the border. Munroe was lashed into an unconscious state for his activities against the Grants.

From Bennington to Burlington the rough-and-ready Green Mountain Boys ranged, dealing out drumhead justice to all New York sympathizers and Tories. Chieftain Ethan Allen won the name, among less complimentary ones, of the "Robin Hood of Vermont," and had a price placed on his head, as did his lieutenants Warner, Baker, and Robert Cochran. Their lusty efforts, however justly they may be criticized and condemned, were the means of breaking New York's claims on the territory, and were the first steps toward statehood. With the approach of the Revolution, the Council of Safety, meeting at the Catamount Tavern, turned its attention to the imminence of a new and greater struggle. In 1775, at the Catamount, Ethan Allen conferred with agents from Massachusetts and Connecticut on the plan of capturing Fort Ticonderoga. A short time later, a stone warehouse for Continental military supplies and provisions was established on the summit, just northwest of where the monument now stands.

The Battle of Bennington

In the summer of 1777, General Burgoyne pushed down the Champlain Valley, taking Ticonderoga and Mount Independence without a struggle. Seth Warner's stubborn rear guard at Hubbardton protected the flight of the main army under St. Clair, but the British drive seemed irresistible and the whole country was alarmed. On July 30, Burgoyne tardily reached Fort Edward on the Hudson, after some days spent in dalliance with his mistress at Skenesboro. It appeared merely a question of time before he would join the British forces at Albany. But Burgoyne needed supplies badly, wanted horses to mount his dragoons, and was fatally overconfident. Learning of a storehouse in Bennington guarded only by militia, he dispatched Colonel Baum, with Riedesel and Fraser, under the following cocksure instructions, ". . . Mount your dragoons . . . send me 1300 horses . . . seize Bennington . . . cross mountains to Rockingham and Brattleborough . . . try affections of country . . . take hostages . . . meet me a fortnight hence in Albany." He expected little or no opposition from the people of the New Hampshire Grants, but he sent Breymann's German regulars to support Baum in case of unexpected developments.

Meanwhile the fear-stricken Colonies were striving to raise volunteers for defense against Burgoyne's advance. Colonel John Stark, veteran of the French War, Bunker Hill, Trenton, and Princeton, had retired to his New Hampshire farm in disgust when Congress promoted undeserving junior officers over his head. He was called back into service and given command of the forces gathered by New Hampshire. On his withdrawal from service, writers of the day had referred to him as "a rustic Achilles sulking in his tent." Now the promise of leadership filled him with eager activity, and he marched his men over the mountains to Bennington, arriving on August 9. On the 12th, Baum started his eastward march, unaware of the increased strength at Bennington. His detachment of eight hundred included musicians, officers' servants, and women camp-followers; his main strength was three hundred and seventy-five dismounted German dragoons, fifty British infantrymen, and some three hundred Indians, Tories, and Canadians.

By the 14th, Stark knew definitely of Baum's advance and moved his militiamen up to meet them, strengthened by volunteers from Bennington and other towns in the Grants and Massachusetts, a total force of eighteen hundred. At Sancoick Mills a vanguard of American riflemen fired on Baum's ranks from the brush, and retreated before the enemy, sniping at uniforms as they fell back. Eleazer Edgerton had stayed behind to burn St. Luke's Bridge over the Walloomsac, and Baum, forced to halt and restore the bridge, took his position on the hill over the river. After some skirmishing, Stark withdrew to plan the attack. On the 15th, it rained hard all day, and fighting was out of the question; sharp-shooting American scouts managed to keep enough powder dry to harass the enemy and pick off some outpost victims. Baum's position, naturally strong, was weakened by his deploying troops to defend the bridgeheads. On the steep hill-shoulder three hundred feet above the Walloomsac River, he built a breastwork of felled trees to bolster his main defense. But the wide scattering of his four detachments was poor strategy.

August 16 was bright and clear after the storm. Wet leaves glistened and the green earth steamed in the sultry sunshine. It is legendary that the lean, grim-mouthed Stark said, "We beat them today, or Molly Stark's a widow." At three o'clock in the hot afternoon, the attack started, with Nichols and Herrick carrying the left and right flanks respectively, the Indians and Canadians fleeing after but little show of opposition. The enemy's front outpost, manned by Tories behind a flimsy barrier of fence rails and loose earth, fell before Hubbard and Stickney. The Tories fled across the river and up the hill, and Stark and Warner launched the big drive at Baum's main defense on the hill crest. Swarming across the bridgeways or splashing through the stream, the Americans clambered up the blazing hillside, a motley army in tattered shirt sleeves and sweaty jackets. Stark and Warner were greeted by a ball from the Hessian four-pounder. "The rascals know we're officers, all right," cried Stark. "They salute us with big guns." A powder explosion threw the poorly manned English redoubt into confusion, and the charge of ragged farmers and tough woodsmen cleared the barricade. Deserted by their allies and hopelessly outnumbered, Baum and his Germans stood firm until their ammunition gave out; then, drawing their great broadswords and led by Baum, they tried to cut their way out. Baum fell, shot in the belly, and the rest, who were still alive and unwounded, either fled or surrendered. By five o'clock the Hessian forces were smashed and broken, and the Americans were scattered in pursuit, in the gathering of plunder, or the herding of prisoners.

In the meantime Breymann, notorious as a brutal drillmaster, was marching five hundred and fifty Germans to the aid of Baum at the rate of only one-half mile per hour, dragging his cannon through the mud, and halting ten times to the mile to dress and re-dress his ranks with eighteenth century Prussian precision. But for these foolhardy parade-ground tactics, Breymann could have been there a day earlier and the issue might have been entirely changed. Instead of meeting Baum's detachment, Breymann ran into a scene of utter confusion and rifle-fire that raked his lines from rail fences and wooded ridges; but he marched doggedly on.

The Americans, scattered and disorganized now, were wearied from their exertions in the August heat, wilted by the scorching sun. It has been said that Stark was in favor of falling back to re-form his ranks and prepare to meet the German reinforcements, but Seth Warner persuaded him to stay and fight it out on the spot. When the tired volunteers turned Baum's cannon on Breymann, Stark had to dismount and show his in-experienced men how to load and fire the guns. The Hessians were fatigued from marching through mud in their heavy equipment, but they were forcing the farmers back when, just before sunset, Warner's com-pany of three hundred and fifty arrived from Manchester. The only fresh men on the field, they again turned the tide of battle and the Continentals surged forward. The German ammunition was running low, and Brey-mann's retreat in the fading light of day was turned into a rout. At dusk the Colonial victory was complete.

Stark took about six hundred prisoners, and over two hundred of the enemy were left dead on the field. The American losses were small, thirty killed and forty wounded. Baum and Tory Colonel Pfister were carried to a farmhouse, where both died of wounds, and were buried on the bank of the Walloomsac. The prisoners, many of them wounded, were paraded along the streets between the log huts of Old Bennington, before being lodged in the original Meeting House, the schoolhouse, and other houses and barns. "With such a base show of rustic contempt was cele-brated the turning of the tide against Burgoyne." (*The Turning Point of the Revolution,* by Hoffman Nickerson, 1928.) The dead soldiers of both sides were interred in the Old Burying Ground.

Bennington was a crushing blow to the British, the beginning of the end for Burgoyne, and it made possible the later decisive victory of Gates and Arnold at Saratoga, which was the true turning point of the Revolu-tionary War. Bennington is one of the few cases in history of improvised troops beating regular trained soldiers. The following excerpt from a letter of Burgoyne's to England, written after the battle of Bennington, reveals how his confidence was shaken by the totally unexpected and stun-ning blow: "The Hampshire Grants in particular — a country unpeopled and almost unknown in the last war — now abounds with the most active and rebellious race on the continent, and hangs, like a gathering storm, on my left."

BENNINGTON village (alt. 672, pop. 8023; 2300 acres) is large enough to be a city but residents prefer the more direct and more democratic town meeting. The village is a modern manufacturing town sprawled on the wide flats of the Walloomsac River. Motivated by southern New England industrialism, the village lacks beauty, in spite of the handsome public buildings that endeavor to alleviate the dullness of brick and wood blocks in the business area. Red factories and smokestacks mark the bottomlands, north and west of the center, where textile plants and paper mills form the industrial core of the town. Bennington is important commercially as well as industrially, serving as a trading center for the entire southwestern corner of Vermont. To the heavy summer tourist traffic, the village offers accommodations, trading, and recreational facilities.

The natural background of Bennington is more level and open than the usual Vermont countryside, although low hills slouch away from the undulant plains in long easy rises, and *Mt. Anthony* (alt. 2345) stands stately guard on the southwest. Northward the ridges close in to narrow and deepen the valley; southward lie the sharply cupped farmlands of Pownal; and to the east is upfolded the wilderness barrier of the Green Mountains. But opening and spreading west and northwest is a clear expanse of softly rolling country, serene and graceful in contour and threaded by the Walloomsac.

What To See and Do

1. The *Norton-Fenton House,* 208 Pleasant St., a large two-family brick house built by Judge Luman Norton in 1838, is of interest for the specimen of Bennington pottery that rests on its porch, and for its history which links the two great names of Bennington pottery. As early as 1793, Captain John Norton and his sons manufactured pottery, plain and useful articles in stoneware and in a mottled brown and yellow ware known as Rockingham. Under the influence of Christopher Fenton, son-in-law of Judge Luman Norton, more delicate and elaborate types were produced. From 1850 to 1858, independent of the Nortons, Fenton turned out specimens of the potter's art now highly prized by collectors, including "Parian," a porcelain that resembled marble, and Fenton's "Flint Enamel." After a century of pottery-making, the enterprise was given up in 1894.

2. The *Vermont Soldiers' Home* (open to visitors), northeast of US 7, at the northern edge of the village, occupies the former estate of Seth B. Hunt, pioneer textile manufacturer, and is maintained by the state with some aid from the federal government. Equipped to house 84 residents, it serves as a home for disabled and homeless veterans. The long yellow

building is set back in spacious pine-shaded grounds, which include a farm of 350 acres, a fine maple grove and a great fountain.

3. The *Post Office,* South and Union Sts., a long low structure of Vermont marble, has a classic severity of line and a portico with six fluted columns.

4. The *Bennington Free Library,* Silver St., contains about 30,000 volumes. This is another of the attractive modern structures that dignify downtown Bennington, of brick trimmed with marble and graced with a rounded white entrance portico and white tower. The reading-room windows are modeled after those of the General Robinson House in Old Bennington, and the lantern over the entrance is a copy of the courthouse lantern.

5. The *Courthouse,* South St., a brick building with marble trim and a white-pillared façade, is the fifth Bennington courthouse. The county has two shire towns: Manchester in the north, and Bennington in the south.

NORTH BENNINGTON (Vt. 67 and Vt. 67A; alt. 600, pop. 1437), an incorporated village, strung out along the shallow, curving valley and centered on a low slanting plateau above the factories that line the valley bottom. Woodworking and wood products are this mill town's chief manufactories. The H. T. Cushman Co., (about 200 workers) manufactures reproductions of Colonial furniture. The *Stone House* (open 9–5 weekdays: Sundays, June–Sept. Free admission) is a show-place of Cushman products.

McCullough Free Public Library in the village center, is a pale brick structure with a white-columned portico, erected in 1922, as a memorial to Vermont Governor (1902–1904) John G. McCullough. North Bennington is a station on the Vt. Ry.

OLD BENNINGTON village (alt. 873, pop. 205), an incorporated vil-lage, is in reality the old historic Bennington inhabited by wealthy, history appreciating Benningtonians and summer residents — mostly Yorkers. Manhattan's fighting District Attorney William Travers Jerome, kin of Sir Winston Churchill's American mother Jennie Jerome, was a longtime summer resident. The area has no commercial establishment. This is the Bennington whose present residents might be shocked at the memory of former resident Ethan Allen who tossed off many a bowl — always preferred drinking from bowls — of that potent Vermont concoction known as a "Stonewall." This consists of six ounces of hard Vermont cider cut with four ounces of 152-proof rum. Both ingredients are hot. Butter and sometimes a slug of maple syrup were added. Old Bennington, the site of the original settlement on a broad sloping rise west of the village center, is a veritable outdoor museum of historic landmarks compactly grouped along Monument Avenue. Old Bennington is now an exclusive summer resort, after the manner of Manchester and Dorset. Grand new mansions are inter-spersed with the eighteenth-century homes built by the founders of the town, and the Colonial tradition is preserved by the new as well as the old. High over the scene of white summer homes, inns, Colonial houses, church and graveyard in a green setting, the clean stone thrust of Bennington Monument cuts the sky.

What To See and Do

1. The *Historical Museum,* Main St., originally the Church of St. Francis de Sales, was acquired by the Bennington Historical Society and converted to its present use in 1927. Built of native fieldstone, with an iron-fenced courtyard opening between it and the smaller building, formerly the priest's house, the structure has an Old World aspect. The museum contains a wide variety of military relics and historical documents, including Stark's flag carried at the battle of Bennington, and a brass cannon captured from the Hessians. There is also an exhibit of Bennington pottery, and of utensils typical of early Vermont days.

2. The *Old Burying Ground,* Monument Ave., faces the Green where the original Meeting House stood. Here were buried the British and American dead from the battle of Bennington, and here lie the fathers of Bennington who laid the foundations of Vermont — the Robinsons, the Fays, the Harwoods, the Deweys, the Fassetts, the Hubbells, and all the rest. Five Vermont governors rest here: Moses Robinson (1789–90); Isaac Tichenor (1797–1807; 1808–9); John S. Robinson (1853–54); Hiland Hall (1858–60); and John McCullough (1902–4). Many of the headstones are ornamented with popeyed, round-headed angels characteristic of the more elaborate Colonial memorials.

3. The *First Congregational Church,* Monument Ave., raises its gracefully graduated tower over the southern edge of the graveyard. The architect was Lavius Fillmore, a close student of the architectural handbooks of Asher Benjamin. It is considered, with Fillmore's Middlebury church, one of the most beautiful in the state. Of white-painted clapboards, with wood quoins, the structure has a Palladian window above the three entrance doors, and Palladian windows in three sides of the square tower, which supports an open belfry. The belfry is surmounted by a "lantern" with oval windows, capped by a weathervane. The church was built in 1806. Services are held here from May to January.

4. The *Jedediah Dewey House,* Monument Ave. (second south of the church), a solid, square-built house painted white, with a huge central chimney, was built in 1763 by the Reverend Mr. Dewey, and is said to be the oldest frame house in the State. Parson Dewey was Bennington's first minister, and an accomplished carpenter as well, a fact attested by the strength and beauty of his home. On the Sabbath before the battle of Bennington, Parson Dewey delivered a rousing war sermon, urging his people to take up arms and fight. That he was a man of willful purpose was shown one Sunday when Ethan Allen, disliking some remark from the pulpit, rose and started to stalk out. Dewey transfixed the bold Allen with a pointed forefinger and shouted: "Sit down, thou blasphemer, and

listen to the Word of God!" And Ethan Allen sat down. At another time Allen gained some measure of jocular revenge. Dewey was preaching a thanksgiving service for the capture of Ticonderoga, and giving rather more credit to God than to Allen for the victory. In the midst of the prayer, Allen interrupted with a voice full of mock pleading: "Parson Dewey, Parson Dewey — please mention to the Lord about my being there!"

5. The *Walloomsac Inn,* Monument Ave., was founded in 1766 by Captain Elijah Dewey, son of the parson. Elijah commonly remarked that "no one lost anything by going to church," and he donated generously to its support. But he did not unite with the church until his last sickness. He served at Ticonderoga, Bennington, and Saratoga during the Revolution.

6. The *Site of Catamount Tavern,* Monument Ave., is marked by the figure of a lithe bronze catamount standing high on a granite base. This inn was founded as the Green Mountain House by Stephen Fay, and was often referred to as Landlord Fay's. Here the Green Mountain Boys gathered over their rum, the Council of Safety laid the groundwork for the future state of Vermont, Allen plotted the move against Ticonderoga, and Stark and Warner planned the defense of Bennington. Before the battle of Bennington, British officers sent a haughty message to the Catamount Tavern, ordering dinner made ready for their triumphal entry. That August evening, when British prisoners, their splendid uniforms torn, dirty, and blood-smirched, shuffled wearily down the street between the ragged and powder-stained backwoodsmen who had beaten them, Landlord Fay stepped forward with a gallant bow and said: "Gentlemen, the dinner that you ordered is ready." Stephen Fay had five sons fighting on Walloomsac Heights that day, and one of them, John, was killed. He was a popular fellow and his death fired the Bennington volunteers with fury. In the assault that followed they swept aside Baum's barricade. Another son, Jonas, was secretary of the Council of Safety and surgeon of the Green Mountain Boys. Benjamin Fay, still another son of the landlord, was the first sheriff in the state.

7. The *Isaac Tichenor Mansion,* west of (behind) the Walloomsac Inn on Vt. 9, is set proudly back on a knoll fenced with white pickets to match the white house. The latter was built prior to 1790 for the handsome Princeton graduate who served as governor of Vermont for eleven years, and had a brilliant career as a Federalist statesman. Fond of hunting and fishing, Tichenor was as much at home in the woods as in the drawing rooms of Washington. One day, while dining at home with friends, he called suddenly for his fowling piece, pointed to a bird in a tree outside the open windows, and from his chair at table brought the bird down with a shot.

8. The *Old Academy Library,* Monument Ave. Situated near the top of the grade of Vermont's most historic avenue, this small red brick building, with recessed double doors and an open bell tower, was erected in 1821

as an academy, to be "the finest building in the state." It served as a secondary school for three-quarters of a century, since which time (1897) it has been used as a library, and now contains 8000 volumes.

9. The *Site of Samuel Robinson's Cabin*, Monument Ave., is plainly marked just north of the Old Academy near the summit. Here the founder of Bennington erected his log cabin in 1761. One night while Captain Robinson was in London as agent of the New Hampshire Grants, 1767, Mrs. Robinson chased wolves away from the cabin door, by dashing out and waving glowing brands. The Friday prayer meetings of the primitive settlement were held in the Robinson home.

10. The *General David Robinson House*, Monument Ave., opposite the Robinson marker, was built by the eighth son of Captain Samuel in 1795. This beautiful Georgian Colonial structure, facing a wide picket-fenced lawn, is framed by giant shade trees. The two-story dwelling is narrow and rectangular, typical of the eighteenth-century houses found in the state and also in the northern Connecticut valley. Its delicate pedimented entrance portico is painted white in pleasing contrast to the soft gray of the clapboarded siding and the dark green of the shutters. Attenuated Ionic pilasters form the most interesting feature of the exterior. Appearing at the corners of the façade and on either side of the portico, they rise in support of a bracketed cornice and central pediment. The distinctive triple-arched window above the entrance, though cramped and ill-placed, is in itself charming.

David Robinson fought as a private at Walloomsac Heights and later became major general of militia. He was a man of great physical strength and courage, once going alone into a hayloft to drag forth a desperate outlaw whom no one else dared approach. The Robinsons were a husky, high-spirited clan, especially given to wrestling, in which they employed a hold that came to be known as the Robinson Lock. One day Governor Moses Robinson (1789–90) was riding through the mountains and stopped by chance at a house-raising. After the raising, the men began to wrestle, and the Governor watched quietly for a while, until the local bully had thrown all comers. Moses then stepped forward with a challenge, and threw the bully quickly and hard. The furious man leaped up for another try, raging at the "spindle-shanked stranger" who had humbled him. They tangled and again Moses slammed the brawny fellow's shoulders to the sod. It was an added shock to the bully when he learned that the talented grappler was governor of the state.

11. *Betsy Robinson's Tomb*, behind the General David Robinson House, is a rude but substantial arch of fieldstones on a little knoll over the open field, built by David Robinson, Jr., son of the general, to receive the coffin of his beloved wife, Betsy. Here young David spent long hours of mourning, but his grief was finally terminated by the advent of a comely widow, who became his second wife.

12. *Seth Warner Statue* stands at the head of Monument Ave., in the shadow of the Battle Monument. The figure is in the uniform of a

Continental Colonel. Less fiery and colorful than Ethan Allen, Warner was perhaps even more respected and trusted by his contemporaries, who often preferred his calm, steady competence to the arrogant swagger of Ethan. Warner's rearguard action at Hubbardton made it possible for the main body of the retreating American army to escape, and his support of Stark at Bennington was invaluable.

13. *Bennington Battle Monument* (1887–91) towers 306 feet above the broad summit of the hill, where stood the storehouse which Burgoyne ordered Baum to capture. At the time of its dedication in 1891 President Benjamin Harrison was present — it was the highest battle monument in the world. It was dedicated on the centennial of Vermont's admission to the Union. Four hundred and twelve steps zigzag up past 34 landings to a lookout which commands marvelous vistas over Bennington, southern Vermont, northwestern Massachusetts and York State. The installation of an elevator provoked considerable comment. Some Vermonters argued that if the Green Mountain Boys and their allies fought the battle the least contemporary Americans could do in appreciation of the victory was to walk up the stairs. (Open daily, spring through November 1, 9–6; rest of year, 10–4. Small admission charge.)

Battlefield Tour *(cumulative mileage)*

Left (west) from the *Seth Warner Statue,* 0 m., the road leads westward to a junction at 0.7 m. Left from this junction the road leads to another junction at 1.3 m., from which the route is left. At 2 m. the road swings sharply right, and at 2.8 m. is a white farmhouse.

Left from this farmhouse the route leads to the *Site of the Breakenridge Farm* (R), 3.1 m., which Sheriff Ten Eyck of Albany with 300 heavily armed henchmen set out to seize, only to be forestalled by the quick gathering of the Bennington mob. Beyond the Breakenridge marker is the *Site of Seth Warner's House* (L), 3.3 m. Shortly beyond this site, at 3.5 m., is the old *Henry House* (1769). This gray clapboarded house with its asymmetrical plan, sweeping shed roof, and wide front porch, is a notable departure from the usual regional type. The tall square columns of the porch with their interesting but crudely molded caps, the casual treatment of trim and detail, the long raked lines of the downspouts, and the generous proportions of the whole produce an effect of charming informality. It is said that Warner's house was identical in design with this one and that both were raised on the same day at a bee attended by most of the prominent figures in early Vermont history. Just beyond the Henry House is the *Old Covered Bridge,* said to be the strongest of its type in the world, and seemingly as staunch and sturdy today as it was when the Green Mountain Boys swarmed here to meet Sheriff Ten Eyck's Yorkers and turn them back toward Albany.

Left from the bridge, the road leads over a hillock to *Stark's Camping Ground* (R), 4.7 m. Here, on August 14, 15, and 16, 1777, were the headquarters of John Stark's militiamen and volunteers, before and during the action at the Battle of Bennington.

At 5.6 m. the route is left on a blacktop road, and at 5.7 m. (R) is the *Site of the House Where Baum and Pfister Died* of wounds on the day following their defeat. Both officers were buried on the bank of the Walloomsac in unmarked graves.

At 6.1 m. is the *New York Line.* Beyond the line at 8 m. the route swings (R) up the slope of *Baum's Hill,* or *Walloomsac Heights,* the scene of the battle.

MT. ANTHONY COUNTRY CLUB (18 holes). Range 115–575 yds; par 70. Scenic course, clubhouse, outdoor swimming pool, restaurant.

VAH — Fairdale Farms, Robert T. Holden, mgr. Dairy farm and milk processing.

VAH — Harwood Orchards, Paul Bohne. Orchard products.

PROSPECT MOUNTAIN SKI AREA (8 miles east of Bennington on Vt. 9); 2850-ft. elevation and 2200-ft. base. T-bar lift serves 1000 skiers hourly. Rope tow for beginners. Ski shop. Patrol and first aid. Ski lodge with lounge, fireplace and restaurant. Parking area. *Information:* Prospect Mountain, P.O. Box 107, Bennington. Phone: Bennington 6467.

BENSON, 7–A (Rutland County, Vt. 22A and Vt. 141; alt. 420, pop. 549; 25,509 acres). Fair Haven stage. Includes: Benson village and Benson Landing.

BENSON, a side-hill village with wooden houses strung along the slope, distinguished by a few antiquated homes. The *Ark,* a private house, has a square-pillared porch and turretlike roof. From the hill crest at the upper end of the village, an eastern valley panorama unfolds. Walter Durfee was the firstcomer to Benson, before the Revolution. Driven away by Burgoyne's invasion in 1777, he returned in 1782 to establish permanent settlement. Benoni Gleason, another early settler, served at Yorktown and saw the surrender of Cornwallis.

In Benson was born Rufus Wilmot Griswold (1815–1857), one of the most influential, if not always most discriminating, of nineteenth-century American editors, critics, and anthologists. After editing the *Vergennes Vermonter,* 1838–39, he succeeded Edgar Allan Poe as editor of *Graham's Magazine* in 1842. He was Poe's literary executor, and his obituary notice and biographical sketch of the poet were frank almost to the point of moral denunciation, extenuating none of the weaknesses that had accompanied and corroded Poe's genius. Griswold's anthologies were an important factor in molding mid-nineteenth-century American taste in verse. Much of his prose was of a polemical nature, and his retaliatory critique of Duyckinck's *Cyclopaedia of*

American Literature is still considered the most destructive book review ever written by an American.

VAH — Trinity Farm, Michael Cunningham. Dairy farm and milk processing (Jersey cattle).

BERKSHIRE, 1–C (Franklin County, Vt. 105; alt. 640, pop. 965; 24,295 acres). Richford stage. Includes: Berkshire village, East Berkshire, West Berkshire.

BERKSHIRE village lies on a plateau overlooking the Missisquoi River Valley. There are six houses, a town hall, white Congregational Church, World War II bronze plaque memorial tablet and a one-room school-house. The general store has been operated for many years by genial Max Jolley.

EAST BERKSHIRE is a T-shaped village, the stem lying across the Missisquoi at right angles to the highway. In 1866, this village was swept by a fire which destroyed 36 buildings including the church. The present stone and brick *Church* is a handsome adaptation of English Gothic style. One of the early leading citizens of East Berkshire was Governor Stephen Royce of Vermont (1854–56). His son Homer, born here, was Vermont congressman (1857–63) and subsequently Chief Justice of the Vermont Supreme Court for twenty-five years. Supplies were once obtained from Boston. Pollard, the local poet, with another tippler, heard that some rum had arrived, and promptly went after it. Finding the door unlocked, but no one at home, Pollard scratched the following doggerel on a piece of bark with a nail, and pinned it to the door:

> *Sir, we've come*
> *And got our rum;*
> *Home we've gone*
> *Through brush and wood*
> *And hope the rum*
> *Will do us good.*

WEST BERKSHIRE has a post office, general store, a two-story school-house and about twelve houses.

BERLIN, 4–D (Washington County, Vt. 12 and Vt. 14; alt. 589, pop. 1380; 20,861 acres). Includes Riverton.

BERLIN'S population is concentrated along Vt. 14 on Barre Road. There are nearly a dozen restaurants catering to tourists, motels and other commercial establishments. Berlin farms are spread over a rolling plateau high above the Winooski River valley.

Barre-Montpelier Airport, located here in Berlin, offers one of the most spectacular views in the state.

RIVERTON (Vt. 12) is an undistinguished hamlet consisting of a church, two stores, a post office, and a small scattering of plain wooden houses. On the bluffs above, several summer homes have been built, one of them being the residence of Herbert Welch, former president of the Indian Rights Association in this country.

Béla Bartók (1881–1945), refugee Hungarian composer, lived here in the summer of 1941 in a decrepit farmhouse above the village. Bartók, considered by many critics to be one of this century's outstanding composers, wrote *Kossuth, Duke Bluebeard's Castle, The Miraculous Mandarin.* His biography *The Naked Face of Genius* was written by Agatha Fassett, who loaned him the farmhouse.

BETHEL, 6–D (Windsor County, Vt. 12, Vt. 14 and Vt. 107; alt. 600, pop. 1356; 24,990 acres). CV/RR and Vt. Transit bus. Includes: Bethel village and East Bethel.

BETHEL lies in a natural basin in the southeastern part of Bethel town at the junction of the Third Branch and the White River. For years the village was a cutting and shipping center for the town's granite quarries, closed since 1925. The village is now a trading and dairying center.

Bethel's early years were dangerous ones. The White River Valley was a favorite raiding route for the hostile Canadian Indians. In 1780, Fort Fortitude was on the site of the present railroad station. Alarmed by an Indian raid upon Barnard in August, Bethel's settlers called upon the Royalton garrison, which in response moved to Bethel.

Bethel was the home of novelist Mary Waller. The scene of her best-loved book, *The Wood-Carver of 'Lympus* (1914), is laid in the southwestern section of the town that is Olympus on all maps and Lympus on all tongues.

Bethel, the first town to be chartered by the new Republic of Vermont, in 1778, bears the same relation to the state that the latter bears to the Union.

In the *McKinstry House* the main front part dates from 1810, the rear ell from the eighteenth century. From its brick-paved butter cellar (a small part of the cellars that underlie the whole house) to its ten-inch-square hand-hewn timbers, this structure is a fine example of the sturdiness and thoroughness with which early builders wrought. The front of the house has a simple but well-designed Palladian window.

"Old Church" was built about 1820, with a small cemetery behind it, both enclosed by a white wood fence. This building, except for the squat turret, is well proportioned. Each large window contains 50 panes.

General Stephen Thomas (1809–1903) *birthplace site.* The small marker commemorating the Hero of Cedar Creek is difficult to locate. Most local residents seem unaware of its location. Try the town clerk's office.

Dearing Farm (side road) for nearly thirty years was the summer home of famed Arctic explorer Dr. Vilhjalmur Stefansson (1879–1962).

Dr. Stefansson, considered by many Arctic experts as the leading Arctic authority and possibly the greatest Arctic explorer, was the first man to travel across the drifting polar pack and to secure food for his party by hunting. All previous explorers believed the polar sea was lifeless. He discovered new land in the polar regions. Dr. Stefansson was the foremost advocate and practitioner of the meat diet. He himself lived on a straight meat diet for several years during his expeditions. For more than a half century he contended the Arctic was a place well adapted to settlement and that it had great natural resources. Unfortunately, for too many years the Soviets paid more heed to his theories and advice than did his fellow Americans. He was the author of many books including *My Life with the Eskimo, Hunters of the Great North, The Friendly Arctic, Unsolved Mysteries of the Arctic, Not by Bread Alone, The Northward Course of Empire, The Adventure of Wrangel Island, Arctic Manual, The Standardization of Error, Greenland, Iceland, the Oldest American Republic, Ultima Thule, Cancer, A Disease of Civilization?, The Fat of the Land.*

His Arctic Library, considered as the most comprehensive in the world, is now housed at Dartmouth College where he spent his final years directing the school's Northern Studies Program.

EAST BETHEL (alt. 570), Vt. 14, sits snugly in a small cutout beside the highway. The *Hexagonal Schoolhouse* was constructed about 1830. The reason for the peculiar construction is a mystery. Early settlers may have thought its shape would better resist the winter winds that roar down the valley with power and fury.

BIG BROMLEY SKI AREA — Peru (see MANCHESTER)
BINGHAMVILLE (see FLETCHER)
BIRDSEYE MT. SKI AREA (see CASTLETON)
BLACK MT. SKI AREA (see DUMMERSTON)

BLOOMFIELD, 2–G (Essex County, Vt. 114; alt. 912, pop. 212; 20,632 acres). Bloomfield holds the minimum temperature record in New England. It was −50°F. on December 30, 1933. This is a small village across from North Stratford, N.H., a junction of the Maine Central and the Canadian National RR's. Its products are lumber and pulpwood. Rogers' Rangers, starving and harassed by Indians, followed the Nulhegan from Island Pond and were heartened at this point by reaching the Connecticut, the waterway that would lead them south to Charlestown, N.H.

BOLTON, 4–C (Chittenden County, US 2 and Interstate 89; alt. 342, pop. 237; 24,102 acres). Vt. Transit bus. Waterbury R.D. Bolton consists of a depot, general store, schoolhouse, and a few homes scattered along the level floor of the valley. Samuel Barnet, an early settler, served as one of Washington's guard in the Revolution, and in the War of 1812 fought at Plattsburg, being 68 years old at the time.

The *Long Trail* crosses the highway just east of Bolton village. The summit of *Camel's Hump* is 6.0 m. south on the trail. The *Chin* of *Mt. Mansfield* lies 17.2 m. north.

BOLTONVILLE (see NEWBURY)
BOMOSEEN STATE PARK (see CASTLETON)
BOMOSEEN P.O. (see CASTLETON)
BONDVILLE (see WINHALL)
BOWLSVILLE (see MT. HOLLY)

BRADFORD, 5–E (Orange County, US 5, 25 and Vt. 25B; alt. 405, pop. 1619; 18,919 acres). B & M/RR. Includes Piermont Station.
   Newspaper: Bradford *United Opinion* (weekly).

BRADFORD, originally called Waitstown, is situated at the junction of Waits River with the Connecticut. Waits River received its name from an incident in the retreat of Rogers' Rangers. Captain Joseph Waite was leading a small foraging squad down the valley, a group of gaunt emaciated men on the verge of starvation. They started a deer on the banks of this stream, just above its union with the Connecticut, and Waite brought the deer down with the timeliest shot of his life. The venison gave them strength enough to continue the journey and reach the stronghold at No. 4.

Bradford Official Information Booth (opposite Perry's Garage in business district).

VHS marker reads: "Home of maker of first globes and birthplace of Adm. Clark. James Wilson, a Bradford farmer and selftaught engraver, in the early 1800's made and sold the first geographical globes in the U.S. Adm. Chas. Clark, born here in 1843, was Captain of the 'Oregon' which sailed around Cape Horn to defeat the Spanish at Santiago Bay in 1898."

VAH — Burgess Farm, Almon C. Burgess. Dairy farm (Guernsey cattle).

VAH — Honey Bee Haven, Byron E. Eastman. Apiary and honey processing.

Bradford today has some of the virility, induced by the advantages of abundant waterpower, that marks the more active villages of the valley.

The culture of strawberries has become significant here, reaching a high degree of perfection on the lowlands of the Connecticut. Main St. extends between well-shaded lawns, brightened by the presence of many red brick houses. The *Low House,* overlooking the Green, is the outstanding structure in the village, built about 1796. The large white mansion is one of late eighteenth-century elegance; its spacious portico is reminiscent of the southern plantation houses. *Wood's Library,* facing the Common and Main St., is an ugly structure of brick and granite in a style resembling "Cattle Baron" Gothic. The *Craft House,* South Main St., with columned portico, was once a stage tavern.

The old stocks and whipping posts once stood on the east side of Main St.; here Colonel Mike Barron, hard-boiled sheriff for 23 years, used personally to lock, and flog with a cat-o'-nine tails, the transgressors of the law. Captain William Trotter, seaman, soldier-of-fortune, and contrabander, came to live in Bradford in 1804, after a storybook career that made him fairly rich. The first U.S. flag ever seen in the harbor of Buenos Aires was raised by Trotter, whose commercial voyages took him often to South America.

PIERMONT STATION is Bradford's depot on the B & M/RR.

BRADFORD GOLF CLUB (within village limits); 9 holes. Range: 93–473 yds.; par 32. Flat terrain along river. Facilities: golf shop, soft drinks. Special family, campers and student memberships.

BRAINTREE, 5–D (Orange County, Vt. 12, Vt. 12A; alt. 777, pop. 536; 22,146 acres). Includes: Braintree Center and East Braintree.

BRAINTREE CENTER has a combined general store and post office, a library and a Baptist church. The industries are lumbering and farming. EAST BRAINTREE (alt. 720) is an undistinguished village built in an S-shape. Its sole product is lumber.

BRANBURY STATE PARK–*Salisbury–Leicester* (see BRANDON)
BRANCH SCHOOL (see HANCOCK)

BRANDON, 6–B (Rutland County, US 7, Vt. 73; alt. 421, pop. 3330; 24,042 acres). Vt. Transit bus. Includes Forestdale.
  Information: Junction US 7 and Vt. 73 in front of library opposite Village Green and Soldiers' Monument.
  Railroad Station: Vt./Ry (freight only).
  Bus Depot: Center Pharmacy (Center St.).
  Accommodations: Inn, motels, tourist cabins, lodging houses.
  Churches: Protestant and Catholic.

Brandon, chartered 1761 as Neshobe, was first settled by David June and John Ambler. Local legend has it that the name Brandon is a corruption of "Burnt Town." The town, or part of it was destroyed by a party of raiding Tories — some were disguised as Indians — in 1777. Local legend is wrong. Brandon is an English name.

Fine post-Revolutionary homes and some of later vintage stand side by side beneath majestic elms and stately sugar maples.

Brandon is a minor winter sports center and a major summer resort. It is a popular overnight stop on fall foliage tours from Boston or New York. Two covered bridges, Dean's and Sanderson's, are still used. Both are less than two miles from the Village Green. The village is the chief trading area for summer visitors to the Lake Dunmore area.

Brandon, once a noted horseback-riding center, is attempting to recapture some of its former fun and business. During the 1920's the U.S. Cavalry Remount Service used Brandon as the headquarters for testing various breeds of horses. Vermont Morgans, of course, won. Riders rode sixty miles a day for five days.

Longtime Brandon resident Quimby Backus designed and manufactured the famed Backus Heater, here. The Backus Heater once a landmark in thousands of Grange Halls, lodge halls, schoolrooms and churches throughout America is still occasionally seen in rural areas.

Birthplace of Stephen A. Douglas (open; right at northern end of village), a small story-and-a-half cottage, white with green trim and a latticed entryway, faces Conant Square. Stephen A. Douglas, "The Little Giant," famous adversary of Lincoln, was born here in 1813. A marble monument before the cottage tells the story of the dynamic Douglas' life. The house is now headquarters of the D.A.R. Republican Brandon voted for Lincoln instead of supporting native son Democrat Douglas in the 1860 presidential contest.

Pearl Street (straight beyond Conant Square), once a military parade ground, was the forerunner of Brandon's wide streets. The *Farrington House* (1799), on Pearl St., is a large frame building, finished with ship-lap siding characteristic of the period, flanked on the south by a long line of neat barns. Captain Daniel Farrington commanded the Canadian border near Rouse's Point in 1808, where smuggling in defiance of the embargo laws was rampant. One smuggling vessel, the *Black Snake,* was pursued for miles down the lake and finally captured near Burlington in a bloody skirmish in which several men were killed and Farrington himself wounded. The incident resulted in Vermont's first state public hanging, when Cyrus Dean of the *Black Snake* was hanged in Burlington, November 11, 1808, to the edification of a crowd of 10,000 people.

A bridge over the Neshobe River reveals *Neshobe Falls,* where John Conant established his iron furnace, after the discovery of bog iron in 1810, and built up a business of manufacturing stoves. Conant's were the first stoves made in Vermont, and his industrial venture gave impetus to the growth of Brandon. Today early Conant stoves are much prized by antique collectors.

The *Town Hall* (1861), has an unusual massive appearance owing to its heavy Roman portico.

The business district flanks its Village Green of pleasant aspect, which lends a cool note to the commercial center, a respite from hot concrete highways and sidewalks. The *Congregational Church* (1831), of brick with a white wooden tower and old fenced-in burying ground, faces the park. The *Ayrshire Breeders' Association National Headquarters* is in the office building across from the Green.

Park Street, behind and east of the Soldiers' Monument, with its wide roadway — once a military parade ground — and tall elms, has many charming houses of the mid-nineteenth century. It is one of New England's loveliest streets. It lends support to the name "Beautiful Brandon."

The *Soldiers' Monument* is a large imposing memorial of granite, the high shaft topped by the figure of a Civil War soldier.

Brandon Training School (just north of the village, off US 7), established shortly before World War I, is a state-supported institution for training the mentally retarded.

Between Brandon and Pittsford to the south there is a continuous mountain view, green-clothed and graceful in contour, the broken line stretching against a blue sky. The grassy valley lies between US 7 and the mountains, a wavering line of trees marking the winding course of Otter Creek which was a most important Indian waterway in the early days. The highway here follows the *Old Crown Point Military Road,* which was extended from Charlestown, N.H. to Crown Point, N.Y., by General Amherst, 1759.

FORESTDALE (3 m. east on Vt. 73), a settlement in Brandon town, is basically one long street with houses of rather undistinguished types. A bronze plaque attached to a granite monument commemorates Williamstown native Thomas Davenport, "inventor of the electric motor." Directly behind the marker is a two-story frame house with a porch across the front, and a sign which reads "Workshop of Orange A. Smalley who invented the electric motor."

Most Davenport supporters maintain that he alone invented the electric motor and that Smalley was merely a mechanic who did Davenport's bidding. Smalley supporters allege that he alone invented the motor and that Davenport only contributed financial support. The truth, at this late date, will probably never be known, but in recent years there has been growing support of Smalley's claim. The sign, putting forth the Smalley claim, was placed there by the late Mrs. Carver "Buttercup" Smalley, widow of a Smalley descendant. She and her husband lived in the house for many years.

NESHOBE GOLF CLUB (off Vt. 73); 9 holes. Range: 167–460 yds.; par 35. Rolling terrain, 4 water holes. Facilities: Clubhouse, pro shop, showers, snack bar.

HIGH POND SKI AREA (6 m. west of Brandon off US 7). Family area: 1400-ft. elevation and 1000-ft base; 1400-ft. T-bar lift; 600-ft. and 300-ft. rope tows; 200-ft. tots' rope tow; 60 acres open slopes; 3 trails for novice, intermediate and expert. Ski hut and snack bar. Two instructors on weekends. Accommodations at Brandon Inn and Blueberry Hill, Goshen. *Information:* Phone Hubbardton, CRestview 3–2173.

Lake Dunmore, circled by Vt. 53, is possibly the most beautifully situated lake in the state. Dominated by Mt. Mooslamoo on the east and by hills on the west, the lake is free of much of the commercialism that is spoiling so many lakes. Small summer cottages mingle with summer camps.

LAKE DUNMORE FISHING ACCESS AREA is located next to Waterhouse's Marina on the west side of the lake. Boats may be launched here.

WATERHOUSE'S MARINA is the modernized version of the lake's oldest establishment. Established in the late 1890's Waterhouse's has served generations of Vermonters and summer visitors. There is a beach, picnic sites, bathhouse, boat docking and mooring facilities. Marine supplies including gasoline are available.

PINKY JOHNSON'S MARINA AND CAMP AREA is located on the east side of the lake. Groceries, gasoline, boats, motors, tent and tent trailer sites are available.

BRANBURY STATE PARK (Brandon R.D., Vt. 53; 98 acres). Given to the people of Vermont in 1945 by Brandon's multimillionaire philanthropist, Miss Shirley Farr. Former site of boys' camp. One of America's most beautiful lake (Lake Dunmore) beaches lies in the shadow of majestic Mt. Mooslamoo (alt. 2659). 1000 ft.-long white sandy beach backed by several acres of grass lawn. Facilities: tent sites, picnic tables and fireplaces, bathing, boating, fishing, refreshments. Easy foot trail up Mt. Mooslamoo (90 min. round trip). Scenic Llana Falls on Sucker Brook (10 min. walk).

BRATTLEBORO, 10–D (Windham County, US 5, Interstate 91, Vt. 9, Vt. 30 and Vt. 142; alt. 260, pop. [town] 11,734; village, 9319; 19,260 acres). Includes: Brattleboro, West Brattleboro.
Railroad Station: B & M RR and CV/Ry., southeast side of town near interstate bridge.
Bus Service: Vermont Transit. People's Brattleboro Transit (local).
Accommodations: Hotels, motels, tourist cabins, lodging houses.

Newspaper: Brattleboro *Reformer* (daily except Sunday).
Radio Stations: WTSA (1450 kc.), WKVT (1490 kc.).
Hospitals: Brattleboro Memorial; Brattleboro Retreat (mental hospital).
Schools: Grammar, junior and senior high schools. Parochial school.
Information: Putney Road (US 5). On the Common.

Brattleboro, Vermont's largest town, has a greater population than most of the state's cities. It has a representative town meeting government. Brattleboro has adopted the slogan "Where Vermont Begins." The phrase might well read, "Where Vermont Began," for the first permanent white settlement in Vermont was made about a mile and a half from the business district. Present Brattleboro, however, is one of a smaller number of Connecticut Valley towns whose varied commercial and industrial activities, while they have brought prosperity and steady growth, are by no means typical of Vermont as a whole.

Brattleboro spreads along the Connecticut from its junction with the West River south to Whetstone Brook, and climbs an irregular chain of plateaus to the west. The rocky wooded height of Wantastiquet Mountain on the New Hampshire shore of the Connecticut presses down upon the town from the east. Main St. passes from the brief charm of the Common into one of the most crowded business sections in Vermont, winds steeply down between darkened brick buildings to the native stone railroad station, south of which lie the yards and factories of the industrial flats along the river. The two islands at this point that formerly afforded sites for a dance hall and baseball park have been reduced to negligible shoals by the backed-up waters of the Vernon Dam, six miles below. From the semicircle of terraces that rise west of Main St., houses look down upon the jumble of shed roofs and smokestacks. One of the plateaus is commanded by the handsomely landscaped Estey estate, with its mansion looking across to the opposite heights where the family fortune was made. With something of the loud, unlovely industrial atmosphere of Bellows Falls, where the Connecticut is even more sharply walled in by hills, Brattleboro nevertheless possesses a greater variety than any of the other busy valley towns. West on Vt. 9 lies a pleasant residential section, while to the north along US 5, from where the Common stands above the sweeping lawns of the Retreat, is a wealthy suburban district with some of the finest domestic architecture in the state.

Brattleboro was part of the land sold to private citizens by Connecticut in 1716, for about a farthing an acre. These lands, ceded to the state by Massachusetts in return for some settled territory that Massachusetts had granted, but which a new survey showed actually to be in Connecticut, were known as the "Equivalent Lands." Massachusetts obtained permission to establish an outpost here, mainly for the protection of the settlement at Northfield, and work was begun under the direction of Lieutenant Governor Sir William Dummer, for whom the fort, completed in 1724, was named (see below).

In 1753 the town was granted by New Hampshire, which had jurisdiction over Fort Dummer, to the original proprietors, and was named for one of them, Colonel William Brattle, a land speculator who never set foot in the town. The first settlers under this grant chose the present site for their cabins because the hill served as a natural watchtower to guard against surprise attacks by the Indians. One such attack occurred, however, in 1758, in which Captain Fairbank Moor(e) and his son were slain and his wife and a four-weeks-old infant made captive and taken to Montreal, where they were later ransomed for $74. Prior to Vermont's admission to the Union, Brattleboro, like the majority of towns in this section, was a Tory stronghold.

Industry and Commerce

In 1771, Bostonian Stephen Greenleaf opened what is believed to have been the first store in the present state. Not of significance in itself, the fact exemplifies the zeal for trade and industry that Brattleboro has always manifested to a degree equaled by few other Vermont towns. Of the many manufacturing firms that came into being during the last century, the most widely known was the Estey Organ Company. This business was begun in 1846, but did not develop until 1855, when it became the sole property of Jacob Estey. It was Estey's perseverance that triumphed over adversaries — his factory was twice destroyed by fire and once devastated by flood — to win pre-eminence for his product in its field. During the latter half of the nineteenth century thousands of American women sewed till the small hours, picked berries under a blazing sun or rented the spare room, and saved their egg money in a cracked teapot on the top shelf with just one goal in mind: a black walnut Estey organ in the parlor.

Brattleboro's commercial products include cotton goods, penholders, brush handles, lacquer, heels, bathroom accessories, finished woods, toys, overalls, paper, soft drinks, and granite monuments and memorials. The printing establishments here are outstanding in the state. American Optical Company, Southbridge, Mass., has a plant here.

Brattleboro was the early home of James Fisk (1834–1872), the jovial, impudent voluptuary and stock manipulator, whose unscrupulous method of making a fortune and spectacular manner of dissipating it outraged and amused the American public. It is just possible that Fisk's disregard of business ethics was partly due to a Brattleboro venture of his father, who opened a temperance hotel here in 1849, but was forced to close the idealistic establishment the following year for lack of patrons.

Water, however, contributed to Brattleboro's fame and prosperity during the years between 1845 and 1870, when the Brattleboro and Hydropathic Establishment, utilizing the mineral springs here, became one of the most fashionable cures in the country, with an elaborate plant accommodating three hundred guests. Under the leadership of Dr. Robert Wesselhoeft, a German political refugee of high intelligence, the institution attracted many persons of literary and artistic talent as well as wealthy neurasthenics.

The national headquarters of the Holstein-Friesian Breeders' Association is here.

Native Sons

Native sons and/or distinguished residents have included: painter William Morris Hunt, architect Richard Morris Hunt, sculptor Larkin Mead and architect William Rutherford Mead. Rudyard Kipling married a Brattleboro girl and lived here for several years. Rutherford Hayes, father of the President and father-in-law of the White House temperance fanatic "Lemonade Lucy," was a Brattleboro man. Alonzo Church, president of the University of Georgia for more than thirty years and Wesleyan College co-founder Wilbur Fisk, were Brattleboro natives.

What To See and Do

1. The *Brattleboro Public Library* (Brooks Memorial Bldg.), 200 Main St., of red brick with an arched portico, contains several collections of interest. The museum upstairs includes early American pioneer utensils, implements, relics, and several items of historical association, among them a suit of armor worn by the Mexican General Santa Anna. A small art collection is headed by a large original canvas of William Morris Hunt. This work, "The Prodigal Son," is an early example of Hunt's narrative painting. In separate rooms are the Loud collection of porcelains and paintings and the Phelps collection of 3000 rare books, documents, and broadsides donated by James H. Phelps in 1888.

2. The *Center Congregational Church,* Main St., the oldest in town (1842), is a white wooden structure, with decorative quoins and a tall graduated tower rising into a spire.

3. The *All Souls Church,* Main St., constructed of stone, is designed in a modified version of Gothic architecture. A marble copy of Mead's "Recording Angel," originally modeled in snow, was placed in this church as a memorial to the sculptor.

4. The *Estey Estate and Brattleboro Summer Theater,* School St. The mansion built by Jacob Estey is an ornate brown-brick structure. The theater itself was remodeled from the Estey coach house. A repertory of professionally acted plays is produced. The advisory committee in the past has included names like Thornton Wilder, Claude Rains and Jane Cowl.

5. The *Brattleboro Retreat,* Linden St. (1836), is a partially state-supported hospital for mental illness. The brick buildings of the large plant, some of recent construction, others dating from the earlier years of the institution, are set in the quiet seclusion of spacious landscaped grounds.

6. *Site of Fort Dummer,* 1.4 m. south of town on Vt. 30. The actual site of Fort Dummer (dismantled in 1763) is covered by the backed-up waters of the Vernon Dam. The granite marker, beside the highway,

was moved 2200 feet northwest of its original site in 1928. Fort Dummer, of which contemporary drawings are extant, was approximately 180 feet square, of yellow pine timber. The wall of the fort was the back wall of all the houses inside it, the roofs sloping up to the top of the fort. Garrisoned by 55 men, including a dozen friendly Indians, the fort was for its first two years in command of Captain Timothy Dwight, whose son was the first white child born in Vermont, and was to be further distinguished as the father of a President of Yale College.

7. *The Book Cellar* (Main St.), one of the state's best bookshops, owned and operated by Stephen Greene who also publishes books on Vermont and New England.

VAH — Thomas Farm, Emerson Thomas. Dairy farm (Holstein cattle).

BLACK MOUNTAIN SKI AREA (turn west off US 5, 2 m. north of Brattleboro or east off Vt. 30 about 0.5 m. past covered bridge); 600-ft. and 900-ft. rope towns on north face of Black Mountain. Warming hut and snack bar. A community project with moderate rates. *Information:* Phyllis Baldwin, Putney, Vt. Phone: ALpine 4–5422.

LIVING MEMORIAL PARK (2.5 m. west of Brattleboro), 1126-ft. elevation; 1400-ft. rope tow; 1 trail. Ski hut and snack bar. Instruction, ski patrol and first aid. A community project. *Information:* Brattleboro Recreation Dept., 207 Main St., Brattleboro, Vt.

HOGBACK SKI AREA (Vt. 9). Taxi service; 2500-ft. elevation and 1900-ft. base; 2250-ft. T-bar lift; 1700-ft. Pomalift; 1000- and 700-ft. tows. Trails: 5 novice (9000-ft), 4 intermediate (6000-ft.), 3 expert (4200-ft); 50 acres ski area. Jim Howard ski school. Ski patrol and first aid. Ski huts and snack bar. Rentals and repairs. *Information:* Box 812, Brattleboro, Vt. Phone: Wilmington, Vt., HOmestead 4–3942.

MAPLE VALLEY SKI AREA (Vt. 30 between Brattleboro and Newfane). Family area especially designed for novices; 900- and 250-ft. rope tows. All open slope. Free ski instruction. Tobogganing and saucers permitted on 250-ft. tow. Warming hut. *Information:* Raymond Severance, Newfane, Vt.

BRATTLEBORO COUNTRY CLUB (Upper Dummerston Road); 9 holes. Range: 155–510 yds. Hilly terrain. Facilities: Clubhouse, golf shop, pro, caddies. Dining facilities open throughout year.

BREADLOAF (see RIPTON)

BRIDGEWATER, 7–D (Windsor County, US 2, Vt. 100; alt. 820, pop. 776; 28,657 acres). White River Coach Lines. Includes: Bridgewater village, Bridgewater Center, Bridgewater Corners, and West Bridgewater.

Vermont's greatest hero, the legendary Ethan Allen

Vermont Development Department

Hubbardton. A major Revolutionary War battle was fought here. *Claire Griffin*

Fort Ticonderoga, New York — captured by Ethan Allen. *Brown Brothers*

Old Bennington Battle Monument. *Vermont Development Department*

Plymouth. America's most colorful inauguration occurred here
Vermont Development Department

John Coolidge behind the lamp
which lighted his father's
swearing-in ceremony
Aldo Merusi

Rygate sheep farm. *Claire Griffin*

Snaking logs in Grafton. *Arthur Griffin*

Wilmington — maple sap for maple syrup. *Arthur Griffin*

BRIDGEWATER is a small village that is given a distinctly industrial accent by the large woolen mills of the *Vermont Native Industries* here. Across the highway from the mill itself is a large showroom where hundreds of tourists annually inspect the many samples of pure woolen fabrics and, if they wish, purchase materials for suits, overcoats, and dresses fresh from the loom. The woolens made here are nationally advertised as "Vermont Tweeds."

Bridgewater was the birthplace of Zadock Thompson (1796–1856). He put himself through the University of Vermont with proceeds from the sale of an almanac which he published annually for several years. One year his printer called to his attention the fact that he had made no weather prediction for July. "Snow about this time," Thompson replied absent-mindedly. And as it happened, it *did* snow considerably in Vermont that July, a natural phenomenon that gave Thompson a tremendous reputation based upon the least worthy of his many talents. His major claim to fame rests upon his original researches into the history and natural history of Vermont and the publication of the results. Without the numerous histories and gazetteers of Zadock Thompson, countless facts concerning the early Vermont towns and the men who settled and inhabited them would have been irrevocably lost.

BRIDGEWATER CENTER (Briggs) is a tiny cluster of houses around an Assembly of God Church.

BRIDGEWATER CORNERS (alt. 855) is a small cluster of houses with a post office.

WEST BRIDGEWATER (alt. 1056) is a small village dominated by woodworking mills, large piles of the products of which can usually be seen weathering outdoors, between the highway and the river.

BRIDPORT, 6–A (Addison County, Vt. 22A and Vt. 125; alt. 321, pop. 653; 25,650 acres). Middlebury stage. Includes: Bridport village and West Bridport.

BRIDPORT village lies on the plain surrounded by sweeping meadows and pastures, where merino sheep and Morgan horses were formerly raised extensively. The noted ram, "Bismarck," and the celebrated Morgan sire "Black Hawk" were products of Bridport farms. Sheep are still raised in the vicinity, but on a lesser scale. This agricultural community spreads about a large open common, the surrounding homes well spaced. A pleasing brick house and a venerable old wooden homestead are landmarks on the village street. The *Congregational Church* (1852) is a brick structure with a portico of white wooden columns and Corinthian capitals, topped by a wooden spire. The *Old Cemetery* beside the church is guarded by an iron picket fence and holds head-stones dated as early as the 1780's. The view from this graveyard sweeps over the meadowlands to distant mountains.

Bridport was settled in 1768 by 21-year-old Philip Stone from Groton, Massachusetts. The Smiths, second family to arrive, came by ox wagon and bateau from New Jersey. The settlement was disrupted by the strife with "York State" and the Revolutionary War, but the pioneers returned after hostilities ceased. It was in 1772 that Ethan Allen and Eli Roberts visited Bridport and nearly fell captive to the Yorkers. New York State had placed a bounty on the head of "Outlaw" Allen and his associates, and six British soldiers arrived in Bridport to capture the fiery Green Mountain Boy. Warned by their hostess, Mrs. Richards, Allen and Roberts escaped by leaping through an open window, and the six soldiers returned to Crown Point empty-handed, cursing Allen and his unruly band.

BRIGHTON, 2–F (Essex County, Vt. 105 and 114; alt. 1191, pop. 1535; 28, 779 acres). CN/Ry. Includes: East Brighton and Island Pond.

EAST BRIGHTON is a station on the CN/Ry.

Island Pond (Brighton) Official *Information Booth* (center of town near walking overpass near upper end of Cross St.), Weekdays: 10–7, Sundays: 11–7.
Newspaper: Essex County Herald (weekly).

ISLAND POND, originally called Random, derives its name from a pond at the southern end of the village which has a 22-acre island in its center, quite similar to Ellen's Isle in the Trossachs. The pond itself strengthens this Scottish impression, its closely wooded shores and grave, secluded beauty rendering the comparison inevitable. There are seven other ponds in the township of Brighton, in which the village is located. Island Pond was settled late, and like most of the towns and villages in Essex County is entirely lacking in examples of interesting early architecture. As the chief commercial importance of the village is due to the fact that it is a division headquarters of the Canadian National RR and a port of entry from Canada, it is fitting that its business district should be dominated by a large brick and granite railway station. A skeletonlike elevated footbridge north of the station and an overhead highway bridge on State 105 just south of it are necessary to convey traffic in safety across the intricate network of tracks and switches spread out to the east, but this does not keep them from aggravating the gaunt bleakness of the scene. Island Pond's proximity to fine lumber country and its railroad facilities have led to the establishment of large furniture and woodworking factories here, though they are for the most part inactive at present.

Roller Coaster Road (Vt. 114 between Norton Mills and Island Pond). This famous eight-mile stretch of highway is a continuous series of sharp rises and dips of varying height and degree that give the motorist a sensation similar to that derived from the amusement-park device for which the road was named. This road, however, was not constructed to that end, but merely follows the natural contours of the land. Heavy cars may take this exhilarating ride at 45 miles an hour, lighter cars at 40 miles an hour, with perfect safety, *if drivers keep to the right when approaching the tops of the steep knolls that shut out the view ahead.* A parking lookout affords a good view of the southern end of *Norton Lake,* with its fantastic jigsaw shoreline, a rarity among the lakes of Vermont. The mountains to the south and east fill the horizon, their profiles overlapping one another, all apparently equidistant from the traveler. One of the scenic delights of this route lies in watching these mountains grow more distinct and assume perspective.

BRIGHTON STATE PARK (Island Pond PO, off Vt. 105 or Vt. 114; est. 1954; 87 acres) is located on the neck of land between Island and Spectacle Ponds with beach front on both ponds. Facilities: picnic tables and fireplaces, tent sites, lean-tos, camp trailers, bathing, boating, fishing.

BRISTOL, 5–G (Addison County, Vt. 17 and Vt. 116; alt. 575, pop. [town] 2157; 21,710 acres). Includes Bristol village, Rocky Dale (formerly Ackworth).

BRISTOL village (pop. 1421), situated on a broad terrace in the shelter of bluff mountains, is a clean pleasant village with well-kept homes and grounds indicating the home-loving character of its people. In orderly arrangement wide maple-lined streets bound the square central Green with its cool-splashing fountain, park benches, old cannon, war memorials, and playground. *Hogback Mountain* (alt. 1850) forms a picturesque high-ridged background on the east, especially beautiful in autumn when the turning leaves transform it into a blazing wall of color.

The *Town Hall* (Holley Hall), West St., an attractive brick structure, was erected in 1884. *The Bristol Inn,* more than a century old, was torn down to make way for a supermarket and parking lot. Once known as the "Coffin Community" Bristol lost its largest industry when the National Casket Company ceased its local operations. There are various woodworking establishments. The largest single employer is the Van Raalte Company of New York City, manufacturers of women's nylon undergarments.

When a party of surveyors came to this section in 1785, they found living here a lone man, a German named John Broadt, who thought himself a fugitive from justice for the killing of a neighbor near Unadilla, New York. For twelve years Broadt had lived like a hermit in the wilderness depths. It developed that the man he had fought with, and supposedly killed, was alive and well, and Broadt was able to return to his home after his years of self-imposed exile. The first permanent settlers here were Samuel Stewart and Eden Johnson, in 1786.

ROCKY DALE (1.0 m. east of Bristol at junction of Vt. 17 and Vt. 116) is a settlement of houses clustered about a bridge over the New Haven River (a first-rate trout stream in this area). Rocky Dale was formerly known as Ackworth.

What To See and Do

1. *Bartlett's Falls* (1.5 m. east of Bristol on Vt. 17) pour with the cool musical rush of white water into a basin that forms a natural swimming pool. Accommodations are provided for picnic parties and general recreation.

2. *Bristol Municipal Airport* (western edge of town just north of Vt. 17). Flying lessons.

3. *Bristol Pond* (alt. 460, 3.5 m. north of town on back road) is a small low-lying body of water almost completely surrounded by marshlands. The pond has a muddy bottom and offers excellent fishing, being especially well stocked with pickerel. The finding of many Indian relics, arrowheads, and spearheads in this vicinity indicates that the Bristol Pond region was once a rendezvous for Indian tribes, and the discovery of many unfinished arrowheads revealed that the implements were made in the locality. Near the north end of the pond early investigators uncovered the skeletons of several Indians buried in sitting positions in a sand bank.

4. *Hell's Half Acre* (2 m. south of town on back road) is the site of old "Spanish Treasure Diggings." Bring your pick, shovel and plenty of groceries. It may take a long time to uncover the great silver horde.

5. *Lawrence Memorial Library* contains 7500 volumes.

6. *Lord's Prayer Rock* (eastern outskirts of village on Vt. 17). Travelers are mildly surprised to find the Lord's Prayer confronting them suddenly from the face of a huge boulder close by the roadside. Buffalo physician Joseph Greene spent his boyhood in this vicinity. He remembered the cursing teamsters who lashed their sweaty horses up the grade, where the road was always muddy. Dr. Greene paid a stonecutter to inscribe the Lord's prayer in large letters as a reminder to passersby.

BROCKWAYS MILLS (see ROCKINGHAM)

BROOKFIELD, 5–D (Orange County, Vt. 14; alt. 1481, pop. 597; 24,472 acres). Randolph stage. Includes Brookfield village, East Brookfield, West Brookfield.

BROOKFIELD village lies 2.5 miles off Vt. 14 at East Brookfield. It is a mountain village in a sprawling irregular setting with a certain amount of cobwebby atmosphere and off-trail charm. The Brookfield Library is the oldest continuously existent library in the state. It was established in 1791.

The 320-ft. long *Brookfield Floating Bridge* is the only one of its kind in Vermont. It spans Colts Pond (Mirror Lake) at the western end of the village. The bridge is buoyed by 380 tarred wooden barrels which act as pontoons. Hinged ramps at either end allow for the seasonal rise and fall of the water level.

The first bridge here was constructed about 1812 when a man was reported drowned while attempting to cross thin ice. The present bridge, the seventh, was formally dedicated in August 1936. When the state offered to build a modern overhead bridge here, the citizens of Brookfield rejected the proposal in a characteristic Vermont manner, saying that they had used a floating bridge for 124 years; it had been good enough, and they figured it would continue to be good enough. But in this case their attitude was not so backward as it might seem, for the Brookfield Floating Bridge attracts many tourists to this little community in the hills. The present bridge, its wood thoroughly soaked in a tar preparation, is expected to last for at least 50 years.

EAST BROOKFIELD (alt. 741), situated in a low point of the valley, is a village with plain residences and stores strung along the highway for some distance.

WEST BROOKFIELD (alt. 1036), off Vt. 12, is an open village centered loosely around a country four-corners.

ALLIS STATE PARK (Brookfield P.O.), via Vt. 14 over interesting Brookfield Floating Bridge or from Vt. 12 the Northfield Gulf road. The 485 acres were given to the people of Vermont in 1931 by native son Wallis S. Allis and were developed into one of the most useful and scenic Vermont State parks by members of the Civilian Conservation Corps (CCC) during the depression-ridden 1930's.

The park includes a road to the 50-ft.-high lookout tower on the summit of Bear Hill (alt. 2000). The lookout tower, south of the large parking area, affords a magnificent view of mountains, forests, farms and valley. White Pond lies directly below on the east, cupped in gently sloping farmlands, with villages beyond, and the White

Mountains of New Hampshire are outlined on the horizon. White church steeples jut against the greenery of nearby mountains.

Facilities: picnic tables and fireplaces, tent sites, lean-tos, camp trailers.

BROOKSVILLE (see NEW HAVEN)

BROWNINGTON, 2–E (Orleans County, 2.5 m. off US 5 at Orleans; alt. 1200, pop. 509). Includes: Brownington Center and Evansville.

BROWNINGTON village and town were named after two Browns who were among the early grantees. The village is scattered along the easy slant of a plateau surrounded by sloping farmlands and farmsteads, with mountain panorama in the distance. At the crest of the slope above the village center stands the *Congregational Church* and grave-yard, the frame building painted white with green-blinded windows. The *Old Stone House* at the crest, a three-storied structure of mor-tared granite blocks, has a grim military aspect. In 1822, the Orleans County Grammar School was established in this sturdy stone building, which now serves as the *Museum* of the Orleans County Historical Society. The museum contains old furniture, tools, weapons, docu-ments, pictures.

A leader in the early days, Brownington fell into lethargy with the shift of population from the hills to the river valleys. Now the ven-erable houses sleep along the gentle slope in their beautiful upland setting.

BROWNINGTON CENTER has a few houses, a general store, Methodist Church and a sawmill.

EVANSVILLE has a general store, Methodist church and a sawmill.

BROWNSVILLE (see WEST WINDSOR)

BRUNSWICK, 2–G (Essex County, Vt. 102; alt. 1000, pop. 53; 20,663 acres). Includes Brunswick Springs (site of Brunswick Mineral Springs).

BRUNSWICK village has one motel-restaurant but no stores or churches. Residents do their "trading" across the Connecticut in North Stratford, N.H., which also provides postal facilities for residents of this tiny town.

BRUNSWICK MINERAL SPRINGS are a short distance from Brunswick village. The six mineral springs for which the town was once noted flow toward the Connecticut River. These springs are said to differ from one another not only in mineral content, in which sulphur pre-dominates, but also — to a proper connoisseur — in taste as well. The springs and the riverbank ridge are well landscaped, as a result of their having been the leading attractions of a succession of resort hotels on this site, the last of which burned years ago.

BUEL'S GORE, 5–C (Chittenden County, McCullough Highway, pop. 1; 2204 acres). Gore affairs are handled by a supervisor residing in Winooski.

BURKE, 3–F (Caledonia County, US 5 and Vt. 114; alt. 830, pop. 992; 23,003 acres). CP/Ry. Includes: East Burke, West Burke, Burke Green and Burke Hollow.

EAST BURKE is a pretty village with an air of sophistication usually found only in larger towns. The *Burke Mountain Club,* the center of the town's social life, was donated in 1919 by the late Elmer A. Darling, a native son of Burke whose benefactions to his birthplace were many. The graceful white wood building houses a varied library, reading and game rooms, and numerous mementoes of its donor and his family. Among the latter the most notable is what was probably the last pass issued by Abraham Lincoln. It reads: "Allow the bearer, A. B. Darling, to pass to, and visit Mobile, if, and when that city shall be in our possession. A. Lincoln. April 13, 1865." A. B. Darling, owner and proprietor of the old Fifth Avenue Hotel in New York City, was the uncle of E. A. Darling. Lincoln, it will be remembered, was assassinated the next evening.

Immediately south of the club building stands the *White School-house,* named for the White family, who were prominent in early Burke history. Built about two miles north of the village in 1817, this building was acquired by the Burke Historical Society in 1895 and moved to its present site and merged with the Burke Mountain Club in 1922–23. It is now a small but widely representative museum of local antiquities, including furniture, china, glassware, costumes, books, and manuscripts. A curator is in charge at the Burke Mountain Club all day.

WEST BURKE is a small trading and milling village in the township of Burke, which was probably named for Edmund Burke, the British statesman. The settlement is haphazard and straggling, its chief appeal lying in a kind of rustic carelessness. West Burke is at the junction of US 5 and 5A.

BURKE GREEN is the site of the first settlement in the town marked by a few cellar holes and an old cemetery on the shady hill, where early settlers sleep under the somber serenity of tall pines. On the eastern skyline Burke Mountain bulks nobly, and to the north is the striking profile presented by the guardian mountains of Lake Willoughby.

BURKE HOLLOW is pervaded by century-old quietude and as charmingly rustic as an etching from rural folk tales. A narrow stream splashes over its rocky bed at the center of the village. The *Old House,* white, high, and constructed with wide clapboards, is said to have been the first tavern. The *Old Union Meeting House* stands white, prim, and delicately spired above the village street, beautiful in its pure simplicity. Built in 1825, the church seats 300 people and remains unaltered; the interior has the old box pews, or "slips," each with an individual door; and behind the high barrel pulpit is a long choir gallery.

BURKE MT. (see below, DARLING STATE PARK)

DARLING STATE PARK (East Burke P.O.), off Vt. 114 at E. Burke; 1726 acres), given to the people of Vermont in 1933 by L. A. and Elmer Darling, includes Burke Mountain (alt. 3267) with a paved road to the summit. Panoramic views from glass-enclosed fire ranger's tower at summit. Facilities: picnic tables and fireplaces, tent sites, lean-tos, skiing (see below, BURKE MT. SKI AREA).

BURKE MOUNTAIN SKI AREA (7 m. north of Lyndonville off Vt. 114); 3267-ft. elevation with 1700-ft. base; 4880-ft. Pomalift. Trails: 1 novice, 2 intermediate and 1 expert. Rope tow, parking, open slopes, ski school. Ski shop with rentals, repairs and sales. Restaurant. Warming huts at base and summit. *Information:* Ski Burke Mountain, Inc., Box 446, Lyndonville.

BURLINGTON, 3–A (Chittenden County, US 2, US 7, Interstate 89; alt. 100, pop. 35,531; 39,960 acres — 36 sq. miles). Shire town.

GREATER BURLINGTON includes the separate communities of: Burlington city, South Burlington, Colchester, Winooski and Essex. Total area pop. about 62,000.
   Information: Junction US 2 and US 7 (cor. Main and So. Willard Sts.).
   Railroad Station: Union (CV/Ry and VT/Ry) Station. Essex Junction is primary Burlington/RR station.
   Bus Terminal: 137 St. Paul St. (Vermont Transit and local lines).
   Airport: Burlington Airport (So. Burlington): Northeast Airlines (Boston), Mohawk (New York City). Charter flights.
   Ferries: Lake Champlain to Port Kent, N.Y.
   Accommodations: Hotel, motels, tourist cabins, lodging houses.
   Hospitals: Mary Fletcher and DeGrosbriand (Catholic) Memorial.
   Newspaper: Burlington *Free Press* (daily except Sunday).
   TV Station: WCAX–Channel 3.

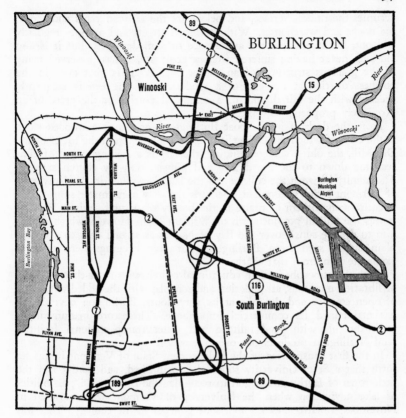

Radio Stations: WMVT (620 kc.), WJOY (1230 kc.), WDOT (1400 kc.).

Schools: Grammar, junior and senior high schools. Parochial.

Colleges: University of Vermont (UVM), Trinity College (Catholic girls). St. Michaels (Winooski).

Vermont State Police Outpost: A Troop. Phone: UNiversity 313435.

Burlington, the "Queen City of Vermont," is beautifully situated on a three-terraced slope rising from the broadest expanse of Lake Champlain. The waterway at its feet, which has contributed so great a part to its commercial prosperity, is one of America's loveliest lakes, stretching far away to the west to the Adirondacks, while on the east, extending north and south, are the Green Mountains.

On the tree-covered summit of the city, flanked by residential districts, stand the buildings of the University of Vermont; the business section occupies the middle terrace, and below are the railroad yards and shops; the docks and warehouses. With its broad streets and avenues regularly laid out, Burlington has the appearance of a modern city, but it is also old and, never having suffered from a great fire, it has preserved many of the gracious structures of an earlier day. So it is, that even in the business district, at the end of a modern vista, the eye is frequently greeted with the fair dignity of a columned portico or the grace of an exquisitely proportioned spire.

From the deck of a lake boat Burlington appears as a wooded slope at the crest of which the University's spires emerge; from the tower of the Old Mill, the oldest college building, the city is a folding carpet of elms reaching down to the broad lake and pierced only by church steeples. The affinity between the college and the lake is typified in the University of Vermont song "Champlain," perhaps the only alma mater song which is entirely an anthem of praise to the beauty of natural setting. Possibly it was the willful provincialism of William Dean Howells which caused him to declare sunset over the Bay of Naples as second only to a Champlain sunset seen from Burlington, but July evenings here tend to exonerate him from that charge.

With the atmosphere of an educational center, with more than its share of libraries, museums, art galleries, and schools; with the added advantage of open country and the lake at its very doors, Burlington nevertheless has maintained its commercial importance. Threescore manufacturing establishments with good railroad and water transportational facilities send Burlington products out over the world.

In the first constitution of the Independent State of Vermont it was set forth that a State University should be established, and hardly had the little town of Burlington begun to recognize the commercial possibilities of lake navigation when the University of Vermont was chartered in November, 1791, one of the first state colleges in the country. That was the year of Vermont's admission to the Union, and, with little else to give it, the state endowed its university with 29,000 acres of wild, forest-covered land, scattered through 120 townships.

Soon Burlington began to win a place as the most important of Champlain ports. Thereafter, through an era of more than fifty years, as grew the city, so grew the University. With the coming of the railroads in 1849 there was a pause for adjustment, but the opening of new markets and speedier transportation brought renewed prosperity both to the city and the college.

History

Burlington was chartered in 1763 by the Province of New Hampshire and settled in 1773. The name derives from the Burling family, landholders in this region. The astute Ira Allen, whose family name is written large in the annals of Vermont, had established a shipyard, building the first local vessel, the schooner *Liberty,* on the Winooski River in 1772.

In the spring of 1775, with the outbreak of the Revolution, most settlers left to join Ethan Allen at Bennington. Practically all activity ceased after 1776, when nearly all who had not answered the first call went south with the retreat of American forces from Canada.

It was not until the close of the war in 1783 that the pioneers returned, their company augmented by the lure of a veritable promised land, with every possibility of a fine fur trade, with vast supplies of standing timber and ample water power — and always the lake for a waterway. Clearing the land, working from the lake front up the hill, was the first necessary task. In 1797, the town of Burlington was organized. Ethan Allen himself came back to the Onion River and passed the last years of his life in lord-of-the-manor fashion on his handsome farm north of town.

A road was put through to Winooski Falls. Pearl Street and Colchester Avenue combine to follow the route of this early thoroughfare, but it is King Street that those interested in the beginning of commercial Burlington will seek out. At the foot of this street, where there were three or four houses comprising the village of Burlington, a rude wharf of logs was chained together and moored. Gideon King (familiarly "Old Gid King"), in whose honor the street was named, was probably the first to grasp the great possibilities of commercial navigation on Lake Champlain. He urged it, he initiated it, he prospered at it, until he was known in all the lake ports and far into Canada as "Admiral of the Lake." John Jacob Astor, at this time founding the Astor fortune in the fur trade, met King, appreciated him as a man of foresight, and chose him to look after his interests.

Also, it was in a room in the sizable home King had built on Battery Street that the law was administered in the early 1790's, but the lumbermen were clearing up the middle area of the town, so that in 1798 what is now City Hall Park was dedicated to the public and the first courthouse was erected.

Meanwhile the "Admiral of the Lake" and those whom he had converted to his enthusiasm were flourishing. With Montreal and Quebec there was already a fine trade. Down the Winooski and Lamoille Rivers floated seemingly endless supplies of logs to be formed into crude rafts and towed, or sometimes sailed, to Canadian destinations. The ever-enterprising Ira Allen had built a sawmill at Winooski Falls and handier rafts of dressed lumber began to appear. Many of these carried cargoes of potash, made from the ashes of wood waste.

Near the foot of King Street was built in 1808 the steamboat *Vermont,* which inaugurated steam navigation on Lake Champlain the following year, and was the second steamboat successfully operated commercially in this country. One hundred and twenty feet over all, of twenty-foot beam and of 167 tons burden, "built and fitted up at great expense for the convenient accommodation of ladies and gentlemen who wish to pass Lake Champlain with safety and dispatch," the *Vermont* set out on her first voyage from Burlington in June, 1809, John Winans in command, scheduled "to make the passage of the lake, 150 miles (to Whitehall), in the short time of twenty-four hours."

Then occurred the outbreak of hostilities with England, and in 1812 Burlington became the Vermont center of military activity. Some four thousand troops were quartered on what is now Battery Park. From here a raiding party went out to attack St. Armand, Quebec, where twenty-five of the enemy were killed or wounded, and one hundred others captured and brought back to Burlington.

The remains of a parapet can be traced along the western border of Battery Park, directly commanding the lake. Here 13 guns had been set up, and when, on June 13, 1813, three British war vessels appeared in the bay and started offensive operations, they were beaten off. After the victory at Plattsburg, naval operations on the lake were discontinued and eighteen months later a treaty of peace was signed between the United States and England. Burlington's merchants resumed trade negotiations with Canada and began to develop the commerce already built up to the south. Steamboats, growing constantly more dependable, appeared in increasing numbers.

In 1823 the opening of the Champlain Canal connected the lake with the Hudson River. Almost at once the course of a large part of Champlain Valley commerce was changed from Canada to New York. With a way open to tidewater from Canada and the lake ports to the Atlantic Ocean, well-financed companies became interested. They built steamers, and not content with single-ship capacity, sent them out at the head of long tows of canal boats which were soon a common sight going up and down the lake.

The canal was a door opening outward for the distribution of products, and swinging inward to admit cheaply, and expeditiously, what was desired. The harbor was busy with craft discharging and loading their cargoes, and shipyards hummed as they labored to supply the demand for more steamboats, more canal boats, more sailing vessels — anything that could bear merchandise over the water. And not only the water was utilized. Enterprising companies or individuals built so-called "landships" — great covered wagons which, laden with diverse commodities and drawn by as many teams of horses as the load required, traded to the east and north, bringing to Burlington the produce of all this section of the state.

Demand for passenger accommodations created lively competition among the steamboat lines. In 1826 the Champlain Transportation Company was chartered and by 1848 it had absorbed all its rivals and was triumphantly running four steamers between St. Johns and Whitehall, two for day and two for night travel (see Transportation). Lake travel attained its peak during the forties, for in the last year of that decade came the railroads and a swift decline in business on the water. Boston, the nearest great city, now accessible by rail, attracted by far the larger part of the commercial trade, and Burlington, recognized as a desirable shipping point, got two railroads almost simultaneously.

The question of the route of the proposed Boston–Burlington railway aroused tremendous feeling. One group of enthusiastic promoters was all for routing it via Rutland; another group held out just as strongly to include Concord, N.H., and Montpelier. Neither side being willing to concede anything, and both having capital, construction of both roads was begun and soon developed into a race to be first to enter Burlington. The Rutland road reached its goal December 18, 1849, and a week later on Christmas Day, its rival, the Central Vermont, was in Winooski.

By this time the once vast timber supply in the vicinity of Burlington was no longer equal to the market demand. But the lumbermen had become busy in Canada, and with great barges of lumber coming in across the lake, with the railroads ready to transport the finished products south, the city became the greatest lumber port in New England and third in the United States.

The Burlington *Free Press,* the oldest daily in the state, was founded April 1, 1848, by De Witt Clinton Clarke, as both a morning and evening paper.

Far to the north of the fighting lines though it was, Burlington's part in the Civil War was an active one. The city sent full quotas in answer to the Government's repeated calls for men; merchants and banks contributed generously; large hospital camps were established for the sick and wounded sent North, and training camps prepared recruits to go to the front. One of these camps was notable as that of the Second Vermont Regiment, which later lost in killed and wounded some forty percent of its men, several times the general ratio of the Northern forces.

Two months before Appomattox, a new era of enterprise and prosperity had begun with a division of the territory of the old town of Burlington, the larger section forming South Burlington while the smaller was incorporated as a city (February 21, 1865). A new unity of civic effort was at once noticeable, and Burlington began to lose the appearance of an overgrown country town and to assume an urban aspect.

Today

The Queen City, long the state's largest city, has had a 40 percent population increase since Pearl Harbor. The expanding UVM student body, with an increased faculty together with the location in the Greater Burlington area of branch plants of International Business Machines Corporation and General Electric Company, has brought in ten thousand people. The population has gradually lost its homogeneous nature through the influx of French Canadians, Germans, Italians, and other races, until Burlington is the most cosmopolitan of Vermont cities.

Outstanding in the state also are the municipal services, including a highly profitable city-owned electric light plant, efficient street, fire, and police departments, and an extensive park system.

The many handsome estates on the higher hill streets, only recently beginning to yield to subdivision, are evidence of the prosperity of fifty years ago, and of the attractions of Burlington for retired wealth.

The University of Vermont, which was united with the State Agricultural College in 1865, has grown steadily if slowly to its present enrollment of 3600 men and women. It includes faculties of Engineering, Medicine, and Education; as well as Agriculture and Arts and Sciences (see Education). The physical plant, first greatly expanded under Vermont's great President Matthew Henry Buckham in the eighties and nineties, has developed rapidly in the last ten years (see below, *What To See and Do*).

Burlington has always faced the sunset. The charm and repose of the city today betoken an economic condition which, if not static, is certainly far removed from the bustling times of the past. Champlain is given over almost completely to the yachtsman and the fisherman.

If and when Vermont's senior US Senator George Aiken succeeds in securing passage of "The Champlain Cut-Off Bill" Burlington would become Lake Champlain's largest and most active port. The proposed cut-off would link New York City and Montreal by water. A canal is needed to complete the link between the Richelieu and St. Lawrence Rivers.

What To See and Do

1. *City Hall,* Main and Church Sts. This large Georgian structure cost more than $600,000 (1926). McKim, Mead and White were the architects. An attractive park lies behind the hall, and a fountain plays near the spot where in the early days a tall pine served as a town whipping post.

2. *Battery Park,* Battery and Pearl Sts., has one of the most beautiful views of harbor and lake, with the Adirondacks in the distant background. It was used by the Government during the War of 1812 as a camp ground with some 4000 men in temporary barracks. In 1813 a battery of 13 guns, firing from behind a parapet erected where the lakeward sidewalk now runs, repulsed three British war vessels. The cannon in the park, presented to the city by the government in 1895, did service in the War of the Rebellion on the U.S. Ships *Constellation, Monongahela, Saratoga, Savannah,* and *Shamrock.*

3. *St. Joseph's Church,* Allen St., two blocks north of Pearl St., of blended Romanesque and Renaissance architecture in light red sandstone, was consecrated in 1901. A cock surmounts the cross atop the church — a weather-vane symbolic of the denial of St. Peter. Rare in the United States, this symbol is common in Canada. It came from the provinces in France from which the ancestors of the present French Canadians migrated.

4. The *Unitarian Church,* Pearl St. and Elmwood Ave., facing the north end of Church St., charmingly closes the vista through the main business district. Erected in 1816 by the First Congregational Society, this

massive red brick structure with its lofty clock tower and crowning steeple is one of the most impressive churches in the state. The design has been ascribed to Peter Banner, an architect of the Park St. Church (1809) in Boston, but it is likely that Bulfinch passed on the plans. The detail of the arched entrance motif at the base of the tower recalls that of Park St. Church. The generous proportions of the body of the church and the almost archaic simplicity of its white trim are pleasing variations from the more elaborate and delicately carved white frame structures usually found in Vermont.

5. *Elmwood Avenue Cemetery*, Elmwood Ave., two blocks north of Pearl St. Here are buried Ethan Allen's wife, Zadock Thompson, Joseph Barron, pilot of Macdonough's flagship, the *Saratoga*, at the battle of Plattsburg, Revolutionary War soldiers, and many early residents.

6. The *First Calvinistic Congregational Church* (1842), S. Winooski Ave. and Buell St., occupies the site of the first building (1812), which was burned in 1839. A brick structure of classic form, designed in Greek Revival style, with portico and Ionic columns, it is surmounted by a belfry, or "lantern" which is a nearly exact copy of the monument of Lysicrates in Athens. Napoleon so admired the original monument as splendid Greek art that he had a terra-cotta copy made for his St. Cloud palace grounds.

7. *Greenmount Cemetery*, Colchester Ave., contains the graves of Ethan Allen and many Revolutionary War soldiers. Over Ethan Allen's grave rises a Tuscan shaft, 42 feet in height, topped by a spirited eight-foot statue of Allen, modeled by Peter Stephenson and cut in Carrara, Italy. The hero is represented as in the act of demanding the surrender of Fort Ticonderoga. The monument, unveiled July 4, 1873, is surrounded by a paling of muskets between posts of cannon.

8. A *VHS* marker reads in part: "The mortal remains of Ethan Allen, fighter, writer, statesman and philosopher, lie in this cemetery beneath the marble statue. His spirit is in Vermont now."

9. *Ethan Allen Park*, 2.5 m. north of City Hall, east of North Ave., is part of what was Ethan Allen's farm, his home at the time of his death. It had belonged to a Tory before the Revolution, was confiscated by the State of Vermont and later sold to Allen. The land was acquired (1902) by the Hon. W. J. Van Patten, Mayor of Burlington (1894–96), who sold most of it to the city for $10,000, donating the proceeds of the sale to the local branch of the Y.M.C.A. Reserved by Van Patten were about 12 acres between the road and the Winooski River, including a rocky cliff some 200 feet in height, known as Indian Rock from the legend that raiding Indians coming down the Winooski Valley spied upon their enemies from here. This tract the Mayor offered to the Society of the Sons of the American Revolution on condition that a substantial stone tower, a memorial to Ethan Allen, be erected on the cliff with a road to give access to it. The tower was built and was dedicated in 1905. From its summit there is an extensive view of country, from Split Rock on the

south to Mount Royal on the north; the lake and Adirondacks on the
west and to the east the Winooski River and the Green Mountains.

10. A *VHS* marker reads: "Park is site of farm owned by Hero of Ticonderoga. Putting behind him the martial deeds of a hero, Ethan came here
in 1787 to till the soil as a peaceful farmer. On Feb. 12, 1789, he died
here after a trip across the ice to South Hero. Memorial Tower was built
on Indian Rock, traditional Algonquin lookout."

11. *VHS* marker (Winooski River Bridge) reads: "Fort Frederick. In
1773, Ira Allen and Remember Baker built a two-storied block fort at
these falls to protect their lands from New York State claimants. With
Ethan Allen and two other brothers they formed the Onion River Co.
to sell Winooski lands."

12. *VHS* marker (South Willard St. near US 2 and US 7) reads: "John
Dewey, philosopher and pioneer in modern education. Born here October
20, 1859, Dewey attended local schools and graduated from the University
of Vermont. World famous as a philosopher and author of many books,
the ideas drawn from his educational doctrines profoundly influenced
American education."

13. *VHS* marker (at Foot of King St. at lake) reads: "Steamer Vermont,
launched here in 1808. John and James Winans built here the second
successful steamboat to operate commercially, only two years after Robert
Fulton made his historic trip up the Hudson on the 'Clermont.' The
Champlain Transportation Co. was one of the oldest steamboat companies
when it suspended operations in 1932."

14. *North* (Municipal) *Beach* (1.5 m. north of City Hall) has swimming, camping, picnic and trailer facilities.

15. The *Fletcher Free Library,* College St., and S. Winooski Ave., founded
(1873) by Mrs. Mary L. Fletcher and her daughter Miss Mary M. Fletcher,
is housed in a building given to the city by Andrew Carnegie (1904).
Opened to the public in 1875 with 9000 volumes, in the old Courthouse
on City Hall Park, the library had far outgrown its quarters by the
turn of the century when Mr. Carnegie offered $50,000 for a new
building on condition that the city supply $5000 for maintenance. Of
red brick relieved with white terra-cotta, on a granite base, the structure
has a most attractive setting, and is fully equipped. It contains more than
75,000 volumes.

16. *Site of the First Jail* (southwest corner College and Church Sts.). In
the log structure built here in 1796, Ethan Allen's brother, Levi, a Tory,
was imprisoned for debt and died (1801). Later the site was occupied by
Lyman King's Hotel, a noted hostelry, till 1823.

17. The *College Green,* University of Vermont. Surrounded and enclosed
by the University buildings and the residences of the faculty, the old
College Green comprises a part of the fifty-acre lot deeded by Ira Allen
as the University site. The first clearing was, however, not made there until
1799, several years after building operations had begun, and then the

builders found it a convenient source for timber. A statue of General Lafayette, in bronze, of heroic size, stands in front of the College of Medicine, and commemorates the fact that Lafayette in 1825 laid the cornerstone of the Old Mill (see below). In the center of the campus is a statue of Ira Allen, founder of the University, the gift of the Hon. James B. Wilbur, and executed by Sherry Fry.

The University which has nearly tripled its student body since World War II is carrying out an almost continual building program. Contemporary design buildings mingle with nineteenth-century structures. Some interesting buildings include:

(A) The *Robert Hull Fleming Museum,* Colchester Ave. (open to public daily, adm. free), erected in 1931 by the University through the generosity of the late James B. Wilbur of Manchester, Vt., Miss Katherine Wolcott of Chicago, Ill., and six other friends of the University. Messrs. McKim, Mead and White were the architects. The museum houses much valuable and interesting material in art, archaeology, ethnology, geology, natural science, and Vermont history, the latter comprising the finest collection of Vermont Indian relics extant, and other material pertaining to early life in the state. The Cannon Oriental collection is a notable one; the Wilbur Room contains a personal library of Vermontiana; and the Geological Room in the Basement shows, among other objects, a relief model of the State. In the Art Gallery there are exhibitions throughout the year, including classical and contemporary paintings.

(B) *Billings Library* (open), University Place, gift of the late Frederick Billings of Woodstock, (1885), is a Romanesque structure of Longmeadow sandstone, a beautiful example of the work of the famous architect H. H. Richardson, who himself said of it, "It's the best thing that I have yet done." Beautifully grained Georgia pine is used for the interior finish and both interior and exterior of the building are rich in ornament. The library contains volumes, the largest collection in the State, including the famous Marsh collection of 13,000 books dealing mainly with philology and European history and literature, the gift of George Perkins Marsh (see WOODSTOCK).

(C) The *Ira Allen Chapel,* University Place (1927), is the gift of James B. Wilbur, and was also designed by McKim, Mead and White. Of red brick, the chapel is built in the form of a Latin cross. A campanile, 20 feet square and 170 feet high, has four clock faces and is topped by a powerful electric beacon, visible at night for many miles.

(D) *Grassemount,* 411 Main St., was built by Thaddeus Tuttle in 1804 and was the home of Cornelius P. Van Ness, Governor of Vermont (1823–26), U.S. Minister to Spain (1829–30). It was also the home of Brigadier General Heman "Chili" Allen, U.S. Minister to Chili (1823–28). Lafayette was entertained here in 1825. The residence was acquired by the University in 1895. Grassemount is perhaps the finest example in Vermont of the American Georgian style of architecture (see *Archi-*

tecture), notable for its grace of detail (as in the arched insets around the windows), and the cupola surrounded by a balustrade. The setting is appropriate — wide lawns, tall elms, and a sweeping lake view.

(E) The *Old Mill,* University Place, dates from 1825 and is the principal recitation building of the University. This was the site of the first college building, begun in the spring of 1801. About 1850, three separate original buildings were joined into the present single structure, and in 1883 the Old Mill assumed its present form through the generosity of John P. Howard. It is of red brick, 250 feet long, 60 feet deep, and four stories in height. From the tower is the finest view in the city of the Champlain Valley and the Green and Adirondack Mountains.

(F) *Morrill Hall,* University Place, is a memorial to Senator Justin Smith Morrill of Vermont, father of the land-grant colleges and universities of the United States. The building was erected in 1907 for the College of Agriculture. A three-story edifice of buff brick, it contains class and laboratory rooms.

(G) *Field House* (1963) cost nearly $3,000,000. The building is 488 × 140 feet and is 53 feet high. There is a 200 × 85-ft hockey rink which doubles in off season for tennis, volley ball and badminton courts. The 234 × 123-ft cage has a regulation baseball infield, golf range and track facilities. The adjacent gymnasium has three basketball courts, handball and squash courts and a swimming pool. The Field House seats 5000 spectators. The huge steel arches — 28 in all — were manufactured in Burlington by the Vermont Structural Steel Corporation.

18. *Missile Products Section & Space Vehicle Department,* General Electric Company's Burlington plant, manufactures the Vulcan aircraft cannon and linkless ammunition feed system, helicopter armament, re-entry vehicles for ballistic missiles and salt water distillation equipment (Free conducted tours).

BURLINGTON COUNTRY CLUB (off South Prospect St.); 18 holes. Range: 141–522 yds.; par 71. Hilly and wooded terrain with some water. Facilities: clubhouse, dining facilities, golf shop, pro, caddies, electric carts.

BURRINGTON HILL SKI AREA (see WHITINGHAM)

CABOT, 4–E (Washington County, US 2; alt. 947, pop. 763; 22,325 acres). Includes: Cabot village, Cabot Plain and Lower Cabot.

CABOT was named by Major Lyman Hitchcock in honor of his fiancée, a Miss Cabot of Connecticut. The Common at the village center is faced by pleasant old houses, by the Congregational Church, and the high school. The *Center Elm,* planted by early settlers at the geographic center of the township, rises from a rocky ledge and is marked by a painted sign. The *Site of the First Meeting House* and the *Site of the*

Whipping Post are across the road from the Center Elm, and the *Old Pound* still stands in good condition, with only a few stones missing from one side. Zerah Colburn, child prodigy and mathematical genius, was born in Cabot, and here he first amazed people with his lightning-fast calculations of involved problems.

CABOT PLAIN is the site of the original settlement on the Hazen Military Road. *Fortification Hill* was prepared for defense against a British advance, which never materialized. Major Whitcomb, who commanded Hazen's scouts here, was a famous fighter and hunter. Whitcomb made a singlehanded invasion of Canada for the purpose of picking off a British general. He lay in ambush outside of Montreal until a British general rode by in glittering regalia, whereupon Whitcomb shot him dead and escaped. The British set a price on Whitcomb's head but never collected.

LOWER CABOT is a few houses strung along the river.

VAH — Cabot Farms Cooperative Creamery. Milk processing and cheese manufacture.

CADY FALLS (see MORRISTOWN)

CALAIS, 4–D (Washington County, Vt. 14; alt. 1080, pop. 684; 21,590 acres). Includes: Adamant, East Calais, North Calais, Kent's Corner, Maple Corner and Pekin.

Calais (pronounced Kal-lus) town, on high fertile plateau land with many lakes and ponds, contains three post offices — Calais, East Calais, and Adamant — and 106 miles of roads. The first settlement was made by Francis West, and the town was named by Colonel Jacob Davis, founder of Montpelier, who here again revealed his fondness for French names. In 1838, Wareham Chase invented an electric motor here, two years after Davenport's and/or Smalley's invention (see BRANDON).

Chase lived to be nearly a hundred without ever going thirty miles from home. The sheer ingenuity of such an obscure, unlearned man is almost incredible. In 1922, the president of General Electric examined Chase's motor in the Historical Society Museum, at Montpelier, and declared it to be more nearly perfect than the Davenport/Smalley motor. Dorman B. Eaton, the founder of Civil Service reform, grew up in Calais. Pardon Janes (1788–1870) came here from Connecticut as a child and showed unusual intelligence and promise as a young man. He was a gifted speaker and represented Calais in the legislature, 1828–31. The latter part of his long life was clouded by a disillusionment, that verged upon madness. He wore for many years a short pitchfork strapped to his hand, so that he need not touch with his flesh any object touched by another human being. The very few things he bought at store — unbleached cotton, salt — he paid for with money that he carried in a tin pail on the end of his pitchfork, the clerks making the change for him. The title poem of "The Devil is a Woman" (1929), by Alice Mary Kimball, treats of Pardon Janes by name, but is a highly colored deviation from the facts.

ADAMANT is a small settlement clustered about the *Adamant Co-operative Store* and post office.

EAST CALAIS is situated on a rise in the valley, with gently ascending hills on either side. The *Community Church* is at one end of the street.

NORTH CALAIS is another settlement in Calais town.

KENT'S CORNER was named after a pioneer Calais family. There are still Kents in Calais. The *Kent Tavern,* restored by a $30,000 bequest from pioneer electric radio manufacturer Atwater Kent, and by other Kents including the late Ira Rich Kent, longtime Houghton Mifflin editor and Calais native. The building is now maintained by the Vermont Historical Society. The two houses adjacent to the tavern were built by Kents in the late eighteenth and early nineteenth centuries.

Kent's Corner is reportedly the "Appleyard Center" of Louise Andrews Kent's *"Mrs. Appleyard"* cookbooks. She also writes children's books.

1 m. South from Kent's Corner stands the *Old West Church,* exactly as it was when erected in 1824, epitomizing the stalwart severity of plain rural meeting-houses of that period. The church is the oldest landmark in Calais Township, and has been the meetinghouse at different times of various sects, including the Millerites. Calais had more than its share of these fanatics, of whom it was estimated that there were about 50,000 in the country. They were followers of William Miller, who demonstrated from Scripture, to their satisfaction, that the world would end on December 31, 1843, with the earth and sea giving up their dead and those who had achieved salvation entering immediately into eternal bliss. On the last evening of 1843, the Old West Church was packed, with both Millerites and those who came to see the show. A large clock was set up near the pulpit. As midnight began to strike, women screamed, and several fainted; that was all. In ten minutes the church was empty.

MAPLE CORNER (Calais P.O.) is what many Hollywood producers might consider the typical Vermont hill village. A few well-kept houses of early Vermont design and construction are clustered about a crossroads. The *Maple Corner Co-operative Store* mails Vermont maple syrup and cheese to customers in many states and countries.

PEKIN, a tiny hamlet, bears an Oriental name but no local resident seems to know why the name was adopted. Between Pekin and Kent's Corner is the former *Gospel Hollow Church,* now the *Calais town hall.*

CALEDONIA COUNTY (Area, 613 sq. miles. Pop., 27,786). Shire town: St. Johnsbury since 1856; original shire town, Danville. County established 1792. Caledonia is ancient Roman name for Scotland. Many early settlers came from Scotland. Includes: Barnet, Burke, Danville, Groton, Hardwick, Kirby, Lyndon, Newark, Peacham, Ryegate, St. Johnsbury, Sheffield, Stannard, Sutton, Walden, Waterford, Wheelock.

CALVIN COOLIDGE STATE FOREST (Bridgewater Corners P.O., US 4 and Vt. 100; est. 1925) includes several separate forested tracts in eastern Rutland and western Windsor Counties. Total acreage: 11,875. Most of the forest lies in Plymouth and is bounded on the south by the Coolidge homestead in Plymouth Notch. Smaller tracts in Bridgewater, Reading, Sherburne, Shrewsbury and Woodstock. Some 400 acres have been reforested. Facilities: picnic tables and fireplaces, tent sites, lean-tos, hunting, refreshments, foot trails, skiing (see KILLINGTON SKI AREA under RUTLAND).

CAMBRIDGE, 3-C (Lamoille County, Vt. 15; alt. 454, pop. 1295). Vt. Transit bus. Includes: Cambridge village, Cambridge Junction, Jeffersonville, North Cambridge, South Cambridge and Pleasant Valley.

CAMBRIDGE, an attractive village situated on a broad intervale of the Lamoille at the northwest base of Mt. Mansfield, has one of the finest natural settings in the state. The unusually wide main thoroughfare gives an orderly, spacious, and parklike aspect to the village. The macadam of Vt. 15 forms the central strip flanked by elm-shaded grassy parkways, which in turn are bordered by unpaved streets fronting the well-spaced brick and wooden homes. This arrangement was made in order that the militia might drill on the main st. without obstructing traffic; practical in origin, it also adds to the attractiveness of the village street. The town was settled in 1783. In the heart of the maple-sugar section, Cambridge has, for nearly 200 years, been a major producer of maple products.

The *Cambridge Inn* was built as the Borough House over a century ago, and stands in the strong security of ancient red brick, the dignity of its old-time charm lingering in line, detail, and the delicate fanlight of the entrance motif. The inn is completely furnished with antiques. The *Congregational Church* has attractive stained-glass windows.

CAMBRIDGE JUNCTION is a small settlement huddled about a creamery.

JEFFERSONVILLE (alt. 480) named in honor of Thomas Jefferson by vote of the citizens in 1827, stretches L-shaped along a wide avenue on the broad flats of the Lamoille, with neat lawns and spacious verandas shaded by elms, inducing an aspect of pleasurable living in quiet comfort. The sawmills and lumber stacks along the river indicate that this is a lumbering center primarily. The *World War Memorial* in the village center is carved from solid rock, an unusually impressive and distinctive memorial. Jeffersonville is the northern terminus of the Smuggler's Notch Road, and the central village of Cambridge Town.

NORTH CAMBRIDGE is the location of a cemetery.

PLEASANT VALLEY is just what the names implies — a pleasant valley.

SOUTH CAMBRIDGE is a tiny hamlet built at a zigzag in the road. The double-cupolaed white *Community House* (1858) is typical of countless others in small communities throughout the state which serve their respective localities in many capacities.

VAH — River Bend Farm, Arthur D. Toof, Jr. Dairy farm (Brown Swiss and Holstein cattle), maple syrup.

SPRUCE MT. SKI AREA (6 miles south of Jeffersonville off Vt. 108). This area connects with Stowe–Spruce Mt.–Mansfield Area; 3200-ft. elevation and 1700-ft. base; 3300-ft. Pomalift with 1000-ft. vertical rise; 2000-ft. Pomalift with 500-ft. vertical rise; 900-ft. lift. Capacity: 2500 skiers hourly. Novice, intermediate and expert trails and slopes. Parking area. Smugglers' Notch trails connect with Spruce Peak area via double chair lift on latter peak. Accommodations in Smugglers' Notch and Jeffersonville. *Information:* Smugglers' Notch Ski-Ways, Inc., Jeffersonville. Phone: MIdway 4-8849.

CAMBRIDGEPORT (see ROCKINGHAM)

CANAAN, G–1 (Essex County, Vt. 102 and Vt. 114; alt. 1042, pop. 1094; 19,025 acres). Includes Beecher's Falls. A port of entry from Canada.

CANAAN is a small village across the Connecticut from West Stewartstown. These river valley towns are duel settlements built up on both sides of the river which in actuality constitute single towns or villages except in matters of government. The Maine Central RR follows the northern Connecticut on the New Hampshire bank, but serves the towns on the Vermont side as well. Canaan is centered about a green Common with a fountain and the inevitable war memorial.

State Fish Hatchery is a white wooden building with a system of cement raceways in front where the young fish, hatched indoors in winter, can be seen during the summer months. Like most Vermont State Hatcheries, this one, since its establishment in 1914, has been devoted almost solely to maintaining and increasing the stock of lake and brook trout in Vermont waters. On the inside walls of the hatchery, what at first appear to be actual mounted fish are in reality wooden models realistically carved from cedar by a former employee.

BEECHER'S FALLS, a village in Canaan town, is another port of entry from Canada. The major industry here is the manufacture of Ethan Allen Early American furniture by a division of the Baumritter Corporation. An interesting sightseeing trip is available to visitors. (Not open Saturdays and Sundays.)

CARINTHIA SKI AREA (see DOVER)

CASTLETON, 7–B (Rutland County, US 4 and Vt. 30; alt. 450, pop. 1902; 23,360 acres). Rutland–Whitehall (N.Y.) bus. Includes: Castleton village, Bomoseen, Castleton Corners, West Castleton and Hydeville.

CASTLETON VILLAGE is a town of historic importance and physical charm. It was here, at Zadock Remington's Tavern, that Ethan Allen, Seth Warner, and their associates planned the successful attack on Fort Ticonderoga, and the town was Hessian headquarters after the battle of Hubbardton.

The many well-preserved examples of early architecture in Castleton reflect the talent of Thomas Royal Dake, a natural genius in building design who came here about 1807 and whose all-too-narrow field of influence was centered here.

The brick and wood *Federated Church,* at the east end of the village, dates from 1833. The *Ransom House,* now the parsonage, across the street, is interesting for its huge Ionic columns, elaborate iron grillwork, and balance of masses. Built in the 1840's, it is as good an example of the Greek Revival style of architecture as there is in the state (see Architecture). The brick *Higley House,* east of the parsonage, bears the date 1811 on the keystone of its doorway arch. The *Harris House,* directly across the road, is forgiven the late and ungainly addition of its porch when the intricate delicacy of its carved festoons and gable decorations is examined. The *Northrup House* (1810) has a remarkable pilastered doorway. The *Meecham-Ainsworth House,* near the center of the village, has a Corinthian-pillared portico in which three distinct types of arch are blended into a beautiful and unified design. The much photographed *Cole House,* built by Dake in 1833, is the most startlingly original example of the devious means by which he attained to his sure goal of architectural grace. The contours of the façade are roughly those of an oxbow, the top toward the road. The portico rises two stories, the outer columns supporting a projection of the roof. On the interior a double archway spans the hall at the foot of an enclosed staircase. The oldest building in Castleton is the diminutive *Brick House* near the west end of the village, which dates from 1787 at the latest, a considerably earlier date being sometimes claimed for it with some justification.

VHS marker (US 4, west of village), *Edwin L. Drake's birthplace.* Drake (1819–1880), "Founder of the oil industry. Drilling the first modern oil well in the U.S. on Aug. 27, 1859, at Titusville, Penn., Drake struck oil at 69 feet and launched one of the world's great industries. On a farm on Drake Road near this spot, he lived as a boy and attended the local schools."

VHS marker (US 4, at Hubbardton Road), Fort Warren (1777–79). "Battle of Hubbardton seven miles north. Directly east is the elevation of Fort Warren, built in 1779 for defense of the northern frontier. The road from the north was route of American retreat before Burgoyne, protected by Colonel Seth Warner's rearguard action at the Battle of Hubbardton, July 7, 1777."

Castleton State College (formerly Castleton Normal School, see Education) lies off the main street from the center of the village. The present institution has developed through a succession of changes from the Rutland County Grammar School, chartered in 1787. The first medical college in Vermont was established here in 1818 and functioned until 1854. The present school plant is largely modern, the older one having been destroyed by fire. The small but pleasant shaded campus and the dignified brick and wood buildings seem fittingly located in this serene and memoried village.

BOMOSEEN (Vt. 30) is the nucleus of this resort region, with large smart hotels along the lakeside, dominating the picture of summer houses, stores, and a church. In season the scene is marked by the ease and gaiety of resort life.

BOMOSEEN GOLF CLUB (off Vt. 30); 9 holes. Range: 155–420 yds; par 35. Slightly hilly terrain with one water hole. Facilities: golf shop, caddies, carts, restaurant nearby. Open 8 A.M.–6 P.M.

BOMOSEEN STATE PARK (Fair Haven R.D. 1, 3 m. north of US 4 at Hydeville; 365 acres). Given to Vermonters in 1959 by Mrs. Martha Warren. The park, formerly the site of slate quarrying, has large waste piles of slate which can be used for paving patios. Facilities: picnic tables and fireplaces, tent sites, camp trailer sites, bathing, boating, fishing.

LAKE BOMOSEEN (Vt. 30) is one of the largest lakes and most highly developed summer areas in Vermont, only a mile and a half wide with an irregular, cedar-fringed length of nearly eight miles. Bomoseen occupies a rocky basin surrounded by low, forested hills and blunted mountains, a fine setting for its cool, clear waters, overlooked by many neat cottages, hotels, and elaborate summer homes. The western shore is overhung by cliffs where slate deposits are quarried. Pineclad Neshobe Island lies at the center of the lake with an area of ten acres: here once dwelt those summer Green Mountain Boys — Alexander Woollcott and Harpo Marx.

CASTLETON CORNERS (alt. 460) is a scattered village at the four-corners junction of US 4 with Vt. 30. At the western end of the long central street are fine pine groves.

HYDEVILLE (alt. 405) is industrially dominated by the slate works located here, as the large heaps of waste material and the use of the stone for common walls and wharfings suggest. The brown *Episcopal Church* near the center of the village has been nominated as the ugliest church in Vermont. The bridge, just beyond, spans a rushing stream, the outlet of Lake Bomoseen.

WEST CASTLETON lies on a Hydeville–Fair Haven loop road. It is a small settlement. The run follows the west side of Lake Bomoseen from which a wide view of the Green Mountains can be seen. Beyond the abandoned slate quarries there are several places at which wide vistas of the Adirondacks can be seen.

BIRDSEYE MOUNTAIN SKI AREA (off US 4). One two-section 2000-ft. Disc (ground contact) lift serves 1-mile novice open slope, 0.75-mile and 0.5-mile open slopes. Separate children's area with rope tow; 40-meter jumping hill. Practice slope for cross country and slalom; 1000-ft. open slope floodlighted for night skiing on Wednesdays, Thursdays and Fridays. Ski school. This family area operates weekends, holidays, school vacations and for night skiing on days listed above.
   Bird Mountain (alt. 2210), one of the noblest of the Taconics, is accentuated by a very steep drop of 300 feet on the southern face. Bird Mountain, sometimes wrongly called Bird's-Eye, was named for Colonel Bird, the first settler in Castleton. Laboring under great handicaps, Colonel Bird built a sawmill, but died so soon after its completion that the first boards sawed were used for his own coffin.

CAVENDISH, 8–D (Windsor County, Vt. 103 and Vt. 131; alt. 929, pop. 1223; 25,140 acres). Vt. Transit bus. Includes: Cavendish village and Proctorsville.

CAVENDISH was settled in 1769 by Captain John Coffin who built a house and later a tavern, on the Crown Point Military Road, and whose hospitality was known to thousands of American troops stopping here on their way from Number Four (Charlestown, N.H.) to the military posts on Lake Champlain. In August, 1754, the Indians burst into the Johnson house at No. 4 and seized the seven inmates, carrying them back to Canada. The first time they camped was in what is now Cavendish, and here Mrs. Johnson gave birth to a child, whom she named Captive. Northeast of Cavendish is the *Site of Twenty-Mile Encampment,* the camping ground used by the soldiers marching on the Crown Point Road. Twenty-Mile Stream, a tributary of the Black River, was named after the encampment, which was about 20 miles from No. 4. The 1927 flood tore a tremendous gorge through the township, in places revealing the fantastic carvings made by the erosion of years ago. Prominent families are the Proctors and the Fletchers. Three Vermont governors were born in Cavendish town: Redfield Proctor (1878-80); Fletcher Proctor (1906-8); Ryland Fletcher 1856-58).

PROCTORSVILLE (off new Vt. 103) was named after the family of marble magnate Colonel Redfield Proctor. The closing of the woolen mills and the rerouting of Vt. 103 around the village have brought a population decline and loss of income. Some residents commute to mills in nearby Ludlow, Windsor and Springfield.

CEDAR BEACH (see CHARLOTTE)
CENTER (see NEWPORT)
CENTER RUTLAND (see RUTLAND TOWN)
CENTERVALE (see ST. JOHNSBURY)
CENTERVILLE (see HARTFORD, *also* HYDE PARK)
CENTRAL (see GUILDHALL)
CENTRAL PARK (see VERNON)
CHARLES DOWNER STATE FOREST (see SHARON)

CHARLESTON, 2-E (Orleans County, US 5A and Vt. 105; alt. 1196, pop. 688; 20,471 acres). Includes: East Charleston and West Charleston.

EAST CHARLESTON is a small village lying at a bend in the highway above the banks of the Clyde River, its sawmills and lumber stacks remaining as vestiges of a once thriving industry.

WEST CHARLESTON is a small mill village in Charleston town, originally called Navy by Commodore Whipple, Revolutionary naval officer and grantee of the town. The highway curves into the village and winds uphill between abandoned mills, general stores, and unkempt houses, an air of crumbling decadence prevailing in the side-hill settlement. An odd stone *Community Church* has an outside brick chimney and wooden belfry. The collapse of the lumber-milling industry left West Charleston dead and empty, and the community has lain dormant since that time. The dammed pond at the northern end of the village is locally known as *Electric Light Pond;* a public utilities power plant generates electricity for many Orleans County communities.

CHARLOTTE, 4–A (Chittenden County, US 7 and F5; alt. 180, pop. 1271; 24,062 acres). Vt. Transit bus. Includes: Charlotte village, East Charlotte, Cedar Beach, and Thompson's Point. Charlotte, for some unknown reason, is pronounced locally as "Shar-*lot*."

CHARLOTTE village. A section of this small community lies at the foot of a hill on the highway, with the main section spreading on the plain of the Champlain Valley toward the lake, an excellent orchard region. The *Congregational Church,* a handsome red brick structure with white-columned portico, was built over a century ago, one of the few evidences of the Greek Revival in Vermont.

EAST CHARLOTTE (2.0 m. east of US 7 at Charlotte village on unnumbered road) is a small crossroads settlement.

CEDAR BEACH (3.0 m. west from Charlotte village on US 7) is a summer colony on the Lake Champlain shore.

THOMPSON'S POINT (3.5 m. southwest from Charlotte village on unnumbered road) is another summer colony on the Lake Champlain shore.

CHELSEA, 5–D (Orange County, shire town, Vt. 110 and Vt. 113; alt. 840, pop. 957; 23,818 acres). Barre–South Royalton stage.

CHELSEA village sits in the valley of the First Branch of the White River sheltered by green mountain walls. An attractive village park, shaded by spreading elms and old maples, makes a pleasing front for the County Courthouse and Congregational Church. The Chelsea Shop was at one time occupied by Charles I. Hood, capitalist and manufacturer of Hood's Sarsaparilla. Beyond the shop is an old type *Gristmill.* Many years ago this gristmill supplied power to the Tinker Chair Shop, which was directly across the street, by means of a leather belt suspended over the roadway. The flapping of the belt frightened passing horses, and that method of transmitting power had to be abandoned. The *National Bank of Chelsea* is one of the oldest in the state. Prominent Chelsea sons include William F. Vilas, Postmaster General (1885–88) and Secretary of the Interior (1888–89), and Brigadier General Napoleon B. McLaughlin (Civil War). While the general exodus of population from the rural to urban centers has impaired the growth of Chelsea, the village remains active as a trading center for the surrounding farm district.

The town was first chartered at Turnersburgh and settled in 1784. The earliest comers packed furniture and provisions on their backs from Tunbridge, approximately eight miles away, exemplifying the pioneer spirit of ever pushing on to new frontiers.

CHESTER, 9–D (Windsor County, Vt. 11 and Vt. 103; alt. 599, pop. 2318; 34,624 acres; settled 1756). Vt. Transit bus. Includes: Chester village, Chester Depot and Gassetts.

Chester Official Information Booth (Main St. near jct. of Vt. 11 and Vt. 103).

CHESTER village, beautifully situated along the Williams River and at a junction of valleys, wears an air of charming gentility over broad streets shaded by great elms and old maples. A long slender green splits the Main St., and gracious homes of wood, brick, and stone are set back on smooth lawns. The *First Baptist Church* (1835), a large structure in cherry-red brick, looms over the stone-walled graveyard which flanks the street with a somber mien. A pale green *Colonial House* adds a distinguished touch, and the western end of the village street is colored by homes of red brick and patterned stone. The big white *Congregational Church* (1829) carries a tower of Bulfinch adaptation, suggesting the Wren traditions in architecture. The gray-green stone, of which many Chester houses were built a century or more ago, was quarried in the nearby hills.

Site of First Log House in Chester. A marble tablet at the roadside above the wide meadows along the stream indicates that these river flats were the site of the first settlement in Chester, when Jabez Sargeant and Thomas Chandler hewed a home out of logs here.

The office and plant of the National Survey Company is located here. National Survey is essentially a mapmaking firm and during World War II was cited for the excellence of its many maps designed for the military.

CHESTER DEPOT, site of the former Rutland Railway depot, has long since become an integrated part of Chester proper.

GASSETTS (alt. 715) is scattered along the open plain of the Williams River south of Proctorsville Gulf, a small settlement in Chester Town, uninteresting but for its odd name.

Parson Flagg of Chester made of his house a Yankee Gretna Green for the convenience of eloping couples from New Hampshire, in the old days. The practice developed to such an extent that New Hampshire elopements came to be known as "Flagg Marriages." Another character was Clarence Brown, a scholar, respected citizen and legislator. When it was discovered that he had been robbing and terrorizing fellow citizens, belated justice cast Brown into prison, but he escaped, it is told, by going into a trance and playing dead so realistically that he was given burial in a cemetery vault, where he was rescued from the casket by a confederate and escaped to Canada.

CHIMNEY POINT (see ADDISON)
CHIPPENHOOK (see CLARENDON)
CHISELVILLE (see SUNDERLAND)

CHITTENDEN, 6–C (Rutland County, off US 7 at Pittsford or Rutland Town or north off US 4 in Mendon; alt. 1160, pop. 460; 46,315 acres). Includes: Chittenden village, North Chittenden, Holden.
Chittenden, originally chartered as Philadelphia, is in area the largest town in the state.

CHITTENDEN village has a church, general store and a few houses. There is the traditional Civil War soldiers' monument.

HOLDEN is a small settlement.

NORTH CHITTENDEN is an area rather than a settlement. Many abandoned farms have been purchased by city folk and remodeled into summer homes.

Chittenden Dam, built by the Central Vermont Public Service Corporation, forms a large lake which is stocked by the Vermont Fish and Game Department. There is a public access area for boats and a sandy beach.
U.S. Fish Hatchery at Holden (visitors). Trout are raised here for release in Vermont's lakes and streams.

CHITTENDEN COUNTY (Area 543 sq. miles. Population 74,425), state's most populous county. Shire town: Burlington. Organized 1787. Includes: Bolton, Buel's Gore, Burlington, Charlotte, Colchester, Essex, Hinesburg, Huntington, Jericho, Milton, Richmond, St. George, Shelburne, South Burlington, Underhill, Westford, Williston, Winooski.

CLARENDON, 8–C (Rutland County, US 7 and Vt. 103; alt. 600, pop. 1091; 19,958 acres). Vt. Transit bus. Includes: Clarendon village, Clarendon Springs, East Clarendon, North Clarendon, Chippenhook, and Pierce's Corner.

CLARENDON (South Flats) (alt. 600) is a low-lying village on the broad flat plains of Otter Creek, with homes scattered about the elm-sheltered valley floor where fine meadowlands merge into stony pastures and ridged mountains rise on the west. Around 1800 Clarendon was a leading town in Rutland County, and previous to that the center of bitter controversy between the patriots and Tories. Nicholas M. Powers (see PITTSFORD), builder of covered bridges, lived here for a time.

CLARENDON SPRINGS (alt. 560). The great brick hotel with its white wooden porches, looms huge and lonely and out-of-place in the forsaken resort village. There is an air of haunting melancholy about any "ghost town," but nothing is more desolate than a ghost resort town. Before the Civil War this was a famous and fashionable watering place, the mineral springs and natural setting attracting people from great distances. Most of the patrons were wealthy southerners, a fact which naturally caused the decline of the resort after the death of the Confederate cause. Today the big hotel stands incongruously on deserted grounds, still kept up by caretakers, which only accentuate its aspect of forlorn emptiness. People continue to visit the place to see the old Clarendon House and sample water from the mineral springs.

EAST CLARENDON (alt. 740) lies along the wild secluded valley of Mill River, dashing along its boulder-strewn bed. The highway twists downhill into the little settlement of obvious antiquity, its wooden houses straggling along the forested and rocky gorge. The home of Benjamin Spencer, a leader of the Yorkers in the vicinity, this village was once the storm center of the strife between the New Hampshire Patriots and the New York Tories. In 1772 Spencer wrote a friend that "one Ethan Allen hath brought from Connecticut twelve or fifteen of the most blackguard fellows he can get, doubly armed, in order to protect him." The *Spencer Homestead,* at the western edge of the village, was the setting for a strange scene on November 21, 1773, when the Green Mountain Boys arraigned Spencer for trial at his own doorstep, the Tory standing before a "judgment seat" upon which were seated Ethan Allen, Remember Baker, Seth Warner, and Robert Cochran, while more than 100 of their heavily armed followers formed a raucous audience. That day Spencer was adjudged guilty, and the Green Mountain Boys literally tore the roof off his house "with great shouting and much noise and tumult," to replace it only after Spencer swore allegiance to the New Hampshire cause. Tory Spencer had little choice other than to yield to the roistering Patriots and watch them restore the roof of his home, with a great deal of rough jesting and merriment. Spencer's treatment was mild compared to that received by other Yorkers, many of whom saw their homes burned to ashes and felt the cutting lash of the beech seal on their bare backs.

Clarendon Gorge is a deep narrow rock-ledged cut through which Mill River foams and boils over a rocky bed. The walls of the sharp craggy defile are lined with evergreen, which brightens the grim gray of the rock, and trees at the top of the gorge lean out dizzily, 200 feet above the white water.

NORTH CLARENDON (North Flats) (alt. 580), lies on the southern outskirts of Rutland, suburban and commercialized for tourist trade with filling stations and wayside cabins among the dull-colored wooden homes.

East from North Clarendon on a country road is *Northam State Picnic Area,* 8 m. (see SHREWSBURY).

West from North Clarendon on a country road is *Wait's Monument,* 0.4 m., in a field behind a barn at the crossroads. This old stone slab bearing the queer effigy of a Revolutionary soldier, and enclosed by an iron picket fence, marks the grave of Colonel Joseph Wait. Member of a prominent early Vermont family, Wait served with Rogers' Rangers during the French and Indian Wars (see BRADFORD) and fought in the Revolution until his death. He was buried by his comrades here where he died on the march, from a wound received at Valcour Island.

CHIPPENHOOK (alt. 840), an antiquated upland village, spreads on a high plateau with higher hills rising above. Chippenhook retains an air of 1790, a wild mountaineer flavor reminiscent of the Tennessee hills. Seldom in New England is such raw rusticity found but a few miles from a main and cosmopolitan thoroughfare; a hillbilly settlement in close proximity to the modern and progressive city of Rutland. The *Oldest House* in the district stands at the entrance to the hamlet, and beyond is the empty shell of an old *Stone Mill* on the Tinmouth River where grist was ground and cider pressed. The *Old Church,* built before 1800, stands in plain severe white at the entrance to the tiny village. Chippenhook was the home of Judge Theophilus Harrington, known for his trenchant reply to an irate slaveowner in a runaway slave case. Judge Harrington declared that the owner's claim to the slave was defective. The owner indignantly demanded to know what was lacking in his legally sound claim. The Judge exploded, "A bill of sale, sir, from God Almighty!"

PIERCE'S CORNER (Junction of US 7 and Vt. 103) is named for the family that has lived over a century in the *Old Bowman Tavern,* a stagehouse in early days.

COLBYVILLE (see WATERBURY)

COLCHESTER, 3–B (Chittenden County, US 2 and US 7, Vt. 116; alt. 274, pop. 4718; 15,000 acres). Includes: Colchester village, Colchester Point and Mallet's Bay.

COLCHESTER, though a separate town, is essentially a Burlington suburb.

COLCHESTER POINT, a former RR station on the now defunct Rutland Railway.

MALLET'S BAY, a large beach and summer resort favored by many Burlington area residents.

CONCORD, 4–F (Essex County, US 2; alt. 860, pop. 979; 27,611 acres). MC/RR and Vt. Transit bus. Includes: Concord village, Concord Corners, East Concord, North Concord and Miles Pond.

CONCORD is an agreeable little village tucked into knobby hills on either side of the Moose River. Its modest houses, stores, and churches are held tightly by the narrow valley. Settled in 1788, Concord has enjoyed an uneventful and fairly prosperous history. The early settlers were bothered by bears. One of the animals, caught in a large trap, was being exhibited to the curious from miles around when he managed to shake himself loose and make for his tormentors. Unfortunately for him, he selected as his prey the child of one Rebecca Morse. Mrs. Morse promptly seized the trap and dispatched the bear with one blow on the head. Bears are still not infrequently slain in this section of Vermont, but by more modern means.

CONCORD CORNERS, a small settlement, east of US 2 from Concord village.

EAST CONCORD, a small village around the Maine Central RR depot. Many residents work in the nearby Gilman paper mills. VHS marker in front of the East Concord Methodist Church reads, "George Lansing Fox, one of four Dorchester chaplains. Called from his Gilman parish to serve in World War II, First Lieutenant Fox died when the Dorchester was torpedoed in the North Atlantic. Giving his life jacket to a soldier, he perished with 3 other chaplains, in one of the most heroic acts of the war."
   VHS marker on US 2 at junction with Concord Corners Road reads: "First Normal School. Pioneer in Teacher Training. The first recognized school in America for the purpose of training teachers was conducted near here by the Rev. Samuel Read Hall, 1823–25. Practice teaching was employed with 'Lectures on Schoolkeeping,' which became in 1829, the first professional book for teachers." (The school is 2.4 m. south at Concord Corner).

NORTH CONCORD is a few houses scattered about a crossroads.

MILES POND is a settlement of cottages and camps along the shores of *Miles Pond*. The Fish and Game Department has a public access area here.

"The most beautiful state house in America," wrote John Gunther
Vermont Development Department

Montpelier — Washington County Court House and Post Office.

Ewing Galloway

Left, above: Town meeting — time for decision
Aldo Merusi

Left, below: A Vermont political convention
Aldo Merusi

Rapidly disappearing from the Vermont scene, the one-room schoolhouse

Arthur Griffin

The University of Vermont, from the belltower of the Ira Allen Chapel

Ewing Galloway

The Unitarian Church in Burlington. Paul Revere cast the bell. *Ewing Galloway*

Old First Church in Bennington. *Vermont Development Department*

Plymouth. Calvin Coolidge worshipped here. *The Costas, Foto/Find*

COPPERFIELD (see VERSHIRE)
COOKVILLE (see CORINTH)

CORINTH, 5–D (Orange County, off Vt. 25 and Vt. 113; pop. 775; 28,863 acres). Bradford stage. Includes: Cookville, Corinth Corners, East Corinth, South Corinth, West Corinth and Goose Green.

The Corinths are all small settlements in *Corinth town*. The *Corinth P.O.* is located in *Cookville*. The settlement with the delightful name *Goose Green* has three rather forlorn-looking houses. The only store is in *South Corinth*. The numerous settlements in Corinth are generally so small that it is difficult to tell when one is in a settlement or the country. The countryside is very lovely in this area.

NORTHEAST SLOPES SKI AREA (10 m. northwest of Bradford on Vt. 25); 1180-ft. elevation and 820-ft. base; 2 tows totaling 1800 feet; 46 acres open slopes. Ski hut and snack bar. Patrol and first aid. *Information:* Eugene Eastman, Corinth. Phone: Idlewood 9–3700.

CORNWALL, 6–B (Addison County, Vt. 30; alt. 370, pop. 756; 17,400 acres). Includes West Cornwall.

This rural community, stretched on a gently rolling terrain, was once a breeding center for merino sheep and Morgan horses. The nucleus of the scattered village is at a small green bearing the usual Civil War Memorial. The *Congregational Church* (1803), with its adjacent graveyard, has the agreeable simplicity of early churches. The *Sampson Memorial Library,* of red brick and white wooden trim, also houses the Mary Baker Allen Chapter of the D.A.R. The settlement, started in 1774, was disrupted by the Revolution, to be resumed again ten years later by thirty Connecticut families. A pioneer named Andrus was captured by Indians, who also took his mare and colt. Andrus was freed and came back to the settlement. A few years later, the lost mare and the colt, now full grown, returned home with another colt, and instead of losing two horses, Andrus gained one.

Henry Norman Hudson (1814–1886), the first American Shakesperean critic to win a high reputation abroad, was born in Cornwall. His twenty-volume *Harvard Shakespeare* (1880–81), now issued with emendations made possible by recent research as the *New Hudson Shakespeare,* is still widely studied. That Hudson's studies of Shakespeare's characters were based on an understanding of his work not merely as great literature, but also as great acting plays, is evidenced by the fact that he was avowed the favorite critic of both Edwin Booth and Sir Henry Irving.

Cornwall is the location of one of the oldest U.S. Weather Bureau reporting stations in the country. Four generations of one family have recorded the weather data daily since May 1886. Henry Lane made the observations for the first year and then the duties were taken over by his son Charles H. Lane who recorded the data until his death in 1928. His widow Sarah E. Lane continued the daily data recording until her death in 1950. Since then her grandson Stuart T. Witherell has continued the observations. "This enviable record of devoted public service at Cornwall results in an exceptionally valuable source of data for climatic investigation," said state climatologist Robert E. Lautzenheiser, director, U.S. Weather Bureau, Boston, Mass. The Lanes receive no financial compensation for their recording and reporting activities.

WEST CORNWALL (2 m. west, Vt. 30) is a small cluster of houses.

South of Cornwall, Vt. 30 rolls along between rail-fenced fields of smooth-sloping contours. Orchards spread on the plain, and in the fall flocks of sheep graze in the meadows.

Old Brick House, high and roomy with end chimneys, has a kind of heavy dignity. The highway drops into a thick-wooded patch of low swampland, the southern fringe of the great Cedar Swamp, which stretches along the western edge of the Otter Creek Valley.

South of the swamp, mountain views range on either side of the open road, the Green Mountains piled on the east, the notched wall of the Adirondacks against the western horizon. Gnarled stump fences outline the wide fields.

COVENTRY, 2–E (Orleans County, US 5; alt. 718, pop. 458; 16,027 acres). Vt. Transit bus.

COVENTRY village, named after Coventry, Connecticut, lies in a green bowl of the valley. The clapboarded *Congregational Church* with cupola and clock faces the narrow Common. The long narrow green contains a *Civil War Monument* and a cannon once owned by the Coventry militia.

CRAFTSBURY, 3–D (Orleans County, Vt. 14; pop. 674; 22,558 acres). Includes: Craftsbury village, Craftsbury Common, East Craftsbury.

CRAFTSBURY, named for original grantee Ebenezer Crafts, lies low in the river valley, built around a lumber mill and dam. This village, though crudely rustic in contrast with Craftsbury Common to the north, is typical of the small mill villages found in Vermont valleys and is industrially the heart of the township. Colonel Ebenezer Crafts opened a road from Cabot to this area and founded the settlement in 1788, becoming veritably the patriarchal head of the little community that grew up in the wilderness. Samuel Crafts, Ebenezer's son, carried on the leadership of Craftsbury and became governor of the state (1828–31). Among the pioneer families were many sturdy Scotch people who left their imprint of clean, thrifty living and sound-minded reliability on the town.

CRAFTSBURY COMMON crowns the broad summit of a high plateau. Everything in the place is white, gleaming in clean paint: the trim-lined houses and churches, the academy buildings, the single-railed wood fence surrounding the smooth broad green of the Common. Here is a quality of airy cleanness and light, a happy blending of tasteful architecture with the charm of natural setting, that combine to make Craftsbury Common memorable among the villages of northern Vermont. The Colonial ideals of simple purity in line and color are emphasized in this spotless village, arranged with orderly spacing about the large level green. Craftsbury Common is the center of the intellectual and social life of the township and locality.

At the south end of the village the *Old Cemetery* lies iron-fenced beside the highway, with stones dating from the 1790's. Across the street a charming trio of white houses in the Colonial tradition stand behind a white picket fence shaded by giant elms. These three structures strike the keynote of Craftsbury Common's appeal and balance the scene about the Common at the north end of the village. The *Congregational Church* (1820) faces the street from across the north end of the Common in attractive white wood and clear-lined simplicity. *Craftsbury Academy,* housed in an ungainly white wooden structure, was established in 1829; among the former headmasters of this reputable little institution was the Reverend Samuel Read Hall (see CONCORD). The *Craftsbury Public Library,* a tiny and unusual stone oblong, resembles a granite vault. The *Old Covenanter Church,* now used as the Academy gymnasium, stands well back from the street in severe white dignity. The vista west from the high plain of the Common reveals the march of rugged mountains against the distant skyline.

The *Congregational Church* on the *Common* is one of the most widely photographed of all Vermont village scenes. Craftsbury was the locale of Alfred Hitchcock's *Wild About Harry.*

EAST CRAFTSBURY. The *Presbyterian Church* stands on the site of the Old Covenanter Church, where, until recent years, the forms of this austere faith were explicitly preserved. For several generations the almost undiluted Calvinism of the Covenanter service and discipline held together those Scotch families of the region who had come up over the Hazen Road from the original settlements on the Connecticut River. The *John Woodruff Simpson Memorial Library,* a pleasing little white wooden structure, was originally the community store. The interior has been retained; counters, shelves, and drawers are now lined with books instead of groceries and spices. The library, endowed and managed by a niece of the Scotch proprietor, contains a diversified collection of books with discrimination. The Simpson family has always been eminent in East Craftsbury.

VAH — Brass Knocker Farm, Jean Simpson, owner, and Morris Rowell, operator. Dairy farm (Jersey cattle).

CRYSTAL LAKE STATE PARK (see BARTON)

CUTTINGSVILLE (see SHREWSBURY)

DANBY, 8–B (Rutland County, US 7; alt. 700, pop. 891; 22,746 acres).
Vt. Transit bus. Includes Danby village and Danby Four Corners.

DANBY village is a pretty little valley community, sheltered by mountain stretches. Attractive homes with patterned lawns and shrubs flank
the street, and the town has an air of prosperity, based on marble
quarrying and dairying. In earlier times lumbering was the chief industry here. A better-than-ordinary *Civil War Monument* stands at
the center, the bronze figure of a soldier surmounting a marble shaft.
The *S. L. Griffith Memorial Library* is constructed of buff brick on a
granite base.

Micah Vail, one of the first settlers, 1765, was a leading citizen and
a prominent Green Mountain Boy during turbulent Revolutionary
times. He and his wife are supposed to have been poisoned to death
by a Tory doctor from Arlington. Many of the early settlers were
Quakers, and the sect remained active here until about the middle of
the nineteenth century. The first town clerk was Thomas Rowley,
celebrated wit and "the Poet of the Green Mountain Boys," the first
important Vermont versifier, and at one time chairman of the Committee of Safety. Silas Griffith, the lumber king and the state's earliest
millionaire, built his fortune from the forests of Danby. A curious
business, the wholesaling of ferns, has been established here, the ferns
being gathered in Mt. Tabor and stored in a refrigerated warehouse
in Danby to be sold to florists during the winter.

DANBY FOUR CORNERS (3.5 m. west on uphill road from Danby village) is a small mountain settlement surrounded by a broad plateau
of fertile farmland. The churchyard of the *Corner Church* is lined
with ancient marble slabs bearing rare old names and quaint spellings.
Well worth a visit. Captain Micah Vail and his wife are buried here
under a double tombstone dated 1777.

DANVILLE, 4–E (Caledonia County, US 2; alt. 1341, pop. 1368; 34,373
acres). St. J & LC/RR and Vt. Transit bus. Includes: Danville village,
North Danville, West Danville and Harvey.

DANVILLE, named for the French Admiral D'Anville, was settled in
1784. Danville Green, as the village is locally called, lies along the
slope of a high airy plateau commanding views of the White Mountains, and is a resort for hay-fever sufferers. The tree-shaded Common,
with bandstand and Civil War Monument, was in early times the
scene of June Training Day celebrations. Until 1855 Danville was the
shire town of Caledonia County, and for the first seventy-five years
of its existence an influential town. The *North Star,* an early news-

paper established here by Ebenezer Eaton, was in large measure responsible for this prominence. The remodeled *Town Hall* was originally the county courthouse, and in 1805 the General Assembly of Vermont convened here. The *Elm House* is over a century old, and a number of plain clapboarded dwellings antedate this hostelry. The small square brick *Caledonia Bank* is now one of the best-protected in the state, modern safety devices having been added after the 1935 holdup of the institution, an event so rare in Vermont as to cause nationwide interest.

Thaddeus Stevens, bitter abolitionist opponent of Lincoln over the question of Reconstruction policy, was born in Danville, in 1792. He was elected to Congress from Pennsylvania as a Whig in 1849, and rose to political power in the anti-slavery cause. Returning to Congress in 1858, he led the fight for the Fourteenth Amendment, and almost succeeded in bringing about the impeachment of President Andrew Johnson. Because of his fanatical devotion to abolitionism, and his harsh view of Reconstruction, Stevens was probably the most hated man in an era of universal animosities.

Danville, for more than eighty years, has been the site of the annual national convention of water dowsers, who locate underground water sources with a "water wand." This is a cut branch which is said to turn downward in the dowser's hand when he comes to underground water.

NORTH DANVILLE, a hamlet north of Danville on unnumbered backroad, includes a church, store and garage.

WEST DANVILLE (US 2) lies at the eastern end of *Joe's Pond*, a wood-bordered sheet of water named for Old Joe, the Indian guide and friend of the pioneers (see NEWBURY). A summer cottage colony has grown up on the shores of the pond. Tiny West Danville now furnishes supplies to summer visitors.

VAH — Sherryland Farm, Henry Sherry. Dairy farm (Holstein cattle).

HARVEY, a tiny settlement south of Danville village on a back road, includes a church, store and garage.

D.A.R. STATE PARK (see ADDISON)

DARLING STATE PARK (see BURKE)

DERBY, 1–E (Orleans County, US 5; alt. 1028, pop. 2499; 28,650 acres). Newport stage. Includes: Derby village, Beebe Plain, Derby Line and North Derby.

DERBY village lies along the high broad level of a plateau that once served as a favorite hunting ground for the St. Francis Indians. The houses flanking the long main street are wood-clapboarded, constructed in the neat plainness of common domestic building, set back from the street and well spaced. The plateau setting and the freshness of a high altitude give Derby a bright cleanness that is appealing.

DERBY LINE, a station on the Quebec Central/RR. The hamlet has a U.S. Immigration Station.

NORTH DERBY, a tiny settlement, has a general store.

BEEBE PLAIN and BEEBE JUNCTION straddle the U.S.–Canadian border.

DORSET, 9–B (Bennington County, US 7 and Vt. 30; alt. 940, pop. 1150; 28,756 acres). Vt. Transit bus and Manchester Ctr. stage. Includes: Dorset village, Dorset Hollow, East Dorset, North Dorset and South Dorset.

DORSET (alt. 940, Vt. 30), a center of art and literature, is perhaps the most distinctive of the southwestern Vermont cultural resorts, which include Manchester and Bennington. The terraced valley, serene in its enclosure of forested marble mountains, is an ideal setting for such a colony, and writers and artists have established winter, as well as summer, homes here. Clean white houses with green blinds sit on landscaped grounds under the shade of elm trees; the purity of white limned against a green background makes a striking picture. Dorset has an elegance that is not pretentious, a charm that is simple and fastidious. Descendants of early settlers share this with intellectuals from the outside world, and the pattern is harmonious.

The *Dorset Inn* is at the center of the village, a gracious hostelry in white wood with a high, square-pillared porch, the interior furnished with old furniture. The *Dorset Memorial Library,* housed in a remodeled tavern built (about 1790) by John Gray, is a square trim structure. Captain Gray opened a marble quarry in Danby Notch after the Revolution, but gave up the venture when a landslide buried his quarry. He then came down from the hills to build the first Dorset tavern. Of five early inns here, the *Cephas Kent Tavern* (1773) was the most important historically. Its foundation stones and timbers are now incorporated in a summer residence. In 1776, the first convention of the New Hampshire Grants was held in Kent's taproom, where the Green Mountain Boys and Patriots first proclaimed the independence of the state. Among the names signed to their declaration of rights were: Thomas Chittenden, Ira Allen, Matthew Lyon, and Seth Warner. Cephas Kent, who became first representative and first treasurer of Dorset, sent four sons to the Revolution. The tiny rustic *Post Office* upholds the white motif that is so pronounced here.

The *Congregational Church* (1911), stands on a side street west of Vt. 30, in the clear beauty of native marble, with a square tower and stained-glass memorial windows. West of the church is *Cheney Woods,* a dense area of natural woodland preserved as a memorial to musician and author Edward Cheney. At the edge of the woods is the *Dorset Playhouse,* built in rustic style of weatherbeaten boards taken from old barns, on a framework of hand-sewn beams. The auditorium seats 225, and has a large, well-equipped stage. During the summer the Dorset Players put on new three-act plays every two weeks; the organization also sponsors the Vermont Little Theater Contest, an annual three-day event. The *Southern Vermont Artists* (see MANCHESTER) originated in Dorset, under the impetus of such painters as Herbert Meyer, Edwin B. Child, John Lillie, and Frank Dixon.

Golf was played on pasturelands here as early as 1893, when cattle furnished many moving hazards, necessitating an intricate system of ground rules.

The *Quarry Swimming Pool* marks the site of the first commercial marble quarry in America, opened in 1758 by Isaac Underhill. In the primitive stage of the industry, when family burying grounds were common, stonecutters often started out in the spring with a wagonload of marble slabs, which they peddled from home to home, stopping off to do the required lettering for their customers. Later, Dorset marble went into the construction of many public buildings around the country. The quarry hole, now filled with pure spring water, makes an excellent swimming place.

DORSET HOLLOW (3 m. east of Dorset), a scattered settlement of summer homes and upland farms, buried deep in the calm, verdant beauty of the remote, tranquil mountainsides.

EAST DORSET (alt. 788, US 7). In this small, quiet village at the base of *Mount Aeolus* (alt. 3185), marble was quarried as early as 1812. On entering from the north, a white *Union Church* and graveyard are seen across the valley. The drabness of the main street is brightened by the flowerbeds. A more pleasant residential street branches left, a street of white houses sitting under old elms. Mt. Aeolus quarries are no longer worked, but they can be visited by turning right from Main St. at the RR station. The New York Public Library is constructed of marble from these quarries. Among the pioneers who settled here was John Manley, husband of Benedict Arnold's half sister. Today, East Dorset slumbers undisturbed but for the traffic on US 7.

NORTH DORSET (US 7). In this wayside hamlet ancient houses are strung along the highway in the narrow valley confined by mountain ridges. The *Old Cemetery,* a fenced-in burying ground on a knoll above the highway, is unusually congruous here. The use of marble for eighteenth-century headstones is a characteristic of the graveyards in southwestern Vermont.

North Dorset Pond (alt. 740, US 7) is a narrow body of water with a wooded island rising from it, the water taking a deep green color from the shadow of the forested mountain on the western shore. Emerald Lake, the pond's other name, is, for once, a truthful appellation.

An *Old Cemetery* lies in a hollow below the highway, the small group of ancient leaning headstones wearing a lost, forgotten look there in the meadow near the rush of traffic along US 7.

SOUTH DORSET (alt. 940, Vt. 30), a scattered rural community is stretched along the highway where ridges narrow the valley.

West from South Dorset on a country road is *Mill Hollow,* with the picturesque ruins of an old marble mill, and a millpond that is fine for swimming, fishing, and skating.

DORSET FIELD CLUB, INC. 9 holes. Range: 100–542 yds; par 71. Varied terrain, woods and water holes. Facilities: clubhouse with shower rooms and lockers, golf shop, tennis courts, dining room, caddies, tennis and golf pros. Course open to members, guests and guests of certain local hotels and motels.

EMERALD LAKE STATE PARK (East Dorset P.O., US 7 at North Dorset; est. 1957; 462 acres). Includes Emerald Lake, surrounded by open fields, forests and beaches. Facilities: picnic tables and fireplaces, tent sites, lean-tos, camp trailer sites, bathing, boating, fishing, refreshments.

DOVER, 10–D (Windham County, Vt. 100; alt. 1860, pop. 369; 22,623 acres). Includes: East Dover, West Dover and Mt. Snow.

DOVER village is a town hall and a contemporary design elementary school located on a mountainside with a wide view toward the southeast.

EAST DOVER (alt. 1100) is a small settlement with a general store, a Baptist Church and a few houses. Williamsville stage.

WEST DOVER (alt. 1720), one of the highest villages in the state, is a small settlement with a general store, Congregational Church and a library. There are a few houses. Wilmington and Williamsville stage.

MT. SNOW within the space of a few years has become one of the most fashionable and popular ski resorts in the East. It is located high up in Vermont's heavy snow belt country. Inns, motels and chalets accommodate more than 3000 skiers.

CARINTHIA SKI AREA (Vt. 100, adjacent to Mt. Snow); 3600-ft. T-bar lift; 800-ft. rope tow. Ski school; warming hut and cafeteria; ski shop with sales, rentals, and repairs. Daily. *Information:* Walter Stugger, Carinthia Ski Area, West Dover, Vt. Phone: HOmestead 4–5461.

MT. SNOW SKI AREA (off Vt. 100); 6 mono-rail chair trams; 3 aerial high-speed double chair lifts including 7600-ft. and 5600-ft. lift; 40 trails and slopes. Mile long Exhibition and South Bowl reportedly provides widest summit in East. Base lodge has outdoor Sauna Swimming Pool, heated outdoor sun terrace and suntan lounge. Indoor skating rink; 3-story ski lodge and restaurant; 3 cafeterias. Observation deck. Parking areas. Harvey Clifford Ski School with 50 ski instructors. "Learn-to-Ski Weeks"; 120-unit Lake Lodge with health pools, tropical gardens. Low-cost accommodations in Snow Barn, American plan. Area open throughout year. *Information:* Mt. Snow, Vt. Phone: HOmestead 4–3333.

DUMMERSTON, 10–E (Windham County, US 5, Interstate 91, Vt. 30; alt. 400, pop. 872; 8675 acres). Includes: Dummerston Town, East Dummerston and West Dummerston.

DUMMERSTON TOWN. Granted in 1753 as Fullam, the town assumed the name of Dummerston in very early days, but the charter was never changed or regranted. Not until 1937 did the legislature confirm the name under which Dummerston had been conducting its affairs for more than a century and a half. The town reached its peak of population in 1810, when it had nearly three times as many people as it has today. From here the father of Rutherford B. Hayes emigrated to Ohio in 1817, five years before the birth of the future president.

President Hayes' grandfather was a Vermont saloonkeeper but his wife, renowned for her temperance activities, was known as "Lemonade Lucy" during her White House years.

EAST DUMMERSTON (off Vt. 30 on US 5) is a tiny hamlet.

WEST DUMMERSTON (Vt. 30), scattered along a slight rise in the valley, has a street marked by two small white churches and a large white *Grange Hall.* First settler John Kathan (1752) cleared 120 acres and built a house, barn, sawmill, and potash works. His daughter was taken into Indian captivity for two and one half years, after which she was ransomed.

Lydia Taft Pratt (public) *Library.*

Frederic Van de Water, author of *The Reluctant Republic, Home in the Country,* and many novels, lives in Dummerston.

DUTTON PINES STATE PARK (Brattleboro R.D., US 5; est. 1937; 0.33 acre). Pine grove with picnic tables and fireplaces. The pines were planted in 1896.

MAPLE VALLEY SKI AREA (7 m. north of Brattleboro on Vt. 30). This family area opened during the 1963–64 season. Double chair lift (1100 per hour); 5-m. novice, intermediate and expert trails. All type slopes. T-bar lift serves 25- and 45-meter jumps. Restaurant, ski shop, ski school. *Information:* Write Terry Tyler, West Dummerston, Vt.

DUTCH HILL SKI AREA (see READSBORO)
DUTTON PINES STATE PARK (see DUMMERSTON)

DUXBURY, 4–C (Washington County; alt. 340, pop. 546; 24,801 acres). Includes: North Duxbury, South Duxbury. This little town has a crossroads store and coal and lumber companies. The First Union Church is in South Duxbury.

CAMEL'S HUMP (alt. 4083), the third highest mountain in the state, was called *le lion couchant* by Vermont discoverer Samuel de Champlain. *Le lion couchant* (the couching or sleeping lion) was frequently mistranslated as the Crouching Lion. Around 1800 it became known by the less romantic name of Camel's Rump. Vermont's Victorians shuddered at the latter designation and changed the name to Camel's Hump. Many lovers of the bald mountain want the name changed back to Couching Lion or its French equivalent.

Spectacular views are seen from the summit of this peak. New Hampshire's Presidential Range, including Mt. Washington, lie to the east. New York's jagged Adirondacks lie along the westward horizon. Owl's Head peak in Canada is visible. Far to the south lies Killington, the state's second highest peak.

CAMEL'S HUMP STATE FOREST includes 7577 acres in the towns of Duxbury, Fayston, Huntington and Waitsfield of which the original 1200 acres were given by the late Colonel Joseph Battell (See RIPTON). Camel's Hump summit (alt. 4083) is in the forest.

MONROE STATE PARK includes the 228 acres of the late Professor Will S. Monroe's *Couching Lion Farm*. Professor Monroe, before and after his retirement from teaching in New Jersey, devoted much of his time to developing the Long Trail. The 30-mile section from Lincoln Gap to Bolton is named the *Monroe Skyline* in his memory. The gentle old man's will stipulated that the park — his farm — must be kept for ever as a bird sanctuary, plant and game preserve. Foot trails lead to the summit of *Camel's Hump*. No other recreational facilities. Take *Monroe State Park road* from North Duxbury.

EAST ARLINGTON (see ARLINGTON)
EAST BARNARD (see BARNARD)
EAST BARNET (see BARNET)
EAST BARRE (see BARRE TOWN)
EAST BERKSHIRE (see BERKSHIRE)
EAST BETHEL (see BETHEL)
EAST BRAINTREE (see BRAINTREE)
EAST BRIGHTON (see BRIGHTON)
EAST BURKE (see BURKE)
EAST CABOT (see CABOT)
EAST CALAIS (see CALAIS)
EAST CHARLESTON (see CHARLESTON)
EAST CHARLOTTE (see CHARLOTTE)
EAST CHITTENDEN (see CHITTENDEN)
EAST CLARENDON (see CLARENDON)
EAST CONCORD (see CONCORD)
EAST CORINTH (see CORINTH)
EAST CRAFTSBURY (see CRAFTSBURY)
EAST DORSET (see DORSET)
EAST DOVER (see DOVER)
EAST DUMMERSTON (see DUMMERSTON)
EAST ENOSBURG (see ENOSBURG)
EAST FAIRFIELD (see FAIRFIELD)
EAST FLETCHER (see FLETCHER)
EAST GEORGIA (see GEORGIA)
EAST GRANVILLE (see GRANVILLE)
EAST HARDWICK (see HARDWICK)

EAST HAVEN, 3–F (Essex County, Vt. 114; pop. 99; 21,600 acres). Lyndonville or Island Pond stage.

EAST HAVEN is a tiny village with a general store, post office, a *Methodist Church* and a burying ground.

EAST HIGHGATE (see HIGHGATE)
EAST HUBBARDTON (see HUBBARDTON)
EAST JAMAICA (see JAMAICA)
EAST JOHNSON (see JOHNSON)
EAST MIDDLEBURY (see MIDDLEBURY)
EAST MONKTON (see MONKTON)

EAST MONTPELIER, 4–D (Washington County, US 2 and Vt. 14; alt. 728, pop. 1200; 17,957 acres). Vt. Transit bus. Includes: East Montpelier Center and North Montpelier.

EAST MONTPELIER CENTER, set apart from Montpelier as a separate township in 1848, lies along an irregular shelf over the Winooski River. Perley Davis, brother of Jacob Davis, who founded Montpelier, was the pioneer father of East Montpelier. The brick *Universalist Church* stands above the highway junction at the north end of the settlement.

Across the fields and beyond an old unfenced graveyard on the open meadow, the *Old Quaker Burial Ground* lies in a tree-grown, fenced-in plot, with chipped and crumbling stones, many of which lean grassward or lie flat on the earth. The oldest legible slate is dated 1797.

NORTH MONTPELIER (alt. 670) lies in a narrow valley at the foot of a long hill descending from the south, with a millpond at its northern extremity. The square lined *Rich House,* standing eminent near the top of the hill, bears the date of its erection, 1805. The *Little Woolen Company Mill* lies on both sides of the highway at the village center, its two sections connected by an overhead wooden passageway arching the road. The mill employs about fifty workmen and is the basic industry of this immediate vicinity. Vermont's "little poetry magazine," *Driftwind,* edited, printed, and published by Walter J. Coates, storekeeper and poet, was once published here.

EAST PEACHAM (see PEACHAM)
EAST PITTSFORD (see PITTSFORD)
EAST POULTNEY (see POULTNEY)
EAST RANDOLPH (see RANDOLPH)
EAST RICHFORD (see RICHFORD)
EAST RUPERT (see RUPERT)
EAST RYEGATE (see RYEGATE)
EAST ST. JOHNSBURY (see ST. JOHNSBURY)
EAST SHELDON (see SHELDON)
EAST SHOREHAM (see SHOREHAM)
EAST THETFORD (see THETFORD)
EAST TOPSHAM (see TOPSHAM)
EAST WALLINGFORD (see WALLINGFORD)
EAST WARREN (see WARREN)

EDEN, 2–D (Lamoille County, Vt. 100 and Vt. 118; alt. 1111, pop. 430; 32,231 acres). Vt. Transit bus. Includes: Eden (Corners) and Eden Mills.

EDEN CORNERS resembles the name locally given it, a rural corner settlement lying rather barren and isolated on the open plain. The horizon to the northwest is marked by the bulk of *Belvidere Mountain* (alt. 3360) with the large asbestos mines whitening an area of its shoulder. Eden was granted to Colonel Seth Warner and associates from his Revolutionary regiment, none of whom ever settled here.

EDEN MILLS (alt. 1198), lies desolately in a narrow ravine below the picturesque ruins of an *Old Mill* (R), crumbled on the banks of the mountain stream. The white *Congregational Church,* which centers the tiny settlement, is open only for summer services when the wild charms of Lake Eden make the district more populous.

Lake Eden (alt. 1239) lies wood-hemmed in the upland wilds, with two long peninsulas almost bisecting the narrow irregular lake. Three mountains are reflected in the clear water of Eden, and its scenic attractions are augmented by the presence of sandy shores forming excellent beaches.

ELMORE, 3–D (Lamoille County, off Vt. 15 and Vt. 100 at Morrisville; alt. 1145, pop. 237); Morrisville stage. Includes: Lake Elmore village.

LAKE ELMORE village is a small settlement along the shores of Lake Elmore.

ELMORE STATE PARK (off Vt. 15A at Morrisville, 545 acres) includes 0.5 m. of beach on Lake Elmore and the summit of Mt. Elmore (alt. 2608). This park was made available to Vermonters in 1936 by a gift of public-spirited residents of Elmore and nearby Morrisville. Facilities: picnic tables and fireplaces, bathing, boating, fishing, scenic views, foot trails and refreshments.

ELY (see FAIRLEE)
EMERALD LAKE STATE PARK (see DORSET)
EMERSON (see ROCHESTER)

ENOSBURG, 1–C (Franklin County, Vt. 105 and Vt. 108; alt. 426, pop. 1321: 27,028 acres). Includes: East Enosburg, Enosburg Center, Enosburg Falls, North Enosburg and West Enosburg.

ENOSBURG FALLS is a distinctive village with an attractive park in its center that strikes a keynote of planned neatness, echoed by the residential sections. The village and the township in which it was located were named for Ira Allen's father-in-law, General Rogers Enos, to whom the township was chartered in 1780 by the independent Republic of Vermont. Isaac Farrar, an early settler, instituted the use of wooden spouts for tapping maple trees. They were soon universally adopted and retained until replaced in recent times by metal ones; Farrar, nevertheless, was accused by his neighbors of "scientific farming," which was not well regarded in those days.

In the latter part of the nineteenth century, Enosburg Falls was known throughout the land as the home of panaceas and patent medicines that were "guaranteed" to cure the ills of both man and beast. At least four major fortunes were amassed by local sons in this business. On a smaller scale, descendants of the original manufacturers are still carrying on.

Susan Mills, founder of Mills College for women in California, was born here.

WEST ENOSBURG (alt. 440) is a small four-corner village of frame houses and one church. Snug and domestic, it is neither attractive nor unattractive; it is like a hundred other similar Vermont hamlets that constitute brief pauses in the panorama of the countryside, like marks of human punctuation in the long poem of the landscape.

LAKE CARMI STATE PARK (Enosburg Falls R.D. 3, off Vt. 105 and Vt. 120 on town roads; est. 1963; 499 acres) has a 2-mile frontage on southeast shore of Lake Carmi (alt. 435). Facilities: picnic tables and fireplaces, tent sites, camp trailer sites, bathing, boating, fishing.

ESSEX COUNTY (Area 611 sq. miles, pop.. 6083). Shire town: Guildhall. Organized 1792. Includes: Averill, Avery's Gore, Bloomfield, Brighton, Brunswick, Canaan, Concord, East Haven, Ferdinand, Granby, Guildhall, Lemington, Lewis, Lunenburg, Maidstone, Norton, Victory, Warner's Grant, Warren's Gore.

ESSEX, 3–B (Chittenden County, US 2A and Vt. 15; alt. 358, pop. 7090; 22,316 acres). CV/Ry., Burlington–Winooski bus. Includes: Essex Junction and Essex Center.

ESSEX JUNCTION is an important junction where three lines of the Central Vermont RR and four highways converge, and is also a busy industrial center. In spite of these factors, Essex Junction remains cleaner and more pleasant than most junctions and industrial towns. The *Congregational Church,* in the simplicity of red brick, exemplifies the local unwillingness to let industrial dominance mar the appearance of the village. From the busy *Railroad Station* rows of shining steel tracks stretch on the plain, and the network of automobile highways makes a hub of the well-kept business district.

Essex's population has doubled within the past two decades. An important local factor was the location of the International Business Machines Corporation plant here. The manufacture of bricks and concrete and cinder blocks is an important industry.

The RR station and the town were immortalized in the poem, "Lay of the Lost Traveller," written in 1865 by the Hon. E. J. Phelps, one of Vermont's noted lawyers and Cleveland's Minister to England (1885). Frustrated by the long delays and baffled by the variety of directions, Phelps spent hours trying to leave the Junction and finally ended back in Burlington whence he had departed that morning bound for Boston.

I hope in hell
Their souls may dwell
Who first invented Essex Junction.

This refrain, which he contributed to a New York newspaper, rendered articulate the despair of generations of Vermonters, and ranks, for Chittenden County people, second only to "In the name of the Great Jehovah and the Continental Congress!" Economic conditions, diverting much of the traffic and almost suspending two of the lines, have in recent years done much to remedy the confusion traditionally associated with the name of Essex Junction.

A beautiful *White House* holds a position of eminence, portraying a type of architecture which embraces more elaborate detail and elegance than is generally seen in Vermont. The homes in general are pleasing and well cared for.

Winooski River Gorge, where the river has cut deeply through the rocks, forms a picturesque gorge that borders on the sensational.

The *Champlain Valley Exposition Grounds* occupy a broad flat expanse on the western outskirts of the village. The fair held annually the week before Labor Day attracts thousands daily.

ESSEX CENTER is a tiny cluster of buildings at a highway junction and a bend. The *Federated Church* is brick built with a belfry and weathervane, and faces an irregular little Common and the fenced-in cemetery across the road. An attractive little buff brick house adds a colorful touch to the small settlement on its rolling plain. That this was once a favorite Indian camping ground has been evidenced by the finding of pottery pieces and flint arrowheads.

VAH—United Maple Products, Frank Rees. Maple Products.

VAH—Wetherbee Poultry Farm, Cedric Wetherbee. Poultry and poultry products.

EVANSVILLE (see BROWNINGTON)

FAIR HAVEN, 7–B (Rutland County, US 4 and Vt. 22A; alt. 400, pop. 2378; 10,123 acres). Rutland–Whitehall bus.

Fair Haven is the center of the only district in the United States producing green, purple, and mottled slates. The main quarries are located near the village, on Scotch Hill. There is a large and closely knit group of Welsh in Fair Haven, descendants for the most part of the slate workers who emigrated here from the quarries of Wales about the middle of the last century. Services at two of the churches in Fair Haven are still conducted in the Welsh tongue.

The extraordinarily large white-fenced Common, bordered by houses and churches, gives Fair Haven somewhat the appearance of an overgrown country village, more especially because the extent of the town's residential section is not apparent from US 4.

Fair Haven's early history was dominated by one man to an extent equaled by few towns in the state. He was Matthew Lyon (1750–1822), a brilliant, headstrong, pugnacious Irishman, who moved here in 1783. Lyon had important political affiliations. He married first the niece of Ethan Allen and second the daughter of Thomas Chittenden. He erected the first sawmill, first gristmill, employed the first teacher, built the first meetinghouse, was the first moderator, established the first printing press, issued the first newspaper, and erected the forge, ironworks, and paper mill that did much to make Fair Haven an early industrial center.

In 1797, after several terms in the state legislature (to which he was elected nineteen times in all), he was sent as Vermont's Representative to Congress. Here he immediately became a center of attack by the Federalists, and was viciously lampooned, along with Jackson and Jefferson, in the Federalist press. On January 30, 1798, goaded by the repeated insults of Roger Griswold, a Congressman from Connecticut, Lyon spat in his opponent's face, the encounter taking place on the floor of the House. Two weeks later, Griswold attacked Lyon from behind with a heavy cane, in the same arena, the incidents being sensationally exploited as "the first breach of decorum in Congress."

Lyon was a bitter foe and outspoken critic of President Adams, and in October, 1798, he was sentenced under the Sedition Act to four months in the Vergennes jail and a fine of $1000, for allegedly treasonable remarks made in his newspaper, *The Scourge of Aristocracy and Repository of Important Political Truth.* He was re-elected to Congress by an overwhelming majority while still in jail and made a triumphant progression of his journey to Washington. In 1801, he moved to Kentucky, which he represented in Congress 1803–11. He was appointed a factor of the Indian Territory in Arkansas and moved to that state, which also elected him to Congress, but he died before he could assume his seat.

Lyon has often been called "the man who elected Jefferson," because in 1801, when the House of Representatives was voting to break the tie between Jefferson and Burr, he cast the decisive vote for Jefferson, on the 36th ballot. Lyon was the only man who has ever been elected to Congress by three different states, and he was the most influential Democrat whose name is associated with Vermont, unless we include in that group Stephen A. Douglas, who was born here (*see* BRANDON).

Prior to the Civil War, Fair Haven was an important "junction" of the Underground Railroad, which helped so many southern slaves escape to Canada. The *Zenas Ellis House* on South Main St., thought to have been the home of Matthew Lyon, was one of the slave depots. *Castle Inn,* Main St., is built on the site of a tavern built by Matthew Lyon. More interesting architecturally, however, is the *Major Tilly Gilbert House* (1806), across the highway from the Common. This house, now an antique shop, is a splendid example of the Georgian architecture, in wood, depending entirely upon simplicity and the rightness of fundamental lines for its effects.

Its proximity to New York and the presence here of a considerable unassimilated foreign element combine to give Fair Haven a personality all its own among Vermont towns of its size.

The *Poultney River* is the boundary line between Vermont and New York State.

FAIRFAX, 2–B (Franklin County, Vt. 104; alt. 349, pop. 1244; 22,433 acres). Burlington–St. Albans bus. Includes: Fairfax village, Fairfax Falls, North Fairfax.

FAIRFAX lies partly in a hollow, at the southern end, rising to a long open plain on the north. Formerly a manufacturing town of some commercial importance, its industries today are chiefly lumbering and dairying. Here is *Bellows Free Academy* (1903), housed in a large brick building set on low ground about a quarter mile west of the central street. The *Baptist Church,* brick on a stone foundation, has latticed towers and an uneven placement of doors. On the northern outskirts of the village, the squat *Stone House* is at least a century old, though the exact date is uncertain. It is an example of pure native building, of mortared stone, with solid irregular lintels over the door and windows, and an asymmetrical arrangement of the windows themselves, boldly proportioned to interior needs rather than exterior patterns.

Fairfax's greatest claim to distinction is its view of Mt. Mansfield to the southeast. No other village in Vermont lives in the continuous presence of its equal in grandeur. Beautiful in the greenery of summer, but even more irresistibly arresting in late fall or winter, when the barren summit is white with snow above the sullen blue of the lower slopes. Mt. Mansfield from Fairfax presents at any time a spectacle too impressive to be interpreted in terms of anything but itself.

FAIRFAX FALLS (Great Falls) is the hydroelectric plant of the Public Electric Light Company, which furnishes electricty for St. Albans, Burlington, and the surrounding countryside, utilizing the natural forces that formerly powered large flour and woolen mills. The river plunges in a series of cascades to the jagged rocks below, attaining a fall of 88 feet in a distance of 30 rods. But the turbulent thundering fury of the waters, fearsome at first glance, seems like a tempest in a teapot when the serene immutability of Mansfield, more noble than ever from this distance, is viewed to the southeast.

NORTH FAIRFAX is a handful of houses built on an S-curve. Here is the *St. Albans City Reservoir,* the waters hidden from the road by the grassed embankment of the dam face.

FAIRFIELD, 2–B (Franklin County, Vt. 36; alt. 500, pop. 1225; 39,360 acres). ST. J & LC/RR. Includes: Fairfield village, Fairfield Station, East Fairfield.

FAIRFIELD village has a peaceful air of seclusion. Though not of high altitude for this state, the view is remarkably wide in three directions. Fairfield is a major maple-sugar production center.

FAIRFIELD STATION is a depot on the St. J & LC/RR.

EAST FAIRFIELD (alt. 424) is a small village in the hollow of a valley. The industries are a maple syrup processing plant, slaughterhouse and a woodworking mill. There are Catholic, Episcopal and Union Churches.
    President Chester A. Arthur Birthplace. The assassination of President James A. Garfield, a one-time Vermont schoolteacher, placed Fairfield native and Vice-President Chester A. Arthur (1830–1886) in the White House. Arthur was defeated for renomination.
    President Arthur was born in a small one-story clapboard frame house which disappeared many years ago. In 1954, the Vermont Board of Historic Sites utilized funds appropriated by the 1953 legislature to construct a replica of the original house. A photograph of the original house was used in the reconstruction. A park of 35 acres adjacent to the house has picnic and parking facilities. The house has been partly refurnished and is open from June to September.

FAIRLEE, 6–E (Orange County, US 5; alt. 430, pop. 569; 11,490 acres). Vt. Transit bus. Includes: Fairlee village and Ely.

FAIRLEE village lies in the shelter of a great rock barrier, the 600-foot *Palisades* towering like a fortress wall over the tranquil river valley. The long wide village street is lined with century-old houses, and interspersed with them are modern shops serving the summer visitors to Lake Morey; the village is now commercially dependent upon summer tourist traffic and guests from the nearby *Lakes Fairlee* and *Morey.*
    It is possible that the world's first steamboat was invented and operated here on the Connecticut by Samuel Morey, Fairlee lumberman and inventive genius. As early as 1793, or 14 years before Fulton launched the *Clermont,* Morey was plying up and down the river in an absurd little craft barely large enough to hold himself, the rude machinery connected with his steam boiler, and an armful of firewood. This was unquestionably one of the earliest steamboats. Morey exhibited his model to Fulton and Livingston, and it is said that Fulton later visited Morey in Fairlee. The details of the affair are clouded and vague. Fulton lives in history as the creator of the steamboat.

Samuel Morey was long since relegated to obscurity, in spite of the fact that he invented many other things.

VHS marker reads "Samuel Morey, pioneer inventor of steam and gas engines lived here. Samuel Morey, resident of Orford and later Fairlee, successfully operated a steamboat on the Conn. River in 1793. Making over 4000 experiments, this early scientist patented an internal combustion engine in 1825 to anticipate the age of the motorcar and airplane."

ELY (Vt. 5, alt. 464) is a P.O. and station on the B & M/RR. Turning-off place for Lake Fairlee. Formerly this was the railway station for the Ely Copper Mines (see VERSHIRE) and here, early one July morning in 1883, five National Guard companies detrained to put down the insurrection of the miners, that was called the "Ely War."

Lake Morey (alt. 416, 506 acres) is a charming little body of water set in an amphitheater of wooded hills. It is a well-developed summer resort of the fashionable type. There are facilities for all summer and water sports in this delightful natural setting. Samuel Morey operated his last steamboat here, and a tragic glamour is added to the scene by the story that, discouraged and embittered by lack of recognition, Captain Morey finally sunk his beloved boat in this lake. Many attempts to locate it have failed, but it may be deeply imbedded in the muddy bottom today.

Lake Fairlee (427 acres) lies in the towns of Fairlee, Thetford and West Fairlee. There is a substantial summer colony along the shores.

Bill Greene's Rare Bird and Animal Farm (US 5), open late May–October, has animals from many countries. Also exotic birds. This is the home of "Queenie" the water-skiing elephant, star of TV and water shows.

LAKE MOREY COUNTRY CLUB (on shore of Lake Morey); 18 holes; par 69. Home of Vermont State Open Championship. Rolling terrain. Facilities: golf shop, pro, caddies, shower rooms, caddy carts. Daily and weekly greens fees.

BONNIE OAKS COUNTRY CLUB (2 m. off US 5 at north end of Lake Morey); 9 holes; par 34. Facilities: clubhouse (lunch), showers, lockers, tennis courts. Lunch, dinners and drinks served at Lodge. Open to members or non-guests.

FAYSTON, 5–C (Washington County, off Vt. 100 north of Waitsfield; alt. 1209, pop. 172; 21,493 acres). Includes North Fayston.

FAYSTON, a tiny hill settlement, exists for skiers. Mad River Glen, a major ski area, is located partly in Fayston and partly in Waitsfield. Fayston has 12 ski lodges, a general store and a burying ground. (MAD RIVER GLEN: see WAITSFIELD)

GLEN ELLEN SKI AREA (4 m. west of Vt. 100 at Irasville [Waitsfield]). Highest vertical drop in the East; 1000-ft. T-bar lift; 2400-ft. double chair lift; 6300-ft. double chair lift (2300 skiers per hour); 10 miles of novice, intermediate and expert trails. All types of open slopes. Ski school, restaurant, equipment rentals, ski patrol. First aid, lounge. Phone: Waitsfield 496-3484.

FELCHVILLE (see READING)

FERDINAND, 2–F (Essex County, Vt. 102; pop. 16; GT/RR. 28,079 acres). Includes Wenlock.
Ferdinand is one of three Vermont towns which never organized town governments. The town's affairs, such as they are, are handled by a supervisor in nearby Island Pond. The town has one motel but no stores or churches.

WENLOCK is the town's railroad depot on the GT/RR.

FERNVILLE (see LEICESTER)

FERRISBURG, 4–B (Addison County, US 7; alt. 218, pop. 1426; 26,825 acres). Vt. Transit bus. Includes: Ferrisburg village, Basin Harbor, North Ferrisburg and Ferrisburg Station.

FERRISBURG sprawls along either side of the main thoroughfare, and trails off on the plain toward Champlain. The town, settled in 1785, was named after grantees by the name of Ferris. The Quaker influence was strong here for many decades. During the War of 1812, Fort Cassin was built at the mouth of Otter Creek in this township, to prevent the enemy from sailing upstream to Vergennes and destroying the vessels being built there.
    Rokeby (open to public May to November), the Rowland E. Robinson Homestead, sets back from the highway in tangled shade and rustic peace, attractive in a simple, venerable, unkempt way. This house was built prior to 1784. In the pre-Civil War times it was an "Underground Railway" station. Robinson's private collection of pictures and antique furniture is here. Rowland E. Robinson (1833–1900) was probably Vermont's most representative and loved writer, and the outstanding Vermont literary figure of the nineteenth century. No other writer in the state has ever translated so accurately and warmly the personality of Vermont people and Vermont landscapes, and in so doing Robinson

pictured a unique little corner of American civilization that has now vanished from even the remotest backwoods sections (see WRITERS).

BASIN HARBOR is a popular Lake Champlain summer resort with cottages and a hotel on the shore looking across the narrowed lake to the mighty Adirondacks of New York State. Close by is the *Site of Old Fort Cassin,* named in honor of the young French lieutenant who led the defense of this fortress, blockading the British fleet's attempt to bottle up Macdonough's flotilla in the waters of Otter Creek. On April 14, 1814, the English attacked Fort Cassin in hopes of gaining entrance to Otter Creek in order to sail upstream and destroy Macdonough's fleet under construction at Vergennes. The British were repulsed after a half-hour encounter, and Macdonough was saved to go on to subsequent Champlain victories.

BASIN HARBOUR CLUB (18 holes) Range: 120–500 yds; Par 72. Facilities: dining room, cocktail lounge, heated swimming pool, pro shop, electric carts. Open to public by reservation.

NORTH FERRISBURG (0.6 m. east of US 7), a hilly, shady village, has queer unpainted old wooden houses stretching eastward from US 7 into a deeper valley. *Allen's Hall* is an old-fashioned opera house, and beyond this the main street passes through an old covered bridge. Trees arch the main street. The gravestones in the large cemetery far outnumber the present inhabitants.

FERRISBURG STATION, a station on the Vermont/Ry.

FLETCHER, 2–C (Franklin County, Vt. 108; alt. 628, pop. 399; 25,629 acres). Includes: Fletcher village, Binghamville, East Fletcher and West Fletcher.

FLETCHER village has a few scattered houses, an IGA store and an abandoned church now used as a town hall.

BINGHAMVILLE has a former church, now a schoolhouse. The school has a square tower with a town clock. Burying grounds are behind the school. The settlement has a half-dozen houses.

EAST FLETCHER, formerly Fletcher Station, has several farms scattered about the former depot.

WEST FLETCHER has one farmhouse, a one-room schoolhouse and a church.

FLORENCE (see PITTSFORD)

FORESTDALE (see BRANDON)
FOXVILLE (see WILLIAMSTOWN)

FRANKLIN COUNTY (Area 659 sq. miles. Population 29,474). Shire town: St. Albans. Organized 1792. Includes: Bakersfield, Berkshire, Enosburg, Fairfax, Fairfield, Fletcher, Franklin, Georgia, Highgate, Montgomery, Richford, St. Albans, Sheldon, Swanton.

FRANKLIN, 1–B (Franklin County, Vt. 108 and Vt. 120; alt. 426, pop. 796; 22,252 acres). Includes: Franklin village and East Franklin.

FRANKLIN was settled in 1789 as Huntsburg, the name being changed by the legislature in 1817. This is a clean and pleasant village, with a modern brick library at the southern end and two white churches, a town hall, and a Civil War Memorial at the northern end. The early settlers of this region did most of their trading in Canada. With the War of 1812 came the embargo, ending their normal state of commercial and social relationship. Smuggling was rife.

This area was the scene of the major battle with the Canadians in the Irish attempt to conquer Canada and set up an independent Irish Republic. The Fenians were the American branch of the Irish Revolutionary Brotherhood, dedicated to the freeing of Ireland from England by force of arms. The odds being too great against the Irish for open warfare in the British Isles, the conquest of Canada was decided upon as a preliminary step. In 1866, some 35,000 Fenian troops entered Canada from several points, including Franklin, and engaged in skirmishes. The movement was frustrated by the intervention of the United States authorities, who seized the Fenian arms and arrested the leaders of the movement for violation of the neutrality laws. In 1870, a second attempt was made, the major force of over 2000 men being concentrated between Franklin and Cook's Corner, just across the border. The purpose of both these attacks was to divert the attention from a main attack launched from Ogdensburg, New York, which also failed. The leaders were again captured by the U.S. government, but were given their freedom by General Grant in recognition of their Civil War services.

Before its settlement, Franklin was a favorite summer hunting ground of the St. Francis Indians of Canada. The meat of the deer and moose killed in the marshes here was dried before being taken back to the Canadian settlements to be consumed during the winter months. Native sons: Orville E. Babcock, Civil War brigadier general and President Grant's secretary, and Governor Charles Gates (1915–17).

EAST FRANKLIN has a general store, church and burying grounds.

LAKE CARMI STATE PARK, to the north of Franklin, includes 500 acres around beautiful Lake Carmi.

GALLUP MILLS (see VICTORY)
GASSETTS (see CHESTER)
GAYSVILLE (see STOCKBRIDGE)

GEORGIA, 2–B (Franklin County, US 7; alt. 385, pop. 1079; 23,732 acres). Vt. Transit bus, CV/Ry. Includes: Georgia Center, East Georgia and Georgia Plain.

GEORGIA CENTER. Sitting well back from the single street, homely old houses and a red brick *Methodist Church* are sequestered under leafy boughs, the whole picture clearly dominated by the great white *Town Hall*, which was erected in 1800 as a Baptist Church, and at that time considered one of the finest churches in the state. Renovating and landscaping was a Works Progress Administration project. Georgia was the scene of hectic strife between smugglers and customs officers in the 1812 era of contrabanding. Patriotic Georgia citizens allied with the customs forces to check the flow of beef cattle being smuggled into Canada to supply British troops, and the smugglers found it so difficult to win their way past Georgia that they called the place Hell's Gate.

EAST GEORGIA is a station on the CV/RY.

Birthplace of General Stannard. A monument marks the site of the farmhouse in which this Civil War hero was born. At Gettysburg when Pickett launched his gallant Confederate charge, Vermont troops held a key position. It was General George Stannard's well-timed counterattack on Pickett's right flank that shattered the charging columns of gray. After Pickett was repulsed, Alabama and Florida brigades advanced in another onrushing wall of steel-tipped gray, but Stannard's Sixteenth Vermont again smashed the enemy back with heavy losses. In this second counteraction, Stannard himself was painfully wounded in the leg, but refused to leave the field until his command was relieved and the wounded safely removed.

GEORGIA PLAIN is a tiny farming community centered around a sawmill on the level plains near Lake Champlain. The inhabitants do their trading in Georgia Center, around which the commercial and social life of the township revolves. In the vicinity of Georgia Plain fossils and trilobites have been found, revealing that this territory was once submerged as the bed of a great prehistoric lake.

VAH — Hillandale Farm, Eric Nye. Dairy farm (Holstein cattle).
VAH — Pierce Farm, Allen Pierce. Turkey farm.

GIFFORD WOODS STATE PARK (see SHERBURNE)
GILMAN (see LUNENBURG)

GLASTENBURY, 10–B (Bennington County, pop. 4; 27,431 acres) became an unorganized town by an act of the 1937 legislature. The population was then seven people. Its present affairs are under the direction of a supervisor in nearby Wilmington. Until its disorganization in 1937, Glastenbury was allotted equal representation in the state legislature with all the other towns, and its three voters biennially dispatched the head of the Mattison family to sit in the House of Representatives in Montpelier with the member from Burlington (pop. 24,780) and the member from Rutland (pop. 17,315). At one time a vigorous lumbering community, Glastenbury is now the clearest example of Vermont's basic problem: hill towns with declining population.

GLENDALE SKI AREA (see NEWFANE)
GLEN ELLEN SKI AREA (see WAITSFIELD)

GLOVER, 2–E (Orleans County, Vt. 16; pop. 683). Barton stage. Includes: Glover village, West Glover and Keene's Corner.

GLOVER, a peaceful little village surrounded by low hills, has a long Main St. with wooden houses set irregularly along either side. The town was settled in 1797 and named for General John Glover, to whom it was presented in return for military services. Many of the original settlers have descendants living here today, which is indicative of the stolid unchanging life of the rural community. There is an interesting taxidermy and gunsmith's shop.

The Old House, a plain white wooden structure, was built sometime before 1800, and was the only house in the valley left standing after Runaway Pond swept through in 1810. Still in excellent condition, this sturdy house contains a loft unchanged from its original state with hand-hewn rafters joined by wooden pegs, as solid and strong as ever. In the basement is a huge square foundation of field stone, built for the fireplaces which no longer exist. This house still serves as a private residence. The trim white *Federated Church,* with green blinds, is the most attractive structure in the village. The *Union House,* a large roomy building with green-and-white porched front, was built in 1846 for a stagecoach hostelry.

WEST GLOVER (pop. 63) has a general store, post office, library and *Congregational Church.*

KEENE'S CORNER is the site of the original settlement made by pioneers from Keene, N.H. This land was sold at a sheriff's sale in Danville, and the records show that one Silas Clark bought 80 acres for $3.59. The *Old Cemetery* is fenced and somewhat cared for, but the oldest stones are illegible. This graveyard and a scattering of poor farms are all that remain to mark the site of the first settlement in Glover.

GOOSE GREEN (see CORINTH)

GOSHEN, 6–B (Addison County, Vt. 73; alt. 1136, pop. 79; 11,133 acres). Brandon P.O. Brandon stage. Includes Goshen village, Goshen Four Corners, North Goshen.

GOSHEN, formerly Goshen Gore, has no stores or post office but it has two burying grounds and a *Methodist Church.* Many of the town's small farms, once noted for Goshen potatoes, have been abandoned or purchased for hunting camps or summer homes.

Thorpe Camp for Crippled Children was founded by the late Reverend Walter Thorpe, longtime pastor of the Brandon Congregational Church. It is now directed by his son-in-law Basil Walsh. This was one of the first summer camps in the United States designed to provide recreation and therapy for crippled children.

GOSHEN FOUR CORNERS is a crossroads with a few houses.

NORTH GOSHEN is not a settlement but the north section of the town. Blueberry Hill is the restaurant and lodge operated by John and Elsie Masterson, authors and/or co-authors of the *Blueberry Hill Cookbook,* novels and tales of Vermont hill country life.

GOULD'S MILLS: (see SPRINGFIELD)

GRAFTON, 9–D (Windham County, Junction Vt. 35 and Vt. 121; alt. 862, pop. 426; 23,246 acres). Townshend and Saxtons River stage.
Grafton is one of Vermont's loveliest small villages. Post-Revolutionary War houses line the tree-shaded streets. The Grafton Tavern is known for its excellent meals.

GRANBY, 3–F (Essex County, off US 2 below Guildhall; pop. 56; 21,898 acres). North Concord stage. One of Vermont's smaller towns, Granby has no store but there is a *Congregational Church* and a library.

GRAND ISLE COUNTY (Area 88 sq. miles — smallest Vt. county; population 2927), least populated county. Shire town: North Hero. Organized 1802. Includes: Alburg, Grand Isle, Isle La Motte, North Hero, South Hero.

GRAND ISLE, 2–A (Grand Isle County, US 2; alt. 160, pop. 624; 10,142 acres). Includes: Grand Isle village and Grand Isle Station.

GRAND ISLE has somewhat more the summer-resort aspect than do other South Hero Island towns, and seems to wear a more modern polish. The road bends into the village past the usual gardens, lawns, and hedges that color every community on the islands and brighten the tidy wooden homes. Grand Isle is near the eastern shore with wide spreading plains under a vast dome of sky, the like of which are found in but one other section of Vermont, that of western Addison County. Alexander Gordon was the first settler here, arriving in 1783 on the same day that Ebenezer Allen landed at the southern end of the island to claim priority on South Hero.

Grand Isle–Plattsburg Ferry is on the island's western shore where Quakers first settled. The view over sparkling Champlain water to the carved grandeur of the Adirondacks is awe-inspiring. Wall on wall the mountain barriers are massed high against the western skyline, shutting in the gleaming stretch of the inland sea that Champlain discovered for the Old World, but which long before that time knew the glide of birch canoes and the thrust of Indian paddles. A network of beautiful drives covers the island, with its rich farmland and great apple orchards. Apple-blossom time is one of fragrant glory and delicate colors in this orchard region.

Hyde Log Cabin (US 2), built by settler Jedediah Hyde, Jr., in 1783, is said to be the oldest existing log cabin in the U.S. The cabin, formerly on another site, was purchased some years ago by the Vermont Historical Society and was then moved here. The Society, lacking funds for restoration, turned the cabin over to the Vermont Board of Historic Sites, which completely restored the cabin, saving as much of the original structure as possible. A new roof was added for protection, and the original fireplace was rebuilt of local fieldstone, as near as possible to the way it was in 1783. In 1956 the cabin was leased over to the Grand Isle County Historical Society. This group now uses the cabin as a meeting place, museum and local information center. The responsibility for the furnishings belongs to them. The cabin is kept open during the summer.

GRAND ISLE STATE PARK (Grand Isle P.O., US 2), est. 1955 (222 acres) on the shore of Lake Champlain (alt. 95), has a new tent site area opened in 1960. Facilities: tent sites, lean-tos, camp trailer sites, boating, fishing. No bathing or picnic facilities.

GRANGERVILLE (see PITTSFORD)
GRANITEVILLE (see BARRE TOWN)

GRANVILLE, 5–C (Addison County, Vt. 12A and Vt. 100; alt. 1013, pop. 215; 28,704 acres). Rochester stage. Includes: (Upper) Granville village, East Granville and Lower Granville.

GRANVILLE (Upper) stretches on the open flat where the White River, Alder Meadow Brook and Kendall Brook unite. The settlement is built around the *Granville Manufacturing Company,* makers of wooden bowls and other wood products. Originally called Kingston for grantee Reuben King, the present name was adopted in 1834. South of Granville the valley broadens, seeming very open and wide after the close confines of Granville Gulf.

EAST GRANVILLE (alt. 850, Vt. 12A) is a tiny rural settlement across the Braintree Mountains from Granville and Lower Granville. It is more than a 50-mile trip by the shortest route from Granville to East Granville. The only industry aside from farming is a small wood products factory. The high ridge beginning about three miles north of East Granville, is wooded almost exclusively with white birches, which grow in greater density here than in any other section of Vermont. Only in early spring or in late autumn, when the other trees, having lost their bright foliage, seem gaunt and bare, do these birches reveal the full beauty of their white arabesques against the dark hills.

LOWER GRANVILLE (alt. 960), scattered along the valley floor, is centered by a general store and white wooden *Methodist Church* with a high blank façade. The setting has a calm serenity in sharp contrast to the wild mountain fastnesses on the north. The White River, increased in size by its two tributaries, bends pleasantly along the valley.

GRANVILLE GULF STATE PARK (Vt. 100 extending south for 6 m. from Warren town line). 1200 acres of which the first 600 — along both sides of road through gulf — were given to Vermonters by former Governor Redfield Proctor in 1927. The Gulf Park lies along the eastern boundary of the Green Mt. National Forest. Beautiful Moss Glen Falls is a major attraction. No picnic tables or fireplaces but picnic lunches (no fires permitted) can be eaten at the turn-out places alongside the highway.

GREEN MOUNTAIN NATIONAL FOREST runs from the Massachusetts line on the south to Mt. Ellen on the north. Its three separate units include more than 630,000 acres of which about 500,000 are suitable for recreational purposes. That portion of the Long Trail which runs through the forest and the shelters are maintained by the U.S. Forest Service. Picnic areas are located at Hapgood Pond (see Landgrove), White Rocks (see Wallingford), Greendale (see Weston), Texas

Falls (see Hancock) and Mooslamoo (see Brandon). Campgrounds are located at Hapgood Pond, Greendale and Chittendenbrook (see Rochester). Campfires cannot be built outside of developed campsites or picnic grounds unless a permit is secured from the district ranger. Offices are located at Manchester Center, Middlebury and Rochester. Forest headquarters are in Rutland.

GREENS CORNERS (see SWANTON)

GREENSBORO, 3–E (Orleans County, off Vt. 16 south of Glover, alt. 1463, pop. 600; 21,268 acres). Includes: Greensboro village and Greensboro Bend.

GREENSBORO, the summer home of many famous writers and scholars, was appropriately named after the Greens, a family of local printers. Beautiful Caspian Lake (alt. 1404) lies at the edge of the hamlet in wood-rimmed shores surrounded by low hills. The high elevation of this lake assures refreshing coolness in summer, and the mountain breezes that blow over the water are keenly exhilarating. The entire setting is a combination of beauty and peacefulness, and it is easily understandable why Caspian has become a haven for the many prominent educators, authors, and professional men who compose the large summer colony here.

The best-known current summer resident is probably John Gunther, author of the famous "Inside" series. He has referred to his summer home here as "my ramshackle, delicious hut" and once described the moon over Caspian as "a lollypop."* Other summer residents have included Harvard's Bliss Perry and Dean Christian Gauss of Princeton.

GREENSBORO BEND (alt. 1248) lies bleakly on unshaded flats where the Lamoille River, the highway and the railroad make wide sweeping bends. The village is a trading center for farmers. The Hazen Military Road passed through Greensboro, and in 1779 a blockhouse was built on the western shore of Caspian Lake. In 1781 four scouts in the blockhouse were surprised by Indians, two of them being slain by the raiders.

Hospital: *Greensboro Memorial.*

MOUNTAIN VIEW COUNTRY CLUB; 9 holes. Range: 146–473 yds.; par 35. Hill, wooded terrain. Facilities: clubhouse open July–August, 9 A.M. to 4 P.M.; 12 noon Sundays. Tennis courts.

GROTON, 4–E (Caledonia County, US 302; alt. 773, pop. 629; 25,100 acres). Vt. Transit bus. Includes: Groton village, West Groton and Ricker Mills.

* *A Fragment of Autobiography* (New York: Harper & Row, 1962).

GROTON, named for Groton, Mass., sprawls on a flat wide section of the valley with the erratic course of the Wells River bisecting the village. Sturdy Scottish people laid the foundation of this settlement, which now bases its subsistence mainly on the industries of lumber and granite. The surrounding country is wild and heavily forested, with Groton State Forest stretching densely for miles. The many ponds and woodland streams provide excellent fishing.

RICKER MILLS, at the foot of *Lund Pond,* is the source of the Wells River. Here the droning burr of a board saw cleaves the pure upland air, the screaming yet sibilant welcome of steel and hemlock. Weather-warped and time ravaged, Ricker Mills still turns out its 150,000 feet of lumber each year — the oldest stationary sawmill in America in continuous operation and the only mill of its character still engaged in the production of soft-wood timber. At one time all the sawed lumber in three counties came from Ricker's. Now the output is dwindling, but the lumbermen expect to continue operating for a long time to come. This mellowed landmark on the shore of the forest-shrouded pond combines the flavor of active utility with genuine antiquity.

The *Old Lake House,* just beyond the mill, was built in 1843 to serve as a boarding-house for the lumberjacks, when this section was being worked by big lumber companies and the woods resounded with the clean, ringing blows of countless axes. This old house and the vicinity was the hangout of "Bristol Bill," notorious bank robber and counterfeiter of the middle 19th century, and here in 1850 this sensational outlaw was finally captured. He was William Darlington of Bristol, England, but two continents knew him as Bristol Bill. It is ironic that, after evading the law in our major cities as well as those of England, Bristol Bill should have been taken prisoner here in the backwoods of Groton. And it was but natural that Bill should make one final gesture of flaming defiance and scorn — in the St. Johnsbury courtroom where he was being sentenced, Bristol Bill stabbed the prosecuting attorney to death with a knife.

VAH — Morse Poultry Farm, Gerald Morse. Hatchery and poultry products.

GROTON STATE FOREST (Marshfield P.O., US 2 or US 302; est. 1919; 15,607 acres) lies in the towns of Groton, Marshfield, and Peacham and contains all or part of Lake Groton (alt. 1078), and the following ponds: Kettle (alt. 1443), Martin's, Niggerhead (alt. 1279), Osmore, Peacham (alt. 1401), Ricker. Lake Groton, formerly Groton Pond, is 3 m. long. Facilities: picnic tables and fireplaces, tent sites, lean-tos, camp trailer sites, bathing, boating, fishing, hunting, scenic views, foot trails, refreshments.

This forest contains four separate recreation areas: New Discovery, Stillwater, Lake Groton, Ricker Pond.

New Discovery facilities: picnic tables and fireplaces, tent sites, lean-tos, camp trailer sites, fishing.

Stillwater facilities: picnic tables and fireplaces, tent sites, lean-tos, camp trailer sites, boating, fishing.

Lake Groton facilities: picnic tables and fireplaces, bathing, boating, fishing, refreshments.

Ricker Pond facilities: tent sites, lean-tos, camp trailer sites, boating, fishing.

GUILDHALL, 3–G (Essex County, Vt. 114; alt. 874, pop. 248; 17,791 acres) is the shire town of Essex County and one of the earliest settled towns (1764) in this part of the state. There is no other place in the world named Guildhall, and research cannot discover why this town was so called.

Early Guildhall settlers were harassed by Indians and Tories, and were apparently of a somewhat aggressive nature themselves. New Hampshire Town Papers preserve a petition dated June 22, 1780, to the Council and Representatives in which one Enoch Bartlett of Northumberland, just across the river from Guildhall, begs redress because in the previous September "a Sort of Banditti" entered his grist- and sawmill, cut and destroyed the wheels and shafts, and "took away all the Iron Works of Said Mills, Mill Stones and other Gear and a Quantity of Boards and Carried them A Cross Connecticut River into the State Called Vermont And improved them for other Mills." Guildhall's claim of having had the first mill in northeastern Vermont is perhaps a clouded distinction.

The village centers about a grass quadrangle bordered by houses and public buildings, the most interesting of which are the *Essex County Courthouse* and the *Guild Hall,* now the Town Hall, dating from 1795. Smallest of Vermont's shire towns, Guildhall is not only dominated by, but almost composed of, the physical appurtenances of local self-government. Its tiny square has not only the charm but the essence of one of New England's most excellent traditions. In summer twilight it is a stage set. A few rods off the road but visible, is the *North Burying Ground,* which was laid out by the selectmen in 1797 and contains stones dating two years earlier. The verse epitaphs in this cemetery are unusually varied and interesting.

VAH — Peaslee Farm, Mrs. Fred Peaslee. Potato and beef farm (Hereford cattle).

GUILFORD, 11–E (Windham County, US 5 and Interstate 91; alt. 400, pop. 823; 23,771 acres). Includes Guilford village, Green River, Guilford Center and Hinesburg.

GUILFORD village. Though no formal pitched battle was ever fought here, the town has probably been the scene of more internal strife and violence than any other in the state. It was granted by New Hampshire in 1754 and governed by committees of its own choosing until May 19, 1772, when its inhabitants voted of their own will that Guilford was in Cumberland County, Province of New York, and chose officers agreeable to the laws of that province. Beginning in 1776, however, an increasing number of residents began to question this jurisdiction, and there followed a period of fifteen years — until Vermont's admission into the Union in 1791 — during which the town was literally in a state of continuous civil war, with intermittent manifestations of physical violence. There were two sets of town officers and two town meetings, both heavily armed and augmented by armed sympathizers from neighboring towns, especially Brattleboro. The record for the May town meeting of 1782 reads in one place: "Then the people met in general and voted to stand against the pretended State of Vermont." That, of course, is from the records of the "Yorker" faction. The Patriots' records no one can quote. They were stolen by the Yorkers and buried under the earth in the town pound for stray animals. When finally recovered, they were in an almost complete state of disintegration, barely recognizable for what they were.

In the summer of 1783, Ethan Allen arrived in Guilford with 100 Green Mountain Boys and issued a proclamation whose language makes the phraseology he used at Ticonderoga seem almost equivocal: "I, Ethan Allen, declare that unless the people of Guilford peaceably submit to the authority of Vermont, the town shall be made as desolate as were the cities of Sodom and Gomorrah, by God." (There is a school of historians that prefers to omit the last comma in the quotation, but they are a minority.) He then established martial law, and the Vermont constable, for the first time, collected taxes from everyone who was supposed to pay them. But Ethan Allen had larger matters in hand than the proctoring of Guilford, and from 1784 to 1791 the town continued in a state that can only be called anarchy. When the authority of Vermont could no longer be questioned or resisted, a large majority of the Yorkers fled to the state to which they had been loyal. Bainbridge, Chenango County, N.Y., was settled almost wholly by Guilford emigrants.

Guilford's early growth was, relatively judged, meteoric, and in 1790, despite the loss of many Yorkers, it was, with 2432 inhabitants, the most populous town in the state. This was partly due to immigration and partly to the large families, exceeding even the norm of that time, that were the rule here. A local census taken in 1772 shows that of the 84 married men living here then, only one, Captain William Bullock, was without issue, a distinction that he later removed. Not even in Vermont is Ethan Allen regarded as a divinely inspired prophet;

and Guilford today, with its tea houses, tourist homes, summer residences, and fertile farms, is far removed yet from the ashes of desolation; still, remembering Ethan's unheeded threat, it is perhaps just worth noting that until 1960 Guilford was the only town in Vermont whose population showed a decrease in every census since the first official one in 1790.

The four-pointed spire of the white *Christ Church* (1817) rises above Route 5. Called the Episcopal "mother church" in Vermont, it is maintained by an annual Old Home Day Service in August.

Governor's Mountain, in the extreme northwestern part of town, is an example of Colonial irony. Governor Wentworth, in the original charter of Guilford, stipulated that 500 acres of land be reserved for him; and so it was — on the only considerable peak in the town, 1823 feet above sea level.

In 1791, Royall Tyler settled in Guilford and began the legal practice that culminated in his becoming, in 1807, Chief Justice of Vermont. Here he probably studied from life models the prototypes of Updyke Underhill, the first true Yankee character in literature and the narrator of Tyler's novel, *The Algerine Captive,* 1797. Another pioneer settler was Benjamin Carpenter. His large marble tombstone, in the western section of town, has a long inscription, listing his many services to the state, which concludes: "Left this world and 146 persons of lineal posterity, March 29, 1804, aged 78 years, 10 months and 12 days, with a strong mind and full faith of a more glorious state hereafter. Stature about six feet — weight 200. Death had no terror." A real Guilford man.

GREEN RIVER (unnumbered road south of Guilford Center or west of Guilford) is a delightful little southern Vermont hill hamlet with a red-painted covered bridge, general store, and Methodist Church.

GUILFORD CENTER has a church (Universalist) and a library. Brattleboro stage.

HINESBURG (not to be confused with Hinesburg town in Chittenden County) is a small village and former P.O. address in Guilford town.

HALIFAX, 10–D (Windham County; alt. 1800, pop. 268; 23,720 acres; P.O. Brattleboro or West Halifax). Brattleboro stage. Includes: West Halifax. Tiny Halifax has a Union Church.

WEST HALIFAX has the Post Office, Baptist Church, and lumber company. Brattleboro stage.

HAMMONDSVILLE (see READING)

East Poultney — the old church seen from the Eagle Tavern steps. *Aldo Merusi*

Richmond — a sixteen-sided church. *Arthur Griffin*

Left, above: State House Senate Chamber
Vermont Development Department

Left, below: Newfane — the classic village green
Arthur Griffin

An odd steeple at Stowe. *Ward Allan Howe, Ewing Galloway*

Left, above: Essex Center Grange Hall
Ewing Galloway

Left, below: The Inn At Weston is what many city folk
think a small Vermont inn should be

Quechee — abandoned farm, buyer wanted. *Ewing Galloway*

The round barn in Irasburg. *Vermont Development Department*

"The Sentinels" by Vermont artist Paul Sample

HANCOCK, 6–C (Addison County, Vt. 100 and Vt. 125; alt. 912, pop. 323; 20,926 acres). Includes: Hancock village and Branch School. Eastern terminus Vt. 125.

HANCOCK village consists of a T-shaped collection of houses, a white-fenced cemetery and a rather unattractive church but there is great beauty in the mountains surrounding the hamlet. The Weyerhaeuser Company, Wood Products Division, at the edge of the village, is an unusually large plant for such a sparsely settled section; about 150 workers are employed here, coming from Hancock, Granville and Rochester.

BRANCH SCHOOL (on Vt. 125 about 2.0 m. east of Vt. 100) is a country settlement of a few houses and a one-room schoolhouse.

TEXAS FALLS RECREATION AREA (Green Mt. National Forest), 3 m. west of Vt. 100 on Vt. 125, then 0.4 m. north. Facilities: picnic tables and fireplaces beside one of Vermont's most beautiful waterfalls.

HANKSVILLE (see HUNTINGTON)

HARDWICK, 3–D (Caledonia County, Vt. 14 and Vt. 15; alt. 861, pop. 2349; 22,402 acres). Vt. Transit bus. Includes Hardwick village, East Hardwick, and Hardwick Street.

HARDWICK, named after Hardwick, Mass., from which the first settlers came, is an unshaded granite and industrial village, with a sloping thoroughfare winding down between the crowded wooden buildings of the business section. In a hurried growth under the impetus of the granite industry and its resultant prosperity, no attempt was made to beautify the village; appearance was sacrificed almost entirely to intensive industrialism. Although granite has suffered a marked decline, Hardwick is still somewhat imbued with the Barre spirit of modern aggressiveness, and is therefore unlike the usual Vermont village of its size. Laid out in a haphazard manner, Hardwick conveys the impression of unplanned disorder, resulting from too much haste in upgrowth and industrial progress rather than from lack of prosperity and civic ideals.

The first settler here was Captain John Bridgam, 1797. The community was mainly agricultural until the discovery of granite, by Henry R. Mack in 1868. Hardwick rose incredibly to become one of the granite centers of the United States and like a raw booming mining town, rode the crest of prosperity. Under the late George H. Bickford, the Woodbury Granite Company became the largest building-granite firm in the world, furnishing stone for the Pennsylvania State Capitol, the Cook County Courthouse in Chicago, and many public buildings in Washington and throughout the country.

The *Memorial Building,* Main and Church Sts., is of Woodbury granite with a Memorial Room of Proctor marble, the walls of which are inscribed with the names of Hardwick soldiers. There is a valuable collection of old coins and paper money. In the main corridor is a World War I Memorial of local granite, and on the second floor is a plaster-of-paris copy of the "Last Supper" by Frederick A. Purdy, a sculptor associated with the Woodbury Granite Company.

The *Jeudevine Memorial Library,* Main St., is a handsome sandstone building. The *Bickford Buildings,* Main St., contain woodwork and paneling from the pews of the first church in town, the French Meeting House. This French Meeting House was named for an early settler, Samuel French, who built it in 1820, after sectarian variances in the town had delayed the erection of a house of worship. He put the inscription "Liberty of Conscience" over the door and allowed all sects the use of the building, which he firmly refused, however, to sell. At one time the French Meeting House was even used by the New Lights, a band of Hardwick fanatics whose short-lived sect, distinguished chiefly by extravagant outward manifestations of inner spiritual light, came into being in 1837.

Hospital: Hardwick.

Newspaper: Hardwick Gazette (weekly).

EAST HARDWICK is a side-hill village, spilling from the level of a plateau down a sharp incline into the valley of the Lamoille. In passing through, Vt. 12 makes two right-angle turns, right and down the hill, then left from the middle of the hill. The settlement is marked only by its peculiar hillside location.

HARDWICK STREET, the original settlement of the town, made in 1795 by Colonel Alpha Warner and others. The long straight street, broad and maple-shaded, is lined with old homes set well back on spacious lawns, many of which are picket-fenced. The scene on this secluded level plain is one of serenity. The *Hazen Road Monument* commemorates the military road which passed through on Hardwick St. and ran northward two miles to Caspian Lake. The *Stage House* was built in 1799 by Alpha Warner, and the original tavern sign still hangs in front of the fine old structure, which now serves as a summer home for descendants of the founder of Hardwick. This is the oldest house left in town and in back of the great fireplace has a "Chimney Room" once used as a secret chamber.

HARMONYVILLE (see TOWNSHEND)

HARTFORD, 7–E (Windsor County, US 5 and US 2; Interstates 89 and 91 have an interchange here; alt. 340, pop. 6355; 14,851 acres). CV/Ry., B & M/RR, Vt. Transit bus, White River Coach Lines. Includes: White River Junction, Centerville, West Hartford, and Wilder.

WHITE RIVER JUNCTION (alt. 340), where rivers, roads, and railways converge, is an appropriately named town that has been commercially enterprising since the early days of locks and canals on the Connecticut. The bleakness inseparable from a railroad center distinguishes White River Junction from other Connecticut Valley villages. Its crowded business center gives no hint of the pleasantly terraced residential districts, but is overshadowed by the proximity of railroad sheds and a network of tracks. Not uncommon in more industrialized sections of the country, this aspect is an unusual one in Vermont, creating something of a shock in contrast with the clean, shady villages characteristic of the valley.

Diners along Main Street are usually crowded with red-faced railroad men in blue overalls and husky truck drivers in leather jackets, while just across the way, taverns and restaurants are thronged with Dartmouth undergraduates. The transient business of White River is extremely heavy, and the resultant pattern of life complex and changing.

The village is a wholesale business center as well as a railroad junction. As a majority of travelers bound for Hanover get off the train at White River, the town is closely linked with Dartmouth College, and is enlivened and brightened periodically throughout the year by this association. On football weekends and other special occasions, White River is invaded by crowds in the holiday spirit, becoming a dull background for colorful scenes of merriment and revelry. Between these high points, the unceasing ebb and flow of transient life saves White River from monotony and inertia. The depot here also serves the resort town of Woodstock (see WOODSTOCK).

Newspaper: Valley News (daily), Lebanon, N.H.

CENTERVILLE, a community of farmsteads strung along both sides of Vt. 14 in the valley that has widened to fertile beauty.

HARTFORD (alt. 400), is a residential suburb of White River Junction, with attractive homes, shrubs and lawns offering a pleasing contrast to the unrelieved industrial and commercial aspect of the Junction. The trees that shade the community spread from the business district to a background of low rounded hills. Uncrowded and undeveloped, Hartford is a model residential section. The town was settled in 1761 by a few families from Lebanon, Conn., and one of the earliest comers was Joseph Marsh, later the first lieutenant governor of the state. Horace Wells, the discoverer of laughing gas, was born here.

WEST HARTFORD (alt. 420), is a small and rather faded hamlet, with all of its business section lying alongside the highway.

WILDER, originally known as Olcutt Falls, is a village of houses strung along US 5.

HARTLAND, 7–E (Windsor County, US 5 — Interstate 91 scheduled, Vt. 12; alt. 416, pop. 1592; 27,912 acres). CV/Ry and Vt. Transit bus. Includes: Hartland village, Hartland Four Corners, and North Hartland.

HARTLAND is the central village in Hartland Town. Originally chartered as Hertford, the name was changed to Hartland by act of legislature in 1782 to avoid confusion with Hartford to the north — a change that strangers sometimes find insufficient still. Hartland village radiates from a highway four-corners. At the junction is a *Soldiers' Monument* that economically commemorates the veterans of three wars. The *Sumner-Steele House* on the knoll around which the highway curves is a dignified expression of the American Georgian style of architecture. The Palladian window is very fine, and the white lawn balustrade that stretches in front of the house, though not the original one, is a rare and authentic feature. The house was built in 1804 by David Sumner, a wealthy merchant and mill owner. It descended to his daughter, the wife of Benjamin Steele, who in 1856 was appointed to the bench of the Vermont supreme court when he was twenty-eight years of age, the youngest man ever to hold that position.

HARTLAND FOUR CORNERS (1.0 m. west of Hartland on Vt. 12) is a small settlement centered about a *Universalist Church, Library* and a country store.

NORTH HARTLAND (RR station Evarts) is a small rustic residential village, formerly the seat of large woolen mills. The falls here at the junction of the Ottauquechee with the Connecticut were the scene of one of the climaxes in the retreat of Rogers' Rangers, 1759 (see NEW-PORT). The four raftsmen headed by Major Rogers were drifting downstream on the rude unwieldy float they had made at the foot of the White River Falls, where they had nearly been swept to death. They landed above the Ottauquechee rapids, faced with the problem of getting past the falls and retaining their raft for the remainder of the voyage, knowing that if this raft was lost it meant the end for them and their comrades waiting upstream for rescue. They were too weary and weak from hunger to endure the labor of building another. While the Rangers held the raft at the head of the rapids, Rogers walked to the foot of the falls and prepared to swim out and board the raft when it came down. The bound timbers hurtled over the falls, and Rogers plunged out and clambered aboard, to fight the current and bring the log craft ashore by paddling with the strength of desperation. He made the riverbank, and the four men camped there overnight, spent and exhausted. In the morning they put out again and rode the current down to a point near Fort No. 4, at Charlestown, N.H. Rogers himself, tireless and indomitable, led the party back upstream with supplies, and most of his men were saved. On the entire expedition, through the most terrible perils and hardships, Rogers lost 50 of the 200 men who started with him from Crown Point.

Hartland was settled by Timothy Lull, who in the spring of 1763 paddled his family up the Connecticut River from Dummerston in a hollowed-out-log canoe. Lull's Brook, in the southern part of town, he christened by breaking a bottle of liquor and spilling the contents in the presence of his family, no trivial gesture to make at that distance from any source of further supply. The settlement grew so rapidly that by 1791 it was the most populous town in the county, having, in fact, about 400 more inhabitants within its borders than it has today. Perhaps it was the friction of overcongestion, by pioneer standards, that caused the men of Hartland to act so "unlawfully, riotously, and routously" as they did on several occasions. In 1786 about thirty of them, with a few additions from Barnard, assembled fully armed at Windsor to prevent the sitting of the county court there. The leader was fined and imprisoned, and the Hartland insurgents assembled again, in greater numbers this time, to rescue him. High Sheriff Benjamin Wait captured twenty-seven of them in an early morning surprise attack on Lull's house, and lodged them in the jail at Windsor. Thereupon more than a hundred sympathizers gathered at Captain Lull's house, and only the hurried assembling of 600 men under arms at Windsor kept this miniature Shays's Rebellion from assuming tragic proportions.

HARVEY (see DANVILLE)
HAZEN'S NOTCH (see WESTFIELD)
HAZEN'S NOTCH STATE PARK (see WESTFIELD)
HEALDVILLE (see MT. HOLLY)
HEARTWELLVILLE (see READSBORO)

HIGHGATE, 1–B (Franklin County, US 7; alt. 127, pop. 1608; 30,574 acres). U.S.-Canadian Customs and Immigration Station. Includes: Highgate Springs, Highgate (center), East Highgate and Highgate Falls.

HIGHGATE SPRINGS (3.2 m. south of the U.S.-Canadian line) is popular as a resort because of its mineral springs and the excellent fishing, swimming, and boating in the nearby bay. The little summer settlement is built around a hotel and dance pavilion and makes no pretense of being other than a tourist place, relying mainly on summer guests for its existence. A queer white *Union Church* stands with a tall narrow façade, high spire and red roof. The pleasant and placid resort aspect of Highgate Springs gives little indication of the border controversies that once were rife here, when bullets and fists flew as smugglers mixed it with the revenue officers.

Between Highgate Springs and Swanton, the highway is separated from Champlain waters by the outthrust of a huge promontory, through which the Missisquoi flows northward to empty into the Bay.

Canadian Boundary. This is one of the most pleasant border crossings, where the customhouses of both nations stand close together in the peace of the open countryside, its serenity unmarred by any barriers, fortifications, or bayoneted rifles. The entrance to Vermont is made at the town of Highgate, which was settled in 1787 by a body of Hessian troops, professional soldiers brought here by the British, who decided to remain in the New World. Under the impression that they were settling in Canada, the Hessians continued to believe so until the establishment of the permanent international boundary proved their mistake. The iron boundary post at this gateway between the Province of Quebec and New England is 52 m., south of Victoria Bridge in Montreal.

U.S. Customhouse is a trim modern structure, built in 1934–35.

Site of the birthplace of John Godfrey Saxe (1816–1887), one of Vermont's outstanding poets, whose verse was in the Longfellow spirit. Lawyer, politician, lecturer, and editor, as well as poet, Saxe's significance in the latter field is supported by the fact that thirteen Saxe pieces are reprinted in Burton E. Stevenson's standard *Home Book of Verse,* a larger number than is given to many other American poets of higher acknowledged standing.

HIGH POND SKI AREA (see BRANDON)

HINESBURG, 4–B (Chittenden County, Vt. 116; alt. 341, pop. 1180; 1180 acres). Burlington bus. Includes: Hinesburg, Mechanicsville, Rhode Island Corners and South Hinesburg. The town of Hinesburg should not be confused with the hamlet of Hinesburg in Guilford town.

HINESBURG, *Windham County* (see GUILFORD)
HOGBACK SKI AREA (see BRATTLEBORO)
HOLDEN (see CHITTENDEN)

HOLLAND, 1–F (Orleans County, north of Morgan Center, alt. 1450, pop. 376; 22,346 acres). Includes: Holland village and Tice. This small village, south of the Canadian frontier, has two churches, a burying ground and a sawmill but no stores.

HUBBARDTON, 7–B (Rutland County, Vt. 30; alt. 480, pop. 238; 16,125 acres). Includes East Hubbardton and the Hubbardton Battlefield.

Once called Hubbard Towne, after grantee Thomas Hubbard, this tiny settlement rests in the valley at the northern end of Lake Bomoseen. Most of the town — as distinguished from the village — is hilly or mountainous. Nine families lived in the town at the time of the battle, July 7, 1777.

Battle of Hubbardton

Here high in the hills on July 7, 1777, Colonel Seth Warner's rear guard, protecting the retreat of General St. Clair from Mount Independence, made a desperate stand against pursuing British forces under General Simon Fraser and Baron von Riedesel. Warner's ragged army of farmers was cooking and eating breakfast on the heights when the British attacked early in the morning, coming in formidable scarlet waves through the gray mists of dawn. The surprised backwoodsmen dropped skillets and grabbed their muskets, deploying to fight Indian fashion in an attempt to check the heavy onrush.

Hale's company, the first to be set upon, fled in a body to the forest, but Warner's Vermonters and Francis' company made a grim and stubborn stand, and Colonel Francis was killed fighting at the head of his men. For a time it looked as if Fraser's British regulars would be beaten back, but the arrival of von Riedesel's Brunswick troops turned the tide. The booming of the German band heralded their approach and killed the rising hopes of Warner's woodsmen. Scattered rifle fire seemed to make no impression on the advancing ranks of red and blue. The Colonials moved down the valley to Castleton and Manchester, where they prepared to join John Stark's New Hampshire militia at the battle of Bennington (see BENNINGTON). Hubbardton was a dearly bought British victory. Big stalwart Seth Warner had accomplished his purpose, inflicting such heavy losses on the enemy that further pursuit of St. Clair and the main Colonial army was impossible. The battle site commands a fine Green Mountain vista of wilderness stretches.

The best account of this battle is in Charles Miner Thompson's *Independent Vermont* (Boston, Houghton Mifflin, 1942).

Hubbardton Battlefield is readily located by a VHS marker, a granite shaft. In the field back of the monument is a slate structure housing the Hubbardton Battlefield Museum (open summers).

HIGH POND SKI AREA (see BRANDON)

HUNTINGTON, 4–C (Chittenden County, 6 m. south of Richmond, alt. 623, pop. 518; 22,174 acres). Richmond stage. Includes: Huntington village, Hanksville and Huntington Center.

HUNTINGTON. The large and busy sawmill at the north end of the village, with its stacks of crude lumber and piles of sawdust, indicates the advantage Huntington has taken of its water-power facilities. Along with lumbering, the dairy business serves as a support of this ordinary-looking upland-valley community. A small triangle centers the village. Huntington Center and Hanksville are small hamlets.

An interesting native son was James Johns (1797–1874), a man of unflagging curiosity and tireless industry. In 1834 he began to pen-print a newspaper, *The Vermont Autograph and Remarker,* which he continued intermittently until three months before his death. He purchased a small hand press, but he used it little, as he could print faster with his quill pen. Johns wrote history, essays, verse, and fiction. The Vermont Historical Society (see MONTPELIER) preserves about 350 items of Johnsiana. Samples from his "Minutes" for 1823–24 and 1860 follow:

1823. "June 15th . . . the F.[reewill] B.[aptist] Qua. M. hold in Richmond, I attended, Saw & heard much noise and wildfire, together with the self contradiction in preaching. peculiar to Arminianism. His Freewill Highness Pope Ziba was present, and tried to see how much noise he could make. . . . September 21d . . . Trespass committed by our worse than no neighbor Roswell Stevens in cutting down a bee tree. on. our land. and taking the honey. The measures which Stevens took to possess himself of the honey, cast. an indelible disgrace upon his name . . . November 10th. Some two legged creatures. who ought to have been abed and asleep. took an old lame horse. (in the night). cut off his ears. mane. and tail. and equipt him with a Side saddle of hemlock boughs. and rope for crupper. and hitched him at Dr Nichols's door. apparently intended for his wife to ride upon. and who. justly fearing he was not sure footed, declined the offer.

> *Twas in the night these subtle wights*
> *This pony did prepare*
> *By taking sheers, to crop his ears*
> *And regulate his hair.*
> *A saddle soft. to sit aloft*
> *Of hemlock boughs they made*
> *That Miss might ride in pompous pride*
> *And hold the horse's head,*
> *The beast so good already stood*
> *In patience at the door*
> *But pride somehow would not allow*
> *Herself on him to soar.'*

1824. "April — on the night between the 5th and 6th John Clark's shop. wherein Taylor had put his potash, was broken open and the potash carried off. Information supposed, or known to have been given the thieves concerning where the potash was given by that most abandoned of all villains. Gail Nichols. the curse and bane of society."

1860. "[December] 21st. Almira Rood died. — It may not be amiss to mention here that the newspapers are ripe at this time with accounts of demonstrations made in South Carolina, of seceders from the Union in which they are abetted and seconded by Georgia, Alabama, Florida and one or two other states, and all this on the foolish contumerous pretext of the election of Lincoln as President!"

First settlers, Jehiel Johns (father of James Johns) and Elisha Bradley, came to Huntington in 1786 from the southern part of the state. The town produced an outstanding soldier in General Emerson H. Liscum, Civil and Spanish-American War veteran, who was killed leading his troops at Tientsin, China, in the Boxer Rebellion.

HYDE PARK, 3–D (Lamoille County, Vt. 100; alt. 660, pop. 1217; 21,210 acres). Includes: Hyde Park village, Centerville and North Hyde Park.

HYDE PARK, named after Jedediah Hyde who made out the charter, is the shire town of Lamoille County. The village is one of simple neatness unmarred by shops or factories. The *Lanpher Memorial Library,* at the junction in the center of the village, is of tan tapestry brick. Directly facing Vt. 100 at its junction with Main St. is the red brick *Courthouse,* ugly and severe. The *Carroll S. Page House* on North Main St. sits well back from the road behind spacious lawns. This house is copied closely from the Henry Wadsworth Longfellow House in Cambridge, Mass. Carroll S. Page, Governor of Vermont (1890–92) and U.S. senator (1909–23), was the largest calfskin dealer in the world, amassing wealth for himself and bringing Hyde Park commercial prominence. Hyde Park pioneers broke the wilderness here in 1787 to make one of the earliest settlements in this region, and here began the white settlers' long friendship with Indian Joe and his squaw Molly, who preceded the white men in choosing this spot for their home (see NEWBURY).

CENTERVILLE is a small settlement.

NORTH HYDE PARK trails along its single street in the narrow valley, a village of plain clapboarded houses and a few stores. The lumber stacks indicate the industrial trend of the community. A calm, pleasant *Millpond* at the north end of the village gives a serene tone to the scene, and diving boards projecting over the placid water show that the pond is popular as a swimming place during the hot months. Novelty products are turned out at the woodworking mills.

HYDEVILLE (see CASTLETON)

IRA, 7–B (Rutland County, Vt. 133 (Horace Greeley Memorial Highway); alt. 830, pop. 218; 11,166 acres). West Rutland stage.

Ira has no village but the old two-story red brick house, now used as a town hall, is the scene of the Rutland County Bar Association's annual

meeting and dinner. The lawyers like the first-rate feed put on by Ira
women.

IRASBURG, 2–E (Orleans County, Junction Vt. 4 and Vt. 58; alt. 947,
pop. 711; 22,498 acres). Orleans stage.

Irasburg, named for Ira Allen, ranges about a large open square on a
level plateau above the Black River valley. The buildings along the north
side of the square, which were razed by a fire, have been replaced by
smaller and more modern structures that still retain an appearance of
drabness. The community depends on lumbering and dairying Once the
shire town of Orleans County, this village was the nucleus about which
the political and business life of the county revolved, and the spacious
square, that today seems so emptily quiet, was generally a busy scene. The
Leach Public Library is a small, neat structure in tapestry brick. A white
high-spired *Federated Protestant Church* graces the southeast corner of the
square. A few uncommon mansard roofs are seen on the dwelling houses,
but the stores and homes ranked around the open square are unattractive
on the whole.

IRASVILLE (see WAITSFIELD)
ISLAND POND (see BRIGHTON)

ISLE LA MOTTE, 1–A (Grand Isle County, Vt. 129; alt. 210, pop. 238;
4476 acres).

ISLE LA MOTTE village rests serenely in scenic beauty and historic
tradition, with clear-lined buildings of stone and brick standing along
gently sloping Main St., and apple orchards stretching to a woodland
background. The people of Isle La Motte are mainly of English and
Scottish descent, all very proud of their peaceful idyllic little island.

What To See and Do

1. *Shrine of St. Ann,* a small chapel and statue in a grove of pines, and
the *Site of Fort Ste. Anne,* is outline marked by cedars and spaced rock
mounds at a commanding point on the lake shore facing across the
water to New York. Here in the calm of shaded lakeside beauty,
French soldiers under Captain de La Motte built a fort in 1666 for
protection against the Mohawks, and here in the essence of Champlain
island loveliness was the scene of Vermont's first, though impermanent,
white settlement. The beauty of Ste. Anne is deepened by history —
the pictures brought to mind of swashbuckling French gallants casting
off uniform-coats to swing axes and ply spades; the solemn-faced Jesuits
in their dark garb; and a garrison of 300 men celebrating mass on this
wilderness isle in the chapel of Fort Ste. Anne, the first mass to be held
in the state. Benedict Arnold, master military strategist on land and
water, anchored his fleet off the western shore of Isle La Motte shortly

before fighting the battle of Valcour Island in 1776. In 1814 Captain Pring landed his British vessel on this shore to protect a position abreast of Little Chazy where supplies were being unloaded; and from this anchorage off La Motte the British fleet went to meet Macdonough in the battle of Plattsburg, September 11, 1814.

2. *Isle La Motte Historical Building* occupies a former schoolhouse of stone structure. Here is the junction with a country road. Left on this road is a *Coral Reef,* running through the pasture of the Gilbert Farm, plainly traceable for nearly a mile. This is said to be the oldest coral reef in the world, and indicates that the territory was once submerged in a sea. Many eminent geologists come here to study the coral formations that bulge through the surface of the pastureland, with a maximum relief of seven feet.

3. *Marble Quarry,* unusually situated on the lake shore, provides Isle La Motte marble, including Champlain Black, French Gray, and Grand Isle Fleuri, extensively used in construction, both interior and exterior. Stone from the quarries on this tiny island has gone into the building of such structures as Rockefeller Center, Brooklyn Bridge, and Victoria Bridge.

ISLE LA MOTTE STATION, former depot on the defunct Rutland Ry.

VAH — Level Land Farm, Harold Kellas and Roy Rowe. Dairy farm (Holstein cattle).

JACKSONVILLE (see WHITINGHAM)

JAMAICA, 9–C (Windham County, Vt. 30; alt. 700, pop. 496) Includes: Jamaica village, East Jamaica and Rawsonville.

JAMAICA lies on Ball Mountain Brook at the eastern point of a triangular valley opening toward the plains of the West River. Hills wedge the village in on three sides. Aloof on the eastern outskirts stands the *Baptist Church,* with a plain front and square belfry. The white *Congregational Church* (1808) is equally undistinguished architecturally. The first minister of the latter church, John Stoddard, was dismissed from his pastorate in 1799 for selling his wife to another man. Mrs. Stoddard, the scandalous and antique rumor relates, was well pleased with the transaction and raised a family for her purchaser. Other public buildings are the churchlike *Town Hall* and the tiny white *Jamaica Memorial Library.* Most of the houses are set close to the street, and the community is irregularly laid out. Lumbering and the manufacture of wood products, are the chief industries.

Ball Mountain (alt. 1745), a solid granite formation, rising north of Jamaica, is more than half enclosed by a great coil of the West River. In 1748, Captain Eleazer Melvin and eighteen scouts were retreating from Lake Champlain by way of Otter Creek and the West River, followed by a band of Abnaki Indians. The scouts followed the West River in its great eastward bend around the bulk of Ball Mountain, and stopped to shoot salmon and replenish their supplies south of the heights. The Indians cut straight through the gap west of the mountain and overtook the little scouting party. The Abnakis opened fire from ambush, and four buckskin-clad scouts went down under the first volley. Stunned by the suddenness of this blow, the other soldiers dived for cover and returned the fire, advancing on the enemy through the tangled brush. Several painted warriors fell before the accurate rifle fire, but after the Indians picked off two more victims, Melvin and his men scattered and fled through the forest toward Fort Dummer. The burial party sent out from the fort found Hayward, Taylor, Dod, and Mann where they had fallen on the bank of the river. The riddled bodies of Petty and Severance were sprawled some distance away in the thicket.

The National Whitewater Canoe Championship races are held here each spring.

EAST JAMAICA (alt. 556) consists of a few houses.

RAWSONVILLE (alt. 1070), a little mountain settlement, is scattered on the uneven plain of the Winhall River surrounded by rough, forested hills. In a fine fish and game region, this hamlet was one of the last settled in Windham County. The *Rawson Monument,* a stone slab ringed by an iron fence, is dedicated to eccentric Bailey Rawson, who founded the settlement, 1810–12. During the Revolutionary War, sixteen-year-old Rawson played the fife for a Massachusetts company. Before settling here, he was a blacksmith, riding horseback from town to town to follow his trade. On one occasion Rawson gathered bags of sorrel seed, which he sold to innocent down-countrymen as "not clover seed." Some people who used the seed in expectance of raising clover, carried the matter to court. Rawson replied: "I sold the stuff for 'not clover seed.' If you can prove that they *are* clover seed, I will pay the damage."

BALL MOUNTAIN DAM RECREATION AREA (east of Vt. 30, north of Jamaica village) has picnic tables, fine view, fishing.

JAY, 1–D (Orleans County, west off Vt. 101, 4 m. north of Troy; alt. 922, pop. 199; 23,040 acres). North Troy stage.

Jay was named for the grantee and statesman John Jay, when the first grant, Carthage, reverted to the state through lack of settlement. This remote little village lies almost in the shadow of Jay Peak, close to the Canadian border.

JAY PEAK (alt. 3861) is the last major summit on the *Long Trail* south of the U.S.-Canadian frontier. A trail leads to nearby Jay village. This is the commanding summit of the Vermont-Canada borderline and northern terminus of the Long Trail. Footpaths twist up the mountainside, a stiff hike, but well marked, to the crest, from which panoramic views sweep over 100 miles in all directions.

On clear days the streets of Montreal are visible from Jay to the north, the Presidential Range of the White Mountains to the east, and Champlain and the Adirondacks to the west in what is one of the most extensive and varied views in eastern America.

JAY PEAK STATE FOREST (4 m. west of Jay village; est. 1954; 1710 acres). Facilities: hunting, foot trails, refreshments, skiing (see JAY PEAK SKI AREA).

JAY PEAK SKI AREA (3 m. south of North Troy or 4 m. north of Troy, junction off Vt. 101. Also 7 m. west of Montgomery Center. Hardtop roads). Double chair lift; 2 T-bar lifts; Pomalift. Capacity: 3000 skiers uphill per hour; 16 trails (22 miles) for novice, intermediate and expert. Certified instructors teach Walter Foeger's Natur Teknik. Ski hut with snack bar. Chalet restaurant. Equipment rental and repairs. Standard and style races throughout season. Mid-December through mid-May skiing on Austrian-designed trails. *Information:* Jay Peak, Inc., North Troy, Vt. Phone: 988-2511. Accommodation offices, North Troy 988-2607.

JEFFERSONVILLE (see CAMBRIDGE)

JERICHO, 3–B (Chittenden County, Vt. 15; alt. 560, pop. 1425; 21,423 acres). Includes: Jericho village and Jericho Center.

JERICHO is a village of well-constructed homes ranked along the level surface of a plain that dips downward at the southern end of the settlement. A few Georgian structures add a touch of dignity and charm to the main street. The *Congregational Church* is a pleasing red brick building, severely plain and gracefully spired, with an old cemetery forming a somber background. The little white *Methodist Church* is less appealing, with the blunt crenellated tower employed widely in religious structures throughout the state. The *Rawson House,* built in 1790, has received accurate restoration, retaining the serene balance and the clear-cut beauty of Colonial buildings expressed in gray brick, with characteristic end chimneys. The *Old Blacksmith Shop,* a low red brick building, was erected in 1810. The main street pitches downhill at the southern end of the village, to a small triangle with a war memorial at the junction of roads. A red brick *Georgian House* stands in trim-lined eminence on a knoll.

The late W. A. Bentley, known as the "Snowflake King," lived in this town for forty-five years and here engaged in his endless photographic studies of snowflakes, which made him the world's foremost authority in that curious field of research. His 5300 microphotos of snowflakes constitute the largest collection of its kind in the world; the flakes, caught on a cold board covered with black velvet, were photographed in Bentley's refrigerated camera room.

Site of the First Settlement in Jericho, marked by a monument commemorating Joseph Brown and family, who hewed a home out of this extreme frontier wilderness in 1774. The Browns were captured here in 1780 by Indian raiders sent out by the British, and taken to Montreal, where they were held until 1783.

JERICHO CENTER is attractively settled around a large elm-shaded square. The *Congregational Church* at the north side of the square was built in 1825, and stands firmly in durable red brick and severe lines, its high white spire rising in clean, towering thrust, visible for miles around. The *Jericho Academy Building,* southeast corner of the square, was also built in 1825, in the white frame style favored at that time for schools. It now serves as a library.

JOHNSON, C–3 (Lamoille County, Vt. 15 and Vt. 100C; alt. 531, pop. 1479; 27,131 acres). St. J & LC/RR. Includes: Johnson village, and East Johnson.

JOHNSON, named for grantee Samuel Johnson, is a small industrial center on the river flats of the Lamoille, where it is joined by the Gihon River from the north. Brown, one of the first settlers in Jericho, originally received this grant, but the Brown family was captured by the Indians, taken to Canada and held prisoners until near the end of the Revolution. In the meantime another grant was made to Samuel Johnson, 1782, and Samuel Eaton opened the settlement two years later. The Lamoille County Grammar School was incorporated here in 1836, and became the *State Normal School* in 1866. The woolen mill is one of the basic industries here; talc manufacturing and woodworking on the river flats constitute the others. The *Masonic Temple,* built in 1855 as a Baptist Church, rests with a quiet mien behind its white-pillared portico.

Johnson State College, formerly the State Normal School (see above), is operated by the state of Vermont (see Education).

EAST JOHNSON is a small settlement and R.D. route out of Johnson.

JONESVILLE (see RICHMOND)
JUDGEMENT RIDGE SKI AREA (see VERSHIRE)
KEENE'S CORNER (see GLOVER)

KENDALL'S CORNERS (see SPRINGFIELD)
KENT'S CORNER (see CALAIS)
KILLINGTON PEAK (see SHERBURNE)
KILLINGTON P.O. (see SHERBURNE)
KILLINGTON SKI AREA (see RUTLAND)
KIMBALL (see WILLOUGHBY under BARTON)

KIRBY, 3–F (Caledonia County, 2 m. east of Concord off US 2), pop. 235; 15,651 acres.

Kirby, a farming region, has no village or trading center of its own. Vermonters remember the town as the home of bachelor Russell Risley, in whom Yankee ingenuity, as applied to domestic economy, reached flood tide. He and his spinster sister worked the home place for many years with a minimum of physical exertion and a variety of labor-saving contrivances. A trapeze slid back and forth on wires between the house and barn transporting Risley to his daily chores; milk pails were carried on similar wires to the waiting sister who handled the emptying end of the process. A self-taught artist and sculptor, Risley created with Renaissance gusto and profusion, covering his barn with charcoal sketches of local notables and carving trees and fence posts.

LAKE CARMI (see FRANKLIN)
LAKE CARMI STATE PARK (see FRANKLIN)

LAMOILLE COUNTY (Area 475 sq. miles. Population 11,027). Shire town: Hyde Park. Organized 1835. Includes: Belvidere, Cambridge, Eden, Elmore, Hyde Park, Johnson, Morristown, Stowe, Waterville, Wolcott.

LANDGROVE, 9–C (Bennington County, 2 m. northeast of Peru off Vt. 11; alt. 1300, pop. 76; 5586 acres). Includes Landgrove village and North Landgrove.

LANDGROVE has no village. Most residents live on a few farms. Samuel Ogden and his family moved to Landgrove about 1930. The former village, about a half-dozen houses, had been abandoned. Ogden, who then had more imagination and brawn than money, took over the abandoned houses. Within a few years he had restored the houses and created a small community by selling the fixed-over homes to friends and friends of friends. The Ogden family entered politics and filled various town offices. They went to the legislature. "Squire" Ogden wrote books and magazine pieces, and established a blacksmith shop in which he was his own blacksmith. Landgrove, once an abandoned hill town, is an example of what can be done with imagination, courage and hard work.

HAPGOOD POND RECREATION AREA, Green Mt. National Forest (2 m. north of Vt. 11). Facilities: camp sites, picnic tables, sandy beach, bathhouse, outdoor fireplaces, sanitary facilities, parking areas, drinking water. This is the most popular recreation area in Green Mountain National Forest.

LARRABEE'S FERRY (see SHOREHAM)
LARRABEE'S POINT (see SHOREHAM)

LEICESTER, 6–B (Addison County, US 7; alt. 359, pop. 551; 11,478 acres). Vt. Transit bus. Includes: Leicester (Four) Corners, Fernville and Leicester Junction.

LEICESTER (FOUR) CORNERS is a little crossroads settlement, with service stations strung like bright red-and-white splotches along US 7, with residents hoping to thrive on travelers. Off the highway stands a brick Nazarene Church among wooden dwellings, softening somewhat the brazen front line of gas pumps, and hinting at the true antiquity of the town, the simple homely houses offering mild rebuke to the commercial front. Settlement started in 1770, was retarded by conflicts between chartists of Leicester and Salisbury. At the first town meeting in Leicester, Jeremiah Parker, seventy-five, first settler, outjumped all comers to win five gallons of brandy. The settlement was broken up during the Revolution, and many Leicester prisoners taken to Canada. John Barker, prominent pioneer, was a veteran of the Revolution and also fought at Plattsburg.

LEICESTER JUNCTION (2.0 m. west of US 7 on unnumbered paved road), once the junction of the Rutland Railroad's main line and Larrabee's Point spur, consists of a few houses huddled around the former railroad depot, now a feedstore, and a dozen houses straggling along the highway. Nearby is an abandoned limestone quarry.

FERNVILLE (Vt. 53) is a half-dozen houses on the south shore of Fern Lake.

LEMINGTON, 1–G (Essex County, Vt. 102; alt. 1011, pop. 112; 20,532 acres). R.D. from Colebrook or North Stratford, N.H. Mail is addressed to Colebrook, N.H.

Lemington is probably best known as the boyhood home of historian Stewart Holbrook (see Writers). There is a burying ground but no stores or churches. Lemingtonites trade across the Connecticut River in Colebrook or North Stratford, N.H.

LEWIS, 2–F (Essex County, Vt. 105, alt. 1711; 21,150 acres). No known residents.

This unorganized town is under the direction of a supervisor residing in nearby Island Pond. There are no roads in Lewis. Travelers wanting to join the "251 Club" — individuals who visit all Vermont towns, cities, grants and gores — will have to visit Lewis either on horseback or afoot.

LEWISTON (see NORWICH)

LINCOLN, 5–B (Addison County, Vt. 17's eastward extension; alt. 971, pop. 481). Bristol stage. Includes: Lincoln village and South Lincoln.

LINCOLN was settled in 1795 by Quakers. The former industrial activity of this community is indicated by the ruins of two old mill-dams; a bobbin factory and creamery are the only remaining industries. *Burnham Memorial Building,* an attractive brick community house, is supported by an endowment of approximately $100,000 left to the town by Walter Burnham, who was born here in 1852. The *Soldiers' Memorial* stands at a highway junction.

SOUTH LINCOLN, a tiny end of the road settlement, served by a Star Route out of Bristol.

LINCOLN-WARREN PASS (Lincoln Gap) is a steep narrow pass cutting through the mountainous wilds with forested slopes towering on all sides. *Lincoln Mountain* (north) is composed of several peaks, one of which, *Mt. Ellen* (alt. 4135), is the third highest in the state. Mt. Abraham, another of its peaks, was known as "Potato Hill" among early settlers, and as such appears in the stories of this region written by Rowland Robinson (see Literature). Scenes from Robinson are brought to mind by these wild forest-clad slopes, where his characters roved with long hunting rifles, and gathered about campfires at night for their inimitable discussions and the telling of tall tales. Rearing high on the south side of the mountain-walled defile are *Mt. Grant* (alt. 3661) and *Bread Loaf Mountain* (alt. 3825). The overshadowing mountainsides are generally wooded with here and there somber gray outcroppings of rock breaking the thick greenery.

The *Long Trail* crosses the highway near the top of the pass (alt. 2424).

By stopping at this point and walking a short way to either side on the Long Trail, vantage-points are attained which reveal views as fine as any in the entire Green Mountain Range — vistas that sweep from the mighty thrust of mountains shouldering the sky over vast forested reaches to open lowland valleys, scenes marked with grandeur. The Champlain Valley in all its picturesque beauty stretches north and south, the lake with its irregular shorelines lying before the Adirondacks.

A magnificent mountain panorama (north) stretches broken green-cloth lines against the horizon, and through a break in the ridge is a glimpse of the Adirondacks, hazily blue in the distance.

This mountain-pass route, the highest in the state, crosses the principal range of the Green Mountains, traversing a wild highland country on the east and the level plains of Addison County on the west, thus combining the rugged beauty of forested heights with the pleasing serenity of broad meadows that sweep toward the waters of Lake Champlain. Of the passes through the central portion of the Green Mountain Range this Lincoln Pass is easily the most scenic. The others have individual merits, but, to the tourist desirous of crossing the mountains in this general region, the present route is recommended for grandeur and scope of outlook. On the Champlain Valley side, the region is rich in connotations of the past from the time of Champlain's visit, the French and Indian Wars, and the Revolution.

LIVING MEMORIAL PARK SKI AREA (see BRATTLEBORO)

LONDONDERRY, 9–C (Windham County, Vt. 11 and Vt. 100; alt. 1400, pop. 898; 18,831 acres). Includes: Londonderry village and South Londonderry.

LONDONDERRY is built along the banks of the West River in a narrow, gully-like valley, hemmed in on the south by forested ridges. Above the dam and gray steel bridge, the river flows in slow smooth retention, darkly placid and deep. The little *Universalist Chapel,* a fairy-story structure, has an old coach lantern hanging on the tiny porch. Londonderry was chartered in 1770 by New York State as Kent, but was confiscated from the Tory proprietors in 1778, and regranted by Vermont in 1780, under the name of Londonderry.

SOUTH 'DERRY, an active village, has industries centered about lumber, woodworking, and dairy products. Here was the northern terminus of the West River RR, only state-owned railroad in Vermont. Now defunct, the line has never justified the $200,000 which was expended on its rehabilitation after the 1927 flood.

Brattleboro–Chester–Manchester stages.

The Londonderry–Jamaica area is a popular winter sports playground.

VAH — Middletown Farm, Edward Janeway. Dairy farm (Guernsey and Holstein cattle).

MAGIC MOUNTAIN SKI AREA (off Vt. 30); 5000-ft. double chair lift with (1000 skiers per hour) 1600-ft. vertical rise; 220-ft. T-bar with 500-ft. vertical rise; 3 large open slopes. Hans Thorner (Swiss and U.S.) Ski School with either small classes or individual instruction. Two-story base chalet with 2 cafeterias. Three-story wing has ski shop with sales, rentals and repairs. Checking department. First aid room. Large sundeck with outdoor dining facilities; 500-car parking area. Ski area village has 15 two-story chalets. Three motel ski lodges. "Learn to Ski Weeks." *Information:* Magic Mountain Corp., Londonderry. Phone: VAlley 4-6373.

LOWELL, 2-D (Orleans County, Vt. 58 and Vt. 100; alt. 996, pop. 617; 33,380 acres). Hyde Park or Newport stage line.

LOWELL was originally granted as Kellyvale, an indication of Irish predominance among the early settlers, of which an element remains, though the French-Canadian immigrants, of whom there has been a steady influx since the turn of the century, now outnumber them. The section of Lowell village that borders the highway is called Lowell Plain, a pleasant plateau upon which are the plain but dignified white *Federated Church* and the Catholic and Protestant burying grounds. The main part of the village lies in the narrow gullylike valley of the stream which once supported busy sawmills and was alive with the droning buzz of steel cutting through wood. This central settlement of one of the largest townships in area in the state now sleeps in a commercial inactivity that seems unlikely to be broken unless the long-projected development of the large asbestos deposits here should become a reality. The French-Canadian families have brought in their own standards and customs, in many ways not unlike those of the earliest settlers, and Lowell's three-sided barrier of mountains helps to preserve them unchanged. Evening gatherings in the general stores are suggestive of the one in Uncle Lisha's shop, pictured in the writings of Rowland Robinson (see Literature).

Vt. 58 runs northwest of Lowell through heavily wooded country, much of the timber being original growth. These are some foothill farms. Between Lowell village and Hazen's Notch the present highway follows quite closely, it is believed, the old Hazen Military Road. *Hazen's Notch* (alt. 1700) is a natural cut in the Green Mountain Range, with sheer rock cliffs rising above the highway in a framework of trees. Here is a marker designating this point as the northern terminus of the uncompleted road that General Hazen built in 1770 for a proposed invasion of Canada. It is believed locally, however, that the road extended a few miles farther, into the township of Montgomery, where traces of an old corduroy road were uncovered many years ago.

The *Long Trail* crosses the highway at the Notch.

LOWER CABOT (see CABOT)
LOWER GRANVILLE (see GRANVILLE)

LUDLOW, 8-C (Windsor County, Vt. 100 and 103; alt. 1064, pop. 2380; 21,763 acres). Vt. Transit bus.

LUDLOW lies Y-shaped in the divergent valleys of the Black River and its tributary Jewell Brook, and is characterized by an industrial virility which originally sprang from the woolen mills, most of which produce reworked wool. The manufacturing of shoddy was introduced after the Civil War to combat the shortage of cloth that existed, and two Black River Valley towns, Ludlow and Springfield (see SPRINGFIELD), were among the pioneers in the field.

Ludlow's loss of its major textile industries has been compensated for by the establishment of a General Electric Company Small Aircraft Engine Parts Plant.

The streets are colored by houses of bright red brick, and *Fletcher Memorial Library* is of red brick facing the small shaded triangle of the green. *Black River Academy,* founded in 1834, is the high school where Calvin Coolidge received his secondary education. The building, in towered red brick, stands on a low hill immediately over the village center. The *Brick House,* prominent at the eastern edge of town, is the home of John Garibaldi Sargent, the boyhood friend whom Coolidge appointed Attorney General in his Cabinet. The very large, homelike, six-chimneyed structure is the only type of house that big "Gary" Sargent could be happy in: solid, spacious, and unpretentious. Ludlow was the home of Abby Maria Hemenway, the prodigious historian who compiled town histories covering the entire state, now available in five volumes totaling 6000 pages.

OKEMO (MT.) STATE FOREST (Ludlow P.O., Vt. 100 and Vt. 103; est. 1935; 4461 acres) is primarily a winter sports area (See OKEMO MOUNTAIN SKI AREA) but the road which once led upward to a parking area may soon be completed to the summit. Foot trail to the summit. Panoramic views of the Green Mountains and the Adirondacks (west and north), White Mountains (east), Berkshire Hills south).

OKEMO MOUNTAIN SKI AREA (off Vt. 103); 5372-ft. top elevation and 1300-ft. base; 5 Pomalifts; 6207-ft. lift with 1540-ft. vertical drop; 3000-ft. lift with 750-ft. vertical drop; 1700-ft. lift with 250-ft. vertical drop. Novice lift; 11 trails for novice, intermediate and expert; 14 acres of open slopes. Ski hut with restaurant at summit and base. Ski shop. Patrol. *Information:* Ludlow-Okemo Assoc., Ludlow. Phone: CAnal 8–5656.

LUNENBURG, 4–G (Essex County, US 2; alt. 844, pop. 1237; 25,882 acres). Includes: Lunenburg village, Gilman and South Lunenburg.

LUNENBURG has the pleasant repose of the upper valley villages, its maple-shaded Green adorned with the almost inevitable Vermont grouping of Civil War monument, cannon, and bandstand. The community cluster of dwellings, small stores, and schoolhouse is enhanced by earlier excellence of line. The old cemetery contains weathered slate markers, some of the inscriptions dating as far back as 1793. Only in sparsely settled Essex County could Lunenburg achieve the rank of second largest township.

Neal Pond is known for its excellent trout fishing.

GILMAN. This company town created by the Gilman Paper interests lies on a hillside overlooking the Connecticut River, its terraced streets lined by identical small white houses. Paternalism has here avoided architectural drabness if not monotony. The company, which employs 500 men and women when in full operation, is the main economic support of Lunenburg township. For 60 years its mills have been busy with Essex County's great timber resources.

SOUTH LUNENBURG, a tiny roadside hamlet, has a general store and a post office.

LYNDON, 3–E (Caledonia County, US 5; alt. 727, pop. 3425; 23,061 acres). CP/RR station. Includes: Lyndon (Corners), Lyndon Center, Lyndonville.

LYNDON (Corners) centers about a sloping bend in the highway. The old stone watering trough that used to mark the corner was removed after a speeding automobile crashed into it. The northern end of the community dips to a level intervale of the Passumpsic.

General William Cahoon House (1800–1805), a sturdy clapboard house, was the first two-story house built in the town, and is now reported to be the oldest house in the community.

LYNDON CENTER (0.7 m. west of Lyndonville; alt. 720, pop. 274). The *Wild Boar Fountain* in the triangle is a copy of the piece by Pietro Tacca that stands in the New Market, Florence. The situation here, on a green shelf over the Passumpsic, is a pleasing one. In the central part of the beautiful cemetery here can be read curious provocative inscriptions in the Ethan Allen tradition, carved by G. P. Spencer (1825–1908), atheist stone cutter. The verses on one side of the stone were so strongly blasphemous that churchly citizens had them obliterated. The old section of the cemetery contains many early tombstones. North of the graveyard are rolling sand dunes, forming a miniature desert unique in Vermont. Reforestation has been undertaken to combat soil erosion here.

Lyndon State College, formerly Lyndon Normal School (1911) with 249 students and 19 teachers, is a state-supported college for the preparation of elementary and junior high school teachers and for general education in the liberal arts. Offers B.S. in education.

Lyndon Institute (1867) is a coeducational college preparatory school. Accommodations for boarding 450 students.

LYNDONVILLE presents its less attractive side on the southern entrance. The business district is concentrated along Depot St., bare and unshaded, but *Powers' Park* gives a cool freshness to the picture, stretching from the village center to the wooded banks of the Passumpsic River. The long wide level main street is residential, running northward between elm trees and comfortable homes. The general impression at the northern end of town is one of rich verdure and heavy foliage. Lyndon was chartered in 1780 to Jonathan Arnold, and named after his son, Josias Lyndon Arnold. Daniel Cahoon, Jr., settled the town in 1788. For a long time Lyndonville was headquarters and terminal for the Passumpsic Division of the Boston & Maine RR, extended here in 1866. It was as a railroad town that Lyndonville reached its peak of prosperity. The imprint left by the many public benefactors whom Lyndonville has been fortunate to have is clearly discernible in the community.

Flanking the entrance to Lyndonville National Bank, Elm St., are bronze reproductions of Donatello's *Il Marzocco* (Lion of the Republic), cast in the original mold. *St. Peter's Episcopal Church,* Elm St., is the architectural work of Henry Vaughan of Boston, with a stained glass chancel window designed by J. & R. Lamb of New York. *People's Methodist Church,* Church St., has "The Children's Window," designed by Miss Jessie Van Brunt.

Cobleigh Public Library, Depot St., a square structure of red brick, contains about 9000 volumes, as well as cabinets of New England birds, Mexican curios, and American and foreign coins and bills. The volumes on art, contributed by Theodore Vail, telephone magnate, constitute the most valuable book collection. Here also is an ancient grandfather's clock, brought to Lyndon in 1798 by Jude Kimball, pioneer settler.

LYNDON OUTING CLUB SKI AREA (0.25 m. east of Lyndonville); 1600-ft. elevation and 800-ft. base; 1500-ft. T-bar lift; 800-ft. electric tow; 20- and 40-meter jumps. Floodlighted open slopes. Ski hut and snack bar. Ski instruction. Ski patrol and first aid. *Information:* Lyndon Outing Club, Box 737, Lyndonville.

MAD RIVER GLEN SKI AREA (see WAITSFIELD)
MAGIC MOUNTAIN SKI AREA (see LONDONDERRY)

MAIDSTONE, G–2 (Essex County, Vt. 102; alt. 875, pop. 78; 16,467 acres). Includes: Maidstone Station.

MAIDSTONE STATION (Maine Central/RR) is a train stop in this thinly settled town which has no stores or churches. Maidstone residents trade across the Connecticut River in North Stratford, N.H.

MAIDSTONE STATE FOREST (North Stratford, N.H., P.O. off Vt. 102 north of Maidstone; est. 1938; 469 acres) includes south shore of beautiful isolated *Maidstone Lake* (alt. 1303). A 5.0 m. approach road (dirt) from Vt. 102 leads through lovely forest of mixed hard and soft woods. Facilities: picnic tables and fireplaces, tent sites, lean-tos, bathing, boating, fishing. Three-mile-long Maidstone Forest is a favorite habitat of the loon whose plaintive cry is a hallmark of a true wilderness.

MANCHESTER, 9–B (Bennington County, US 7, Vt. 11 and Vt. 30; pop. 2753). Vt. Transit bus. Half shire town. Includes: Manchester village, Manchester Center and Manchester Depot.

Manchester *Information Booth:* American Legion Park, Manchester Center (US 7).

Newspaper: Manchester Journal (weekly).

Manchester Village (alt. 694) is the foremost of Vermont summer resorts wearing an air of rich and cultured living. Lying in the shadow of the broad noble heights of *Mt. Equinox* (alt. 3816), the elm-bowered streets of Manchester align historic Colonial structures and fine modern summer homes, set far back from the pavement, their white-pillared porches fronted by smooth-shaven lawns. The sidewalks are of sawed marble slabs. The world of affairs, art, letters, and social registers has invaded Vermont and established here a stronghold, cosmopolitan and exclusive, enhanced by the beauty of the Vermont natural background, but otherwise unrelated to the state.

The first Council of Safety met in Manchester, unofficial capital, and Ira Allen announced his plan to finance Vermont's Revolutionary activities by confiscation of Tory property. Mrs. Abraham Lincoln and Mrs. U. S. Grant were accustomed to spend summers here, and Robert Todd Lincoln, the President's favorite son, died here on the Lincoln estate. Presidents Taft and Theodore Roosevelt were Manchester visitors.

Mark Skinner Library, a memorial to an outstanding early family, stands at the entrance to the village from the north, in buff brick with red tile roof, surrounded by trim lawns. The interior is beautifully finished and contains a fine collection of books.

Burr and Burton Seminary (1829) stands on a hill at the base of Mt. Equinox, an old gray-stone building, austere in its simplicity. The red brick *Gymnasium* is the scene of the Southern Vermont Artists' Exhibition held every summer in August.

Soldiers' Monument, on the narrow village green, topped by the figure of a Revolutionary soldier, honors the fighting men of Vermont and heads the long, scrupulously cared-for main street. Incorporated in the *Equinox House,* a resort hotel, is the wall of a pre-Revolutionary building. The *Hoyt House,* a long, low yellow structure of one story, is dated 1769, and its simple dignity of line authenticates its age, with allowances for restoration.

Site of Seth Warner's Camping Ground (south of the Country Club entrance) slants gently up from the highway; here a regiment under Colonel Warner encamped for a few weeks, after the Battle of Hubbardton and before proceeding to the Battle of Bennington. Recently a soldier's hatchet was found embedded in a tree here, where it had been stuck a century and a half, the tree having grown entirely around it.

Johnny Appleseed Bookshop is owned by poet Walter Hard, author of *The Connecticut River* in the Rivers of America Series.

Charles F. Orvis Company (1856) manufactures what are probably the finest bamboo fly and spinning rods made in America. Bamboo, of the type used in high-quality rods, is no longer obtainable because the Communists have taken over those countries which grow the best bamboo. The Orvis Company has a twenty-year supply of bamboo which is stored in several different sites as a measure against destruction of the entire supply by fire. The Orvis people also operate a store which is frequently called "The Vermont Abercrombie & Fitch."

A *VHS* marker is located in front of the estate of the late *Robert Todd Lincoln,* son of the president, and onetime president of the Pullman Car Company.

Southern Vermont Art Center (west off US 7 in Manchester Village. Follow Art Center signs. Open late May–mid-Oct.) The former 28-room house was converted after its purchase in 1950 by the Southern Vermont Art Center. The Music Pavilion built in 1956 seats 450. The Art Center holds and sponsors several art shows during the season. Concerts, ballet, and other dance-music productions are held in the Music Pavilion. Classes in the dance, sculpture and painting are held regularly. Special classes for children. Details for the current season on the Art Gallery, Study Program and Music Pavilion may be obtained by writing the Director, Southern Vermont Art Center, Manchester, Vt.

Equinox Country Club (Manchester Village, off US 7). 18 holes. Blue tees: 124–517 yds., 6558-yds., par 72. White tees: 114–483 yds., 6039–yds., par 70. Course extends to 6750 yds. for tournament play. U.S. Golf Association rules apply except where modified by local rulings. Facilities: clubhouse, pro, pro shop, bar, lounge.

This is one of the best and most beautiful courses in the Northeast. Playing privileges primarily restricted to guests of the Equinox House, members and guests of members.

The course was constructed during the late 1890's. It has been and still is the scene of many regional and some national tournaments.

Manchester and environs have many excellent restaurants. The *Toll Gate* (off Vt. 11, 4 m. east of the Center) offers cuisine comparable to many first rate New York restaurants. The *Wilburton Inn, Equinox House, Reluctant Panther* and *L'Auberge* (US 7 in Sunderland) offer fine food. The *Quality Restaurant* (Manchester Center) despite its pedestrian name is a popular luncheon rendezvous.

The *Mad Tom Paperback Book Shop* (2 m. north of Manchester Center on US 7) is the state's outstanding paperback book shop.

Skiing

Manchester, a leading ski area, is popular with New Yorkers. *Big Bromley, Snow Valley, Magic Mountain* and *Stratton* are readily accessible. Lodgings for skiiers are available in both Manchester and at the ski areas.

MANCHESTER CENTER (alt. 940) is a forerunner of the beautiful villages to the south. Trim white buildings, clean shady lawns, and multicolored flower gardens ranged along the broad entrance from the north merge agreeably with the immaculate if uninteresting business center at the double-bend of the highway. Manchester Center ushers the traveler into the most worldly section of Vermont, at once the oldest and most smartly modern district in the state, a fashionable resort superstructure over a foundation of historical tradition inseparable from the birth of Vermont. Known as Factory Point until late in the nineteenth century, this village was the industrial nucleus of the town and still retains an air of activity about its business section, though the old industries are dead. The *Colburn House* stands on the site of the first house in the village.

MANCHESTER DEPOT (Vt. 11) lies about the Vt/Ry. tracks. It is primarily a commercial area.

BARNUMVILLE is a rural locality off US 7 and Vt. 11.

Area Points of Interest

The following area points of interest may be reached in approximately 30 minutes driving time:

Mt. Equinox Skyline Drive (May–Oct.)
Bromley Mt. chair lift to summit (June–mid-Oct.)
Summer Theater, Dorset
Summer Theater, Weston
Vermont Country Store, Weston
Bennington Battle Monument
Bennington College Summer Music Festival
Covered bridges, Arlington

VAH — Bryant Farm, Clyde Bryant. Dairy farm and maple products.
VAH — Wilcox Brothers Dairy. Milk and dairy products.

BIG BROMLEY SKI AREA (on Vt. 11 off either US 7 or Vt. 103). Taxi service. Elevation 3260 ft. and 1860-ft. base; 5700-ft. double chair lift with footrests provides express service to summit in 12 minutes. Five J-bar and 1 Pomalift with 17,200 travel. Novice, intermediate and expert trails from summit terminal of chair lift. All trails and slopes reported skiable on 4 inches packed snow. Trails: 7 intermediate and

4 expert. Novice slope with 1 lift. Intermediate slope with 4 lifts and 1 expert with lift. Large parking area. Restaurant capacity 1000. Approved ski school with 40 instructors. Ski patrol. Ski shop with rentals, sales, gifts and repairs. Lounge. *Information:* Big Bromley, Box 368, Manchester Center, Vt. Phone 315.

SNOW VALLEY SKI AREA (8 miles east of Manchester on Vt. 30). Taxi service; 3180-ft. T-bar lift; 1450-ft. Pomalift services; 2 novice slopes. Beginners' rope tow. Trails: 1 novice (2.5 miles), 3 intermediate (3.0 miles) and 2 expert (2 miles). Fifteen acres of open slopes. Ski huts, meals, Ski shop for sales, rentals and repairs. Patrol and first aid. Instruction. *Information:* Snow Valley, Manchester. Phone 92 or 93.

MAGIC MOUNTAIN SKI AREA (see LONDONDERRY)

MAPLE CORNER (see CALAIS)

MARLBORO, 10–D (Windham County, Vt. 9; alt. 1736, pop. 347; 26,435 acres). Brattleboro stage.

Marlboro was named for the Duke of Marlborough. The *Congregational Church* (1932), a simple wooden structure with a seating capacity of 350, duplicates the first Congregational meetinghouse here, which was built in 1819 and destroyed by fire in 1931. On Sunday, June 26, 1748, in the northern part of Marlboro town, Captain Humphrey Hobbs with 40 soldiers from Fort No. 4 at Charlestown, N.H., was attacked by a large band of Indians under a half-breed named Sackett. The soldiers took cover behind tree trunks, boulders, and logs, and poured a scorching fire into the onrushing braves to halt the charge. Failing to carry by direct assault, Sackett deployed his redmen in a half circle to make the advance from tree to tree. The fight lasted four hours. In such a snipers' duel, the superior marksmanship of the whites offset the advantage in numbers that the enemy possessed. Hobbs and Sackett, both famed on the frontier as fearless fighters, knew one another and constantly exchanged taunts and threats. Sackett shouted that if Hobbs refused to surrender, his whole outfit was doomed to torture and the tomahawk. Hobbs roared back a lusty invitation to "Come on in and get us! If you're afraid, Sackett, send your red dogs of hell in after us!" Driven by their furious leader, the Abnaki warriors made thrust after thrust, but each was shattered and repulsed by the sharpshooting riflemen, until the forest floor was strewn with brown bodies. After suffering severe losses in the four-hour engagement, Sackett withdrew his forces, carrying off the dead and wounded. Hobbs lost but three men, Mitchell, Scott, and Green; three other scouts were wounded.

Marlboro College, a small liberal arts school with high scholastic standards, rescued Marlboro town from becoming another "ghost town." The college sponsors the annual Marlboro Summer Music Festival directed by pianist Rudolf Serkin.

MARSHFIELD, 4–D (Washington County, US 2; alt. 1140, pop. 891; 25,783 acres). Vt. Transit bus.

Marshfield was named for Captain Isaac Marsh, who bought the land from the Stockbridge Indians in 1789, the Indians having received the grant from the General Assembly of Vermont in 1782. The village is situated on a sharp-tilted plane above the Winooski valley, and the main street is a long hill dipping in a southwesterly direction. The *Brick House,* facing the small triangle at the north end, dates from about 1820 and is shaded by century-old maples. The wooden *Federated Church,* above the triangle at the crest of the main street, bears the date, 1829. From the church, the highway pitches downward between clapboarded houses and stores to the level bottomlands of the Winooski.

McINDOE FALLS (see RYEGATE)
MECHANICSVILLE (see HINESBURG, Chittenden County)

MENDON, 7–C (Rutland County, US 4; alt. 1000, pop. 461; 23,130 acres). White River Coach Lines. Mendon is a long scattered village, overlooking from its higher level, the distant city of Rutland. This was the home of General Edward Ripley, commander of the Union forces which occupied Richmond in 1865. The view, directly to the west, is broad and very beautiful at sunset.

MIDDLEBURY, 5–B (Addison County shire town, US 7; alt. 366, pop. 5405, includes about 1300 Middlebury college students, village 3788).
Hospital: Porter Memorial.
Bus Depot: Sargent House, Vt. Transit.
VT/Ry (freight only).
Information: Middlebury Official Information Booth (opposite Addison County Courthouse and Middlebury Inn).
Newspaper: Addison *Independent* (Thurs.).
Accommodations: Hotels, motels, cabins, tourist homes.
State Police Outpost: Troop A, Phone DUdley 8–4919.
MIDDLEBURY is a charming college town. To its natural beauties and the appeal inherent in its relics and buildings expressive of the more gracious aspects of early Vermont, the presence of Middlebury College here for more than a century and a quarter has added a patina of intellectualism.

The town lies on both sides of Otter Creek, in the friendly shelter of Chipman Hill on the northeast, and spreads to the gentle slopes that border the valley. The village is centered by the parklike Common, west of which, on narrow Main St., is the compact business district, where stores of the type common to a village of this size alternate with shops that cater to the more sophisticated tastes of town and gown.

Middlebury was granted in 1761, together with Salisbury and New Haven, and received its name from the fact that it lay midway between the other two. Benjamin Smalley was the first settler who came with his family and the first to build a log house, near the southern limit of the township, in 1773. The several families who had joined him by 1778 were in that year forced to evacuate their homes before a raiding party of Indians and Tories. Burying their pewter and all but a few provisions, and bidding farewell to their unharvested crops, the pioneers fled south to Pittsford, then a military post. Not until the spring of 1783 did they begin to return to Middlebury, which during the interval was a Colonial ghost town.

Middlebury College was chartered in 1800, on the foundation of the Addison County Grammar School (1797). The desire for an institution of higher learning among the early settlers, led by Gamaliel Painter, was quickened into decisive action by a visit here in 1800 of Timothy Dwight, president of Yale College and son of the first white child born on Vermont soil. Seldom has an educational institution come into being with such wholehearted support of the community. There was less unanimity, however, on the matter of a choice of location, one faction wanting it east of the river, another, west. The question was settled by competitive bidding in the form of contributions to the college, those who could not make cash offerings giving building materials and labor.

President Dwight pushed the establishment of Middlebury College in hopes its intended religious influence would offset the University of Vermont that had been sponsored by the "ungodly Allens."

Sharry Underwood School of the Dance, located here, is directed by Mrs. Wynn Underwood, a former Broadway musical star.

Industry

Middlebury village might almost be said to rest on a marble foundation, and it was here, in 1803, that the first extensive marble quarrying was begun in the state by Eben Judd, who had discovered the deposits the year before and obtained a lease to "dig" in them for 999 years. The quarries were closed when it became no longer profitable to operate them with modern quarrying techniques. Eventually, the marble mills were shut down.

Isaac Markham discovered, or rediscovered, the method of sawing marble with sand and water and toothless saws that Pliny says was practiced by the ancient Ethiopians and that is still in use today. In 1799–1800, Josiah Nichols, Daniel Pettibone, and Ezekiel Chapman, working together in Nichols's blacksmith shop, discovered a practical method of welding cast steel. Norman Tupper and his associate mechanics, of East Middlebury, evolved the first machinery for the manufacture of doors and window sashes. In the number and scope of its inventions, Middlebury probably ranks second only to Windsor in this state.

Middlebury factories turn out wood products, plastics, and business forms.

Native Sons and Other Notables

Emma Hart Willard (1787–1870), one of the leading pioneers in American female education, began her work when she came here from Connecticut in 1807 to take charge of the Middlebury Female Academy. She married Dr. Willard in 1809 and gave up the school, but in 1814, her husband having suffered financial reverses, she opened the Middlebury Female Seminary as a private institution. Her most famous school, at Troy, New York, was begun in 1821. Emma Hart Willard did more than any other one person to demonstrate that women were capable of mastering the subjects studied by men in schools of higher learning and to secure the establishment of institutions wherein they might study them. Her verse includes one remembered poem: "Rocked in the Cradle of the Deep."

Native sons include: William Slade, governor of Vermont (1844–46) and one of its ablest historical scholars; John W. Stewart, governor of Vermont (1870–72); and Edward J. Phelps. Educated at Middlebury and the Yale Law School, Phelps practiced law here. He was president of the American Bar Association. Cleveland appointed him to be James Russell Lowell's successor as United States Minister to Great Britain. His diplomatic achievements included the settlement of American fishing rights in Canadian North Atlantic waters; the resolution of the Bering Sea fur-seal question; the settlement of the boundary dispute between Great Britain and Venezuela; and the negotiation of an extradition treaty (see ESSEX).

What To See and Do

1. The *Middlebury College Campus,* west of the business section, is a charming parklike area, with many trees shading its rolling surface. The well-spaced buildings are not so homogeneous architecturally as those of some modern campuses, because Middlebury has never had huge sums with which to build a new plant all at once. Its buildings suggest, rather, the history of the enthusiasm with which it was supported in its early years, the depressions through which it subsequently passed, and its recent expansion. Dominant on the western crest of the main slope is *Mead Memorial Chapel* (1917), which translates the lines of a Colonial church into white marble, bulwarking the simple beauty of the design with lasting and almost symbolical strength. *Hepburn Hall* (1916), a men's dormitory in buff tapestry brick, stands beside it. *Painter Hall* (1816), the oldest, is in the tradition of dormitory architecture established by Harvard's "Old Massachusetts." It was given by Gamaliel Painter, who has more right than anyone else to be called the father of Middlebury College, and of whom its students sing:

He left us Painter Hall,
Noblest monument of all.

Starr Hall (1861), a dormitory, completes this harmonious group. The *Egbert Starr Library* (1900, additions 1928) is built in a simple classic style of six varieties of Vermont marble. The pleasant, well-appointed interior is conducive to random browsing or scholarly research. The main library contains more than 100,000 volumes. The Julian W. Abernathy Library of American Literature, in the east wing, is a growing special collection of some 12,000 volumes. The many first editions of American authors include one of the best collections anywhere of Thoreauiana: manuscripts, letters, relics, and first editions of Henry D. Thoreau. North of the older part of the campus is the women's campus, or "the other side of the hill." The two main buildings here are *Forest Hall* (1936), a sandstone dormitory for women, and the *Château* (1925), a large brick and stucco building in the French château style of architecture. Much less elaborate than most examples and copies of this mode, the Château escapes being anomalous by being architecturally appropriate to its functions. During the college year it is used for all French classes and as a women's dormitory. In the summer it houses the French School.

2. The *Congregational Church,* facing the Common from the north, was built in 1806–1809. In its main lines this impressive building resembles the First Congregational Church in Bennington, but the 136-foot tower is more elaborate and graceful in design. The broad façade consists of a central projecting bay with pediment. Over the well-proportioned entrance is a Palladian window typical of much post-Colonial architecture in Vermont. Two arched doorways flank the main entrance. The tower rises in four stages to a delicately detailed eight-sided belfry surmounted by a short spire. Among the finest churches in Vermont, the building is an excellent example of early nineteenth-century architecture. It is based upon a design by Asher Benjamin published in his famous book, *The Country Builder's Assistant.* The interior has a large central dome supported by four Ionic columns. The original plan of the auditorium had the pulpit in the center, surrounded by circular pews.

3. *Sheldon Art Museum,* Main St. (open daily except Sunday, 10–5, June 1 to Oct. 15. Winter hours: Tues. and Thurs., 1–5). This varied collection of curios, relics, and pictures is housed in a three-story brick building dating from 1829, the gift of Henry J. Sheldon. The interior is furnished with early American furniture, china, glass, and utensils. There are exhibits of old maps and newspapers, firearms, Indian relics, and early portraits. On the third story is an authentic restoration, even to a rum bottle, of the room of a Middlebury College student in the early nineteenth century. In an adjacent building is a collection of old tools and vehicles, including the two-seated surrey used by President Monroe during his visit to Middlebury.

4. The *Wainwright House,* Court St., was built by Gamaliel Painter in 1807. It is an excellent example of Federal architecture, its simple, strong main lines relieved by detailed decorations. The roof balustrade is typical. Especially noteworthy is the intricate interlacing of the carved frieze, a striking addition to a classic background of a motif in the Adam tradition, that could be properly executed only in wood.

5. The *Community House* (open to inspection), corner of Main and Seymour Sts., was built in 1816 by Horatio Seymour, United States Senator from Vermont, 1821–33. It is of yellow-painted brick, with a hooded entrance, roof balustrade, and gable ends projecting above the roof incorporating the four end chimneys.

VAH — Champlain Valley Apiaries, Charles Mraz. Honey production and processing.

Area Points of Interest

The following area points of interest may be reached in the approximate driving time listed:

(30 *minutes*)
Branbury State Park and Lake Dunmore (see BRANDON)
D.A.R. State Park & Lake Champlain (see ADDISON)
Gen. John Strong Mansion (see ADDISON)
Lake Champlain Bridge (see ADDISON)
(45 *minutes*)
Burlington City (see BURLINGTON)
Fort Ticonderoga, N.Y. (see SHOREHAM)
Lincoln-Warren Pass and Long Trail (see LINCOLN)
Rutland City (see RUTLAND)
Shelburne Museum (see SHELBURNE)
Ski Areas of Pico-Killington (see RUTLAND)

EAST MIDDLEBURY (Vt. 125 off US 7 south of Middlebury; alt. 474; stage from Middlebury) is one long street. Located here is the *Waybury Inn.* The late Robert Frost, summer resident of nearby Bread Loaf in Ripton, occasionally walked here for dinner. One of Vermont's few secondhand bookstores is operated and owned by Miss Harriet Proctor.

MIDDLEBURY COLLEGE GOLF CLUB; 9 holes. Range: 140–472 yds.; par 36. Hilly and lightly wooded terrain. Facilities: clubhouse, golf shop, pro, caddies. No dining facilities. Open to visitors 8 A.M. to dusk.

MIDDLESEX, 4–D (Washington County, US 2 and Vt. 100; alt. 560, pop. 770; 22,651 acres). Vt. Transit bus. Includes: Middlesex village and Middlesex Center.

MIDDLESEX village is set on a hummock in the valley. Stone rip-rapping on the riverbanks by CCC workers has prevented serious erosion at the bend in the river above the village. The white *Community House* and the white *Methodist Church* with its red roof stand south of the highway. The little *Depot* faces across the railroad tracks to a sidehill cemetery, beyond which is the abrupt rise of hill spurs.

First settler Thomas Mead tramped up the wilderness valley to this spot in 1783. Mead's feat of shooting three bears in one forenoon gave him the reputation of a master hunter.

MIDDLESEX CENTER is a few houses spread along an unnumbered road north of its junction with Interstate 89 and US 2.

MIDDLETOWN SPRINGS, 8–B (Rutland County, Vt. 140; alt. 887, pop. 382; 13,587 acres).

MIDDLETOWN SPRINGS, a famous health resort of the late nineteenth century, shows obvious decline. Only one of the four churches is used. Numerous empty houses line the streets of this tiny crossroads village which still retains a rural charm. Middletown's springs of iron and sulphur brought visitors from all over the U.S.

MILES POND (see CONCORD)
MILL VILLAGE (see RUTLAND)

MILTON, 3–B (Chittenden County, US 7; alt. 320, pop. 2020; 27,804 acres). Vt. Transit bus and CV/Ry. Includes: Milton village, Checkerberry village, Miltonboro and West Milton.

MILTON, named after the poet, John Milton, lies in the Lamoille Valley, in the heart of one of the finest dairying districts in the state. A green iron bridge over the Lamoille leads into the small business center with its brick buildings and Civil War Monument. A residential street climbs to a low pleasant plateau above the valley, and here is the *Milton Public Library* housed in late nineteenth-century brick. A large cooperative creamery constitutes the chief industry, drawing its members from several neighboring towns and handling great quantities of milk from the extensive dairy farms of the region. The southern end of the village street lies under a canopy of spreading elms.

SANDBAR STATE PARK (Milton R.D. 1, US 2; est. 1933; 20 acres) is where the Sandbar Bridge crosses from the mainland to Grand Isle County. Facilities: picnic tables and fireplaces, tent sites, camp trailer sites, bathing, boating, fishing, refreshments.

MOLLY STARK STATE PARK (see WILMINGTON)

Country horseback riding is a popular sport

Vermont Development Department

Lake Bomoseen near Rutland

Left, above: Groton State Park
Vermont Development Department

Left, below: Scenic Mt. Mansfield is the backdrop
for Barre's golf course. *Vermont Development Department*

A typical Long Trail shelter. *Vermont Development Department*

Right, above: Skiing Vermont's winter wonderland
Vermont Development Department

Right, below: Woodstock — beagles for bunnies
Arthur Griffin

Wallingford auction. *Aldo Merusi*

Left: Horse-pulling at the Tunbridge World's Fair
Arthur Griffin

. . . and a cattle parade
Claire Griffin

Hartford — spring fishing. *C. M. Abbott, Foto/Find*

MONKTON, 4–B (Addison County, 4 m. south of Hinesburg off Vt. 116; alt. 533, pop. 551; 21,376 acres). Bristol stage. Includes: Monkton Ridge, East Monkton and Rockville.

MONKTON RIDGE, the principal village in Monkton town, is one street lying along a narrow ridge. Grand views are obtained of the Adirondacks to the west and of the Green Mountains to the east. The principal industry is dairying.

MONTCALM LANDING (see ORWELL)

MONTGOMERY, 2–D (Franklin County, Vt. 118; alt. 533, pop. 876; 30,846 acres). East Berkshire stage. Includes: Montgomery village and Montgomery Center.

MONTGOMERY is a postal and trading center, its well-shaded streets radiating from a highway three-corners. The first settler was Captain Joshua Clapp, a Revolutionary soldier who came here in 1793. William B. Clapp, born in Montgomery, was the first man to can meat successfully in this country. At one time the town specialized in the growing of fine timothy grass seed for exportation, but its agriculture now, as in most Franklin County towns, is centered around the dairying industry.

West of Montgomery village the land becomes even more level, the farms larger and more prosperous-looking, with well-kept, modern buildings. The most interesting architectural features of this immediate section, however, are the numerous covered bridges that span Trout River as it interlaces the road between Montgomery and East Berkshire.

MONTGOMERY CENTER is a quiet residential village and trading center, one of two in this fine agricultural township. Trout River, which, as its name implies, is a fine fishing stream, is seen here.

MONTPELIER, 4–D (Washington County, US 2, Interstate 89 and Vt. 12; alt. 523, pop. 8,782).
Information: State House lobby.
Railroad Depot: Barre & Montpelier/RR (freight only), CV/Ry (passengers) near State House.
Bus Depot: Vermont Transit.
Airport: Barre-Montpelier (Berlin) Northeast Airlines (Boston-Burlington).
Accommodations: Hotels, motels, tourist cabins, lodging houses.
Newspaper: Times-Argus (daily except Sunday).
Radio Station: WSKI (1240 kc.).
Hospital: Heaton.

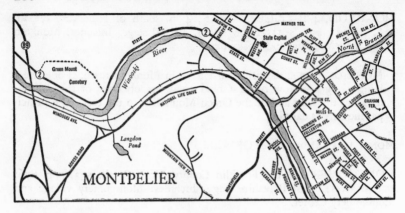

Schools: Grammar, junior and senior high and parochial.
College: Vermont Junior College.

MONTPELIER, the State Capital, was established as such in 1805, when
the legislature probably had in mind merely a convenient valley site near
the geographical center of the state. It was a happy choice, for this small
gap city on the main pass through the Green Mountains is cupped in
wooded hills and lines the banks of peaceful streams, thus properly representing the state of valley towns. The granite State House stands domi-
nantly above State St., squarely backed by one wooded hillside and facing
another across the narrow valley. Thus, close-guarded and confined, its
clean Doric simplicity emphasized in native stone, this capitol has for
Vermont something of the symbolic character which Edinburgh Castle
holds for Scotland. From nearby hill roads in summer, the gold dome,
gleaming through thick greenery, alone reveals the presence of a city.

Three principal streets follow the Winooski River and its tributary,
North Branch. Generations of school children were taught to chant the
name of the Vermont Capital as "Montpelier on the Onion River," by
which name the watercourse was known until Vermonters reverted to the
Indian word for onion, Winooski. Main, State, and Elm Sts. are the
arteries from which unplanned side streets diverge to climb the hillsides
banking the valley. The shopping section of Main St., with its crowded
brick and wooden buildings, a grain elevator towering over Clothespin
Bridge, and the buff bulk of City Hall reared above the squat brick fire
station, is much like the business district in any town of comparable size.
The upper reaches of Main St., however, have the dignity and charm of
gracious homes set back under great elms in the best residential tradition,
enhanced by the graceful ascendancy of church spires.

State St., heterogeneously lined with old and modern structures, marked
by the three imposing edifices of Capitol Square, is the heart of Montpelier. Here the life-insurance offices lie in the shadow of the State

House, embodying the two fundamental forces that have built the city. The smooth sweep of terraced lawns rising to the elm-shaded dignity of the Capitol is flanked on one side by the severely simple Supreme Court Building and on the other by a state office building. High on the hilltop back of the State House, the skyline is sentineled by the picturesque watchtower of Hubbard Park.

Elm Street, the third main thoroughfare, slants off State and runs parallel to the North (Worcester) Branch, progressing from a row of shabby wooden houses, set on stonewall foundations built directly up from the water's edge, to a more pleasant residential section. Tree-lined streets branch irregularly to slant along hillsides and spread on summits, with homes set at all levels. In general the domestic architecture of the city is mixed and unrelated, with little Colonial color, yet many of the homes have dignity, and a certain unpretentious charm.

Closely interwoven in Montpelier's financial, economic, and social pattern are two prime strands — state affairs and the life-insurance business. At noontime and at four o'clock when the state offices and the insurance offices turn a flood of humanity into State Street, the city fairly swarms with a brief punctual life, that swiftly subsides to leave the streets quiet and empty.

Settlement

Colonel Jacob Davis, Revolutionary veteran and leader among the pioneer settlers, named the town after the French city, Montpellier (by analogy, *mont* — hill; *peler* — to strip, make bald). It is sometimes thought that the presence of a bare hill looming over the site inspired this choice of name, but it is doubtful if the translation figured in Davis' selection, for he elsewhere demonstrated his fondness for French names (see CALAIS). In 1788, with ringing axe blade, Colonel Davis cleared land along the North Branch and down the Onion River. Court St., which today leads to the east portal of the State House, was the first road laid out by Davis and his followers. In the fall of 1807, State St. was opened between fields of waving corn, and the foundation of the original Pavillion Hotel was laid to house members of the legislature. The first State House was occupied in 1809. As some old historian has said: "There was manifested some degree of hope and courage by the people of Vermont, when they named this spot in the heart of the hills and depths of the forest as the place of making laws."

The situation of Montpelier, on converging main roads at a junction of watercourses, made the town an important trading-center from the start.

In 1827, enterprising citizens started drilling for salt — until, after penetrating through layers of slate limestone to a depth of eight hundred and fifty feet, the drill stuck and the venture was abandoned, a failure. The development of the granite industry proved a very important factor in the city's growth, and brought in a large foreign element of stoneworkers, who live chiefly in the Barre Street district, adjacent to the long gray granite sheds on the flats of the Winooski at the eastern edge of Montpelier.

In November, 1927, flood waters roared in yellow torrents through Montpelier streets, sweeping to second-story heights in ravaging progress. The city was shut off from the outside world and suffered immense property losses and damages. Recurrence of this disaster in 1936 was prevented by the federal government dams at Wrightsville and East Barre.

What To See and Do

1. *The Capitol,* State St. The first State House, designed by Sylvanus Baldwin, was an odd three-storied wooden structure and served its first session of the legislature in 1809. This crude building sufficed until 1836, when it was replaced by a beautiful Capitol of Barre granite, designed by Ammi B. Young. The magnificent Doric portico, modeled after the Temple of Theseus in Athens, is retained in the third and present structure and remains the most striking architectural feature. Constructed of native Vermont granite, its design exemplifies the simplicity of the Greek Revival mode. Its solemn dignity lightened by the gilt dome, its clear lines etched against the green curtain of a hillside, the Capitol rises above State Street, a fitting embodiment of the solid strength of a rugged state and its people. The interior of the second building was destroyed by fire in 1857, but the portico and granite walls withstood the flames. Renovations on the present State House were completed in 1859 by J. R. Richards. The edifice follows the general style and proportions of its predecessors, but stands larger and higher, a central structure with two wings, in the form of a Greek cross. The gleaming dome, visible for miles around, is leafed with pure gold and surmounted by a statue of Ceres, Goddess of Agriculture, the work of Larkin Goldsmith Mead (see Artists). This same Vermont sculptor made the marble statue of Ethan Allen, which stands within the portico and represents Allen demanding the surrender of Ticonderoga. On the other side of the portico is a brass cannon captured from the Hessians in the battle of Bennington.

The colonnaded façade is fronted by tall elms shading the broad smooth lawns that descend to State St. Flanking the third terrace are two steel Krupp guns taken from the Spanish cruiser *Castilla,* sunk in Manila Bay, May 1, 1898, by the guns of Dewey's fleet. The lobby of the Capitol is stately and serene, with tessellated marble floor, Ionic columns, ornate hand-carved woodwork, and coffered panels in the ceiling. The walls are hung with portraits of Coolidge, Admirals Clark and Dewey, and memorials to other famous sons of Vermont. Mead's bust of Lincoln occupies a central place facing the main entrance. Along with Representatives' Hall and the Senate Chamber, the usual state offices are housed in the building. The Hall, treated in the Corinthian order, is semicircular in plan with the rear wall serving as a background for the dais of the Speaker's chair. The Chamber, the finest room in the building, and in the State, is graced by a gallery supported by classic columns. In the Reception Room to the Governors' Suite, a large painting by Julian Scott depicts the Old Vermont Brigade in action at Cedar Creek (Civil War). An ancient carved English clock (c. 1720) stands in an opposite corner, and portraits of former governors line the walls. The second-floor lobby contains the battle flags of Vermont regiments in the Civil, Spanish, and World Wars, with silver plaques listing the engagements in which they were carried. Here also is a portrait of Judge Daniel P. Thompson, author of the *Green Mountain Boys,* painted by Thomas Waterman Wood, Montpelier artist.

2. *Supreme Court Building,* State St. This severe gray structure of Barre granite stands at the eastern edge of the Capitol lawn, its clear plain lines at once harmonizing with and accentuating the eminence of the State House.

3. *State Administration Building,* formerly the national headquarters of National Life (Insurance) Company, now houses various state departments including the Highway Department. The building is a dignified and impressive six-story structure of gray Rock of Ages Memorial granite, with an interior finished in Vermont marble.

4. Vermont Historical Society Museum (admission free) first floor of the former National Life Insurance Company of Vermont's office building.

The Vermont Historical and Antiquarian Society was incorporated at Barnet in 1838, through the efforts of Henry Stevens, and moved to Montpelier in 1851, where it occupied a room in the Capitol for many years. The modern name was adopted in 1857. The museum contains an unusually fine genealogical and town history library, an excellent collection of geological specimens, exhibits of stuffed animals and birds, fascinating displays of old historic weapons, uniforms, tools, coins, relics, and manuscripts.

Unusual items include the following: the Bennington Declaration; the works of Royall Tyler, author of "The Contrast," the first professionally staged comedy written in America; the sword used by Lord Byron in Greece; a full-length portrait of Washington, a rather remarkable copy of a Stuart; the first geographical globes made in America, by James Wilson.

5. *Pavilion Hotel,* State St. The original hotel, which entertained Lafayette in 1825, was built (about 1807–1808) to accommodate the legislature, and the present Pavilion, constructed in 1876, still furnishes quarters for the members and remains practically a state institution. The present hotel occupies the same site, and is roughly modeled after the original, although a great deal larger. The appearance and atmosphere of the huge rambling red brick structure, with its white double porches and mansard roof, are reminiscent of the taste and politics of the General Grant era.

6. *Washington County Court House,* State St., erected in 1832, is a long red brick structure with a white-pillared portico and clock tower, in the post-Colonial tradition of public-building architecture. The clean contrast of red and white and the trimness of line add much to the character of State Street. The old courtroom retains its original design, and the

fireplaces, which once heated the building, remain as ornamental features in every room. The original Bulfinch-style tower, destroyed by fire in 1879, was replaced by the present one, which is bulky and decidedly inferior.

7. *Christ's Church*, State St. (1867), across from the courthouse, built of granite in the Victorian Gothic style, tempers the complex nature of State Street with a religious note.

8. The *Chester Wright House* (private), 159 State St., built in 1809 by Montpelier's first minister, has been carefully restored and stands on an elevation over the western end of State St., facing the Winooski River. A large white house topped by a huge central chimney and surrounded by great elm trees, its modern additions conform to the original lines, so that the whole structure is a pleasing architectural unit.

9. The *Dewey House* (private), State St., birthplace of Admiral George Dewey, the hero of Manila, is a simple wooden house of a story-and-a-half with a steep-pitched roof. In this modest home, originally standing almost in the shadow of the Capitol but since moved westward on State St., Dewey was born in 1837. After graduating from Norwich and Annapolis, he served with Farragut's fleet at the capture of New Orleans (Civil War), and later distinguished himself in the attack on Fort Fisher. In 1897, when trouble with Spain became imminent, Dewey was given command of the Asiatic squadron and eventually dispatched to Manila. On April 30, 1898, Dewey steamed his flagship *Olympia* into Manila Bay at the head of the American squadron and proceeded to wreck the Spanish fleet anchored there, without loss of a single American life. The Spanish boats were all sunk, burned, or deserted, and the shore batteries were silenced. George Dewey became a great national hero.

10. *Bethany Congregational Church*, Main and School Sts., built in 1867 of reddish-brown sandstone, is said to be one of the finest examples of Gothic architecture in the state, and a direct copy of an English original.

11. The *Kellogg-Hubbard Library*, Main St., a square solid building of rough-surfaced granite with superimposed loggias in the entrance pavilion.

12. The *Davis House* (private), 91–93 Elm St., the first frame house in Montpelier.

13. The *Wood Gallery of Art*, 94 State St., was established in 1895 by Thomas Waterman Wood (1823–1903), the best of nineteenth-century Vermont painters, in cooperation with Professor John W. Burgess of Columbia.

The spacious main gallery is, rightly, above all else a memorial to the talent of Wood himself, and is dominated by his self-portraits and his genre paintings of nineteenth-century American — sometimes specifically Vermont — life. In addition, Wood was a copyist, and his many copies (one critic has called them "translations") of the great painters of the past, particularly of Rembrandt van Rijn are done with a distinction and a reverence that capture much of the beauty as well as the inner meaning of the originals. Wood became President of the American Water Color

Society in 1878 and President of the National Academy of Design in 1891. His well-known Negro painting "The Contraband, Recruit and Veteran," is hung in the Metropolitan Museum.

The Wood Gallery is more than a memorial to one man, however. In recent years the trustees have purchased, as extensively as their funds permitted, representative canvases of the best contemporary Vermont painters, including Lillie, Schnakenberg, Lucioni, and Meyer. In time this section of the gallery should become the best permanent collection of paintings, watercolors, and etchings executed by Vermont artists, and interpretive, in part at least, of the scenic and social background of the state.

14. *Athenwood* (private; visitors welcome), Northfield St., a brown churchlike structure of the Swiss chalet type, the summer home of Thomas Waterman Wood, stands high on a ledge on the southern outskirts of the city, overlooking the Winooski River. The unusual lines of the building and the eminence of its position make it an outstanding landmark. The name Athenwood, engraved on the front door, was given in honor of Mr. Wood's wife, whose name, Minerva, suggested the Greek synonym, Athena. Built before 1850, the peak-roofed house was designed by Mr. Wood himself and contains six rooms of odd and angular shape. Close by, the artist erected a small studio in the same style of architecture, and there some of his best painting was done.

15. National Life Insurance Company Building, National Life Drive (off Northfield St., Vt. 12 or State and Winooski Ave., US 2). National Life Insurance Company of Vermont, founded by Dr. Julius Dewey, father of Manila Bay hero Admiral George Dewey, is the 9th oldest and 23rd largest life insurance company among the nation's 1400 life insurance firms. The building, one of the most beautiful contemporary structures in the state, is situated high on a hill overlooking Montpelier and the Winooski valley. There is a magnificent view of the Green Mountain range. The building has a mural fifty feet long and eight feet high by noted American artist Paul Sample depicting major events in the state's three and one-half century history. The building is open Mondays through Fridays (8:00 A.M.–3:30 P.M.) throughout the year; free guided tours are available May 1 through October 31.

VAH — Morse Farm, Sydney and Harry Morse. Dairy farm and maple products.

MONTPELIER LODGE OF ELKS #924 AND COUNTRY CLUB (2 m. east of city on US 2);9 holes. Range: 194–520 yds; par: 35 (men), 38 (women). Hilly terrain. Facilities: clubhouse, golf shop, food. Greens fee, $2 daily. Open to visitors from 10 A.M. to dusk.

MORETOWN, 4–C (Washington County, Vt. 100; alt. 620, pop. 788; 23,348 acres). Moretown is well barricaded by the lumber stacks and log piles that loom along the Mad River. Vibrant with the whine of saws and flavored by the smell of raw lumber, Moretown is a fitting introduction to a section dominated by the lumber industry. A neat high school building of white-painted wood is the most attractive structure on Main St. The first "pitches" here were probably made by Haseltine and Munson around 1790. The early settlers were frequently molested by bears and wolves, many of which were shot in the vicinity. In 1830 the terrific general flood that swept the State, tore through this valley destroying lives and property.

VAH — Bis-May Farm, Everett Maynard. Dairy farm (Holstein cattle).

MORGAN, 1–E (Orleans County, Vt. 111; alt. 1384 pop. 260; 18,415 acres). Newport–Island Pond stage. Includes: Morgan village and Morgan Center.

MORGAN sprawls in barren rusticity around a simple white *Methodist Church* and a general store on the easy sloping hillside above Lake Seymour. Originally called Caldersburgh, this sparsely settled village was founded around 1800 in an outlying wilderness region of good fishing and hunting. The frontier aspect is still much in evidence.

MORGAN CENTER forms a ragged crescent of crude wooden houses and primitive stores at the northeastern corner of the lake shore. This rude outlying frontier settlement seems far removed from the modern world, and some of its inhabitants show a tendency to regard all "outsiders" with distrust. The setting of the lake, in a broken wooded terrain against mountain horizons, has a wild, barren type of beauty, but the little village itself is interesting only as an example of hinterland settlements that still exist in rural Vermont.

Lake Seymour (1723 acres) lies enclosed by an irregular wooded shoreline against a backdrop of forested hills, dominated by a sharp wooded knob on the immediate southern shore. A long beach stretches across the northern end of the lake beside the highway. Seymour is noted for its fishing, but has been developed very little as a resort.

MORRISTOWN, 3–D (Lamoille County, Vt. 15A and Vt. 100; alt. 681, pop. 3347; 29,292 acres). Vt. Transit bus and St. J & LC/RR. Includes: Morrisville, Morristown Corners and Cady Falls.

MORRISVILLE is sprawled along a terrace above the Lamoille River and clouded with the smoke of industry, its business enterprises being concentrated in lumber and dairy products. The river flats at the northern end of the village, hold long, drab, factory sheds overhung with smoke from the tall stacks of Plant 4 of the Atlas Plywood Corporation. The long Main St. with its brick business section is distinguished only by the handsome and imposing *People's Academy* building which faces the street from a commanding rise at the head. This is a long, rectangular, flat-roofed, two-storied structure of red brick, with granite facings and portico, fronted by a circular cement drive. It is excellently equipped, including an observatory.

The first academy in the town was incorporated in 1847, and was for several years called "Poor People's Academy," the reason for this being that the wealthier families had been sending their children to schools even as distant as Burlington that they might receive more adequate instruction. The present building was given to the town by Alexander H. Copley (1929), a native son who was financially successful in real estate and chain drugstore ventures. To his philanthropy Morrisville is also indebted for the *Copley Hospital,* located on a plateau southeast of the village. This is a rambling white structure of two buildings connected by a passageway, with a porch at the front, surmounted by a balcony. The location is ideal for an institution of this kind.

Morrisville is nationally known as one of the half-dozen best examples of municipal ownership of public utilities. Wise management has preserved for the citizens the advantages of plentiful local power supply, and the municipal electric light and power company (which operates two plants) has been an outstanding success for the past twenty years. Not only have the rates been kept at a consistently low level, but the profits have paid village taxes since 1934. Morrisville's fine display of cement streets and many other civic improvements were financed by these profits derived from selling electricity at reasonable rates on a cooperative basis.

Newspaper: Morrisville (weekly) *News and Citizen.*

MORRISTOWN CORNER, a tiny corner of Morristown, has a store and nearby houses.

Cady Falls is site of artificial dam which creates Lake Lamoille.

COPLEY COUNTRY CLUB (within village limits); 9 holes. Range: 160–523 yds; par: 33 (men), 38 (women). Flat open terrain surrounded by woods. Facilities: clubhouse, pro shop. No food. Restaurant nearby.

MOSCOW (see STOWE)

MT. HOLLY, 8–C (Rutland County, Vt. 103 and Vt. 155; alt. 1540, pop. 517; 29,338 acres). Vt. Transit bus. Includes: Mt. Holly village, Belmont, Bowlsville, Healdville, Mt. Holly Station and Summit.

MT. HOLLY, a small cluster of wooden buildings on the slope of an upland plain, surrounded by stone-walled fields and outlying farmsteads. The open heights are breezy and fresh, with a "top of the world" feeling. The surrounding mountains, heaped and piled against the horizon on all sides, seem but little higher than the sloping plateau of this settlement. The land, cleared by the ringing axes of early settlers, is fine for grazing. Little cultivation is attempted.

BELMONT (alt. 1840), formerly called Mechanicsville, is located in a depression of the highlands at the southwest corner of *Jackson Pond.* Belmont traditionally claimed the highest elevation of any village in the state. For years the town's representative in the state legislature boasted that he came from Mt. Holly, "where the church steeple points nearest to God!" A recent survey, however, revealed that both Windham and Woodford are higher in altitude than Belmont, Woodford being the highest village in Vermont. The mildly discredited Belmont steeple adorns the slate-gray *Federated Church* on a knoll in the center of the town. A maple-guarded stone wall flanks the Main Street, and the whitewashed brick *Georgian House,* with end chimneys and recessed windows, has been marred but not wholly spoiled by a porch addition. The long plain I.O.O.F. Hall (left above the village) was originally a toy factory, contributing much to the financial stability of the little community. A remote highland air and sequestered peace pervade Belmont; these characteristics, with the quiet waters of Star Lake, attract a few summer folk.

BOWLSVILLE (alt. 1300), a little group of homes beside the highway in Mt. Holly Town, received its name from the factory which once made wooden bowls and other articles of wooden ware here.

HEALDVILLE (alt. 1432) is a small settlement with a post office and general store. G. A. Crowley's famous Vermont cheese is manufactured here.

SUMMIT, highest point on the former Rutland RR (alt. 1415). This lonely outpost was the scene of one of the most important events in the history of transportation in Vermont. Here, the last spike was driven, completing the line, and winning the race between the Rutland and the Vermont Central for the first train from Boston into Burlington. On December 18, 1849, to celebrate the victory, trains from Burlington and Boston, with directors and other officials on board, met here at the summit of the pass, were united and drawn by a flag-decorated engine named Mt. Holly. With speeches and cannon salutes, water from Boston Harbor was mingled with water from Lake Champlain, and less symbolic liquid flowed freely from a barrel of New England rum. A prior incident in the construction of the line near Summit had been the uncovering by workmen of several bones, teeth, and tusks which Louis Agassiz pronounced to be those of an extinct species of elephant (doubtless buried by some prehistoric Democratic landslide). Mt. Holly's fragmentary elephant is now on display in the Vermont Historical Society Museum, Montpelier.

MT. TABOR (Rutland County, east off US 7 at Danby; alt. 700, pop. 165; 23,995 acres). Danby stage.

This hill town lies within the *Green Mountain National Forest.* Its primary industry is the collection of ferns for florists. There is also a gristmill and a general store. The country is wild and mountainous, excellent for hunting and fishing.

NEW BOSTON (see NORWICH)
NEW DISCOVERY RECREATION AREA (see GROTON STATE FOREST)

NEW HAVEN, 5–B (Addison County, US 7 and Vt. 17; alt. 454, pop. 922; 24,059 acres). Vt. Transit bus and VT/Ry. Includes: New Haven village, New Haven Junction, New Haven Mills, and Brooksville.

NEW HAVEN (0.6 m. east on Vt. 17 off US 7 at New Haven Junction), known locally as New Haven Street, the principal village of the town, consists of a single street running north and south across Vt. 17. Early New Haven settler Solomon Brown was reported to have been the first Minuteman to drop a Lobsterback on Lexington Green. The most notable native son was probably Sir Curtis Miles Lampson, deputy governor of the Hudson's Bay Company, who was knighted by Queen Victoria for his services as vice-president of the company that laid the transatlantic cable.

NEW HAVEN JUNCTION (US 7 and Vt. 17) is a small settlement on the Vermont Railway, an irregular blotch on the valley floor. *Lathrop's Gun and Sporting Goods Store* is a good place to secure information about local game and fish conditions.

West of New Haven Junction, Vt. 17 runs along the northern base of *Snake Mountain,* (alt. 1271), sometimes called Grand View Mountain. The lookout tower at its summit commands a view described by Bayard Taylor, writer and traveler, as unexcelled by anything in Europe. From that elevation the long sweep of Lake Champlain is seen lying before its background of Adirondacks on the west, while to the east stand the Green Mountains in superb array.

Spring Grove Camp Ground (3.0 m. west of New Haven Junction on Vt. 17 and 1.3 m. north on unnumbered road) was once the scene of stirring old-time camp meetings and fanatical revival services, drawing large crowds from many area towns. Wild-eyed, arm-swinging, hollering speakers strove with fiery words to whip their audiences into religious fervor.

NEW HAVEN MILLS is more of a locality than a settlement.

BROOKSVILLE is a few houses along a section of US 7 which has been by-passed with a new section of highway.

NEWARK, 2–F (Caledonia County, 3 m. off US 5 above West Burke; alt. 700, pop. 151; 22,047 acres; P.O. address West Burke). This hill hamlet with no stores or churches has a State Fish Hatchery (open to public).

NEWBURY, 5–E (Orange County, US 5 and US 302; alt. 418, pop. 1452). B & M/RR. Includes: Newbury village, Boltonville, Newbury Center, South Newbury (Conicut), West Newbury and Wells River.

NEWBURY village, the first settlement north of Charlestown, New Hampshire, on the Connecticut River, lies in the heart of the *Coos Country,* where great double bends in the river leave broad expanses of lush meadowland — the *Ox-Bow Meadows,* that were once loved by the Abnaki Indians as they since have been by the whites. Coos Country was variously translated by the Indians, as meaning Crooked River, Wide Valley, Place of Tall Pines, Great Fishing Place, and so on. Here the Abnakis had a permanent settlement, and to this day Newbury plows occasionally turn up tomahawk blades and flint arrowheads. For a long time Newbury was the northern outpost of pioneer settlements on the eastern side of the state. The grave composure of age, with a beautiful Connecticut Valley setting, gives Newbury a gracious charm.

In the long rectangular common surrounded by dignified old buildings at the village center is the *Jacob Bayley Monument,* dedicated to the founder of Newbury, who was a leader in the settlement and development of the whole eastern side of Vermont. The Bayley family, in fact, played in this region a rôle similar to that performed by the Allens on the other side of the Green Mountains. The rear wooden section of the *Ox-Bow Antique Shop,* at the south end of the village, was Jacob Bayley's residence. Bayley was plowing on the day that the British lieutenant, Pritchard, and his Tory followers came to capture him. Thomas Johnson, on parole from the British, was aware of the plot but unable to warn his friend personally, because the Tory ambuscade overlooked the Bayley meadow. Johnson contrived the warning by sending another man to the field, not to speak to Bayley, but to drop a slip of paper bearing the following message: "The Philistines be upon thee, Samson." Bayley escaped across the river to Haverhill, but that evening Pritchard took four prisoners from the Bayley home, including one of Jacob's sons. But for the courage of a defiant housemaid who barred their entrance, the British would have seized more captives.

The *Congregational Church* (1794) is of white wood, with a double entrance under its pillared portico, and a spire rising to a point from a square base — one of the most satisfying examples of early Vermont church architecture.

The northern and oldest section of the village is known as the Ox-Bow. The *Isaac Bayley House* (just off US 5), a white-painted frame structure with a flat balustraded roof, was built (1790) by Jacob Bayley for his son. Since it has always remained in the family, the interior has been excellently preserved. Necessary renovations have carefully harmonized and in woodwork, furniture, wallpaper, and other details the house consistently retains the charm of the period in which it was built. The parlor is distinguished by recesses on either side of the fireplace, one known as the "courting alcove," the other as the "marriage arch." That this design had a truly functional value is attested by the marriage record rapidly accomplished by the eight lovely daughters of Isaac Bayley. The *Colonel Thomas Johnson House,* a square tan building of severe lines, was built in 1775 by the man whose leadership was on a par with that of Jacob Bayley. There is a brave gesture toward refinement in the quoins, modillioned cornice, and paneled entrance of this house.

SOUTH NEWBURY (Conicut) is a group of clapboarded houses on the highway, and a railway station that also serves West Newbury. Maple products are manufactured here.

The *Ox-Bow Cemetery,* at the northern edge of Newbury, one of the oldest and most beautiful in the state, contains slate headstones dating from 1761. Old Joe, the Indian guide, who, with his squaw Molly, befriended so many white settlers in various sections of Vermont, is buried here. Joe was a peaceful Indian and a favorite among Newbury pioneers; he received a magnanimous $70-a-year pension from the state for his services to the early settlers.

Captain John, another Newbury Indian, was quite the opposite of Joe. A fierce and bloody warrior of the St. Francis tribe, John had fought against Braddock, and boasted that he tried to shoot young Washington during the engagement. Later John had fought with the Americans against Burgoyne. When a young Newbury savage named Toomalek attempted to kill the Indian who had taken the squaw he loved, his bullet killed the squaw instead. Captain John, presiding as judge at the trial, decreed that Toomalek was no murderer, inasmuch as he had not intended to slay the woman. Toomalek then tomahawked the man whom his bullet had missed, and again John acquitted him. But the third victim of Toomalek was John's own son. In this case there was no question raised as to the killer's guilt, and Captain John acted as executioner with grim satisfaction.

WELLS RIVER (alt. 395), lying at the junction of the Wells River with the Connecticut, is the industrial village of Newbury Town, and an important gateway between the White Mountains and the Green Mountains. At the southern end of the brisk little community an attractive white frame *Congregational Church* lifts its graceful spire above the treetops. The modern business section is rather bare and crowded, but the residential streets are shady and pleasant. Wells River enjoys a great deal of activity for a village of its size, owing to a strategic position for mill sites and on transportation lanes.

The village was once the head of navigation on the Connecticut River, New England's principal artery of commerce before the railroads. In 1830 a steamboat made the run from Hartford, Conn., to Wells River, and the following year a steamer, the *Adam Duncan,* was launched here. With the coming of the railroads, the village became a busy junction of the Boston & Maine and Montpelier & Wells River roads. The B & M station remains here, but the offices and bulk of business have been transferred to Woodsville, New Hampshire, just across the river. Wells River was the starting point of the Hazen Military Road, 1779, which was intended to open the way for an invasion of Canada, but in reality served as a path for early settlers to follow northward in extending the frontier. A celebrated criminal-chaser of the middle nineteenth century, John Bailey (descendant of Jacob Bayley of Newbury), made his home here.

NEWFANE, 10–D (Windham County, Vt. 30; alt. 560, pop. 715; 23,510 acres). Includes: Newfane village, South Newfane and Williamsville.

NEWFANE village (pop. 146) was originally chartered (New Hampshire) as Fane, for Thomas Fane, according to tradition, who was a follower of Sir Thomas Wyatt in 1553 in the movement to place Lady Jane Grey on the British throne in place of Queen Mary. The village proper was first called Park's Flats, for pioneer Jonathan Park, and then Fayetteville, in honor of Lafayette. Situated on a level valley floor banked by soft-sloping terraces, its handsome greens distinguished by town hall, church, courthouse, and old inns, Newfane stands with Woodstock as one of the most charming villages in southern Vermont. Newfane remains the shire town of Windham County, in spite of the greater size and affluence of Brattleboro and Bellows Falls. This is a rare instance in the state in which the county seat is retained in a small village instead of being transferred to a larger center. It is also a gratifying instance, for the Newfane setting is a lovely one.

An early settler was lawyer Martin Field who came to Newfane in 1800 after having secured degrees from Williams and Dartmouth Colleges. His grandson, poet Eugene Field, a Chicago newspaperman, spent several summers here and is reported to have based several of his delightful poems on his Newfane residence as a barefoot boy.

The broad open *Common,* outlined by elms, has the *Jonathan Park Memorial,* honoring the first settler who gave the land that is now the village nucleus. Park, with Stedman and Dyer, came here in 1776, to begin the original settlement on Newfane Hill. Lieutenant Park led Newfane volunteers to fight at Bennington. The smooth square forms a pleasant plaza.

Across the street is another shaded green, dignified by three fine white structures. *Union* (Town) *Hall* was built as a Union Church in 1832. The *Congregational Church* (1839), set back between town hall and courthouse, is white and pure of line with a high, graceful spire. The *County Courthouse* was erected in 1825 when the center of town shifted from Newfane Hill to the valley flats, and is the most beautiful in Vermont. In white wood with a four-pillared portico, handsome windows, and a red-capped tower, the building shows the Greek Revival trend. The Courthouse is one of the buildings most photographed — by tourists — in the state.

Across Route 30 is the white building housing the sheriff and the county jail.

The Newfane Inn (1793), an attractive white building, is said to be the second oldest hostelry in the state. In recent years, the Inn, now operated by a Frenchman and his wife, has gained a widespread reputation for its excellent continental victuals (*vittles* to Vermonters).

A red brick building contains the museum of the Windham County Historical Society.

Windham County Jail is the two-and-one-half story building across the street from the Courthouse. This jailhouse was once the most famed county jail in the country. It was a combined jail and hotel. Prisoners on good behavior (trusties) ate their meals at the same tables or at tables adjacent to the hotel's guests. The latter almost invariably wrote letters to their friends on the hotel stationery which was marked "Windham County Jail, Newfane Vt."

This unique institution, whose dual role ended shortly after World War II, had its origin about 1900. The 36-mile-long West River Railroad had steep hills and small steam engines. During Windham County Court sessions most people having business with the civil and criminal sessions of the court came in on the railroad from Brattleboro, the county's largest town. The train full of passengers could not make the steep grades, and at several places along the way it was necessary to sidetrack all but the engine and one passenger car. The engine then pulled the one passenger car up the grade and then made a trip back for each of the remaining passenger cars. This process had to be repeated several times between Brattleboro and Newfane. Everybody cussed the delays. About 1900 the decision was made to accommodate travelers, mostly people with court business but anyone could stay there, in the jail. Frugal Vermonters saw no necessity for providing separate dining facilities when "fair to middlin' vittles" were already served prisoners in the jail's mess hall. This room became the hotel dining room.

Most prisoners were either awaiting trial or were serving short terms for offenses like intoxication, wife beating or horse stealing. When county authorities decided to abandon the five decades long hospitality of the jailhouse, it was a cause of lament among many past guests.

NEWPORT City, 1–D (Orleans County shire town, US 5 and Vt. 100; alt. 723, pop. 5025).

Railroads: Canadian Pacific and Quebec Central (Main St.).

Bus Depot: Vermont Transit, Quebec Central Bus, Verreault Bus.

Airline: Northeast Airlines (summer service to Boston), Newport Flying Service (charter).

Accommodations: hotels, motels, tourist cabins, lodging houses.

Newspaper: Newport *Daily Express* (daily except Sunday).

Radio Station: WIKE (1490 kc.)

Hospital: Broadview.

Schools: Grammar, junior and senior high. Parochial high school.

State Police Outpost: Troop B (Derby). Phone: Derby 766-2211.

Customs Port: Port of Newport.

U.S. Immigration Service: U.S. Border Patrol unit.

Newport lies on a sloping promontory that juts across the southern end of Lake Memphremagog, with its outer fringes spread along the irregular hilly shoreline. The only incorporated city in northeastern Vermont, Newport is known as the Border City, and is one of the most popular gateways between Canada and New England. Memphremagog (Indian, "Beautiful Waters") was a fishing ground and avenue of travel for the Indians, whose birch canoes skirted the wild, ragged shores long before the white settlers came. Newport in the nineteenth century was the base of operations for a big lumber business, but this fell off with the general slump in lumbering, and today the little city is a vacation resort and trading center. During the summer months heavy traffic between the eastern United States and Montreal flows unceasingly through Newport, impregnating the town with changing life and color. Many travelers, impressed by the cleanliness and beautiful setting of Vermont's northernmost city, stop over here to enjoy the freshness of lake and mountain vistas opening directly from the streets of this modern community.

The sloping breadth of Main St. is lined with stores, which serve patrons from outlying towns. Residential sections stretch along the waterfront and ascend quiet, shady streets to the hills overlooking the lake. There is a marked contrast between the busy confusion of Main St. and the serene northward sweep of Memphremagog's waters between woodland shores and jagged mountains overshadowed by the rugged bulk of *Owl's Head* (alt. 3360), named for an Indian chief. The lake is thirty miles long, from one to four miles wide, and its surface is picturesquely broken by forested islands and headlands.

The railroad played a prominent part in the development of the town. A railway junction near the international border; the southern terminus of the Quebec Central RR; a Canadian Pacific station on the main line between Montreal and Boston; and an important customs port of entry, Newport is naturally a railroad center. The large yards near the depot, while less active than in the past, are still a busy scene, and ruddy-faced railroad men in blue overalls are familiar figures around the foot of Main

St. Much of the city's industry still hinges upon the waning lumber business, led by the old firm of Prouty and Miller, which once was among the biggest lumber companies east of the Mississippi (headquarters, Taunton, Massachusetts). When lumbering was at its peak, the bay was choked with logs rafted up the lake to the humming saws of the Prouty and Miller plant. The decline in the lumber trade and the railroad business left Newport faced with the necessity of developing its natural advantages as a summer resort. A fashionable colony has grown up around Camp Elizabeth at the pine-shaded Bluffs, north of the city on the eastern lakeshore.

Lake Memphremagog has a charm for sportsmen devoted to boating, swimming, and fishing. Each spring scores of fishermen and spectators crowd the railway platform, and lines are dropped into the bay a scant hundred feet from the traffic of Main St. Ragged boys with makeshift poles rub shoulders with expensively outfitted anglers from the metropolitan districts, and the spectators cheer when some tousle-headed urchin hauls in the best catch of the day. Summer train passengers may see on one side a car-crammed concrete street, and on the other skilled diving exhibitions by tanned youngsters plunging from the cinder-blackened platform rail into the cool calm water of 'Magog. This contrast is the secret of Newport's charm.

The first known white visitors here were Rogers' Rangers, returning from a daring and successful offensive against St. Francis village in Canada, in 1759. Major Robert Rogers left Crown Point, Sept. 13, with 200 green buckskin-clad Rangers, sailing down to the north end of Lake Champlain, and from there marching through the wilderness. Scouts told him his boats and supplies, left at Missisquoi Bay, had been taken by the enemy, and that a powerful body was in pursuit of his Rangers. He kept this information from his men and pushed forward, sending scouts back to Crown Point with the word that his retreat would be down the Connecticut and that he must be met there with provisions. On the night of October 4 they reached St. Francis. Lord Jeffrey Amherst had given orders to fight Indian fashion and show no mercy to the tribe that had so long terrorized the white settlers. The Rangers attacked the sleeping village at 4 A.M. Rogers ordered that women and children be spared, but when the pale morning light fell on hundreds of white scalps hanging from poles above the houses, there was no restraining the Rangers, who slaughtered men, women, and children and burned the entire village. Two hundred Indians were killed and 20 taken prisoners. The Rangers lost one man and six were wounded.

Rogers's plan was to follow the St. Francis and Magog Rivers to Lake Memphremagog, and thence cross to the Connecticut. They were harassed by pursuing Indians, but in 10 days they reached Memphremagog. They voted to split up into smaller parties, against Rogers's inclination. On the eastern side of the lake one squad was overtaken and wiped out. The other parties, suffering from hunger, exposure, and constant strain, made for the Connecticut. Their foraging route through a dense wilderness is paralleled almost exactly by the modern automobile route, US 5. A good description of this expedition is in *Northwest Passage,* by Kenneth Roberts (1937).

The first house in Newport was built by Deacon Martin Adams (1793) and by 1800 there were eleven families in the settlement. The charter was granted under the name of Duncansboro, for the chief proprietor, and the present name was adopted in 1816. Two prominent brothers were born here: Charles A. Prouty, longtime member of the Interstate Commerce Commission; and George H. Prouty, Governor of Vermont (1908–10).

Points of Interest

1. The *Federal Building,* Main St., stands at the crest of the sloping thoroughfare with other public buildings. Constructed of granite and brick, it houses the post office, and others, the most important of which is the U.S. Immigration Headquarters Office for District No. 1, including Maine, New Hampshire, Vermont, and New York border territory as far west as the Oswego County Line.

2. *Orleans County Court House,* Main St., in somber red brick, has been the center of judiciary life since the county seat was shifted from Irasburg to Newport.

3. *Goodrich Memorial Library,* Main St., dedicated in 1899, is a baroque structure in red brick with granite base and trim. Here are over 20,000 volumes, an excellent coin collection, and exhibits of stuffed animals and birds.

4. The *Catholic Church* (Ave Maris Stella), Prospect Hill, with twin granite towers flanking an arched portico, stands proudly above the city and lake. The view of Memphremagog from here is one of the finest obtainable, sweeping northward over the far reaches and islands of the long narrow lake with its broken shoreline and mountain background.

NEWPORT COUNTRY CLUB; 9 holes. Range: 130–505 yds; par 35. Rolling terrain overlooking Lake Memphremagog. Facilities: clubhouse with showers, golf shop, caddies. Restaurant open 8 A.M. to midnight.

VAH — Petit Farm, Laurier Petit. Dairy farm (Holstein cattle).

NORTH BENNINGTON (see BENNINGTON)
NORTH CALAIS (see CALAIS)
NORTH CAMBRIDGE (see CAMBRIDGE)
NORTH CHITTENDEN (see CHITTENDEN)
NORTH CLARENDON (see CLARENDON)
NORTH CONCORD (see CONCORD)
NORTH DANVILLE (see DANVILLE)
NORTH DORSET (see DORSET)
NORTH DUXBURY (see DUXBURY)
NORTH ENOSBURG (see ENOSBURG)

NORTH FAIRFAX (see FAIRFAX)
NORTH FAYSTON (see FAYSTON)
NORTH FERRISBURG (see FERRISBURG)
NORTH GOSHEN (see GOSHEN)
NORTH HARTLAND (see HARTLAND)

NORTH HERO, A-2 (Grand Isle County, US 2; alt. 120, pop. 328; 8033 acres). Includes: North Hero village and North Hero Station.

NORTH HERO, the shire town of Grand Isle County, faces Lake Champlain across a shoreline Main Street, with the attractiveness of neat wooden houses enhanced by flowers and hedges, shadowed under tall elm trees. This village, sometimes rather incongruously called Island City, has a delightful location on the eastern shore, with slow waves washing almost at the base of its single street, and clean fresh breezes blowing in from the water. The sheltered bay is closed in by wooded points of land forming a natural harbor, and the *Catholic Church* was originally a store standing near the old dock where the steamers landed. The *Courthouse* was built in 1824 of Isle La Motte marble. North Hero was the home of the Rockwell family, which for a century furnished Lake Champlain steamers with captains.

John Knight Inn stands on the home site of the first settler on North Hero Island. Enos Wood, accompanied by two other men, came in 1783 to stake a claim here at the southern end of the island, and later in the year came Mrs. Wood, the first white woman to step on this shore. John Knight subsequently acquired this land and his descendants still live here.

The bridge linking the islands of North Hero and South Hero has a magnificent view from the bridgeway that embraces all the manifold charms of island scenery. Between these two islands on the night of October 10, 1776, the British fleet anchored. The next morning it sailed southward along the shores of North and South Hero, unaware that Arnold was lying in wait behind the high bulk of Valcour Island on the New York side. Arnold showed the enemy a few boats to draw them into pursuit, and the Battle of Valcour Island was on as the British tried to beat into the bay where the American fleet waited to greet them with the blasting roar of cannon (see PANTON).

NORTH HYDE PARK (see HYDE PARK)
NORTH LANDGROVE (see LANDGROVE)
NORTH MONTPELIER (see EAST MONTPELIER)
NORTH ORWELL (see ORWELL)
NORTH PAWLET (see PAWLET)
NORTH POMFRET (see POMFRET)
NORTH POWNAL (see POWNAL)
NORTH RANDOLPH (see RANDOLPH)

NORTH SHELDON (see SHELDON)
NORTH SHERBURNE (see SHERBURNE)
NORTH SHREWSBURY (see SHREWSBURY)
NORTH SPRINGFIELD (see SPRINGFIELD)
NORTH THETFORD (see THETFORD)
NORTH TROY (see TROY)
NORTH TUNBRIDGE (see TUNBRIDGE)
NORTH UNDERHILL (see UNDERHILL)
NORTH WALDEN (see WALDEN)
NORTH WARDSBORO (see WARDSBORO)
NORTH WESTMINSTER (see WESTMINSTER)
NORTH WILLISTON (see WILLISTON)
NORTH WINDHAM (see WINDHAM)
NORTHEAST SLOPES SKI TOWS (see CORINTH)

NORTHFIELD, 5–C (Washington County, Vt. 12; alt. 760, pop. 4511; 24,564 acres). Vt. Transit bus and CV/Ry. Includes: Northfield village, Northfield Center, Northfield Falls and South Northfield.

NORTHFIELD is near the geographical center of the state. As the home of Governor Charles Paine, one of the projectors and financial backers of the Central Vermont Ry., Northfield became an important railroad center (see Transportation). The railroad shops that gave the town its main business impetus were removed to St. Albans after Governor Paine's death. The large red brick depot is on the west side of the small central square, which is dominated by a Civil War memorial monument. Today the numerous granite and monument shops are the most important of the several industries in the town, which include also two textile mills, a hosiery mill, a handkerchief mill, and several saw-mills and woodworking shops.

Norwich University is located here (see Education). It is an interesting sight, for many visitors, to watch the marching cadets at this oldest private military college in the U.S.

Hospital: Mayo Memorial.

Library: Brown Public Library. Northfield University Library.

Newspaper: Northfield News and Advertiser.

NORTHFIELD FALLS (alt. 680) is a small residential village, the houses of which are set unusually close to the street, resulting in a noticeable absence of the green, shaded lawns that often constitute the chief charm of settlements of this size and type. On the southern outskirts of the village, however, a neat modern cemetery has received the landscaping that the private homes lack. A road leads west from the center of the village to outlying farms.

SOUTH NORTHFIELD (alt. 839) is a small straggling village.

NORTHFIELD OUTING CLUB (off Cross St.); 600-ft rope tow. Novice slope; 10-meter jump (20-meter jump nearby). Operated weekend afternoons and on other non-school days. Use limited to club members but public can utilize facilities for small membership fee. *Information:* Ronald Davis, 4 Warren Ave., Northfield.

NORTHFIELD COUNTRY CLUB (3 m. north of Vt. 12A); 9 holes. Range: 142–460 yds. Hilly terrain. Facilities: clubhouse, dining room and golf shop.

NORTON, 1–F (Essex County, Vt. 114; alt. 1252, pop. 241; 22,174 acres). GT/RR. Includes Norton Mills.

NORTON MILLS is a scattered village with three churches, a hotel, and a *Customhouse,* 0.5 m. from the line. As its name suggests, the settlement was originally the center of large lumber mills, which no longer operate. Norton Town was one of the latest to be settled in the state (1860), and the northern section of this route dates from the present century, as there was no highway communication between Norton and the rest of Vermont for 50 years, except by way of Canada.

From the Norton Mills customhouse a good road ascends gradually to a higher level, from which at 1 m. there is a fine view of massed mountains to the south. The route continues through mediocre farming country to *Great Averill Lake,* 4.4 m., all but the northwestern tip of which lies in the unorganized town of Averill (see AVERILL).

NORWICH, 6–E, (Windsor County, US 5; alt. 536, pop. 1790; 25,365 acres). B & M/RR. Includes: Norwich village, Lewiston, New Boston, West Norwich and Pompanoosuc.

NORWICH Village was chartered by New Hampshire as *Norwhich* but the first h was soon dropped. Resting cool-shaded under the dense foliage of maples, the village has a venerable charm. Old frame houses sit back of spacious lawns, and the scene is pervaded with the atmosphere of Old New England. Norwich University was founded here but removed to Northfield in 1867 (see NORTHFIELD and Education). The original Norwich Military Academy Building once occupied the present public school site. A strong and active feud was carried on between Norwich students and those from Dartmouth just across the river in Hanover. In the *Old Burying Ground* there are stones dating to 1770. Many have curious inscriptions.

U.S. Navy Rear Admirals George Colvocoresses, George Converse and Stephen Rand were born here. Boston music and dramatic critic Philip Hale was a Norwich native. The village has become a popular residence for Dartmouth faculty members. Hanson Carroll, noted for his *Vermont Life* magazine photographs, lives here.

LEWISTON is a half-dozen houses at the Vermont end of the *Ledyard Bridge*. John Ledyard, whose name is given to the bridge, is Dartmouth's patron saint of the great outdoors. Ledyard had no interest in getting a sheepskin from Dartmouth. Less than two years sufficed to satisfy his yearning for President Wheelocks' cultural program. At an all-night session with himself in the midwinter of 1773 on the snow-covered Velvet Rocks of Balch Hill, three miles northeast of Hanover, he decided to listen to the call of the open and leave college. It probably was no surprise to the president, for that gentleman had already had a display of the wildness of the youth when he proposed such an unheard-of use of leisure time for students as "stepping the minuet." Selecting a towering pine growing on the bank, just north of the present bridge, Ledyard secretly hewed out a dugout canoe, 50 feet long and 3 feet wide, and with some dried venison, an Ovid and a Greek Testament, he pushed out into the Connecticut River bound for a larger and less restricted world. Ledyard's passion for wandering led him, a few years later, to sail with Captain Cook on his third voyage; and still later to attempt, at the request of Thomas Jefferson, an exploration of the American Northwest via Siberia. He died in Egypt.

The present bridge, a low steel structure, replaced a fine old covered one built in 1859; the first bridge across the river here was erected in 1796.

NEW BOSTON, is a section of Norwich high in the hills east of Norwich village.

POMPANOOSUC (alt. 392), lying near the junction of the Ompom-panoosuc with the Connecticut, consists of pastureland and cornfields with a few straggling homes, a lattice-type covered bridge, and a railroad depot. The main part of the settlement is west of the highway.

WEST NORWICH, a section of Norwich, is west of Norwich village.

OKEMO MT. STATE FOREST (see LUDLOW)
OLD BENNINGTON (see BENNINGTON)
OLYMPUS (see BETHEL)

ORANGE COUNTY (Area 690 sq. miles. Population 16,014). Shire town: Chelsea. Organized 1781. Includes: Bradford, Braintree, Brookfield, Chelsea, Corinth, Fairlee, Newbury, Orange, Randolph, Strafford, Thetford, Topsham, Tunbridge, Vershire, Washington, Williamstown.

ORANGE, 5–D (Orange County, US 302; alt. 1500, pop. 430; 20,515 acres). Barre stage. Includes: Orange village and East Orange.

ORANGE is strung pleasantly along the roadway with wide meadow-lands flowing smoothly away to the south, situated at a high altitude where at one time extensive sheep-raising was carried on. The clean, white *Congregational Church,* whose spire dominates the village, is attractive and well kept. From the hillcrest on the western edge of Orange is a splendid view of the great *Granite Quarries* on the heights above Barre, where broken and massive ramparts of gray stone piles stand out from the wooded hillsides like ruined fortresses.

EAST ORANGE has a few houses, general store, burying ground and a *Baptist Church.*
Library: Ada Richardson.

ORLEANS COUNTY (Area 715 sq. miles. Population 20,143). Shire town: Newport (moved from Irasburg). Organized 1792. Includes: Albany, Barton, Brownington, Charleston, Coventry, Craftsbury, Derby, Glover, Greensboro, Holland, Irasburg, Jay, Lowell, Morgan, Newport, Troy, Westfield, Westmore.

ORLEANS (see BARTON)

ORWELL, 6–A (Addison County, Vt. 22A and Vt. 73; alt. 385, pop. 826; 24,394 acres). Includes: Orwell village, Beeman's Corner, Montcalm's Landing and North Orwell.

ORWELL, well laid out, with an eye toward spacious planning, lies along the gentle slope of a plain rising to the east, the easternmost houses in the shadow of the woods at the crest. This orchard and dairy community centers with a pleasant airy quality about a large sloping green with the white-and-green *Town Hall* (original Baptist Church, 1810) and the *Congregational Church* (1843), red brick with white wooden trim, overlooking the Common and Main St. *St. Paul's Catholic Church* (on the hill) was erected 1860, of red brick with a crenellated white wood steeple. The first settler was an eccentric Scotchman named John Charter, who brought his family down from Montreal several years before the Revolution. Long before any settlement was made, armed men ranged this region concerned with Mt. Independence and Ticonderoga, keystones of the gateway to Champlain.

Orwell for many years was one of the leading sheep-raising centers in the Champlain Valley.

BEEMAN'S CORNER, at the western edge of Orwell village is a junction of Vt. routes 22 and 73.

MONTCALM'S LANDING, named for the French general who was whipped at Quebec by General James Wolfe, is a ferry landing.

NORTH ORWELL is a tiny hamlet.

PANTON, 5–A (Addison County, 3 m. west of Vergennes; alt. 200, pop. 352; 9345 acres). Vergennes stage.

PANTON, also known as Panton Four Corners, is reported to have been named after Lord Panton. This low-lying sparsely settled town was burned by the British in 1777 when "Gentleman Johnny" Burgoyne's forces swarmed down the Champlain Valley until they were delayed at Hubbardton (see HUBBARDTON), whipped at Bennington (see BEN-NINGTON) and counted out at Saratoga.

Arnold Bay (4.8 m. straight north from Panton on unnumbered road) is a tiny cove on the larger *Button* (originally Button Mould) *Bay*. The cove owes its name to the final scene of a stirring and gallant chapter in Revolutionary history. Here it was that in October, 1776, Benedict Arnold ran his flagship *Congress* and four smaller boats aground under the guns of the British fleet after the battle of Valcour Island. Arnold set fire to the ships and let them burn with colors flying rather than yield them to the enemy. The rotted hulks and beams are still visible in low water; cannon-balls and countless relics have been found here. *Valcour Island* is a high hog-backed island off the New York shore across the lake from South Hero. An overpowering British fleet was ready to sail southward against Ticonderoga and Mt. Independence when Arnold put his fleet in anchorage on the New York side of Valcour to hide and surprise the enemy. When the British fleet hove into sight, Arnold left the main strength of his fleet in the bay, and swung four boats around before the enemy to lure them after him. Following Arnold back into the narrow-mouthed bay, the Britishers ran into the concerted fire of the American fleet, and the mili-tary genius of Benedict Arnold had completely outmaneuvered the English admiral, Carleton. The two fleets pounded away at each other until night-fall, with the Americans having the advantage. During the night Arnold pulled another coup, sailing his fleet out under cover of darkness and escaping southward. The British followed when daylight showed that their quarry had flown. Arnold, with the *Congress* and a small flotilla of supporting vessels, fought a rearguard action that allowed the main part of his fleet to reach Ticonderoga in safety while the rear guard was being hammered to pieces by the overwhelming forces of the English. Hope-lessly smashed and beaten, Arnold put to shore in Buttonmould Bay, carried his wounded to the land and fired the battered boats. While Valcour Island was technically a British victory, Arnold had accomplished his purpose, that of delaying the English advance another year. Before the British could recover and get another naval offensive under way, winter had set in and Lake Champlain was closed to navigation. There is an excellent account of this battle in *Rabble in Arms* by Kenneth Roberts.

BUTTON BAY STATE PARK (4.8 m. north of Panton) is a 206-acre park with undeveloped (1964) facilities. Future facilities will probably include: picnic tables and fireplaces, tent sites, bathing, boating and fishing.

PASSUMPSIC (see BARNET)

PAWLET, 8–A (Rutland County, Vt. 30 and Vt. 133; alt. 680, pop. 1112; 22,040 acres). Granville, N.Y., stage. Includes: North Pawlet and West Pawlet.

PAWLET village lost its tiny fenced-in green and Revolutionary War cannon when the fence decayed and was not replaced, and the cannon were donated to a World War II scrap drive. The monument to Pawlet's Revolutionary War soldiers still stands on the fenceless green.

Pawlet, whose industries in the 1830's rivaled those of Rutland, is the classic Vermont rural village of the movie and TV scripts. Storekeeper Johnny Mach, an enterprising and transplanted Yankee who came to Pawlet in 1936, rebuilt the village millpond and constructed a waterwheel to generate electricity for his store and home. The 27-foot diameter and 4-foot-wide waterwheel was designed and built by Frank Gibson of Reading. Mach extended the rear of his store over the old millworks and Flower Brook. He cut a hole through his store floor and covered it with glass so that customers or visitors obtain a most interesting and unusual view.

PEACHAM, 4–E (Caledonia County, off US 5 near Barnet; alt. 1908, pop. 500; 29,579 acres). Includes: Peacham village, East Peacham and South Peacham.

PEACHAM. Smooth-flowing hills darkened by woodland patches surround the village with pleasant seclusion, which increases its favor as a summer home for college professors and others seeking rest, quiet, and comfort. The *Congregational Church,* dating from the 1790's, is clean-cut and white, with a high tapering spire; crumbling horse sheds flank the clapboard structure. *Peacham Academy* was founded in 1795 as the Caledonia County Grammar School. The first newspaper in the county, *The Green Mountain Patriot,* was published here in 1798. Peacham was influential in early Vermont history and intellectual life.

Deacon Jonathan Elkins was the father of the town, coming with a few followers in 1775, and making a permanent settlement the next year. The *Elkins Tavern* (1787) stands halfway between Peacham and South Peacham on a branch road. The Hazen Military Road went through Peacham, and was a great convenience and main thoroughfare for the pioneer settlers. The caliber of the Peacham pioneers is suggested by the following story: A band of Tories and Indians hovered in the woods preparing to attack a crew of woodchoppers. When the woodcutters left their axes and went to lunch, the raiders descended, but they halted in awe at the sight of the great axes. "No, no," said an Indian. "We no fight men who use such big axes. We no fight." And the raiders withdrew. Thaddeus Stevens, violent abolitionist and foeman of the Confederacy during the Civil War and Reconstruction, spent his boyhood on a farm at East Hill, east of the village. George Harvey, editor of *Harper's Weekly* and Ambassador to England under Harding, was born in Peacham. He was a leader in the fight against Wilson's peace plans, and was influential in the nomination of Harding.

A historical flask turned out in the early 1860's celebrated Flora Temple, foaled in Peacham, and the first horse in the world to trot a mile under 2.20 — time, 2.19¾.

EAST PEACHAM is a tiny settlement around a lumber mill.

SOUTH PEACHAM (alt. 1000), a typical small rural corner village, has an atmosphere of stolid unchanging comfort and seclusion. The houses are scattered haphazardly around a bridged stream and general store. The abandoned *Mill* employed three stones in grinding its grist. The first millstones were brought to Peacham by Colonel Thomas Johnson of Newbury, who hauled them in on an ox sled, March 6, 1781. Johnson stayed that night with Jonathan Elkins. At midnight both men were surprised by Pritchard's Tories, taken prisoners, and marched off to Canada. Johnson was paroled, but Elkins was taken to England to await an exchange of prisoners.

PEACHAM COMMUNITY SKI AREA (5.0 m. S.W. of Danville and US 2 or 8 m. northwest of Barnet and US 5); 1500-ft. elevation and 1350-ft. base; 700-ft. rope tow; 25 acres open slopes. Ski hut and snack bar. Open weekends, holidays and by appointment. Nearby accommodations. Stevens Valley Men's Club, Peacham.

PEKIN (see CALAIS)
PERKINSVILLE (see WEATHERSFIELD)

PERU, 9–C (Bennington County, Vt. 11 and Vt. 30; alt. 1660, pop. 164; 20,977 acres). Manchester stage.

Peru lies high in the mountains, under the dominance of Bromley Mountain (alt. 3260). This hill village has a clean well-groomed aspect, refuting the general ideas regarding the slovenly backwardness of mountain settlements. Many of the homes and buildings are painted white, and the general scene is one of neatness and quiet pride. The *Community House* contains the town library. The *General Store and Post Office* is so much the neat model of such common rural arrangements that it resembles a movie-lot setup, even to the rustic sign hanging above the entrance. The *Congregational Church* (1846) exemplifies in the plain severity of white-painted wood a simple effectiveness of church building, with double entrances, green-blinded windows, and square bell tower. The interior contains four hanging oil lamps, corner stoves with overhead pipes for winter heating, and a large painting of Bromley Mountain behind the pulpit. An appropriate quotation from Psalm 121 is on the wall: "I will lift up mine eyes unto the hills." The *Bromley House* is early nineteenth century, a square roomy-looking structure of white-painted brick, with an outside fireplace on the porch. Peru was settled in 1773 and first took the name of Bromley. John Stark's forces cut a road through this town on their way to the battle of Bennington.

PICO PEAK SKI AREA (see RUTLAND)
PIERCE'S CORNER (see CLARENDON)

PITTSFIELD, 6–C (Rutland County, Vt. 100; alt. 892, pop. 254; 13,296 acres). Vt. Transit bus.

PITTSFIELD, named for Pittsfield, Mass., from which the first settlers came, lies pleasantly deep in the hills at another junction of rivers. The north end of the little village is marred by burnt-out cellar holes, but the center is pleasing with its long narrow strip of tree-studded green.

PITTSFORD, 7–B (Rutland County, US 7 and Vt. 3; alt. 560, pop. 2225; 26,333 acres). Vt. Transit bus. Includes: Pittsford village, East Pittsford, Florence, Grangerville and Pittsford Mills.

PITTSFORD, noted for pine-scented mountain air and pure water, was once the site of two sanatoriums. The long main street curves under shade trees between rows of comfortable homes. In many cases brick has been employed as the building material, coloring the cool green of the street. *Old Cemetery* is a shaded sidehill graveyard at the entrance to the village, its ancient headstones dating back to 1774. The *Drake Homestead,* Main St., a small cottage over a hundred years old, is where the mother of President Millard Fillmore was born. *Walker Memorial Library,* facing the triangle as US 7 bends left, stands in the plain security of red brick. Nicholas M. Powers, who built lattice-type covered bridges throughout Vermont and New Hampshire, was born in Pittsford. Many of his sturdy and picturesque structures remain as useful memorials to him and links to the past.

Site of Fort Vengeance (US 7) is marked by a marble shaft beside the climbing roadway. A soldier was killed by Indians when the fort was first occupied, 1780, and his comrades, in swearing vengeance, so named the fort.

Colonial Stone House (US 7) is a compactly built, picturesque struc-
ture with an interesting old fireplace and bake oven. The ford on Otter
Creek behind this house was called Pitt's Ford, after Prime Minister
William Pitt, and from this evolved the name of Pittsford.

PITTSFORD MILLS, formerly a busy industrial section where mill wheels
were turned by Furnace Brook, is now simply the southern residential
section of Pittsford, a continuation of the village street.

PROCTOR–PITTSFORD COUNTRY CLUB (see PROCTOR)

PITTSFORD MILLS (see PITTSFORD)
PLEASANT VALLEY (see CAMBRIDGE)

PLYMOUTH, 8–D (Windsor County, Vt. 100; alt. 1420, pop. 308;
27,249 acres). Ludlow–Woodstock stage. Includes: Plymouth Notch,
Plymouth Union and Tyson.

PLYMOUTH (NOTCH), the *Birthplace of Calvin Coolidge,* is a country
store at the crossroads in this tiny hamlet buried in the mountains. On
Independence Day, 1872, Calvin Coolidge was born in the cottage
attached to the rear of the combination store and post office. He was
educated at Black River Academy (see LUDLOW) and Amherst. As
mayor of Northampton, Massachusetts, he started his political career,
becoming governor of that state, and then Vice-President of the United
States under Harding. Coolidge was at home with his family in Plymouth on August 3, 1923, when he was awakened at 2 A.M. by the
news of Harding's death, and sworn in as President by his father,
Colonel John Coolidge, on the worn family Bible under the yellow
flicker of a kerosene lamp. Calvin Coolidge finished that term and
served another full term. Known as "Silent Cal," he was looked upon
by the world as a typical Vermonter, taciturn, unsmiling, penurious —
a solemn man, thin and sharp as a scythe, without humor, without
emotions. He never lost the harsh farmer's twang in his voice. It was
as a simple homespun person that he appealed to people. The fact that
a peak of prosperity was attained in the Coolidge regime lifted him to
almost legendary heights for a brief stay. "Keep Cool with Coolidge"
was the slogan, and the country looked upon him as a safe, sane balance-
wheel. Coolidge died in 1933, and now sleeps in the sidehill cemetery
at Plymouth beneath a severely simple stone.

PLYMOUTH UNION is a few houses strung along Vt. 100 in a narrow
irregular valley. *Crown Point Military Road Marker* (Vt. 100), a high
stone slab, indicates the course followed by the historic trail between

Charlestown, N.H., and Crown Point, N.Y., stating that the site of the 26-mile encampment is one quarter mile west of the monument.

Lake Amherst is a beautiful natural memorial to Lord Jeffrey Amherst, the military commander under whose direction the Crown Point Road was laid through the wilderness. Wooded shores rise sharply from the clear water, and the highway skirts the western edge of the wood-ringed little lake. It is likely that the builders of the old road camped by this quiet body of water, rough brawny axemen and lean, sharp-eyed riflemen resting from their labors on the shore of the peaceful lake.

Echo Lake, less closely confined by forested slopes, is similar to Lake Amherst in unspoiled quiet beauty of natural setting.

TYSON is a small summer settlement at the southern end of Echo Lake. A neat concrete bridge with built-in lampposts conducts a road over the Black River to the summer homes along the eastern shores of Echo and Amherst.

Rescue Lake is the southernmost and largest of this chain of pretty lakes through which the Black River flows. Its shoreline is much more broken and irregular.

POMFRET, 7–D (Windsor County, off Vt. 12 and Vt. 14; alt. 1220, pop. 600; 23,429 acres). West Hartford stage. Includes: Pomfret (Center) village, North Pomfret and South Pomfret.

POMFRET CENTER is named after Pomfret, Connecticut, from where the settlers came in 1770. Scarcely any evidence of a settlement is left here at the central village buried high in the hills. The first pioneers to penetrate these mountain wilds found evidences of a terrific hurricane which had ravaged the slopes long before the coming of the white man.

NORTH POMFRET (alt. 894) is a small settlement sprawled along a tree-shaded road.

SOUTH POMFRET (alt. 736), the chief village of the town, is a pleasant little community resting in the small valley. The *Abbott Memorial Library,* a neat little building of unorthodox style, contains a museum of many local historical items.

Former foreign correspondent Graham Peck, author of several books on China, lives here.

POMPANOOSUC (see NORWICH)
POST MILLS (see THETFORD)
POTTERVILLE (see WOLCOTT)

POULTNEY, 8–B (Rutland County, Vt. 30 and Vt. 140; alt. 430, pop. 3009; 25,396 acres). D & H/RR. Includes: Poultney village, East Poultney and South Poultney.

Library: Poultney Public Library.

Newspaper: Poultney Herald.

POULTNEY lies on the level plain of the Poultney River near the New York borderline, a neat clean village in the heart of the district that produces unfading green, purple, and mottled slates. The streets are orderly and well planned; the unpretentious brick and wooden houses with slate roofs, and here and there traces of Colonial dignity, are well kept. In spite of the fact that the depression caused slate to be widely replaced by cheaper materials, thus undermining the industrial foundation of the town, Poultney has maintained a brave and attractive front. The population includes a large proportion of Welsh, who left their native slate quarries in Wales for this new quarrying field. Hooker and Son opened the first quarry in Poultney.

Green Mountain Junior College, at the western end of Main St., was founded in 1836 by the Methodist Episcopal Church as Troy Conference Academy, became Ripley Female College for a time, and took its present name and status in 1931. The fine red brick buildings with white trim are set back on an elm-shaded campus, and center around Ames Memorial Hall, with its rounded, white-pillared portico. The athletic field is behind the school. This is one of the oldest and most respected secondary schools in Vermont (women only).

The town was settled in 1771 by Thomas Ashley and Ebenezer Allen; the latter subsequently moved north to Grand Isle. Both of these pioneers, with other Poultney settlers, were with Ethan Allen and Benedict Arnold at the capture of Ticonderoga. The origin of the name Poultney is not definitely known, but it is thought to derive from Lord Poultney, a friend of Governor Benning Wentworth.

Two Editors Inn on the village green is named after Horace Greeley and George Jones (see EAST POULTNEY). The Inn (open to the public) is owned by the college.

The *U.S. Post Office* (1962), built of local slate, is one of the most attractive post offices in the state.

EAST POULTNEY follows the valley of the Poultney River and has a triangular Green in the midst of austere old houses. On the Green is the *Old Baptist Church* (1802–5), with three entrances, Palladian windows, and a large square clock tower, in white-painted wood (restored by Poultney Historical Society). The *Eagle Tavern* (private), an old stagecoach inn (about 1790), is a handsome wide-clapboarded structure, painted pale yellow with tall two-story columns of white, and a deep porch. Reminiscent of southern Colonial buildings, it has marked distinction. Horace Greeley boarded here for two years. The tavern was the scene of many gay dinners and balls in post-Revolutionary times, and on one occasion Captain William Watson raised his glass in this toast: "The enemies of our country! May they have cobweb breeches, a porcupine saddle, a hard-trotting horse, and an eternal journey." Other houses of Colonial purity in line harmonize with the scene here at the Green triangle where the settlement of Poultney was begun. Heber Allen, brother of Ethan and Ira, was an early settler, and is buried in the *Old Cemetery* here.

Horace Greeley spent four years in East Poultney (1826–30), and learned the printing trade as a typesetter in the tiny office of the Poultney *Gazette*. Working in the same office with Greeley was another young lad, George Jones, who was later one of the founders of the New York *Times* (1851), ten years after Greeley had founded the *New York Tribune*. The house in which Greeley lived stands on the east side of the triangle, a plain white structure. At the age of fourteen, Greeley made his first political speech in the old Poultney schoolhouse.

SOUTH POULTNEY is a small settlement with a country store and a Welsh Presbyterian Church.

ST. CATHERINE STATE PARK (Poultney R.D. 2, Vt. 30; est. 1953) is a 16-acre site on the east shore of Lake St. Catherine. Facilities: picnic tables and fireplaces, bathing, boating, fishing, refreshments.

LAKE ST. CATHERINE COUNTRY CLUB (4.0 m. west of Poultney on Vt. 30); 9 holes. Range: 165–530 yds; par 36. Varied terrain. Facilities: golf shop, pro and sandwich shop during July–August.

POWNAL, 11–B (Bennington County, US 7; alt. 594, pop. 1509; 26,903 acres). Vt. Transit bus and B & M/RR. Includes: Pownal village, Pownal Center and North Pownal.

POWNAL spreads over the Hoosic Valley floor west of US 7, its wooden houses scattered on the plain, a white church spire lifting above the treetops, and the Boston & Maine RR running through the village. Pownal is supposed to have been settled as early as the 1720's by Dutch squatters who remained but a short while. Permanent settlement was made in 1766 by Rhode Island pioneers. Pownal, uniquely located in the corner of Vermont between New York and Massachusetts, is the scene of a Christopher Morley tale, "Blythe Mountain," which appeared first in his column and later in book form.

POWNAL CENTER (alt. 986) is built on a knoll in the valley, with a shaded *Old Cemetery* facing stores, garage, and gasoline pumps across the bare cement thoroughfare, an incongruous contrast. The old *Union Church* was erected in 1789, but has been restored and renovated. The white, double-porched structure nearly opposite the church incorporates portions of the *First Tavern* in town.

NORTH POWNAL (alt. 602) is a small village near the New York borderline. Born in this hamlet, the son of a peddler whose nine-cart caravan jolted over early New England, was Jubilee Jim Fisk, railroad magnate, Wall Street operator, and nationally known playboy. Fisk achieved ownership of the Erie RR, staked his fortune against Jay Gould's for a corner on the gold market, bought an opera house in New York for his lady-of-the-moment to star in, and careened through a gaudy-colored career in the 1880's and 90's with the sky the limit. A reckless gambler, free-spender and high-liver of the Diamond Jim Brady school, Fisk died as suddenly and violently as he had lived, shot to death by Ed Stokes in the elegance of the Broadway Central Hotel in New York, the victim of a love triangle.

Two presidents, Vermont-born Chester A. Arthur and Ohio native James Garfield, taught school in the old Oak Seminary. Arthur (see FAIRFIELD) was removed by Garfield when the former was U.S. Customs Collector for the Port of New York. Later Garfield and Arthur were running mates in the election of 1880. Arthur became President when Garfield died from a crank's bullet.

Green Mountain Raceway (1963) is Vermont's first and only parimutuel race track.

Kreigger Rocks are seen (westward) across the deep valley from the road swinging high over the eastern valley edge, an unusual rock formation rising in a perpendicular ledge and having the structural appearance of a large fortress wall. Geologists say that this was part of a natural dam that formed glacial Lake Bascom. Looking toward Kreigger Rocks from US 7, there is presented a valley-and-mountain vista of sharp grandeur, the valley floor far below stretching smoothly westward to the mountain flanks that rise beyond the ramparts of this great natural dam of a prehistoric era.

PROCTOR, 7–B (Rutland County (Vt. 3 off US 7 at Pittsford or off US 4 at Center Rutland; alt. 477, pop. 2105; 2102 acres). VT/Ry.
Hospital: Proctor Hospital.
Library: Proctor Free Library.

PROCTOR, named after Redfield Proctor, is the "Marble Center," built around the headquarters and finishing plants of the Vermont Marble Company. Lying in the narrow Otter Creek Valley, Proctor is pervaded with the pleasing cleanness of its famous building stone, exemplified in neat homes and the marble of public buildings. In places even the sidewalks are of marble. The picture is glacial white against a green background.

The business center of the trim, well-kept village is dominated by

Silver Lake in Barnard. *Vermont Development Department*

Brattleboro, Main Street. *Ewing Galloway*

Bennington College for Women. *Ewing Galloway*

The Old Mill Pond in East Jamaica

Old mill with water wheel in Dorset Hollow

Vermont Development Department

Left, above: Grand Isle — the oldest log cabin in the United States
Vermont Development Department

Left, below: Barnard. "Big House," the longtime residence of novelist Sinclair
Lewis and his journalist wife Dorothy Thompson. *John L. Warner*

Haying in East Corinth. *Claire Griffin*

Green River covered bridge. *Vermont Development Department*

Floating bridge in Brookfield. *Vermont Development Department*

the great long marble mills and yards piled high with marble slabs, the whole scene neat and orderly. From the narrow valley floor residential streets wind up the shady hillsides with houses strewn irregularly at all levels, and mountains closing in on every side of the gap.

Water power is furnished by beautiful *Sutherland Falls* (right from bridge near center), which drop a sheer 118 feet in roaring foaming cascades. The falls were named for John Sutherland, an early settler who built a sawmill and gristmill here. Marble was first quarried in the vicinity, 1836, when it was a part of Rutland (see RUTLAND). In 1870 Redfield Proctor took over the Sutherland Falls Marble Company, rapidly absorbed other firms, and welded together the mighty Vermont Marble Company. Redfield Proctor as governor of Vermont, 1878–80, instituted the nearest thing to a capitalistic dynasty that the state has ever known. Today Vermont Marble operates quarries throughout the state, as well as in Colorado, Montana, and Alaska, and the central offices make Proctor virtually the center of the marble world. An elaborate *Marble Exhibit* (open to the public from May 1 to November 1, admission free, guide service furnished) is held in the company display room.

Wilson Castle, north off US 4 in Center Rutland or West Proctor Rd. from Proctor Village (open daily 10–6. Fee). This mid-18th century built castle cost a reported one million dollars. The 150 acre estate with 16 buildings includes the 32 room Castle. Interesting furnishings, paintings and sculpture. Antique guns, swords and armor.

PROCTOR-PITTSFORD COUNTRY CLUB (Corn Hill Road 1.0 m. off US 7 in Pittsford or 3 m. from Proctor); 9 holes. Range: 173–415 yds. Mostly hilly terrain with one water hole. One of most scenic courses in New England. Facilities: marble clubhouse with showers, golf shop, practice putting green. Course open 8 A.M. to sundown.

PROCTORSVILLE (see CAVENDISH)
PROSPER (see WOODSTOCK)

PUTNEY, 10–E (Windham County, US 5 and Interstate 91; alt. 580, pop. 1177; 17,669 acres). Vt. Transit bus.

PUTNEY is the home of U.S. Senator George Aiken, and former governor of the state. This quiet community is the site of Windham College, the Putney School and the Experiment for International Living. The townspeople have never quite recovered from the shock of having been the site of John H. Noyes' "Bible Communism" experiment (see Chapter 12). There are still standing in Putney village several houses where Noyes' "Perfectionists" lived — three and four families to the house — but they are not designated by any plaques or markers, and the casual visitor might be well advised not to inquire as to their location. It is only within the past few years that Putney summer residents have been allowed to wear shorts.

VAH — Harlow Orchards, Frank Harlow. Orchard products.

VAH — Ranney Farm, George Ranney. Dairy farm (Jersey cattle) and maple products.

QUECHEE (see WOODSTOCK)
QUECHEE GORGE (see WOODSTOCK)

RANDOLPH, 6–D (Orange Couny, Vt. 12 and Vt. 12A; alt. 694, pop. 3414; 28,712 acres). CV/Ry and Vt. Transit bus. Includes: Randolph village, Randolph Center, East Randolph, North Randolph and South Randolph.

Hospital: Gifford Memorial.
Library: Kimball Public Library.
Newspaper: White River Valley Herald.

RANDOLPH is a trim and prosperous-looking village. It is unusually well provided with public buildings to meet all civic and social needs, though uninteresting architecturally. The village is divided almost equally in two by the Central Vermont Ry., the main business section lying north of the tracks. Farm implements of several types, rubber stamps, furniture, and sheet gelatin are manufactured in Randolph, and its location in one of the leading dairy districts of the state has led to the establishment of three creameries here. In the high, quiet residential section at the southern end of the village are a *Hospital* that serves a wide radius and the *Old Ladies' Home* maintained by the Vermont chapters of the Order of the Eastern Star.

RANDOLPH CENTER. This quiet hilltop village, one of the highest in the state (alt. 1384), was the earliest settled part of Randolph town, once its business as well as its geographical center, and was seriously considered in the opening years of the nineteenth century for the state capital. Montpelier was the final choice instead (in 1805), and in the succeeding decades the population and trade of Randolph Center — as in so many Vermont hill communities — were drawn to the valley, where there were streams to turn the wheels of the mills and, after 1850, railroads to carry their products away.

Randolph Center is best known as the seat of the Vermont Agricultural and Technical Institute, established by act of legislature in 1910 on the site of the Orange County Grammar School (1806), the original building of the latter school being still in use as a recitation hall. The curriculum is designed to include courses in scientific farming and practical farm management for young Vermonters. The neat yellow-

and-white recitation halls and dormitories dominate the east side of the one wide shady street. Behind them lies the large modern farm that is operated chiefly by student labor — a great outdoor laboratory. Records show that more than 80 percent of the alumni of this school have remained in Vermont and that the greater part of them are engaged in agricultural work. The value of such an institution to a predominantly agricultural state is self-evident.

Of the several century-old houses set back from the broad street, the most noteworthy is the Chase, or Parrish, House, *Maple Grove* (1804), one of the finest remaining examples of Adamesque adornment in Vermont. The delicate white grace of its door, fanlights, pilasters, and cornice carvings, shining through the shade and between the trunks of some dozen large maple trees planted soon after the house was built, is a sight not soon forgotten. If Randolph Center had been selected as the Capital site, as many hoped it would be, Maple Grove was to have been the Governor's Mansion. For a time the house sheltered Salmon P. Chase, Chief Justice of the United States (1864–73), who lived here and studied law with his uncle, Judge Dudley Chase, until the latter advised him to abandon it, as it was foreign to his talents.

EAST RANDOLPH (alt. 606) is another attractive little hamlet at rest in the serenity of the valley.

NORTH RANDOLPH (alt. 671), similar in general appearance and background to East Brookfield, is an agreeable village in a meadowland setting.

SOUTH RANDOLPH (alt. 563) is simply the center of a scattered rural settlement with a general store, gasoline pumps, and antique shop on the main thoroughfare. The *Antique Shop* is located in a low brown frame house, which was built in 1781 by Experience Davis; it was the first house put up in Randolph Town and the oldest structure encountered on this route. Randolph suffered from Indian raids soon after that time, but Experience Davis' house escaped the torch, and has since withstood all the vicissitudes of nature and time. The Duke of Kent (who became father of Queen Victoria) stayed overnight in this house on his trip through Vermont about 1791. For some time the building was used as a tavern, and around 1830 it served as tollhouse for the old toll road, the route of which Vt. 14 approximately follows today. The original clapboards, handmade nails, beams, and sills of Experience Davis' construction remain, and the house is substantially as it was when built, quite properly housing what collectors consider one of the best antique collections in the state, including one of the two best privately owned collections of historic china in New England.

MONTAGUE GOLF CLUB (0.2 m. from CV/Ry. station) 9 holes; range: 145–375 yds; par 31. Level terrain. Facilities: clubhouse and pro shop.

VAH—Vermont Agricultural and Technical Institute Farm. Dairy farm (Jersey cattle), poultry, fruit, farm products processing.

RAWSONVILLE (see JAMAICA)

READING, 8–D (Windsor County, Vt. 106; alt. 754, pop. 472; 26,912 acres). Windsor stage. Includes Felchville, Hammondsville and South Reading.

FELCHVILLE (P.O. Reading, 18 m.), a pleasant, uncommercial village consisting mainly of one long maple-shaded street, is the chief settlement in Reading Town. There is an unusually fine *Library* here and a commodius but rather bleak-looking *Town Hall* with an auditorium and stage equipment, both the gifts of native sons. Reading has always been theatrical-minded. For twenty-five years after the Civil War the Whitmore and Clark Minstrels of Reading traveled all over New England, eastern New York, and the Provinces with perennial success. Azro ("Hank") White, the leading comic, was regarded by scattered thousands as the finest natural comedian of his time. In Reading also was born, in 1853, Henri Wilkins, whose extravagant melodramas, written as a very young man, were widely successful. His *Three Glasses a Day, The Reward of Crime,* and others seem crude today, but they delighted the audiences of the 1880's.

HAMMONDSVILLE is a tiny hamlet stretched along one side of the highway. *Graystone Inn* (1820), is another good example of the sturdy native stone houses that are found in considerable numbers in Reading, Cavendish, and Chester. Preserved records show that the man who quarried all the stone used in building this house — from the hill facing it across the narrow valley — received as his total payment one heavy winter overcoat. The *Grange Hall* just north of the inn is well over a century old. That it is not more interesting architecturally is doubtless due to the fact that it was built in haste and discouragement to replace a much finer structure, a tavern, that burned soon after its completion. In this building lived for many years the woman known as Sleeping Lucy, who later, in Boston and other cities, became one of the best-known spiritualistic mediums in New England.

SOUTH READING, a small village built roughly in the shape of a triangle. The *Schoolhouse* (1835) and the one *Church,* of approximately the same date, are excellent and well-preserved examples of early building in native gray stone. This little settlement once supported a

map-making industry that had branch offices in New York, Cleveland, and Montreal.
Library: Reading Public.

READSBORO, 11–C (Bennington County, Vt. 100 and 8; alt. 1180, pop. 783; 23,961 acres). Hoosic Tunnel and Wilmington RR. Includes: Readsboro village, Heartwellville and Readsboro Falls.

DUTCH HILL SKI AREA (10 m. north of North Adams, Mass., on Vt. 8 and 100). Taxi service; 2740-ft. elevation with 1900-ft. base; 2000-ft. T-bar lift; 1300-ft. J-bar lift; 400-ft. rope tow. Capacity 1700 hourly. Trails: 1 novice (1.25 miles), 2 intermediate (2.25 miles), 2 expert 1.0 mile). Five-acre open slope for novice and intermediate. Ski huts, food, rentals, repairs. First aid and ski patrol. Three instructors. *Information:* Madelon Mulroney, Heartwellville, Vt. Phone: Readsboro, Vt., GArfield 3–5312.

RHODE ISLAND CORNERS (see HINESBURG)

RICHFORD, 1–C (Franklin County, Vt. 105; alt. 504, pop. 2316; 26,168 acres). CP/RR and CV/Ry. Includes: Richford village, East Richford and Stevens Mills.
Newspaper: Richford Journal-Gazette (Thursday).

RICHFORD is approximately in the center of the northern end of the Green Mountain Range and is consequently extremely hilly, the main thoroughfare rising in sharp ascent from both banks of the Missisquoi River, which divides the village north and south. The connecting bridge, which seems much larger than necessary to span a stream usually so small and placid, was designed to resist the traffic forces of the Missisquoi at high flood: forces which have time and again swept away the bridge at this point, leaving the two parts of the village without means of communication. Richford's Main St. is dominated by the *Federal Building,* containing the post office, and the *Town Hall,* which was remodeled from the Advent Church (1871). In addition to the usual town offices, the Town Hall houses the *A. A. Brown Public Library.* Facing the central three-corner intersection is the *Roman Catholic Church,* overlooking from a slight eminence a small triangular Common with an ornate iron fountain. Formerly on the site of the church, the *Union House* now stands across the street and is used as a rectory, an architectural hybrid built in 1820, but interesting for the unrelieved slope of its roof and the wide front verandas on both stories.
Because of the abundance and good quality of the timber near Richford, woodworking in its various branches is the town's main industry. Power for the present mills, however, is transmitted electrically from Newport, 30 miles away. From the upper reaches of the village the

view is unusually impressive, with Jay Peak to the east, its slender, clean-cut cone commanding this part of the Green Mountain Range, and the wide-spreading Champlain Valley to the west. Especially scenic is the location of the Richford Country Club, 1.2 m. northeast of the village, whose 9-hole course has one of the most magnificent settings in the state. Richford has suffered many adversities. Fires and floods have greatly retarded its growth. But the steady persistence and tenacious spirit of its inhabitants have prevailed over all disasters to achieve the present status of commercial prosperity.

EAST RICHFORD is a small cluster of houses to the left of the highway, all but hidden by a railroad embankment.

The route becomes hard-surfaced at this point and roughly parallels the Canadian Pacific Railroad to Richford.

STEVENS MILLS consists of a railroad depot and a few scattered dwellings. The village derived its name from the owner of a sawmill.

RICHFORD COUNTRY CLUB; 9 holes. Range: 130–467 yds.; par 37. Moderately hilly terrain. Facilities: clubhouse with snack bar.

RICHMOND, 4–B (Chittenden County, US 2 and Interstate 89; alt. 319, pop. 1303; 18,123 acres). Vt. Transit bus and CV/Ry. Includes Jonesville.

RICHMOND is a small crossroads village at the junction of US 2 and Vt. 124. Located in a good farming region, it has a large cooperative creamery and a shirt factory. In 1908 fire destroyed the entire business part of the village and even today that section is bare and unshaded. Richmond's chief attraction is the *Old Round Church,* across the river about half a mile from US 2. Completed in 1813, this building has been called the first Community church in the country. It was the joint undertaking of five sects — Congregationalists, Universalists, Baptists, Christians, and Methodists. For many years all the denominations held services here, but they broke away one by one and the structure reverted to the town, eventually becoming the Town Hall. It is actually sixteen-sided, rather than round, with an octagonal belfry, and is painted light brown. The interior contains the original box pews, pulpit, and gallery. Henry Ford at one time wished to buy the Round Church, for removal to Dearborn, but the town refused to sell. Since 1918 an annual Pilgrimage has been held here each summer, with religious services revived for one Sunday in the year.

West of Richmond the valley is broad, terraced, and serene. The backbone of the Green Mountains is on the east, and the Winooski is scrolled in great swinging bends as it curves northward and flows nearer the plain of the Champlain Valley. *Chamberlain Hill* was named for John Chamberlain, who, with Amos Brownson, began the settlement of Richmond in 1775. Although driven away by Indians, they returned after the close of the Revolutionary War to become permanent settlers.

JONESVILLE (alt. 326), a village in the town of Richmond named for the pioneer Jones family that settled here, is marked by an active lumber mill and a handful of wooden houses. The eastern end of the hamlet is guarded by a rock ledge that rears close above the highway.
   Birthplace of Senator George F. Edmunds (1828–1899). Appointed to the Senate at the age of thirty-eight, Edmunds served for twenty-five years until 1891, twenty years of which he was chairman of the Judiciary Committee. He has been considered by some historians the most outstanding representative the state has sent to Washington.
   Library: Richmond Free.
   VAH — Riverside Farm, R. M. Conant. Dairy Farm (Jersey cattle).

RICHVILLE (see SHOREHAM)
RICKER MILLS (see GROTON)
RICKER POND RECREATION AREA (see GROTON STATE FOREST)

RIPTON, 6–B (Addison County, Vt. 125; alt. 1017, pop. 135; 25,840 acres). Middlebury stage. Includes: Ripton village and Bread Loaf.

RIPTON is a small hill village of old frame houses, a church, and a community house. Somewhat decrepit in outward appearance, it is in noticeable contrast to the sophistication against a rural background that Bread Loaf embodies. On the western edge of the village is the old home of Daniel Chipman, a founder of Middlebury College, professor of law and Vermont Congressman (1815–17). This house was built (1833) after Chipman had retired from public life and disposed of his more pretentious estate in Middlebury village. Ripton is of interest to geologists because of the large number of glacial boulders that were deposited here. It was the summer home of the late Robert Frost.

BREAD LOAF is a unique upland settlement centered around Bread Loaf Inn, established in 1866 by Joseph Battell. Mr. Battell left the imprint of his dictatorial but generous personality upon this whole section. His farm at Bread Loaf was a pioneer headquarters for the development of pure-blooded Morgan horses. His love of horses and of mountain peace made him the most aggressive opponent of automotive transportation that this state has ever known. For years before his death, Mr. Battell devoted one page of each issue of his weekly newspaper, the Middlebury *Register,* to gruesome accounts of motor accidents all over the country, hoping that such reprints might at least restrain the local citizens from purchasing those infernal contraptions which seemed destined to supplant his beloved Morgans. Those of his many guests who owned automobiles were met by his men, with horses, at Ripton Hollow, three miles from the undefiled environs of Bread Loaf. Mr. Battell's two-volume *Morgan Horse and Register* is, as might be expected, a thoroughly authoritative labor of love. His 800-page pseudo novel, *Ellen, or the Whisperings of an Old Pine,* is an incredible hodgepodge, consisting chiefly of discussions of theology, philosophy, and all the sciences between Ellen, a spritelike Vermont girl, and the Old Pine, who vaguely represents Mr. Battell himself. Published at his own expense, the book did not, of course, sell, and copies of it can still be found scattered about Bread Loaf Inn, where they serve as casters and doorstops.

Bread Loaf has few rooms for transients because it is the seat of the *Bread Loaf Summer School of English,* conducted by Middlebury College. Here each year distinguished teachers, writers, and critics serve as guest faculty, offering courses in the creation and the appreciation of literature that draw students from all parts of the country. No laboratory of the fine arts could have a more suitable setting than this pastoral haven in the foothills of the Green Mountains. The physical plant includes not only the Inn proper, but several adjacent cottages and dormitories, a library building, and a little theater.

Started in 1920, the School of English has drawn students from all states and many colleges. The six-week session of the school is supplemented by a Writers' Conference (last two weeks in August), when a selected group of prospective writers are brought into contact with leading figures in the professional writing world, including critics, editors, and literary agents.

From Bread Loaf Inn there are a number of short, marked foot trails that wend pleasantly through the woodlands. All are worthwhile, but particularly so is the one to the Widow's Clearing, from which is a superb view of Bread Loaf Mountain. From the Widow's Clearing in summer the picture is one of sharply contrasting color and beauty — on clear days the sky is intensely blue, lightly bannered with fragile white clouds; the deep green blanket of treetops stretches away almost interminably; the open fields around the Inn are yellow with grain, and beyond is the blue-purple bulk of the mountains. By late August there are scattered patches of brilliant red and yellow and brown, from the frosted leaves of birches and maples.

A short distance west of Bread Loaf Inn is the summer home of William Hazlett Upson, the creator of Earthworm Tractor salesman, Alexander Botts.

RIVERTON (see BERLIN)
ROBINSON (see ROCHESTER)

ROCHESTER, 6–C (Windsor County, Vt. 73 and Vt. 100; alt. 837, pop. 879; 30,533 acres). Bethel stage. Includes: Rochester village, Emerson, Robinson and Talcville.
Library: Pauline Manning.
Newspaper: White River Valley *Herald.*

ROCHESTER village was awarded the prize at the Jamestown Exhibition (1907) as the Model Town of the United States. The highway curves in on the northern end past close-set wooden dwellings to the large broad level green, evenly shaded and attractive at the village center. The white wooden *Congregational Church,* gracefully spired, faces the square across Main St. Rochester's industrial virility in no way mars its gracious and orderly appearance.

Rochester District headquarters of the Green Mt. National Forest are located here. Campfire permits for undeveloped areas within the National Forest can be obtained from the District Ranger.

Rochester lost some of its industry when the White River Valley RR closed down. Current industries turn out marble by-products, sawmill machinery and plywood, along with dairy products, by the banks of the White River, separated from the residential sections which sit back in quiet dignity on the natural terraces east of the watercourse. The mountain horizon to the west is commanded by *Mt. Horrid* (alt. 3120). Rochester's setting and general character appeal to an increasing number of summer visitors.

EMERSON (Vt. 100) consists of a few houses strung about the highway about 1.0 m, below Talcville.

ROBINSON (Vt. 73), is a settlement of half a dozen houses huddled together in the eastern section of Rochester town.

TALCVILLE (alt. 825) was once a vigorous mining community, built around the talc mine. Its deserted buildings now rest in idle disrepair on the hillside, unsightly shells of a dead industry.

CHITTENDEN BROOK RECREATION AREA, Green Mt. National Forest (east of Brandon off Vt. 73 or west of Rochester off Vt. 100 on Vt. 73). Facilities: Camp sites, fireplaces, sanitary facilities, drinking water, tables. There is excellent trout fishing in Chittenden Brook.

ROCKINGHAM, 9–E (Windham County, US 5, Interstate 91, northern terminus of N.H.–Mass. 12, a southern terminus of Vt. 103; pop. [town] 5704; 26,020 acres). Includes: Bellows Falls, Bartonsville, Brockways Mills, Cambridgeport, Rockingham, Saxtons River.

BELLOWS FALLS, (incorporated village: alt. 309, pop. 3831).

Bellows Falls Official Information Booth: Adjacent to Red Barn below Westminster line (US 5).

Railroad Station: B & M/RR (also formerly R/Ry), Union Station.

Bus Depot: Town Hall Bldg., Vermont Transit.

Hospital: Rockingham Memorial.

Vermont State Police Outpost: Troop D. Phone: HOmestead 3–4554.

Accommodations: Hotel, motels, cabins, tourist homes.

Newspaper: Bellows Falls *Times.*

Bellows Falls lies on one of the most sharply defined series of terraces that the Connecticut River has cut throughout its long course. On the New Hampshire side towers Mt. Kilburn, stark and craggy; to the west rise the green hills of Vermont. Bellows Falls is definitely divided into three levels; the bottomlands, shaped into an island by a canal, are occupied by industry and a railroad; the middle level is the business mart; the upper sections are residential. The main thoroughfare, Westminster Street, is hemmed in by the bluff covered by homes and the industrial flats along the river. The height of the two- and three-story brick buildings packed on either side is accentuated by the extreme narrowness of the street. The tall brick tower of the Town Hall overshadows this canyon; projecting signs hang over narrow sidewalks, and store windows reflect the jam of pedestrians and automobiles. Compressed between the walls of vari-shaded brick, the small central square makes a peaceful oasis in the most crowded business district of the state. A concrete stairway, an unusual device for Vermont, climbs from Westminster to the level of School Street. From the flats below, the smoke of factories and locomotives rises to shroud the defile made by the river and hangs in a gray pall over the dark bulk of Mt. Kilburn, standing grimly like a backdrop for the Bellows Falls drama of concentrated industrialism and commercialism. The scene has a strong similarity to that of Brattleboro, and, less marked, to that of Windsor.

The town's most distinctive scenic feature is the falls, originally called Great Falls and named, like the town itself, for Colonel Benjamin Bellows, of Walpole, an early proprietor. The falls are divided at their verge by a large rock, which at low water diverts the whole flow into the sixteen-foot western channel below, the narrowest point in the river's entire length. During a freshet the waters dash against the rock, rise high into the air, and fall in smashing sheets fifty feet below to drive through both channels with a violence that has altered the nearby landscape several times. Usually destructive, these freshets have occasionally been beneficial, as when the one of 1797 created the riverbank sites of several of the town's present factories by filling a worthless swamphole with alluvial deposits.

At least a dozen persons have gone over these falls and lived. The first of whom there is any record was an Abnaki squaw, whose adventure was celebrated in print as early as 1781. Carelessly allowing her canoe to be drawn to a point where she could not paddle against the current, the squaw drank a bottle of rum that she was taking to her brave and lay down in the canoe to await her fate. She was fished out below the falls, quite safe and quite drunk. The latest person known to have made the brief but perilous trip was Captain Paul Boyton, who passed over the falls in a rubber suit in 1879 before a crowd of two thousand people.

The falls occasioned the construction here, between 1792 and 1802, of the first canal in America upon which work was actually begun, though not the first completed for navigation. Built by John Atkinson of London, it was retained until 1858, though little used after 1840. Nine locks were necessary to lift the barges, rafts, and small steamers over the falls. In the early 1830's the *William Hall* made a trial trip up the river. The trip ended at Hartland and was never repeated, for the *William Hall,* a side-wheeler, was bigger than any boat the canal builders had visioned and had to be drawn past the falls by means of ox-power, via the village street. After the late 1840's the railroads soon destroyed all commercial navigation on the northern Connecticut, and the shrill blasts of their locomotives, instead of the merry, rowdy songs of the boatmen, were flung against the gaunt sides of Mt. Kilburn to reverberate with piercing intensity over the town.

The first bridge across the Connecticut River, and for eleven years the only one, was built here in 1785 by Colonel Enoch Hale, and was conducted as a toll bridge until 1840. It stood very near the site of the present concrete bridge south of the falls. In 1912 this bridge, a painting of which is fortunately preserved in Rockingham Library, was chosen by an executive committee of the American Society of Mechanical Engineers as one of the eight best and most important wooden bridges ever built in this country. The steel bridge north of the falls was built in 1904–5. Its 540-foot eastern span is one of the longest highway arch spans in the east and one of the few that have a suspended floor. The double-arch stone bridge of the Fitchburg division of the Boston & Maine Railroad has a notably low rise in proportion to the length of its span: twenty feet to one hundred and forty, for each arch.

Industry

The same natural spectacle that has given the town its name, an amusing store of anecdotes, and a minor distinction in the history of American transportation has, more significantly, furnished the water privilege that chiefly accounts for its industrial development and well-being. From the earliest days, the power of the falls has been utilized for a multitude of manufactures, beginning with the inevitable saw- and gristmill. In 1802, Bill Blake moved here from Alstead, New Hampshire, and established one of the first paper mills in Vermont. The stock was rags, which were sorted at tables by girls and cut upon discarded scythes set into the tables. This early venture lasted until 1846. In 1869, William A. Russell, of Lawrence, Massachusetts, later first president of the International Paper

Company, established a mill here where was conducted one of the first successful attempts to manufacture paper from pulp. Since that time Bellows Falls has been one of the largest paper-producing towns in the country.

A curious deviation from the stable and suitable industrial development of the town occurred between 1835 and 1845, when a number of local business and professional men undertook the production of silk. The exotic industry prospered for a time, and the company refused an offer of $20,000 for its mulberry groves, which were shortly afterwards killed by a severe winter. There are still preserved in town a number of articles made from Bellows Falls silk.

Bellows Falls, though not a permanent settlement, was a favorite camping ground of the Abnaki Indians, many of whose relics and implements have been uncovered here. Near the foot of the falls was formerly one of the two most interesting series of Indian rock carvings in the state, the figures of which have become almost entirely covered or obliterated. One reason for the popularity of the spot was the great number of shad and salmon that were to be found at the foot of the falls. Another was the commanding view of the surrounding country from Mt. Kilburn. During the French and Indian Wars both the English Colonies and the French in Canada offered bounties for the scalps of their enemies, and many Colonial scalping parties foraged through this section in search of Indian scalps, for which the Governor of Massachusetts paid bounties up to £100. Extant records show that Mt. Kilburn here, Mt. Wantastiquet at Brattleboro, and Mt. Ascutney at Windsor were among the eminences where the scouts "lodged on ye top and viewed for smoaks" of Indian fires. The last Abnaki Indian seen in Bellows Falls was an aged chieftain who came here to die in 1856 and lies in an unmarked grave in Restland Cemetery. The "smokes" viewed from Mt. Kilburn now are chiefly those of the mills where millions of pounds of paper have been produced, enabling another generation to indulge in such scalpings as are done with printer's ink.

What To See and Do

1. *The Former Home of Hetty Green* (cor. School and Westminster Sts.), the Witch of Wall Street, is a dingy house of faded yellow brick, more interesting for its associations than for its uninspired architecture. It is also the former home of Edwin H. Stoughton and Charles B. Stoughton, two brothers who came here from Chester in 1853 and both of whom became brigadier generals in the Civil War. The house is primarily noted, however, as the home for many years of Henrietta Howland Robinson Green (1834–1916), who married Edward H. Green, a successful Bellows Falls businessman, in 1867. Hetty Green personally managed and greatly increased the large fortune and worldwide enterprises that she inherited from her father, a prominent figure in nineteenth-century whaling and China trade. She was long known as the richest

woman in America and was probably the most astute woman financier who has ever lived. She was almost the only great financier who foresaw the panic of 1907 in time to convert most of her investments into cash, by means of which she increased her own wealth at the same time that she saved many others from ruin. She was undoubtedly somewhat penurious personally — partly as a result of the countless importunings that disturbed the quiet, simple life she desired; but local tales, such as that of her storming out of a milliner's shop in a fury because she couldn't find a becoming hat for less than three dollars, should be taken, if at all, with several grains of salt.

2. The *Immanuel Church* (Episcopal), Church St., was founded by John Atkinson, builder of the Bellows Falls Canal. The present church building, in a modified Gothic style, dates from 1867. The bell, which was part of the first church built in Bellows Falls, was cast in the Paul Revere foundry. Hung in 1819, it was for 30 years the only church bell in town and was used as a fire alarm, for curfew at 9 P.M., and to announce the death of any resident within the village limits. The death knell was three strokes for a man, two for a woman, followed by strokes to the number of the dead person's years. One Sunday morning in the 1830's pious worshipers were outraged to find that a sign from the entrance to the river canal had been nailed firm and high over the door of the Immanuel Church reading, "All Enter Stern Foremost."

3. The *Bellows Falls High School* (1927), School St., is built of gray brick and concrete. On the ground floor, just inside the entrance, is a fine mural painting by Steven Belaski, a local artist, commemorating the encampment north of town near the mouth of the Williams River of a large party of Indians and 112 white captives taken in a raid on Greenfield, Mass., in 1704. The day was Sunday, and the Reverend John Williams, for whom the river was later named, preached what is thought to have been the first Protestant sermon ever delivered on Vermont soil.

4. The *Rockingham Free Public Library,* 65 Westminster St., is of yellow brick with granite trim. There is a museum of relics, oddities, and a few paintings on the second floor. One of the paintings shows the original toll bridge built in 1785 by Colonel Enoch Hale.

5. The *Bellows Falls Hydro-Electric Corporation* (open to inspection), Bridge St., a subsidiary of the New England Power Co., is housed in a large (1928) brick structure, its bright and spotless interior matched by neat terraced lawns outside. The use of natural waterpower for the development of electrical energy, for consumption here or transmission elsewhere, was made possible by the reconstruction of the dam and canal in 1926–28 at a cost of more than $4,000,000.

BELLOWS FALLS COUNTRY CLUB (5 miles north of Bellows Falls on Vt. 103); 9 holes. Range: 137–467 yds.; par 35. Hilly terrain with 1 water hole. Facilities: clubhouse, golf shop, food.

BARTONSVILLE (P.O., Vt. 103; alt. 487) is a tiny settlement with brick homes flanking the road about a church and a lumberyard. The main part of the settlement lies on the eastern bank of the highway off Vt. 103.

BROCKWAYS MILLS is a former station on the Rutland Ry. just east of Vt. 103.

CAMBRIDGEPORT (Junction of Vt. 35 and Vt. 121 about 6 m. northeast of Bellows Falls) is a small settlement surrounding a Congregational Church and cemetery. Stage daily from Saxtons River.

ROCKINGHAM (alt. 480, pop. 5704, off Vt. 103), a quiet little settlement drowsing in the gentle roll of hills, gave its name to a township whose population is swollen by the inclusion of Bellows Falls and Saxtons River. The tiny hill-cloistered village lies under the dominance of the *Rockingham Meeting House* on the knoll, a severely plain white structure erected in 1787, one of Vermont's earliest churches. The Puritan simplicity of this building, without steeple or decoration, gives it a distinctive charm. It was renovated, painted, and landscaped with FERA funds. In the shadow of the meetinghouse are the tombstones of the old burying ground, adding to the reverent dignity of the picture. The interior of the church, retaining the straight-backed solemnity of old box pews, complements the Colonial restraint so evident in the clean lines of the exterior. Rockingham, but a few miles from the clamoring activity of Bellows Falls, rests in complete rural peace.

Between Rockingham and the junction with US 5, Vt. 103 winds and dips along the Williams River Valley, shaded by great old trees. In 1704, near the mouth of the Williams River, 240 Indians returning from a raid on Greenfield, Massachusetts, with 112 prisoners, stopped to camp. It was Sunday and among the prisoners was Rev. John Williams, who preached a sermon to his fellow captives. His text was Lamentations I:18: "The Lord is righteous; for I have rebelled against his commandments. Hear, I pray you, all people, and behold my sorrow; my virgins and my young men are gone into captivity."

SAXTONS RIVER (Vt. 125, alt. 920, pop. [village] 725). Stage from Bellows Falls. This pleasant village is situated in the Saxtons River Valley. The white Baptist Church is gray trimmed with a slate roof. The *Congregational Church* lifts its needle spire from a square base over the head of Main St.

Vermont Academy (1876), originally co-educational, was reorganized in 1931 as a boys' college preparatory boarding school. It was Vermont Academy headmaster James P. Taylor who back in 1911 founded the Green Mountain Club that built the Long Trail. The

School's red brick buildings stand above the maples and elms that shade the greensward of the campus: Jones Hall. The original academy building, and Alumni Hall, flank Fuller Hall, the administration and recitation building. To the rear are Proctor Dining Hall, the small stone Wilbur Library, and the gymnasium, with the athletic field and Bowl Pond in the background. The setting is pleasant, and the atmosphere of the school is friendly and homelike. Classes are small and informal. The majority of students come from outside the state. Extracurricular activities of a diversified nature are strongly encouraged, with stress on both athletic and cultural interests. Emphasis is placed on friendliness and a familylike environment. A pioneer in the field of winter sports, Vermont Academy was instrumental in the development and spreading fame of the Dartmouth Winter Carnival.

ROCKVILLE (see MONKTON)
ROCKY DALE (see BRISTOL)

ROXBURY, 5–C (Washington County, Vt. 12A; alt. 1007, pop. 364; 23,631 acres.) VC/Ry. Includes: Roxbury village and East Roxbury.

ROXBURY is a quiet country village of one main street and a side street leading to the Roxbury–Warren Gap Road. There are no alarums and excursions in Roxbury today (except possibly in camping season), yet one of its earliest settlers was Captain Benjamin Sampson, the boy who rang the Lexington church bell to call out the Minutemen on April 19, 1775. Part of Roxbury Township lies on a height of land from which water flows to both the St. Lawrence Bay and Long Island Sound. The Central Vermont Ry. here reaches the highest point on its line.

On a ridge, half hidden by the pines sit the many cottages of *Teela-Wooket,* a summer camp for girls. Adjacent are the tennis courts and golf links and the stables for the fine saddle horses for which this camp is noted.

EAST ROXBURY has an interesting little cemetery.
Library: Roxbury.

ROYALTON, 6–D (Windsor County, Vt. 14; alt. 513, pop. 1388; 23,928 acres). CV/Ry. and Vt. Transit bus. Includes: Royalton village, North Royalton and South Royalton.

ROYALTON is peculiarly situated along a curve in the highway, hemmed in closely by the gaunt encroachment of a high bluff and the smooth-flowing sweep of the White River. *Cascadnac Inn,* built in 1792 and remodeled in 1810, has such architectural oddities as Holy Lord hinges on the doors, witch crosses built into the doorframe to keep evil spirits away, handmade shutters, and strange archways. Lafayette and President Monroe were one-time guests here. The *Old Lyman House* is of the same period as the inn.

The *Granite Monument* in the small parkway commemorates the burning of Royalton by Indian raiders in 1780, the most calamitous raid in the history of the state. From Tunbridge to Royalton, 300 red marauders under an English lieutenant attacked home after isolated home and settlement after settlement, plundering and burning, taking white prisoners and slaughtering cattle, desolating the valley with torch, tomahawk, and gun. It was no massacre, although a few of the white men were killed. In many cases women and children were let go free. The object of the raid seemed to be the taking of prisoners and the terrorizing of the settlers with wanton destruction of homes and property. Zadock Steele, one of the men taken prisoner to Canada, wrote a long and detailed account of the raid and his captivity, after he was released. The *Whiting House* dates from about 1800; the *Congregational Church* and the *Episcopal Church* belong to a somewhat later period. The *Academy Building* was formerly a Methodist meeting-house, and now houses a grammar school. From the old Royalton Academy many famous men were graduated, including Salmon P. Chase, Senator, Secretary of Treasury during the Civil War, and Chief Justice of the United States; Truman Henry Safford, mental marvel who accomplished unbelievable feats of memory and lightning calculation; Albert M. Billings, co-builder of New York's first elevated railway; and the eminent lawyer family of Denisons. The *Denison House,* built around 1800, is a large handsome white structure surrounded by a white fence.

Library: Royalton Memorial.

NORTH ROYALTON (alt. 520) is a neat little settlement enclosed in the narrow valley, where the Second Branch flows into the White River.

At the southern end of the village is the old brick *Fox Stand,* where Lafayette stopped overnight on his visit in 1825. From here Vt. 14 follows the White River in a southwesterly direction.

SOUTH ROYALTON (west off Vt. 14), the chief village in Royalton, is pleasantly situated along the broad river flats.

The landscaped village green has a fountain, cannon, Civil War Memorial, and the *Handy Memorial Arch,* a marble archway at the entrance to the green that pays tribute to the memory of Hannah Hunter Handy. Facing the Indian raiders of 1780 with courage, she succeeded in rescuing nine children from the red warriors, whose amazement was equaled only by their respect for this white woman's dauntless manner. A real saga of pioneer spirit is the story of Hannah Handy, snatched out of her home by Indians and knocked down by a gun butt, only to rise and persist in snatching children from the invaders' hands until they yielded to her with the savage's admiration for sheer courage. The memorial also bears an inscription in honor of Phineas Parkhurst, who was shot during the attack, but escaped to fling himself on to a horse and ride madly down the White River Valley with a bullet in his side, warning settlers along the way as far as Lebanon, New Hampshire.

Industrial activity here revolves mainly around the woodworking shops. The village is a trading center for outlying farms and smaller communities.

RUPERT, 9–B (Bennington County, Vt. 30 and Vt. 153; alt. 814, pop. 603; 23,312 acres). D & H RR. Includes: Rupert village, East Rupert, North Rupert and West Rupert.

RUPERT is a placid little village on the White Creek, that retains the atmosphere of the past. Many of the scattered wooden houses are more than 100 years old, and the simple *Congregational Church* is nearly 200 years old. The patent asthma remedy made here is sent to many parts of the world. Abandoned by the first settlers during the Revolution, Rupert became a Tory hangout for two or three years.

EAST RUPERT (alt. 840) is a collection of wooden dwellings at a bend in the highway. Near here, in 1785, Reuben Harmon acquired the sole right of minting copper coins for the independent state of Vermont, and maintained the right for a decade. The face of his first coin depicted a sun rising over the hills, a plow in the foreground, and the legend *Vermontensium Res Publica, 1786;* the reverse was a radiated eye surrounded by thirteen stars. These coins are now prized by collectors.

WEST RUPERT (alt. 760) is a small community near the New York boundary, where wood novelties are produced.

VHS marker, just east of the New York–Vermont frontier, reads: "West of village Lt. Col. Robert Cochran Revolutionary Hero Settled Here 1769. Condemned to death by the N.Y. Assembly Col. Cochran fought the Yorkers for Vermont land grants. Joining the Green Mt. Boys, he was with Ethan Allen at Ticonderoga and Seth Warner at Crown Point. Later he commanded Continental forces in the Mohawk Valley Campaigns and undertook dangerous espionage duties in Canada for the American cause."

VAH — Graf Farm, Robert Graf. Dairy farm (Holstein cattle).

RUTLAND COUNTY (Area 929 sq. miles. Population 46, 719). Shire town: Rutland (moved from Tinmouth in 1784). Organized 1781. Includes: Benson, Brandon, Castleton, Chittenden, Clarendon, Danby,

Fair Haven, Hubbardton, Ira, Mendon, Middletown Springs, Mount Holly, Mount Tabor, Pawlet, Pittsfield, Pittsford, Poultney, Proctor, Rutland City, Rutland Town, Sherburne, Shrewsbury, Sudbury, Tinmouth, Wallingford, Wells, West Haven, West Rutland.

RUTLAND CITY, 7–C (Rutland County, US 4 and US 7; alt. 560, pop. 18,325; 4300 acres).

RUTLAND TOWN (Rutland County, US 4 and US 7; alt. 550, pop. 1541; 11,336 acres). Includes: Mill village and Center Rutland.

Rutland city and Rutland town, for all but political purposes, are a single unit. The city is completely surrounded by the town.

RUTLAND (Rutland County shire town).

Information Booth: Corner of West and Main Sts. at Park (summers only).

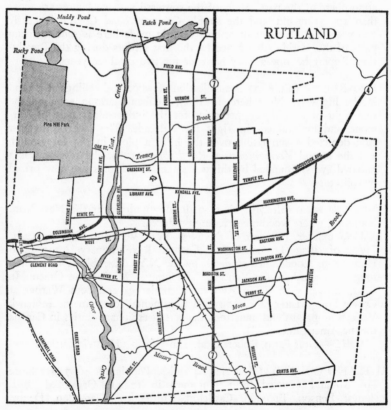

Bus Depot: Merchant's Row.

Railroad (freight only): VT/Ry. and D & H.

Airport (6 m. south on US 7): Mohawk Airlines to Burlington, Albany and N.Y.C. Flights daily. Charter planes available.

Hospital: Rutland.

Newspaper: Rutland *Herald* (daily except Sunday).

Radio Stations: WSYB (1380 kc.) and WHWB (1000 kc.).

State Liquor Stores.

Schools: High school, junior high and grammar schools. Parochial school. Rutland Business College.

State Police Outpost: C Troop. Phone PRospect 3–1901.

Rutland is set in the lovely widened Otter Creek Valley. Vermont's second largest city is the trading area for 80,000 people from the surrounding towns and farms. It is a center for nearby summer resorts and on winter weekends accommodates hundreds of skiers unable to find lodgings in the Pico-Killington ski areas.

Once known as the "Marble City" and now as "The Gateway City" Rutland retains its vigour despite a major shift in the community's economy. The Rutland Railroad, long the city's major traffic lifeline and a prime industry, was abandoned in 1962 after years of losses and two strikes.

The gradual shift from marble as a major building stone and tombstone material closed down or greatly reduced the operations of marble plants. The nationally famous Howe Scale Works which came to Rutland from Brandon in 1877, provides work for several hundred Rutlanders and commuters from nearby "bedroom" towns. The opening of a Tampax and General Electric plant has created several hundred new jobs.

The natural setting is relatively unaffected by industrial progress. The tree-bordered streets of the residential district blend into the meadows of the fertile valley. Pico, Killington, and Shrewsbury, three of the most striking Green Mountain peaks, rise sharply to the east, while the Taconic Range is thrown against the western sky.

The visitor entering the city along US 7 drives through a residential district flanking the long, attractive Common, now known as Main Street Park, but called in early days "Federal Square," a well-preserved survival of eighteenth-century Rutland. Side streets dip westward down the hill to the business section, and beyond to the factories and the railroad yards. To the north lies another residential development near the country club.

Otter Creek had always been a favorite route for Indian travel, and was known as rich beaver country. A fur trader, James Cross, on an expedition from Fort Dummer in 1730, gives in his journal the first recorded description of the falls on the Otter at this point and the fertile adjacent territory. During the French and Indian War travel through here must have been considerable, for the site of the present city was a junction on the Crown Point Military Road which General Amherst ordered built across the mountains to connect the Champlain forts with the Connecticut Valley. Rutland was chartered in 1761 by Governor Benning Went-worth of New Hampshire. The first grantee, John Murray, of Rutland, Mass., was responsible for the name of the town. Actual settlement was begun by James Mead, who brought his wife and ten children up over the mountains from Manchester in 1770 and established them in a log house near the falls which now bear his name. He was able shortly to build here a gristmill and sawmill, and in a few years Rutland was an active frontier community.

> *West of the Mountains Green*
> *Lies Rutland fair;*
> *The best that e'er was seen*
> *For soil and air.*
>
> .   .   .   .   .
>
> *We value not New York,*
> *With all their powers;*
> *For here we'll stay and work,*
> *The land is ours.*

In such verse, appropriately crude, Thomas Rowley of Danby, who was the minstrel of the Green Mountain Boys, celebrated the fierce resistance to New York authority which the inhabitants of the New Hampshire Grants were making in the early years of Rutland's existence. Into the midst of this land controversy was thrust the graver issue of the dispute with Great Britain; and Rutland became a northern outpost of the Revolutionary War in Vermont. Fort Rutland was built in 1775, Fort Ranger (at Mead's Falls) in 1778, and in the latter year the town was made the headquarters for state troops. The cycle of early Vermont history — settlement, the building of a primitive self-sufficient economy, the struggles over title to land, the warfare with England — all this, in the case of Rutland, was telescoped into less than a decade.

In 1784 the county seat was moved from Tinmouth to Rutland, one of the five post offices of the independent Republic of Vermont was estab-lished here the same year, and from 1784 to 1804 various sessions of the legislature were held in Rutland. Vermont's admission to the Union in 1791 was enthusiastically greeted by an all-day celebration in Federal Square. In that era of innumerable and eloquent toasts, this occasion supplied a memorable one — "The Union of Vermont with the United States: May it Flourish like our Pines and Continue as unshaken as our Mountains."

Among the early notables of Rutland the Reverend Samuel Williams, author of the first history of the state (*Natural and Civil History of Vermont,* 1794), is perhaps the most impressive figure. A brilliant mem-ber of the Harvard faculty, honored both here and abroad for his scholar-ship, he resigned from his college position under a cloud and left Cam-bridge at the age of forty-five for what was then the frontier of New

England, becoming in 1789 the minister of the Rutland Congregational Church. In 1794 he was one of the founders of the *Rutland Herald* which, becoming a daily in 1861, has had a continuous record of publication for almost a century and a half. Williams was active in promoting the University of Vermont, and, although disappointed at its final location in Burlington rather than Rutland, he lectured for two years, 1807 to 1808, on natural philosophy and astronomy.

Between 1800 and 1850, the town of Rutland grew from 2124 to 3715, an increase of 75 percent; in the next thirty years the population more than tripled, reaching 12,149 in 1880, passing Burlington (which in 1850 had been twice the size of Rutland), and becoming, for the first and only time, the largest community in Vermont. The sudden shift in the fifties from a long period of normal growth to one of quick expansion was a result of two things — the arrival of the railroad and the subsequent boom in the marble business. The Rutland and Burlington Railroad, the first line to connect western Vermont and Boston, was completed in 1849 (see Transportation). Later known as the Rutland Railroad, it has been extended several times, has changed hands frequently, but has always maintained its headquarters here.

After the Civil War, Colonel Redfield Proctor returned to Rutland and set about transforming the marble business, which had been operating on a small scale for a generation, into one of the nation's great industries. The marble deposits in the western part of the town were among the richest in the world, and their efficient exploitation soon brought prosperity to Rutland and power to the Proctor family. The Vermont Marble Company continued to expand until it controlled a major portion of the marble business in the country (see PROCTOR).

By 1886, the Proctor influence in Vermont had reached a point which made possible the partitioning of Rutland. Strongly urged by Redfield Proctor (who had been Governor from 1878 to 1880), bills were put through the state legislature creating two new townships, Proctor and West Rutland. Public opinion in Rutland was aroused against the change, the opponents protesting that 97 percent of the property in Proctor was owned or controlled by the Proctor family. In 1892, a further partition took place, when the city of Rutland was organized, making four subdivisions of the original town.

The homogeneous nature of the population in the early days was of course definitely altered by Rutland's growth. With the building of the railroad came a large Irish group, and the marble business brought in new racial strains, including Italian, Polish, and Swedish.

Proximity to New York State, strategic railroad and highway location, and industrial activity have given Rutland an atmosphere of urban complexity more common to southern New England communities than to Vermont. But the transition, which came so quickly, after the Civil War, when the railroad and the marble business joined hands to build the modern city, has nevertheless not obliterated the old town. Colonial and

Revolutionary Rutland are still visible despite the prominence of the shopping district and the presence of the big manufacturing plants.

Modern Rutland is a retail trading center and an industrial community. Next to the marble business the most important manufacturing interest in Rutland's history has been that of the Howe Scales, which rank with the Fairbanks Scales of St. Johnsbury in national reputation. Moving to Rutland from Brandon in 1877, the company has operated here continuously since that time.

Rutland has contributed its share of public men to the state and nation. Seven governors of Vermont were residents of Rutland: Israel Smith (1807–8), Charles K. Williams (1850–52), John B. Page (1867–69), Redfield Proctor (1878–80), John A. Mead (1910–12), Percival W. Clement (1919–21), and Charles M. Smith (1935–37). To this list might justly be added Fletcher D. Proctor (1906–8), and the younger Redfield Proctor (1923–25), although both were residents of Proctor.

There are only three places in Vermont which a visitor will feel to be cities; and whereas Barre remains a mining town tempered and restrained by its Vermont matrix and Burlington, with all its air of a great port and a university seat, still wears her queenliness with a sunset charm, Rutland alone maintains the vigor which her railroad gave. Rutland, more typically than either of her rivals, is the small American city — her roots sunk deep in the land and in her history, she yet has a keen eye on the main chance.

What to See and Do

1. *Temple House* (1812), 64 N. Main St., is a dignified, white-painted brick structure, backed by terraced gardens and topped with huge chimneys. Its graceful entrance motif marks it as Georgian. It was the home of several generations of the Temple family. (Private.)

2. *Aiken House,* 1 Aiken Place. At the end of an elm-shaded avenue stands the *First Congregational Parsonage,* built in 1849. A plain white wooden frame house, with rambling ells, it retains the old brick oven, Christian doors, and other interesting details of the period. (Private.)

3. *Main St. Park,* a quiet green, was once the site of the courthouse jail, pillory, and whipping post. Here the hastily recruited troops drilled in Revolutionary days. Here, in 1791, was staged the all-day celebration when news came of Vermont's admission into the Union. The *Statue of the Green Mountain Boy,* with musket and powder horn, alert on a pinnacle of natural rocks, poised as if watching for attack, and a large *Boulder,* with bronze inset bearing the names of Rutlanders who served in World War I, were both placed here by Ann Story Chapter, D.A.R. Between Center and Washington Sts., the park widens to form the old parade ground. Here a white *Marble Bench* with tall entablature has been placed as a memorial to General Clarence Edwards, by the Yankee Division, A.E.F., on the occasion of their Third National Reunion, June 24, 1934.

4. *Sycamore Lodge,* Main St. near Park, was the home of Governor John B. Page, prominent in banking and railroad affairs and state treasurer during the Civil War. President Rutherford Hayes was a visitor at the Page home. (Private.)

5. *Pond House,* 27 S. Main St., is a mellow buff-painted brick house with gabled façade. The small-paned windows are framed by brick arches painted white, and the wide marble sills accent the design. This was the home of Solomon Foot, president of the monster Whig Convention of 1840, later Congressman, and president of the Senate during the 36th and 37th Congresses. Associate and adviser of President Lincoln, he was an outstanding war senator. (Private.)

6. *Kilburn House,* Main St. near Park. A swinging tavern sign, dated 1794, marks the home of the Reverend Samuel Williams, historian and scholar. This simple frame homestead, white clapboarded, with chimneys abutting the side elevations, has lost some of its characteristic beauty through alteration. The house was originally gambrel-roofed, with large central chimney. (Private.)

7. *Morse House,* cor. Main and Madison Sts., was the home of Moses Strong, one of the great landholders of early Rutland. The large, square house, painted white and set in spacious grounds, surmounted by a captain's walk, still retains the charm of the Georgian style, although the classic simplicity of the entrance and the delicacy of the cornices have been destroyed somewhat by the addition of a veranda.

8. *Church of Christ the King* (1929), Main St., is a native white marble structure of English Gothic design. The statue of Christ the King, placed above the entrance under a window of delicate tracery, the heavy wooden doors with their massive hinges, the ornamentation and craftsmanship of the interior, all reflect modern rendering of the early Gothic tone. The sanctuary with three marble altars is separated from the nave by a carved marble rail, extending from north to south transept. Above the main altar are the four Evangelists, while north and south transept windows portray the Transfiguration and the childhood of Christ. The Stations of the Cross are cloisonné work in warm subdued colors. The simplicity of beams and columns, the carved oak organ loft, unite the entire structure into homogeneous design.

9. The *Congregational Church* (1860), Court St., is a large cream-painted brick structure with an impressive spire. Set on an elevation, with pleasant greensward broken by flagged walks, it is a dominant feature of the hill section.

10. *Rutland Free Public Library,* Court St. The old Federal Building designed by Ammi B. Young, and restored with Civil Works Administration funds, is built of pressed brick, and painted buff. Its arched windows and doorways lend distinction, and the interior has all the appurtenances of a modern library. It contains 40,000 volumes and a notable collection of Vermontiana.

11. The *Federal Building,* West St., follows the modified classical style

typical of government construction in the 1930's. Native white marble forms the first story, while the upper three stories are of brick with marble trimmings and quoins. The central pedimented pavilion is in the Corinthian order. Six murals, done by Steven Belaski, under the Federal Art Project, W.P.A., portray outstanding events in the history of Vermont. The building was completed in July, 1933. Post Office, courtroom and offices of the U.S. District Court, the U.S. Navy Recruiting Station, and other federal agencies are located here.

12. *The Synagogue* (1889), Grove St., originally the Baxter Memorial Library, is built of rock-faced gray marble from the West Rutland quarries, in the Romanesque style of architecture.

13. *Riverside,* the State Reformatory for Women, State St., is a group of red brick buildings situated on the green terraces which rise from East Creek. Here a unique experiment in correctional methods has been conducted, and has attracted wide attention among penologists. The absence of bars, the homelike atmosphere of the living quarters, the quiet and beauty of the chapel, and the freedom of the open grounds surrounding the buildings, through which the inmates go about their tasks unguarded, are the subject of an article written by Dorothy Canfield Fisher and Sarah Cleghorn, entitled "Miss Ross's Girls." The system, inaugurated by the superintendent, the late Lena Ross, is founded upon her philosophy: "The prison should be a hospital for body, mind, and soul, a place where one can return when out of a job or needing advice." (Visitors.)

14. *The Maples,* Dorr Road. Built on a high knoll overlooking Otter Creek, this is one of the notable residences of Rutland. A large plain, roomy house, enclosed by a stone wall, backed by wooded hills, and reached by a winding driveway, it was the home of Julia C. R. Dorr, poet. Here she was frequently hostess to Emerson, Longfellow, Lowell, Holmes, and other New England literary figures. *Fern Cottage,* a modern villa built on the estate, was the home of her artist daughter, Zulma DeLacy Steele, and her grandson, Frederick Dorr Steele, illustrator.

15. *Gookin House,* west of the cemetery, built in 1781, on the site of the log church of the first settlers is an old house in excellent preservation. The French wallpaper in the front hall, imported from England soon after 1812, is of Oriental design.

16. *Site of Fort Ranger,* Center Rutland. On the high bluff directly opposite the site of the marker, Fort Ranger was built in 1778 as headquarters for the state troops under the command of Captain Gideon Brownson. In 1781 the garrison was moved to Castleton, and the fort was used as a gathering-place for the people of the settlement.

17. *Center Rutland Falls,* US 4. This is locally known as Mead's Falls, after the first settler, who built his gristmill on the banks of the Otter, and his log house within a half mile of the stream to the west. During the flood of 1927, Otter Creek swept away the railroad bridge which crosses the stream at this point, undermined the highway bridge, and carried nearby houses down the stream.

18. *VAH* — Thomas Dairy, Orin A. Thomas & Sons. Dairy farm, milk bar and milk processing.

19. *Chaffee Art Gallery,* (US 7) Main St. (open June 6–Oct. 21, Mon.–Sat. 12–5, Sun. 1–5, Tues. & Thurs. 7–9:30 P.M. Small fee). Changing exhibits of paintings, sculpture, prints. Vermont crafts.

VHS marker (West St.) notes the site of the former state house. Rutland on several occasions during the late 18th Century was the temporary seat of the legislature.

PICO PEAK SKI AREA (9 m. east of Rutland & US 7, on US 4). One of few major ski areas dating back to the World War II era. A 4000-ft. double chair lift serves new novice and intermediate areas; 1700-ft. T-bar lift for intermediate area. Double chair, 2 T-bars and J-bar lifts. Capacity: 3000 skiers hourly; 9 trails above 2000-ft. elevation; 5 slopes. Karl Acker Ski School. Ski shop with sales, rentals and repairs. Ski patrol. Ski lodges. *Information:* Pico Peak Corp., Rutland. Phone: PRoctor 3-7140.

KILLINGTON BASIN SKI AREA (15 m. east of Rutland and US 7 off US 4). Highest ski elevation in Vermont, Killington Peak; elevation 4241 ft. and 2500-ft. base; 2 double chair lifts; 5 Pomalifts; 6600-ft. double chair lift. Sixteen miles of trails for novice, intermediate and expert. Top Pomalift services peak which usually has November to May skiing. Slow-moving base Pomalift for novices and children. Ski lodges with restaurants. Ski shops with sales, rentals and repairs. Two warming huts. Ski school. Patrol and first aid. Social programs. "Learn to ski Weeks." Overnight accommodations for 3000 guests. *Information:* Sherburne Corp., Killington, Vt. Phone: Sherburne 422-3333.

RUTLAND COUNTRY CLUB (1.25 m. north of business section on North Grove St.); 18 holes. Range: 150–550 yds. Rolling terrain with 3 water holes. Facilities: clubhouse, golf shop, pro, caddies and restaurant. Open 8:30 A.M. to sundown.

RYEGATE, 5–E (Caledonia County, US 5 and US 302; alt. 464, pop. 895; 21,658 acres). Vt. Transit bus and CV/Ry. Includes: Ryegate Corners, East Ryegate and McIndoe Falls.

RYEGATE CORNERS (East, 2.4 m. off US 5 from East Ryegate), a farming community on an upland plateau commanding a wide view of the White Mountains to the east. Ryegate was founded in 1773 by a colony of Scots from Glasgow, led by James Whitelaw and David Allen, who purchased the territory from Dr. Witherspoon, president of Princeton. When they arrived on the tract, they found one of their countrymen already engaged in building a house there. An excerpt from

Whitelaw's journal says: "So we helped him up with it both for the conveniences of lodging with him till we built one of our own, and also that he might assist us in building ours." The following April they made 60 pounds of maple sugar. The next year other families from Scotland came to increase the little wilderness outpost, and to begin the making of oatmeal. Later, dairying was developed until Ryegate butter became well known in the dairy markets. James Whitelaw, six feet ten inches tall, was the founder of the town, the first surveyor in the State, and rated one of the best surveyors and mapmakers in early New England. His surveying spyglass is now in the St. Johnsbury museum. The novel *Safe Bridge,* by Frances Parkinson Keyes, deals with the Ryegate setting and characters. *Blue Mountain* (alt. 2379), rising northwest of the village, is nearly solid granite in structure, with quarries on the southern slopes. South of the village is a pretty little lake named *Ticklenaked Pond.*

VAH — White Farm, Mr. and Mrs. Reginald White. Dairy farm (Jersey cattle).

SADAWGA SPRINGS (see WHITINGHAM)

ST. ALBANS CITY, 2–B (Franklin County shire town, US 7 and Interstate 89; alt. 409, pop. 8807; 1009 acres).

ST. ALBANS TOWN (Franklin County, pop. 2305). Area 22, 681 acres. Includes St. Albans Bay.
Railroad: CV/Ry depot.
Bus Depot: Hotel Kelley. Vt. Transit and Greyhound.
Accommodations: Hotels, motels, lodging houses, tourist cabins.
Schools: Grammar, junior and senior high schools. Parochial.
Newspapers: St. Albans *Messenger* (daily); St. Albans *Leader* (weekly).
Radio Station: WWSR (1420 kc.).
Hospitals: St. Albans; Kerbs Memorial.
Vt. State Police Outpost: A Troop. Phone: LAkeview 4-5993.

St. Albans, the shire town of Franklin County, is rightly known as "The Railroad City." Containing the office headquarters, yards, and shops of the Central Vermont Railway (Canadian National subsidiary), it owes much of its vigorous growth to its transportation facilities and its prosperity to the employment of residents by the railroad.

Yet St. Albans is largely free from the clamor, smoke, and smudge that more often than not detract from the physical appearance of railroad centers. The railroad yards and shops are separated from the business and residential sections. The natural setting is beautiful. The city stands on the gentle slope of an amphitheater formed by Green Mountain foothills. Its floor stretches over wide meadows to island-dotted Lake Champlain, behind which bulks the immutable purple of the northern Adirondacks. From the high eastern residential districts, or from nearby hills, St. Albans seems to rest submerged beneath a green sea of elms, from which rise only the slender spires of churches, like constant periscopes. This view caused Henry Ward Beecher to write that St. Albans was "a place in the midst of a greater variety of scenic beauty than any other I can remember in America."

From 1664 to 1763, St. Albans was part of the French seigniory La Douville. In 1763 it was included in the New Hampshire Grants. Eleven years later, first settler Jesse Welden, a half-breed Indian, came from Connecticut. He made an extensive clearing on Ball Island, in St. Albans Bay, but disappeared during the Revolution, not to return till 1785. By this time the St. Francis Indians were friendly, and Welden cleared and cultivated 70 acres near the center of the present city. He was joined by settlers, from the lower Connecticut Valley of present Vermont, and in 1788 a town was formally organized. An early comer was Levi Allen (brother of Ethan), who laid claims, later invalidated, to so great a part of the town that he addressed his wife, in a letter, as "Duchess of St. Albans." He was a Tory.

Because it was the northernmost sizable community in western Vermont, St. Albans has been the scene of violent events. Between 1807 and the War of 1812, it was the largest base of smuggling operations on Lake Champlain. The most elusive smuggling craft, the aptly named *Black Snake,* was employed by a St. Albans merchant to transport potash into Canada. The *Black Snake* was finally captured after an encounter in which three federal officers lost their lives. So bitter was the resentment of Vermonters against Jefferson's embargo — which prevented the disposal of what was often their only salable product (potash) at the only profitable market (Montreal) — that only one of the smugglers involved in the affray was hanged and those imprisoned were all subsequently pardoned (see BRANDON).

In 1814, when Gov. Martin Chittenden declined to call out the state militia to resist the imminent invasion of upper New York, 80 volunteers from St. Albans made up their own company and proceeded to Plattsburg, where they took active part in the land engagement of the decisive battle of September 11. St. Albans residents gathered on the hills east of town from which the smoke of the naval engagement was visible. Upon the sudden cessation of cannonading, they returned sadly home, convinced that Macdonough's Vermont-built fleet, smaller than that of the enemy, had been defeated. Not until sunset did a galloping horseman bring news of the complete victory that had been won when

> *The Vermontese*
> *As thick as bees*
> *Came swarming o'er the lake, Sirs.*

St. Albans, with Swanton, was one of two Vermont towns seriously affected by the backwash of the rebellion of the Canadian-French population against British rule in the "Papineau War" of 1837. Many rebels found sympathetic haven here, and feeling ran dangerously high. At a mass meeting of 2000 people held in St. Albans on December 19, 1837, supposedly reputable witnesses gave affidavits that public threats had been made by men of southern Canada to burn both St. Albans and Swanton to the ground. No major incidents occurred before Generals Wood and Scott (U.S. Army) arrived to clear up the situation.

The Confederate Raid

The most memorable day in the history of the city was October 19, 1864, the day of the St. Albans Raid, the most northerly engagement — if it can be called that — of the Civil War. Twenty-two Confederate soldiers, in civilian clothes, had insinuated themselves into the city over a period of several days. At three o'clock in the afternoon of the 19th, working with speed and precision, they entered all banks simultaneously, killed one man and wounded others, and fled northward with more than $200,000, firing Sheldon Bridge behind them. The leaders were caught and tried in Canada, but acquitted on the ground that the raid was legitimate warfare. This verdict caused so much international ill feeling that the Canadian Parliament appropriated $50,000 in gold to help defray the financial loss. Vermont became taut with excitement upon receipt by telegraph of news of the raid, the extent of which was at first greatly exaggerated; its effect was, in fact, more important than the money involved.

In June, 1866, large numbers of Fenians, an Irish organization dedicated to the capture of Canada by arms and the establishment of an independent Irish State there, arrived in St. Albans by rail on their way north, as many as three hundred coming in on one train. Many of them slept on the St. Albans Common and in unoccupied buildings. Most of the Irish troops returned through this city after their ineffectual advance some six miles into Canada. The Green was occupied by U.S. troops under General Gordon Meade, sent by President Johnson to preserve neutrality. The soldiers remained for two weeks, escorting tired and disillusioned Irishmen to the special trains the government provided for them, and delighting St. Albans with open-air band concerts in the evening.

The establishment of direct connection by rail with the outside world through the Central Vermont Railway was the turning point in the industrial history of St. Albans, which had almost no importance as a shipping point during the heyday of water commerce on Lake Champlain. Construction of the road was begun in 1848 at Essex Junction, but was suspended when about half completed because of lack of funds. President Smith and other incorporators borrowed the needed money on their personal credit and saved the project from failure. The first train entered St. Albans on October 18, 1850, a diminutive wood-burning locomotive named "Abigail Adams" having pulled it all the way from Montpelier.

With some of the bitter opposition that had marked the development of the new project withdrawn, the Central Vermont grew rapidly and the growth of the city coincided with it. In 1860, the general offices, originally at Northfield, were removed to St. Albans, and the machine and car shops soon followed. Today, with buildings and yards covering an area of 135 acres, the Central Vermont employs nearly two thousand townspeople.

In conjunction with its facilities for transportation, St. Albans has developed a number of thriving industries, including the manufacture of poultry and cattle feeds, maple sugar and sugar-making equipment, canned goods, and lime. It is also an important production and distribution center for dairy products.

The internationally known Eveready flashlight batteries are made here in the *Union Carbide Consumer Products Plant* (free tours).

What To See and Do

1. *Taylor Park,* the city's large central Common, was named for Halloway Taylor, who deeded it to public use in 1799. Its shaded lawns are a contrast to the busy streets. At the northern end is a handsome bronze fountain, the gift of the late governor John Smith. On the southern lawn stands a World War memorial statue. A grim reminder of old-time "justice" is the foundation of the old town whipping post.

2. *Bellows Free Academy,* S. Main St. (1930), was the gift of Hiram Bellows, who left to the city property the proceeds of which, after fifty years, were to be used for the building, equipment, and support of a public academy.

3. The *Elizabeth Fisk Looms,* S. Main St. Housed in a picturesque cottage are two large hand looms operated by women who have successfully revived the technique of weaving intricate designs into linen and of making vegetable dyes. A widely known example of their work is the woven coat of arms of Vermont in the State House at Montpelier, a duplicate of which is in the headquarters of the Federation of Women's Clubs in Washington.

4. The *St. Albans Free Library,* Maiden Lane, occupies the lower floor of a handsome brick and Longmeadow sandstone structure that was one of Governor Smith's many gifts to the city. Among the volumes is the Frank L. Greene Collection of Vermontiana, containing some 300 books and pamphlets, many of them rare.

5. The *Hoyt House,* N. Main St. (1793), the oldest in St. Albans, was built by Silas Hathaway, who though he died poor, at one time owned so much land that he was generally known as Baron Hathaway. Though of utilitarian plan, the house exhibits the instinctive feeling for symmetry possessed by so many early builders. The chief ornamental detail is a pleasing four-pillared entrance portico. During the early nineteenth century the building was used as the Franklin County Courthouse.

6. The *Scoffield House,* N. Main and Hoyt Sts. (1798), is another

eighteenth-century dwelling of almost boxlike plainness except for its pillared entrance.

7. The *Campbell House,* Congress St. (1830), is a satisfying example of late Federal architecture, its brick sturdiness set off by a delicate Ionic portico.

ST. ALBANS BAY STATE PARK (Vt. 36 off US 7; est. 1935; 45 acres) is a sandy beach 0.5 m. long. Facilities: picnic tables and fireplaces, bathing (200-ft.-long stone bathhouse), boating (315-ft.-long L-pier with catwalks and tie-ups for 30 boats). Electricity, gasoline and water available. Fishing. Refreshments.

CHAMPLAIN COUNTRY CLUB (9 holes). Range: 145–570 yds. Flat course. Facilities: clubhouse, pro shack, food.

ST. CATHERINE STATE PARK (see POULTNEY)

ST. GEORGE, 4–B (Chittenden County, Vt. 116A; pop. 110; 2184 acres). Burlington stage. St. George has an 18-hole golf course and a burying ground but no schools, stores or churches. One out of every four St. George residents holds a town political office. Most of these posts pay no salary or fees.

ST. JOHNSBURY, 4–F (Caledonia County, US 2 and US 5, alt. 655, pop. [village] 6809, pop. [town] 8869). Includes: St. Johnsbury city, St. Johnsbury town, Centervale and East St. Johnsbury.
Railroads: St. J & LC, Maine Central, CP/Ry.
Bus Depot: Vermont Transit.
Accommodations: Hotels, motels, lodging houses, tourist cabins.
Schools: Grammar, junior and senior high schools. Parochial.
Newspapers: Caledonia Record (daily except Sunday). *Vermont Union Journal* (weekly).
Hospitals: St. Johnsbury; "Brightlook."
Radio Station: WTWN (1340 kc.).
Vt. State Police Outpost: B Troop. Phone: PIoneer 8-3111.
    St. Johnsbury, the shire town of Caledonia County, is the home of the Fairbanks-Morse Scales and Cary Maple Sugar, and a gateway between the Green Mountains of Vermont and the White Mountains of New Hampshire. Although in recent years it has assumed national leadership in the maple-sugar industry, St. Johnsbury has been as clearly a one-family town as any in the state. The Fairbanks family have left their stamp on St. Johnsbury more conspicuously than has the railroad in St. Albans, and the great rambling factory dominates the western entrance to town. The two finest public buildings on Main Street were given by the Fairbanks family.

Situated at the confluence of the Passumpsic, Moose, and Sleeper's Rivers, St. Johnsbury stretches along the three valleys and surmounts the dividing hills, having an exceptionally broken terrain. The two main divisions in the central section of this vigorous village are marked by a sharp difference in elevation. The principal business district is concentrated along Railroad Street in the central (Passumpsic) valley, typical of active shopping sections in a trading center, with close-set buildings of brick and stone fronted by signs and show windows. On a broad plateau known as the Plain, high above that level, wide, shaded Main Street runs roughly parallel to Railroad Street. Main Street and environs on the Plain constitute the most attractive part of St. Johnsbury, with fine homes set back on shaded lawns, and the outstanding landmarks arrayed here in gracious setting. The two main thoroughfares are connected by steep, winding Eastern Avenue, which is also lined with business places. Across the valley from Depot Park at the foot of Eastern Avenue, a stern wooded bluff overlooks the Passumpsic and the lower parts of town.

The largest town in northeastern Vermont, St. Johnsbury exhibits a broader scope of interests than is common to communities in this section of the state. Devotion to athletics is balanced by an appreciation of the arts and sciences traceable to the presence of an exceptional museum and attractive art gallery. The dominance of relatively stable industries over a long period has had its effect upon the social life as well as the physical appearance of the town. Interest in all branches of athletic sport is keen: the usual clubs are socially active; bowling alleys boom until closing time; the many dances are well attended; restaurants, beer taverns, and theaters are adequately patronized.

The territory was first granted by King George in 1770, under the name of Bessborough, and later Dunmore, but no settlement was made until 1786, when Jonathan Arnold and associates of Rhode Island received a charter from Governor Chittenden. Named in honor of Saint-Jean de Crèvecœur, French consul at New York, author of *Letters of an American Farmer*, and friend of Ethan Allen, it is the only town in the world bearing this name. In 1792, St. Johnsbury and other towns were set off from Orange County to form the new county of Caledonia, which took its name from the ancient Roman term for Scotland, out of deference to the Scottish colonies in Barnet and Ryegate. In 1856 the county seat was transferred from Danville to St. Johnsbury.

Much of the history of St. Johnsbury is coincident with the history and munificence of the Fairbanks family. In 1830, Thaddeus Fairbanks, inventor of the first lever scale, took out his initial patent, and from that time the town dates its material growth and prosperity. Between 1830 and 1870, St. Johnsbury tripled in population, its growth during this period accounting almost entirely for the increase registered by Caledonia County as a whole. For his invention, Thaddeus Fairbanks was knighted by the Emperor of Austria, and to the Fairbanks dynasty, whose members were always philanthropic, St. Johnsbury owes much of its present beauty. Today Fairbanks Scales are shipped to all parts of the world.

The first airplane flight in Vermont was made in 1910 at the Caledonia County Fair in St. Johnsbury.

What To See and Do

1. *Arnold Park,* Main St., a shaded green at the head of Main, faces the length of the broad beautiful street along which church spires rise above the treetops of the Plain. A tablet on a boulder memorializes Dr. Jonathan Arnold, the Providence, R.I., surgeon who founded St. Johnsbury, and was principal proprietor of Lyndon and Sutton.

2. *North Congregational Church,* Main St., Gothic style, is built of Isle La Motte stone, with ornamental red granite pillars, interior woodwork of native cherry.

3. *Museum of Natural Science,* 81–85 Main St., presented by Colonel Franklin Fairbanks in 1891, is the best architectural work in town. Constructed of Longmeadow red sandstone in the Richardson Romanesque style, it is modeled somewhat after the Billings Library at the University of Vermont (see BURLINGTON), which Richardson considered representative of his finest work. The guardian lions by the entrance are strikingly rendered. Exhibits include a complete collection of Vermont flora; a large bird collection; mammals, reptiles, fish, and insects, shells, minerals, fossils, and ethnological specimens from abroad; relics from early history and various wars; old china, pewter, and glassware. Vermont agriculture is illustrated by agricultural implements. The museum, in cooperation with the public schools, sponsors an educational program. Such a museum is unusual for a town the size of St. Johnsbury, its only competitor in the State being the Fleming Museum at the University of Vermont (see BURLINGTON).

4. *Civil War Statue,* Main St., stands in Court House Square over the junction of Eastern Ave. with Main, a figure representing *America,* carved from Carrara marble by the Vermont sculptor, Larkin Goldsmith Mead (see Artists).

5. The *Athenaeum,* 30 Main St., dedicated in 1871 by Horace Fairbanks (Governor of Vermont, 1876–78), houses a public library and museum in a building designed by J. D. Hatch of New York. W. F. Poole, bibliographer, supervised the selection of books. The Art Gallery, featured by Bierstadt's "The Domes of the Yosemite," has 56 other paintings and several pieces of statuary. Each New Year's Eve when Horace Fairbanks was alive, the Athenaeum was opened for a general reception, the social event of the year. The guests of honor at receptions included Admiral Peary and Henry M. Stanley. From the east balcony, President Harrison in 1891, and President Taft in 1912, addressed thousands of Vermonters.

6. *South Congregational Church,* Main St., constructed of wood painted white, is the most pleasing of the churches. A conical spire rises from the

Little Church at Road's End, McIndoe Falls

Vermont Development Department

Montpelier. Ceres, goddess of agriculture, tops the State House dome
Vermont Development Department

Rawsonville — winter logging. *John H. Harris*

The Shelburne Museum on the former J. Watson Webb estate is one of the most interesting and popular museums of its type in the United States

Photo at left: *Einars J. Mengis*

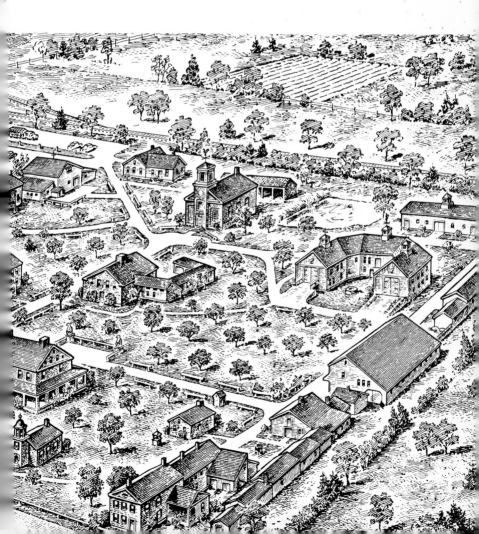

Village of Stowe. *Claire Griffin*

Lower left: Slalom!
Vermont Development Department

Below: Après ski. *Arthur Griffin*

Pownal Center. *Gustav Anderson, Ewing Galloway*

open bell tower, which rests on a square base with clock faces. Three tall entrance doors open from the severe façade. In the interior broad-backed pews and the wide mahogany pulpit are reminiscent of early houses of worship.

7. *St. Johnsbury Academy,* Main St., founded in 1842 by Sir Thaddeus Fairbanks and brothers, Erastus and Joseph, is a private and endowed school, serving as a high school for local students through special tuition arrangements with the town. The trim red brick buildings form an imposing group near the southern end of Main Street.

8. The *Fairbanks-Morse Scale Works,* Western Ave., is the outgrowth of Thaddeus Fairbanks' invention of a device for weighing hemp in a factory where the fiber was cleaned and prepared for market. Investigation and experimenting with the principle of levers in a weighing machine resulted ultimately in the development of the platform scale in 1830. Now all types and sizes are produced here, from the delicate apothecary's scale to enormous ship and railroad scales. The red brick factory buildings are neat and clean. *St. Johnsbury Vocational School* is operated in connection with the plant, high school curricula being combined with practical training.

9. The *Methodist Episcopal Church,* Central St., has a beautiful memorial window, "Annunciation to the Shepherds," by Tiffany.

10. The *Octagon House,* Eastern Ave. (private), was built of brick in 1852, and has on its estate two subsidiary houses of the same peculiar shape, one of brick and one of wood, forming a triumvirate of eight-sided structures on shady landscaped grounds near the heart of the business district.

11. The *Century House,* at the Four Corners (private), was erected in 1798 by William C. Arnold, much of the interior finish being hauled by ox-team from Connecticut. The handmade clapboards are fastened with old hammered nails. On the second floor is one remaining corner of the original ballroom, the floor marked in gray and yellow diamonds, which knew the stately grace of many a minuet.

12. The *Cary Maple Sugar Co.,* Portland St. (visitors welcome), had a modest start fifty years ago as a pioneer in the maple industry, and is now the largest maple-sugar plant in the country. The brick plant and storehouses occupy five acres, and every department is well-equipped. Each spring several million pounds of syrup are purchased and shipped here for processing and packing. *Maple Grove, Inc.,* a subsidiary of Cary, manufactures a wide variety of maple candies, and its attractive candy kitchen here is open for inspection.

ST. JOHNSBURY COUNTRY CLUB (5 m. north on US 5); 9 holes. Range: 150–530 yds; par 35. Rolling terrain. Facilities: clubhouse with showers, lounge, locker rooms; golf shop, pro, caddies. Open 8 A.M.–11 P.M.

SALISBURY, 6–B (Addison County, old US 7 and Vt. 53; alt. 340, pop. 575; 16,863 acres). Vt. Transit bus. Includes: Salisbury village and Lake Dunmore.

SALISBURY was named after Salisbury, Conn., early home of the Allens and other prominent Vermont pioneers. The sidehill village is built along the sharp-curving highway above riverbanks in a narrow valley, and is best known as the southern junction of the Lake Dunmore road. Amos Story first settled the town in 1774, but was killed under a falling tree before he could bring his family here. Mrs. Story, a woman of great strength and courage, came with her brood of small children, to carry on the work of the farm. She remained in Salisbury during the Revolution, when nearly all the settlers fled. Her home was burned by Indians, but the dauntless woman soon had it rebuilt, and it became a popular stopping place for the Patriots in the stirring times when it was the Green Mountain Boys against the world. A monument to her memory was erected in 1905.

Governor (1927–31) John E. Weeks was born here.

VAH — Foster Farm, Howard A. Foster. Dairy farm and maple products.

VAH — Maple Meadows Poultry Farm, George Devoid. Poultry products.

LAKE DUNMORE (see BRANDON)

SANDGATE, 9–B (Bennington County, off Vt. 313 in West Arlington; alt. 820, pop. 94; 23,040 acres). Includes Sandgate village.

SANDGATE, a tiny hill town, has excellent deer hunting. The nearby Battenkill River is one of the nation's finest trout streams. The town's one industry is a woodworking plant. There is a Methodist Church, a burying ground and an inn.

WEST SANDGATE has a Union Church, a burying ground and a few houses.

SAXTONS RIVER (see ROCKINGHAM)

SEARSBURG, 11–C (Bennington County, Vt. 9; alt. 1760, pop. 73; 12,247 acres). Wilmington stage.

Searsburg is a mountain settlement of a half-dozen houses along the high, narrow valley of the Deerfield River, buried in the ridged hills of a great wilderness tract. Once washboards and bedsteads were manufactured here, but lumber-milling ventures died out. The streams that thread the neighborhood afford fine fishing and attract many sportsmen. New England Electric System's hydroelectric plant is located here.

SHAFTSBURY, 10–B (Bennington County, US 7 and Vt. 63; alt. 833, pop. 1939; 24,255 acres). Vt. Transit bus. Includes: Shaftsbury village, Shaftsbury Center and South Shaftsbury.

SHAFTSBURY village (off US 7 north of Shaftsbury Center), formerly a station on the Rutland RR, lost much of its commercial importance when US 7 was routed around the community. The town was settled in 1763 by pioneers from Rhode Island. Some of the leading Green Mountain Boys lived here during Vermont's struggle with Yorkers over land titles. Vermont had only a few Tories during the Revolution but one of them was a former Yorker sheriff. He was John Munroe who with the aid of a large posse captured Remember Baker of the Green Mountain Boys. The nude saber-wielding Baker was captured after a hard fight in a snowbank. He was wrapped in bearskin robes and thrown into Sheriff Munroe's sleigh. Jubilant at the prospect of collecting the price on Baker's head (it was later cut off by an Indian), the Yorkers headed for Albany. A large posse of Green Mountain Boys chased the Yorker posse and forced Baker's release. The affair went into Vermont Legend and rhyme:

> *Old Munroe and all his Yorker train*
> *Picked Remember Baker up*
> *But put him down again.*

The first Baptist Church in Vermont was erected here in 1768.

SHAFTSBURY CENTER (alt. 1480), locally known as Center Shaftsbury, is a scattered, undeveloped settlement strung along either side of the highway, characterized by open lots and tourist places. The chief landmark is the *Governor Galusha House,* a white Colonial structure notable for its beautiful entrance detail, the trinity window above the entrance, and the lunette windows in the gables. Lavius Fillmore, who built the Old Bennington and Middlebury churches, is said to have constructed this house, and the clean true lines reveal the handiwork of a master architect. Jonas Galusha, who lived here, was a Revolutionary captain and nine times governor of Vermont (1809–13; 1815–20).

A *VHS* marker (US 7, north of village) reads: "The birthplace, 1805, of Jacob Merritt Howard. Moving west, Howard became Senator from Michigan and wrote resolutions adopted by the Convention at Jackson, July 6, 1854, on which the Republican Party was founded. He was also the sole author of the 13th Amendment to the Constitution. His birthplace stands about 2 miles to the east."

SOUTH SHAFTSBURY (alt. 740) lies on a flat alongside the highway, lightly shaded by maples. Here is the home of the *Eagle Square Manufacturing Company,* the basic industry of the township, employing 100 in producing steel squares of a wide reputation. The *Old Stone Mill*, where the first steel square was made, has been renovated into a strikingly handsome residence. *Cole Hall* was erected in 1834 as a Universalist Church.

The *Monroe-Hawkins House* graces the north end of the village of South Shaftsbury, a perfect Georgian type of structure with an unusually beautiful entrance. Here again it is felt that the art of Lavius Fillmore, follower of Sir Christopher Wren, is apparent in the architectural details. The imposing white front has entrance pilasters and pediment with a trinity window over the doorway. On the interior are 24 spacious rooms, polished floors, soapstone-backed fireplaces, and a vaulted wine cellar. Here is found one of the earliest examples in Vermont of marble lintels above fireplaces. Constructionally the house approximates perfection for its period, about 1820.

Mary Monroe Hawkins Memorial Library for schoolchildren.

SHARON, 7–E (Windsor County, Vt. 14; alt. 500, pop. 485; 26,654 acres). Vt. Transit bus and CV/Ry. Library.

Sharon lies in a little valley walled in on three sides by mountains and situated on the outside curve of a wide bend in the White River. The white *Congregational Church* and the brick *Town Hall* are both nearly 150 years old.

Site of Joseph Smith's birthplace (entrance to road in Royalton just north of Sharon town line, 2.2 m. to birthplace). The *Guest House* (free admission), an attractive little bungalow sitting on a green-lawned knoll, contains pictures, books and documents relating to the Mormon Church, and the original hearthstone from the birthplace of Joseph Smith. The *Monument* honoring the founder of the Mormon faith stands behind the cottage, nearly 60 feet in total height. The shaft proper is a granite monolith from the Barre quarries, 38½ feet in height and 39 tons in weight. Each foot represents a year of the prophet's life. The briefer of the two inscriptions is as follows:

SACRED

TO THE MEMORY OF

JOSEPH SMITH,

THE PROPHET.

BORN HERE

23d DECEMBER, 1805;

MARTYRED,

CARTHAGE, ILLINOIS,

27TH JUNE, 1844.

In a mellow June twilight, tall, fearless Joseph Smith and his brother, Hyrum, were shot to death against the well curb at the Carthage Jail in Carthage, Illinois, by an enraged mob, which had risen from the storm of hatred against Smith's Nauvoo Legion and the Mormon faith.

Born here on an isolated farm, Joseph Smith spent the first ten years of his life in these hills. It was as a farmer boy of fourteen that he had his first visitation while wandering in the forest near Palmyra, New York. From there he moved to the Middle West, and, in Nauvoo, Illinois, founded the Mormon Church.

SHEFFIELD, 3–E (Caledonia County, Vt. 122; pop. 342; 18,511 acres). Lyndonville stage. Library.

SHEFFIELD, named for Sheffield, England, is an old mountain village well off the main thoroughfares of travel. It has time-mellowed houses, many over a century old and still serving sturdily as homesteads in the highland community. The manufacture of pot- and pearl-ash was an important early industry, but at the present time dairying and lumbering on a small scale are the means of livelihood. The general aspect in Sheffield is one of quiet antiquity in a wild upland setting, remote from the rush of modern times. The *Old Church on the Hill* (Federated), standing above the village, in simple white wood, has an annual "Old Home Day Service." The first blacksmith in town was a Bunker Hill veteran, Captain Joseph Staples. Another Sheffield pioneer, Alexander Berry, sent six sons to the Union Army in the Civil War.

SHELBURNE, 4–B (Chittenden County, US 7; alt. 174, pop. 1805; 14,906 acres). Includes Shelburne village, Shelburne Falls and Shelburne Harbor.

SHELBURNE village lies in restful shade along the highway, with neat hedges bordering velvet lawns. The village center clusters about a small green oval, faced from the south by the attractive *Pierson Free Library* of yellow brick with white-pillared façade. The *Episcopal Church,* a miniature English abbey in local red sandstone, was given by W. Seward Webb (see below), the town's benefactor, who also maintained a rector in residence at the adjacent parsonage. The brick *Town Hall* (right beyond village Green) is further evidence of Webb's generosity. Its graceful Georgian exterior, and well appointed interior provide Shelburne with one of the best community buildings to be found in Vermont among towns of comparable size. The red brick High School serves an area much larger than the town limits. Shelburne's only industry is the Cooperative Creamery.

Shelburne was settled in 1768 by two Germans, who engaged in lumbering for the Canadian market. According to the legend they were killed for their money by soldiers sent from Montreal, supposedly to protect the lumbermen from Indians. In 1778, two Shelburne settlers were slain by raiding Indians and Tories, and the small garrison would have been burned by the attackers, if a timely hogshead of home-brewed beer had not served effectively as fire extinguisher. John L. Barstow, Governor of Vermont (1882–84), was born here.

Shelburne Museum (west side US 7) is open from late May into October. This museum, comparable in some ways to Ford's Dearborn Village near Detroit and Sturbridge Village in Massachusetts, should be visited by all tourists, and Vermonters, too, who are interested in the nation's past. The museum, a nonprofit affair, is located on part of the estate of the late Watson Webb, and was established by the Webb family.

The museum includes more than forty buildings representing about all of America's past major architectural forms. There is also an interesting art museum. The buildings were moved to their present location from wherever they were found. The Webbs purchased the *Ticonderoga,* the last steamboat to operate on Lake Champlain, and moved the large craft inland to the museum — a considerable engineering feat. Museum visitors should plan on spending an entire day if they wish to take in and fully appreciate all the various houses, old-time stores and other structures.

SHELBURNE FALLS (east of US 7 at Shelburne village), a settlement around Shelburne Falls on the River La Platte.

SHELBURNE HARBOR (4.9 m. west off US 7 north of Shelburne village). Macdonough's fleet was anchored here during the winter of 1812–13. Part of the hull of the USS *Philadelphia* was raised in the harbor.

KWINIASKA GOLF CLUB (Spear St., 1 m. off US 7); 18 holes. Range: 174–552 yds.; par 72. Men's course, 6832 yds., Women's course, 5979 yds. Tournament play, 7019 yds. Facilities: clubhouse, pro shop, snack bar, putting green, driving range, caddies, handcarts.

Kwiniaska, the Indian name for Shelburne, means "Long elbow in the river's course."

SHELDON, 1–C (Franklin County, Vt. 105; alt. 374, pop. 1281; 23,040 acres). CV/Ry. Library. Includes: Sheldon village, East Sheldon, Sheldon Junction, North Sheldon and Sheldon Springs.

SHELDON village was chartered as Hungerford and settled in 1790 by a son of Colonel Sheldon and a Scotchman named MacNamera. Colonel Sheldon was of the Light Horse Dragoons and a close friend of Washington. The first birth in town was a colored child born to a servant of Colonel Sheldon. The village is built on two parallel ridges. In the valley between flows the narrow, swift waters of the Black Creek. By the bridge connecting the two parts of the village stands an *Old Mill* with a stone base. As early as 1708 iron kettles were manufactured at Sheldon, the ore being mined and smelted here. This industry attained a high state of production, people placing their orders far in advance and coming from miles around to procure them. Iron was referred to as "Sheldon Currency." Dairying was also of major importance in the township with herds ranging from 25 to 100 head. During this period Sheldon was one of the leading centers of cheese production in the state.

EAST SHELDON, a tiny settlement, is an R.D. route of Enosburg Falls.

SHELDON JUNCTION is a post office and station on the CV/Ry.

NORTH SHELDON is a small dairy community.

SHELDON SPRINGS lies on a sloping hillside by a bend in the Missisquoi. The town is economically dependent upon the large mill of *Standard Packaging Company* at the foot of the hill. Many houses, though built in a uniform style, of brown-stained shingle, are well spaced and landscaped. In the pine grove at the foot of the hill flows the *Mineral Spring* for which the village was named and noted. In this now deserted glade, the Missisquoi, a hotel of 100 rooms, with $35,000 invested in the furnishings alone, once accommodated the hundreds of visitors who came here annually to drink the Spring waters. Now the quiet is broken only by the villagers who come down over the hill in the cool of the evening to fill their jugs.

SHERBURNE, 7–C (Rutland County, US 4; alt. 1240, pop. 265; 26,108 acres). Vt. Transit bus. Includes: Sherburne (Killington P.O.) village, North Sherburne and South Sherburne.

SHERBURNE is a small village of a church and a few undistinguished houses built on a highway three-corners. In the sparsely populated town of Sherburne, about five miles south of the highway, is *Killington Peak* (alt. 4241), the second highest mountain in Vermont. It was from the summit of Killington that the Reverend Samuel Peters, a Connecticut clergyman, claimed to have christened the state by a variant (Verd-Mont) of its present name, in 1763, when he took a horseback trip through this territory, preaching and baptizing. The ceremony, assisted in by many of the proprietors of nearby townships, included the breaking of a bottle of spirits on a rock, and the pronouncing of such sentiments as "a new name worthy of the Athenians and ancient Spartans, which new name is Verd-Mont, in token that her mountains and hills shall be ever green, and shall never die." Later

Peters criticized the accepted form of the state's name. "Since Verdmont became a state in union with the thirteen states of America, its general assembly have seen proper to change the spelling of *Verd-mont,* Green Mountain, to that of *Ver-mont,* Mountain of Maggots. Both words are French: and if the former spelling is to give place to the latter, it will prove that the state had rather be considered a *mountain of worms* than an evergreen mountain!" Peters did not assert his claim, however, until 1807, and it is demonstrable that he lied in print more than once, as when he assumed an LL.D. from the "University of Cortona in Tuscany," which never existed. Nevertheless, Samuel Peters was one of the first Protestant clergymen to enter what is now Vermont, and he was certainly elected the first Bishop of Vermont, at a convention of Episcopal clergymen at Rutland, in 1794, though the Archbishop of Canterbury refused to consecrate him.

NORTH SHERBURNE is a few houses scattered about a tourist camp.

SOUTH SHERBURNE consists of a few houses along the highway.

GIFFORD WOODS STATE PARK (Sherburne P.O., Vt. 100; est. 1931; 108 acres) has been expanded from the original 40-acre sugar bush tract given Vermonters by W. K. Barrows. The tree-shaded area with its relative high elevation provides a cool picnic and camp site. Facilities: picnic tables and fireplaces, tent sites, lean-tos, camp trailer sites and foot trails.

KILLINGTON BASIN SKI AREA (see RUTLAND)

SHOREHAM, 6–A (Addison County, Vt. 22A and Vt. 74; alt. 396, pop. 786; 25,130 acres). Brandon stage. Includes: Shoreham village, Larrabee's Point, Shoreham Center and East Shoreham.

SHOREHAM lies mainly west of Vt. 22A around a large sloping open common, on the high western edge of which stands two trim brick buildings: the *Congregational Church* (1846) and a *Masonic Temple* (1852), the latter having been built and used for many years as a Universalist Church. This village reveals a careful and spacious planning evident in its fellows of the region, which may be traced to the availability of large level tracts of land, seldom found anywhere else in Vermont. The *St. Genevieve Catholic Church* (at the junction of the roads) was built in 1873 and stands in the clear-lined eminence of white-painted wood, facing west toward the main part of the village and the broad open green. A *War Memorial* is found in a little plot near the hotel.

The town was founded by Ephraim Doolittle, a captain under Amherst in the French and Indian War, 1755, and present at Amherst's capture of Ticonderoga and Crown Point, 1759. While engaged in opening the Crown Point Military Road, Colonel Doolittle became impressed with the beauty and fertility of the Shoreham section, and in 1766 headed a party of some fourteen men in settling the town. Nearly all the early comers were veteran fighting men from the French War. Doolittle and his followers established settlement on a "share the profits" basis, undoubtedly one of the first cooperative ventures in America.

Library: Platt Memorial.

Hands Cove Monument (4.0 m. west of Shoreham village) commemorates the pretentious daring of the Green Mountain Boys in crossing the lake to seize Fort Ticonderoga from the unwary British garrison. Northwest from this marker is *Hands Cove,* where on May 10, 1775, Ethan Allen and his lieutenants gathered their motley little backwoods army in readiness to strike at the stronghold on the York State side of Champlain. Here it was that Benedict Arnold arrived, handsomely uniformed and fully commissioned to head the attack, and here the proud Arnold and the dynamic Allen disputed as to who should take command, finally compromising to share the honor. The fact that they took Ticonderoga with such ridiculous ease does not detract from the willful courage and high purpose that motivated them. The prodigiousness of their feat is amply realized on viewing the beautiful restoration of Fort Ticonderoga, seemingly impregnable on its commanding site over the lake.

LARRABEE'S POINT on Lake Champlain. The *First Store* in Shoreham Town, stands near the water's edge, a strong solid structure of stone built in 1823 by John Larrabee and Samuel Holley, of stone carried across the lake from Fort Ticonderoga. The building was used as a store and warehouse, and resembles more the latter. A brief line of cottages along the shaded shore forms a little lakeside group. A beautiful quality of black marble is found near the Point.

Across the lake by ferry is *Fort Ticonderoga* (The fort is open to the public). Ticonderoga stands on a bold promontory commanding Lake Champlain, both north and south, as well as the outlet of Lake George. Recognized from earliest history as the key position, the gateway of Champlain Valley, Ticonderoga has served as military theater for the forces of France, Great Britain, and the United States, being captured, held, and lost by one after another, once without a shot being fired, again after furious fighting which cost over 2000 lives.

A splendid job has been done in restoring the fort, which was originally constructed with the characteristic thoroughness and finish of the French manner, incredibly elaborate for an eighteenth-century outpost in the wilderness. The grimness of gray cannon-guarded walls is relieved by the red-roofed barracks surrounding the central Place d'Armes. Properly garrisoned, the outworks well manned, Ticonderoga was practically impregnable, as was indicated in 1758 when 3500 Frenchmen under Montcalm shattered and repulsed with heavy losses

15,000 attacking Britishers, who never even carried the outer lines of French defense. Each time the fort was taken, it was taken from a small and unprepared garrison, or else abandoned without a fight.

On May 10, 1775, Ethan Allen landed in the early morning darkness with 83 Green Mountain Boys, clubbed down a surprised sentry on their unopposed entry to the fort, routed out the sleeping British Commander La Place and informed him that Ticonderoga was taken. This easily won victory was significant in that it offered moral courage to the Colonies and exemplified the audacity of the Green Mountain Boys.

The restored South Barracks contains an excellent Museum collection, displaying uniforms, firearms, armor, powderhorns, celebrated paintings, etchings, drawings, valuable documents, and books. The West Barracks, restored as an Armory, holds hundreds of firearms and weapons of all description. Many war relics have been unearthed here, identified, classified, and labeled for display.

SHOREHAM CENTER (formerly Richville) is a few houses on the banks of Lemon Fair River.

EAST SHOREHAM, an area rather than a community, has a burying ground surrounded by farms.

SHREWSBURY, 8–C (Rutland County, Vt. 103; alt. 1640, pop. 445; 28,127 acres). Vt. Transit bus. Includes: Shrewsbury village, Cuttingsville and North Shrewsbury.

SHREWSBURY (alt. 1640) is a small agricultural community known for the production of excellent butter. Captain Lemuel White was the first settler, and became captain of the first militia, kept the earliest tavern, and was the first representative, although he could neither read nor write. When a neighbor asked to borrow White's harrow, White replied that if the man brought his land over he might use the harrow on it. Another early arrival was John Kilburn, coming from North Walpole, N.H., where Kilburn and three other men, aided by their womenfolk, had made a heroic stand against attacking Indians. On August 17, 1775, Kilburn and an eighteen-year-old son, with Peak and his son, were going home to dinner from the field, when one of them saw the bare legs of Indians among the alders, "as thick as grasshoppers." The four whites raced to the Kilburn cabin and prepared to defend it. The war whoops rang and the savages started the assault, but the straight-shooting pioneers repulsed them time after time, the women loading the spare guns, and the men keeping the rifle barrels hot. From noon until sundown the siege went on, until at sunset the painted warriors withdrew, leaving the little log stronghold battered but unyielding. Peak was wounded by a ball through the hips, and died five days later from lack of surgical care. John Kilburn lived to see his fourth generation enjoy the land he had helped to free from primitive dangers.

CUTTINGSVILLE (alt. 1040), named after pioneer Cutting who settled here, is the principal village and railroad station of Shrewsbury Town. A green-painted steel bridge spans Mill River at the center of the settlement, which extends from the narrow valley floor up the hillside to the south. About the middle of the nineteenth century copperas was mined, at *Copperas Hill* (alt. 1861) rising east of the village. The section is excellent dairying country, and two Cuttingsville factories manufacture cheese. In the Laurel Green Cemetery on the hilltop is the curious *Bowman Memorial,* a marble and granite mausoleum resembling a miniature Greek temple, with granite busts of the deceased wife, daughter, and small child inside the temple, and a life-sized figure of John P. Bowman, the mourner, outside the door. In the late nineteenth century Cuttingsville had a popular resort inn, the old Finney Tavern.

NORTH SHREWSBURY, a tiny hamlet sometimes called Northam, lies 5 m. north of Shrewsbury.

Northam State Picnic Area is located at the foot of Shrewsbury Peak (alt. 3737).

SILVER LAKE STATE PARK (see BARNARD)
SIMONSVILLE (see ANDOVER)
SNOW VALLEY (see MANCHESTER)

SOMERSET, 10–C (Windham County, Somerset Reservoir rd., north of Vt. 9; alt. 2000, pop. 4; approx. 18,000 acres) became an unorganized town by act of the 1937 legislature.

SOUTH ALBANY (see ALBANY)
SOUTH ALBURG (see ALBURG)
SOUTH BARRE (see BARRE TOWN)
SOUTH CAMBRIDGE (see CAMBRIDGE)
SOUTH CORINTH (see CORINTH)
SOUTH DORSET (see DORSET)

SOUTH HERO, 3–A (Grand Isle County, US 2; alt. 140, pop. 614; 8455 acres). Includes: South Hero village and Keeler's Bay.

SOUTH HERO is spread on a more hilly and uneven terrain than are the northern villages, and consists of two sections, Keeler's Bay on the north, South Hero proper on the southeast. Over the northern part a high church spire rises from a red brick *Catholic Church,* with a tall narrow façade. On the shores of the bay red-roofed cottages are seen among the trees, but in general the village inclines toward the dullness of scattered old wooden or brick houses. The *Old Stone Inn,* at the crossroads in the village center, was built in 1829 and known as the Island House, a favorite stopping place in early days for farmers en route to sell their produce in Montreal. Bunks were built around the walls of the lobby to accommodate the overflow. The rafters in the upstairs dance hall often resounded to music and laughter, as travelers reveled with the natives to break the monotony of slow journeys and rural isolation. Fossils found in the stone walls of this inn support the contention that the islands were once under water, for the stone was quarried locally.

Site of the Ebenezer Allen Tavern, now occupied by an ordinary farmhouse built over, or around, the remains of the old inn. It is thought that some portions of the inn are incorporated in the present structure. Ebenezer Allen, cousin of Ethan and the pioneer settler of South Hero, came in 1783, landing his raft at this southernmost tip of the island, which became known as *Allen's Point.* For many years Ebenezer Allen operated a ferry from the point which bears his name, and in 1787 he enlarged his original homestead to serve as a tavern, and entertained, among many travelers, Prince Edward of England, on his way from Montreal to Boston. On February 10, 1789, Ethan Allen came here from his Burlington farm after a load of hay. It is quite likely that in the course of a long conversation recounting exploits of the Green Mountain Boys, strife with the Yorkers, Revolutionary days, etc., a great many bottles of rum were opened and emptied after the custom of men of action the world over; and so it is not unlikely that Ethan, as legend tells us, was rather full when he started the tedious trip homeward late in the winter night. At any rate, it was Ethan Allen's last expedition. One version is that he was taken sick and died on the way home. Another, and usually discredited one, is that injuries received in falling from the hay-load led to the death of the fiery, arrogant chieftain of the Green Mountain Boys.

In all directions from South Hero village are branch roads that penetrate acres of apple orchards and fertile farmland, and reveal wide vistas of island scenery, Champlain water glimmering away into the distance, mountain peaks guarding the far horizons.

Library: Arthur Hall Langdon Memorial.

VAH — Allenholm Farm, Ray Allen. Apple Orchard and Dairy Farm (Guernsey cattle).

SOUTH NORTHFIELD (see NORTHFIELD)
SOUTH PEACHAM (see PEACHAM)
SOUTH POMFRET (see POMFRET)
SOUTH POULTNEY (see POULTNEY)
SOUTH RANDOLPH (see RANDOLPH)
SOUTH READING (see READING)
SOUTH ROYALTON (see ROYALTON)
SOUTH SHERBURNE (see SHERBURNE)
SOUTH STARKSBORO (see STARKSBORO)
SOUTH STRAFFORD (see STRAFFORD)
SOUTH TUNBRIDGE (see TUNBRIDGE)
SOUTH VERNON (see VERNON)
SOUTH VERSHIRE (see VERSHIRE)
SOUTH WALDEN (see WALDEN)
SOUTH WARDSBORO (see WARDSBORO)
SOUTH WHEELOCK (see WHEELOCK)
SOUTH WINDHAM (see WINDHAM)
SOUTH WOODBURY (see WOODBURY)
SOUTH WOODSTOCK (see WOODSTOCK)

SPRINGFIELD, 9–E (Windsor County, US 5, Interstate 91, Vt. 10, Vt. 11 and Vt. 106; alt. 410, pop. [village] 6600, pop. [town] 9934; 28,210 acres). Includes: Springfield village, Gould's Mill, Kendall's Corner and North Springfield.

Railroad: Springfield Terminal/RR (connect with B & M RR at Charlestown [Fort No. 4], N.H.).

Bus Line: Vermont Transit.

Accommodations: Motels, tourists cabins, lodging houses.

Schools: Grammar, junior and senior high schools.

Newspaper: Springfield *Reporter* (weekly).

Radio Station: WCFR (1480 kc.).

Hospital: Springfield.

Airport: Harkness Municipal (charter flights).

Vt. State Police Outpost: D Troop. Phone: HOmestead 3–4554 (Bellows Falls).

SPRINGFIELD, the first of many towns named for Springfield, Mass., has attained high rank in machine toolmaking and a general industrial prominence not usually looked for in Vermont towns. Notable as this industrial development is, still more notable is the manner in which resultant prosperity has been directed into the proper channels. Industrial leaders have made it possible for Springfield to ride the crest of large-scale manufacturing without creating the sooty slough that submerges so many mill towns. Inventive ability of employees has been fostered by employers who give their subordinates full credit, and even go to the extent of helping set them up in business. Keen minds and cultural tastes have left their mark.

The hills on which Springfield is built rise sharply on both sides of a narrow valley; residential sections overlook the strong-flowing Black River and the large plants along its banks. From the brick-built business center, crowded compactly about a small open square, streets diverge steeply, curving erratically up the hillsides between trim stone walls, with houses set at all levels along the slopes, looking down over roofs and treetops to the machine shops and mills on the valley bottom. Pleasant homes, lawns, and shade trees along the tranquil streets balance the compressed bleakness of the central square and the vibrant hum of manufacturing.

History

About 1750, a tribe of Abnaki Indians lived on French Meadows, near the mouth of the Black River. In 1752 they were joined by an outcast white man named John Nott, who was accepted because of his half-breed Indian wife. Other white squatters came later. The eastern end of the Crown Point Military Road was started on the Springfield side of the Connecticut, and a blockhouse was erected (1 mile north of Cheshire Toll Bridge) for the protection of the soldiers working on this strategic highway, which linked the waterways of the Connecticut River, and Lake Champlain, and outpost No. 4 at Charlestown, N.H., with Crown Point, N.Y. The first real white settlement was begun in 1772 at Eureka, a hilltop site on the Crown Point Road, the pioneers avoiding the marshy lowlands of the Black River to break the soil back in the hills.

It was in 1774 that William Lockwood bought the land around the falls in the Black River, dammed the west branch stream, and put up a sawmill. Others followed the call of waterpower in the churning roar of Lockwood Falls, and the inevitable trend of population from the hills to the valleys was under way. In 1808, Isaac Fisher came from Charlestown, N.H., and secured rights along the river, utilizing the waterpower to operate a cotton mill, an oil mill, a carding shop, a foundry, and a woolen mill, thus establishing himself as the father of industrial Springfield. Fisher's primitive machine shop was a forerunner of the great plants that now stretch along the river flats.

The nineteenth century was drawing to a close when Springfield inventiveness burst upon the machine-tool world with new processes and vastly improved machines that were transmitted over America and Europe to the Far East. Mechanical geniuses who made these contributions were: Amasa Woolson, Adna Brown, James Hartness, E. R. Fellows, W. LeRoy Bryant, Fred Lovejoy, and Ralph E. Flanders.

Springfield has also been a leader in amateur astronomy, and here again James Hartness (governor of Vermont, 1921–23) played a part. Hartness already had a private observatory on his estate, when he came in contact with Russell W. Porter, who possessed an intense interest in astronomy and telescope-making, but no funds for experimentation. There followed a notable instance of a rich man's hobby and a poor man's ardor uniting in a scientific contribution. The Springfield Telescope Makers' organization, founded by Porter in 1923, maintains a fine observatory, Stellafane (3 miles west, off Vt. 11), where amateur astronomers and telescope makers convene. In aviation Hartness was also a pioneer, soloing at fifty-five years of age as Vermont's first licensed pilot.

A strong foreign element has left its imprint on the community, bringing the color and flavor of eastern Europe. People of Polish and Russian extraction comprise nearly one-third of the population, and of no small importance have been their offerings to industry, music, art, and athletics. A good sporting town, Springfield's athletic teams are made up largely of Poles and Russians, and when men gather in the Community House lounge, drugstores, or beer gardens, talk of touchdowns and base hits is likely to prevail with that of the machine shops.

The Springfield Terminal Railway Company, the last electric railroad in northern New England (replaced by diesel trains), was instrumental in the town's industrial rise.

What To See and Do

1. The *Jones and Lamson Machine Co.,* Clinton St. (visitors welcome), occupies immense sheds on the river flats at the eastern edge of the village, a plant so huge as to seem misplaced in Vermont. James Hartness, superintendent in 1889, became part owner, and under the impetus of his inventive genius, "J & L" rode to the forefront in American machine toolmaking, and developed a large foreign business as well. Before the turn of the century the Hartness Flat Turret Lathe and the Fay Automatic had spread over America and Europe to remote China and India. The later growth of J & L has been steady but less spectacular. It has always been a training school for inventors, from which talented young men branch out to establish firms of their own, on the strength of innovations made in the J & L shops, and with the backing of J & L owners — a series of storybook careers in the Horatio Alger vein.

J & L was for many years headed by former U.S. Senator Ralph Flanders, who entered the company in the 1890's as a draftsman. He married the daughter of J & L President James Hartness.

2. The *Fellows Gear Shaper Co.,* River St. (visitors welcome). The former head of this big plant, E. R. Fellows, was chief draftsman for Jones and Lamson when he discovered a new and superior process for cutting gear teeth. As the merits of his process came to be recognized, the automobile industry began its expansion, and quiet gears were in great demand. Fellows' gear shaper shot to prominence, and now the machines which cut the majority of automobile gears, and gears for other machinery, come from this factory.

3. The *Bryant Chucking Grinder Co.,* Clinton St. (visitors welcome), was founded by W. LeRoy Bryant, who made his invention while working as

chief draftsman under Mr. Hartness at Jones and Lamson, and then organized his own business.

4. The *Community House,* S. Main St., originally a Jones and Lamson factory building, is now a spacious club, founded in 1919 by industrialists to serve the community. The first, and by far the most successful, venture of its kind in the state, it is the center of social and recreational life in the village.

5. The high *Falls Bridge* (1917) spans the chasm into which the Black River drops. The Indians used to fish for salmon in this deep pocket in the rocks. The first bridge was built in 1774 by William Lockwood, who felled hemlock trees across the gap. It is legendary that a blind man, when the rude bridge was being rebuilt, crossed unknowingly on a single stringer, while onlookers held their breath. Another story is that the town's first doctor rode up to the dismantled bridge one dark night, urged his horse forward and made the crossing on one strand in the jet blackness, blithely unaware of his peril until it was too late to turn back. In 1836 a sixteen-year-old girl deliberately emulated blind man and horse, walking one stringer over the gorge to settle a dare.

6. *St. Trinity Greek Orthodox Church,* Park St., at the top of Seminary Hill, was erected in 1909, high above the valley. Its architecture is undistinguished, but it is interesting for the picturesque and symbolic rites of prerevolutionary Russia, preserved by the Russian families of Springfield. The Christmas and Easter ceremonies are particularly impressive. At Midnight Mass on Easter, the congregation light candles at the altar and bear them around the church in a stately procession.

7. The *Old House,* Park St., a former tavern, was built in 1802, and is one of the oldest houses in the village proper. Most of the older homes were built back in the hills or near the Connecticut.

8. The *Spafford Library,* Main St.

9. The *Congregational Church,* Main St., a red brick structure with white-columned portico and high white spire, was erected in 1833 and remodeled in 1927.

10. The *Catholic Church,* Mansion Hill, completed in 1930, is constructed of Vermont marble in the Italian Romanesque style of architecture.

11. *Miller Art Center,* Elm Hill (open Mon.–Fri. 10 A.M.–5 P.M. Sat. and Sun. by appointment only). This excellent art center which opened in 1956 is the only one within a 40 mile radius. Rutland and Manchester are nearest. The center is housed in a former private home built during the 1860's but extensively remodeled. Art exhibits are changed monthly. Exhibits may be done by local painters of talent or by nationally known painters. There are a small but excellent art library, local historical items and a general library. Painting, ballet and early American decoration classes are held for both adults and children throughout the year.

VAH — Idlenot Dairy, North Springfield. Dairy products and dairy bar.

SPRINGFIELD SKI AREA (2.5 m. west of US 5 on Vt. 11 and 106); 1000-ft. elevation; 800-ft. tow. Novice and intermediate slopes and trails. Ski hut. *Information:* Springfield Chamber of Commerce, 1 Main St. Phone: TU 5-2779.

CROWN POINT COUNTRY CLUB (Weatherfield Center Road); 18 holes. Range: 140–548 yds.; par 72. Rolling terrain with some water and woods; 10,000 sq. ft. putting green and practice fairway. Facilities: clubhouse with lockers, golf shop, dining room (lunch and dinners), pro and caddies.

GOULD'S MILL and KENDALL'S CORNER are hamlets in Springfield town.

STAMFORD, 11–B (Bennington County, Vt. 100 and Vt. 8; alt. 1131, pop. 513; 25,191 acres). R.D. from North Adams, Mass. This village has three churches and a general store.

STAMFORD VALLEY GOLF COURSE (Vt. 8 and 100); 9 holes. Range: 165–500 yds.; par 35. Facilities: snack bar, pro shop, bar. Scenic course with three state view.

STANNARD, 3–E (Caledonia County, off Vt. 15, 2 m. east of Vt. 16 north of Hardwick; alt. 1700, pop. 113; 6499 acres). This tiny town has three burying grounds and a Methodist Church but no stores. It was named in honor of General George Stannard, the Vermont-born hero of Gettysburg (see ST. ALBANS).

STARKSBORO, 4–B (Addison County, Vt. 116; alt. 612, pop. 612; 24,415 acres). Includes: Starksboro village and South Starksboro.

STARKSBORO stretches along one street on a plain slightly above the river valley to the west, while the eastern terrain climbs to blunt hills. The Mountain View Creamery typifies the principal industry of the region; the large dairy herds may be seen along the route. Two old white houses, with end chimneys and projecting window lintels add a pleasant distinction to the otherwise rather commonplace village street. Among the pioneers who broke the soil here in 1788 were several staunch members of the Society of Friends; their descendants still cling to the faith and conduct services in the Quaker meetinghouse at South Starksboro. The town was named after General John Stark, hero of the Battle of Bennington.

SOUTH STARKSBORO has a Quaker Church and burying ground.

STEVENS MILLS (see RICHFORD)

STILLWATER RECREATION AREA (see GROTON STATE FOREST)

STOCKBRIDGE, 7–C (Windsor County, Vt. 100 and Vt. 107; alt. 734, pop. 392; 25,600 acres). Vt. Transit bus. Includes Stockbridge village and Gaysville.

STOCKBRIDGE is a simple crossroads settlement on a little hummock in the valley with a pine-wooded ridge standing sober guard on the east. South of the village Vt. 100 swings sharply right over the White River and leaves that stream behind to follow the Tweed River directly west for an interval.

GAYSVILLE is a post office and general store surrounded by a few houses. *Belcher Library.*

STOWE, 4–C (Lamoille County, Vt. 100; alt. 723, pop. 1904; 39,973 acres). Includes: Stowe village, Lower Village, Moscow and Mt. Mansfield (settlement).

STOWE quite probably deserves its self-"be-stowed" title "Ski Capital of the East." This small mountain village with several night clubs, more than 50 resorts accommodating more than 3000 skiers, is Vermont's most sophisticated community. Stowe is a "smart" place to be seen and many Stowe snowtime visitors are not skiers.

Stowe, one of the nation's largest and oldest ski areas, owes much of its pre-eminence to its location on the slopes of Vermont's highest peak — Mt. Mansfield. The saying "There's always snow in Stowe" has considerable truth. The average ski season lasts from mid-December through late April, and there has been May skiing in Stowe. Its high altitude places it in the heavy (120 inches or more) snow belt. The large mountain provides adequate space for many miles of ski trails and many acres of open slopes.

Back around 1900 when most Vermonters believed — many still do — "The only way to keep warm in winter is to dress warm and stay inside next to the stove," a few hardy Stowe residents were skiing on barrel-stave skis. Several Swedish families moved here about 1912 but their skiing was a means of transportation, not sport. About 1000 people attended a Washington's Birthday Winter Carnival to watch ski jumping in 1921.

One of the first modern ski trails in America was built in 1933 by former Harvardman Albert Gottlieb. He was then in charge of a CCC (Civilian Conservation Corps) Camp. In 1934 he designed and his crew built the famous Nose Dive Trail. Gottlieb has long been director of Vermont's State Forests.

The Nose Dive Trail received national attention when it was skied by members of the American Women's Ski Team who had returned from Europe. The team was brought to Stowe through the influence of Roland Palmedo, president of the influential Amateur Ski Club of New York, who visualized the development of the area. Bruce Trail, the first local racing trail, was designed by engineer Charles Lord, then a CCC camp boss. Visiting members of the Women's Ski Team told Palmedo that while Mansfield was wonderful, a lift was needed to tote people up the mountain. A rope tow had already been constructed by Frank E. Griffin, a Burlington businessman who moved to Stowe about 1928. He built the Toll House, the area's first real — and fancy — ski lodge. In 1936 Griffin hired a native Austrian professional skier, Sepp Ruschp, to head one of the nation's first ski schools. Ruschp, by the mid-1960's as president of the Mt. Mansfield Corporation, was the leading figure in the Stowe area ski business. This company controls the trails, lodges and lifts on Mt. Mansfield. It is a multimillion-dollar business employing several hundred people.

The first single chair lift was installed in 1940. A T-bar lift was added in 1946. Adjacent Spruce Peak has also been developed by the Mt. Mansfield Corporation.

The Mt. Mansfield Ski Club, one of the oldest in the country, has probably done more to promote and to assist America's international skiers than any other organization. It selects and trains many American skiers for international events including the Olympics. Many American Olympic ski champions were once Stowe High School students, including: Billy Kidd, America's 1964 Olympic medalist; Marilyn Shaw McMahon, who skied at three and won the Women's National Championship at sixteen; Marvin Moriarty, who won five sports letters at Stowe High in one year, won the National Junior Ski Title at fourteen and in 1963 became the first American to defeat European professionals.

Stowe in 1963 celebrated the 200th anniversary of its town charter. The charter granted by New Hampshire Governor Benning Wentworth was issued in the name of Stow. The letter "e" appeared for the first known time in the 1838 town meeting notice. Three of the town's original grantees came from Stow, Mass. Stowe has been in four different Vermont counties. It was originally in Chittenden County. In 1810 it became part of the newly organized Jefferson County. In 1814, Vermont legislators, disgusted with the War of 1812 and Jefferson's Embargo Act, changed the name to Washington County. In 1835 Stowe became part of Lamoille County.

The village itself, though plain and domestic in its architecture, is uncommonly neat in appearance. The *Community Church* has a four-pillared portico, and perhaps the most beautiful spire in Vermont. The *Akley Memorial Building,* of red brick with white Corinthian columns, houses nearly all the public institutions of the town: post office, library, museum, and a savings bank.

LOWER VILLAGE is that section of Stowe which lies along Vt. 100 south of Stowe Village.

MOSCOW is a small settlement 0.5 m. west of Vt. 100. There are a few houses, general store and post office and an elementary school. Moscow is said to have been named at a school meeting in 1839. Someone hit a large saw blade and the sound was believed by someone present to have resembled church bells in Moscow, Russia!

MT. MANSFIELD is a settlement near the summit of the mountain. Its most notable, and almost only feature, is the Mt. Mansfield House, a summer inn dating back nearly a century. The toll road leads from near Stowe to the hotel.

MT. MANSFIELD AND SPRUCE PEAK (Stowe) 6 m. from Stowe on Vt. 108. Top, alt. 4000; bottom, alt. 1500. Three T-bar lifts and 3 chair lifts. Uphill capacity: 5300 skiers per hour. Largest ski area west of the Rockies. Novice, intermediate and expert slopes and trails. More than 50 ski lodges and motels in area. Ski school. Restaurants, snack bars, nightclubs, cocktail lounges. Ski patrol. Ski shops, rentals and repairs (see CAMBRIDGE).

STOWE COUNTRY CLUB; 18 holes. Range: 120–540 yds. Facilities: club house, pro shop, dining room, outdoor cafe, lockers. This is a private course open to guests of member motels, hotels and lodges.

STRAFFORD, 6–E (Orange County, Vt. 132; alt. 960, pop. 548; 24,957 acres). Sharon and Pompanoosuc stage. Includes: Strafford village and South Strafford.

STRATTON, 10–C (Windham County, West of Vt. 100 at West Wards-12,490 acres). Brandon stage. Library.

STRATTON village includes the "Old Stratton Church" founded in 1806 and "moved to this site in 1840." There are two houses. No stores or other facilities. Most of the town's residences are summer homes.

SUDBURY, 6–B (Rutland County, Vt. 30 and Vt. 73; alt. 572, pop. 249; 12,490 acres). Brandon stage. Library.
Sudbury is situated on the edge of a very narrow plateau overlooking Lemon Fair River valley to the west. The jagged Adirondacks are outlined against the western horizon. The river's name is reported to have grown out of an Indian massacre that occurred on its banks; the settlers referred to the occasion as "a lamentable affair," and through constant usage this was shortened to Lemon Fair. Another legend traces the name to "leman fair," the Old English phrase for "mistress fair." During the

editor's childhood in the area he and other children were told that a little boy while coming home from the store with a bag of lemons stopped to fish and the bag of lemons dropped into the river, thus giving the water a yellowish tint.

The *Congregational Church* has a double entrance and an imitation Gothic tower of wood. The *Old Stone Schoolhouse* (1829) is made of stone blocks and has a wide arched doorway and a slate roof. Early settlers prospered in dairying and Merino sheep-raising.

Lake Hortonia (alt. 484), formerly Horton's Pond, was named after the Horton family, once prominent in local affairs. It lies in a wild setting of low hills, with an irregular forested and open shoreline and little islands give it an undefiled charm. Summer cottages are being built along its shores. This spring-fed lake is a popular ice-fishing spot.

SUMMIT (see MT. HOLLY)

SUNDERLAND, 10–B (Bennington County, east off US 7 below Manchester; alt. 649, pop. 566; 28,443 acres) has a general store, sawmill and a *Free Baptist Church.* The town was named after Peleg Sunderland, a Green Mountain Boy.

VAH — Hill Farm, Early Hill. Dairy farm (Holstein cattle).

SUTTON, 3–E (Caledonia County, west off US 5 at West Burke; alt. 1050, pop. 476; 21,973 acres. CP/RR. Library. Includes: Sutton village and Sutton station.

Sutton, a secluded little hill town atop the Connecticut and St. Lawrence watershed systems. The village is touched with quiet and charm. Several Revolutionary War soldiers are buried in the cemetery. One inscription reads:

> *Death like an overflowing stream*
> *Sweeps all away; our life's a dream,*
> *An empty tale, a morning flower*
> *Cut down and with'd in an hour.*

Sutton, granted to Colonel Jonathan Arnold in 1782, was originally called Billymead after Arnold's son, Billy. The name was changed by resentful townsmen when Billy turned out to be a bullying drunkard.

SWANTON, 1–B (Franklin County, US 7; alt. 155, pop. 3946; 27,454 acres). Vt. Transit bus. CV/Ry. and St. J & LC/RR. Includes: Swanton village, Greens Corners and East Swanton.

Newspaper: Swanton *Courier* (weekly).

SWANTON was named for a British captain in the French and Indian Wars, and centers pleasantly around the shaded green of Swanton Park, a long rectangular common. These village greens, almost standard equipment for Vermont towns, serve to differentiate them from their Canadian neighbors. Trim lawns, neat shrubs and colorful flower patches are enclosed by picket fences of wood and iron, shaded by old maples, elms, and willows. The well-spaced and cared-for homes, largely of wood, wear an aspect of comfortable and leisurely living. *Walls of 1812 Barracks* are incorporated in the present Prouty Market, facing the head of the park. The *Old Taquahunga Club* was once the home of Ethan Allen's widow and her daughter, Fanny Allen, who became a nun. *Swanton Library* is a brick structure with white-columned portico. Merchant's Row spread around the head of the park, and a red stone *Episcopal Church* stands at the foot of the elm-shadowed green.

The St. Francis Indians occupied this area before the white men and prior to 1700 built a chapel under the guidance of the French Jesuits, which was the first church erected in the territory that is now Vermont. These Indians participated in many depredations against the whites, most terrible of which was the Deerfield Massacre, 1704, at which time they stole the Deerfield bell to use in their chapel at Swanton for many years. After France lost this new country to England, the Indians moved their beloved chapel stone by stone to St. Hyacinth on the Yamaska River. It was the repeated and bloody raids made by the St. Francis warriors that led in 1759 to the daring drive of Rogers' Rangers against the village of St. Francis, in which the Rangers attacked in Indian fashion, killing and burning without mercy to wipe out the entire settlement.

The French made a settlement in Swanton township about 1700, but an interesting legend places white visitors at a far earlier date. The legend grew out of the discovery of a lead tube on the banks of the Missisquoi, in 1835, which held a piece of paper bearing this message: "Nov. 29 A D 1564 — This is the solme day I must now die this is the 90th day since we lef the Ship all have Parished and on the Banks of this River I die to farewell may future Posteritye know our end — John Graye." The theory was that a last survivor of one of Martin Frobisher's expeditions wrote this farewell message, but indications in general consign this discovery to the limbo of nineteenth-century forgeries. The lead tube has vanished but the manuscript is in the Highgate Library.

In 1765, an Englishman named Robertson established a lumber business here at the falls in the Missisquoi, but the first permanent white settler was John Hilliker, who came in 1779. In the early nineteenth century when border smuggling was at its height, soldiers were sent to Swanton to halt the activities of the contrabanders, and the vicinity was the scene of many thrilling hide-and-seek games and running gunfights between the smugglers and border guards. Smuggling has always been a major business along the Vermont-Canada borderline, and the twentieth-century bootleggers who defied prohibition in roaring high-powered automobiles laden with liquor were the occupational and temperamental, if not the lineal, descendants of those early Vermont smugglers who drove plodding cattle across the line into Canada to sell to the starving British troops. In the War of 1812 English gunboats landed in Maquam Bay and dispatched a force of 600 to burn the Swanton barracks, which had been built to quarter American soldiers sent to protect the border.

The long defunct Robin Hood Ammunition Company (formerly Robin Hood Powder Co.) produced millions of rounds of 8mm Lebel rifle ammunition for the French Army during World War I. The firm was purchased during the middle of the war by Remington Arms of Bridgeport, Conn. The plant was closed at the end of the war. Specimen cartridges are today highly prized by ammunition collectors.

Once known for "Swanton Marble," the town today produces lime products, burlap bags and assorted lumber products.

GREEN'S CORNERS is a section of Swanton.

EAST SWANTON is a depot on the CV/Ry and the St. J & LC.

VAH — Vallee Farm, R. L. Vallee. Dairy farm (Holstein cattle).

TAFTSVILLE (see WOODSTOCK)
TALCVILLE (see ROCHESTER)
TEXAS FALLS RECREATION AREA (see HANCOCK)
THE ISLAND (see WESTON)

THETFORD, 6–E (Windsor County, US 5; alt. 939, pop. 1049; 23,379 acres). B & M/RR. Includes: East Thetford, Thetford Center, Post Mills, Thetford Hill, North Thetford and Union Village.

EAST THETFORD (alt. 408) is a scattering of houses along US 5. *Coombs House,* (2 miles west of East Thetford) is a simple white farmhouse with green blinds, a story-and-a-half with a long pitch roof and low-hung eaves. This unpretentious structure achieved fame through a photograph of it, taken by New York artist Clara Sipprell, that won first prize in the International Gold Medal Contest.

THETFORD CENTER (alt. 668) is a little hamlet near *Lake Abenaki* (alt. 840), which is an elongated body of water enclosed by hills. A girls' camp is situated on the lake. Thetford Center was once a milling village, but now the deserted mills have crumbled and fallen into decay, leaving nothing but a general store, town hall, and a handful of wooden houses.

Childs Pond, a small nearly round pond with no inlet or outlet, is on a plateau 143 feet above the level of the Connecticut, and resembles a great mirror lying face-up on the level earth. The fact that the water is almost flush with the flat banks gives it this strange artificial appearance.

The pond is 60 feet deep and contains carp and hornpout. Across from the pond is an *Old Graveyard,* where forgotten tombstones overlook the Connecticut River. The level tract just north of Childs Pond once served as a racetrack, and also as a drill field for the Thetford militia.

THETFORD HILL (alt. 939), an attractive and secluded upland village, with an air of quiet refinement in the white houses, church, and school surrounding the irregular elm-shaded green. The atmosphere is enlightened by a kind of intellectual awareness, not usual to such a small rural village in the hills. The *Old Congregational Church,* erected in 1787, is the oldest church in the state in continuous use since construction. The tower and bell were added in 1830, and further remodeling was done in 1858. The Reverend Asa Burton (1752–1836), prominent among the ministers of his time, served this church for fifty-seven years. As a boy Burton helped clear the Dartmouth campus of trees, and was later graduated from that institution. *Thetford Academy* (1819), one of the few in the state to remain a private institution, also serves as a high school for local students, through tuitional arrangements with the town. *Latham Memorial Library* was founded in 1877, another evidence of the spirit prevailing in this picturesque hill town.

Richard Wallace was Thetford's Revolutionary hero; in 1777 with Ephraim Webster of Newbury, Wallace volunteered for the hazardous mission of swimming across Lake Champlain from Ticonderoga to Mt. Independence, to deliver important dispatches. The British fleet lay in the middle of the lake. It was late in the fall and swimmers had to follow a zigzag course in order to avoid the blockade. The men passed so close to the enemy boats that they clearly heard the lookout's call, "All's well." They swam naked with their clothes bound behind their necks by cords across the forehead. It was a night swim of two miles in ice-cold water past the British fleet, but the dispatches were delivered. Wallace's health was permanently impaired by the chill and strain of the effort. His wife, a true pioneer woman, worked the farm singlehanded while Wallace was away in the army.

NORTH THETFORD (alt. 399) is typical of the small clean Connecticut Valley villages, with US 5 passing through on the Main St. between the elm-shaded hedges, lawns, and flowerbeds that front the dwellings. White frame houses with green trim are predominant, while several handsome stone structures lend a diversifying touch. The neat white *Congregational Church* harmonizes with the general scene. During the 1936 flood the village was completely inundated, but escaped permanent damage and quickly regained its immaculate appearance.

UNION VILLAGE (alt. 440), a settlement in Thetford Town, was once an active little mill village; it is now a sleepy hamlet stretched under mighty elms in the lee of a bare ridge that shelters the Ompompanoosuc valley. The brick-built *Methodist Church* was dedicated in 1837.

UNION VILLAGE DAM (Ompompanoosuc River) is part of the system of reservoirs and land-protection works for the control of floodwaters in the Connecticut River drainage basin. The dam was constructed under the supervision of the U.S. Army Engineer Division, Corps of Engineers, and is operated by that unit. The dam, constructed 1947–50, cost $4,010,000. If it had existed in the time of the March 1936 flood most of the $6,000,000 property losses could have been averted.

The dam is 1100 feet long and is 170 feet high. The base is 970 feet thick and it is 30 feet wide at the top. Its maximum capacity is 12,400,000 gallons and it covers 720 acres, or more than one square mile. The spillway is 388 feet long.

Picnic tables are located near the base and at the top of the dam. This is a very scenic and pleasant site.

POST MILLS is about a dozen houses surrounding the Malmquist Wood Products Company, a general store, Odd Fellows Hall and the Peabody Library.

THETFORD HILL STATE FOREST (1.0 m. west of US 5 off Vt. 113A; est. 1931; 262 acres) was given to Vermonters by Dwight Goddard. A fine auto road leads to summit (alt. 1160). Good views of White Mountains and Connecticut River valley. Facilities: picnic tables and fireplaces.

THOMPSON'S POINT (see CHARLOTTE)

TINMOUTH, 8–B (Rutland County, Vt. 140; alt. 1263, pop. 228; 17,227 acres). West Rutland stage. Library.

TINMOUTH is reached after a scenic climbing drive. The first county seat of Rutland County, Tinmouth was once the home of iron furnaces and forges, but the enterprise was abandoned in 1837. Nathaniel Chipman, later one of Vermont's foremost jurists, built a forge here for the manufacture of bar iron, 1781. This hill town has long been known as a dairying community, producing excellent cheeses. During the Revolution patriotic spirit burned high in Tinmouth. John Irish was shot down by three local soldiers, who suspected him of being a Tory spy and who apparently decided to shoot first and ascertain the facts later. At the present time the town reposes in its upland setting, a simple peaceful farming community.

Tinmouth Pond is becoming a popular vacation cottage site.

TOPSHAM, 5–E (Orange County, Vt. 25; alt. 2000, pop. 638; 29,145 acres). Barre–Bradford stage. Includes: East Topsham, West Topsham and Waits River.

WEST TOPSHAM (Vt. 25), Barre-Bradford stage, is the principal settlement of this farming town. Some residents live in the tiny village clustered about a Methodist Church, general store/post office and firehouse, but most Topsham folk live on farms in the surrounding country.

EAST TOPSHAM is a locality on an unnumbered back road.

WAITS RIVER is a tiny settlement along the banks of Waits River.

TOWNSHEND, 10–D (Windham County, Vt. 30; alt. 574, pop. 643; 26,387 acres). Saxtons River stage. Library. Includes: Townshend village, Harmonyville and West Townshend.

TOWNSHEND is close-girded by abrupt, rocky hills that on the north rise from the very backyards of the houses. The handsome stucco *Town Hall* is impressive for a tiny village, with its columned portico, clock tower and belfry surmounted by an American Eagle weathervane (this concession to Federalism being suggested by the presence of the post office in the building). The *Dutton Gymnasium,* a neat brick structure, is another improvement that was made after a fire razed the eastern side of the street. *Leland and Gray Seminary,* founded in 1834 as "The Leland Classical and English School of Townshend," is now a high school housed in a red towered building (1894). The first president of the board of trustees was the Hon. Peter R. Taft, the grandfather of William Howard Taft, President of the United States.

The maple-shaded Common at the village center, with a brown wooden glassed-in World War Honor Roll and a fountain, is pleasantly surrounded by white houses. It is difficult to realize that this fine level Green was once so rough and rocky that "an ox cart could not be drawn across it without being capsized." The *Congregational Church* (1790), white with green blinds, enhances the attractiveness of the Common; from a square tower and belfry, the conical spire lifts its weathervane above the treetops.

Joseph Tyler started the settlement in 1764, dragging his possessions on a hand-sled through the wilderness from Brattleboro. Prominent among the early settlers was Samuel Fletcher, soldier and blacksmith, who served in the French and Indian War, faced the British redcoats from the earthworks on Bunker Hill, and fought under Arnold at Saratoga. For eighteen years after the war, this seasoned veteran was high sheriff of Windham County.

HARMONYVILLE (alt. 461) lies along Mill Brook above its junction with the mother stream, a string of large, rambling wooden houses and a sawmill in the township of Townshend. About 1830 Townshend village allegedly grew jealous of the progress made by its little southern neighbor, and fastened on it the name of "Tin Pot." In retaliation the then busy hamlet gave Townshend the title of "Flyburg," and nailed bold signs on its own bridge, proclaiming itself to the world as Harmonyville. Brash invaders from Townshend promptly tore down the signs, but the name has been retained.

WEST TOWNSHEND (alt. 606), situated mainly on a low plateau above a wide oxbow bend in the West River, stretches L-shaped from the lowland flats to its raised shelf. The southern entrance is along a stone-walled street marked by the trim tan stucco of the *Seventh-Day Adventist Church*, neat and new in contrast to its neighbors. Rude old sheds give a rustic air to the bridge, which is at the elbow of the L. The road curves sharply from the bridge, climbing to the village center where old wooden houses and the white *Congregational Church* are set on the tilted slope.

TOWNSHEND RESERVOIR RECREATION AREA (2 m. north of Townshend or 3 m. south of West Townshend along Vt. 30. Drive across top of dam. Turn right.) Recreational facilities provided through the U.S. Army Corps of Engineers include: sandy bathing beach, bathhouse, boat launching site and picnic tables. No fee.

TOWNSHEND STATE PARK (Same directions as for Townshend Reservoir Recreation Area but turn left instead of right at far end of dam top road.) Park is 2 m. from dam site. Facilities provided by the Vt. Dept. of Parks include: campsites, picnic tables, fireplaces. Swimming in West River. Fee.

VHS — Scott Covered Bridge (leads off Vt. 30) — not open to traffic — is owned and maintained by the Vermont Board of Historic Sites.

TROY, 1–D (Orleans County, Vt. 105, alt. 764, pop. 1613; 22,616 acres). Includes: North Troy and Troy village.

NORTH TROY is an industrious community with well-shaded streets bordered by clapboarded residences. Being a gateway between the United States and Canada, it has had a turbulent border history. The early settlers were a high-spirited, reckless lot with a strong love for excitement. They lacked the more staid and regular habits of some of their neighbors to the south. In May, 1812, when an invasion from Canada seemed imminent, a special town meeting was held at which the selectmen were authorized to purchase muskets, bayonets, powder, and a hundredweight of lead for the town's defense. The men of Troy were ready for a fight, whatever the odds, but the British never came. The Weyerhaeuser Company manufactures plywood products. It is one of the largest industrial plants in this section.

1.1 miles north of North Troy, is the *U.S. Customhouse.*

TROY village lies on a slight elevation of an open plain in the eastern Missisquoi valley, its drab houses radiating from a small triangular common. The red-fronted garage that faces the green on the west was originally a church, as its lines reveal. The Grange Fair held annually in this village is an event of local importance. Since there are no special grounds, the straight, level Main St. serves as both midway and race track. Lacking in major or distinctive attractions of sophisticated appeal, this fair is truly festive in a kitchen junket way, a real community celebration. A Kraft cheese factory and a creamery are the sole industries.

Troy Falls, a beautiful natural cascade in the Missisquoi River. The falls are seen best from the high rocky promontory that rises precipitously above the boiling white waters of the deep gorge below. A favorite spot locally for summer picnics and autumn corn roasts is the small adjacent grove, out of sight from the falls, but still within sound of their cool music.

Site of the Boston and Troy Iron Mine, its old stone blast furnace still standing on the bank of the Missisquoi. Though it is beginning to crumble now, this furnace, 24 feet square and 30 feet high, is still suggestive of the magnitude of the iron industry that once existed here. Despite the excellent quality of the products of this mine and blast, it was finally abandoned as being too far from the markets for profitable operation. The iron markers set on the international boundary line between Vermont and Canada were cast here.

TUNBRIDGE, 6–D (Orange County, Vt. 110; alt. 640, pop. 743; 26,384 acres). South Royalton–Chelsea stage. Library. Includes: Tunbridge village, North Tunbridge and South Tunbridge.

TUNBRIDGE lies along the highway in the valley of the First Branch, above the deep level bowl which, as the annual Fall scene of the Tunbridge World's Fair, has imbued the little rustic community with a picturesque aura of interest, color, and significance as a living monument to the rural life of the past. The setting and atmosphere are reminiscent of frontier times. When dusk descends from the stern wild mountains into the deep valley, pictures are conjured of lonely log cabins, open campfires, prowling Indian scouts, and bearded men with long rifles. In October, 1780, 300 Indians under the command of English Lieutenant

Horton proceeded down the valley of the First Branch and fell upon Tunbridge, killing two settlers and taking many prisoners, before heading south to continue their depredations in Royalton.

The *Fairgrounds,* low-lying green meadowlands in a wide bend of the First Branch shadowed by rugged mountains, form an ideal setting for a true country fair, the fame of which has circulated so widely that more than 15,000 paid admissions have been recorded for a single day. With other fairs throughout the state discontinued in the face of depression, Tunbridge's little World's Fair persisted in maintaining the traditions of its origin, until it became the seasonal objective of people from all over the state as well as of autumn tourists from many parts of the country. It grew to be a fashionable fad, quite the thing to visit, and in 1936 the highway was clogged for miles either side of Tunbridge, while the green bowl on the banks of the First Branch was jammed solid with surging humanity. In former years it is said that at three o'clock in the afternoon all sober persons were rounded up and herded off the grounds, as undesirable. The tradition of insobriety is still carefully preserved. The carnival spirit runs rampant, but in all goodwill and friendliness, with government-labeled bottles being passed about in place of the pewter jugs of old. The elaborate antique department is of particular interest and sets the keynote for the fair. Housed in a low pine-slab building are extensive and curious exhibits from pioneer days; an early combination store and post office; a loom and full equipment for carding, spinning, weaving; a blacksmith shop with a bellows-forge; etc. The yard outside is filled with ancient agricultural implements and vehicles of transportation. At intervals during the day, old-fashioned square dances are given by local people in costume. Horse racing and livestock exhibits attract many, and the long midway is constantly packed with merry milling throngs. People from all walks of life are jostled together in the gay riotous turmoil that is Tunbridge Fair — back-country folk of the soil mingle with people from the metropolitan districts; world travelers eat hot dogs at the same booth with native Vermonters; schoolteachers from Iowa, lumbermen, truck drivers, state officials, country storekeepers, college boys, schoolgirls, bankers, and laborers are caught alike in the hilarious whirl.

West from the covered bridge at the north end of Tunbridge on an uphill dirt road is the junction with the Old Turnpike at 4 m. Right on the Old Turnpike and left on the first side road are *Brocklebank Hill and Quarries* (alt. 2120), 5.2 m. The quarries have not been worked for years, but the view from the heights here is superb, ranging over the grandeur of the major Green Mountain peaks from Mansfield south to Killington.

NORTH TUNBRIDGE (alt. 640) consists of a few brick and frame houses and a plain white *Baptist Church* bordering the highway. The sole industry here is lumbering.

SOUTH TUNBRIDGE (alt. 542) is a small farming community, with a red brick *Methodist Church* sitting in the midst of the well-stocked farmsteads.

TYSON (see PLYMOUTH)

UNDERHILL, 3–C (Chittenden County, Vt. 15; alt. 796, pop. 730; 31,292 acres). Vt. Transit bus. Library. Includes: Underhill Flats, Underhill Center and North Underhill.

UNDERHILL (Flats) lies along a level plain, centered around a small tree-studded triangle surrounded by stores, homes, and a small light tan church with a shuttered belfry and spire. A stone fountain plays in the triangle. Mt. Mansfield overshadows the village on the northeast, its broad heights carved high against the skyline. Underhill was settled in 1786, and one of the firstcomers, Udny Hay, had been commissary general of a Revolutionary division.

UNDERHILL CENTER is a pleasing little hamlet on the lower western slope of Mt. Mansfield. The *Catholic Church* dominates the village center, the largest church in the district, containing a number of excellent stained-glass windows.
The former U.S. Army Artillery Range, a 4600-acre tract, was used when the 7th Field Artillery was stationed at Fort Ethan Allen in pre-World War II days. The range is now used for testing the rapid-fire Vulcan aircraft cannon made by General Electric's Burlington plant.
Beyond Underhill Center on another road is a white schoolhouse and right from here on a climbing branch road is the *Stevensville Summer Colony,* a mountain resort in the shadow of Mansfield.
Beyond the white schoolhouse is the junction with a third branch road at 4.2 m. Right on this climbing road is a *Rustic Shelter* and *Free Camp Site,* established by the State Forestry Department. The *Halfway House,* is a summer inn and refreshment shop, the "jumping-off" place for the hike up Mount Mansfield. One foot trail leads directly up the mountain-side to the hotel on the summit. The Sunset Trail runs diagonally to the Chin of Mansfield. Either trail may be taken, but the usual procedure is as follows: climb straight up the summit on the direct route; proceed north along the summit ridge on the Long Trail; and descend the Sunset Trail to the Halfway House.

UNDERHILL SKI BOWL (20 m. from Burlington on west slope of Mt. Mansfield); 800-ft. rope tow. Open slopes. Ski hut and snack bar. Night skiing on floodlighted slope. *Information:* Underhill Ski Bowl, Underhill Center. Phone: Essex TR 8-2836.

UNION VILLAGE (see THETFORD)

VERGENNES, 5–B (Addison County, US 7 and Vt. 22A; alt. 203, pop. 1923; 1200 acres). Vt. Transit bus.

VERGENNES, the third oldest city in New England and one of the smallest incorporated cities in the world, one mile square, was settled in 1766 and incorporated 1788. It was named after Count de Vergennes, French minister of foreign affairs. Large dairy plant at the northern entrance, with the accompanying railway water tanks and freight cars, indicate the city's industrial foundation. The blocky wooden houses with mansard roofs are characteristic of the late nineteenth-century trend in architecture. An attractive central square, with a *Monument to Macdonough,* opens placid and shaded from the compact business district, its green surrounded by the red and white of pleasing homes.

From the business center, the main street slants sharply down to the level of Otter Creek and the falls where, during the War of 1812, forges and furnaces produced 177 tons of cannonballs. Here on the banks of the Creek, Macdonough's flagship *Saratoga* and entire flotilla were constructed in the record time of forty days, for their attack on Plattsburg, 1814 (see History).

Colonel Reid of New York laid claims to land here in 1766, but was dispossessed in 1772 by the New Hampshire proprietors. Reid then engaged Scotch emigrants to settle his claims in Vergennes, but the Yorkers were driven out by Allen, Warner, and Baker at the head of 100 Green Mountain Boys, who ruthlessly burned the huts of Reid's envoys and tore down their gristmill at the falls, 1773.

Bixby Memorial Library, Main St., built of buff brick with a pillared entrance, is one of the finest small libraries in New England

The *Weeks School,* North Water St., the state reformatory for wayward boys and girls, is situated on a plateau above Otter Creek. *U.S. Arsenal* (1828), a grim gray-stone structure, is now employed as one of the school buildings.

General Strong House, Main St., was built in 1793 by Samuel Strong, second son of John Strong of Addison, and has remained in the family since that time. It is a large handsome white structure in the clean simplicity of the best Colonial tradition, and is considered one of the finest in Vermont.

VERNON, 11–E (Windham County, Interstate 91 and Vt. 140; alt. 280, pop. 865; 11,652 acres; Vt. C/Ry) is Vermont's most southeastern town.

SOUTH VERNON, a few scattered homes, is located just north of the Massachusetts line, along Vt. 140. The corner of Vermont, Massachusetts and New Hampshire meet in the Connecticut River in the town's southeast corner.

Vernon Dam (hydroelectric power) across the Connecticut River provides a lake for swimming and boating.

PINE TOP SKI AREA (9 m. south of Brattleboro off Vt. 142 or 3 m. north of East Northfield, Mass.). Three tows totaling 2200-ft service novice, intermediate and expert slopes and trails; 4500 feet of trails. Tiny Tot Tow. Ski hut and snacks. Patrol and first aid. Instructors. Ski shop sales, rentals and repairs. Local residents provide accommodations. *Information:* Pine Top Ski Area, South Vernon. Phone: Vernon 992.

VERSHIRE, 6–E (Orange County, Vt. 113, alt. 1200, pop. 236; 21,817 acres). Thetford–Chelsea stage. Includes: Vershire village, Vershire Center, South Vershire and Copperfield.

VERSHIRE, settled in 1780, was once called Ely. Here in the Vershire Hills are the headwaters of the Ompompanoosuc River, which flows to the Connecticut. Looking at this mountain settlement with its few old frame and brick dwellings resting in an air of tranquillity, it is difficult to realize that around 1880 the great Ely Copper Mines here supported a population of 2000, and in one year produced and shipped three million pounds of copper, then worth more than 20 cents per pound. At the peak of production, the Ely Mines turned out three-fifths of the entire copper output of the United States.

In July, 1883, the "Ely War" occurred, with 300 unpaid miners rising in insurrection to attempt collection, by force of arms if necessary, of the $25,000 back wages owed them by the company. The rioting miners seized arms and ammunition, stopped the water pumps to flood the workings, tore down a few buildings, and threatened to dynamite the works and destroy the villages of Ely and West Fairlee unless they were paid by the following afternoon. Governor Barstow called out five companies of the National Guard to go to Ely by special train in answer to the appeal of civil authorities. The troops arrived in the early morning, and were conveyed from the station to the mining villages in coke wagons while the unsuspecting miners were still sleeping. Rudely wakened in the wan gray morning light, twelve of the leading strikers opened their eyes to face bayoneted rifles, and when the other miners awoke, their leaders were under guard and the streets were full of uniformed militiamen with fixed bayonets. This procedure was followed at both Ely and West Fairlee, the strike was broken, and the Ely War was ended. The mine manager paid the men all the money he had left, about $4000, but the industrial tragedy was complete, for the mines never again operated, and three townships in the vicinity were desolated.

VERSHIRE CENTER (alt. 1700) lies on the remote upland slopes of "The Highlands," from which the eastern range of the Green Mountains stands out in sharp perspective. A few old farmhouses, some of them long since abandoned, are scattered on the gusty hillsides.

Methodist Church in Union Village. *C. M. Abbott, Foto/Find*

South Windham, a typical hill village. *Arthur Griffin*

Left: Weston — interior of Vrest Orton's "original"
Vermont Country Store

Lake Woodbury is really a pretty pond. *Vermont Development Department*

Suicide Six in Woodstock, America's first commercial ski slope
Vermont Development Department

SMUGGLERS' NOTCH
Forbidden Trade with Canada
passed through here, 1808-14

The Notch gained its name after
Jefferson's Embargo Acts of 1808
and the War of 1812. when cattle
were driven north and Canadian
goods were smuggled into New
England through this picturesque
gap beside majestic Mt. Mansfield.
remote from revenue officers.

Smuggler's Notch. Rum was popular contraband. *Ewing Galloway*

Left: Sunderland — the Chiselville covered bridge
Claire Griffin

Apple blossom time in Grand Isle. *Vermont Development Department*

JUDGEMENT RIDGE SKI AREA (36 m. northwest of Hanover, N.H. on Vt. 113); 2000-ft. elevation; 3 trails and open slopes. Ski hut. Snowshoeing. *Information:* Richard Wright, Chelsea, Vt. Phone: OVerland 5-3871.

VICTORY, 3–F (Essex County, off US 2 north of Concord, alt. pop. 46; 23,930 acres). North Concord stage and R.D. Includes: Victory village and Gallup Mills.

VICTORY has a burying ground but no stores. Children attend school in Concord. The many deserted sawmills, or what is left of them, explain Victory's decline from a peak population of nearly 600 residents in 1890. Hunting and fishing are excellent in the woods surrounding this mountain-hemmed hamlet.

GALLUP MILLS is a small deserted-looking hamlet in the northeastern part of the town of Victory. Gallup Mills was formerly the site of important sawmills, which were built when this great timber region was cut for the first time. The St. Johnsbury and Lake Champlain RR (Victory Branch) once went through this settlement and two and a half miles north to other mills.

WAITSFIELD, 5–C (Washington County, Vt. 100; alt. 698, pop. 658; 13,631 acres). Middlesex stage. Includes: Waitsfield village and Irasville.

WAITSFIELD received its name from General Benjamin Wait who founded the settlement in 1789. Eleven of the thirteen pioneers who followed Wait were veterans of the French & Indian War and the Revolution, and it is traditional that six of these eleven soldiers were among the Minutemen at Concord Bridge and Lexington Green. Wait had a long career as a soldier, starting under Amherst at the age of eighteen, and fighting in 40 battles before he was twenty-five. In the Revolution he served as a captain under Washington, being raised to the rank of colonel by the close of the war, and then becoming a general of militia. After coming to Waitsfield this hardened campaigner devoted himself to religion and led an exemplary life.

An amusing story is told of Deacon Moses Fisk's barn-raising in 1821, at which the deacon declared that, contrary to the usual custom, no liquor was to be drunk at his raising bee. When the time came to raise the ridgepole, or "rum pole" as it was called, the workers went on a strike, informing the deacon that they could not lift the ridgepole until they were strengthened by rum. But the stubborn old deacon refused to yield, and after a time the men, grumbling or joking as was their nature, completed the task without the aid of stimulants.

The village lies along the river flats walled in by hills. Dairying and lumbering are the industries. The *Federated Church,* a nice white structure with a tall clean spire, adds attractiveness to the village street. *Joslin Memorial Library* is built of brick painted yellow. At the south end of the settlement a rock ledge rears close above the highway as the western ridge encroaches on the valley.

IRASVILLE (alt. 789) is a small hamlet on a plateau banked by high hills.

MAD RIVER GLEN SKI AREA (16 m. south of Waterbury and 4 m. west of Vt. 100 at Waitsfield). Taxi service; 3600-ft. elevation and 1600-ft. base; 5640-ft.-long single chair lift with 2000-ft. vertical rise; 4400-ft.-long double chair lift with 1400-ft. vertical rise; 1500-ft. T-bar with 300-ft. vertical rise. Trails: 4 novice (4.5 miles), 3 intermediate (2.5 miles) and 5 expert (3 miles). Wide practice slopes. Ski huts at summit and base. Restaurant, ski shop with sales, rentals and repairs. Ski school Patrol and first aid; 35 chalets, ski lodges and guest homes. *Information and reservations:* Mad River Glen, Waitsfield. Phone: Waitsfield 496-3397.

WAITS RIVER (see TOPSHAM)

WALDEN, 3–E (Caledonia County, Vt. 15; alt. 1656, pop. 427; 22,242 acres). Vt. Transit bus. Includes: Walden Heights, North Walden and South Walden.

WALDEN consists simply of a few wooden buildings clustered raggedly at a rural corner and bridge, and lying at the high altitude for which Walden Heights is known. The Hazen Military Road passed through the town, and the blockhouse built here was garrisoned under the command of Major Walden, whose name was given to the town. The blockhouse, which remained standing for many years, and housed early settlers and the first school, was the scene of the first religious services, the first birth, and at one time served as a homestead for Mr. and Mrs. Gideon Sabin and their twenty-six children. Today this is a purely agricultural community, with land under cultivation at an altitude of 1671 feet, one of the highest elevations at which agriculture is carried on in the state. Prominent among Walden citizens have been the Bell family, descendants of John Austin, the Glasgow artisan who invented the tulip-shaped bell now in common use, for which he was knighted by Queen Elizabeth and took the name of Bell.

Lyford Pond, named after Lieutenant Lyford of a Hazen Military Road detachment, is shaped like an oxbow and lies low in the fringe of trees that mark its shoreline.

Scenic View, one of the finest in northern Vermont, not only shows the main range of the Green Mountains nobly prominent, stretching almost 100 miles down the center of the state, but the Worcester Mountains rising sharp and clear in the middle distance.

NORTH WALDEN is a tiny hamlet.

SOUTH WALDEN is another tiny rural corner settlement built around a sawmill on the banks of a mountain stream. The *Stage Tavern,* a long white double-porched building with green trim and three chimneys, was a stagecoach inn about the middle of the nineteenth century; the stone hitching post stands by the roadside. On the hill a white tin-roofed *Methodist Church* with belfry stands over the little mill settlement.

WALLINGFORD, 8–C (Rutland County, US 7 and Vt. 103; alt. 580, pop. 1439; 24,621 acres). Vt .Transit bus. Includes: Wallingford village, East Wallingford and South Wallingford.

WALLINGFORD is typical of the more attractive New England villages, with a broad main street running under a tunnel of green boughs arched from lofty elms, fine, large houses set back on trim lawns, and a scrupulous cleanness everywhere. Shrubbery frames immaculate columned porches, and a gracious quality of peace permeates the whole scene. The *True Temper Tool Factory* of the American Fork and Hoe Company, one of the large plants operated by this firm, the biggest manufacturers of hand garden tools in the world, dominates the entrance on the north. Flower gardens brighten the general cleanness of the factory, in contrast to the industrial dinginess that might be expected.

The small house bearing the date 1818 was the *Boyhood Home of Paul P. Harris,* founder of Rotary International. Though Michigan-born, Harris spent most of his early years in Vermont and attended the University of Vermont. The organization which he created has acquired possession of this, his grandfather's home, and a portrait of Harris is displayed within.

Another *Brick House,* built by William Fox, who was a sixteen-year-old soldier in the Revolution, embodies the compact security and clarity of line associated with its type and age. The *Wallingford Inn* centers the village street, the slender white pillars giving it a pseudo–Mt. Vernon aspect. The *Boy and Boot Fountain* is an unusual landmark in front of the inn, with water flowing from the toe of a boot held by a boy. The *Gilbert Hart Library,* a brick and granite building, contains 7000 volumes. The *Old Stone Shop* was the original mill building of the fork factory, established in 1836 by Lyman Batcheller, and stands picturesque and sturdy, beautifully remodeled and tastefully fitted with old furnishings to serve as a tea room.

Green Hill Cemetery. This attractive terraced graveyard rises from the roadside at the southern edge of Wallingford, with a fountain playing at its base, the grounds well cared for and colored with flowers. The landscaping is such as to impart a slightly incongruous Versailles atmosphere. The first man to be buried here was a Tory killed by Wallingford patriots.

WHITE ROCKS PICNIC AREA, Green Mt. National Forest (2 m. southeast of Wallingford on short spur off Vt. 140). Facilities: picnic tables, fireplaces, sanitary facilities, drinking water. Short trail to lookout.

VAH — Skyfield Farm, C. Edgar Stevens. Dairy farm (Ayrshire cattle).

EAST WALLINGFORD (alt. 1240, off Vt. 103 at junction of Vt. 140 and Vt. 155), a comparatively recent settlement, owed its existence largely to the late Rutland RR. The village occupies a fairly wide place in the valley of Mill River, with plain domestic houses stretching from the riverside up the gradual slope to the west. A creamery and cheese factory constitute the industries. The white *Baptist Church* is neat and attractive in an ordinary way, as is the white school building. The cemetery occupies a hill with a stonewall base, on the eastern edge of the hamlet.

SOUTH WALLINGFORD (alt. 620) was something of a mill town and a small industrial center in the middle nineteenth century, but this activity has died out, leaving only a hamlet stretched along US 7 above the banks of the Otter Creek. The *Union Church* is of white wood, with an odd crenellated tower.

Old Cemetery lies on a knoll over the highway. Among the old tombstones is one marking the grave of Jerathmiel Doty, Revolutionary soldier who died at the age of ninety-three in 1858, the last survivor of Lafayette's escort on the Marquis' return to France.

WALTHAM (Addison County, US 7; alt. 450, pop. 186; 5464 acres). Vt. Transit bus.

Waltham has no stores or schools. There is no village. Residents do their trading in nearby Vergennes.

WARDSBORO, 10–D (Windham County, Vt. 100; alt. 920, pop. 322; 17,943 acres). Includes: North Wardsboro, Wardsboro Center, South Wardsboro and West Wardsboro.

The legislature of the Republic of Vermont granted the Wardsborough (sic) charter, November 7, 1780, to William Ward of nearby Newfane and 62 associates. In 1788 Wardsborough was divided into a North and South District. In 1810 the Southern District was removed from Wardsborough's jurisdiction to create the new town of Dover.

Frederick Baldwin, inventor of the automatic lathe, was born in this hill town.

NORTH WARDSBORO, called Wardsboro by its residents, is a tiny settlement with two stores, two churches and a post office (Wardsboro P.O.). In years past the Catholic Church, *Our Lady of Hope,* served as a meetinghouse and as a Protestant church. It is still adorned with the original cupola. A cross is perched atop the front peak. The post office is located on the first floor of a two-story dwelling. The railing on the second-story porch is often used as a clothesline. It is a singular sight to see washing dangling above the American flag of the post office. In the mid-1960's one preacher served the Methodist Church in North Wardsboro, Baptist Church in West Wardsboro and the Congregational Church in South Wardsboro.

WARDSBORO CENTER consists of about two dozen houses strung along a narrow valley. There are a few hunting shacks and summer cottages.

SOUTH WARDSBORO has a few scattered houses, a Congregational Church and a burying ground.

WEST WARDSBORO has a few houses clinging to the hillside and clustered along the valley floor. There is a general store, a Baptist Church (organized 1792) and the West Wardsboro P.O.

WARNER'S GRANT, 1–F (Essex County, no road, no reported residents).

WARREN, 5–C (Washington County, Vt. 100; alt. 893, pop. 469; 21,655 acres). Middlesex stage. Library.

WARREN is another lumber milling town which has taken on a new life with the advent of a major ski area within the town (see SUGARBUSH below). Motels, ski chalets and inns are adding an Old World touch to this tiny mountain village and environs. Warren occupies an even terrain in the mountains between (east) *Warren Pinnacle* (alt. 1700) and (west) *Sugarloaf Mountain* (alt. 2120). Woodworking mills lie along the Mad River below the village street with puffs of white steam blowing from the pipes and fading against stacks of fresh timber. From early times lumbering has been the primary activity, and the inevitable accidents that accompany the trade took the lives of many pioneer lumberjacks, killing them under falling trees and in log jams. The *United Church,* on a knoll with a stonewall base, commands the unpainted homes of the street.

South of Warren the Mad River twists and turns through a rocky gorge, grim, jagged and picturesque. The *Natural Bridge of Stone* here has a 12-foot arch, and thus has been much photographed. The ruins of abandoned mills are seen along the way, and higher ridges over-shadow the narrowing valley.

EAST WARREN has a few houses and a cemetery.

SUGARBUSH VALLEY SKI AREA (3.2 m. off Vt. 100). Taxi service; 4013-ft. elevation and 1625-ft. base. Enclosed (9300-ft.) European gondola tramway is longest single spanlift in U.S. with greatest vertical rise (2300-ft.) in East. Trails ranging from 1.75 to 3.25 miles long for novice, intermediate and expert. Two open practice slopes served by T-bar lift; 5000-ft. double chair lift serves network of "expert only" trails about summit of Lincoln Peak. Warming lodge at summit. Valley Lodge at base with restaurant. Ski shop, lounges and first aid room. Peter Estim Ski School. Luxury lodge, chalets, bunkhouses. Lift operates daily December–April. Gondola operates July 1 to mid-October. *Information:* Jack Murphy, Sugarbush Valley Corp., Box 10, Warren, Vt.

SUGARBUSH GOLF COURSE (designed by Robert Trent Jones); 18 holes. Par 72. Length: 5760 yds. (women), 6400 yds. (men), 7050 yds. (championship). Clubhouse, pro shop, practice tee and green, restaurant with lounge. Open from late May or early June through late October.

WARREN'S GORE, 1–F (Essex County, no reported roads or residents). Area: 5678 acres. Station on GT/RR.

WASHINGTON COUNTY (Area 708 sq. miles. Population 42,860). Shire town: Montpelier. Organized 1810. Includes: Barre, Berlin, Cabot, Calais, Duxbury, East Montpelier, Fayston, Marshfield, Middlesex, Montpelier, Moretown, Northfield, Plainfield, Roxbury (center of state), Waitsfield, Warren, Waterbury, Woodbury, Worcester. This county was organized as Jefferson County in 1810 but in 1814 the name was changed to Washington. Many Vermonters, for business reasons, detested Jefferson's Embargo Act and they opposed the War of 1812.

WASHINGTON, 5–D (Orange County, Vt. 110; pop. 565; 22,956 acres). Barre–Chelsea stage.

WASHINGTON was originally called Kingsland under a New York grant, being the shire town of Gloucester County, which included the entire section of the state, but the Yorker jurisdiction was short-lived, and the Vermont legislature regranted the territory in 1780, the first settlers coming five years later. The little village is neat and charming with clean-painted houses and two white churches, all having a well-kept appearance. A granite *Civil War Monument* stands at the village center. Stanley C.

Wilson, governor of Vermont (1931–35), was born here. The community subsists on dairying and lumbering.

Library: Calef Memorial.

WATERBURY, 4–C (Washington County, US 2 and Interstate 89; alt. 425, pop. 4306; 37,788 acres). Vt. Transit bus and CV/Ry. Includes: Waterbury village, Colbyville and Waterbury Center. Population includes about 1200 inmates of the Vermont State (Mental) Hospital.

WATERBURY, named for Waterbury, Conn., stretches along an intervale made by the Winooski in a southward bend, its beauty of setting intensified by the deep cleft to the north between the Worcester Mountains and the highest elevations of the main Green Mountain Range. The mile-long main street, pleasantly shaded, is broken by a small Green near the railroad station and by the intersection with Vt. 100. Waterbury's industrial activity consists largely of dairy products and woodworking, the latter business impressing itself upon the visitor as he enters the town from the east past a factory bearing the formidable sign "Scythe Snaths." Architecturally Main Street is marked by several elaborate red brick homes of the more pronounced General Grant style, in contrast to which the *Carpenter House* reveals the graceful restraint of the American Georgian. Built in 1816, the house is notable for its excellent proportions, for its fanlight, and other decorative details.

The *Vermont State Hospital,* S. Main St., a group of brick buildings set back on a wide level sward of trimmed green, is the state hospital for the insane, with over 1200 inmates. The spacious grounds are well kept, shaded by spreading boughs and ornamented with shrubbery. Several farms in connection with the institution supply all the milk and vegetables, and the hospital has its own laundry, cannery, sewing room, and like departments.

The *Congregational Church,* N. Main St., is a white clapboarded structure erected in 1824, with arched windows of stained glass, and a needle spire rising from a square tower. The old cemetery behind the church is excellently preserved. The *Waterbury Public Library* has 10,000 volumes, and a museum containing shell and basket collections, swords, guns, and documents.

WATERBURY CENTER (alt. 655) lies mainly to the east of the highway on a small plateau. The *Federated Church,* red brick with wood trim, stands close to the roadside at the northern end of the little settlement. The radio tower of WDEV, one of the leading broadcasting stations in Vermont, rises from *Blush Hill* above the highway, in slender skeleton outline. The hill also holds the scenic 9-hole course of the Waterbury Country Club.

Between Waterbury Center and Colbyville, Vt. 100 twists along a narrow valley whose downward slant is diversified by small ridges and hummocks.

COLBYVILLE is a scattering of wooden dwellings dotting a crest in the highway.

BLUE HILL COUNTRY CLUB; 9 holes. Range: 145–378 yds; par 33. Hilly terrain. Facilities include: Clubhouse, drinks for members, pro shop. Course open 9 A.M.–9 P.M.

WATERFORD, 4–F (Caledonia County, Interstate 93 and Vt. 18; alt. 816, pop. 460; 23,806 acres). St. Johnsbury stage. Includes: Lower Waterford and West Waterford.

LOWER WATERFORD, often called the "White Village" from the color of its houses, library and church, is one of Vermont's most charming villages. This hillside village overlooks the reservoir behind Moore's Dam on the Connecticut River. The white spired Congregational Church (1798) has a square double-decked cupola. Next door is the Waterford Memorial Library, a white two-story house with a double-decker porch. The half-dozen houses are fine examples of immediate post-Revolutionary War architecture.

WEST WATERFORD is a tiny settlement on an unnumbered back road.

WATERVILLE, 2–C (Lamoille County, Vt. 109; alt. 394, pop. 332; 9880 acres). Jeffersonville stage. Library.
Waterville, with its score of houses strung along the main street, is known for its boat oars, lawn furniture and other lumber products. The first settler (1797) was Timothy Brown and his wife.
The white *Town Hall* with the square cupola has an unusual town clock in that the face is white and the numerals black. This is the reverse of the traditional Vermont town clock. There is a covered bridge west of the main street. An old-fashioned covered bandstand stands before the Town Hall.

WEATHERSFIELD, 8–E (Windsor County, US 5, Interstate 91 scheduled, Vt. 106 and Vt. 131; pop. 1254; 25,259 acres). Vt. Transit bus. Includes: Amsden, Ascutney(ville), Downer's, Greenbush, Murderer's Gulch, Perkinsville, Weathersfield Bow, Weathersfield Center.

AMSDEN is a tiny hamlet 6 m. west of Ascutney.

ASCUTNEY (formerly Ascutneyville, US 5; alt. 412), was named for the mountain in whose shadow it lies — a quiet, shady four-corner village relatively untouched by the streams of traffic that flow through it.

Ascutneyville is the chief trading center in the eastern part of the township of Weathersfield. This town had as many inhabitants in 1791 as it has today and was commercially thriving during the greater part of the nineteenth century, chiefly in connection with the lime and soapstone deposits in the western section of the town. Among the earliest settlers were several Revolutionary soldiers who showed a spirit of individual independence amounting almost to a disregard for all authority. William Dean, son of Captain William Dean of Windsor, moved here before the Revolution. In 1769, he and his brother and their father were arrested and taken to New York City for violating the charter restrictions against cutting the tall white pines that were reserved for masting the King's navy. The Deans were convicted and spent several months in the New York jail. The affair of the "Dean boys" became something of a Colonial *cause célèbre* and was actually of significance in the contest between New Hampshire and New York for the jurisdiction over what is now Vermont. Jonathan Allen, who came here from Connecticut, took part in the battle of Bunker Hill — too eager a part: a portion of one of his ears was cut off with a saber by his own commander for shooting a British officer before the order to fire was given.

Isaac Eddy, Vermont's first known engraver, was born here. Research has revealed but sparse details of his life. In 1814 he took over the Stephen Daye press in Windsor. He was apparently a man of considerable learning. His engravings, though eagerly sought today, were somewhat crude. Typical of his work are the plates he did for the first Vermont Bible, published in Windsor in 1812, in which all of the characters are depicted with extravagantly Hebraic features.

DOWNER'S (intersection Vt. 106 and Vt. 131) is the site of the old eighteenth-century Downer's Tavern, a hostelry so widely known for many years that until recently it was marked on many Vermont maps simply as "Downer's."

GREENBUSH (Vt. 106) is a tiny cluster of houses, chiefly memorable for the pleasant name.

MURDERER'S GULCH, a rural section of Perkinsville, reportedly so called because a wealthy farmer was slain by a hired man.

PERKINSVILLE (Vt. 106; alt. 591, pop. 161) is a typical backcountry Vermont trading center with a post office. The small central common is surrounded by comfortable houses and a rather grim steepleless church (1832). Stage to Springfield.

WEATHERSFIELD BOW (US 5, alt. 362) is a small settlement that gets its name from the oxbow bends in the Connecticut River at this point.

WEATHERSFIELD CENTER (Springfield R.D. #2) is notable chiefly as the headquarters of the Weathersfield Historical Society.

VHS marker reads, "William Jarvis, consul to Lisbon was first to import Merino sheep to U.S. In 1811 Consul Jarvis brought from Spain to his farm in Weathersfield Bow the prized Merino sheep, whose longer fiber revolutionized the woolen industry and stimulated sheep raising throughout the East. In the 1830's Merinos were the state's principal livestock."

Jarvis bred Merinos here for forty-eight years. It has been reported that he resorted to "Yankee trickery" to obtain his 400 sheep.

WILGUS STATE PARK (Ascutney P.O., US 5; est. 1931). Colonel William J. Wilgus gave Vermonters the 129 acres for this park. Facilities: picnic tables and fireplaces. Scenic view. Camping permitted 3 miles north of Ascutney State Forest.

WEBSTERVILLE (see BARRE TOWN)

WELLS, 8–B (Rutland County, Vt. 30; alt. 502, pop. 419; 12,493 acres). Granville, N.Y., stage.

WELLS (settled 1768) is on the level plan of Wells Brook, sheltered by the rocky Taconics on the east. Two churches, *St. Paul's Episcopal* and the *Methodist* about a triangular Green mark the north end of the village. The *Village Library,* once a church, stands in the center of the green. A marble monument lists Wells' World War II veterans.

Lochlea Little Theatre (1932) is an attractive building (250 seats) where the Wells Little Theatre Society presents plays. The theatre is also the community social center. The village proper straggles along tree-lined streets on the flats south of *Little Pond* (southern extension of Lake St. Catherine).

The white two-story building with a second-story porch (next to the post office) houses the Fraser Publishing Company, publishers of the "Contrary Opinion Library" and the Fraser-Neill Contrary Opinion newsletter on Wall Street operations.

WELLS RIVER (see NEWBURY)
WEST ADDISON (see ADDISON)
WEST ARLINGTON (see ARLINGTON)
WEST BARNET (see BARNET)
WEST BERKSHIRE (see BERKSHIRE)
WEST BOLTON (see BOLTON)
WEST BRAINTREE (see BRAINTREE)
WEST BRATTLEBORO (see BRATTLEBORO)

WEST BRIDGEWATER (see BRIDGEWATER)
WEST BRIDPORT (see BRIDPORT)
WEST BROOKFIELD (see BROOKFIELD)
WEST BURKE (see BURKE)
WEST CASTLETON (see CASTLETON)
WEST CHARLESTON (see CHARLESTON)
WEST CORNWALL (see CORNWALL)
WEST DANVILLE (see DANVILLE)
WEST DOVER (see DOVER)
WEST DUMMERSTON (see DUMMERSTON)
WEST ENOSBURG (see ENOSBURG)

WEST FAIRLEE, 6–E (Orange County, Vt. 113, alt. 752, pop. 331; 13,429 acres). Chelsea-Thetford stage. Includes: West Fairlee village and West Fairlee Center.

WEST FAIRLEE is a score of undistinguished houses strung along the main street. Facilities include a general store, a Masonic Temple (Bean Hall), the West Fairlee Congregational Church with a short white steeple, a library and burying ground.

The village is a supply base for summer camps on Lake Fairlee (see FAIRLEE). Camp Beenadeewin (girls), Camp Billings (YMCA), Camp Wyoda (girls), Camp Passumpsic (boys), Aloha Hive (girls), Idlepine Lodge (adults).

WEST FLETCHER (see FLETCHER)
WEST GLOVER (see GLOVER)
WEST HALIFAX (see HALIFAX)
WEST HARTFORD (see HARTFORD)

WEST HAVEN, 7–A (Rutland County, off 22A north of Fair Haven; alt. 380, pop. 220; 15,423 acres). Fair Haven stage.

WEST HAVEN is a little hamlet around the *First Baptist Church* (1831), in a hilly region where the sparse population subsists on dairying and lumbering.

This is one of the very few Vermont towns where rattlesnakes are regularly found. The state pays a one dollar bounty per rattlesnake. Some West Haven farmers add to their income by bounty hunting.

WEST MILTON (see MILTON)
WEST NEWBURY (see NEWBURY)
WEST NORWICH (see NORWICH)
WEST PAWLET (see PAWLET)
WEST RUPERT (see RUPERT)

WEST RUTLAND, 7–B (Rutland County, US 4 and Vt. 133; alt. 500, pop. 2302; 9570 acres). Whitehall (N.Y.) Bus Co.

WEST RUTLAND lies on a level plain at the foot of guarding mountains and is visible for nearly a mile before it is reached from the east. The township was set off from Rutland proper in 1886. Here is located America's most famous marble deposit. Quarrying began here on a small scale about the year 1844. In recent times from 400,000 to 600,000 cubic feet of marble have been removed each year, and the quantity yet available appears to be unlimited. Without including the various grades of blue marble, which lie west of the white deposit at West Rutland, this vein produces fifteen different grades of marble for monumental and building purposes. These range from the almost pure white to the dark greens, such as Verdoso and Olivo. Right from the center of the town in an extremely marshy region is a new quarry, where caissons have been sunk to keep out the water.

The village has a relatively small business section and is composed chiefly of one long residential street, which US 4 crosses. The public buildings of West Rutland confute the saying that the shoemaker's children go without shoes: the *Memorial* on the school Common, the *Catholic Church* (1860), the *West Rutland High School,* and the really handsome *Library* are all constructed of native marble.

WEST TOPSHAM (see TOPSHAM)
WEST TOWNSHEND (see TOWNSHEND)
WEST WARDSBORO (see WARDSBORO)

WEST WINDSOR, 8–E (Vt. 44; alt. 689, pop. 540; 14,752 acres). Windsor stage.

BROWNSVILLE, the chief settlement in West Windsor, has less than a dozen houses clustered about a general store, the *Mary L. Blood Memorial Library* and a *Methodist Church.* Many dairy farms are scattered through the valley.

WEST WOODSTOCK (see WOODSTOCK)

WESTFIELD, 2–D (Orleans County, Vt. 100; alt. 825, pop. 347; 21,402 acres). Newport bus.

WESTFIELD is spread on the gentle slant of the plain with a small, maple-shaded green in its center. The former *Church,* erected in 1818 but now in a poor state of preservation, no longer serves a religious purpose. The *Hitchcock Memorial,* a square white building with a clock tower, combines the local library with a museum of natural history that is quite unusual in a village of this size. During the War of 1812 the inhabitants of Westfield, like those of most of the towns in northern Vermont, were rightly apprehensive of a British invasion from Canada. The barn of Captain Medad Hitchcock was converted into a blockhouse refuge, but fortunately never had to be defended. Today the village is made up of people who, having led a rugged, strenuous life on the nearby hill farms, have sought the well-earned comfort and sociability of village life in their declining years. In the houses along Westfield Street of a winter's evening are heard tall tales of the exploits with plow, pitchfork, and axe of a whole race of agricultural Paul Bunyans who are no more.

HAZEN'S NOTCH STATE PARK has 140 acres around Hazen's Notch.

WESTFORD, 3–B (Chittenden County, Vt. 128; alt. 464, pop. 680; 23,193 acres). Burlington stage.

WESTFORD was granted by Hampshire Province Governor Benning Wentworth in 1763. The first settler, Hezekiah Parmlee, came in 1787.
Tiny Westford has the classic New England village Green. The white-spired *Congregational Church* (founded 1801, present structure built 1840) stands on a hill overlooking the rectangular green. There is a Grange Hall, one-room schoolhouse, red brick *Baptist Church* (founded 1810) and a small library building. This 12 × 10 feet square library must surely be the smallest library building in the state and one of the smallest in the country. A covered bridge spans Brown's River just off the northeast corner of the green.
Captain John W. Woodward (1839–1863), 1st Vt. Cavalry, is probably the town's most noted hero. After Gettysburg he was killed in an engagement at Hagerstown, Md.

WESTMINSTER, 10–E (Windham County, US 5 and Interstate 91; alt. 314, pop. 1602; 24,640 acres). Vt. Transit bus. Includes: Westminster village, North Westminster, Westminster Station and Westminster West.

WESTMINSTER is a restful-looking village lying on the mile-wide plain of one of the most beautiful of the many terrace formations on the Connecticut. Its present serenity gives no hint of the violence and strife that made Vermont history here in Revolutionary and pre-Revolutionary days. Westminster was granted, probably in 1735, as Number One. The land was divided into 63 allotments; a sawmill and at least one house were built; and roads were laid out. Most important among the latter was the die-straight two-mile stretch known from the earliest days as *The King's Highway,* which runs through Westminster village northward to Westminster Station. Its unusual width (originally ten rods, now six), which contributes so much to the charm of Westminster, was due to its being designed as a training ground for the early military companies of this section. The first settlement was abandoned in

1740, when the decision on the northern boundary line of Massachusetts excluded Number One, or New Taunton, as it had come to be called, from that province.

The town was regranted by Governor Wentworth of New Hampshire in 1752, and within fifteen years more than fifty families had located here. In 1772 was built the courthouse in which the then Cumberland County (N.Y.) Court held its sessions. Loyalty to New York had never been universal, however, even in this section, and that province's refusal to adopt the resolves of the Continental Congress increased the dissatisfaction. On March 13, 1775, an armed party of local men took possession of the courthouse, refusing admittance to the court officials. The latter procured a sheriff and an armed force, and that night fired into the building, killing one William French (see below) and wounding several others, at least one of whom died of his wounds. This was the "Westminster Massacre." Since the British were at most only indirectly responsible for it, it is not rightly to be called, as it often is, the first engagement of the Revolution. It was important, however, because of the temper it displayed and the resentment it aroused. It was at a convention held in Westminster that Vermont, on January 15, 1777, declared itself a free and independent state.

The first printing office in Vermont was established at Westminster in 1778 by Judah Paddock Spooner and Timothy Green. In 1781, they issued here the state's first newspaper, *The Vermont Gazette,* or *The Green Mountain Post Boy.* Their press was the Stephen Daye press, the first one used on this continent north of Mexico and now preserved in the museum of the Vermont Historical Society (see MONTPELIER).

The brick *Community Hall* (officially Westminster Institute) dominates the center of the village. It was built in 1923, the gift of G. A. Dascomb, a local philanthropist who left $250,000 for its erection and maintenance. It contains a gymnasium-auditorium, various clubrooms, children's rooms, the Butterfield Library (public), and a *Museum* (open daily; adm. free). The Museum preserves many relics pertinent to Westminster's florid and vivacious past, including copies of *The Green Mountain Post Boy;* a drum used in the Revolution; a door panel with a bullet hole made, it is stoutly maintained, by one of the bullets that killed William French; a Revolutionary cannon ball embedded in a tree; a large number of letters and original documents; and a sizable collection of rocks and minerals.

William French is buried in the old *Cemetery* at the north end of the village. His headstone, with a long inscription telling how he was shot "by the hands of cruel ministerial tools of George ye 3rd," is an exact copy of the original one, which was destroyed when the old church here in which it had been placed burned many years ago. Here is buried also Judge Thomas Chandler, except for whose duplicity the Westminster Massacre would probably never have taken place. Chandler died in a debtor's cell in the very courthouse he caused to be fired upon.

Because of a legal technicality regarding burial, it was several days after his death before his body, in a rough wooden box, was dragged to the jail wall and thrown into a hole that had been dug in a slanting direction into the cemetery. Beside the road across from the cemetery is a curious white stone *Monument,* in the form of a wide chair, to the memory of William French and the old courthouse (razed in 1806) in which he inadvertently became, if not a hero, at least a remembered name to the posterity of this state.

A *VHS* marker at this site reads, "Westminster 'Massacre.' Northward stood the Cumberland County Court House, seat of New York's colonial administration. Opposition to holding a court session led to the 'Massacre' of March 13, 1775. Here the New Hampshire Grants on Jan. 16, 1777 declared their independence as 'New Connecticut', later Vermont."

WESTMORE, 2–E (Orleans County, US 5A; alt. 1200, pop. 179; 20,091 acres). Orleans stage.

WESTMORE. This scattered settlement, basically rural and agricultural under its resort superstructure, is centered here at a combination general store and town clerk's office on the eastern shore of the lake, a few dwellings clustered about it. The native population lives mainly on farms back in the hills. A local expression states that the community is "Willoughby Lake in the summer, and Westmore in the winter."

Long Pond (alt. 1835), cupped in a pocket of wooded mountains at the foot of *Bald Mountain,* a rounded helmetlike dome. This is a favorite rendezvous of fishermen and hunters, and a few camps lie around the shores, built by sportsmen who prefer the wild seclusion offered here. A forested island rises in the middle of the pond, and the whole scene is one of wilderness beauty.

WESTON, 8–C (Windsor County, Vt. 100; alt. 1300, pop. 442; 20,397 acres). Includes: Greendale, The Island and Weston village.

This tiny hill town with its delightful green, is quite possibly Vermont's best-known town. More than 100,000 tourists come here annually. They are drawn by the Vermont Country Store owned and operated by writer Vrest Orton. The store, opened during the 1930's, was the first of many such stores designed to supply old-time atmosphere, such as cracker barrels along with native products. A first-rate restaurant specializing in "Vermont vittles," also operated by Orton, is adjacent to the store. The store's atmosphere seems more authentic than does the atmosphere of its numerous imitators.

Weston is a beautifully restored hill village sitting at the north end of West River Valley, high-banked on all sides by forested mountain walls. The village center is ranged attractively around the shaded oval green of Farrar Park, which was a shallow frogpond previous to the Civil

War. The modern awakening of Weston was essentially a revival of interest in the past with an understanding of present needs, and the results are highly gratifying. The restoration of old houses, the establishing of a fine museum, and the transformation of an old church into a modern little theater, are some of the steps in restoring beauty and cultural interests to an isolated little village lost in the mountain wilds. In transition, Weston is not emulating the hustle of commercialism in the 1860's nor the sterile indolence of the early 1900's, but is seeking a new and more vital life, the tangible results of which point to a better social and economic idealism for Vermont villages.

The *Farrar-Mansur House,* north end of the Common, was built as a tavern in 1797 by Captain Farrar, housed the first town meeting in 1800, and served long as the nucleus of social and political life in Weston. This commodious and distinguished structure has been carefully restored to its original state and is now a local museum filled with antiques that express the provincial life of a century ago. Here are seven fireplaces; a kitchen full of early iron and brass utensils, pewter and chinaware; the taproom with its old grill bar; the council room with rare inside window-shutters; and a top floor ballroom containing exhibits of furniture, books, pictures, etc.

The Weston Playhouse, one of Vermont's first summer theaters, was rebuilt after a disastrous fire. The original playhouse, reconstructed from an abandoned Congregational Church, was a handsome white-pillared structure modeled in the style of the Greek revival period in early American public architecture. It was called the most beautiful small playhouse in New England. The new playhouse, designed by Weston Architect Raymond Austin, is also a beautiful structure.

Weston Priory (4 m. north of village on Vt. 100 and 155) is a Benedictine Monastery of the Dormition Abbey in Jerusalem. Guests are welcome at the Priory and at Chapel services.

WEYBRIDGE, 5–B (Addison County, Vt. 23; alt. 180, pop. 430; 9993 acres). Middlebury stage. Includes: Weybridge village and Weybridge Hill.

VAH — University of Vermont Morgan Horse Farm, Luther Kenney, supt. Morgan horses, Columbia and Southdale sheep, Aberdeen Angus cattle. This experimental station, formerly operated by the U.S. Dept. of Agriculture, is primarily devoted to experimental work in improving livestock for farmers.

WHEELOCK, 3–E (Caledonia County, pop. 246; 23,400 acres). Lyndonville stage. Includes: Wheelock village and South Wheelock.

WHEELOCK (Hollow) was named after President John Wheelock of Dartmouth College. This mountain hamlet, similar in general to Sheffield, lies low in an upland valley with broad-sloping sides, and is interesting for its connection with Dartmouth. The General Assembly of Vermont granted the township to Dartmouth College and Moor's Charity School at Hanover, N.H., an unusual instance of a state granting territory for the support of a college in another state. As late as 1815 the rental paid by Wheelock settlers comprised at least one-half of the permanent funds of both the college and the school. The township still pays a small sum to the college, and in 1930 the trustees of Dartmouth voted full tuition scholarships to sons of Wheelock, by birth or residence, who present adequate preparation and suitable recommendation.

The *Revolutionary Soldiers' Monument* is a simple plaque on a millstone taken from the first gristmill in Wheelock. The 1793 *Gristmill* still stands beside its dammed river, and across the stream in early times was a sawmill employing the old up-and-down type saws, as well as a tannery. The *Sulphur Spring* is strongly mineral. It is housed under a wood canopy, and its waters are free. The *Colonel Chase Inn,* a small plain white house with wide clapboards, was the first tavern in town, established in 1812. It is no longer an inn. The *Old Caledonia Spring House,* a large red brick structure with a double porch, was once a popular resort and watering place, but is now abandoned. The mineral water from Caledonia Springs is said to be of exceptionally high quality. At one time a venture was made to bottle and sell the water, but it failed. Over a century old, the hotel remains in good condition even though deserted. The Town Hall, church and school are at the southern end of the village, fronted by a grove of tall pines. The *Old Cemetery* contains the grave of Revolutionary soldiers. Wheelock has an unusual military record: early settlers included 31 Revolutionary veterans; 13 men enlisted for the War of 1812; 96 citizens served in the Civil War, and 12 in the World War. Erastus Fairbanks (Governor of Vermont, 1852–53, 1860–61) was the first postmaster here in Wheelock Hollow. From 1810 to 1930, the town population dropped from 964 to 412.

WHITE RIVER JUNCTION (see HARTFORD)

WHITING, 6–B (Addison County, Vt. 30; alt. 391, pop. 304; 7769 acres), named for grantee John Whiting of Wrentham, Mass., is a rural crossroads village on the plain of the Otter Creek. The *Free Public Library* is a plain churchlike building of wood. The *Congregational Church,* white-painted wood, has a pleasing clarity of line. The *Town Hall* is a formidable brown structure of cement blocks with a slate roof. A creamery constitutes the lone industry of the community. According to historian Crockett, when Ethan Allen wished to inform his scattered Green Mountain Boys of the proposed attack on Ticonderoga, he dispatched blacksmith Gershom Beach of Whiting as messenger. In twenty-four hours long-legged Beach ran 64 miles through the wilderness to spread the call that gathered the backwoods clan for its bold venture across Lake Champlain.

Between Whiting and Sudbury, the countryside becomes a bit more rolling and broken, with a stern, rugged barrier of mountains on the east, and smooth plains extending westward, their boundaries outlined by rows of trees.

WHITINGHAM, 11–C (Windham County, Vt. 8; alt. 1400, pop. 838; 23,040 acres). Brattleboro–Readsboro stage. Includes: Whitingham village, Jacksonville and Sadawga Springs.

WHITINGHAM (Sadawga Springs), the birthplace of empire builder Brigham Young (1800–1877) who led his people west into Utah, after Joseph Smith was killed in Illinois (see SHARON). Young's father was a poor basketmaker in Whitingham.

The town was chartered (New York) in 1770 to Colonel Nathan Whiting, from whom it took its name. The mineral springs here are believed to have remarkable curative qualities, especially for diseases of a cutaneous nature. The Chase family of Whitingham descended from an ancient English family, and one of the forebears was sergeant-at-arms to King Henry VIII, the much-married monarch. The *Baptist Church*, built in 1850, has the bell from the first Whitingham church (1798–1806).

JACKSONVILLE is situated in a glen at the southwestern corner of Jacksonville Pond, in Whitingham Town. The manufacturing of wood products and syrup cans is carried on here, and the nearby presence of Sadawga and Whitingham Lakes increases activity during the tourist season. *Sadawga Lake* (alt. 1660) was named for an Indian who lived on the shore, and who was drowned in the Deerfield River. The small lake is popular for boating and swimming.

VAH — Coombs Farm, Robert Coombs. Maple processing and packing.

BURRINGTON HILL SKI AREA (off Vt. 9); 1000-ft Stabilski lift; 600-ft. rope tow; 6 completed trails ranging from 1200 to 2600 feet, suitable for novice and intermediate. Open slopes for novice and practice. Ski instruction. Lodge. Toboganning. Floodlighted skating pond. *Information:* Chet Page, Whitingham, Vt. Phone: Jacksonville, EMpire 8–2309.

WILDER (see HARTFORD)
WILGUS STATE PARK (see WEATHERSFIELD)

WILLIAMSTOWN, 5–D (Orange County, Vt. 14; alt. 872, pop. 1553). Vt. Transit bus. Includes: Williamstown village and Foxville.

WILLIAMSTOWN sits along the broad floor of a pleasant valley with smooth-sloped hills rising on each side. The major part of the village lies compactly beside the attractive main street. The *Thomas Davenport Monument* (see BRANDON), Main St., is brightened by beautiful landscaped flower gardens on the slope of a hill. The *Congregational Church* is spired with unusual grace, and the huge *Civil War Monument,* erected in 1869, is surmounted by a stone eagle. The *Town Hall* is a good example of the New England town halls of the middle nineteenth century.

FOXVILLE, a settlement which serves neighboring quarries in Williamstown and bears the stamp of a granite community.
Library: Ainsworth.

WILLISTON, 4–B (Chittenden County, US 2; alt. 501, pop. 1484; 18,463 acres). CV/Ry. Library. Includes: Williston village and North Williston.

WILLISTON, named for grantee Samuel Willis, is stretched along the broad plain of a plateau. The long village street is distinguished by houses of clean-cut Colonial design and sober red brick structures. The large brick *Bingham House,* built by the Millers, who were among the first settlers, has entrances on front and side fashioned in the Greek Revival spirit. The *Federated Church* is white clapboarded, with a tall spire. Standing side by side at the western end of the street are three simple one-story red brick buildings, almost identical in construction — a former church, a Woodmen's Hall, and the Town Hall.

In the farming region south of Williston village, Ringling Brothers Circus once bought a number of farms, on which they planned to keep their cold-weather animals during the winter months. Their plans did not materialize, and the farms passed into other hands.

Old Williston Graveyard, contains the *Chittenden Monument* over the grave of Vermont's first Governor.

Site of Thomas Chittenden's House, beautifully situated on a natural terrace overlooking the broad sweep of the Winooski with a background that is sharply dominated by those two major summits of the Green Mountains — Mansfield on the northeast, Camel's Hump on the southeast. Here, in 1774–76, Thomas Chittenden, the first governor of the state, established his home, and Colonel Jonathan Spafford built a house on the adjoining tract of land. The beauty of the setting would seem to indicate that rough, sincere, practical Chittenden had an eye for the charms of nature, as well as for the intricacies of government. Chittenden and his fellow settlers moved southward during the Revolution, but the governor returned at its close, and lived here until his death. His mansion was destroyed by fire and only the cellar hole remains.

WILLISTON GOLF AND COUNTRY CLUB (7 m. east of Burlington on US 2); 18 holes. Range: 115–460 yds; par 68. Facilities: clubhouse, golf shop, food.

WILLOUGHBY (see BARTON)

WILMINGTON, 11–D (Windham County, Vt. 9; alt. 1580, pop. 1245; 26,023 acres). Brattleboro–Bennington stage. Includes: Wilmington village and East Wilmington.

WILMINGTON lies at a junction of valleys in the rough shape of a cross, a picturesque village of homey wooden houses in the miscellany of domestic building, with many second-story porches overhanging the streets, and four church spires rising above the shingled roofs. It is said that Clarence Budington Kelland studied here the original of his widely known character, Scattergood Baines. The center of the village is a true four-corners, and the high white *Baptist Church* (1833) stands close beside the green front of a little chain store, just north of the intersection. Along the stream at the western edge of the community are the industrial projects of Wilmington, concentrated in woodworking and veneer mills that formerly accounted for a relatively high degree of prosperity and that still make the village the only substantial settlement between Brattleboro and Bennington.

Library: Petee Memorial.

Revolutionary Major Jonathan Childs was outstanding among the pioneer settlers, and his descendants have been prominent in the later life of the town. The Reverend Zephaniah Swift was the first person born in Wilmington (1771). One stormy night, when the pastor was comfortably in bed, there came a loud and insistent pounding on his door. The Reverend Mr. Swift poked his reluctant head out in the gusty rain, and found below a young couple that wanted to be married. Calling them close beneath the window, Zephaniah made brief of the ceremony, shouting these words into the teeth of the storm-rent darkness:

> *Under this window, in stormy weather,*
> *I join a man and woman together;*
> *Let none but Him who made the thunder,*
> *Ever put this man and wife asunder!*

Lake Whitingham, a large reservoir formed by the Harriman Dam. The caved-in ruin of a railroad trestle extends partway across the water, and the high concrete smokestack of a submerged mill thrusts strangely above the surface of the artificial lake. Here is the junction of two northern branches of the Deerfield River. Picnic sites and boat launching facilities.

MOLLY STARK STATE PARK (Vt. 9; est. 1940; 158 acres on western slopes of Mt. Olga; alt. 2438). Firetower offers fine views. Facilities: tent sites, lean-tos, camp trailer sites, foot trails.

WINDHAM COUNTY (Area 793 sq. miles. Population 29,776). Shire town: Newfane. Organized 1781. Includes: Athens, Brookline, Brattle-boro, Dover, Dummerston, Grafton, Guilford, Halifax, Jamaica, London-derry, Marlboro, Newfane, Putney, Rockingham, Somerset (unorganized), Stratton, Townshend, Vernon, Wardsboro, Westminster, Whitingham, Wilmington, Windham.

WINDHAM, 9–D (Windham County, Vt. 11 and Vt. 121; alt. 1980, pop. 135; 15,697 acres). Chester or West Townshend stage. Library. In-cludes: Windham village, North Windham and South Windham.

WINDHAM, named for Windham, N.H., a small community maintained by lumbering and talc-mining activities. This is the second highest village in Vermont, most of the people living at an altitude around 2000 feet above sea level. The white wooden *Congregational Church* sits on the mountainside overlooking the rustic settlement, a landmark for the surrounding country. Its needle spire points "closer to God" than that of the Belmont church, thus refuting the representative from Mt. Holly. But this Windham steeple is topped by the spike tower of a little church in Woodford.

NORTH WINDHAM consists of a few plain wooden farmhouses and apple orchards scattered on the plain at a highway junction.

WINDSOR COUNTY (Area 965 sq. miles — largest county. Popula-tion 42,483). Shire town: Woodstock. Organized 1781. Includes: An-dover, Baltimore, Barnard, Bethel, Bridgewater, Brownsville, Cavendish, Chester, Hartford, Hartland, Ludlow, Norwich, Plymouth, Pomfret, Read-ing, Rochester, Royalston, Sharon, Springfield, Stockbridge, Weathersfield, Weston, West Windsor, Windsor, Woodstock.

WINDSOR, 8–E (Windsor County, US 5; alt. 354, pop. 4468; 11,311 acres). Vt. Transit. B & M/RR and CV/Ry.
Railroad: CV/Ry. depot.
Bus Depot: Windsor House.
Accommodations: Inn, motels, tourist camps.
Schools: Grammar, junior and senior high schools.
Hospital: Windsor.
Newspaper: Vermont Journal (weekly).
Windsor, the birthplace of Vermont, is an incongruous combination of the historic and antique with the industrial and modern; of the placidly reminiscent with the nervously aggressive. The town remains static and

indigenous despite external influences toward change, yet the successive impacts of industrial developments and foreign influxes have left permanent marks.

Windsor is admirably situated on a terrace of the Connecticut River, with the green hills of Cornish to the east and dark Ascutney on the western horizon. The village is compact. Main St., with residential sections at both ends and the business district in the middle, runs north and south along US 5. State St., the other leading artery, runs west from the business section. Machine shops and uniform frame houses lie unobtrusively on lower ground between Main St. and the river.

Windsor was granted on July 6, 1761, by Governor Wentworth, of New Hampshire. A second grant was allowed by York Province, March 28, 1772, to Colonel Nathan Stone, who for several years had been legally the sole owner of the town, having been deeded all lands by the other proprietors and settlers that he might easily and effectively represent the town's interests before the York court.

Settlement began in 1764; in 1791 the population was 1542; and in 1820, Windsor, with 2956 inhabitants, was the largest town in the state.

On July 2, 1777, delegates from the New Hampshire Grants met here to discuss and adopt a constitution for an independent republic, their address to the Continental Congress of 1776 having been unfavorably regarded. The convention remained in session seven days. On July 8, the new constitution was adopted and a Council of Safety of twelve members was appointed to conduct the affairs of the republic until the first legislature could convene. There was a dramatic crisis in the state's history July 8, 1777. A messenger from Colonel Seth Warner appeared before the convention with the disquieting news of General Burgoyne's army on the western side of the state. The constitution was undergoing a final reading, yet so great was the excitement and general alarm, especially among the delegates from the invaded territory, that the meeting was on the point of breaking up with its work unfinished. Suddenly a terrific thunderstorm broke; "the road became a river, the yard became a strand." The storm, whether a token of divine intervention, as many have believed, or merely a fortunate coincidence, compelled the men at Windsor to remain, to reconsider, and to complete the reading and adoption of the document that continues to serve as the bulwark of Vermont government nearly two centuries after Burgoyne and his 8000 men left the state.

The General Assembly frequently convened here until Montpelier became the permanent capital in 1805. Between 1781 and 1794, Windsor was the shire or half-shire town of the county.

Industry

The industrial history of Windsor is vitally concerned with the inventive genius of a few men who have lived here. Early industries included several woolen mills that naturally followed the intensive breeding of merino sheep in this section; but Windsor's first real boom period occurred in the middle decades of the nineteenth century as a result of contracts for the manufacture of firearms during the Mexican, Crimean, and Civil Wars. The second such period, dependent upon the production of automatic machinery, occurred during and after the World War.

The Vermont *Journal and Advertiser,* published at Windsor, was the third newspaper in the state and is now the oldest, having appeared continuously since 1783. During the late eighteenth and early nineteenth centuries, Windsor was one of the leading towns in the state in the number of books and pamphlets issued from its presses. Here was printed in 1812, on the Stephen Daye press, the first Vermont Bible, now a bibliographical rarity, which included seven elaborate copper-plate engravings by Isaac Eddy, Vermont's earliest engraver (see WEATHERSFIELD).

Since 1800, when Asahel Hubbard came to Windsor from Connecticut and built his experimental pump, the town has been the scene of more inventions and the home of more inventors than any other in the state. Hubbard's hydraulic pump was patented in 1828. In 1829, the National Hydraulic Company was organized and its shop installed at the State Prison here, of which Hubbard had conveniently been made warden through the political influence of his partner, Jabez Proctor, father of Senator Redfield Proctor. Agencies were established throughout the settled parts of the country and in Mexico. An early order was for a twenty-horsepower pump for the first city waterworks of St. Louis, Mo.. Hubbard delivered the pump and installed it. The St. Louis company did not have enough money to pay for it. He accepted as part payment a pure white saddle horse, upon which he rode into Windsor several months after his departure and which was long known to the old inhabitants as "the St. Louis horse."

In 1833, Hubbard sold the right to manufacture his pump in the state of Rhode Island to David Fales and Alvin Jenks, and today, more than a century later, the Fales and Jenks Machine Company of Pawtucket makes Hubbard pumps, unchanged in principle. George Hubbard, Asahel's nephew, invented the coffee percolator in 1876, and four years later patented a glazier's point and driver, which revolutionized the setting of window glass. In 1858, the manufacture was begun here of a sewing machine, locally designed. The business was sold after a few years to the White Sewing Machine Company.

Firearms

Gunsmith Nicanor Kendall took his fiancée, the daughter of pump-maker Hubbard, for a sleigh ride. Sighting a squirrel, he reached under the buffalo laprobe for his percussion rifle. The weapon accidentally discharged, the ball passing through Kendall's hand and through his fiancée's top hair. Kendall went back to his shop and designed an under-hammer rifle which many considered as the safest sporting rifle of the era. Father-in-law Hubbard financed the manufacture of the rifle. The first large order for Kendall rifles came from the Republic of Texas in 1836

— the year of Goliad and the Alamo. Kendall and Hubbard received 2000 acres of Texas land as partial payment for the weapons.

Kendall entered into a partnership with Richard Lawrence. The latter designed and constructed machinery which, for the first time, largely eliminated handwork in the manufacture of firearms. Lawrence initiated the development of the first successful repeating rifle — the Jennings — though he himself did not actually invent the rifle.

Christian Sharps, first mass-produced rifles were manufactured by Lawrence and Kendall. Lawrence later went to Connecticut where he assumed control of the Sharps plant. It was Lawrence, not Sharps, who perfected the long-range Sharps rifle which more than any other rifle wiped out the buffalo. The first real Winchester rifle, the Henry, was invented and designed by Lawrence employee B. Tyler Henry.

Windsor, more than any other American town, was the "Cradle of the American firearms industry."

Windsor has a greater percentage of foreign population than most Vermont mill towns. The cotton mills that superseded the firearms factories in the 1870's brought French Canadians, most of whose decendants have departed or become assimilated. Present day foreign millhands are predominantly Slavic.

Native sons of Windsor include Vietts Rice, inventor of the roller process for the manufacture of flour; Carlos Coolidge, governor of Vermont (1848–50); Jonathan Hubbard, congressman from Vermont (1809–11); James Whitcomb, senator from, and governor of, Indiana; and William H. H. Stowell, three times congressman from Virginia.

What to See and Do

1. The *Old Constitution House* (1772?) North Main St. (open) is the building in which the Constitution of the Vermont Republic was framed and adopted. It was then (1777) a public tavern. It originally stood near the RR station. The building is owned and maintained by the Old Constitution House Association, to which it was presented on July 10, 1914, by Mrs. Caroline S. Fay and her children with the provision that it be "restored, maintained, and preserved as an historic relic and be devoted to historical, literary, and social usages." Every room in the building contains relics and documents significant to its own history or that of the state. The controversy as to just which room was occupied by the Constitutional Convention is not likely to be settled, though present opinion favors the north upstairs room now used by the Windsor chapter of the D.A.R.

2. The *Vermont State Prison and House of Correction,* State St. (open to visitors). Windsor has been the seat of the Vermont State Prison since its inception in 1807. There is no adequate history of the penal institutions of this state, but the first five years of the prison's history are well covered in *An Authentic History of the Vermont State Prison,* by John Russell, Jr., (Windsor, 1812). Russell was nineteen when he wrote this work, and his only motive, he admits, was "the aid that the sale of the

copyright would afford the author in obtaining a collegial education."
Imprisonment during those early years was usually for one of three crimes:
counterfeiting, horse-stealing, and highway robbery. As early as 1809
prisoners were employed in the manufacture of shoes for marketing on a
commercial scale. This practice has been discontinued. The prison population is now employed in maintaining the prison plant and farm and in
labor of a noncompetitive nature, such as the manufacture of auto tags
and highway signs.

3. The *Covered Toll Bridge,* 0.1 m. east of the four-corner intersection on
South Main St. (US 5) (1866) is the longest covered bridge in, or partly
in, Vermont. The first bridge (1796) here, replaced a ferry. Here,
Lafayette entered Vermont, June 28, 1825, for his brief tour of the state.
The records (1811-40) of the earlier toll bridge here have been preserved,
though in private hands, and make suggestive reading. On November 12,
1837, for instance, there passed "Gen'l Lyman Mower" with "1 wagon,
1 sulky, 1 horse & rider, 600 sheep, 127 cattle." The only possible conclusion is that there passed also, toll-free, some dogs.

4. The *Old South Church* (Congregational), Main St., was built (1798),
presumably after a design by Asher Benjamin (see below). It is a graceful
white wooden structure, and its spacious lawns, unusual for a church
centrally located in a busy commercial community, enhance its beauty.
Before this church was built, Windsor Congregationalists held meetings
in one another's houses. From 1768 to 1774 they listened every third
Sunday to the Reverend James Wellman, a Harvard graduate, who
preached other Sundays at Cornish, across the river. After fording the
Connecticut on horseback, he would enter his "pulpit" in some private
home dripping wet.

5. The *Harriet Lane House* (1804), North Main St. The attenuated
Ionic pilasters, the delicately carved festoons on the friezes of the window
heads, and the graceful Palladian window, are executed in striking similarity to the decorative patterns of the Adam brothers. This house was
designed by Asher Benjamin, who worked in Windsor for five years
(1800-1804). He was the best-known architect in the Connecticut Valley,
and later, after he established himself in Boston, his reputation, enhanced
by his popular architectural books, became even greater. His work, like
that of McIntire, was a variation, an elaboration, upon the style developed
by the Adam brothers. His use of miniature fluted columns, Ionic pilasters,
festooned carvings over windows and beside doors, and his repetition of
entrance details in the second story resulted in houses that are, at their
worst, slightly florid, at their best, superlatively handsome. Windsor's
industrial growth has prevented the preservation of several of these houses.
The Fullerton House (1800), the finest of all Benjamin houses, which
stood just north of the post office, was razed in 1935 to make room for a
filling station, its interior and exterior decorative details being incorporated in a house of similar design in New Canaan, Conn.

6. The *Green House* (1791), Main St., now owned by the local Masonic

Lodge, overlooks the business district from the brow of a hill. It is a plain two-story frame structure, somewhat marred by a later porch. The north front room downstairs preserves the original eighteenth-century wallpaper, probably of French origin. Early in the 19th century this house was a school for girls. Salmon P. Chase, later Chief Justice of the United States, who was born across the river, obtained special permission as a very little boy to attend it in company with his older sisters.

ASCUTNEY STATE PARK (Windsor P.O., Vt. 44 off US 5; est. 1935; 1547 acres) has 4-mile-long hard-surfaced road leading from entrance (alt. 600) to Mt. Ascutney summit (alt. 3144). Large parking area at summit. Maximum grade 15 percent. One of New England's most scenic highways. Facilities: picnic tables and fireplaces, tent sites, lean-tos, camp trailer sites, foot trails.

MOUNT ASCUTNEY SKI AREA (5 m. west of Windsor, and US 5, on Vt. 44). Two T-bar lifts carry 2400 skiers hourly; 2250-ft. open slope with 620-ft. vertical drop. Snow maker on 2250-ft.-long, 250-ft.-wide slope. Trails for novice, intermediate and expert. Parking area, ski hut and snack bar. Ski shop for sales, rentals and repairs. Certified instructors, ski patrol and first aid. *Information:* Mt. Ascutney Ski Area, Box 44, Windsor, Vt. Phone: Reading, Vt., 2711.

WINDSOR COUNTRY CLUB (North Main St., US 5); 9 holes. Range: 127–465 yds. Hilly terrain. Facilities: clubhouse with showers, golf shop, caddies.

WINHALL, 9–C (Bennington County, Vt. 30; alt. 1220, pop. 245; 27,071 acres). Includes Bondville.

BONDVILLE is the only village in sparsely settled mountainous Winhall Town, strung along narrow Winhall River valley in the hills. Pioneers first penetrated these dense mountain wilds about 1780. *Methodist Church* (1850). The Bondville Fair, held each autumn when the ridges are burning with the flame-red of maples and the golden haze of birches, is a picturesque back-country pageant.

Between Bondville and the junction with Vt. 11, the highway traverses the mountain wilderness of Winhall Town with views sweeping over forests so dense that they resemble thick green mosses carpeting the earth. The mountain scenes are dominated by the broad-capped dome of Bromley on the north. To the south stretches a vast area of forest-shrouded mountains. Several ski lodges are located in the area.

WINOOSKI, 3–B (Chittenden County, US 7 and Interstate 89; alt. 200, pop. 7428; 795 acres). Burlington Rapid Transit Busline. Library.

WINOOSKI (alt. 200), the Mill City, was founded in 1787 by Ira Allen and Remember Baker, who foresaw the advantages in utilizing the tremendous waterpower available at the lower falls of the Winooski River. Winooski was predestined from the start to become one of the few industrialized towns in Vermont. This industrial atmosphere, unrelieved and unadulterated, marks Winooski today. Winooski resembles on a small scale the manufacturing towns of southern New England, such as Fall River, and so seems misplaced in northern Vermont. The manufacturing plants, textile and woodworking in the main, are in the sharp-cleft valley of the Winooski, and the major part of the city lies on the sidehill sloping up from the northern banks of the strong-flowing stream. The bridge at the foot of Main St. was constructed to replace the one washed out in the raging flood of 1927; from the bridge is a fine view of the great power-distributing dam. The *Site of Fort Frederick* is on Main St. at the bridge; here once stood a blockhouse built by Ira Allen for protection against the Indians, and one of the earliest military structures in this region. The strictly industrial aspect of Winooski is tempered by its close proximity to Burlington and Lake Champlain, which permits Winooski people to enjoy the scenic, cultural, recreational and educational advantages of the largest and most beautifully located city in the State.

The development of the manufacturing directly responsible for the city's growth and virility began as early as 1835, when a woolen mill was established on the falls. A large and significant industry is the Vermont Furniture Manufacturing Co. The city's largest industry was once textile manufacturing. One of the largest textile plants in the country was once operated here by the American Woolen Company.

St. Stephen's Church, Platt St., is built of Vermont marble in the Gothic tradition. *St Francis Xavier Church,* Weaver St., is one of the oldest French-Canadian churches in Vermont. St. *Michael's College* (see Education) is just east of the city limits. There is a very large French-Canadian population in Winooski and the Catholic influence is predominant, coloring the contemporary pattern of community life.

WOLCOTT, 3–D (Lamoille County, Vt. 15; alt. 720, pop. 633; 20,376 acres). St. J & LC/RR. Includes: Wolcott village, Potterville and North Wolcott.

WOLCOTT was once the home of the *"Largest Country Store in the World,"* opened 1886 by Charles E. Haskell and now operated by Gilman and Seavey.

Wolcott, settled in 1789, was named after General Oliver W. Wolcott, a signer of the Declaration of Independence. The population has remained practically stationary for over a century. The drab main street, dominated by the big country store, is characterized by second-story wooden porches protruding from nearly every house.

POTTERVILLE, a little sawmill settlement of rude unpainted houses in the narrow valley, owes its existence to the mill, surrounded by log piles and lumber stacks. In the town of Wolcott, this is really an outlying industrial part of Wolcott village.

WOODBURY, 3–D (Washington County, Vt. 14; pop. 317; 20,680 acres). Hardwick stage. Includes: Woodbury village and South Woodbury.

WOODBURY straggles sleepily along the valley, a small collection of nondescript wooden houses with a ragged central grass plot before a country store. Several rather dilapidated structures here, now serving various purposes, resemble rude churches. Lumber milling on a small scale is now the main means of subsistence of a hamlet that flourished in the days when its granite industry was at its height. The *Antique Shop,* plain and commodious, is the oldest building in the village, constructed about 1815. The shop is upstairs in the old ballroom, which still has the original bandstand. Woodbury claims to have furnished more Civil War soldiers per capita of population than any other Vermont town. There are 28 lakes and ponds in the township, and a peculiar feature is that no water flows into the township, all the streams flowing outward.

SOUTH WOODBURY. A high-façaded wooden *Congregational Church* dominates the small cluster of buildings on the highway, facing the plateau across the valley where the weatherbeaten backs of houses constitute an oddly arranged pattern. Under drooping shade trees on the low plateau, faded homes and overgrown lawns lie quietly remote, a scene untouched by modern times.

Between South Woodbury and Woodbury, the highway twists and turns in endless sharp curves through a wild wooded country of rugged barrenness.

Woodbury Lake is an attractive body of water, stretching in irregular outline between wooded shores, with jutting points and shady islands diversifying the scenery with wild beauty. Affording fine boating and canoeing, this has become a popular summer resort.

Woodbury Mountain and *Granite Quarries.* This mountain is believed to be the largest deposit of building granite in the world. Mammoth quarries are here, with great gray piles of waste granite massed everywhere. The deposit is so uniformly good, and in such deep veins, that the quarrying is done horizontally, cutting into the mountain side rather than penetrating vertically down. The nine-mile railroad that connected these quarries with Harwick ran high along the mountain flank, one of the highest railways in New England. The president of this line, seeking an exchange of passes with the president of the New York Central, admitted that his line was shorter than the Central, but insisted "It's just as wide." Woodbury Mountain was the source of building stone that lifted Hardwick to eminence in the granite world. The view from this height is superbly far-reaching.

WOODFORD, 11–B (Bennington County, Vt. 9; alt. 2215, pop. 207; 26,977 acres). Bennington–Brattleboro stage.

Woodford is the highest village in Vermont, despite the tenacious claims of Belmont (alt. 1840) and Windham (alt. 1980). The short spiked tower of the plain white *Union Church* is the one that points "closer to God" than any other steeple in Vermont, to use the expression oft repeated by the Mt. Holly representative, who was unaware that both the Windham Congregational and the Woodford Union have spires that reach higher than that of his Belmont church.

The feeling of altitude is emphasized by the cleared summit land that stretches in a broad, gradual rise to the thick-wooded backbones of even greater heights: *Prospect Mountain* (alt. 2740) on the south, and *Maple Hill* (alt. 2740) on the north. Large iron deposits were discovered in Woodford, and at one time several forges manufactured bar iron here. During Jefferson's administration, Woodford forges turned out anchors for use on American gunboats.

One of America's most influential industrialists was born in Woodford. He was Franklin W. Olin (1860–1954). Farm boy Olin studied engineering at Cornell University and in the early 1890's devised new and more efficient methods of gunpowder manufacture. He founded Western Cartridge Company in East Alton, Ill. Olin, in the 1930's, together with his sons John and Spencer, took over the bankrupt, historic Winchester Repeating Arms Company, New Haven, Conn. Winchester-Western were decisive factors in America's arms and ammunition superiority in World War II. The Olins secured control of the Mathieson Brass Company and created Olin Mathieson Chemical Corporation. Today, Olin Industries is one of America's greatest industrial complexes.

WOODSTOCK, 7–D (Windsor County, US 4; alt. 705, pop. 2786; 27,384 acres). Includes Woodstock village, Prosper, Quechee, Taftsville, South Woodstock and West Woodstock.

Railroad Station: CV/Ry station located 15 m. east at White River Junction.

Bus Service: White River Coach Lines (White River Junction–Rutland)

Accommodations: Inns, motels, tourist cabins.

Schools: Grammar, junior and senior high schools. Woodstock Country (private) and Doscher's Country School of Photography (private).

Hospital: Mary Hitchcock Memorial (Hanover, N.H.)

Newspaper: Vermont Standard (weekly).

Woodstock, one of the state's loveliest villages, has preserved both the physical and spiritual flavor of an earlier day. Long one of the favorite summer resorts in the state and a winter sports center, Woodstock has nevertheless retained the somewhat astringent quality of its native personality. Its instinctive reaction to change is negative: it has no factories and wants none and it saw its railroad discontinued without regret. If Woodstock places sentiment above progress, if it is — as its rustic neighbors say — too smug in its own well-being, it is perhaps by these very tokens a microcosm of the state to which, culturally, intellectually, and politically, it has contributed so much.

Woodstock is one of the most charming villages in New England. Lying on the banks of the Ottauquechee, it is overlooked from the north by Mt. Tom, on other sides by lesser hills, some of which include parts of the residential sections. Its broad streets are lined with houses and public buildings, beautiful not merely because they are old, but because they were built in a tradition of grace and beauty. The business square, neat and compact, centers the village. West of the square is the long slender oval of the Green, probably the most widely known village common in Vermont. Throughout two-thirds of the last century — and to this very day by some of the oldest inhabitants of nearby towns — the village was called Woodstock Green, or simply "the Green." One of the first lots to be cleared in the village, the Green assumed its present shape in 1830, about seventy years too early to justify the harmless legend sometimes told to visitors that it was laid out in the shape of the flagship of Admiral Dewey, who spent his summers here during the latter part of his life.

The town, granted in 1761, was settled four years later by Harvardman Timothy Knox. The first clergyman was Harvardman Aaron Hutchinson, one of the best Biblical and classical scholars in 18th-century New England and the man whose preaching at Bennington had such a powerful effect on Ethan Allen, who was not notably susceptible to the clergy. It was men like these who from the very beginning sounded an intellectual pitch that has never ceased to vibrate.

In 1786, Woodstock became, with Windsor, half-shire town of Windsor County, and in 1794 shire town, which it has remained ever since and for which its central location in the county well qualifies it.

Woodstock was one of the leading publishing centers of the state prior to 1850. The famous Stephen Daye press, the first press operative on this continent north of Mexico (see MONTPELIER), was in use here for a time, subsequent to its ownership by the Spooners and Isaac Eddy in Windsor. The large bibliography of Woodstock presses includes broadsides, verse, hymns, sermons, children's chap-books (the rigidity of the moral instructions matched by the stiffness of the woodcut figures), and the first Greek lexicon printed in North America. Since 1805 Woodstock has always had at least one newspaper, and at one time (1830) as many as five were published here contemporaneously.

The best-known medical school in Vermont of its time was established here in 1827 and operated until 1856. A faculty schism led to two separate advertisements in the local papers, one by each faction, which caused someone to remark that Woodstock was the only place in the country except Philadelphia with two medical schools.

From 1846 to 1932, Woodstock was the seat of the Windsor County Fair, which was at the time of its discontinuance the oldest county fair in New England.

It has been claimed that the first U.S. express line ran between Woodstock and Windsor in the 1820's. Alvin Adams, who came here as a hostler's assistant at the old Bowker Tavern, began on a small scale the business he later developed into the worldwide Adams Express Company.

The list of prominent men closely associated with Woodstock either as native sons or through long residence is a proud one.

Jacob Collamer (1791–1865), born in Troy, N.Y., was graduated from the University of Vermont in 1810 and made Woodstock his permanent home after 1836. He was Representative in Congress (1842–49), Postmaster General (1849–50), and U.S. Senator (1855–65). During the Civil War, Collamer was a close friend and personal adviser of Lincoln, and it was he who drafted the bill, enacted July 13, 1861, which gave the war its first Congressional sanction and invested the President with new and necessary powers.

George P. Marsh (1801–1882) was one of the most distinguished scholars and most accomplished diplomats ever produced by this state. From 1844 to 1849 he was a Vermont congressman. After serving (1849–54) as U.S. Minister to Turkey, he lectured at Columbia University and Lowell Institute. That established him as one of the leading philologians. In 1860, Lincoln appointed him first U.S. Minister to the new kingdom of Italy, where for twenty-one years he remained the close friend and consultant of King Victor Emmanuel and a beacon light of American culture. Matthew Arnold said, after meeting him, that he had found a man whose culture was so deep and so universal that it made him forget about Yankeeism and rejoice only in the bond of race. Marsh was a lifelong collector in diverse fields. Two of his collections (reptiles and engravings) are in the Smithsonian Institution, and another is in the Billings Library at the University of Vermont (see BURLINGTON). Of his twenty books, ranging in subject from philology and zoology to art and philosophy, the greatest is *Man and Nature*, (1864), revised in 1874 as *The Earth as Modified by Human Action*. This book is the fountainhead of the conservation movement; it first suggested "the possibility and the importance of the restoration of disturbed harmonies and the material improvement of waste and exhausted regions." A great many of the conservation and restoration programs in which the national government has interested itself most actively in recent years were advanced by George P. Marsh a century ago.

Hiram Powers (1805–1873), born on a hill farm near Woodstock, became in the middle decades of the last century the most famous of American sculptors. (see Artists)

Past residents of Woodstock include Frederick Billings, president of the Northern Pacific Railroad and the man who saved it in the panic of 1873 and secured its extension beyond Dakota; James A. Mower, major general in the Mexican and Civil Wars; Peter T. Washburn, Julius Converse, and Franklin S. Billings, all governors of Vermont; Charles L. Dana, president of the New York Academy of Medicine and one of America's greatest neurologists; and John Cotton Dana, the man who did more than anyone else to expand the function of the public libraries of America and to educate the public to take advantage of them. Despite the year-round stream of guests, Woodstock has completely avoided the brazenness of much resort appeal. Even transient visitors recognize this as the town's most potent charm. The grace of Woodstock's heritage, scenically, architecturally, and culturally, and the ceaseless care with which it has been preserved leave little cause to wonder why the Vermont poet, Daniel L. Cady, in his oft-quoted line, "It beats a day on Woodstock Green," made a visit to this place the very yardstick of human felicity.

PROSPER is a small three-corner settlement of a few houses and an old mill.

QUECHEE, the main village lying below in the valley of the Ottauquechee, powers the large woolen mills that are its chief industry.
Quechee Gorge, one of the outstanding natural spectacles of the state. The highway bridge here, on the site of the former railroad bridge, once the highest one in the East, is 165 feet above the Ottauquechee River which, dwarfed to a turbulent thread, flows below at the bottom of the jagged gorge it has cut from sheer rock in the course of the ages. Mosses and an occasional wind-sown tree grow on the sides of the canyon, but they merely emphasize the fact that here is a landscape which Nature in an extravagant and Gothic mood endowed with a grim majesty that neither growing things nor the power of man can soften or subdue.

TAFTSVILLE (alt. 668) is a small village on the high left bank of the Ottauquechee. The river is dammed here.

SOUTH WOODSTOCK (alt. 1055) is a drowsy little village with a Colonial air, a fitting transition between the rustic vigor of Reading and the urbane reserve of Woodstock itself. The white churchlike building on the knoll across the brook was the seat of the *Green Mountain Liberal Institute* (1848), which has been closed for many years but was once the leading preparatory school of this section. The countryside around South Woodstock is largely given over to summer homes where artists, writers, and other out-of-state people spend a part of each year. Author Anne Bosworth Greene was once a year-round resident, as those who have read her charming book *The Lone Winter* (1923) will remember.

The headquarters of the Green Mountain Horse Association are located here. Horses for hire. The annual 100-mile trail ride starts and ends here. Riders ride 40 miles daily for two days and 20 miles the final morning.

WEST WOODSTOCK, a small hamlet, was once the summer home of Ed Payne, originator of the "Billy the Boy Artist" cartoons, one of the earliest comic strips.

What to See and Do

1. *Norman Williams Public Library* faces the east end of the Green from the south. This fine Richardsonian, Romanesque building was completed in 1885, the gift of E. H. Williams in memory of his father, Norman Williams, Vermont Secretary of State. The book collection is surpassed only by Burlington and Brattleboro public libraries. Rare items include one of the largest files of 18th- and early 19th-century Vermont newspapers.

2. *Williams Collection of Japanese Art,* in the Norman Williams Library, comprises choice examples of ceramics, ivories, bronzes, and prints. The collection is notable for the wide range and infinite finesse of modern Oriental craftsmanship.

3. *Windsor County Courthouse* (1855), first building west of the Library, is a good example of a Vermont courthouse in the Georgian tradition: red brick, with white trim, quoined corners, and an arch-supported domed belfry.

4. *Old White Meeting House* (Congregational), Elm St., the town's church (1808), has been renovated. The restoration is not perfect, since the original front entrance was eliminated, but the present balance of porticoed entrance is pleasing. The graceful Bulfinch tower, white against the surrounding elms, houses a bell cast by Paul Revere. The *Christian* (1816) and *Universalist* (1835) *Churches* have bells by the same patriot bell founder, as does also the modern *Episcopal Church.*

5. *Hutchinson House* (1794) is part of the White Cupboard Inn. Its outline is relieved by the ample-pillared side porch on the east. The end façade facing the bank has a fine third-story pediment whose arrangement of windows and shuttered openings, asymmetrical from that of the first two stories, makes a happy architectural climax.

6. *Johnson House* (1809), on Elm St., is the best example of the late Georgian Colonial or Federal style of architecture in town. It has a distinguished Ionic-pillared portico, roof balustrade, and four end chimneys. The yew hedge surrounding the large lawns and gardens is matchless within the state.

7. *General Lyman Mower House* (1823), Woodstock's most imposing residence (across street from Woodstock Inn), is the private home and

antique shop of the John Martins. Note the four tall hooded chimneys and the delicate Palladian shutters over the third story end windows. The delicately formed four columns of the front doorway, and the rest of the entrance, were added about 1860. The Martins' antique shop is considered by many collectors to be the best antique shop in the state and one of the finest in New England.

VAH — Billings Farm, Harold Corkum, mgr. Dairy farm (Jersey cattle) and dairy products.

VAH — Sunset Farm, Thomas W. Rutherford. Dairy farm (Brown Swiss cattle) and dairy products.

VAH — Wood Apiary, Clyde N. Wood. Honey production and honey processing.

SUICIDE SIX SKI AREA (3 m. north of Woodstock along Vt. 12 and north Pomfret Rd). First ski tow in America established here in 1933–44; 2000-ft. Pomalift with 500-ft. vertical drop. Capacity: 1000 skiers hourly; 70 acres open slopes; 3 miles of trails for intermediate and novice. Ski hut with snack bar and first aid room. Parking area. *Information:* Claude Gaudin, Woodstock. Phone: 649.

MT. TOM SKI AREA (on Vt. 12); 2000-ft. Pomalift; 500-ft. slow-speed Baby Poma for children and novices. Open slopes. Snow-making equipment. Ski school. Patrol and first aid. Ski shop with sales, rental and repairs. Ski hut with fireplace and snack bar. Excellent area for novices and intermediate. Parking area. Ski Week Plans. *Information:* Claude Gaudin, Manager. Phone: Woodstock 649.

WOODSTOCK COUNTRY CLUB. (redesigned course in 1964); 18 holes. Clubhouse, pro shop, tennis courts, food.

WORCESTER, 4–D (Washington County; pop. 417, 23,456 acres; Montpelier stage) is a few houses scattered along a valley floor. There is a general store, post office and a white-spired *Methodist Church*. Agriculture and a fur farm are the principal industries.

Chronology

1609 Samuel de Champlain discovered lake which bears his name.

1666 French build fort and shrine to Saint Anne on Isle La Motte.

1690 First settlement at Vernon; British build Chimney Point Fort.

1704 Indians passed through Vermont on way to Deerfield raid; Rev. John Williams preached to the captives the first English sermon in Vermont.

1724 Dutch settled Pownal temporarily; Fort Dummer (Vernon) built by Massachusetts Colony.

1726 Timothy Dwight, first known white child born in Vermont (Fort Dummer).

1749 Bennington granted by Governor Wentworth of New Hampshire.

1752 First maple sugar made by whites — Samuel Robinson of Bennington.

1754 "Captive" Johnson born at Reading following an Indian raid.

1759 Rogers' Rangers destroy St. Francis Indian village.

1759–1760 Crown Point Military Road built.

1762 First church organized, Bennington.

1763 Treaty of Paris; French relinquish Vermont claims.

1764 Connecticut River boundary between New Hampshire and Vermont proclaimed by George III.

1765 First settlers' convention held at Bennington relative to jurisdiction controversy.

1768 Cumberland County first county within limits of state, established by New York.

1769 First act of revolution against New York when surveyors were turned back in Bennington.

1770 Green Mountain Boys organized.

1773 Fort Frederick, at Winooski River Falls at Burlington, built by Ira Allen and Remember Baker.

1775 "Westminster Massacre," armed seizure of the courthouse considered by some Vermonters as first act of the Revolution.

1775 Ethan Allen captured Ticonderoga and Seth Warner, Crown Point.

1776 Battle of Valcour Island. Hubbardton Military Road built.

1777 Dr. Thomas Young of Philadelphia made the first use of the name "Vermont."
Constitution adopted making Vermont an independent republic.
Battles of Hubbardton and Bennington fought.

1778 Thomas Chittenden elected first Governor of Vermont.

1779 Bayley–Hazen Road completed.

1780 Clio Hall in Bennington incorporated as first secondary school.
Royal Raid by Indians.

1781 First Vermont newspaper at Westminster — *Vermont Gazette* or *Green Mountain Post Boy.*

1781–1783 Haldimand negotiations looking toward the neutrality of Vermont.

1783 Pioneer log cabin built at Grand Isle by Jedediah Hyde, Jr.

1784–1785 First bridge across the Connecticut River — toll bridge at Bellows Falls.

1785 Legislative grant to Dartmouth College of town of Wheelock.
First marble quarry in United States at East Dorset.

1787 Royall Tyler wrote *The Contrast,* the first popular American play by an American author, later settled in Guilford and became Chief Justice of the Vermont Supreme Court.

1788 Vergennes incorporated; oldest and now claimed as the smallest incorporated city in New England.

1789 Ethan Allen died in Burlington.

1790 New York's claims settled for $30,000.
First U.S. patent granted to Samuel Hopkins of Pittsford for a process of manufacturing pot and pearl ashes.

1791 Vermont admitted to the Union as 14th State.
Morgan Horse ancestor first brought to Vermont by Justin Morgan.
First library at Brookfield; University of Vermont chartered.

1792 Thaddeus Stevens, Reconstruction Congressman from Pennsylvania, born in Danville.

1793 First Bennington pottery manufactured; copper discovered in Strafford.
After years of original experimenting, Samuel Morey successfully operated a steamboat on the Connecticut River, fourteen years before Fulton's voyage of the *Clermont* on the Hudson River.

1797 Legislature ordered towns to support schools.

1798–1799 During winter, Matthew Lyon, founder of Fair Haven, re-elected to Congress while serving jail term at Vergennes.

1800 Middlebury college chartered.

1801 Brigham Young, successor to Mormon Leader Joseph Smith, born in Whitingham.

1802 First canal in United States built at Bellows Falls.

1803 State flag established.

1805 Montpelier became the State Capital.
Joseph Smith, founder of Mormonism, born in Sharon.

1806 First state bank chartered — Vermont State Bank with first branches at Woodstock and Middlebury.

1808 SS *Vermont* launched on Lake Champlain — second regularly operated commercial steamship in the world.

1809 State Prison established in Windsor.

1810 Introduction of Merino sheep into the United States by Consul Jarvis at Weathersfield.

1813 First glass factory at Salisbury; State medical society incorporated.
Stephen A. Douglas born at Brandon.

1814 Battle of Plattsburgh won by Macdonough.
Death of Ira Allen.

1814–1819 Collegiate instruction for women started by pioneer educator Emma Willard at Middlebury.

1816 "Year without a summer."

1819 Norwich University chartered.

1823 First Normal School in America established at Concord; Champlain Canal opened.

1824 Levi P. Morton, banker and vice president under Benjamin Harrison, 1888, born in Shoreham.

1825 General Lafayette toured the state.

1826 Royall Tyler, famed dramatist and poet, dies at Brattleboro.

1827 State Board of Commissioners for Common Schools.

1828 George F. Edmunds born in Richmond. Distinguished lawyer and lawmaker.

1830 Invention of platform scale by Thaddeus Fairbanks.

1833 Rowland E. Robinson, writer of Vermont folklore, born near Ferrisburg village.

1836 Bicameral legislature adopted; Senate replaced Council.

1837 Electric motor invented by Thomas Davenport of Brandon.

1838 Second State House erected.

1848 First railroad, Central Vermont, White River Junction to Bethel opened.

1857 Second State House destroyed by fire.

1859 John Dewey, philosopher and educator, born at Burlington. Vermont-born Edwin L. Drake successfully drilled first modern oil well at Titusville, Pennsylvania.

1861 Civil War began — Vermont the first state to offer troops to Lincoln.

1862 Morrill land grant college act passed by Congress.

1864 Confederate raid at St. Albans.

1865 Snowflake Bentley, pioneer microphotographer of frozen crystals, born in Jericho.

1866–1870 Fenian raids — those sympathetic to the Irish cause attempted to invade Canada from Vermont.

1868 Death of Daniel P. Thompson, writer, author of *Green Mountain Boys.*

1870 Biennial sessions of the legislature began; district school system abolished.

1872 Calvin Coolidge born in Plymouth, later became 30th President.

1881 Chester A. Arthur, born in Fairfield, became 21st President upon the death of President James A. Garfield, onetime Vermont schoolteacher.

1891 Bennington Monument dedicated with President Harrison present.

1893 First electric railway — Winooski to Burlington.

1896 Rudyard Kipling leaves Vermont for England, after authoring the two *Jungle Books* and *Captains Courageous* at Brattleboro home.

1898 Vermont-born Admiral Dewey victorious at Manila Bay; Vermont-born Admiral Clark brings the USS *Oregon* around the Horn (to defeat Spanish at Santiago Bay).

1909 Champlain Tercentenary, President Taft present.

1910 First airplane flight in Vermont at St. Johnsbury.

1910–1929 Long Trail built through efforts of James Taylor.

1923 Calvin Coolidge inaugurated President of the United States at Plymouth Notch, Vt.

1926 Death of Robert Lincoln, President's oldest son at summer home in Manchester.

1927 The Great Flood. (Occurred November 3rd.)

1931 State income tax adopted.

1933–34 First ski tow in the United States at Woodstock.

1936 President Roosevelt visited flood-control project in Vermont.

1938 Hurricane caused death of five persons and twelve million dollars damage on September 21.

1941 World War II. Vermont, by defining "armed conflict" on September 11, virtually declared war on Germany before the United States.

1943 One of Four Immortal Chaplains who perished in torpedoing of SS *Dorchester* was George Lansing Fox from Gilman, Vermont.

1946 Senator Warren A. Austin appointed the first U.S. Delegate to the United Nations Security Council.

1954 First woman Lieutenant Governor, Consuelo Northrop Bailey.

1959 Vermont celebrates 350th Anniversary of the Discovery of Lake Champlain.

1962 Vermonters elect Philip Hoff, the state's first Democratic governor in more than a century.

1964 Vermont votes for President Lyndon Johnson. This is first time the state has voted for a Democratic candidate since the formation of the Republican Party in the 1850's. Governor Hoff re-elected. Democrats also sweep other top state offices.

U.S. Supreme Court orders reapportionment of Vermont legislature.

1965 House votes to reapportion itself. Membership reduced from 246 to 150 members. Representation to be based on total population. Senate votes to retain its 30 members but to reapportion on basis of registered voters. Federal court approves reapportionment plans.

Vermont Books

THIS BRIEF bibliography is of necessity only a selective working list. It is by no means the complete record of sources consulted in the preparation of this book. It was not prepared for the student of books as books, though a few early imprints that might interest him are included. Books mentioned in the text are not for that reason included here unless they have a pertinence beyond that which the text indicates. Cross references are omitted entirely. Unless a book has undergone revision that makes a later issue more authoritative or informative, the date given for each entry is that of the first edition. The novels listed are those that have a Vermont background.

WE-LIKE-VERMONT BOOKS

Crane, Charles Edward, *Let Me Show You Vermont*. New York, Knopf, 1937.
  Somewhat outdated in parts, this is still one of the better essayistic interpretations of pre-World War Two Vermont and Vermonters.
———, *Winter In Vermont*. New York, Knopf, 1941.
  Interesting history about Vermont's early winter sports events.
Fisher, Dorothy Canfield, *Vermont Tradition: The Biography of an Outlook on Life*. Boston, Little, Brown, 1953.
  Biography, essays, history and essays on Vermont and Vermonters.
Hard, Walter and Margaret, *This Is Vermont*. Brattleboro, Stephen Daye Press, 1936.
  An outdated but chatty informal tour through the state.
Lee, W. Storrs, *The Green Mountains of Vermont*. New York, Henry Holt, 1955.
  A variety of Vermont lore and history.
Van de Water, Frederic, *A Home in the Country, An Adventure in Serenity*. New York, John Day, 1937.
  A New York writer moves to Vermont. He calls Vermonters Yanks.
——— *We're Still in the Country*. New York, John Day, 1938.

HISTORY

Allen, Ira, *The Natural and Political History of the State of Vermont*. London, J. W. Myers, 1798. Reprinted in Vermont Historical Society Collections, vol. 1, 1870.
  Vermont's early struggles, viewed — not always impartially — from within.

Benedict, George, *Vermont in the Civil War*. 2 vols. Burlington, By Legislative Authority, 1886.

> The definitive account of Vermont's infantry, cavalry and sharpshooters and sailors in the War Between the States.

Bogart, Walter T., *The Vermont Lease Lands*. Montpelier, Vermont Historical Society, 1950.

> The one and only complete study of Vermont's interesting lease lands. Must reading for every serious student of Vermont history — and for all Vermont lawyers.

Chittenden, Lucius E., *The Capture of Ticonderoga*. Montpelier, Vermont Historical Society, 1872.

> Probably the best account of the taking of Ticonderoga.

Coolidge, Guy O., "French Occupation of the Champlain Valley." *2 Proceedings of the Vermont Historical Society,* New Series, vol. VI, No. 3 (Sept. 1938), pp. 144–313.

> The best published account of the French in Vermont.

Crockett, Walter H., *History of Vermont*. 5 vols. New York, Century History Co., 1921.

> Inadequate by modern scholarship standards, Crockett's *Vermont* is still the most complete record written by one person of what happened in Vermont and who was responsible for its happening. Hundreds of thumbnail profiles are woven into the text.

Daniels, Thomas E., *Vermont Indians*. Orwell, Mrs. Thomas Daniels, 1963.

> Longtime game warden Tom Daniels, part Indian himself, devoted his life to studying Vermont Indians. This is his partial report.

Force, Peter, *American Archives,* vol. II, 4th Series. Washington, D.C., 1837.

Hall, Hiland, *The History of Vermont From its Discovery to Its Admission into the Union in 1791*. Albany, N.Y., Munsell, 1868.

> An excellent study but somewhat outdated by later scholars.

Jones, Matt Bushnell, *Vermont in the Making*. Cambridge, Mass., Harvard University Press, 1939.

> This is a legal study of the Vermont-Yorker controversy. Native Vermonter Jones, onetime president of New England Telephone and Telegraph Co., uncovered many basic documents during his long research. Copies are on file with the Vermont Historical Society.

Muller, Charles G., *The Proudest Day, McDonough on Lake Champlain*. New York, John Day, 1960.

> How Vermonters whipped the Limey sailors in the battle of Lake Champlain. This was one of America's greatest naval victories — and still is.

Sheldon, Harold P., and others, *Vermont in the World War*. Montpelier, By Legislative Authority, 1928.

> A competent official history.

Slade, William, Jr., *Vermont State Papers: Records and Documents Relative to the Early History of the State*. Middlebury, J. W. Copeland, 1823.

> Valuable source material.

Thompson, Charles Miner, *Independent Vermont*. Boston, Houghton Mifflin, 1942.

> This is the best general history of Vermont's fourteen years as an independent republic. Thompson was the grandson of Vermont novelist Daniel Pierce Thompson. Dorothy Canfield Fisher in her book *Vermont*

Tradition incorrectly called Mr. Thompson the son of D. P. Thompson. *Independent Vermont* should be reprinted.

Thompson, Zadock, *History of Vermont, Natural, Civil and Statistical.* Burlington, Chauncey Goodrich, 1842.

This enlarged edition of earliest works is invaluable to researchers in several fields. It has reliable population, livestock and industrial statistics for every town in the state.

Van de Water, Frederic, *Reluctant Republic 1724–1791.* New York, John Day, 1941.

A somewhat more exciting but less reliable account than Thompson's *Independent Vermont,* although Van de Water covers a longer span of years.

Walton, E. P. (editor), *Records of the Governor and Council.* 8 vols. Montpelier, By Legislative Authority, 1873–80.

Records cover 1775–1836. Basic material.

Wardner, Henry Steele, *The Birthplace of Vermont.* New York, Charles Scribners's Sons, 1927.

Ostensibly a history of Windsor, but in reality it covers state-wide history until 1781. Somewhat anti-Allen and pro-Yorker.

Williams, Samuel, *The Natural and Civil History of Vermont.* Burlington, S. Mills, 1809.

This is a two-volume enlargement of the single-volume 1794 edition. Many competent critics consider it the best eyewitness narrative of early state history.

Williamson, Chilton, *Vermont in Quandary 1763–1825.* Montpelier, Vermont Historical Society. 1949.

Scholarly account of Vermont's difficult years. Excellent work.

Woodward, Florence M., *The Town Proprietors in Vermont: The New England Proprietorship in Decline.* New York, 1936.

A first-rate account of how Vermont proprietorship functioned.

BIOGRAPHY

Allen, Ethan, *A Narrative of Col. Ethan Allen's Captivity.* Philadelphia, Robert Bell, 1779.

Sabin says this is the first edition. Other editions, many of them pirated, appeared during the next seventy-five years. This is Allen's personal account of how he captured Fort Ticonderoga and then appropriated its rum stores "for the refreshment of the thirsty soldiery." Allen was as vigorous a writer as he was tosspot, orator, fighter, leader and propagandist.

Allen, Ira, "Autobiography." The uncompleted manuscript was published as part of Wilbur's *Ira Allen,* pp. 1–59. (See Wilbur, S. B.).

Allerton, Robert, *A Yankee Saint: John Humphrey Noyes and the Oneida Community.* New York, G. P. Putnam's Sons, 1935.

An interesting biography of the Vermont-born "wife swopper" who founded this nation's only successful socialistic community.

Anonymous, *Vermont Biographical Encyclopedia — 19th Century.* Boston, Metropolitan Publishing and Engraving Co., 1885.

More than one hundred biographies — with family tree — of Vermonters who made good.

Beardsley, Harry M., *Joseph Smith and His Mormon Empire*. Boston, Houghton Mifflin, 1931.

The first real biography not written by a Mormon of the man who perhaps influenced the lives of a larger number of people than has any other Vermonter that ever lived.

Brodie, Fawn M., *No Man Knows My History, The Life of Joseph Smith*. New York, Knopf, 1946.

Brown, W. G., *Stephen A. Douglas*. Boston, Houghton Mifflin, 1902.

Probably the best Douglas biography. It should be reprinted or a new one written.

Chipman, Daniel., *A Memoir of Thomas Chittenden, First Governor of Vermont*. Middlebury, 1849.

Thomas Chittenden, a first-rate man, deserves a first-rate biography.

Crockett, Walter H., *Vermonters, A Book of Biographies*. Brattleboro, Stephen Daye Press, 1931.

Short but interesting sketches of famous and some not so famous but interesting Vermonters.

Davenport, Walter Rice, *Biography of Thomas Davenport*. Montpelier, Vermont Historical Society, 1929.

This one-sided account gives the credit for inventing the electric motor to Thomas Davenport instead of Orange Alonzo Smalley, the real inventor.

Dewey, Adelbert M., *The Life and Letters of Admiral Dewey*. New York, Woolfall, 1899.

This uncritical biography, written by a relative, nevertheless contains some interesting Dewey material, not found elsewhere.

Duffus, Robert Luther, *Williamstown Branch, Impersonal Memories of A Vermont Boyhood*. New York, Norton, 1958.

The author was a longtime *New York Times* newsman.

Evans, John Henry, *Joseph Smith, An American Prophet*. New York, Macmillan, 1933.

This biography mentions only one of the Prophet's twenty-seven wives.

Hill, Ralph Nading, *Contrary Country, A Chronicle of Vermont*. Brattleboro, Stephen Greene Press, 2nd ed., 1961.

A miscellany of interesting Vermonters.

Holbrook, Stewart H., *Ethan Allen*. New York, Macmillan, 1940. Reprinted 1958 by Binfords and Mort, Portland, Ore.

This biography, despite small-minded critics, brings vividly alive the exciting years of Vermont's greatest hero far better than any of the other half-dozen biographies.

Kent, Dorman B. E., *Vermonters*. Montpelier, Vermont Historical Society, 1937.

A later edition of the author's *One Thousand Vermonters*. Despite many inaccuracies and shortcomings the book provides a concise handy reference list of 1500 prominent men and women born in Vermont. The division is by towns. Names are indexed. A new and more comprehensive edition of this book is badly needed.

Lee, John Parker, *Uncommon Vermont*. Rutland, Tuttle, 1926.

Poorly written profiles of little-known Vermonters. Interesting.

Lee, W. Storrs, *Town Father, A Biography of Gamaliel Painter.* New York, Hastings House, 1952.
> Painter, a shrewd rascal, was a founder of Middlebury College. He was a Congregationalist, Federalist and didn't like Ethan Allen.

Lowenthal, David, *George Perkins Marsh, Versatile Vermonter.* New York, Columbia University Press, 1958.
> Perkins well may have been the most versatile Vermonter. He was certainly one of the most extraordinary.

Lutz, Alma, *Emma Willard, Daughter of Democracy.* Boston, Houghton Mifflin, 1929.
> She was one of Vermont's most influential females.

McLaughlin, James Fairfax, *Matthew Lyon, The Hampden of Congress.* New York, Wynkoop, Hallanbeck and Crawford, 1900.
> This is the best biography to date of Lyon. All biographies since have derived much of their material from McLaughlin.

Noyes, George Wallingford (editor and compiler), *John Humphrey Noyes and the Putney Community.* Oneida, N.Y., 1931.
> Letters and documents pertaining to "Complex Marriage" as evolved by Noyes while still a Putney resident.

Parker, Wyman W., *Henry Stevens of Vermont: An American Bookdealer in London 1845-86.* Amsterdam, Netherlands, N. Israel, 1963.
> The definitive biography, to date.

Pell, John, *Ethan Allen.* Boston, Houghton Mifflin, 1929.
> Possibly a more factual but less exciting biography than Holbrook's *Ethan Allen.* Holbrook wrote with fire in his belly.

Rice, Howard C., *Rudyard Kipling in New England.* Brattleboro, Stephen Daye Press, 1936.
> The story of Kipling's feud with his brother-in-law. The feud finally drove Kipling and his Vermont-born wife to England. Compare Rice version with Kipling's autobiography *Something of Myself.*

Sparkes, Boyden, and Samuel Taylor Moore, *The Witch of Wall Street: Hetty Green.* New York, Doubleday, Doran, 1935.
> She married a Vermonter, poor fellow!

Swanberg, W. A., *Jim Fisk: The Career of an Improbable Rascal.* New York, Charles Scribner's Sons, 1959.
> The story of Vermont's most successful scalawag.

Tupper, Frederick, and Helen Tyler Brown (editors), *Grandmother Tyler's Book, The Recollections of Mary Palmer Tyler.* New York, G. P. Putnam's Sons, 1925.
> By the wife of the first really important Vermont writer, Royal Tyler, this realistic book is the closest thing to Jane Austen that ever came out of the state.

Werner, M. R., *Brigham Young.* New York, Harcourt Brace, 1925.
> This is still the best biography of the Whitingham boy who became the Moses of Mormonism — and incidentally, one of America's great empire builders.

Wilbur, James Benjamin, *Ira Allen, Founder of Vermont.* 2 vols. Boston, Houghton, Mifflin, 1928.
> This will probably remain the definitive biography despite its prejudice in favor of Ira.

Woodburn, J. A., *The Life of Thaddeus Stevens.* Indianapolis, Bobbs-Merrill, 1913.

Radical Republican Stevens, leader of House Abolitionists, was directly responsible for much of the ill feeling postwar Southerners had — some still have — for Yankees.

EDUCATION

Andrews, Edward D., "The County Grammar Schools and Academies of Vermont." Montpelier, *Proceedings,* Vermont Historical Society, New Series, vol. IV, no. 3, 1936.

An abridgement of a long-needed study of Vermont's lower grade nineteenth-century schools.

Ellis, William A., *A History of Norwich University (1819–1911).* Montpelier, Capital City Press, 1911.

An updated edition is needed.

Lee, W. Storrs, *Father Went to College.* New York, Wilson-Erickson, 1936.

An informal history of Middlebury College.

Richardson, Leon B., *History of Dartmouth College.* Hanover, N.H. (formerly Dresden, Vt.), Dartmouth College Publications, 1932.

Dartmouth was Vermont's first college. It was supported with grants by Vermont government.

Stone, Mason S., *History of Education, State of Vermont.* Montpelier, published by the author, 1934.

Poorly arranged and somewhat evangelical, this account is still fairly complete and is rich in interesting sidelights that might have been excluded by a more orderly and formal plan.

REGIONAL BOOKS

Hall, Benjamin, *History of Eastern Vermont.* New York, Appleton, 1858.

A first-rate thorough anti-Allen account of goings on in Vermont's Connecticut River Valley up to 1800.

Hard, Walter, *The Connecticut* (Rivers of America Series). New York, Rinehart, 1947.

A considerable portion of this book is devoted by Vermonter Hard to Vermont.

Hayes, Lyman S., *The Connecticut River Valley in Southern Vermont and New Hampshire.* Rutland, Tuttle, 1920.

History and yarns.

Hemenway, Abby Maria (compiler and editor), *Vermont Historical Gazetteer.* 5 vols. Burlington, published by the editor, 1871.

A priceless hodgepodge of town history, biography and anecdote collected, preserved and published by the indomitable and unselfish enthusiasm of one Vermont spinster. Windsor County is lacking. Miss Hemenway deposited the manuscript as a security for a debt. After her death it was destroyed by fire just a few days before it was to have been redeemed by the Vermont Historical Society.

Hill, Ralph Nading, *The Winooski* (Rivers of America Series). New York, Rinehart, 1949.
> Hill incorrectly calls the Winooski the longest river in the state. All reports from Ira Allen to current state documents list the Big Otter, also known as Otter Creek, as the longest river lying entirely within the state's boundaries.

SOCIAL STUDIES

Green, Mason A., *Nineteen-Two in Vermont*. Rutland, Marble City Press, 1912.
> A biased but informative boom on the fight for local option and the repeal of Vermont's prohibition.

Horton, Guy B., *History of the Grange in Vermont*. Montpelier, Capital City Press, 1926.
> Incomplete to publication date but still the only extended account of an organization which in the past exerted considerable influence on the rural social life of this state.

Ludlum, David M., *Social Ferment in Vermont 1791–1850*. New York, Columbia University Press, 1939.
> The best account extant of the various social forces at work in Vermont during the first sixty years of statehood.

Stilwell, Lewis D., *Migration from Vermont*. Montpelier, Vermont Historical Society, 1948.
> This excellent study details town by town and decade by decade nineteenth-century migration from Vermont.

Wilson, Harold Fisher, *The Country of Northern New England*. New York, Columbia University Press, 1936.
> By far the best book in its field, and its field is very wide: the economic history of the three northern New England states between 1790 and 1930. The references to Vermont probably equal the sum of those to Maine and New Hampshire, for this is the state that the author knows best.

TRAVEL AND TRANSPORTATION

Carman, Bernard R., *Hoot, Toot & Whistle*. Brattleboro, Stephen Greene Press, 1963.
> A delightful history of the Hoosac Tunnel and Wilmington R.R., better known from its initials H. T. & W.

Hill, Ralph Nading, *The Mad Doctor's Drive*. Brattleboro, Stephen Greene Press, 1964.
> How Colonel Jackson of Burlington made the first trip across the United States in a motorcar.

Morse, Roy, *36 Miles of Trouble, The Story of the West River R.R.* Brattleboro, Stephen Greene Press, 1959.

Perkins, Rev. Nathan, *A Narrative of a Tour Through the State of Vermont from April 27 to June 12, 1789*. Woodstock, Elm Tree Press, 1920.
> A classic tour. He didn't like Vermont or Vermonters.

Shaughnessy, James, *The Rutland Road.* Berkeley, Calif., Howell-North, 1964. This superbly illustrated volume with nearly 500 photographs is one of the best railroad histories produced to date.

Wilgus, William J., "The Economic Background for Transportation Growth in Vermont." *Vermont Quarterly,* New Series, vol. XII, no. 2 (April, 1944), pp. 67–90.

INDEX

Index

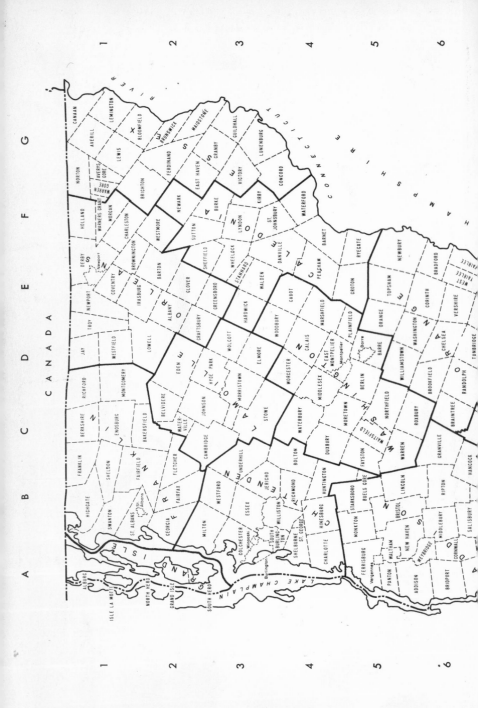